# THE
# COLLEGE
# PRESS
# NIV
# COMMENTARY

## MINOR PROPHETS
### VOLUME 2

# THE
# COLLEGE
# PRESS
# NIV
# COMMENTARY

## MINOR PROPHETS
### VOLUME 2
Nahum–Malachi

## MARK ALLEN HAHLEN, PH.D.
## CLAY ALAN HAM, PH.D.

### Old Testament Series Co-Editors:

Terry Briley, Ph.D.
Lipscomb University

Paul Kissling, Ph.D.
Great Lakes Christian College

COLLEGE PRESS
PUBLISHING COMPANY
Joplin, Missouri

The Library of Congress issued the following CIP jointly to *Minor Prophets Volume 1* (author Harold Shank) and *Minor Prophets Volume 2* (authors Clay Ham and Mark Hahlen).

**Library of Congress Cataloging-in-Publication Data**

Shank, Harold.
    Minor Prophets/Harold Shank.
      p.   cm. — (The College Press NIV commentary. Old
  Testament series)
    Includes bibliographical references.
    ISBN 0-89900-895-X
    1. Bible. O.T. Minor Prophets—Commentaries.   I. Title.
  II. Series.
BS1560.S47 2001
224'.9077—dc21

                                          2001037121

# A WORD
# FROM THE PUBLISHER

Years ago a movement was begun with the dream of uniting all Christians on the basis of a common purpose (world evangelism) under a common authority (the Word of God). The College Press NIV Commentary Series is a serious effort to join the scholarship of two branches of this unity movement so as to speak with one voice concerning the Word of God. Our desire is to provide a resource for your study of the Old Testament that will benefit you whether you are preparing a Bible School lesson, a sermon, a college course, or your own personal devotions. Today as we survey the wreckage of a broken world, we must turn again to the Lord and his Word, unite under his banner and communicate the life-giving message to those who are in desperate need. This is our purpose.

# ABBREVIATIONS

*1 En.* . . . . . . . . *1 Enoch*
*1QpHab* . . . . . *Pesher Habakkuk*
*1Qs* . . . . . . . . *Rule of the Community*
*AB* . . . . . . . . *The Anchor Bible*
*ABC* . . . . . . . *Assyrian and Babylonian Chronicles*
*ABD* . . . . . . . *Anchor Bible Dictionary*
*ACCS* . . . . . . . *Ancient Christian Commentary on Scripture*
*Adv. Jud.* . . . . . *Against the Jews.* Tertullian
*Ag. Ap.* . . . . . . *Against Apion.* Josephus
*Anab.* . . . . . . . *Anabasis.* Xenophon
*ANEP* . . . . . . . *The Ancient Near East in Pictures Relating to the Old Testament*
*ANESTP* . . . . . *Ancient Near East: Supplementary Texts and Pictures Relating to the Old Testament*
*ANET* . . . . . . . *Ancient Near Eastern Texts Relating to the Old Testament*
*Ant.* . . . . . . . . *Jewish Antiquities.* Josephus
*ARAB* . . . . . . . *Ancient Records of Assyria and Babylonia*
*ARI* . . . . . . . . *Assyrian Royal Inscriptions*
*AUSS* . . . . . . . *Andrews University Seminary Studies*
*b.* . . . . . . . . . . . *Babylonian Talmud*
*BA* . . . . . . . . *Biblical Archaeologist*
*BASOR* . . . . . . *Bulletin of the American Schools of Oriental Research*
*BBC* . . . . . . . . *Broadman Bible Commentary*
*BDB* . . . . . . . . Brown, Driver, and Briggs, *A Hebrew and English Lexicon of the Old Testament*
*BerOl* . . . . . . . *Berit Olam*
*BHK* . . . . . . . . *Biblica Hebraica*, ed. by R. Kittel
*BHS* . . . . . . . . *Biblia Hebraica Stuttgartensia*
*BI* . . . . . . . . . . *Biblical Illustrator*
*Bibl. Hist.* . . . . *Bibliotheca historica [Library of History].* Diodurus Siculus

*BJRL* . . . . . . . . *Bulletin of the John Rylands University Library*
*BLS* . . . . . . . . . *Bible and Literature Series*
*BRev* . . . . . . . . *Bible Review*
*BT* . . . . . . . . . *The Bible Translator*
*BWANT* . . . . . *Beiträge zur Wissenschaft vom Alten und Neuen Testament*
*CBC* . . . . . . . . *Cambridge Bible Commentary*
*CBET* . . . . . . . *Contributions to Biblical Exegesis and Theology*
*CBQ* . . . . . . . . *Catholic Biblical Quarterly*
*Cels.* . . . . . . . . *Against Celsus.* Origen
*CEV* . . . . . . . . *Contemporary English Version*
*Comm. Matt.* . . . *Commentary on Matthew*
*ConBOT* . . . . . *Coniectanea biblica: Old Testament Series*
*DBI* . . . . . . . . . *Dictionary of Biblical Imagery*
*Dem. ev.* . . . . . *Demonstration of the Gospel.* Eusebius
*DJG* . . . . . . . . . *Dictionary of Jesus and the Gospels*
*DOTHB* . . . . . *Dictionary of the Old Testament: Historical Books*
*DOTP* . . . . . . . *Dictionary of the Old Testament: Pentateuch*
*ErIsr* . . . . . . . . *Eretz Israel*
*ESV* . . . . . . . . . *English Standard Version*
*FOTL* . . . . . . . *Forms of the Old Testament Literature*
*GKC* . . . . . . . . *Gesenius' Hebrew Grammar,* 2nd ed., ed. by E. Kautzsch
*GTJ* . . . . . . . . . *Grace Theological Journal*
*HALOT* . . . . . *The Hebrew and Aramaic Lexicon of the Old Testament*
*HAR* . . . . . . . . *Hebrew Annual Review*
*HAT* . . . . . . . . *Handbuch zum Alten Testament*
*HBD* . . . . . . . . *HarperCollins Bible Dictionary*
*Hist.* . . . . . . . . *Histories.* Herodotus
*HSM* . . . . . . . . *Harvard Semitic Monographs*
*HTR* . . . . . . . . *Harvard Theological Review*
*HUCA* . . . . . . . *Hebrew Union College Annual*
*IBC* . . . . . . . . . *Interpretation: A Bible Commentary for Teaching and Preaching*
*IBHS* . . . . . . . . *An Introduction to Biblical Hebrew Syntax*
*ICC* . . . . . . . . . *International Critical Commentary*
*IDB* . . . . . . . . . *Interpreter's Dictionary of the Bible*
*ISBE* . . . . . . . . *International Standard Bible Encyclopedia*
*ITC* . . . . . . . . . *International Theological Commentary*
*JAOS* . . . . . . . . *Journal of the American Oriental Society*

*JBL* . . . . . . . . . *Journal of Biblical Literature*
*JETS* . . . . . . . . *Journal of the Evangelical Theological Society*
*Jos. Asen.* . . . . . . *Joseph and Asenath*
*Jov.* . . . . . . . . . *Against Jovinianus.* Jerome
*JSOT* . . . . . . . . *Journal for the Study of the Old Testament*
*JSOTSupp* . . . . *Journal for the Study of the Old Testament: Supplement*
                    *Series*
*JSS* . . . . . . . . . *Journal of Semitic Studies*
*JTS* . . . . . . . . . *Journal of Theological Studies*
*J.W.* . . . . . . . . *Jewish Wars.* Josephus
*KJV* . . . . . . . . . *King James Version*
*Lev. Rab.* . . . . *Leviticus Rabbah*
*Liv. Pro.* . . . . . *Lives of the Prophets*
*LXX* . . . . . . . . *Septuagint*
*Mart. Ascen. Isa.* . . *Martyrdom and Ascension of Isaiah*
*MSJ* . . . . . . . . . *Master's Seminary Journal*
*MT* . . . . . . . . . *Masoretic Text*
*NAC* . . . . . . . . *New American Commentary*
*NASB* . . . . . . . *New American Standard Bible*
*NBD* . . . . . . . . *New Bible Dictionary*
*NCB* . . . . . . . . *New Century Bible*
*NDBT* . . . . . . . *New Dictionary of Biblical Theology*
*NEAEHL* . . . . *The New Encyclopedia of Archaeological Excavations in*
                    *the Holy Land*
*NEB* . . . . . . . . *New English Bible*
*NET* . . . . . . . . *New English Translation*
*NIB* . . . . . . . . . *New Interpreter's Bible*
*NICOT* . . . . . . *New International Commentary on the Old Testament*
*NIDOTTE* . . . *New International Dictionary of Old Testament*
                    *Theology and Exegesis*
*NIV* . . . . . . . . . *New International Version*
*NJB* . . . . . . . . . *New Jerusalem Bible*
*NJPS* . . . . . . . . *New Jewish Publication Society Bible*
*NKJV* . . . . . . . *New King James Version*
*NLT* . . . . . . . . *New Living Translation*
*NRSV* . . . . . . . *New Revised Standard Version*
*NTM* . . . . . . . . *New Testament Monographs*
*NTTS* . . . . . . . *New Testament Tools and Studies*
*OTL* . . . . . . . . *Old Testament Library*

*Pesiq. R.* . . . . . *Pesiqta Rabbati*
*Protr.* . . . . . . . *Exhortation to the Greeks.* Clement of Alexandria
*RevExp* . . . . . . *Review and Expositor*
*RTJ* . . . . . . . . *Reformed Theological Journal*
*SBLDS* . . . . . . *Society of Biblical Literature Dissertation Series*
*SJT* . . . . . . . . *Scottish Journal of Theology*
*S. 'Olam Rab.* . . . *Seder 'Olam Rabbah*
*Strom.* . . . . . . . *Stromata.* Clement of Alexandra
*T. Ab.* . . . . . . . *Testament of Abraham*
*TLOT* . . . . . . . *Theological Lexicon of the Old Testament*
*TNIV* . . . . . . . *Today's New International Version*
*TOTC* . . . . . . . *Tyndale Old Testament Commentaries*
*TWOT* . . . . . . *Theological Wordbook of the Old Testament*
*VT* . . . . . . . . . *Vetus Testamentum*
*VTSupp.* . . . . . *Supplements to Vetus Testamentum*
*WBC* . . . . . . . . *Word Biblical Commentary*
*WEC* . . . . . . . . *Wycliffe Exegetical Commentary*
*WMANT* . . . . . *Wissenschaftlichen Monographien zum Alten und Neuen Testament*
*ZAW* . . . . . . . . *Zeitschrift für die alttestamentliche Wissenschaft*
*Zebah.* . . . . . . . *Zevahim, Babylonian Talmud*

# Simplified Guide to Hebrew Writing

| Heb. letter | Translit. | Pronunciation guide |
|---|---|---|
| א | ʾ | Has no sound of its own; like smooth breathing mark in Greek |
| ב | b | Pronounced like English B *or* V |
| ג | g | Pronounced like English G |
| ד | d | Pronounced like English D |
| ה | h | Pronounced like English H |
| ו | w | As a consonant, pronounced like English V or German W |
| וּ | û | Represents a vowel sound, pronounced like English long OO |
| וֹ | ô | Represents a vowel sound, pronounced like English long O |
| ז | z | Pronounced like English Z |
| ח | ḥ | Pronounced like German and Scottish CH and Greek χ (chi) |
| ט | ṭ | Pronounced like English T |
| י | y | Pronounced like English Y |
| כ/ך | k | Pronounced like English K |
| ל | l | Pronounced like English L |
| מ/ם | m | Pronounced like English M |
| נ/ן | n | Pronounced like English N |
| ס | s | Pronounced like English S |
| ע | ʿ | Stop in breath deep in throat before pronouncing the vowel |
| פ/ף | p/ph | Pronounced like English P *or* F |
| צ/ץ | ṣ | Pronounced like English TS/TZ |
| ק | q | Pronounced very much like כ (k) |
| ר | r | Pronounced like English R |
| שׂ | ś | Pronounced like English S, much the same as ס |
| שׁ | š | Pronounced like English SH |
| ת | t/th | Pronounced like English T *or* TH |

Note that different forms of some letters appear at the end of the word (written right to left), as in כָּפַף (*kāphaph*, "bend") and מֶלֶךְ (*melek*, "king").

Vowels in Hebrew (except where the ו is used to represent a vowel sound), are represented by "vowel points" added to the consonant. For example: הַ (*ha*, "the"). The letter *yod* (י, *y*) also becomes a *part of* certain vowel sounds, as in the conjunction כִּי (*kî*, "that"). Originally, Hebrew was written as "unpointed" text, with just the consonants. For convenience, the different vowel points are shown below on the letter Aleph (א).

| | | |
|---|---|---|
| אָ | ā | Pronounced not like long A in English, but like the broad A or AH sound |
| אַ | a | The Hebrew short A sound, but more closely resembles the broad A (pronounced for a shorter period of time) than the English short A |
| אֶ | e | Pronounced like English short E |
| אֵ | ē | Pronounced like English long A, or Greek η (eta) |

| | | |
|---|---|---|
| אִ | i | Pronounced like English short I |
| אִ | î | The same vowel point is sometimes pronounced like אִי (see below) |
| אָ | o | This vowel point sometimes represents the short O sound |
| אֹ | ō | Pronounced like English long O |
| אֻ | u | The vowel point ֻ sometimes represents a shorter U sound and |
| אֻ | ū | is sometimes pronounced like the וּ (û, see above) |
| אֵ | ê | Pronounced much the same as אֶ |
| אֵי | ê | Pronounced much the same as אֶ |
| אִי | î | Pronounced like long I in many languages, or English long E |
| אְ | ə | An unstressed vowel sound, like the first E in the word "severe" |
| אֳ, אֲ, אֱ | ŏ, ă, ĕ | Shortened, unstressed forms of the vowels אָ, אַ, and אֶ, pronounced very similarly to אְ |

# PREFACE

Since 1992 we have both served on the faculty of Dallas Christian College, Dallas, Texas. During that time, some fourteen years now, we have worked jointly on various projects. Together we have taught classes, written curriculum, prepared exams, hired adjunct professors, interviewed graduates, and played in student-faculty games. So this commentary stands among (and perhaps beyond) these other joint efforts. It is a work that has developed at an intersection of our common research, since one of us did doctoral work in Habakkuk and the other in the use of Zechariah in Matthew. If someone had chronicled our lunch conversations over the years about issues relating to biblical exposition, recurrent topics would certainly concern these two books. We would dare say so frequently that some of our students have intentionally avoided selecting texts from Habakkuk and Zechariah for their exegetical papers in our classes.

Several people merit our thanks. We are grateful to our teaching colleagues at Dallas Christian College for listening and entering into our discussions about these six prophetic texts. We are indebted to our church friends who prayed for us and asked often about our progress and to our wives and children who frequently altered their plans to accommodate our writing schedules. We are thankful for our students from Dallas Christian College, Louisville Bible College, and Lakeview Bible Seminary; indeed they are the joy of our academic ministry. Among these students, we especially appreciate the members of the "Special Topics: Nahum–Malachi" class for being the initial audience for much of our research and Timothy Jenkins for his interest in the project and for preparing research notes on Zechariah 1–9. Special thanks goes to Diane Ham for reading the entire manuscript and suggesting ways that the work would communicate better to its intended audience and to Dru Ashwell of College Press for his patient and constant encouragement.

17 July 2006<br>
Mark Allen Hahlen<br>
Clay Alan Ham

To our students at

Dallas Christian College,
Louisville Bible College,
and
Lakeview Bible Seminary

# GENERAL INTRODUCTION

## PURPOSE

The act of reading and interpreting the Bible requires contemporary readers to traverse from their world to the world of the text. However, a cultural distance between the two worlds complicates this journey. Biblical authors use images from ancient agriculture and warfare that are distant to modern readers. They refer to events, circumstances, geographical entities, and socio-political realities familiar to the text's original audience but not part of a frame of reference for contemporary readers. They allude to earlier biblical texts not immediately recognizable and may occasionally use literary forms unfamiliar to the reader. Because of this, the prophetic literature of the Bible has become, for many readers, "a closed corpus, incomprehensible and therefore largely neglected except as a quarry from which to mine a few choice messianic nuggets or moral admonitions."[1]

Both general Bible readers and others doing in-depth biblical research should find helpful this volume for diminishing or closing the distance between the biblical audience and contemporary readers. As a result, they may better read, understand, and be challenged by the messages of the prophets Nahum, Habakkuk, Zephaniah, Haggai, Zechariah, and Malachi. The contents of this commentary provide information regarding the historical, sociocultural, and theological milieu of the texts, discuss words and literary forms employed, and analyze the relationship between the studied texts and the remainder of biblical literature. The Selected Bibliography provided for each book and those sources cited in footnotes offer resources for further technical research or for comparing interpretive options.

---

[1]J.J.M. Roberts, *Nahum, Habakkuk, and Zephaniah*, OTL (Louisville, KY: Westminster/John Knox Press, 1991), p. 9.

# FORMAT

This volume is a commentary on the last six of the Minor Prophets (Nahum, Habakkuk, Zephaniah, Haggai, Zechariah, Malachi) using the New International Version (NIV) translation[2] as the starting point. Following this General Introduction, each book is treated individually in its canonical order. The first part of each treatment consists of an introduction discussing the book's authorship, historical background, date, literary features, theology, and message. An outline of the book's content then follows as well as Selected Bibliography for further research. The ensuing comment on the biblical text itself follows the versification common to most English translations of the Bible. Here, a short description of the literary form and content of each major section precedes the more detailed discussion of the individual verses in each section.

# TERMINOLOGY

Every field of study has its technical or specialized vocabulary; the same is true with biblical studies. The nonspecialist may require definitions for some terms appearing repeatedly in this volume. Nahum, Habakkuk, Zephaniah, Haggai, Zechariah, and Malachi are the final six books in a twelve-book collection often referred to as the Minor Prophets. This name refers to their relative brevity as opposed to their diminished significance. They circulated together with the first six books of the collection (Hosea, Joel, Amos, Obadiah, Jonah, and Micah) in an anthology known to the Jews as the Book of the Twelve, the final book in the section of the Hebrew Scripture known as the *Nevi'im* or Prophets. The Hebrew Old Testament upon which the NIV and this commentary are based is known as the Masoretic Text (MT). The version of this text commonly studied by the scholarly community is the *Biblia Hebraica Stuttgartensia* (*BHS*). The Dead Sea Scrolls, sometimes called the Qumran Scrolls, also bear testimony to the contents of the original biblical texts. Though Hebrew is the language in which the majority

---

[2]See the Preface to the New International Version for information regarding translation theory, policies, and methods for the NIV translation.

of the Old Testament is written, study of early Greek translations such as the Septuagint (LXX) also aids in ascertaining the original intention and wording of the authors. Helpful also are the Targums, Aramaic paraphrases or interpretive translations of the Old Testament.

The NIV and most other English translations of the Bible use the designation "LORD" (in small caps) to render the personal name of the Hebrew God, which is often called the Tetragrammaton because it consists of four Hebrew letters (יהוה, *YHWH*). Since biblical Hebrew was written without vowels before the fifth century A.D. and since the practice of not pronouncing the personal name Yahweh developed out of reverence for God, knowledge of the exact vowels used in the name has been lost. Older translations, commentaries, devotional literature, and songs, influenced by older German language and practice, render the name "Jehovah," but recent scholarship has argued for the more likely rendering "Yahweh" used here.[3] The NIV renders as "Lord" a different Hebrew name for God (אָדוֹן or אֲדֹנָי, *'ādôn* or *'ădōnay*).

## THE FUNCTION AND FOUNDATION
## OF THE PROPHETS

Because the books of Nahum through Malachi are part of the corpus of Old Testament prophetic writings, a brief discussion of the role of the prophet is in order. The English word "prophet" is derived from the Greek noun προφήτης (*prophētēs*), designating one who speaks forth or proclaims. In the LXX, *prophētēs* translates the Hebrew נָבִיא (*nābî'*). One use of *nābî'* in Exodus 7:1-2 highlights the relationship among Yahweh, the prophet, and the people. There Yahweh informs Moses, "See, I have made you like God to Pharaoh, and your brother Aaron will be your prophet. You are to say everything I command you, and your brother Aaron is to tell Pharaoh to let the Israelites go out of his country." The prophet proclaims to the audience the words Yahweh desires them to hear. A similar anal-

---

[3]For more information on the meaning, translation, and significance of the Tetragrammaton, see G.T. Manley and F.F. Bruce, "God, Names of," *NBD*, pp. 420-422, and "Tetragrammaton," *TBD*, pp. 1248-1249.

ogy occurs in Exodus 4:15-16. Yahweh promises to give words to Moses with which Moses instructs Aaron. Aaron, in turn, speaks to the Israelites as if Moses is God and Aaron, his mouth.

Though contemporary readers often think of prophets as predictors whose primary task is to tell the future, the biblical prophets are primarily "forthtellers." Yahweh calls them to proclaim a message to their own generation so that the people may be reformed in the present, not simply informed regarding the future (Deut 18:14-19; 2 Kgs 17:7-23). Even in those times when the prophets "foretell" things Yahweh is going to do in the near or distant future, their primary objective is to elicit from the original audience trust in and obedience to Yahweh.

The beginning point and centerpiece of the prophets' message is the Torah or Law and the covenant relationship to which that literature testifies. The use of Torah by later prophets is exemplified by the words of Moses in Deuteronomy 30:11-20. Moses has previously set before Israel a recollection of Yahweh's dealings with them in delivering them from Egypt, giving them the Law, and leading and providing for them in the wilderness in spite of their continual sin. He has laid before the nation the blessings that Yahweh has promised should they be obedient to Torah and the curses that result if they are unfaithful to the covenant with Yahweh. Then, on the basis of the history of their covenant relationship with Yahweh and of Yahweh's promises for the future, Moses calls them to choose life by choosing to obey Yahweh and Torah.

Three early prophets set the agenda for the later prophets. Moses gives the prophets their preaching text, the Torah, and confronts the people with the covenant obligations attendant to their being the people of Yahweh. Samuel models the role of Yahweh's spokesman to the people and the king during times of crisis and uncertainty. Elijah epitomizes the prophetic role of protector and enforcer of the covenant, admonishing the people to a single-minded and complete devotion to Yahweh that forsakes all other gods and loyalties.

One finds within the prophetic literature the constant influence of or allusion to three covenants that form its foundation. The covenant with Abraham (Genesis 12; 15; 18; 22) promises Abraham and his descendants land, nationhood, and prominence. Most significant, however, is the promise that they are a means of blessing for the world (Gen 12:3; 18:18; 22:18); this promise forms the basis for later prophetic oracles that anticipate the worship of Yahweh by the nations.

The Mosaic or Sinaitic covenant (Exodus 19–24; Leviticus 26; Deuteronomy 4–5; 28–29) establishes Israel as the nation that fulfills the promise to Abraham. It articulates the promise of Yahweh's presence among Israel (Lev 26:11-12), of the bestowal on Israel of a special status among the nations (Exod 19:5-6; Lev 26:13), and of divine blessing on the land of Israel (Lev 26:9-10; Deut 28:1-14). In response to these promises, Israel must serve Yahweh totally and faithfully by observing the covenant stipulations (Exod 20:1-17,22-26; 21:1–23:19; Deut 5:1-21; 6:4-5). Failure to do so results in covenant curse (Lev 26:14-46; Deut 27:9-26; 28:15-68). This interplay between obedience and disobedience to demands of covenant determines that the outworking of covenant blessing or curse is the focal point in the majority of the prophetic literature.

Second Samuel 7 and its parallel in 1 Chronicles 17 narrate the making of Yahweh's covenant with David. Following the conquest of Jerusalem and the solidification of his kingdom among the neighboring nations (2 Samuel 5), David announces to the prophet Nathan his intent to build a house (i.e., a temple) for Yahweh as a suitable place for Yahweh's throne and the ark of the covenant (2 Sam 6:1-19; 7:1-4). Yahweh intervenes, however, and pledges rather to establish a house or dynasty for David. The Davidic house is an enduring dynasty that rules over the covenant people of Yahweh (2 Sam 7:5-16). The place of Jerusalem and of the temple is a prevalent theme throughout the prophetic literature, so also is the anticipation of a future Davidic figure that brings salvation and blessing to Israel and the nations. In many respects, messianic prophecy involves how Yahweh works within the history of Israel to fulfill the promise that through the family of Abraham the whole world is blessed and through a Davidic descendant the promised kingdom comes.

## HISTORICAL BACKGROUND

Found within the introductions of the individual books are more detailed discussions of the historical contexts for the prophets

Nahum, Habakkuk, Zephaniah, Haggai, Zechariah, and Malachi. Nevertheless, some broad observations may be beneficial to place the books within their general contexts. Nahum, Habakkuk, and Zephaniah function within the last century of the kingdom of Judah's existence. These days preceding the fall of Judah in 586 B.C. see tremendous shifts in power within the ancient Near East. During the ninth century, Assyrian rulers extend their empire from northwest Mesopotamia into the lands west of the Euphrates River. The military successes of Assyria often are accompanied by the brutalization of those they conquer, perhaps to foster terror and thus submission among those whom they subjugate. By the eighth century, the northern kingdom of Israel has become one of Assyria's western vassals.

Nevertheless, the sway of Assyria over the region subsides as civil war leads to a three-quarter-century eclipse of Assyrian power. During this period, Jeroboam II (793–753 B.C.) restores Israel to political and military prominence in the region (2 Kgs 14:23-29). This decline is short-lived, when Tiglath-Pileser III (745–727 B.C.), also known as Pul (cf. 1 Chr 5:26), reasserts imperial power and launches an effort to reestablish Assyria as a world empire. He subjects Israel to tribute and takes large amounts of the northern kingdom's territory. He also extends Assyrian influence over Judah when its king, Ahaz, asks Pul for protection from Aram and Israel (ca. 734–732 B.C.; cf. 2 Kings 16). The Assyrians are a constant threat to Israel and Judah over the next three decades. Indeed, Samaria falls to them in 722/721 B.C., and the Assyrians fiercely retaliate when Judah's king Hezekiah reverses the pro-Assyrian policies of his father Ahaz in 701 B.C. Only a miraculous delivery by Yahweh rescues Judah (2 Kings 18–19; 2 Chronicles 32; Isaiah 36–37).

The following century sees both Assyria's zenith and decline. Ashurbanipal (669–627 B.C.) brings Assyrian power and culture to a climax in 663 B.C. through a successful campaign in Egypt. Nevertheless, decline begins as the region of Babylon rebels and drains the resources of the empire. During this time, Josiah (640–609 B.C.) enacts religious and political reforms in Judah (2 Kings 22–23; 2 Chronicles 34–35) that effectively repudiate Assyrian control. The Babylonians eventually join the Medes in a coalition and renew the Babylonian revolt. This culminates in the destruction of the old Assyrian capital of Asshur in 614 B.C. and then Nineveh in

612 B.C. The anticipated fall of the Assyrian capital Nineveh is the focal event of the book of Nahum.

The opening verse of the book of Zephaniah locates the ministry of that prophet "during the reign of Josiah son of Amon king of Judah" (1:1), a period spanning from 640 to 609 B.C. Josiah seeks to reverse an escalation of Canaanite baalism and devotion to Mesopotamian astral deities that has occurred within the kingdom over the previous half century. Josiah's devotion to Yahweh leads to two major periods of reform, the first beginning in 628 B.C. (2 Chr 34:3-7) and the second following the discovery of a copy of the Book of the Law within the temple in 622 B.C. (2 Kgs 22:3–23:27; 2 Chr 34:8–35:19). The book of Zephaniah likely reflects the period between these two reform movements (see Zephaniah Introduction: Date).

During this period, Egypt responds to Assyria's troubles in Mesopotamia by attempting to expand its presence into Palestine. In 609 B.C., Egypt joins with Assyria to fight the Babylonians at Haran. Josiah tries to stop this alliance but is defeated on the plain of Megiddo in a battle that costs the king his life (2 Kgs 23:29-30; 2 Chr 35:20-24). The Assyro-Egyptian alliance loses to the Babylonians at Haran and at Carchemish (605 B.C.). Assyria then disappears as a power in the ancient world, Egypt retreats, and Carchemish in northwest Mesopotamia becomes the dividing line between the powers of Egypt and Babylon. With Josiah's death comes Judah's last good chance for lasting repentance and reform. Judah is subjected to a succession of evil kings who lack the leadership skills of Josiah and who reverse his religious reforms. The writer of Kings (2 Kgs 23:34-37), the Chronicler (2 Chr 36:5-8), and Jeremiah (Jer 22:13-19; 26:20-23; 36:1-32) characterize the eleven year reign of Jehoiakim (609–598) as one of injustice and intolerable evil. This period is the likely setting for the book of Habakkuk.

After his victory at Carchemish and the death of his father the king, the Babylonian general Nebuchadnezzar takes control of Babylon. He then seeks to expand Babylonia's control over the lands on the eastern coast of the Mediterranean. Daniel 1:1-3 indicates that the Babylonians besiege Jerusalem around 605 B.C. and carry treasures and captives to Babylon. Daniel is taken as a part of this deportation (Dan 1:1-6). The Babylonians return in 597 B.C. This time they spare the city but carry the young king Jehoiachin, the queen mother, craftsmen and artisans, nobility, young men of ability like Ezekiel, and treasures to Babylon (2 Kgs 24:8-16; 2 Chr 36:9-10). The Babylonians install on the throne a third son of Josiah, Jehoiachin's uncle Mattaniah, whose name is changed to Zedekiah. His reign, characterized by indecision, sedition, and ill-founded reliance upon Egypt for protection from Babylon, ends in a protracted siege following a rebellion by Zedekiah. The Babylonians conquer Jerusalem, destroying the city and the temple in 586 B.C. (2 Kgs 24:18–25:10; 2 Chr 36:11-20).

The Babylonians carry a large number of Judah's inhabitants into exile in keeping with the warnings of preexilic prophets (Isa 39:6-7; Jer 20:4-6; 25:9-11; 27:1-22; Ezek 5:1-12; 6:1-10; 24:22-27; Micah 4:10). Their fortunes change, however, when a coalition of two groups from the Iranian Plateau east of the Tigris River, the Medes and the Persians, supersedes the Babylonian Empire. After Cyrus ascends to the Persian throne in 550 B.C., he overthrows the Median king Astyages and then conquers Lydia (546 B.C.). The Medo-Persians grow in power and territory until Babylon surrenders to Cyrus in 539 B.C.

In the following year, Cyrus issues an edict that emancipates captive peoples living in the Babylonian exile. This policy crafted by Cyrus for dealing with conquered peoples differs greatly from that of earlier Near Eastern empires. By allowing captive peoples to return to their homelands and to rebuild destroyed sanctuaries, Cyrus likely seeks to avoid unnecessary friction with the subjected peoples and to present the new monarchy as the liberator from Babylonian oppression. Second Chronicles 36:23, Ezra 1:2-4, and Ezra 6:2-5 present recollections of the version of the Decree of Cyrus published among the Jewish community. The Persians grant the Jews permission to return to their homeland, to rebuild the temple, to offer sacrifice, and to bring back to Jerusalem the gold and silver articles that the Babylonians had taken during the destruction and sacking of the temple in 586 B.C. The Persians also provide financial assistance from the Persian treasury for these enterprises.

Nevertheless, no Jewish return to Palestine *en masse* occurs, in part, because the exiles have followed Jeremiah's instructions (Jer 28–29) and have become economically established in Babylon. Instead, a small group numbering around fifty thousand makes the

nine-hundred-mile journey back to Jerusalem in 538 B.C. (Ezra 2:1-
66). They begin reconstruction of the temple (Ezra 3:8) in the second year of their return (536 B.C.). Hostility and opposition arise
from the neighboring peoples of the land who misinterpret its construction as an attempt to reconstruct the city's defenses, and the
work ceases shortly thereafter. This political opposition, together
with economic hardships linked to inflation, drought, and crop failure (Hag 1:6,9,11), make the task too daunting for the small community of the return. Work does not recommence for sixteen years.
The prophets Haggai and Zechariah come to the forefront at the
close of this period (520 B.C.) to encourage the people to begin
anew the temple.

Events in the larger Persian Empire during this period of inactivity contribute to an environment conducive for the resumption of
the work. When the successor of Cyrus, Cambyses, dies suddenly
while returning from a campaign in Egypt in 522 B.C., a struggle for
power ensues from which the Persian general Darius arises. The early
years of Darius's reign are marked by outbreaks of resistance and
revolts with which Darius must contend before consolidating power
by his second year (520 B.C.). Darius resumes the benevolent policies
of Cyrus and supports the rebuilding of the temple (Ezra 6:3-12),
probably to establish Judah as a buffer against Egypt at the western
fringe of the empire. Through the encouragement of Haggai and
Zechariah (especially Zechariah 1–8) and under the leadership of
their governor Zerubbabel and high priest Joshua, the Jews complete
the second temple (Ezra 6:15) in the sixth year of Darius (516 B.C.),
some three-and-a-half years after they begin building again.

At the close of Darius's reign, the Greeks have begun to instigate
rebellion on the western fringe of the Persian Empire. The rout of
Persia in the battle of Marathon (490 B.C.) leads the Persians to take
aggressive actions to preempt rebellion in the west. The escalation
in international turmoil, the multiplication of military garrisons in
Palestine, and the precarious political situation of postexilic Israel in
the closing years of Darius and early years of his son Xerxes (called
by his Hebrew name Ahasuerus in some English translations) provide a plausible backdrop for the latter half of Zechariah (chs. 9–14).

Xerxes' early military successes against the Greeks are reversed
in a monumental naval battle at Salamis. Continued losses to the

Greeks bring to an end all hopes for a western expansion of the
Persian Empire. Artaxerxes I (Longimanus) succeeds Xerxes in 465
B.C. The Persians' grip on their empire continues to loosen through
his reign, while the Greeks support various rebellions. A desire to
ensure loyalty from local leaders in case of a border war may explain
the emperor's support of the ministries of Ezra (Ezra 7:6-9,21-26;
458 B.C.) and Nehemiah (Neh 1:1,11; 2:5; 5:14; 445 B.C.).[4] A rapid
succession of emperors after the death of Artaxerxes I (424 B.C.)
culminates in Alexander the Great conquering the weakened state
and control of the region passing into Greek hands by 330 B.C.

The prophet Malachi addresses a decline in the spiritual state of
Israel during this era that matches the decline of the Persian Empire
outside the borders of Israel. Since the presence of the rebuilt temple in Jerusalem does not bring about a new, autonomous, and prosperous Jewish kingdom ruled by the Davidic house, religious fervor
begins to decline in the community. The laxity of the priests in fulfilling their duties (Mal 1:8-13) as well as the community's neglect in
paying the tithe (Mal 3:8-10) evidence a waning spiritual fervor.
Diminished commitment to Yahweh and the law is exacerbated
when those Hebrews emigrating to Palestine encounter non-Hebrew
residents in the land (Ezra 10:2; Neh 13:3,23; Mal 3:5) and strict obedience to the law comes into conflict with movements toward assimilation with Gentile culture.

---

[4]Jon L. Berquist, *Judaism in Persia's Shadow: A Social and Historical Approach* (Philadelphia: Fortress, 1995), p. 26.

# SELECTED BIBLIOGRAPHY

Achtemeier, Elizabeth. *Nahum–Malachi*. Interpretation: A Bible Commentary for Teaching and Preaching. Atlanta: John Knox, 1986.

_____ . *Preaching from the Minor Prophets: Texts and Sermon Suggestions*. Grand Rapids: Eerdmans, 1998.

Bentzen, Aage. *Introduction to the Old Testament*. 2 vols. Copenhagen: Gad, 1948–1949.

Boadt, Lawrence. *Reading the Old Testament: An Introduction*. New York: Paulist, 1984.

Bruce, F.F. *New Testament Development of Old Testament Themes*. Grand Rapids: Eerdmans, 1968.

Calvin, John. *Habakkuk–Malachi*. Vol. 15. *Calvin's Commentaries*. Trans. by John Owen. Grand Rapids: Baker, 1984.

Childs, Brevard S. *Introduction to the Old Testament as Scripture*. Philadelphia: Fortress, 1979.

Chisholm, Robert B., Jr. *Interpreting the Minor Prophets*. Grand Rapids: Zondervan, 1990.

Cohen, A. *The Twelve Prophets*. 2nd ed. Rev. by A.J. Rosenberg. Soncino Books of the Bible. New York: Soncino, 1994.

Dillard, Raymond B., and Tremper Longman, III. *An Introduction to the Old Testament*. Grand Rapids: Zondervan, 1994.

Dorsey, David A. *The Literary Structure of the Old Testament: A Commentary on Genesis–Malachi*. Grand Rapids: Baker, 1999.

Duguid, I.M. *Ezekiel and the Leaders of Israel*. VTSupp 56. Leiden: Brill, 1994.

Dumbrell, William J. *The Faith of Israel: Its Expression in the Books of the Old Testament*. Grand Rapids: Baker, 1988.

Eissfeldt, Otto. *The Old Testament: An Introduction*. Trans. by Peter R. Ackroyd. New York: Harper & Row, 1965.

Ferreiro, Alberto, ed. *The Twelve Prophets*. ACCS. Downers Grove, IL: InterVarsity, 2003.

Floyd, Michael H. "The מַשָּׂא (*maśśā'*) as a Type of Prophetic Book." *JBL* 121 (2002): 401-422.

──────── . *Minor Prophets: Part 2*. Forms of Old Testament Literature 22. Grand Rapids: Eerdmans, 2000.

Gaebelein, Frank E., ed. *Daniel – Minor Prophets*. In *Expositor's Bible Commentary*. 12 vols. Grand Rapids: Zondervan, 1985.

Gottwald, Norman K. *The Hebrew Bible: A Socio-Literary Introduction*. Philadelphia: Fortress, 1985.

Harrison, R.K. *Introduction to the Old Testament*. Grand Rapids: Eerdmans, 1969.

Hill, Andrew E., and John H. Walton. *A Survey of the Old Testament*. Grand Rapids: Zondervan, 1991.

House, Paul R. *Old Testament Theology*. Downers Grove, IL: InterVarsity, 1998.

──────── . *The Unity of the Twelve*. JSOTSupp 97. BLS 27. Sheffield: Almond Press, 1990.

Kaiser, Walter C., Jr. *The Messiah in the Old Testament*. Studies in Old Testament Biblical Theology. Grand Rapids: Zondervan, 1995.

Keil, C.F. *Minor Prophets*. Vol. 10 of *Biblical Commentary on the Old Testament*. By C.F. Keil and R. Delitzsch. Trans. by James Martin. Reprint, Grand Rapids: Eerdmans, 1988.

McComiskey, Thomas Edward, ed. *The Minor Prophets: An Exegetical and Expository Commentary*. 3 vols. Grand Rapids: Baker, 1993.

McConville, Gordon. *A Guide to the Prophets*. Vol. 4, *Exploring the Old Testament*. Downers Grove, IL: InterVarsity, 2002.

Newsome, James D., Jr. *The Hebrew Prophets*. Atlanta: John Knox, 1984.

Sandy, D. Brent. *Plowshares & Pruning Hooks: Rethinking the Language of Biblical Prophecy and Apocalyptic*. Downers Grove, IL: InterVarsity, 2002.

Smith, James E. *The Minor Prophets*. Old Testament Survey Series. Joplin, MO: College Press, 1996.

Smith, Ralph L. *Micah–Malachi*. WBC 32. Waco: Word, 1984.

Soggin, J. Alberto. *Introduction to the Old Testament: From Its Origins to the Closing of the Alexandrian Canon.* Trans. by John Bowden. Rev. ed. Philadelphia: Westminster, 1980.

Sweeney, Marvin A. *The Twelve Prophets.* BerOl: Studies in Hebrew Narrative and Poetry. Collegeville, MN: Liturgical Press, 2000.

# THE BOOK OF
# NAHUM

# INTRODUCTION

## AUTHORSHIP

The prophet's name derives from a Hebrew word meaning "comfort," "consolation," or "compassion." Prominent biblical names related to the same root are Noah and Nehemiah. The prophet's name (נַחוּם, *naḥûm*) and the word, translated "avenging" (נָקַם, *nāqam*) in Nahum 1:2, sound alike. The plausibility of such an intended wordplay may be further demonstrated by the similar sound of the prophet's hometown Elkosh (אֶלְקֹשׁ, *'elqōš*) and the divine epithet "avenging God" (אֵל קַנּוֹא, *'ēl qānô'*) also in 1:2.[1] Nahum's name matches the intent of the book's message as the prophet's words bring comfort to Judah and, more specifically, to those loyal to Yahweh within Judah.

Next to nothing is known about the prophet. Some have suggested that Nahum is a cult prophet, that is, a prophet whose ministry is linked to the temple festivals, rituals, and sacrifices.[2] Such a designation, however, denigrates the prophet since it suggests that he functions simply to support the status quo of the temple authorities. Generally, three reasons are offered in support of this supposition: the call to Judah to keep her festivals and vows (1:15), the appearance of an alleged acrostic psalm in chapter 1, and the lack of judgment speeches against Israel and Judah. This view of Nahum as a cult prophet fails at each of the previously mentioned lines of evidence. First, while the command to keep festivals and vows and the

---

[1]Tremper Longman III, "Nahum," in *The Minor Prophets: An Exegetical and Expository Commentary* (Grand Rapids: Baker, 1993), 2:766.

[2]E.g., Otto Eissfeldt, *The Old Testament: An Introduction*, trans. by Peter R. Ackroyd (New York: Harper & Row, 1965), p. 415; contra Brevard S. Childs, *Introduction to the Old Testament as Scripture* (Philadelphia: Fortress, 1979), pp. 441-442.

implied freedom to do so would pertain to those associated with the temple, such concerns would also resonate with others in Judean society. Second, the opening passage of the book does not likely constitute an acrostic psalm (see comments on chapter 1). Even if it does, its existence would not necessitate a cultic (i.e., a temple or worship) setting for the book; biblical acrostics also arise in prophetic (Lamentations 1–4) and wisdom (Psalms 37; 112; Prov 31:10-31) circles. Finally, it is erroneous to insist that true prophets of the pre-exilic period would speak only messages of judgment against Israel and Judah.[3] Moreover, the announcements of salvation in Nahum 1:12 and 2:2 imply a previous judgment on Judah's sin.

Nahum is identified as an Elkoshite (1:1), but no firm evidence exists for the site of the city of Elkosh. Four major proposals have been advanced. One, Jerome (ca. A.D. 450) places it in Galilee in the territory of the former northern kingdom at a site called El-Kauzeh or Elkesi. Two, a possible etymology of "Kepher Nahum" or "Nahum's city" suggests the identification of Elkosh with the New Testament town of Capernaum on the northern shore of the Sea of Galilee. Yet, two factors challenge both of these identifications. The northern kingdom has already fallen to the Assyrians by the time of the prophet (see comments on the date below), and the affirmation in Jesus' day that "a prophet does not come out of Galilee" (John 7:52) contradicts a northern location.

Three, an eastern medieval tradition identifies Elkosh as an Assyrian city located on the site of the Iraqi town al-Kush, some fifty miles north of modern-day Mosul on the Tigris River opposite the ruins of Nineveh. This tradition holds that Nahum descended from northern Israelites who had been carried captive to Assyria and that he wrote the book in Assyria to be sent to Judah.[4] Nestorius, the Patriarch of Constantinople from A.D. 428–431, mentions an alleged tomb of Nahum at this site as does an Islamic tradition dating from the sixteenth century. Benjamin of Tudela (twelfth century A.D.) locates the tomb of Nahum in Mesopotamia, but he claims to have seen the tomb of Nahum south of Babylon rather than in the former Assyrian territory. Favoring an Assyrian location for Elkosh is also

---

[3]Marvin A. Sweeney, *The Twelve Prophets*, BerOl (Collegeville, MN: Liturgical Press, 2000), 2:420.

[4]Longman, *Nahum*, p. 765.

the author's apparent acquaintance with various aspects of Nineveh, including the temples of Nineveh (1:14), her walls (2:5), and river gates (2:6). Nahum alludes to Nineveh's army and its battle tactics (2:3-5; 3:2-3) and is conversant with the city's wealth (2:9; 3:16) and her wickedness (1:11; 2:12). Although an Assyrian location is possible, it is far from certain. The aspects of Nineveh's geography and Assyrian military methods alluded to in the text would have been general knowledge in the prophet's era and do not prove a Mesopotamian provenance or location for Elkosh.[5] Although long-standing, the tradition of the Assyrian location does not extend back into the Old Testament period. Its basis may be less in fact than in the similarity in sound between Elkosh and al-Kush and the prominent role of Assyria within the book's contents.

Four, the strongest proposal locates Elkosh in Judah. A first-century A.D. pseudepigraphal collection of folk stories and legends about prophetic characters, "The Lives of the Prophets," locates the town in Judah near modern Beit Jibrin about twenty miles southwest of Jerusalem.[6] Three main reasons support this proposal. First, names of towns in Judah such as Eltekon and Eltolad (Josh 15:30,59) are somewhat parallel to the name Elkosh. Second, Elkosh may contain the name of the Edomite god Qaush, which also appears in the names of Edomite kings of the era. Moreover, the geographic proximity of Judah to Edom makes the incorporation of Qaush into place names more likely in Judah than in the northern kingdom or Assyria. Third, the text addresses Judah in Nahum 1:15 and seeks to encourage the southern kingdom.

## HISTORICAL BACKGROUND

The anticipated fall of the Assyrian capital Nineveh is the centering event of the book and therefore necessitates a survey of the Assyrian dealings with the biblical world preceding its demise. During the early ninth century, Ashurnasirpal II (884–859 B.C.)

---

[5]Richard D. Patterson, *Nahum, Habakkuk, Zephaniah*, WEC (Chicago: Moody, 1991), p. 7.

[6]Raymond B. Dillard and Tremper Longman III, *An Introduction to the Old Testament* (Grand Rapids: Zondervan, 1994), p. 404.

extended Assyrian rule from its homeland in northwest Mesopotamia to the north and east. His son, Shalmaneser III (858–824 B.C.), then conducted numerous campaigns into lands west of the Euphrates River. On one of these, he forced Jehu, king of the northern kingdom of Israel (841–814 B.C.), to pay tribute. Later, Adad-nirari III (810–782 B.C.) claimed Israel as one of his western vassals. The military successes of Assyria often were accompanied by the brutalization of those they conquered, perhaps to foster terror and thus submission among those whom they ruled.

Nevertheless, the sway of Assyria over the region subsided as civil war led to a three-quarter's century eclipse of Assyrian power. During this period Jeroboam II (793–753 B.C.) restored Israel to political and military prominence in the region (2 Kgs 14:23-29), and the preaching of Jonah prompted a repentance in Nineveh that led to Yahweh sparing the city (Jonah 1–4). Tiglath-Pileser III (745–727 B.C.), also known as Pul (cf. 1 Chr 5:26), however, reasserted the power of the throne over that of court nobles and launched an effort to reestablish Assyria as a world empire. He subjected Israel to tribute during the reign of Menahem (752–742 B.C.; cf. 2 Kgs 15:17-20) and took large amounts of the northern kingdom's territory in the days of Pekah (752–732 B.C.; 2 Kgs 15:29). Assyrian authority soon extended over Judah when its king, Ahaz, asked Pul for protection from Aram and Israel (ca. 734–732 B.C.; cf. 2 Kings 16).

The Assyrians were a constant threat to Israel and Judah over the next three decades. Samaria fell to Shalmaneser V in 722/721 B.C., and a later attempt by Hezekiah in Judah to reverse the pro-Assyrian policies of his father Ahaz elicited a fierce retaliation by Sennacherib (704–681 B.C.) in 701 B.C. Only a miraculous delivery by Yahweh rescued Judah (2 Kings 18–19; 2 Chronicles 32; Isaiah 36–37). The same Sennacherib with whom Hezekiah dealt had razed Babylon after putting down a rebellion there. He also made Nineveh the centerpiece of the Assyrian empire. He nearly tripled the size of the city and made it his capital, constructing a magnificent palace there and beautifying the city with parks, a botanical garden, and a zoo.[7]

The following century saw both Assyria's zenith and decline. Esarhaddon (681–669 B.C.) rebuilt Babylon, firmed up control in the

---

[7]Andrew E. Hill and John H. Walton, *A Survey of the Old Testament* (Grand Rapids: Zondervan, 1991), p. 397.

west, and extended Assyrian influence into Egypt. During his reign, Manasseh of Judah attempted a failed rebellion (ca. 652–648 B.C.; cf. 2 Chr 33:10-13). Esarhaddon's son Ashurbanipal (669–627 B.C.) then brought Assyrian power and culture to a climax in 663 B.C. by his capture of Egypt's ancient capital No Amon, also known as Thebes. Nevertheless, decline began in 652 B.C. as Samash-shum-ukin, who had been appointed king of Babylon by Esarhaddon, rebelled against his brother Ashurbanipal. Although Ashurbanipal was eventually victorious, the conflict drained the empire's resources, and increased weakness characterized the latter years of Ashurbanipal's reign. During this time Josiah of Judah (640–609 B.C.) enacted religious and political reforms in Judah (2 Kings 22–23; 2 Chronicles 34–35) that effectively repudiated Assyrian control.

The Babylonians eventually allied themselves with the Medes, and, in 626 B.C., Nabopolassar renewed the Babylonian revolt that culminated in the destruction of the old Assyrian capital of Asshur in 614 and then Nineveh in 612. The ancient historians Diodorus of Siculus and Xenophon relate that Nineveh fell when the waters of the Tigris were diverted, flooding the city, though Diodorus (*Bibl. Hist.*, 2.27.1) mistakenly identifies the river as the Euphrates. Some ambiguity exists in the Babylonian sources, but it appears that the Medes actually destroyed the city. Babylonian documents suggest the Babylonians were careful to distance themselves from the general looting of the city and its temples, but later took possession of the city when the Medes grew either uninterested or unable to keep it for a permanent possession.[8]

# DATE

Nahum ministered and wrote against the backdrop described above, and internal evidence within the text establishes the limits between which one must date the book. The allusion to the destruction of Thebes indicates a date after 663 B.C., and the anticipation of Nineveh's destruction points to a time before 612 B.C. Thus, the book falls somewhere in the reign of Manasseh (697–642 B.C.) or of

---

[8]Dillard and Longman, *Introduction*, p. 405.

Josiah (640–609 B.C.).[9] Two lines of evidence may support a date in the reign of Josiah. One, the decline of Assyria in the latter years of Ashurbanipal and after his death (627 B.C.) would provide a plausible setting for the book's vibrant anticipation of Assyria's demise. Two, the call for Judah to celebrate her festivals (Nahum 1:15) may anticipate the observance of Passover during the Josianic reforms (2 Kgs 23:21-23). These factors, however, do not preclude an earlier date. The Babylonian rebellion of 652 had already demonstrated weakness in the empire and had kindled hopes among its subjugated peoples. Moreover, the call for Judah to observe her festivals would have held importance during any period of Assyrian oppression.

An earlier date in the reign of Manasseh accounts for several features in the text. First, the fall of Thebes (Nahum 3:8) occurred in 663 B.C. when Ashurbanipal led Assyria's greatest penetration into Egypt. After 663 B.C., however, the Assyrians had to withdraw from Egypt to attend to problems at home. This withdrawal allowed the formation of the twenty-sixth dynasty in Egypt (655–525 B.C.), and the retaking of Thebes by the Egyptians in 654 B.C. would have significantly lessened the power of Nahum's recollection of its fall to Assyria. Second, Nahum 1:12, 2:13, and 3:1 picture Nineveh as fairly secure, so it is likely the book was penned before Assyria began to show signs of permanent decline. Third, the reassurance that Yahweh would destroy Assyria would have greater impact in the earlier part of the span between 663 and 612 B.C. because Assyrian power over the southern kingdom would have been stronger. Fourth, the book does not specifically identify the enemy who would vanquish the Assyrians (cf. 2:1). Failure to mention the Babylonians and Medes seems out of place if the book were written near 612 B.C., and a time before the Medo-Babylonian alliance had gathered

---

[9]A third hypothesis, offered by those within the critical tradition, discounts the book as a prophetic revelation of the future fall of Nineveh. Instead, they treat the book as a text written after the fall of Nineveh to be used for the first time in a liturgical setting that celebrated Nineveh's fall during the New Year's festival in 612 B.C. This view has two major difficulties, according to R.K. Harrison, *Introduction to the Old Testament* (Grand Rapids: Eerdmans, 1969), p. 929. One, it assumes a New Year's festival for which there is no conclusive evidence; two, the denunciations in Nahum 2:4–3:17 are anticipatory rather than reflective.

strength is implied. Fifth, the promise of Nahum 1:9 that "trouble will not come a second time" may reflect the aftermath of the brief revolt by Manasseh (see comments on 1:9) that occurred sometime between 652 and 648 B.C. in conjunction with the Babylonian insurrection against Ashurbanipal (cf. 2 Chr 33:14-16). Together, the preceding arguments suggest a date for the book somewhere between 663 and 645 B.C.

## LITERARY FEATURES

The title of Nahum (1:1) describes the prophetic work with three words: oracle, book, and vision. The word "oracle" signifies a particular type of prophetic pronouncement, in which the prophet answers doubts about the involvement of Yahweh in a particular historical situation. For Nahum, that circumstance is the oppressive presence of Assyria (1:12-13), which Yahweh will now eradicate (1:14-15). The word "book" may indicate that the contents of Nahum are a literary prophecy rather than an anthology of sermons first given orally. The word "vision" refers to Yahweh as the source of the prophecy and to the prophetic means of certain portions of the book, namely, the visionary reports in 2:3-10 and 3:2-3.

The book consists of two major sections: 1:2-15 and 2:1–3:19. Nahum 1:2-15 focuses on Yahweh who delivers Judah by defeating Nineveh. The passage contains a poem descriptive of Yahweh's justice and power (1:2-3a), a theophany depicting Yahweh's power compared with natural phenomena (1:3b-10), and a proclamation of Yahweh's vindication of Judah from their oppressor, Nineveh (1:11-15). Nahum 2:1–3:19 focuses on the destruction of Nineveh, claiming it as a manifestation of Yahweh's intent and justice. The section contains an announcement of the attack upon Nineveh (2:1-10), a taunt over the fall of Nineveh and its king (2:11-13), an announcement of the punishment against Nineveh (3:1-7), a comparison of Nineveh's vulnerability and destruction to that of Thebes (3:8-13), and a report that Nineveh's destruction has left the city defenseless and defeated (3:14-19).

Nahum contains several prophetic forms or genres. For example, 2:1-10 exhibits the form of a prophetic sentinel report, in which the prophet functions like a sentry announcing the approach of an enemy and urging preparations for battle. Nahum 2:11-13 ironically contrasts the impending devastation of Nineveh with its previous power using a lion motif. This unit may be identified as a taunt, that is, a sarcastic challenge against one Yahweh opposes. Nahum 3:1-7 exhibits the form of a prophecy of punishment against a foreign nation and contains the two major features of a prophecy of punishment: accusation (3:1-4) and announcement (3:5-7).

Prominent among Nahum's themes or motifs is that Yahweh is an avenging God who judges the ungodly. For Nahum, the application of this theme regards Nineveh and its complete destruction by fire (1:6,10; 2:3-4,13; 3:13,15) and by flood (1:8; 2:6,8). Such devastation encompasses the Assyrian military (1:12,14-15; 2:1,3-5,13; 3:2-3,8-11,12-15,19), the Assyrian monarch (1:14; 2:6,11-13; 3:18-19), the city itself (1:8-11,14; 2:1,5-10; 3:1-3,7-17), and the city's population (1:8; 2:1,7-8; 3:7,11-18). Nonetheless, the destruction of Nineveh also brings vindication for Judah (1:3,7,12-13,15; 2:2).

Notable images in Nahum include the lion (2:11-13), the harlot (3:4-6), and the locust (3:15-17). The lion imagery reverses one of the favorite metaphors the Assyrians use to portray themselves; they no longer prey on others, but they are prey themselves. The harlot imagery depicts Assyria's destruction with punishment appropriate for the public humiliation of prostitution. The locust imagery portrays Assyria's complete devastation from enemy invasion and the desertion of the Assyrian nobility before the city's fall. Certain images are associated with the theophany in 1:3-8, namely, storm, drought, earthquake, flood, and darkness. Some of the book's images are auditory, the crack of whips and the clatter of wheels (3:2); others, visual, such as charging cavalry, flashing swords, and glittering spears (3:3). Still other images describe physical responses to the destruction of Nineveh, namely, hearts melt, knees give way, bodies tremble, and faces grow pale (2:10); these connote loss of courage, inability to escape, and tremendous terror. The completeness and inevitability of Nineveh's destruction is portrayed with images of entanglement, intoxication, and consumption (1:10) and with images of a staggering drunk, a hiding fugitive, a shaken fig tree, defenseless women, and a city with wide open gates (3:11-13).

Various rhetorical features are also evidenced in Nahum, a work that may be unequaled in this regard among the Minor Prophets.

The book begins with the threefold repetition of the statement, "avenging is Yahweh" (1:2-3). Wordplays link sections together. For example, the phrases "make an end" and "bring to an end" link the theophany of 1:3-8 with the following verses (cf. the words "victims" and "prey" which link 2:11-13 with 3:1-3). Wordplays also mark the beginning and ending of sections. For example, the words "evil" and "wicked" (actually the same Hebrew word) mark the limits of 1:11-15. Similar sounding words, "ravaged, wrecked, ruined" (NJB), appear in 2:10. The prophet directly addresses Nineveh (1:11-12,14; 2:1,5-8; 3:13-17), Judah (1:15), and the king of Assyria (3:18-19). The prophet also speaks commands as if directed to the people of Nineveh; yet, these instructions are rightly understood as ironic in nature (2:1; 3:14-15). Three times the first person singular (1:12-14; 2:13; 3:5-7) emphasizes the involvement of Yahweh. Once is used the messenger formula, "this is what the Lord says" (1:12); twice, the oath formula, "declares the Lord Almighty" (2:13; 3:5). Several rhetorical questions (1:6; 2:11; 3:8,19) punctuate the work. These questions invite the reader to consider Yahweh's power and justice and to reconsider Nineveh's illusion of invincibility, and the last one exposes the cruelty of Nineveh.

## THEOLOGY

The English name of the book and prophet follows the Vulgate (the Latin Bible authorized by the Roman Catholic Church at the Council of Trent held from A.D. 1545 to 1563) that translates the LXX title, Ναούμ (*Naoum*). Nahum is the seventh book in the Masoretic version of the Book of the Twelve (also called the Minor Prophets). Though it follows Jonah in the LXX, Nahum follows Micah in the MT (the traditional text of the Hebrew Bible), Peshitta (the Syriac translation of the Bible written around the fourth century A.D.), and Vulgate. The Micah–Nahum sequence in the MT bolsters Micah's presentation of Yahweh's plans to restore Judah and Jerusalem as a dominant force at the center of the nations following a time of punishment. Nahum comforts Judah with a pronouncement of Assyria's ultimate downfall, and this downfall begins a series of historical events through which Yahweh works out the divine purpose. The following books of Habakkuk, Zephaniah, Haggai, Zechariah, and Malachi portray future stages in the rest of the process.[10]

Major themes in Nahum connect the book with themes in all three divisions of the Hebrew Old Testament: *Torah* (Law), *Nevi'im* (Prophets), and *Kethuvim* (Writings). The portrayal of Yahweh that leads to judgment on Nineveh reflects earlier portrayals of Yahweh in the *Torah*, especially in Exodus. Nahum 1:2 replicates the second commandment in describing Yahweh as a "jealous God" (Exod 20:5). The second and third commandments go on to describe this jealous God as one who punishes sin yet shows love to those loyal to Yahweh, and one who does not hold guiltless those who misuse the divine name (Exod 20:5-6). This characterization, in turn, forms the foundation for Nahum's description of Yahweh as one who "takes vengeance on his foes and maintains his wrath against his enemies" (Nahum 1:2) but who also is "a refuge in times of trouble" and who "cares for those who trust in him" (Nahum 1:7).

Nahum plays a vital role within the *Nevi'im* by announcing that earlier pledges of punishment against Assyria and of deliverance from her (Isa 10:12; 11:11-16; 27:13; 30:31; 31:8; 52:3-8; Hos 11:11; Micah 5:6) are about to transpire. If Yahweh is faithful in these promises, then one can also trust Yahweh to bring about the Davidic promises and the promises of Yahweh's eternal reign over a re-created creation.[11]

The books of Jonah and Nahum are inherently linked by their mutual focus on Nineveh. The connections, however, go beyond that. Like the book of Jonah, Nahum ends with a rhetorical question. This surely is a conscious contrast (cf. Nahum 3:19; Jonah 4:11).[12] Yahweh had earlier shown concern for the repentant generation of Nineveh; now Yahweh will demonstrate concern for those whom later generations of Nineveh have brutalized.

Several theological and thematic similarities may be identified between Nahum and the earlier work of Isaiah.[13] Particularly striking

---

[10]Sweeney, *The Twelve Prophets*, pp. 420-421.

[11]Paul R. House, *Old Testament Theology* (Downers Grove, IL: InterVarsity, 1998), p. 373.

[12]Dillard and Longman, *Introduction*, p. 407.

[13]Carl Armerding, "Nahum," in *Expositor's Bible Commentary* (Grand Rapids: Zondervan, 1985), 7:453-456. Unitary authorship of Isaiah in the late eighth and early seventh century is here assumed. For discussion of the

is a sequence of parallels between Nahum 1:12-15 and Isaiah 51:21–52:7. Judah is Yahweh's "afflicted one" (Nahum 1:12; Isa 51:21) whom Yahweh will now defend and whose fortunes Yahweh will now reverse (Nahum 1:13; Isa 51:22). The wicked will no longer invade Judah (Nahum 1:15; Isa 52:1); therefore she can celebrate (Nahum 1:15; Isa 52:1). These sections then both end with the unique phrase "on the mountains, the feet of one who brings good news, who proclaims peace" (Nahum 1:15; Isa 52:7). These parallels between Nahum and an Isaianic text that precedes a messianic text (Isa 52:13–53:12) may indicate that Nahum understands the fall of the Assyrian empire to be part of Yahweh's greater messianic purposes.[14]

Another motif shared by Nahum and Isaiah is the theme of Yahweh's anger. Although a common theme throughout the Old Testament, these books connect it to Assyria and depict it using fire and other natural imagery.[15] Nahum's announcement of the coming wrath on Assyria expands Isaiah's earlier promise that after Yahweh has used her to punish Judah, Yahweh will punish Assyria for her arrogance (Isa 10:5-27).

Nahum's treatment of Nineveh links with the *Kethuvim* when it mirrors the frequent calls for the destruction of the wicked found in the Psalms (Ps 5:4-6; 58:6-11; 109:1-31; 137:7-9). Like the psalmists, Nahum shares Yahweh's hatred of sin and longs to see Yahweh and the people belonging to Yahweh vindicated. He acknowledges that Yahweh is righteous and will, according to the divine plan, work vengeance upon wicked foes. In the end, those who trust in Yahweh will be vindicated. They must wait as Yahweh works the divine purposes.[16] The opening stanza of Nahum (1:2-8) is reminiscent of hymns of victory in the Psalter (Psalms 68, 97, 98, 114, 124, 125) as it celebrates the mighty God who will avenge evil.[17]

The connections between Nahum and the New Testament are less overt. Paul provides the closest thing to a New Testament quotation or allusion to the book in Romans 10:15. But there the apostle is probably quoting Isaiah 52:7 rather than Nahum 1:15, a text

issues of authorship and date of Isaiah, see Dillard and Longman, *Introduction*, pp. 268-275.

[14]Patterson, *Nahum, Habakkuk, Zephaniah*, p. 15.

[15]Armerding, *Nahum*, 7:455.

[16]Patterson, *Nahum*, pp. 15-16.

[17]Longman, *Nahum*, 2:769.

which itself reflects Isaiah. Nevertheless, Nahum's image of Yahweh as the divine warrior (Nahum 1:2-8; 2:13) anticipates the New Testament's depiction of Jesus Christ coming as a conquering king who judges the wicked and rescues his people (1 Cor 15:24-27; Col 2:15; 2 Thess 1:6-10; Rev 11:15-19; 17:14; 19:11-16).[18]

# MESSAGE

The most apparent message of the book is that the days of Assyrian rule will soon end at Yahweh's hands. This event will be neither an accident of history nor the result of a natural course of events. Yahweh is actively moving against Nineveh to punish her (Nahum 2:13; 3:5). The sovereign God who directs history and commands all armies has announced Nineveh's doom. The prophet announces the fall of the city even before the event has occurred, and the messengers are already on their way to bring the glad tidings of Nineveh's fall (1:15). The twice-used affirmation "I am against you" (2:13; 3:5) focuses on Yahweh as the one who brings judgment upon Nineveh as does the absence of a mention of a human enemy. The prophet does not name the Babylonians and the Medes as the eventual conquerors of Assyria. Instead, Nahum 2:1 announces only that "an attacker" is advancing against Nineveh and its king. The two sets of Yahweh speeches that surround this announcement make it clear that ultimately the attacker is Yahweh; the later Medo-Babylonian coalition is only Yahweh's instrument.

The imminent actions of Yahweh against Nineveh will be more than acts of justice; they will constitute acts of deliverance and restoration for Yahweh's people. The promise in Nahum 2:2 that "The LORD will restore the splendor of Jacob like the splendor of Israel" seems, at first, to be an awkward insertion into an ominous description of the coming battle. It acts, however, as a statement of purpose for the judgment of Yahweh against Assyria; through it Yahweh will deliver and restore the people of Yahweh.[19]

The book's message of judgment and salvation is rooted in Yahweh's self-revelation at Sinai as a God of judgment and mercy.

---

[18]Dillard and Longman, *Introduction*, p. 408.
[19]Kevin J. Cathcart, "Nahum: Theology of," *NIDOTTE*, 4:964.

The opening pericope (1:2-6) echoes this affirmation and forms the basis for the remaining verses of the book as well as transforming the historical particularity of Nineveh's destruction into a type of "larger and recurring phenomenon in history in which Yahweh exercises his eternal power and judgment."[20]

Yahweh is sovereign over nature (1:4-6,8) and nations (1:11-12,15; 2:1-2,3-7,8-13; 3:5-19). Yahweh controls history (1:12; 2:13; 3:5-7). Although patient (1:3) and good (1:7), Yahweh judges foes who are guilty of the sin Yahweh abhors (1:2-3,8-10,14; 2:13; 3:5-7,11-19) and rightly judges that sin (3:4-6,19). Yahweh, nevertheless, will save and restore those who trust in Yahweh (1:7-8,12-13,15; 2:2).[21]

Earlier critical biblical scholarship often dismissed Nahum as a nationalistic prophet who condemned Nineveh merely out of hatred and vengeance and who did not call Judah to repentance.[22] Such a judgment inadequately reads the text and insufficiently assesses the reality of evil in the world and the necessity of Yahweh's wrath. While the prophet may not emphasize Judah's sin or call the people to repentance, Nahum 1:12 acknowledges that Yahweh had already used Assyria to punish Judah. An adequate moral judgment on the Assyrians does appear in 3:1 and 3:19, and the nations stand under Yahweh's judgment.[23] The destruction of Nineveh, moreover, is explicitly linked with the nature of Yahweh rather than originating from the author's personal hatred of the Assyrians.[24] The joy of those who have suffered under the hands of Assyria (3:19) reveals the wickedness of Nineveh rather than any faulty attitudes within the oppressed peoples. One could no more expect them to mourn over Nineveh's fall than one could regret the fall of a Hitler, Stalin, or Idi Amin.[25] The book reminds the reader that the God of Israel is just, and evil will not have the final word.

---

[20]Childs, *Introduction*, p. 444.

[21]Patterson, *Nahum*, pp. 14-15.

[22]See, for example, Artur Weiser, *The Old Testament: Its Formation and Development* (New York: Association Press, 1961), p. 258.

[23]Norman K. Gottwald, *The Hebrew Bible: A Socio-Literary Introduction* (Philadelphia: Fortress, 1985), pp. 391-392.

[24]Childs, *Introduction*, p. 443.

[25]House, *Old Testament Theology*, p. 375.

# OUTLINE

# SELECTED BIBLIOGRAPHY ON NAHUM

Armerding, Carl. "Nahum." In *Expositor's Bible Commentary*, vol. 7. Ed. by Frank E. Gaebelein. Grand Rapids: Zondervan, 1985.

Ausín, Santiago. "Nahum." In *The International Bible Commentary: A Catholic and Ecumenical Commentary for the Twenty-First Century*. Ed. by William R. Farmer. Collegeville, MN: Liturgical Press, 1998.

Baker, David W. *Nahum, Habakkuk, Zephaniah: An Introduction and Commentary*. TOTC 23b. Downers Grove, IL: InterVarsity, 1988.

Barker, Kenneth L., and Waylon Bailey. *Micah, Nahum, Habakkuk, Zephaniah*. NAC. Nashville: Broadman & Holman, 1999.

Bruckner, James. *Jonah, Nahum, Habakkuk, Zephaniah*. The NIV Application Commentary. Grand Rapids: Zondervan, 2004.

Cathcart, Kevin J. "Treaty-Curses and the Book of Nahum." *CBQ* 35 (1973): 179-187.

Charles, J. Daryl. "Plundering the Lion's Den—A Portrait of Divine Fury (Nahum 2:3-11)." *GTJ* 10 (1989): 183-201.

Coggins, Richard J., and S. Paul Re'emi. *Israel among the Nations: A Commentary on the Books of Nahum, Obadiah, and Esther*. ITC. Grand Rapids: Eerdmans, 1985.

Longman, Tremper, III. "The Form and Message of Nahum: Preaching from a Prophet of Doom." *RTJ* 1 (1985): 13-24.

_____ . "Nahum." In *The Minor Prophets: An Exegetical and Expository Commentary*, vol. 2. Ed. by Thomas Edward McComiskey. Grand Rapids: Baker, 1993.

Patterson, Richard D. *Nahum, Habakkuk, Zephaniah*. WEC. Chicago: Moody, 1991.

Roberts, J.J.M. *Nahum, Habakkuk, and Zephaniah: A Commentary.* OTL. Louisville, KY: Westminster John Knox, 1991.

Robertson, O. Palmer. *The Books of Nahum, Habakkuk, and Zephaniah.* NICOT. Grand Rapids: Eerdmans, 1994.

Wiseman, D.J. "'Is It Peace?' Covenant and Diplomacy." *VT* 32 (1982): 311-326.

# NAHUM

## I. TITLE (1:1)

¹**An oracle concerning Nineveh. The book of the vision of Nahum the Elkoshite.**

**1:1** The title of the book of Nahum is unusual. It lacks a phrase that is typically found among the opening words of a prophetic book: "the word of the LORD" (Jer 1:2; Ezek 1:3; Hos 1:1; Joel 1:1; Jonah 1:1; Micah 1:1; Zeph 1:1; Hag 1:1; Zech 1:1; Mal. 1:1). It also lacks the naming of a king, either Hebrew or foreign, who is contemporary with the prophet (see Isa 1:1; Jer 1:2-3; Hos 1:1; Amos 1:1; Micah 1:1; Zeph 1:1; Hag 1:1; Zech 1:1). Instead, Nahum 1:1 begins with three descriptions of the work: oracle, book, and vision.

The word **oracle** (מַשָּׂא, *maśśā'*) occurs eighteen times in the prophetic books (the word is translated "prophecy" in the TNIV). It stands at the beginning of individual speeches (e.g., Isa 13:1; 14:28; 15:1; 17:1; 19:1; 21:1; 22:1; 23:1; 30:6; Ezek 12:10; Zech 9:1; 12:1) and entire books (Hab 1:1; Mal 1:1). It can address a specific nation, city, people, or historical circumstance. Generally *maśśā'* indicates a particular type of prophetic pronouncement.[1] The oracle answers those in the Israelite community who may doubt or wonder about Yahweh's intended action in a particular historical situation. Specifically, an oracle asserts Yahweh's involvement in the historical situation, clarifies any previous prophecy about the situation, and provides a basis for an appropriate response. For Nahum the topic of the oracle is the fall of Nineveh, and the oracle addresses both the community of the faithful (Judah) and the object of divine action (Nineveh). While Nineveh has been allowed to punish Judah (1:12-

---

[1]Richard D. Weis, "Oracle," *ABD*, 5:28-29; Michael H. Floyd, "The מַשָּׂא (*maśśā'*) as a Type of Prophetic Book," *JBL* 121 (2002): 401-422.

13; cf. Isa 10:5-11), Yahweh will now act in accordance with the earlier command about Nineveh (1:14) and destroy Nineveh's power (cf. Isa 10:12-19). For this divine judgment against Nineveh, Judah should rejoice (1:15).

The oracle is preserved as a **book** (סֵפֶר, *sēpher*). Although the usual meaning of *sēpher* is "book" (Neh 8:1; Esth 2:23; Ps 69:28), it can refer to scrolls (Isa 29:11-12; Jer 36:2-8; Dan 12:1-4; Mal 3:16), letters (Isa 37:14; Jer 29:1), deeds (Jer 32:10-16), certificates (Jer 3:8), other writings (Dan 1:4,17), or even Scripture (Dan 9:2). Applied to Nahum, "book" is an unusual designation and may indicate that the contents are a literary prophecy that was not first given by oral proclamation. The word may also emphasize the certainty of the fulfillment of the oracle against Nineveh (cf. the use of "book" in Jer 30:2 and "scroll" in Jer 36:2,4,8,10,11,13,18, and 32).

The basis of the answer Nahum receives about Nineveh is his **vision** (חָזוֹן, *ḥāzôn*). In the prophetic literature, the term *ḥāzôn* has both a broad and a narrow sense. It could refer to the totality of revelation received by and communicated by the prophet (Isa 1:1; Obad 1:1), or it could refer to a more specific means of prophetic revelation (Isa 29:7; Dan 8:1). The latter, more restricted sense is represented by Nahum 2:3-10 and 3:2-3, and these passages may be the reason why the word *ḥāzôn* appears in the title. By calling his prophecy a vision, Nahum underscores that his words are not merely his invention; they have their source in Yahweh rather than in his observations (cf. Num 24:4,16; 2 Chr 32:32; Isa 2:1).

The title also identifies the oracle's topic, **Nineveh**, and the oracle's prophet, **Nahum**. The mention of Nineveh in the superscription is significant because without it one would not know against whom the judgment is directed until 2:8, the otherwise first explicit mention of Nineveh in the Hebrew text (see the commentary below on the NIV's reading "Nineveh" in 1:8,11,14; 2:1). The final phrase of the title identifies the writer as **Nahum the Elkoshite**. Amos, Micah, and Jeremiah are the other prophets identified by their hometown. The name "Nahum" means "comfort" and may be an abbreviated form of "Nehemiah," which means "the LORD is my consolation." Nahum's message brings comfort to Judah but not to Nineveh (cf. 3:7). Nahum's hometown is Elkosh, whose exact location is unknown (see Introduction above).

## II. NINEVEH'S JUDGE (1:2-15)

Nahum 1:2-15 focuses on Yahweh who delivers Judah by defeating Nineveh. The passage contains a poem descriptive of Yahweh's justice and power (1:2-3a), a theophany depicting Yahweh's power compared with natural phenomena (1:3b-10), and a proclamation of Yahweh's vindication of Judah from their oppressor, Nineveh (1:11-15). The section presents a theological description of Yahweh, drawing on language from Exodus and images of Yahweh as warrior, and poses a kind of prophetic confrontation. Based on the implications of Yahweh's nature, the readers are asked to remember that opposing Yahweh is futile, to reconsider what constitutes an enemy of Yahweh, to reaffirm their trust in Yahweh, and to rejoice at the defeat of Nineveh.

### A. THE LORD'S VENGEANCE ON ENEMIES (1:2-10)

[2]The LORD is a jealous and avenging God; / the LORD takes vengeance and is filled with wrath. / The LORD takes vengeance on his foes / and maintains his wrath against his enemies. / [3]The LORD is slow to anger and great in power; / the LORD will not leave the guilty unpunished. / His way is in the whirlwind and the storm, / and clouds are the dust of his feet. / [4]He rebukes the sea and dries it up; / he makes all the rivers run dry. / Bashan and Carmel wither / and the blossoms of Lebanon fade. / [5]The mountains quake before him / and the hills melt away. / The earth trembles at his presence, / the world and all who live in it. / [6]Who can withstand his indignation? / Who can endure his fierce anger? / His wrath is poured out like fire; / the rocks are shattered before him.

[7]The LORD is good, / a refuge in times of trouble. / He cares for those who trust in him, / [8]but with an overwhelming flood / he will make an end of ⌊Nineveh⌋; / he will pursue his foes into darkness.

[9]Whatever they plot against the LORD / he[a] will bring to an end; / trouble will not come a second time. / [10]They will be entangled among thorns / and drunk from their wine; / they will be consumed like dry stubble.[b]

[a]9 Or *What do you foes plot against the LORD ? / He*     [b]10 The meaning of the Hebrew for this verse is uncertain.

Nahum 1:2-8 is sometimes described as an acrostic poem arranged according to the first half of the Hebrew alphabet (א [aleph] to כ [kaph]) (see the arrangement of the passage in the New Jerusalem Bible. Other examples of acrostic poems in the Old Testament include Psalms 9; 10; 25; 34; 37; 111; 112; 119; 145; Prov 31:10-31; Lamentations 1–4). Such an arrangement is suggested by Nahum 1:2 which opens with the first letter of the Hebrew alphabet (aleph) and by the presence of some of the subsequent letters (through kaph) at or near the beginning of succeeding lines.[2] However, several factors argue against any hypothesis of the acrostic arrangement of this section.[3] One, only two letters occur in their expected position (aleph in 1:2a and ב [beth] in 1:3b). Two, the text must be rearranged to find lines beginning with four letters (ד, ז, י, and כ [daleth, zayin, yodh, and kaph]). Three, even with such rearrangement, several lines seem extraneous to or do not fit the alphabetic sequence (e.g., aleph receives six lines, while no other letter receives more than two). Four, the arrangement ignores the contextual connection between Nahum 1:2-8 and 1:9-10 with the repetition of the same phrase ("he will make an end" and "he will bring to an end"). Therefore, the text as it stands probably does not represent an acrostic poem.

This poem introduces the main theme of the book of Nahum: Yahweh is an avenging God who judges the ungodly. The poem also provides a theological interpretation of Nahum's oracle against Nineveh, whose destruction serves as an example of how Yahweh exercises power and judgment against any opposing enemy. Nahum 1:2-10 balances a description of Yahweh's jealousy and vengeance with the tempering qualities of patience (v. 3a) and goodness (vv. 7-8a) toward those who trust Yahweh. The middle section of the poem (vv. 3b-6) offers a frightening depiction of Yahweh's power. Both the middle section and the final description conclude with rhetorical questions (vv. 6a and 9a) and reinforcing images (vv. 6b,9b-10).

Verses 2-10 also reiterate several divine qualities found in earlier texts, especially from Exodus. Yahweh is jealous (v. 2; Exod 20:4-5) and takes vengeance on enemies (v. 2; Deut 32:43). Yahweh is slow

---

[2]Patterson, *Nahum, Habakkuk, Zephaniah*, p. 18.
[3]Michael H. Floyd, *Minor Prophets: Part 2*, FOTL 22 (Grand Rapids: Eerdmans, 2000), pp. 38-39.

to anger (v. 3; Exod 34:6) and great in power (v. 3; Exod 14:31; 32:11) and will not leave the guilty unpunished (v. 3; Exod 34:7). Yahweh rebukes the sea and dries it up (v. 4; Exod 14:15-31). Before Yahweh the mountains quake and the earth trembles (v. 5; Exod 19:18; cf. Ps 18:7). Yahweh possesses a burning anger (v. 6; Exod 15:7).

**1:2** The four lines of verse 2 are dominated by the threefold repetition of the words "**avenging** is Yahweh" (נֹקֵם יהוה, *nōqēm YHWH*). This triple use of the covenant name of God with the participle "one who takes vengeance" occurs in the midst of two expressions, **a jealous God** (אֵל קַנּוֹא, *'ēl qannô'*) and **filled with wrath** (בַעַל הֵמָה, *ba'al hēmāh*). While these two expressions describe Yahweh, they evoke the names of the ancient Canaanite gods, El (*'ēl*) and Baal (*ba'al*). The poem begins, then, as if invoking the power and presence of Yahweh against pagan gods and nations.

The four lines describe Yahweh's jealousy, vengeance, and wrath. The first of these four lines begins with the only occurrence of the divine name "God" (אֵל, *'ēl*) in Nahum; *'ēl* appears frequently with adjectives that express divine attributes (e.g., Deut 7:21; Neh 9:32; Hos 1:10; Jonah 4:2). Here the adjective is "jealous" (translated "passionate" in the NJPS). The specific word "jealous" (*qannô'*) appears elsewhere only in Joshua 24:19, but Yahweh is described as a jealous God often in the Old Testament with the related adjective (קַנָּא, *qannā'* in Exod 20:5; 34:14; Deut 4:24; 5:9; 6:15) and noun (קִנְאָה, *qin'āh* in Deut 29:20; Ps 78:58; 79:5; Isa 9:7; 37:32; 42:13; 59:17; Ezek 5:13; 23:25; 36:5-6; 38:19; Zeph 1:18; 3:8). Notably the theme of Yahweh as a jealous deity appears first in the Ten Commandments (Exod 20:5) The word does not implicate Yahweh with petty envy. Instead, it speaks to Yahweh's rightful demand for exclusive loyalty from the people in the context of covenant. The first and second commandments (Exod 20:5; Deut 5:9) derive from this demand, and the self-description of Yahweh as "jealous" forms the basis for the demand of exclusive worship (Exod 34:14). In the context of Nahum, the word represents Yahweh's determination to defend zealously the people who belong to Yahweh and to retaliate forcefully against Yahweh's enemies who plot against Yahweh. In this way, Yahweh's vengeance and wrath emerges from Yahweh's jealousy for exclusive loyalty.

The threefold repetition of *nōqēm YHWH*, translated "The LORD is . . . avenging" and **The LORD takes vengeance** in the NIV, emphasizes this divine attribute over that of Yahweh's jealousy. The word "vengeance" is easily misunderstood, since it appears to lack any ethical legitimacy whether it comes from deity or humans. Generally humans are warned against taking vengeance (Lev 19:18; Deut 32:35; cf. Rom 12:19; Heb 10:30). Most references of the word reserve vengeance for Yahweh alone (Gen 4:15; Lev 19:18; 26:25; Deut 32:43; Judg 11:36; 1 Sam 24:12; 2 Sam 22:48; Ps 18:47; 94:1; 99:8; 149:7; Isa 1:24; Jer 5:9,29; 9:9; 11:20; 15:15; 20:12; 46:10; 50:15,28; 51:6,11,36; Ezek 25:14-15,17). Theologically vengeance relates to Yahweh's holiness, which cannot allow sin and rebellion to go unpunished. In this sense, vengeance is the action that measures out justice. Without divine justice, divine mercy would lose its meaning. Yahweh takes vengeance in at least two ways: punishing those who break the covenant by sinning (Lev 26:24-26) and avenging the people of God against their enemies (Psalm 94).[4] This latter sense is clearly supported in the present context of Nahum.

Two other phrases in verse 2 describe Yahweh acting justly in judgment against sin and injustice. One, the wording "filled with wrath" (cf. the TNIV's "vents his wrath") translates a Hebrew phrase that could be rendered "master of wrath." Yahweh is thus depicted as one entitled to wrath or anger but one who does not exercise it with impropriety. However, the expression may have a wider connotation, since the word "master" (*ba'al*) most often names the Canaanite storm god Baal in the Old Testament. Nahum may use *ba'al* in his description of Yahweh as a veiled attack on the pagan god, insisting that Yahweh is true master of the storm (see vv. 3-4). Two, in the statement **maintains his wrath**, the word "maintains," when it does not occur in agricultural contexts (e.g., S of S 1:6; 8:11-12), generally refers to the persistent indignation of Yahweh against those who do evil (Ps 103:9; Jer 3:5,12).

**1:3** Verse 3 identifies those who are objects of Yahweh's wrath in the previous verse as **the guilty**. Yahweh shows a temporary forbearance toward them (see Jonah 3:10; 4:2), but this is not born of weakness; instead, Yahweh's great power legitimizes the promise that the guilty will be punished (this contrast of forbearance and power is better noted with the TNIV's "but"). By placing this traditional confessional formula **The LORD is slow to anger** (Exod 34:6;

---

[4]Elmer B. Smick, "נקם," *TWOT*, 2:598-599.

Num 14:18; Neh 9:17; Ps 86:15; 103:8, 145:8; Joel 2:13; Jonah 4:2) in a context emphasizing Yahweh's wrath and power, the prophet emphasizes the inescapable judgment for those who oppose Yahweh.

The second part of the verse begins with a theophany depicting Yahweh's great power in frightening natural phenomena. The word "theophany" comes from two Greek words meaning "God" and "appearance," thus the word refers to a manifestation of God. Here, as elsewhere in the Old Testament (see Job 38:1; Ps 18:7-15; 68:4; 77:16-19; 104:3-4; Hab 3:8-13), Yahweh is personified in the forces of nature. In Nahum 1:3b-5, this personification includes three primary images: storm, drought, and earthquake.

The images of **whirlwind**, **storm**, and **clouds** depict divine activity in a realm between heaven and earth. In the ancient Near East, the gods are often portrayed as storm deities who use the wind and clouds as vehicles in battle contexts. In the Old Testament the psalmists and prophets appropriate this imagery to assert that Yahweh, not Baal nor the Assyrian storm-god Hadad, is the one who controls weather and war (cf. Deut 33:26; 2 Sam 22:10-11; Ps 68:4,33; 104:3; Isa 19:1; 29:6; 66:15; Zech 9:14). Similarly, verse 3 depicts Yahweh as a warrior who rides storm clouds into battle. The image of clouds being **the dust of [Yahweh's] feet** may also be a part of the divine warrior motif since it suggests the image of a warrior momentarily raising dust as he runs to battle. Furthermore, although the lines "His way is in the whirlwind and the storm, and clouds are the dust of his feet" may utilize images originally connected with Baal mythology, they no doubt also allude to the exodus events of Yahweh's guiding the Israelites (Exod 13:21-22), Yahweh's parting of the Red Sea (Exod 14:19–15:21), and Yahweh's speaking the commandments to Moses (Exod 19:16–20:21).

**1:4** The allusion to the exodus continues into the next verse, which mentions Yahweh's rebuke of the sea (Exod 14:21; 15:8; 2 Sam 22:16; Ps 18:15; 104:7; 106:9; Isa 50:2; cf. Jesus' stilling the storm in Mark 4:39). The word **rebukes** (גָּעַר, gāʿar) and the related noun "rebuke" (גְּעָרָה, gᵊʿārāh) can denote forceful and destructive blasts of air accompanied by loud and frightening noises (cf. 2 Sam 22:16; Ps 18:15).[5] A series of passages in Isaiah place gāʿar and

---

[5]John E. Hartley, "גער," *NIDOTTE*, 1:884-885.

$g^ə'ārāh$ in close connection with the wrath of Yahweh, whose rebuke is often expressed with meteorological language (Isa 50:2; 51:20; 66:15). In Canaanite mythology, the sea and river stand as cosmic enemies of Baal, the storm god. So too, the Old Testament uses the "sea" (Job 38:8-11; Jer 5:22) and the "river" (Ps 114:3-5; Hab 3:8-15) to symbolize forces that threaten Yahweh and creation. However, here the **sea** and **rivers** simply **dry** up at the rebuke of Yahweh and offer no resistance to Yahweh. This rebuke of the sea and rivers also anticipates later references to the role of water in the demise of Nineveh (Nahum 2:6,8).

The image of drought envisions the withering of even the most fertile areas of Syria-Palestine. While the NIV translates the same Hebrew word with two different English words, **wither** and **fade**, other versions, such as the ESV, NASB, and NJB, use only the one word "wither" (cf. Isa 16:8; 24:4,7; 33:9; Jer 14:2; Joel 1:10,12). **Bashan** is the mountainous region east of the Sea of Galilee known for its fertile plateau with pastures and trees (Deut 32:14; Ps 22:12; 68:15; Ezek 27:6; 39:18). **Carmel** is the lush mountainous promontory jutting into the Mediterranean Sea west of Galilee where Yahweh defeats the prophets of Baal (1 Kgs 18:19-20,42). **Lebanon** is the mountainous range north of Galilee known for majestic cedars, the source of lumber for Solomon's temple (1 Kgs 4:33; 5:6,9,14). In the Old Testament, each of these localities appear as metaphors for blessing (Ps 29:6; 72:16; 92:12; 104:16; S of S 7:5; Isa 35:2; 60:13; Jer 50:19; Micah 7:14) and for judgment (Ps 29:5; Isa 2:13; 10:34; 14:8; 33:9; Ezek 31:15; Amos 1:2; 4:1; 9:3; Zech 11:1-2). The only other text where all three places appear is Isaiah 33:9, a text like Nahum 1:4 that depicts divine judgment. To inflict these lush and fertile areas with drought depicts the great power of Yahweh.

**1:5** In contrast with connotations of chaos elicited by the earlier references to the sea, the evoking of mountain and hill imagery connotes stability and permanence. The Assyrian king Ashur-nasir-apli II (ca. 883–859 B.C.) claims that at his approach "all lands convulse, writhe, (and) melt as though in a furnace."[6] Yet, the figure of divine shaking of the **mountains** and melting of the earth is a standard feature in theophanies in the Old Testament (Judg 5:4; 2 Sam 22:8; Ps

---

[6]A.K. Grayson, *Assyrian Royal Inscriptions*, Record of the Ancient Near East (Wiesbaden: O. Harrassowitz, 1972–1976), 2:184.

18:7; 46:2-3; 60:2; 68:8; 77:18; Isa 13:13; 24:18; Jer 10:10; Ezek 38:19-20; Joel 3:16; Amos 9:5; Micah 1:4; Hab 3:6,10; Hag 2:6,21; cf. 2 Pet 3:12). The great power of Yahweh overwhelms all of creation. If the **earth melts before** the divine presence, how much more will the palace in Nineveh collapse ("collapse" in Nahum 2:6 translates the same Hebrew word as the one translated "melt" here; cf. Ps 46:6; 75:3; 97:5; Amos 9:5,13).

**1:6** The poetic description and theophany of Yahweh in verses 2-5 leads to the rhetorical questions of verse 6, which underscore the awesomeness of Yahweh with a series of synonyms for divine wrath. These questions address those who may think they can stand before Yahweh, and they prepare for the prophet's announcement of judgment on Nineveh (vv. 8-9). If the mountains tremble at the divine presence, then neither can Nineveh **withstand** the attack of Yahweh's wrath. The image of Yahweh pouring out wrath on enemies appears frequently in the Old Testament (2 Chr 12:7; 34:21,25; Ps 79:6; Jer 6:11; 7:20; 10:25; 42:18; 44:6; Lam 2:4; 4:11; Ezek 7:8; 9:8; 14:19; 20:8,13,21,33-34; 21:31; 22:22,31; 30:15; 36:18; Hos 5:10; cf. Rev 16:1), but the comparison to the pouring out of **wrath like fire** is unusual (Lam 2:4). The geological imagery of **rocks shatter**ing might suggest volcanic activity as the controlling image. Another possibility is that it refers to the pouring of hot substances on an enemy's head (see Ezek 22:20-22).[7]

**1:7** In contrast to the previous verse, Nahum 1:7 affirms positive aspects of Yahweh's character. In this way, the frightening image of Yahweh's wrath is balanced with reassuring statements about Yahweh's goodness and care. This language has many parallels in the Psalter. The opening phrase **The LORD is good** appears in Psalms 34:8; 100:5; 135:3; and 145:9, and frequently the worshiper is enjoined to seek refuge in Yahweh (Ps 2:12; 5:11; 7:1; 11:1; 16:1; 17:7; 18:2,30; 25:20; 31:1,19; 34:8,22; 36:7; 37:40; 57:1; 61:4; 64:10; 71:1; 91:4; 118:8f; 141:8; 144:2). In the present context, the rhetorical goal of such language is to affirm that which may have been doubted by the original recipients. When the people of Yahweh are oppressed by enemy armies (cf. **times of trouble** and its various translations in Ps 37:39; Isa 33:2; Jer 14:8; 15:11; 16:19; Obad 12), the people have a **refuge** in Yahweh. This contrast, in effect, makes

---

[7]Longman, *Nahum*, 2:791.

Judah the literary foil of Nineveh and Yahweh's judgment of Nineveh an expression of divine mercy toward Judah. Both the words **care for** (עָדַ֫ע, *gādāh*) and **trust** (חָסָה, *ḥāsāh*) are covenantal terms. The first, which has the primary meaning "to know" but by extension means "to care about," often describes the superior's obligations to the faithful vassals; the second, which means "to take refuge," signifies the covenant loyalty of the people to Yahweh, frequently in contrast to rebellion (Ps 2:12; 5:11; 31:10; 34:22).

**1:8** While the NIV begins verse 8 with the phrase **but with an overwhelming flood**, other versions take the phrase as a continuation of verse 7. For example, the NRSV reads, "He protects those who take refuge in him, even in a rushing flood" (cf. NJB). One may not need to decide between the two readings, since this may be an example of a hinge (sometimes called Janus) parallelism. This literary feature looks at a word or phrase from opposite directions, that is, it may be read one way as a continuation of the preceding material and another way with the section that follows. Thus, verse 7 envisages Yahweh as the high place where people find refuge from the waters of the flood, while verse 8 pictures the overwhelming flood as the means by which Yahweh destroys Nineveh. Flood (שֶׁ֫טֶף, *šeṭeph*) appears most frequently in a metaphorical sense (Ps 32:6; Prov 27:4; Dan 9:26; 11:22) and in view of Genesis 6–9 testifies to Yahweh's power and justice, but the ancient testimony of the destruction of Nineveh by water might suggest a literal reference as well (Diodorus, *Bibl. Hist.* 2.27.1; cf. Isa 8:7-8; Nahum 2:6,8).

The thematic relationship of the preceding poem descriptive of Yahweh's justice and theophany depicting Yahweh's power (vv. 2-8) to the following judgment oracle against Nineveh is highlighted by the use of the words עָשָׂה (*ʿāsāh*) and כָּלָה (*kālāh*), translated **make an end** in verse 8 and "bring to an end" in verse 9. When used together, these words typically describe the complete destruction or annihilation of something or someone by Yahweh (Neh 9:31; Isa 10:23; Jer 4:27; 5:18; 30:11; 46:28; Ezek 11:13; 20:17; Zeph 1:18). Here that *someone* is identified as **Nineveh** in the NIV, an insertion marked by enclosing "Nineveh" in brackets (but the TNIV removes these brackets throughout 1:8–2:1). Actually, the word "Nineveh," which appears first in verse 1, is not found again in the Hebrew text until 2:8. The NIV has evidently taken the Hebrew word מְקוֹמָהּ (*mᵉqômāh*), translated "its site" in the NASB and "her place" in the NJPS, to refer to Nineveh, a reading that makes sense in the context and one that particularizes the city as an enemy of Yahweh. The NRSV reads "his adversaries," which may reflect the LXX's τοὺς ἐπεγειρομένους (*tous epegeiromenous*), meaning "those who rise up," and may provide a suitable parallel to "his foes" in the following line.

These **foes** Yahweh **pursues into darkness**. Here, darkness may refer either to the land of death (cf. Job 10:20-22; 17:13; 18:17-18) or serve as an image for Yahweh's relentless pursuit of enemies to bring judgment upon them (Exod 10:21-23; Josh 24:7; Isa 8:22; 13:10; 60:2; Ezek 30:18-19; 32:7-8; Joel 2:2,31; Amos 8:9; Zeph 1:15). Verse 9 probably points to the latter. While darkness is a part of the concealing or covering of Yahweh in Old Testament theophanies (Exod 20:21; Deut 4:11; 5:22-23; 2 Sam 22:10-12; Ps 18:9-11; 97:2) and a means by which Yahweh protects the Israelites (Josh 24:7), it cannot hide from Yahweh those who do evil (Job 34:21-22).

**1:9** The very first line of verse 9 should be read as the question in the NJB, "What are your thoughts about Yahweh?" (cf. ESV, KJV, NRSV, NJPS), rather than as the statement in the NIV, **Whatever they plot against the LORD** (but see the NIV text note). Several reasons confirm this.[8] The word מָה (*māh*) ordinarily functions as the interrogative pronoun "what" or "why" and rarely as an indefinite pronoun (Num 23:3; 1 Sam 19:3; 2 Sam 18:22-23).[9] The LXX translates the Hebrew with an interrogative pronoun. The following verb is clearly second person plural ("you") and not third person plural ("they"). The use of rhetorical questions elsewhere in Nahum supports the presence of one here (1:6; 2:11; 3:8).

This question invites the reader to consider Yahweh's power and justice presented in the previous poem and theophany. While the same verb "plot" (חָשַׁב, *ḥāšab*) is used again in verse 11 to speak of planning against Yahweh, its use there differs considerably, since it occurs with a different preposition, "against," and a different noun, "evil." While the NIV translates prepositions in both verses "against," verse 9 contains the spatial preposition "about" (אֶל, *'el*), and verse 11 uses the oppositional preposition "against" (עַל, *'al*). The form of the verb *ḥāšab* in verse 9 may better be translated "think" or "consider" (Lev 25:27,50,52; 27:18,23; 2 Kgs 12:16; Ps 73:16; 77:5; 119:59; 144:3; but cf. Hos 7:15).

---

[8]For the opposing view, see Patterson, *Nahum*, p. 40.
[9]*HALOT*, pp. 550-551.

Verse 9 repeats the previous verse's use of the verb "make" (*'āśāh*) and the noun **end** (*kālāh*), but it adds between them an emphatic pronoun to underscore that it is Yahweh who completely annihilates Nineveh (cf. NJB). The reference to a **second time** may recall that Yahweh does not permit the Assyrians a second victory over the Israelites. The first is the fall of Samaria (722–721 B.C.), but the second is cut short when Sennacherib withdraws after invading Judah in 701 B.C. (2 Kgs 19:35-36; 2 Chr 32:21; Isa 37:36-37).[10] Or, "second time" may suggest a recent experience of Assyrian hostility toward Judah. If so, the brief exile of Manasseh to Babylon after his defeat by the commanders of the Assyrian king (650–648 B.C.) might be in mind (2 Chr 33:10-13). In either case, **trouble** does not come a second time because the destruction of Nineveh is complete (no evidence exists of any occupation on the site of Nineveh for at least three hundred years after its fall) and because Yahweh is a refuge for Judah in times of "trouble" (v. 7).

**1:10** Three striking images (entanglement, intoxication, and consumption) constitute this verse, which is one of the more difficult in the Old Testament. There is difficulty in ascertaining the precise meanings of the words involved and of the first two images: **entangled among thorns** and **drunk from wine** (the latter of these two is perhaps an allusion to the cup of Yahweh's wrath; cf. Isa 51:17; Jer 25:15). Then the meaning of the first two images must be related to the third image that speaks of consumption **like dry stubble**. In general, all three seem to share the theme of total consumption. The bush is entangled with thorns, the drunk is drunk with drink, and the stubble is consumed totally with fire. The use of the verb "consume" or "eat" (אָכַל, *'ākal*) heightens the sense of the fullness of consumption (i.e., punishment).

## B. THE LORD'S JUSTICE FOR NINEVEH AND JUDAH (1:11-15)

[11]**From you, ⌊O Nineveh,⌋ has one come forth / who plots evil against the Lord / and counsels wickedness.**

[12]**This is what the Lord says:**

---

[10]Cf. *ANET*, p. 288.

"Although they have allies and are numerous, / they will be cut off and pass away. / Although I have afflicted you, ⌞O Judah,⌟ / I will afflict you no more. / ¹³Now I will break their yoke from your neck / and tear your shackles away."

¹⁴The LORD has given a command concerning you, ⌞Nineveh⌟: / "You will have no descendants to bear your name. / I will destroy the carved images and cast idols / that are in the temple of your gods. / I will prepare your grave, / for you are vile."

¹⁵Look, there on the mountains, / the feet of one who brings good news, / who proclaims peace! / Celebrate your festivals, O Judah, / and fulfill your vows. / No more will the wicked invade you; / they will be completely destroyed.

Nahum 1:11-15 contains a proclamation of Yahweh's vindication of Judah from their oppressor, Nineveh. This vindication is evidenced in a reversal of fates for Nineveh and Judah. The beginning of the section is signaled by a shift from second and third person plural in verses 9-10 to second person singular in verses 11,12,13, and 15 (with exception of v. 14). Whereas the second and third person plural forms of verses 9 and 10 probably refer to the residents of Nineveh, the second-person singular form at the beginning of verse 11 may suggest the city of Nineveh as a whole. The stitch word "plots" (vv. 9 and 11) connects this section with the preceding one, and the word "wicked[ness]" (בְּלִיָּעַל, *bᵊlîyā'al*) in verses 11 and 15 forms bookends around it.

The section is unique among the prophets since it intertwines salvation oracles directed to Judah (1:12-13,15) with judgment oracles concerning Nineveh (1:9-11,14). The same interchange continues into 2:1-2. However, some ambiguity exists regarding who is addressed at various points. The section heightens dramatic suspense by delaying the identification of the recipients of both salvation and judgment. The Hebrew text does not mention Judah until verse 15, and direct reference to Nineveh is completely absent from the section. The NIV attempts to clarify this ambiguity by inserting "Nineveh" in verses 11,14 and "Judah" in verse 12 and marking them with brackets (cf. the arrangement in the NJB).[11]

---

[11]Santiago Ausín, "Nahum," in *The International Bible Commentary: A Catholic and Ecumenical Commentary for the Twenty-First Century*, ed. by

**1:11** The major difficulty of this verse is the identification of the referents. Even though the verse addresses the antagonist directly (**from you**), it does not do so with the certainty which the NIV's insertion of **O Nineveh** effects. Most commentators identify the subject of **has one come forth** to be either Sennacherib (705–681 B.C.), who leaves Assyria to lay siege against Judah in 701 B.C. (2 Kgs 18:13–19:36)[12] or some other Assyrian king, such as Ashurbanipal (669–627 B.C.) to whom Manasseh submits as a vassal (2 Chr 33:11-33).[13] Others, however, see the first clause of the verse depicting Yahweh's departure from the sinful city of Nineveh and the next two clauses as further appellations of the city, modifying "you."[14] Yahweh abandons the city and leaves it open to destruction (cf. such a description of Jerusalem in Lam 2:7). While the latter is possible, the former is probably preferred.

Two verbal phrases describe the figure who has emerged. The first, **who plots evil against the LORD**, is a common combination of words (Gen 50:20; Esth 8:3; Ps 21:11; Jer 18:8,11; 26:3; 36:3; 48:2; Micah 2:3). The second, who **counsels wickedness**, is unique. The word *bᵊlîyā'al* may be translated "wickedness" (as in the NIV) or "worthless" (as in the ESV). It usually appears in a construction with a preceding noun, most frequently "son of" (בֵּן, *bēn*; Judg 19:22; 20:13; 1 Sam 2:12; 10:27; 25:17; 1 Kgs 21:10,13; 2 Chr 13:7). It denotes a reprobate life (Deut 13:13; 2 Sam 23:6; Prov 6:12; 16:27; 19:28), and eventually it becomes a name for Satan himself (2 Cor 6:15).

**1:12** Verse 12 abruptly introduces an oracle of salvation, a form in which a prophet announces restoration for an individual or for an entire nation. It begins with the messenger formula **This is what the LORD says** (כֹּה אָמַר יהוה, *kōh 'āmar YHWH*). While the formula is used over forty times in the Book of the Twelve and almost two hundred times in the Major Prophets, this is its only use in Nahum, giving more gravity to the pronouncement to which it is attached.

Even though the word of salvation is directed to Judah, it incorporates an announcement of judgment against Nineveh. The con-

---

William R. Farmer (Collegeville, MN: Liturgical Press, 1998), p. 1166, argues that the entire section of Nahum 1:11-15 is directed to Judah.

[12]Cf. *ANET*, p. 288.

[13]E.g., Armerding, *Nahum*, 7:466.

[14]E.g., Longman, *Nahum*, p. 797.

cessive conjunction **although** begins a conditional statement describing the strength and number of the Assyrian forces. The adjective שָׁלֵם (*šālēm*) has the basic meaning "complete," hence the sense "full strength" represented in such versions as the ESV, NASB, NRSV, and NJPS. The NIV follows a study that calls attention to *šālēm*) as a reference to military **allies**.[15] The NIV also ignores the particle "thus" (כֵּן, *kēn*) which appears twice in the Hebrew text; the NASB translates the first occurrence as "likewise," and the second, as "even so": "Though they are at full *strength* and likewise many, Even so, they will be cut off and pass away." The word **cut off** (גָּזַז, *gāzaz*) is generally used for shearing sheep (Gen 31:19; 38:12-13; Deut 15:19; 1 Sam 25:2,4,7,11; 2 Sam 13:23-24) or for cutting human hair (Job 1:20; Jer 7:29; Micah 1:16). Isaiah uses it metaphorically in the Fourth Servant Song to speak of the servant's submission to his oppressors (Isa 53:7). The word **pass away** (עָבַר, *'ābar*) has the basic idea of movement, either in a simple (Num 22:26; Josh 1:2) or symbolic sense (Deut 17:2; Job 30:15). It does appear with some frequency in contexts descriptive of complete destruction and military defeat, especially involving the image of water or flooding (Ps 42:8; 124:4-5; Isa 8:8; 23:10; 54:9; Jonah 2:4; Hab 3:10; Zech 10:11), a sense apparent from its use in verse 8 ("overwhelming"), verse 12 ("pass away"), verse 15 ("invade"), and 3:19 ("felt").

While the prophet may not emphasize Judah's sin or call the people to repentance, Nahum is certainly aware that Judah's predicament is due to Yahweh's punishment. Yahweh has used Assyria as a rod of divine anger in the time of Ahaz (Isa 10:5-11) and again in the time of Manasseh (2 Chr 33:10-13). The word **afflict** (עָנָה, *'ānāh*) is used in contexts of Yahweh's judicial punishment of the people (Deut 8:2-3,16; 1 Kgs 8:35; 11:39; 2 Kgs 17:20; 2 Chr 6:26; Ps 88:7; 90:15; 119:75; Isa 64:12; Lam 3:33). However, the time of punishment and affliction is over; Yahweh now delivers **Judah** from Nineveh, a promise which may presuppose Isaiah 10:5-34. The oracle of salvation offers the reassurance that Yahweh will afflict the people **no more**. The four uses of "no more" or "no longer" (1:12,14-15; 2:13) heighten the eschatological effect and point to a destined and decisive deliverance, the final removal of an Assyrian threat.

---

[15]D.J. Wiseman, "'Is It Peace?' Covenant and Diplomacy," *VT* 32 (1982): 311-326.

**1:13** Isaiah prophesies earlier that Yahweh would **break** the **yoke** of Assyria from Judah's **neck** (Isa 14:25). Nahum envisions the impending fulfillment of that promise. The temporal adverb **now** (עַתָּה, *'attāh*) gives verse 13 a note of immediacy. In addition to its temporal meaning, when combined with the conjunction ("and" in the ESV and NRSV), it has an emphatic use. It denotes the next stage in an argument. In the prophets, the adverb *'attāh* often introduces the imminent actions of Yahweh either in blessing or in curse (e.g., Isa 33:10; 43:19).[16]

The yoke refers to that worn by oxen, but often symbolizes political vassalage, especially when coupled with **shackles** (Jer 5:5; 27:2). Together "yoke" and "shackles" constitute a powerful metonymy for oppression. The masculine form "yoke" (מוֹט, *môṭ*) appears only four times (Num 4:10,12; 13:23; Nahum 1:13), but the feminine form (מוֹטָה, *môṭāh*) occurs ten times (Lev 26:13; 1 Chr 15:15; Isa 58:6,9; Jer 27:2; 28:10,12,13; Ezek 30:18; 34:27). More common for "yoke" is עֹל (*'ōl*; e.g., 1 Sam 6:7; 1 Kgs 12:4; Isa 9:4; Jer 27:8). In Jeremiah, the prophet uses *môṭāh* to portray Judah's looming submission to Babylon and her destruction by the Babylonians' hands. Its three uses in Isaiah pertain to sins of oppression.

**1:14** In previous verses, both Judah and Nineveh are referred to with the second person feminine singular (vv. 11,12), but in verse 14 a new addressee is signaled by the shift to second person masculine singular. Even though the NIV inserts **Nineveh** as the addressee, the transition from feminine to masculine probably directs the words of the verse to the king of Assyria, similar to the change in 3:18-19. Such identification is confirmed by the three clauses that follow the statement of **the LORD's command**, each assailing the king's dynastic power. One, the king will **have no descendants to bear [his] name**. That the king's name will not be sown, a common metaphor for having descendants (cf. the KJV), refers to the extermination of the king's family (cf. Deut 7:24; 9:14; 12:3; 1 Sam 24:21; 2 Sam 14:7; Isa 14:22). Two, Yahweh **will destroy the . . . images and . . . idols** in the king's **temple**. The practice of desecrating temples belonging to a conquered people is common in the ancient Near East (cf. 2 Kgs 25:8-17; 2 Chr 36:18-19). The destruction of the **carved images** and **cast idols** undermines the theological foundation of the king's claim

---

[16]Allan Harman, "Particles," *NIDOTTE*, 4:1031.

to rule by the authority of his **gods**. Moreover, the destruction of the temple where these gods resided exposes their inefficacy. Three, the king will die in disgrace. While the NIV reads, **I will prepare your grave**, the Hebrew text may be read as the NJB, "I shall devastate your tomb." The desecration of the royal tomb shows disdain for the king and repudiates the impotent Assyrian gods. A causal clause closes the verse and may be read as the NIV's **for you are vile**, as the NJB's "for you are accursed," or, according to a recent linguistic study, with the preceding pronouncement, "I will make your grave a refuse heap."[17]

**1:15** The last verse of chapter 1 (v. 15 is actually 2:1 in the Hebrew text; cf. the versification of the NJB and NJPS) sets the following description of the conquest of Nineveh (2:1-10) in the context of Yahweh's deliverance of Judah, who is explicitly addressed for the first time in Nahum. It offers a proclamation of salvation and judgment as does 3:19 at the conclusion of the book. The first word **Look**, a typical beginning for a salvation speech (Joel 2:19; 3:7; Amos 9:13; Zeph 3:19; Zech 2:9-10; 3:8-9; 8:7; 9:9; Mal 3:1), signals a sudden transition from judgment to salvation and introduces the close of the book's first major section. While the NIV translation of **one who brings good news** is appropriate in its context, it diminishes the sense of suspense existing in the Hebrew text. The verse begins merely informing the reader that a messenger is **on the mountains**; the next line clarifies that the messenger brings a message of peace rather than ill (cf. NJB, which reads: "See on the mountains the feet of the herald! 'Peace!' he proclaims"). The literary image of **the feet of one who brings good news** is a synecdoche, where the part ("feet") stands for the whole ("messenger"). This declaration of **peace** that results from the imminent destruction of Assyrian power alludes to the language of the announcement of deliverance in Isaiah 52:7 (cf. Rom 10:15).

The people of **Judah** are commanded to **celebrate** the **festivals** and to **fulfill** their **vows**. The promise that Judah will have peace and freedom to celebrate the appointed festivals (v. 15) is later fulfilled when Josiah leads Judah in Passover celebration during the reforms of 622 B.C. (2 Kgs 23:21-25; 2 Chr 35:1-19). Even vows taken during prayers for deliverance are to be kept with utmost seriousness (Num

---

[17]Kevin J. Cathcart, "Nahum, Book of," *ABD*, 4:998.

30:2; Deut 23:21-23; Ps 61:5,8; 77:11; Jonah 2:9). The NIV omits the
causal conjunction ("for") that introduces the last two lines of the
verse and thereby the reason Judah can celebrate in peace (cf. ESV,
KJV, NASB, NJB, and NRSV). Assyria, identified as the **wicked**, a
word used earlier in verse 11 and translated in the NJB here as
"Belial," **will no more invade** Judah. The NIV's **they will be completely destroyed** translates the final two-word clause of the section
(כֻּלֹּה נִכְרָת, *kullōh nikrāth*), which may be rendered "all of him has
been cut off." The brevity of the line matches the quick and thorough nature of Yahweh's actions which the prophet anticipates.[18]

## III. NINEVEH'S JUDGMENT (2:1–3:19)

Nahum 2:1–3:19 focuses on the destruction of Nineveh, claiming
it as a manifestation of Yahweh's intent and justice. The section contains an announcement of the attack upon Nineveh (2:1-10), a taunt
over the fall of Nineveh and its king (2:11-13), an announcement of
the punishment against Nineveh (3:1-7), a comparison of Nineveh's
vulnerability and destruction to that of Thebes (3:8-13), and a report
that Nineveh's destruction has left the city defenseless and defeated
(3:14-19). In various ways, the section reiterates things that are said
previously in Nahum 1:1-15. It also presents a kind of narrative
sequence that begins before the fall of Nineveh (2:1) and ends after
it (3:18-19), two passages which are connected by the use of the
word "scatter."

### A. ANNOUNCEMENT OF THE ATTACK UPON NINEVEH
### (2:1-10)

[1]**An attacker advances against you, ⌊Nineveh⌋. / Guard the
fortress, / watch the road, / brace yourselves, / marshal all your
strength!**
[2]**The LORD will restore the splendor of Jacob / like the splendor of Israel, / though destroyers have laid them waste / and have
ruined their vines.**

---

[18]Patterson, *Nahum, Habakkuk, Zephaniah*, p. 52.

³**The shields of his soldiers are red;** / **the warriors are clad in scarlet.** / **The metal on the chariots flashes** / **on the day they are made ready;** / **the spears of pine are brandished.**ᵃ / ⁴**The chariots storm through the streets,** / **rushing back and forth through the squares.** / **They look like flaming torches;** / **they dart about like lightning.**

⁵**He summons his picked troops,** / **yet they stumble on their way.** / **They dash to the city wall;** / **the protective shield is put in place.** / ⁶**The river gates are thrown open** / **and the palace collapses.** / ⁷**It is decreed**ᵇ **that ⌞the city⌟** / **be exiled and carried away.** / **Its slave girls moan like doves** / **and beat upon their breasts.** / ⁸**Nineveh is like a pool,** / **and its water is draining away.** / **"Stop! Stop!" they cry,** / **but no one turns back.** / ⁹**Plunder the silver!** / **Plunder the gold!** / **The supply is endless,** / **the wealth from all its treasures!** / ¹⁰**She is pillaged, plundered, stripped!** / **Hearts melt, knees give way,** / **bodies tremble, every face grows pale.**

ᵃ*3 Hebrew; Septuagint and Syriac* / *the horsemen rush to and fro*     ᵇ*7 The meaning of the Hebrew for this word is uncertain.*

Nahum 2:1-10 exhibits the form of a prophetic sentinel report in which the prophet functions in a manner similar to that of a sentry. (Other examples of prophetic sentinel reports include Isa 21:6-10; 52:7-10; Ezek 3:17-21; 33:2-9; Hab 1:5-11; 2:1.) The prophet speaks as a watchman who announces the approach of an enemy and urges preparations for battle (2:1). The prophet explains Yahweh's (theological) purpose for the attack, namely, to restore the splendor of Israel and to reverse the fortunes of their plundering foes (2:2). Then the prophet provides almost a narrative description of Nineveh's defeat (2:3-10); this description shows how the defensive measures of 2:1 happen to no avail. The unit begins and ends with references to "faces," translated "against you" (2:1; i.e., "over against your faces") and "every face grows pale" (2:10) and to "loins," translated "brace yourselves" (2:1; cf. the NRSV's "gird your loins") and "bodies tremble" (2:10; cf. the ESV's "anguish is in all loins").

**2:1** The word translated **attacker** (מֵפִיץ, *mēphîṣ*) appears elsewhere only in Proverbs 25:18. The translation of the word in that context as "club" may explain some renderings of the word in this verse, such as "dasheth" in the KJV or "shatterer" in the NRSV; otherwise, such renderings reflect the meaning of the similar word "war club" in Jeremiah 51:20. A related word (פוּץ, *pûṣ*) refers to the scattering of armies (Num 10:35; 1 Sam 11:11; 2 Kgs 25:5; Jer 52:8) or the scattering of nations; the word frequently represents the scattering of Israel among the nations by Yahweh (Gen 11:8-9; 49:7; Deut 4:27; 28:64; 30:3; Neh 1:8; Isa 24:1; Jer 9:16; 13:24; 18:17; 30:11; Ezek 11:16; 12:15; 20:23; 22:15; 29:12; 30:23,26; 36:19). These uses of *pûṣ* suggest that "scatterer" might be a better translation here and one which retains the verbal connection with "scattered" in 3:18, an occurrence that signifies the thorough defeat of Nineveh. In retrospect, Nineveh's enemies are appropriately called a "scatterer." After the fall of Nineveh in 612 B.C., the Assyrians disperse and survive to fight only two more battles against the Babylonians (Haran in 609 and Carchemish in 605).

The addressee, **you**, is not explicitly identified in the verse. While a particular historical figure such as Neco or Sennacherib may be in view, the singular feminine probably points to the city of **Nineveh** as the addressee. If the addressee is Nineveh, the attacker may be identified as the Assyrians' historical enemy, the Babylonian and Median alliance of Nabopolassar and Cyaxares, or it may even point to Yahweh. Whereas Judah sees a messenger approaching with good news (1:15), Nineveh sees coming destruction. The military use of the phrase **advance against** occurs more than twenty times in the Old Testament (Josh 22:12; 22:33; Judg 18:9; 1 Kgs 14:25; 15:17; 16:17; 20:1,22; 2 Kgs 6:24; 16:5; 17:3; 18:9,13,25; 1 Chr 14:10; 2 Chr 12:2,9; 16:1; 24:23; 36:6; Isa 7:1; 36:1; Jer 37:5; 50:3,9,21; Ezek 26:3).

The prophet speaks four instructions to encourage the city to prepare for the enemy onslaught: **guard the fortress**, **watch the road** (cf. 2 Sam 13:34; Jer 48:19), **brace yourselves**, and **marshal all your strength** (cf. Amos 2:14). Nevertheless, the instructions are ironic in nature and ultimately ineffectual; rhetorically they emphasize the futility of any resistance. Here the image "brace yourselves" ("gird your loins" in the NRSV) connotes preparation and strength (cf. Deut 33:11; 1 Kgs 12:10; Prov 31:17); in verse 10, the image "bodies tremble" ("anguish is in all loins" in the ESV) connotes dread and grief (cf. Ps 66:11; Isa 21:3).

**2:2** This verse almost intrudes in its context because the wording is more prosaic than those that surround it. For this reason, some versions, such as the NRSV and NJB, set the verse off in parentheses. An initial conjunction, "for," omitted in the NIV, introduces the verse and thus the reason why Nineveh faces destruction. The verse stands in contrast to the preceding one where the prophet announces the coming destruction of Nineveh; instead, it declares that Yahweh **will restore** Judah to its previous greatness, an event which is seen as so certain that the Hebrew text presents it as if it were a past event (cf. the wording in the KJV, NJB, and NJPS). The word "restore" appears frequently in the phrase "restore the fortunes of," an idiom for the termination of captivity and restoration of a previous position of blessing (e.g., Jer 29:14; 30:18; 32:44; 33:7). The phrases **the splendor of Jacob** and **the splendor of Israel** are unexpected, since in other contexts the word translated "splendor" (גָּאוֹן, *gā'ôn*) has negative connotations and normally expresses "the pride of Judah" or "Israel's arrogance" (Jer 13:9; Ezek 33:28; Hos 5:5; 7:10; Amos 6:8; 8:7). Here *gā'ôn* with "restore" is used positively.

The designations "Jacob" and "Israel" may specifically name the northern kingdom (Micah 1:5,13), the southern kingdom (Micah 3:8-9; 6:2), or the whole covenant people (Micah 2:12; 5:2). The preposition translated "like" may be comparative, indicating a movement from a humbled (Jacob) to an honored status (Israel), or it may be taken as emphatic, using parallel phrases to identify Judah (cf. NJB and NRSV). Here the prophet probably refers to a desire to see the totality of Israel restored, using Jacob as a natural name and Israel as a spiritual name (cf. Jer 31:31-34; Ezek 37:15-23; Zech 10:6-12). Furthermore, the prophet may use both Jacob and Israel as honorific titles for Judah (cf. Isa 14:1-4), asserting that the nation will become worthy of its exalted calling (cf. Gen 49:8-12) and its foundational role for the renewed people of Yahweh. Such restoration of splendor is needed because of the devastation that has befallen Israel. The image of **ruined vines** provides a powerful portrayal of destruction (Ps 78:47; 105:33; Jer 5:17; Hos 2:12; Hab 3:17) for a people who depend on the vine as a basis for their economy (Lev 19:10; Deut 24:21; Judg 9:27; 1 Sam 25:18) and who regard it as a symbol of their identity as a nation (Ps 80:8-16; Isa 5:1-7) and of divine blessing (1 Kgs 4:25; 2 Kgs 18:31; Micah 4:4; Zech 3:10).

**2:3** Verses 3-10 are a visionary report of the attack upon Nineveh.[19] The section envisions a brief siege followed by a decisive

---

[19]J. Daryl Charles, "Plundering the Lion's Den—A Portrait of Divine Fury (Nahum 2:3-11)," *GTJ* 10 (1989): 186.

attack against the city, which is unable to offer any substantial resistance. The prophet uses effectively the cherished symbols of Nineveh to depict their own defeat: war materials (vv. 3-4), water deluge (vv. 6-7), the palace (v. 6), the temple cult of Ishtar (v. 7), military plunder (v. 9), and the reaction of the helpless to the siege and fall (v. 10). Chapter 3, in the form of a woe pronouncement, also describes the fall of Nineveh but emphasizes the reasons for the city's fall rather than its nature. While verse 1 urges preparation for battle, verse 3 begins a description of the siege of Nineveh (vv. 3-6) and of the consequences of the attack for Nineveh (vv. 7-10). The vivid nature of narration has led to the supposition that the material originates after the events of the fall of Nineveh in 612 B.C., but the basic stock of battle images are readily available both before and after the fall of Nineveh.

The antecedent of "his" appears to be the "attacker" of verse 1, but it is unclear whether the pronoun refers of the city's defenders or attackers (or perhaps even the LORD from v. 2). The ambiguity may be intentional to reflect the confusion that exists in most warfare. If the verse describes an advancing army, the **red shields** and **scarlet** dress suggest a well-equipped and well-trained army with red uniforms not yet bloodied in battle. Ezekiel 23:14 indicates that the Babylonian army wears bright red. Or, Isaiah 9:5 refers to warriors' garments rolled in blood, intimating that the garments are covered with the blood of earlier skirmishes. **Chariots** are built of different kinds of wood for speed and maneuverability. They have fittings of leather and **metal** that **flash** with reflected light (cf. 1 Macc 6:39). The driver in the typical four-man crew is equipped with a long spear and a round shield. Polished cypress **spears** (cf. ESV) can give off a reddish appearance. The word translated **brandished** means "to shake" (cf. KJV), suggesting that the horsemen are eager for the attack (cf. the NJB's "the horsemen are impatient for action").

**2:4** The scene shifts from outside the city walls to within the city **streets** and **squares**. While the **chariots** may be those of the Assyrians who attempt in vain to defend themselves (cf. the ambiguity of "his" in the preceding verse), the chariots are more likely those of the enemy already described. The enemy's chariots penetrate the city's defenses, rushing back and forth through the squares. In this context, the word "squares" does not denote an open area outside the city walls (cf. the NJPS's "meadows"); instead, it refers to the wide open places within a city such as a plaza often used for public assemblies (e.g., Deut 13:16; Judg 19:15; Ezra 10:9; Neh 8:1; Esth 4:6). The prophet uses two similes to describe the appearance and movement of the chariots: **they look like flaming torches**, and **they dart about like lightning**. The images are consistent with the earlier theme of Yahweh's wrath being poured out like fire (1:6); here the agents of that fiery wrath are the chariots of the invaders.

**2:5** At least one commentator understands the first two lines of verse 5 to refer to the king of Assyria and to his troops (cf. the TNIV's insertion of "Nineveh"). If this is correct, they do so in satirical fashion, since the besieged king suddenly "remembers" (cf. the ESV and NASB which render זָכַר [zākar] with its basic meaning rather than its extended meaning **summon**) he has choice **troops** at his disposal. These troops, however, **stumble** to the wall while the attackers put the siege covering in place.[20] This reading may be assumed in the NIV because it begins the second line with "yet," even though the conjunction does not actually appear in the Hebrew text. The context of the preceding verses suggests, however, that these first two lines probably also refer to the attackers rather than the defenders of the city. Thus, the commander of the enemy army calls upon his picked troops (עַדִּיר, 'adîr), a word with the basic meaning of superiority or majesty. In similar contexts, it refers to rulers or nobles (2 Chr 23:20; Jer 30:21; Nahum 3:18) and is used once in parallel with the "mighty," translated as "warriors" in NASB and NJPS (Judg 5:13). If those stumbling then are the picked troops, perhaps they stumble in their extreme haste to reach **the city's wall**, or they have difficulty making their way through streets cluttered with the corpses of their victims. **The protective shield** is a mantelet (cf. NASB and NJB), which is a moveable defensive shield or shelter used to protect soldiers approaching the city walls of a besieged city. Two walls built by Sennacherib surround Nineveh. The outer wall is named "The Wall That Terrifies the Enemy"; the inner wall, "The Wall Whose Splendor Overwhelms the Enemy." The Greek historian Xenophon describes the walls of Nineveh as being fifty feet wide, one hundred feet tall, and about twenty miles in circumference.[21]

---

[20]O. Palmer Robertson, *The Books of Nahum, Habakkuk, and Zephaniah*, NICOT (Grand Rapids: Eerdmans, 1994), pp. 89-90.

[21]Xenophon, *Anab.* 3.4.10-11.

**2:6** "The **gates** of the **river**" probably refers to the sluice gates (cf. NJB) created by Sennacherib to control the waters of the Khosr River, a tributary of the Tigris which flows close to the walls of Nineveh, and to irrigate the city and its surrounding farmland. Perhaps the prophet envisions a scenario in which the river is dammed above the city and then suddenly released to cause a collapse or breach of the walls. Even though the *Babylonian Chronicles* does not mention the use of flood waters in the destruction of Nineveh, the classical written sources do.[22] The image may also be used metaphorically to describe the enemy troops pouring through the walls like water from open sluice gates.[23] **The palace** may be the north palace constructed by Ashurbanipal or the south palace built by Sennacherib and restored by Ashurbanipal. However, the word translated "palace" (הֵיכָל, *hêkāl*) may also refer to a temple (e.g., Jonah 2:4; Micah 1:2; Hab 2:20; Zech 6:12). If it does so here, it may denote one of the major temples of Ishtar, the goddess of war, or Nabu, the god of wisdom and writing, renovated by Ashurbanipal and destroyed in the city's fall (see the comments on v. 7 below). The word **collapse** has the basic meaning of "melt" (cf. the NJB's "the palace melts in terror"). This "melting" of the palace may refer either to the mounting fear of the palace's inhabitants or to the collapsing of the palace walls, although the NIV favors the latter. Certainly, the repetition of the word here mirrors its use in 1:5 and links the destruction of Nineveh in chapter 2 with the theophany of Yahweh in chapter 1.

**2:7** Attention now switches from the attackers to the city after its downfall. Indeed, the next four verses depict the consequences of the attack: Nineveh is defeated, and its riches plundered. The first word of the verse in the Hebrew text (הֻצַּב, *huṣṣab*) is difficult, and some versions merely render the Hebrew word with English letters and so speak of "Huzzab" being led away as captive (cf. KJV and NJPS). The NIV translates the word, **It is decreed**, taking the word to be related to the verb נָצַב (*nāṣab*), "to stand or be placed" (the verb form is found only in Gen 28:12, translated "resting," and Judg 9:6, translated "pillar"). Other versions translate the word, "beauty"

---

[22]Diodorus, *Bibl. Hist.* 2.27.1.
[23]J.J.M. Roberts, *Nahum, Habakkuk, and Zephaniah: A Commentary*, OTL (Louisville, KY: Westminster John Knox, 1991), p. 66.

(cf. NJB), based on an emendation of the spelling of the Hebrew word that adds to it the letter ' (*yod*). Although such an emendation is hypothetical, it likely represents a correct understanding of the word as referring to either the city personified (cf. NET), Nineveh's queen (cf. CEV), or, more likely, Nineveh's patron goddess Ishtar (cf. ESV). The NIV adopts the first of these three options when it adds the words **the city** in half brackets; the TNIV identifies the city as "Nineveh" (cf. the depictions of Babylon in Isa 47:1-5 and Jerusalem in Lam 1:1-4).

For this reason, the NIV also translates the next verb, **be exiled** (גָּלָה, *gālāh*), in a way parallel with the verb, **carried away** (cf. KJV, NJB, NJPS, and NRSV). However, the word *gālāh* may be rendered "stripped," as in the ESV and NASB, and both meanings, "to uncover" and "to go into exile," are well attested.[24] Any decision between these two options is predicated upon an understanding of *huṣṣab* above and the context that follows, namely, the verb "carried away" and the mourning of the slave girls. If *huṣṣab* refers to the city, the deportation of its inhabitants signals Nineveh's final defeat. If *huṣṣab* refers to the queen, the removal of her clothing is a way of humiliating her. If *huṣṣab* refers to the image of Ishtar, the removal of the statue from its pedestal is a way of dishonoring the goddess.

When *huṣṣab* is exiled/stripped and carried away, the **slave girls moan** and mourn. Perhaps these maidservants serve Ishtar, the goddess of love, as sacred prostitutes; if so, they now mourn Ishtar's abandonment of Nineveh in the moment of military defeat. The sound of the moaning dove suits the human lamentation compared to it (cf. Isa 38:14; 59:11; Ezek 7:16), and **beat**ing on **the breast** is a common image for sadness and sorrow (cf. Isa 32:12; Luke 18:13; 23:48).

**2:8** The simile compares **Nineveh** and its population to water. The city is built on the east bank of the Tigris, where the river Khosr falls into the Tigris. A Silician account of the city's fall claims that a sudden rise of the Khosr caused a stretch of the city's wall to collapse.[25] Perhaps the image envisions such a demise of the city. Or, the language may depict in a less literal manner the frightful flight of a defeated army and people as they stream out of the city to avoid capture. No command can cause their return to the city. While the

---

[24] *HALOT*, pp. 191-192.
[25] Diodorus, *Bibl. Hist.* 2.27.1.

verb translated **draining away** typically refers to the flight of humans (e.g., Exod 14:25; Deut 19:3; Josh 8:5; 2 Sam 4:4; Jer 46:6; Zech 14:5), it is applied to water in Psalm 104:7 and 114:3-5. Such an image is rooted in the theophanic representation of Yahweh as the divine warrior from whom the unruly waters of chaos flee (cf. 1:4).

**2:9** In the absence of any defenders, the invaders ransack the city. The verse imagines the cry of the enemy commander, "**Plunder the silver! Plunder the gold!**" The double imperative no doubt corresponds to the double imperative in the previous verse, "Stop! Stop!" Nineveh's **treasures** include more than gold and silver; its **wealth** possesses no end and comprises an abundance of goods "from every kind of desirable object" (NASB). A synonym for "plunder" appears earlier in verse 3, "destroyer" (both words occur in Isa 24:3). What Nineveh has done to Israel (and other nations) now happens to Nineveh. The word translated **endless** is also used in 3:3 denoting countless casualties, and in 3:9 touting the strength of Cush and Egypt. It occurs again only in Isaiah 2:7, a text with remarkable similarities with Nahum 2:9.

**2:10** The vivid and imaginary description of the fall of Nineveh that begins in verse 3 now concludes with a rush of word pictures. The first three are similar sounding words that play on the repeated sounds of the Hebrew letters ב (*beth*) and ק (*qoph*) as if to pronounce a curse upon the defeated city. The NRSV and NJPS attempt to render the wordplay in English, as does the NJB, "ravaged, wrecked, ruined." The *Babylonian Chronicles* confirms the great quantity of plunder taken from Nineveh after its fall.[26] The last four express physical responses of the destruction of Nineveh. **Hearts melt**ing suggests that the people of Nineveh have lost all courage to fight (cf. Deut 1:28; Josh 2:11; 5:1; 7:5; 2 Sam 17:10; Isa 13:7; 19:1; Ezek 21:7). **Knees giv**ing **way** insinuates that they are not able to escape their captors. **Bodies trembl**ing implies that they have no physical strength left (see comments on v. 1 above). **Faces grow**ing **pale** connotes tremendous terror (cf. Joel 2:6). This final image is difficult. The LXX renders it, "all faces are like a burning pot," and KJV reflects this reading, "the faces of them all gather blackness." Nonetheless, faces turning black does not convey the proper under-

---

[26]A.K. Grayson, *Assyrian and Babylonian Chronicles*, Texts from Cuneiform Sources (Locust Valley, NY: J.J. Augustin, 1975), p. 94.

standing of the biblical idiom in modern Western culture, for which a dark face generally connotes sadness. Verse 1 offers four instructions to prepare for battle; here these four expressions of bodily imagery show that such preparations are to no avail. The once powerful and insolent Nineveh is now seen as devastated and terrified.

## B. TAUNT OVER THE FALL OF NINEVEH (2:11-13)

[11]**Where now is the lions' den, / the place where they fed their young, / where the lion and lioness went, / and the cubs, with nothing to fear? / [12]The lion killed enough for his cubs / and strangled the prey for his mate, / filling his lairs with the kill / and his dens with the prey.**

[13]**"I am against you," / declares the LORD Almighty. / "I will burn up your chariots in smoke, / and the sword will devour your young lions. / I will leave you no prey on the earth. / The voices of your messengers / will no longer be heard."**

Nahum 2:11-13 introduces a new metaphor that ironically contrasts the impending devastation of Nineveh with its previous power. The interrogative particle, "Where," begins the unit and introduces the taunt (cf. Jer 2:28), that is, a sarcastic challenge against one Yahweh opposes. The lion motif ties the literary unit together. Of its seven lines, the first four convey the metaphor itself; the last three mix the metaphor with another. The word "behold," not translated in the NIV (cf. ESV, KJV, NASB), introduces the last three lines and shifts the section from a metaphorical description to a divine pronouncement. Thus, the derisive utterance first accuses the city of enriching itself by exploitation of other nations (vv. 11-12) and then announces to the city that Yahweh Almighty will soon destroy it (v. 13). The taunt functions not so much in anticipation of what happens to Nineveh but to identify what happens as divine action. The section shares similarities with 3:1-7, which compares Nineveh to an alluring prostitute and states Yahweh's opposition ("I am against you"), and with 3:8-13, which contains a rhetorical question ("Are you better than Thebes?") and depicts Nineveh's downfall.

**2:11-12** The word **Where** (אַיֵּה, 'ayyēh) most often occurs in rhetorical questions and is used by people disputing the existence and power of Yahweh or other gods (Judg 6:13; 2 Kgs 2:14; 18:34; Job 35:10; Ps 42:3,10; 79:10; 89:49; 115:2; Isa 33:18; 36:19; 63:11,15; Jer 2:6,8,28; 17:15; Joel 2:17). In Nahum, rhetorical questions give a sense of certainty and heightened satire (1:9; 2:11; 3:8). Here the question begins a taunt against Nineveh in the form of an extended metaphor whose image is quite appropriate. Several Assyrian kings tout their military prowess and brutality by comparing themselves to lions,[27] and they decorate their palaces with lion sculptures and lion hunting scenes. Lions appear frequently in the iconography of the Assyrian gods; Ishtar, the goddess of love and war, is often accompanied by a lion, and the sun god Shamash is often portrayed as a winged lion. Other Old Testament prophets also apply the image to Assyria (Isa 5:29; Jer 50:17). The verses use four different words for lion: "lion," "young lion," "lioness," and "cub," perhaps to represent the whole family or pride of lions. The leonine vocabulary may also represent certain Assyrians, namely, the king, his army, his queen, and Nineveh's inhabitants.[28] The question **Where is the lion's den?** may allude metaphorically to the portrayal in verse 6 of the palace's collapse. Since the Assyrian kings portray themselves as lions, the prophet satirically portrays the collapse of the palace in the center of the city as the disappearance of the lion's den.[29] The phrase, **with nothing to fear**, is used in covenant blessings (Lev 26:6; Jer 30:10; 46:27; Ezek 34:28; 39:26; Micah 4:4; Zeph 3:13) but also in covenant curses (Deut 28:26). The action of strangling prey is evidenced when lions occasionally kill their prey by placing both paws on the victim's throat. This then is the gist of the prophetic comparison: as a lion brings back his kill to feed his pride, the Assyrian king has filled Nineveh with the spoils of conquered nations. Thus, Nahum turns one of Assyria's favorite images back upon them, for now Yahweh will prevent Nineveh the power to prey on other nations.

**2:13** Nahum uses the particle, "behold" (הִנֵּה, *hinnēh*), as a transitional device at strategic points in the book (1:15; 2:13; 3:5,13). Its use here with the indictment, **I am against you**, is found also in 3:5, but the NIV does not translate the word in either of these instances.

---

[27]Daniel David Luckenbill, *Ancient Records of Assyria and Babylonia* (Chicago: University of Chicago Press, 1926–1927), 2:129.

[28]Roberts, *Nahum, Habakkuk, and Zephaniah*, p. 67.

[29]Sweeney, *Twelve Prophets*, 2:440.

"Behold, I am against you" is an example of a "challenge formula" in which one party calls another out to battle or duel (1 Sam 17:45; Jer 21:13; 50:31; 51:25; Ezek 5:8-9; 13:8-9; 21:3; 26:3; 28:22; 29:3; 35:3; 38:3; 39:1). Here, it issues the challenge of Yahweh as divine warrior against Nineveh. The force of this declaration is further magnified by the oath formula, **declares the LORD Almighty** (נְאֻם יְהוָה צְבָאוֹת, *nᵉ'um YHWH ṣᵉḇā'ôth*). The name *YHWH ṣᵉḇā'ôth* appears some two hundred sixty times in the Old Testament (e.g., 1 Sam 1:3; 17:45; Ps 24:10; Isa 1:9; Jer 2:19; Hos 12:5; Amos 3:13; Micah 4:4; Hab 2:13; Zech 2:9; Hag 1:2; Zech 1:3; Mal 1:4) and is also translated as "the LORD of Hosts" (ESV, KJV, NASB) or "Yahweh Sabaoth" (NJB). Its use as a title for Yahweh may relate to the appearance of "the commander of the army [צָבָא, *ṣāḇā'*] of the LORD" in Joshua 5:13-15. The noun *ṣᵉḇā'ôth* refers to an army organized for war or warfare in general; consequently, the title designates Yahweh as God of War or God of the Armies. It portrays Yahweh as sovereign not only over creation but over nations and history. The Assyrian army is now opposed by the LORD of Armies.

In addition, the following series of first person pronouns emphasize Yahweh's personal involvement against Nineveh and mix the metaphors of martial imagery (vv. 1-10) and leonine imagery (vv. 11-13) together. It thus structurally unites the chapter, brings it to a conclusion, and highlights several of Nahum's themes before they find their final expression in chapter 3: Yahweh will completely annihilate Nineveh, the arrogant lion. Yahweh will consume Nineveh's military might and vigorous army. The picture here of the **young lions** being devoured reverses one of the favorite metaphors the Assyrians use to portray themselves; they **no** longer **prey** on others, but they are prey themselves. No more will the Assyrian **messengers** threaten, as the field commander threatens king Hezekiah of Judah (the position is translated as the personal name "Rabshakeh" in various versions of 2 Kgs 18:17-37 and the parallel Isa 36:1-22); their **voices will no longer be heard**. Four uses of "no more" (1:12,14-15; 2:13) point to a coming, decisive deliverance for Judah.

## C. ANNOUNCEMENT OF PUNISHMENT AGAINST NINEVEH
### (3:1-7)

¹Woe to the city of blood, / full of lies, / full of plunder, / never without victims! / ²The crack of whips, / the clatter of wheels, / galloping horses / and jolting chariots! / ³Charging cavalry, / flashing swords / and glittering spears! / Many casualties, / piles of dead, / bodies without number, / people stumbling over the corpses— / ⁴all because of the wanton lust of a harlot, / alluring, the mistress of sorceries, / who enslaved nations by her prostitution / and peoples by her witchcraft. / ⁵"I am against you," declares the LORD Almighty. / "I will lift your skirts over your face. / I will show the nations your nakedness / and the kingdoms your shame. / ⁶I will pelt you with filth, / I will treat you with contempt / and make you a spectacle. / ⁷All who see you will flee from you and say, / 'Nineveh is in ruins—who will mourn for her?' / Where can I find anyone to comfort you?"

Nahum 3:1-7 exhibits the form of a prophecy of punishment against a foreign nation (cf. Zeph 2:5-15; Zech 9:1-8).[30] As such, it contains the two major features of a prophecy of punishment: accusation (vv. 1-4) and announcement (vv. 5-7). The accusation against an unidentified city, "city of blood" (Nineveh is not named until v. 7), begins with the word "woe" (v. 1) and returns to a narration similar to the prophetic report of 2:1-10. But now the city has fallen, and the fighting has ended; the enemy rushes about, looting and massacring (vv. 2-3). The city is charged with actions comparable to prostitution (v. 4), and accordingly the charge makes the lament sarcastic. The announcement of punishment by Yahweh is introduced by "behold" (see comments on 2:13 above) and challenge ("I am against you") and oracle ("declares the LORD Almighty") formulas (3:5). Verses 5-6 describe the punishment with metaphors appropriate for the public humiliation of a prostitute (cf. Hos 2:9-10). Such punishment is confirmed as just, since no one mourns for the ruin of Nineveh (v. 7). The unit begins and ends with references to mourning, "woe" (v. 1) and "mourn" (v. 7). Thus, Nahum 3:1-7 describes the defeat of Nineveh and the humiliation of those who

---

[30]Floyd, *Minor Prophets*, p. 71.

survive the city's attack. The unit presents such humiliation as a deserved fate and one indicative of Yahweh's justice.

**3:1** The accusation against an unidentified city begins with the word **woe** (הוֹי, *hôy*), a word that is associated with laments (e.g., 1 Kgs 13:30; Jer 22:18; 34:5). In these instances the interjection is followed by an explanation of the recipients' relationship to the deceased. More common is the use of the word in connection with the woe oracle, where the word is followed by an identification of the recipient of Yahweh's wrath and a description of their reprehensible behavior (e.g., Isa 5:11-14,18-19,20,21,22-25; 10:1-3; 28:1-4; 29:1-4,15; 31:1-5; Amos 5:18-20; 6:1-7; Micah 2:1-5; Hab 2:6-17; Zeph 2:5-7). In these contexts, *hôy* does not express grief but rather threat or curse (as expressed in the NJB's translation of *hôy* as "disaster"). The verse identifies the recipient of the woe oracle only as **the city of blood**, a phrase used in Ezekiel to describe Jerusalem (Ezek 22:2) and Babylon (24:6,9). The descriptive word, "blood" or "bloodshed" (as in the NRSV), intensifies the images that follow and connotes the guilt of the city responsible for carnage, deceit, exploitation, and tyranny.

The phrases that follow *hôy* describe Nineveh's evil, acts which justify her punishment. While the phrase **full of plunder** refers to Nineveh's abuse of subject nations, the description as deceptive or **full of lies** may point to diplomatic practices. One biblical example is Nineveh's dealings with Judah during the Syro-Ephraimic War (ca. 734 B.C.) in which Tiglath-Pileser comes to the aid of Ahaz and Judah, but he seizes the opportunity to heavily subjugate Judah as a vassal (2 Kgs 16:7-8; 2 Chr 28:20).[31] The word, "victims," in the NIV (translated "plunder" in the NRSV) alludes to the previous leonine imagery. The mention of prey (טֶרֶף, *ṭereph*) in verse 1 links this section with the preceding one which uses the related verb, "to tear flesh and consume" (טָרַף, *ṭāraph*), in 2:12. The NIV's **never without victims** understands the noun *ṭereph* as the direct object and takes the city as the unexpressed subject. However, "victims" is actually the subject of the verb יָמִישׁ (*yāmîš*, "he departs"), which is unexpressed in the NIV. The verb shows a masculine subject, yet "city" is a feminine noun. Whereas the NIV renders the sense of the clause

---

[31]Cf. Assyria's dealings with Hezekiah in 2 Kings 18:15-37 and the vassal-treaties of Esarhaddon in *ANET*, pp. 534-541.

well, the NASB better reflects the Hebrew clause itself, "*Her* prey never departs," that is, "the prey never runs out."

**3:2-3** No transition statement comes between the woe-oracle and the short vision account which follows. Verses 2-3 contain nine short exclamations that return to the scene of Nineveh's devastation in 2:9. There the prophet depicts the invasion of the city; now the invaders turn from plunder to slaughter. These two verses present a progression of images. The first images, **the crack of whips** and **the clatter of wheels**, are auditory. The next images, **galloping horses and jolting chariots** and **charging cavalry, flashing swords and glittering spears**, are visual. That is, Nineveh's inhabitants hear the chariots before seeing them. The final images, **Many casualties, piles of dead, bodies without number, people stumbling over the corpses**, represent the numerous fatalities from the attack. From the noise and motion of battle arises the silence and stillness of vast piles of carnage.

Verse 3 expresses the gruesome results of the battle with three different terms for the bodies of those slain. "Casualties" is derived from the verb "to pierce" (חָלָל, *ḥālāl*). It does not necessarily connote fatal wounds (Prov 26:10) and can thus denote those wounded to various degrees. At least four times, it refers to those wounded but not yet dead (Job 24:12; Jer 51:52; Ezek 26:15; 30:24). Ezekiel 32:22-23 uses *ḥālāl* to describe the dead of Assyria. The noun, "dead" (פֶּגֶר, *peger*), is related to a verbal root that means "to grow faint, be exhausted." It can thus describe the body near death or soon after (Num 14:29,32,33; 2 Kgs 19:35; 2 Chr 20:24-25; Isa 37:36). "Bodies" and "corpses" are actually the same Hebrew word (גְּוִיָּה, *gᵉwiyyāh*); it refers to corpses in several contexts (1 Sam 31:10,12; Ps 110:6) but elsewhere denotes bodies that are alive (Gen 47:18; Ezek 1:11,23; Dan 10:6; Neh 9:37). Its use to speak of corpses no doubt is derived from its basic meaning of "body," that is, the lifeless person is merely a body. All three words are used to depict judgment on the wicked (Ps 110:6; Isa 34:3; 66:16,24; Jer 25:33). The prophet may also play on similar sounding Hebrew words, "piles" (כֹּבֶד *kōbed*) in verse 3 and "wealth" (כָּבֹד, *kābōd*) in 2:9; Nineveh now has piles (*kōbed*) of dead instead of wealth (*kābōd*). The use of "stumble" may allude to 2:5. There the attacking soldiers stumble over one another in their haste to reach the city walls; here they stumble over fallen defenders. The picture of piles of corpses is reminiscent of Assyrian accounts of their destruction of cities in which they leave behind piles of bodies and thus is apropos for their own defeat.[32]

**3:4** Verse 4 explains both the destruction described in the previous verses and the judgment pronounced in the following verses. The word "harlot" (זָנָה, *zānāh*) introduces a new image; the underlying root of the word appears three times, translated as **wanton lust**, **harlot**, and **prostitution**. The Old Testament uses prostitution as a metaphor for Israel's worshiping gods other than Yahweh (Exod 34:15-16; Deut 31:16; Judg 2:17; 1 Chr 5:25; Ps 106:39) and portrays unfaithful Israel as a prostitute (Jer 3:1-8; Ezekiel 16, 23; Hosea 1–3). In the Old Testament, the archetypical harlot is Jezebel, infamous for her idolatry and sorcery (1 Kgs 18:19; 2 Kgs 9:22) and exploitation of the defenseless (1 Kgs 21:1-16).

Nahum 2:11-13 compares Nineveh to a lion; now the city is likened to a seductive harlot who enslaves people through prostitution and **witchcraft**. Any actual events to which these offenses may refer are unknown. Perhaps the imagery refers to Assyria's political alliances to aid other nations in exchange for their submission as vassals. For example, Tiglath-Pileser III, also known as Pul, takes tribute from Menahem, king of Israel, in 2 Kings 15:19 and from Ahaz, king of Judah, in 2 Kings 16:7-9. Perhaps the imagery refers to Ishtar, the goddess of war and love, whose rituals involved explicit sexual activity. The city of Nineveh's connection with the goddess makes more significant the section's blending of war (vv. 1-3) and harlot (vv. 4-6) imagery. However, the language of enslavement may also suggest a more literal referent for the harlot imagery, since Assyria frequently took as slaves peoples from nations defeated in battle.

The city is described as **alluring**, possessing majesty and splendor; it impresses with its military strength, its art and architecture, and its ostentation. Whereas Nahum 1:2 calls Yahweh the master of wrath (translated "maintains his wrath" in the NIV), here Nineveh is named **the mistress of sorceries**. The description affirms the Assyrians' interest in divination and sorcery, practices clearly condemned in the Old Testament (Lev 19:26-31; Deut 18:9-13; 1 Chr 10:13-14; 2 Chr 33:6; Jer 27:9-10; Ezek 13:18-20). Both sorcery and harlotry attempt to control by illicit and clandestine means; they

---

[32]See *ARAB* 1:146, 156; 2:219-220.

appear together in other texts (2 Kgs 9:22; Isa 57:3; cf. Gal 5:19-20; Rev 21:8; 22:15).

**3:5** Because Nineveh has used wealth and power to seduce and enslave other peoples, she is now represented as a whore publicly disgraced. The introduction to this speech is identical to that in 2:13, including both the challenge formula, "Behold, **I am against you**," and the oath formula, **declares the LORD Almighty** (see comments above). Seven times verses 5-7 refer to Yahweh in the first person, one time with the pronoun in the challenge formula, six times as the subject of verbs, and one time in the rhetorical question. Yahweh alone is in charge of the humiliation of Nineveh, not Judah or Nineveh's enemies. The absence of Judah as an agent of Nineveh's humiliation argues against characterizing the book as a nationalistic expression of hatred and revenge. The public exposure of **nakedness**, expressed by the action of **lift**ing **skirts over** one's **face**, is indicative of **shame** and humiliation (Gen 9:22-23; Exod 20:26; Isa 47:3; Jer 13:22; Ezek 16:8; Amos 2:16) and thus appropriate for the punishment for prostitution, whether physical or religious (Isa 57:8; Lam 1:8; Ezek 16:36-37; 23:18; Hos 2:3,10). The motif continues the harlot metaphor from the previous verse, but in other contexts it may also extend to other dehumanizing actions, especially the brutal treatment of a conquered people (Isa 47:1-3). For example, Isaiah 20:3-4 describes the king of Assyria leading away captives of Egypt and Cush with bared buttocks.

**3:6** Three more statements describe the public exposure of Nineveh. The word for **filth** means that which is detestable or abominable; it is used elsewhere in contexts dealing with aspects of idolatrous worship and thus is connected with that which repulses Yahweh (Deut 29:17; 1 Kgs 11:5,7; 2 Kgs 23:13,24; 2 Chr 15:8; Jer 4:1; 7:30; 13:27; 32:34; Ezek 5:11; 7:20; 11:18,21; 20:7-8,30; 37:23; Hos 9:10). The word **contempt** has the basic meaning of "foolish," but the verb form used here generally carries the idea of treating another as a fool or with disdain or disrespect (Deut 32:15; Jer 14:21; Micah 7:6). The word **spectacle** refers to something seen openly (1 Sam 16:12; Job 7:8; 33:21) and here with contempt, not unlike the way in which the Assyrians expose their captives to public ridicule.

**3:7 All who see** the spectacle of Nineveh's ruin **flee from** her, leaving the city to mourn her fate alone. A wordplay between two words from the same root word, "spectacle" and "all who see," links

verses 6 and 7. The NIV omits the verse's introductory clause, translated "and it shall come to pass" in the KJV; the frequent expression
characteristically announces prophetic fulfillment (e.g., Isa 2:2; Jer
3:9; Ezek 21:12; Hos 1:5; Joel 3:1; Amos 6:9; Micah 4:1; Zeph 1:8;
Zech 8:13) and does so here. The word "flee" can indicate flight
from the threat of danger (Ps 31:11; 68:12; Isa 10:31; 16:3; 21:14-15;
22:3; 33:3; cf. Nahum 3:17). Nineveh's devastation is so great that
those who see it shrink back in terror. Diodorus claims that the city
of Nineveh is leveled to the ground.[33] Nineveh stands in ruins but
receives no sympathy, for Assyria has ravaged other nations for centuries. Two rhetorical questions heighten the ridicule of Nineveh.
Those who see **Nineveh's ruins** ask **who will mourn for her**. The
word for "mourn" means "to shake the head" and is thus an appropriate gesture of grief (Job 2:11; 16:4; 42:11; Isa 51:19; Jer 15:5;
48:17). Furthermore, in the prophetic writings the word is often
linked with the tragedy engendered by divine judgment (Isa 51:19;
Jer 15:5; 18:16; 31:18; 48:17,27). Yahweh's voice ends the section
with an unanswerable question. The question may play on the meaning of Nahum's name, which is based on the word **comfort**.

## D. DESTRUCTION OF NINEVEH WILL BE LIKE THEBES
### (3:8-13)

[8]**Are you better than Thebes,[a] / situated on the Nile, / with
water around her? / The river was her defense, / the waters her
wall. / [9]Cush[b] and Egypt were her boundless strength; / Put and
Libya were among her allies. / [10]Yet she was taken captive / and
went into exile. / Her infants were dashed to pieces / at the head
of every street. / Lots were cast for her nobles, / and all her great
men were put in chains. / [11]You too will become drunk; / you will
go into hiding / and seek refuge from the enemy.**
  [12]**All your fortresses are like fig trees / with their first ripe fruit;
/ when they are shaken, / the figs fall into the mouth of the eater. /
[13]Look at your troops— / they are all women! / The gates of your land
/ are wide open to your enemies; / fire has consumed their bars.**

[a]*8 Hebrew No Amon*    [b]*9 That is, the upper Nile region*

---

[33]Diodorus, *Bibl. Hist.* 2.28.7.

Nahum 3:8-13 has the character of a prophetic interrogation, similar to 1:2-10; it combines a rhetorical question (v. 8) with comparative statements from which its answer may be inferred (vv. 9-13). The rhetorical question invites the addressee, still Nineveh from the previous section (v. 7), to consider her perceived invincibility. Verses 8-10 recall the fall of Thebes, a city defended by water and one which ruled over Egypt and other neighboring peoples. Although powerful, Thebes suffers a tragic defeat to the Assyrians in 663 B.C. Verses 11-13 assert a similar fate for Nineveh. Although once powerful, Nineveh is now ripe for destruction and wide open to invasion, defended by troops who are drunken cowards unable to stand against the enemy. While the unit is ostensibly addressed to Nineveh, it conveys to the reader that no political power should assume itself invincible to defeat. Thebes fell and so too will Nineveh.

**3:8** The section (vv. 8-13) begins with a rhetorical question, calling on Nineveh to consider her illusion of invincibility. Earlier taunts in 2:11-13 and 3:4-7 are based on lion and harlot metaphors, but here Nahum uses the historical analogy of the fall of Thebes, a city defeated by the Assyrians under Ashurbanipal in 663 B.C.[34] The Hebrew words נֹא אָמוֹן (*nō' 'āmôn*) appear to be a transliteration of the Egyptian name for the city of **Thebes**, generally known in English by this Greek name. Several versions, including the KJV, NASB, and NJB, retain the transliterated name, "No Amon," which means "the city of (the god) Amon." The Greeks also refer to Thebes as Διόσπολις (*diospolis*), "city of (the) god." Elsewhere in the Old Testament, "Thebes" is designated only as *nō'* and without inclusion of the divine name Amon in the identification of the city (Jer 46:25; Ezek 30:14-16). The ancient city, the great capital of Upper (southern) Egypt for much of its history, is located several hundred miles south of Memphis on the Nile River. Like Nineveh, Thebes is a sacred city, dedicated to the god Amon, and a well-protected city. Before Ashurbanipal brings it down, Thebes seems unconquerable, since it is protected by a strong defensive wall and an extensive system of moats and other defenses. The verse depicts the latter with a fourfold mention of water: **Nile**, **water**, **river**, and **waters**. The last two of these translate the Hebrew word typically rendered "sea" (יָם, *yām*). While the word "sea" (cf. the rendering in the ESV, KJV,

---

[34]*ANET*, pp. 294-297.

NASB, NJB, NRSV, and NJPS) seems incongruent with the actual location of Thebes (i.e., Thebes is nowhere near a sea), in other contexts *yām* refers to major rivers, the Nile in Isaiah 18:1-2 and the Euphrates in Jeremiah 51:36, and likewise here the word denotes the Nile and the other waters that **surround** the city like a fortress.

**3:9** Thebes also has North African allies; nevertheless, none render aid when the Assyrians attack. Cush is the ancient designation of the territory on the Upper Nile, south of Egypt, sometimes translated Ethiopia in other versions (Gen 2:13; Esth 1:1; 8:9; Job 28:19; Ps 68:31; 87:4; Isa 11:11; 18:1; 20:3-5; 37:9; Ezek 38:5; Zeph 3:10). Egypt is the ancient civilization of the Nile River valley in northeast Africa, called the "gift of the Nile" by the Greek historian Herodotus. Egypt figures prominently in the history of Israel, particularly as regards events associated with Abraham (Genesis 12–13), Joseph (Genesis 37–47), Moses (Exodus 2–15), Solomon (1 Kings 3), and other of the kings (1 Kings 14; 2 Kings 17–18, 23–24). The pairing of **Cush and Egypt** reflects the political situation in the seventh century during which the two are united under the reign of the Sudanese (or Twenty-Fifth) Dynasty (712–663 B.C.) and Thebes becomes quite wealthy. The exact location of **Put** is not clear, but it may be that Put is the Hebrew name for the same territory as **Libya** or a territory nearby (Isa 66:19; Jer 46:9; Ezek 27:10; 30:5; 38:5). However, Nahum's distinction between Put and Libya seemingly rules out a simple identification of the two. An identification of Put with modern day Somaliland may be possible as the biblical name "Put" resembles "Punt," the Egyptian designation of the east African nation. Libya is the Greek name for the territory in northern Africa along the coast west of Egypt (2 Chr 12:3; 16:8; Ezek 30:5; Dan 11:43).

**3:10** This verse depicts the brutal enslavement and exile of the people of Thebes. In 2 Kings 24:15-16, the same word, **taken captive**, describes the removal of Jehoiachin, king of Judah, by Nebuchadnezzar, king of Babylon, from Jerusalem to Babylon (2 Kgs 24:15-16). The words "taken captive" and **exile** also appear together in the lists of those exiles returning from Babylonian captivity (Ezra 2:1; 8:35; Neh 7:6). The destruction of cities and peoples in ancient warfare often includes the practice of killing **infants**, who are likely unable to survive the journey of deportation (2 Kgs 8:12; Ps 137:9; Isa 13:16-18; Hos 10:14; 13:16; cf. Matt 2:16-18). Neither do **nobles** or officials escape enslavement or exile; they are traded off as slaves and for sexual pleasures (Ezek 24:6; Joel 3:3; Obad 11). In the record of Assyrian campaigns against Arabia, Ashurbanipal puts a dog collar on the defeated king of Arabia and places him like a watchdog at the city gate of Nineveh.[35]

**3:11-13** Nahum depicts Nineveh with five different images in verses 11-13: a staggering drunk, a fugitive from an enemy, a shaken fig tree, defenseless women, and a city with wide-open gates. The conjunction גַּם (*gam*), which is found four times in verses 10-11 (translated as "yet," "also," "too," and "too" in the NASB; the NIV translates only the first and third occurrences of the word), heightens the dramatic comparison of the two cities and emphasizes the certainty that Nineveh will share the same fate as Thebes. The image of **becom**ing **drunk** is an instance of a frequent image used in texts speaking of military threats (Jer 25:27; Lam 4:21; Ezek 23:33; Hab 2:16) and one which characterizes the stupor of Yahweh's enemies earlier in 1:10. (Diodorus remarks that the Assyrian troops, because of overconfidence from earlier victories, banquet and carouse the night before Nineveh falls.[36]) The anticipation that Nineveh **seeks refuge** (מָעוֹז, *mā'ôz*) in vain contrasts with the portrayal of Yahweh as a refuge (also *mā'ôz*) in 1:7. The simile of a **shaken** tree and the eating of **figs** connotes how readily Nineveh's defenses fall and the enemy's eagerness to plunder the riches of the Assyrian city (cf. Isa 28:4; Jer 24:2; Micah 7:1). The pejorative comparison of Nineveh's **troops** to **women** speaks to the troops' cowardice or, more likely, their inability (cf. "weaklings" in the TNIV) to defend successfully the city (cf. Isa 19:16; Jer 50:37; 51:30). The Hebrew word (עַם, *'am*) refers mainly to people but occasionally to troops (Num 20:20; 21:23; 1 Sam 11:11; 1 Kgs 20:10; Ezek 17:15; Dan 11:15). If *'am* should mean "people" here (as translated in the KJV, NASB, and NJB), the image may merely refer to decimation of the men of the city, leaving only noncombatant females (cf. Isa 3:25–4:1). Earlier the prophet envisions the collapse of the city resulting from the opening of the river gates (2:6); now the **gates** guarding entrance into the land are **wide open to** Nineveh's **enemies**. The bars mentioned here are the bars of city gates (cf. TNIV); they are destroyed by **fire**, a familiar motif in Nahum (1:10; 2:13; 3:15).

---

[35]*ANET*, p. 298.
[36]Diodorus, *Bibl. Hist.* 2.26.4.

## E. DESTRUCTION OF NINEVEH WILL BE COMPLETE
## (3:14-19)

[14]**Draw water for the siege, / strengthen your defenses! / Work the clay, / tread the mortar, / repair the brickwork! / [15]There the fire will devour you; / the sword will cut you down / and, like grasshoppers, consume you. / Multiply like grasshoppers, / multiply like locusts! / [16]You have increased the number of your merchants / till they are more than the stars of the sky, / but like locusts they strip the land / and then fly away. / [17]Your guards are like locusts, / your officials like swarms of locusts / that settle in the walls on a cold day— / but when the sun appears they fly away, / and no one knows where.**

[18]**O king of Assyria, your shepherds[a] slumber; / your nobles lie down to rest. / Your people are scattered on the mountains / with no one to gather them. / [19]Nothing can heal your wound; / your injury is fatal. / Everyone who hears the news about you / claps his hands at your fall, / for who has not felt / your endless cruelty?**

[a]*18* Or *rulers*

The switch to frantic orders for the defense of Nineveh in verse 14 distinguishes verses 14-19 as a section separate from verses 8-13. The first part of the section (vv. 14-17) addresses the city Nineveh with the second person feminine singular; the second part (vv. 18-19) addresses the king of Nineveh with the second person masculine singular. Verses 14-17 exhibit the form of a prophetic sentinel report, similar to the earlier section of 2:1-10. It contains ironic commands followed by assertions of their ineffectiveness and metaphors involving locusts with various variations. Verses 18-19 have the character of a dirge, that is, a song of grief fitting for a funeral, but the unit announces, rather than mourns, the death of the king, the one who personifies the nation of Assyria. The prophet is so confident of Nineveh's fall that he composes a dirge as if the king's death has already taken place (cf. Isa 14:4-23; Amos 5:1-3); furthermore, the dirge substitutes for grief the joy of those who witness the demise of Assyria, whose fate is inescapably tied to that of their king. The section identifies for the readers the futility of Nineveh's defense, the internal factors which have made Nineveh vulnerable, and the imminent death of the king, for which the readers will participate in the joyous response of the nations.

**3:14** After verses 12-13, verse 14 is clearly ironic. It contains a series of five imperative verbs; these commands to make ready for a **siege**, however, are followed by assertions that such preparations come too late and only prove ineffective (vv. 15-17). The verse has similarities with 2:1, where the prophet also speaks as a watchman (2:1-10). The commands themselves represent the normal preparations for withstanding a siege, **draw**ing **water** to fill cisterns and maintaining the brickwork of the wall and other fortifications. Nineveh's **defenses** have been **strengthen**ed by several of the Assyrian kings, who build an extensive aqueduct system to supply water for the city and a daunting pair of walls to surround the city. The references to trampling in the mud and making bricks may recall Israel's slavery in Egypt (Exod 1:11-14); thus Yahweh now enslaves Assyria.[37] The word **repair** (חֲזַק, *ḥāzāq*) has the idea of "make strong" and is used to speak of the repair to the temple in the days of Joash (2 Kgs 12:7-8), Hezekiah (2 Chr 29:3), and Josiah (2 Kgs 22:5-6) as well as the restoration of Jerusalem's walls under Nehemiah's leadership (Neh 3:4-32).

**3:15-17** The next three verses use the locust metaphor in various ways to portray the futility of Nineveh's defense and the finality of Nineveh's demise. While the words "grasshopper" and "locust" in the NIV refer to basically the same kind of insect, these words, along with two others, may indicate various stages in the life cycle of a migratory locust.[38] The word "grasshopper" translates the Hebrew word יֶלֶק (*yeleq*) and denotes a young, wingless locust that is unable to fly or walk (Jer 51:14,27; Joel 1:4; 2:25; Nahum 3:15-16; Ps 105:34). Two other words may describe intermediate stages of development. The Hebrew word חָסִיל (*ḥāsîl*) denotes a locust with partially developed wings and jaws and is sometimes translated "grasshopper" or "young locust" in the NIV (1 Kgs 8:37; 2 Chr 6:28; Ps 78:46; Isa 33:4; Joel 1:4; 2:25), and the Hebrew word גָּזָם (*gāzām*) refers to a locust with fully developed jaws and dry wings and is sometimes translated "gnawing locust" in the NASB (Joel 1:4; 2:25; Amos 4:9). The word "locust" translates the Hebrew word אַרְבֶּה (*'arbeh*), a general term for a fully developed, winged locust (Exod 10:4-19; Lev 11:22; Deut 28:38; Judg 6:5; 7:12; 1 Kgs 8:37; 2 Chr 6:28; Job 39:20; Ps 78:46;

---

[37]Sweeney, *Twelve Prophets*, 2:444.
[38]Robert C. Stallman, "אַרְבֶּה," *NIDOTTE*, 1:492.

105:34; 109:23; Prov 30:27; Jer 46:23; Joel 1:4; 2:25; Nahum 3:15-17).
Although some texts speak of locust in a literal sense (e.g., Lev
11:22; Deut 14:19-20; cf. Matt 3:4; Mark 1:6), locusts are a standard
biblical image for judgment beginning with the exodus narrative
(Exod 10:1-20; Deut 28:38-42; 1 Kgs 8:37; 2 Chr 7:13-14; Ps 78:46;
105:34-35; Joel 2:1-11,25; Amos 4:9; Rev 9:3-11). Specifically, the
locust imagery in verses 15-17 depicts the complete devastation from
the enemy invasion, the impossibility of defending the city by increasing its population, the internal demise of the city caused in part
by the exploitation of its merchants, and the desertion of the
Assyrian nobility before the city's fall.

**3:15** The destruction of Nineveh comes by **fire** and by **sword**,
when the enemy like locusts sweeps through Nineveh leaving the
city thoroughly devastated. The Old Testament uses locusts as a fitting metaphor for an invading army, especially in terms of its infinite
number (Judg 6:5; 7:12; Jer 46:23; 51:14),[39] its thunderous approach
(Joel 2:5; cf. Rev 9:9), its unbroken advance (Prov 30:27; Joel 2:5-8),
and its unabated destruction (Joel 1:4; Amos 7:1-2). The metaphor
is commonly associated with destruction by fire as it is here (Joel 1:4;
2:3,5). Both fire and sword consume (**devour** and **consume** translate
the same Hebrew word) the people of Nineveh, an image which
plays on the voracious appetite of locusts. The language also corresponds with the recurring expression, "the edge of the sword" (cf.
ESV and NASB), where "edge" translates the Hebrew word for
"mouth" (Gen 34:26; Exod 17:13; Num 21:24; Deut 13:15; 20:13;
Josh 6:21, and others). The NIV completely omits the idiom in the
Old Testament; it appears only in Hebrews 11:34. The prophet
turns from comparing the destructive power of Nineveh's enemies
to that of locusts to calling upon the city to multiply its populace like
locusts. The notion of a large numerical increase extends from the
image's connotation of an infinite number (Judg 6:5; Jer 46:23).
Thus, the two lines that end verse 15 sarcastically urge Nineveh to
**multiply like locusts**, but, in view of the devastation described previously, such rapid reinforcement of troops is impossible.

**3:16** Nineveh has expanded the **merchant** class within the city,
an **increase** which has actually decreased the city's ability to defend

---

[39]Cf. the use of the image in the Ugaritic legend of King Keret in *ANET*,
pp. 143-144.

itself. The presence of innumerable traders (1 Kgs 10:15; Neh 3:31-32; 13:20; S of S 3:6; Ezek 17:4; 27:3,13,15,17,20,22-24) testifies to the immeasurable wealth within the city, but these same traders take their goods and flee in the face of trouble, depriving the city of needed provisions and deserting a city of needy people. **Like locusts [that] strip the land and then fly away**, the merchants have satisfied their own greed for profit, perhaps through exploitation. The NIV reads, "but like locusts they strip the land"; however, the verb פָּשַׁט (*pāšaṭ*) may refer to the stripping off of the locust's outer layer as it emerges from its larval stage (cf. the use of the word for skinning animals; e.g., Lev 1:6; 2 Chr 29:34; 35:11). If so, the reading in the NRSV, "The locust sheds its skin," may be preferable. The word *pāšaṭ* most often refers to stripping off a garment (Gen 37:23; Lev 6:11; 16:23; 1 Sam 18:4; Neh 4:23; Ezek 26:16), but it may mean "to raid" or "to rob" (1 Sam 23:27; 27:8,10; 30:1,14; 1 Chr 14:9,13; 2 Chr 28:13,18; Job 1:17; Hos 7:1). Both senses, shedding and raiding, suit the locust metaphor, since locusts devour everything in their path and, upon shedding their skins, leave quickly. Both also suit the actions of the merchants, who satiate their craving for economic gain, flee the city, and leave nothing of value behind.

**3:17** In verse 17, the locust imagery portrays the sudden flight of certain administrative or military officials. Both **guards** and **officials** are difficult words for determining their precise meaning; the word "guard" appears only here, and the word "officials," elsewhere only in Jeremiah 51:27. Whereas some translations (e.g., the NIV and NRSV) render the first word as "guards," other suggested meanings include "courtiers."[40] Likewise, the second word translated "officials" may denote an administrative official or a military commander (cf. Jer 51:27 and the use of a similar word in 2 Kgs 25:19; 2 Chr 26:11; Jer 52:25). However, one recent study notes the use of related Assyrian words and suggests that both designations refer to "palace officials," including astrologers and magicians.[41] If so, the words name those officials whose responsibility it is to provide advice to the king and guidance for his actions. Thus the ones who foresee the signs of the coming destruction of Nineveh flee the city at their first opportunity, here signified by the appearance of the

---

[40]*HALOT*, p. 601.
[41]Cathcart, "Nahum," *ABD*, 4:998.

sun **on a cold day**. The phrase **swarms of locusts** translates yet two
other terms for locust (גּוֹב גֹּבָי‎, *gôb gōbāy*); they indicate not a different kind of locust but a group ready to swarm (Amos 7:1). The word
used to denote the departure of the locusts is used elsewhere for
people fleeing from the voice of Yahweh (Ps 68:12; Isa 33:3; cf. Hos
7:13; 9:17) and for soldiers or rulers retreating from battle (Isa
21:14-15; 22:3; cf. Nahum 3:7). Nineveh's officials are numerous like
locusts, but they also resemble locusts by their sudden flight from
the city. They disappear without a trace. Diodorus speaks of how the
king sends away his three sons and two daughters before the city is
attacked,[42] and the *Babylonian Chronicle* seems to indicate that the
Assyrian king escapes from Nineveh before its destruction.[43]

**3:18** For the first time, the **king of Assyria** is addressed explicitly, and the address highlights the battle between the Assyrian
monarch and Judah's true king, Yahweh. The change of tone from
a feverish narration of Nineveh's demise (2:1–3:17) to a mournful
dirge over the king's death (3:18-19) serves as a literary device that
points back to the description of the inescapable judgment of
Yahweh to which the opening hymn testifies (1:2-8).[44] Several parallels also appear between 1:12-15 and 3:18-19. Both address the king
of Assyria and refer to his victims' celebration of his demise (1:15;
3:19). A messenger brings good news on the mountains (1:15), but
the Assyrian people are scattered there (3:18). Both passages utilize
the verb עָבַר‎ (*'ābar*, translated "pass away" in 1:12, "invade" in 1:15,
and "felt" in 3:19) and the root שׁבר‎ (*šbr*) (translated "break" in 1:13
and "wound" in 3:19).[45]

In his address to the king, the prophet pronounces the fate of
three groups: the death of Nineveh's leaders and troops and the
scattering of its populace. In the ancient Near East, **shepherd** is frequently used as a metaphor for "rulers" or "kings" to denote their
responsibility to lead and protect the people.[46] In the Old Testa-

---

[42]Diodorus, *Bibl. Hist.* 2.26.8.

[43]*ANET*, pp. 303-304, but cf. *ABC*, p. 94.

[44]Childs, *Introduction*, p. 445.

[45]Robert B. Chisholm, Jr., *Interpreting the Minor Prophets* (Grand Rapids:
Zondervan, 1990), p. 167.

[46]See Joyce G. Baldwin, *Haggai, Zechariah, Malachi: An Introduction and
Commentary*, TOTC 24 (Downers Grove, IL: InterVarsity, 1982), p. 171; and
F.F. Bruce, *New Testament Development of Old Testament Themes* (Grand

ment, the word "shepherd" generally refers either to Yahweh (Gen 49:24; 48:15; Ps 23:1; 80:1; Isa 40:11) or some earthly ruler. If the latter, it may denote national leaders in Israel (Num 27:17; 2 Sam 7:7), nobility in Israel (Jer 2:8; 23:1-2; 25:34-36), Gentile military commanders (Isa 44:28; Micah 5:5-6), or the Messiah (Ezek 34:23-24; 37:24-25).[47] Thus, here the designation refers to the political or military leaders of the city. The word **nobles** appears earlier in 2:5, where it refers to "picked troops" (see comments above; cf. the NJB's "bravest men"). The image of sleep may perform a double function here at the end of Nahum. On one level is depicted an exhausted and disorganized army unable to rally to the battle; on a second level is invoked the common biblical metaphor of sleep for death (Ps 13:3; 76:5; Job 3:13; 14:12; Jer 51:39,57; Dan 12:2). The parallel image of the nobles lying down to rest points to the former since this image is seldom used for death unless with explicit reference to lying down in death or in the grave (cf. Isa 26:19). If so, it refers to the negligence of Assyrian leadership. However, the presence of the metaphor in the conclusion of the book may suggest that slumber here refers to the sleep of death. In either case, the metaphor reverses the image of Assyria found in Isaiah 5:27, "not one slumbers or sleeps." Although the word translated "people" normally refers to people in general, it may be understood as "troops" (see comments on v. 13 above). Nevertheless, the image of **people scattered** and without a shepherd, a common metaphor in the Old Testament (Num 27:17; 1 Kgs 22:17; 2 Chr 18:16; Ezek 34:5-6; cf. Matt 9:36), favors rendering the word here as "people." While elsewhere Yahweh promises to gather a remnant of the people from captivity and from among the nations (Deut 30:3-4; 1 Chr 16:35; Ps 106:47; Isa 11:12; 13:14; 66:18; Ezek 20:41), here the people of Nineveh have **no** leader **to gather them.**

**3:19** Like Nineveh's leaders and troops, the king also dies. The language describing his demise is common among the prophets for the collapse of a kingdom (Isa 30:26; 51:19; Jer 4:6,20; 6:1; 48:3,5;

---

Rapids: Eerdmans, 1968), p. 100, for examples from Assyria, Babylonia, Canaan, Egypt, and Sumeria.

[47]I.M. Duguid, *Ezekiel and the Leaders of Israel*, VTSupp 56 (Leiden: Brill, 1994), pp. 39-40; J.G. Thomson, "The Shepherd-Ruler Concept in the Old Testament and Its Application in the New Testament," *SJT* 8 (1955): 406-412.

50:22; 51:54; Lam 2:11,13; 3:47-48; 4:10; Ezek 32:9). More specifically, the same vocabulary used here, namely, **wound**, **injury**, and **fatal**, elsewhere describes catastrophe that results from invasion (Jer 10:19), just punishment that results from grievous sin (Jer 30:12), and exile that results from excess and oppression (Amos 6:6), each of which are appropriate for Nahum's depiction of Nineveh's destruction. Nineveh finally falls to a combined attack of Medes, Babylonians, and Scythians in 612 B.C. in the fourteenth year of Nabopolassar, king of Babylon (626–605 B.C.); the city is destroyed such that it is not rebuilt. Nineveh's reigning king at the time of its fall is Sin-Shar-Ishkun (623–612 B.C.). One tradition maintains that, when the king sees that the city is beyond rescue, he sets his palace on fire, killing himself;[48] another tradition offers that the king escapes.[49] The images of the incurable wound and fatal injury anticipate the demise of the Assyrian monarchy that survives for only three years after the fall of Nineveh. Because of endless cruelty, Nineveh lies in endless ruin.

Once again, Nahum utilizes a rhetorical question (cf. 1:6,9; 2:11; 3:7,8). Only two prophetic books conclude with a rhetorical question; both of them involve Nineveh. In Jonah, the question extends compassion toward Nineveh (Jonah 4:11). In Nahum, the question exposes the cruelty of Nineveh (v. 19). (As an example, the Assyrian king Shalmaneser III [858–824 B.C.] boasts of erecting four pyramids of heads in front of the gate of a defeated city.[50]) Both Nahum and Jonah draw upon Exodus 34:6-7 to comment on the character of God. Jonah is troubled by Yahweh's compassion (Jonah 4:2), but Nahum is comforted by Yahweh's justice (1:3). Yahweh now reverses the Assyrian domination originally intended to punish the people of Yahweh (see Isaiah's earlier anticipation of this in 10:5-17). The image of **clap**ping **hands** is an act of derision (Job 27:21-23; 34:37; Lam 2:15; Ezek 25:6). Those who hear about the destruction of Nineveh rejoice that Yahweh has made an end of that great city.

---

[48]Diodorus, *Bibl. Hist.* 2.27.2, but cf. *ABC*, p. 94.
[49]*ANET*, pp. 304-305.
[50]*ARAB*, 1:219-220.

# THE BOOK OF
# HABAKKUK

# INTRODUCTION

## AUTHORSHIP

The extent of certain knowledge of the prophet comes from the scant information in the book's opening verse. The LXX renders his name Αμβακούμ (*Ambakoum*) and the Latin Vulgate *Habacuc*. His name may derive from an intensive stem form of the Hebrew verb to embrace or hug (חָבַק, *ḥābaq*). But it is unclear whether the connotation of the name's meaning be taken as active or passive. Is then Habakkuk an "embracer" or the "embraced"? Martin Luther takes it in the active sense and sees Habakkuk as one who embraces his people to comfort and uphold them. Jerome sees Habakkuk as one who embraces the problem of divine justice in a wicked world. Others prefer the passive sense and picture Habakkuk as one whom Yahweh embraces as a child and messenger.[1]

The name more likely originates from an Akkadian word *habbaququ* that refers to a garden plant. Hebrew personal names derived from plant names exist (e.g., Tamar, Elon, Keziah, Hadassah), and one would expect the presence of Akkadian loan words in Hebrew given the Assyrian domination of the region in the eighth century.[2] An Akkadian plant name may indicate a childhood in the reign of Manasseh (697–642 B.C.). During that general era the use of non-theophoric names increases, for example, Huldah ("mole"), Achbor ("spider" or "mouse"), and Shaphan ("rock-badger").[3]

---

[1] J. Ronald Blue, "Habakkuk," in *The Bible Knowledge Commentary: An Exposition of the Scriptures*, ed. by John F. Walvoord and Roy B. Zuck (Wheaton, IL: Victor Books, 1983–1985), 1:1505; James Bruckner, *Jonah, Nahum, Habakkuk, Zephaniah*, NIV Application Commentary (Grand Rapids: Zondervan, 2004), p. 199.

[2] J.J.M. Roberts, *Nahum Habakkuk, and Zephaniah: A Commentary*, OTL (Louisville, KY: Westminster John Knox, 1991), p. 86.

[3] P.J.M. Southwell, "Habakkuk: Theology of," *NIDOTTE*, 4:688-690.

The lack of biblical data no doubt has led to several conjectures about Habakkuk's identity. The superscription of the apocryphal book Bel and the Dragon, an addition to the book of Daniel in the LXX, identifies Habakkuk as the son of Joshua of the tribe of Levi. Yet, another tradition found in the *Lives of the Prophets*, a pseude-pigraphal work written during the first century A.D., identifies him as a member of the tribe of Simeon.[4] Bel and the Dragon gives a fanciful account of an angel catching up Habakkuk by his hair and transporting him to Babylon where Habakkuk meets Daniel in the lions' den. There he feeds Daniel some stew and bread he has originally prepared for a group of reapers in Judah.[5] A late (ca. 1300 A.D.) rabbinic tradition cites the use of the verb חָבַק (*ḥābaq*) in 2 Kings 4:16 to identify Habakkuk as the son born to the Shunammite couple whose life Elisha saved.[6] This notion is doubtful, since Elisha ministers at least a century before the earliest proposed dates for Habakkuk's ministry (see comments on Date below).

Both superscriptions found within the book (1:1 and 3:1) identify Habakkuk as "the prophet" (הַנָּבִיא, *hanābî'*). No other preexilic prophet is introduced that way in a superscription, but the term is used in the superscriptions of the postexilic books of Haggai and Zechariah. Nonetheless, the presence in the book of lament forms, a salvation oracle (1:5-11) in response to a petition or lament (1:2-4), theophanic imagery, musical notations (3:1,19), and the assertion that "Yahweh is in his holy temple" (2:20) lead to the suggestion that Habakkuk is a "cult prophet," a prophet or Levite employed by the temple who delivers oracles within temple worship settings.[7] Those who entertain this possibility appeal to 1 Chronicles 25:1 for support.[8] There the temple staff is said to include those who prophesy

---

[4]*Lives of the. Prophets* 12.1.

[5]Vv. 33-39; cf. *Liv. Pro.* 12.6-7.

[6]*Sefer ha-Zohar* 1.7; 2.44-45.

[7]Theodore Hiebert, "Habakkuk," in *NIB*, ed. by Leander E. Keck (Nashville: Abingdon, 1996), 7:627.

[8]F.F. Bruce, "Habakkuk," in *The Minor Prophets: An Exegetical and Expository Commentary*, ed. by Thomas Edward McComiskey (Grand Rapids: Baker, 1993), 2:832; C.F. Keil, *Minor Prophets*, vol. 10 of *Biblical Commentary on the Old Testament*, by C.F. Keil and R. Delitzsch, trans. by James Martin (Grand Rapids: Eerdmans, 1988 reprint), p. 49; Bruckner, *Jonah, Nahum, Habakkuk, Zephaniah*, p. 202.

(נָבָא, *nābā'*) with lyres, harps, and cymbals. Such lyres and harps would correspond to the stringed instruments spoken of in Habakkuk 3:19. Even though this data may allow for the argument that Habakkuk is more connected with the cult than are his contemporaries Nahum and Zephaniah, it remains equally plausible that he is not formally connected to the temple. Most Israelites would have been conversant with the musical phenomena cited above, and strong conclusive evidence to affirm a cultic setting is wanting.[9] Moreover, neither an affirmative nor a negative answer contributes significantly to an understanding of the text.[10]

## HISTORICAL BACKGROUND

The general setting of the book of Habakkuk is like that of the book of Jeremiah and possibly Zephaniah (see Date below). It is a tale of a whirlpool of change in the centers of power of the ancient Near East and of the tiny kingdom of Judah caught up in that swirl. The beginning and middle of the seventh century B.C. see the zenith and decline of Assyrian power in the region (see "Nahum Introduction: Historical Background" for detailed information). A contributing factor and complement to Assyria's decline is the rise of the neo-Babylonians (hereafter Babylonians). The NIV, NET, and NLT identify the Chaldeans (כַּשְׂדִּים, *kaśśᵊdîm*) in the Hebrew text of Habakkuk 1:6 as "Babylonians," whereas the ESV, KJV, NASB, NRSV, NJB, and NJPS retain the term "Chaldeans." The NIV uses the term "Chaldeans" to refer to the residents of southern Mesopotamia who live northwest of the Persian Gulf during the patriarchal era (Gen 11:28,31; 15:7; Neh 9:7; Job 1:17), to identify Babylon as the "land of the Chaldeans" (Ezek 12:13), and to name a specific ethnic group within the broader Babylonian alliance (Ezek 23:23). The Assyrian king Shalmaneser II, like others in the ancient Near East, uses it to identify a number of tribes in the region.[11] By the time of Daniel, the term had come to designate astrologers who were sum-

---

[9]Gordon McConville, *A Guide to the Prophets*, vol. 4, *Exploring the Old Testament* (Downers Grove. IL: InterVarsity, 2002), p. 212.

[10]Roberts, *Nahum, Habakkuk, and Zephaniah*, p. 85.

[11]Charles W. Draper, "The Chaldeans," *BI* 30 (2004): 35.

moned by Nebuchadnezzar along with magicians, enchanters, and sorcerers to interpret a dream (Dan 2:2-4).

Shortly after 2000 B.C. Amorite kings like Hammurabi bring Babylon to prominence as the political seat of southern Mesopotamia. Hittites conquer it around 1595 but soon withdraw. Into the political vacuum that ensues come the Kassites. Over four centuries, the Kassites help Babylon reach new cultural and international prestige. An Elamite invasion around 1160 B.C., however, destroys the Kassite dynasty. A later fourth dynasty comes to power when the Elamites withdraw in the wake of Nebuchadnezzar I's victory over them in the late twelfth century B.C.

Through the next several centuries, Babylonian power waxes and wanes in contrast with the power of the Assyrians to their northwest. Repeatedly during the seventh and sixth centuries B.C. Babylonian tribal leaders gain control of northern Babylonia and then lose control of it to the Assyrians. Assyria's spreading conquests in the eighth and seventh centuries B.C. become her undoing as she could not defend the frontiers of the empire against persistent enemies on her frontiers like Babylon. When Thebes in Egypt falls to Ashurbanipal II in 663 B.C., Assyria merely moves farther west the frontiers of a kingdom she could not adequately control (see "Introduction to Nahum: Historical Background" for more detailed information). Babylon finally wins supremacy over Assyria in a series of victories under Nabopolassar and his son Nebuchadnezzar II. Nabopolassar gains control of Babylon by 626 B.C. Both Calah and Nineveh fall to a coalition of Babylonian, Mede, and Scythian forces in 612 B.C. This conquest has been preceded by the fall of Asshur to the Medes.

Judah, under Josiah, removes itself from Assyria's control and exists as an autonomous state until 609 B.C. During this period, Egypt responds to Assyria's troubles in Mesopotamia by attempting to expand its presence into Palestine. In 609 B.C. Pharaoh Neco joins with Assyria to fight the Babylonians at Haran. Josiah tries to stop this alliance, but is defeated on the plain of Megiddo in a battle that cost the king his life (2 Kgs 23:29-30; 2 Chr 35:20-24). Even with Egyptian help, the Assyrians lose their battle with Babylon and disappear as a power in the world. Egypt retreats and Carchemish in northwest Mesopotamia becomes the dividing line between the powers of Egypt and Babylon.

After the unfortunate death of Josiah in 609 B.C. (See "Zepha-niah Introduction: Historical Background" for more detailed infor-mation regarding the religious reforms of Josiah) Judah is subjected to a succession of evil kings who lack the leadership skills of Josiah and who reverse his religious reforms. Jehoahaz, Josiah's son, reigns only three months before being deposed by the Egyptians. Egypt assesses the land a heavy tribute, takes Jehoahaz into captivity (2 Kgs 23:31-34), and places on the throne another son of Josiah, Eliakim whose name they change to Jehoiakim. The writer of Kings (2 Kgs 23:34-37), the Chronicler (2 Chr 36:5-8), and Jeremiah (Jer 22:13-19; 26:20-23; 36:1-32) characterize his eleven year reign (609–598) as one of injustice and intolerable evil.

Further shifts in power occur in 605 B.C. The Babylonians led by their general Nebuchadnezzar defeat the Egyptians at Carchemish. After his victory at Carchemish and his father's death, Nebuchadnezzar takes control of Babylon. He then seeks to expand Babylonia's control over the lands on the eastern coast of the Mediterranean. Judah's king, Jehoiakim, changes his loyalty to the Babylonians and becomes Nebu-chadnezzar's vassal king (2 Kgs 24:1). Daniel 1:1-3 indicates that the Babylonians besiege Jerusalem around 605 B.C. and carry treasures and captives to Babylon. Daniel is taken as a part of this deportation (Dan 1:1-6). Jehoiakim dies suddenly in 598 — perhaps in a palace assassina-tion (Jer 22:19; 36:30). His eighteen-year-old son Jehoiachin then reigns for three months and ten days before surrendering. The Babylonians spare the city, but carry Jehoiachin, the queen mother, craftsmen and artisans, nobility, young men of ability like Ezekiel, and treasures to Babylon (2 Kgs 24:8-16; 2 Chr 36:9-10). The Babylonians install on the throne a third son of Josiah, Jehoiachin's uncle Mattaniah, whose name is changed to Zedekiah. His reign, characterized by indecision, sedition, and ill-founded reliance upon Egypt to protect Judah from Babylon ends in a protracted siege following a rebellion by Zedekiah. The Babylonians conquer Jerusalem, destroying the city and the temple in 586 B.C. (2 Kgs 24:18–25:10; 2 Chr 36:11-20).

## DATE

The book of Habakkuk does not place the prophet's ministry within the context of a Hebrew or international ruler, and it offers little concrete data upon which to construct an historical setting. It does provide clues that lead to proposals falling into three time periods: the reign of Manasseh (697–642 B.C.), the reign of Josiah (640–609 B.C.), and the reign of Jehoiakim (609–597 B.C.).[12] Although obviously the prophet sees unrestrained oppression of helpless victims, the only descriptions he gives of the parties involved are non-specific terms like "the wicked" and "the righteous" (1:4,13; 2:4; 3:13). The one concrete political reference is to the Chaldeans (1:6), a term used elsewhere in the biblical literature to refer to the Neo-Babylonians (2 Kgs 25:1-13; 2 Chr 36:17; Jer 21:4; Ezek 23:23). The Neo-Babylonians first become a major force in the ancient Near East under the rule of Nabopolassar (626–605 B.C.), the father of Nebuchadnezzar II (605–562 B.C.).

The clearest textual indication of the book's date in 1:6 speaks of the "rousing" or "raising up" of the Babylonians. This seems to point to a time after 626 B.C. when Babylon is becoming the dominant power of the ancient Near East as Assyria is declining. The prophet's claim that the Babylonians' advance would amaze his audience (1:5) indicates that the setting of the oracle in 1:5-11 must predate Nebuchadnezzar's first and second incursions into Judah in 605/604 B.C. (Dan 1:1-2) and 597 B.C. (2 Kgs 24:8-17). Because the prophet's description of the circumstances within Judah (1:2-4) seems similar to

---

[12]A fourth theory in critical scholarship denies the unity of the book and considers chapter 3 to be a postexilic addition to an earlier collection. Reasons cited for this theory are the distinct differences in form and content between chapters 1–2 and chapter 3 and the failure of the commentary on Habakkuk among the Dead Sea Scrolls from Qumran (1QpHab) to comment on chapter 3. Most contemporary scholars, however, point to several links in content between the closing psalm and the first two chapters to conclude the entire book is indeed the work of Habakkuk. The Qumran community may not have commented on chapter 3 because it does not suit their sectarian purposes. The presence of chapter 3 in the LXX would argue for a longstanding tradition of its linkage to the book. Proposed emendations of the Hebrew word for "Chaldeans" or "Babylonians" (הַכַּשְׂדִים, *hakkaśdîm*) to read as the Hebrew word for "Kittim" or "Greeks" (הַכִּתִּים, *hakkittîm*) in support of a late postexilic date also have found little support. For a full discussion of the issue of the unity of the book, see Otto Eissfeldt, *The Old Testament: An Introduction*, trans. by Peter R. Ackroyd (New York: Harper & Row, 1965), p. 421; Ralph L. Smith, *Micah–Malachi*, WBC 32 (Waco: Word, 1984), p. 95; Alberto J. Soggin, *Introduction to the Old Testament: From Its Origins to the Closing of the Alexandrian Canon*, trans. by John Bowden (Philadelphia: Westminster, 1980, rev. ed.), p. 278.

the evils of the days of king Jehoiakim, the date of Habakkuk's ministry may be narrowed to the time between 609 and 605 B.C. Thus, his ministry comes after Babylonian power rises in the east (see 1:6-11) following victories over the Assyrians at Nineveh (612 B.C.) and Haran (610 B.C.) but before the Babylonian victory over the Assyrians and Egyptians at Carchemish (605 B.C.) shows Babylon to be a clear threat to nations on the east Mediterranean coast.[13]

While the scene described in 1:5-11 accords well with the evils of the reign of Jehoiakim which begin in 609 B.C., the characterization of Babylon in 1:11-17 seems more fitting for an audience that has witnessed firsthand or has already heard about Babylonian military practices. Therefore, the book may be understood as a collection of sequentially ordered oracles, some dating from 609–605 B.C. and others from around or after 597 B.C.[14] Although the reign of Jehoiakim is the generally accepted date for Habakkuk's ministry, an earlier date in the reign of Josiah (640–609 B.C.) is possible. Since Josiah attempts to prevent Egypt from assisting Assyria against Babylon, he may have considered Babylon a lesser threat to Judean security. This could explain the amazement at Yahweh's raising of Babylon (1:5-6). The evils spoken of in 1:2-4 could also describe a time when the reforms of Josiah have waned or a reality in which official government policy does not trickle down to the society at large.

The prophet's ministry may date to the days of Manasseh (697–642 B.C.),[15] since the coming of the Babylonians may not have seemed such an unbelievable thing in either the days of Josiah or Jehoiakim. In addition, the narrative accounts of Manasseh's reign mention that Yahweh sends prophets to speak against the evil practices of Manasseh's day (2 Kgs 21:10-16; 2 Chr 33:10).[16] The possible identification of the wicked in Habakkuk 1:2-4 as the Assyrians rather than evil residents of Judah may further argue for a date in the time of Manasseh or Josiah.[17]

---

[13]Robert Bergen, "Habakkuk: The Man and His Times," *BI* 30 (2004): 9-10.

[14]Carl Armerding, "Habakkuk," in *Expositor's Bible Commentary*, ed. by Frank E. Gaebelein (Grand Rapids: Zondervan, 1985), 7:493; Bruce, "Habakkuk," p. 834; Roberts, *Nahum Habakkuk, and Zephaniah*, pp. 82-83.

[15]A tradition supported by the rabbinic historical treatise *S. 'Olam Rab.* 20.

[16]Keil, *Minor Prophets*, p. 52.

[17]Brevard S. Childs, *Introduction to the Old Testament as Scripture* (Philadelphia: Fortress, 1979), p. 449; Soggin, *Introduction to the Old Testament*, p. 279.

Ultimately, the arguments for an earlier date during the reigns of Manasseh or Josiah fail to displace those for a setting in the days of Jehoiakim. Although the reforms in the latter part of Manasseh's reign (2 Chr 33:15-16) and the extensive reforms of Josiah (2 Chronicles 34) may not have completely removed evil from Judah, Habakkuk's complaint (1:2-4) points to a period when lawlessness and violence are rampant on all levels in Judah. Nor required is a date when Babylonian power is completely unknown. The disbelief referred to in Habakkuk 1:5 may merely describe the reaction to Yahweh's use of such a sinful nation to judge the wicked in Judah rather than the surprise at the emergence of a new power in the region. Moreover, the covenant language of 1:2-4 indicates the wicked belong to Judah rather than Assyria.

## LITERARY FEATURES

The book of Habakkuk is unique among the prophetic books in its extended use of a dialogue format to record the prophet's quest for an understanding of Yahweh's holiness and justice in a world where unrighteousness and injustice seemingly prevail.[18] Its first major section (1:2–2:20) consists of a dialogue between the prophet and Yahweh that alternates between prophetic complaint and divine response. A prophetic complaint in 1:2-4 gives rise to a divine response in 1:5-11. This divine response then elicits a second prophetic complaint (1:12-17) followed by a second divine response (2:1-20). The second major section (3:1-19) continues this alternating pattern. It begins with a prophetic initiative followed by a divine revelation or response that gives way to a concluding prophetic response. The divine revelation is not a word from Yahweh *per se* but is, instead, a theophanic vision with revelatory character.[19]

The larger structure of the book corresponds to the elements of the lament form. As it appears in the Psalms, the lament form contains a six-part structure: address to God, complaint or distress, confession of trust, petition, words of assurance often in the form of

---

[18]*DBI*, p. 357.

[19]Robert B. Chisholm, Jr., *Interpreting the Minor Prophets* (Grand Rapids: Zondervan, 1990), p. 185.

some oracle of salvation, and vow of praise (e.g., Ps 6; 12; 28; 31; 55; 60; 85).[20] These elements may be identified within the book of Habakkuk as follows: address to God (1:2), complaint (1:3-17), words of assurance (2:2-5), confession of trust (2:6-20), petition (3:2), words of assurance (3:3-15), and vow of praise (3:16-19).[21] This structure moves away from a complaint toward a vow of praise and thus focuses on a decisive move of faith from a context of disorientation ("How long, O Lord, must I call for help, but you do not listen?") into a new orientation ("Yet I will wait patiently for the day of calamity to come on the nation invading us").

Whereas most prophetic books consist of an anthology of oracles that can be read and understood independently of others in the book, Habakkuk consists of a varied sequence of literary forms that must be read sequentially to understand the message of the book.[22] This sequence includes laments or complaints (1:2-4,12-17), a salvation oracle (1:5-11), a series of five woe (*hôy*) oracles (2:6-20), and an epic poem consisting of a theophanic narrative (3:3-7) and a victory psalm (3:8-15).

Numerous rhetorical features enhance the literary artistry of the book. Powerful similes depict the Babylonian threat and create a mood of terror. The Babylonian forces are swifter than leopards and fiercer than evening wolves. They gather up captives like eagles or vultures (see notes on 1:8) seize upon their prey, and the desert winds pick up sand (1:8-9). Enemies capture with hooks and dragnets the humanity that Yahweh has made like helpless fish of the sea (1:13-15). The arrogant attacker is as greedy as the grave or *Sheol* and as unrelenting as death.

Other devices present include rhetorical questions (1:12; 2:13,18; 3:8); synecdoche in which tents and dwellings represent the whole nation (3:7); proverb (2:6); anadiplosis, the repetition of the ending of a sentence or clause in the beginning of the next (3:2; cf. NASB); paronomasia with the phrase "idols that cannot speak" built on an

---

[20]Bernhard W. Anderson, *Out of the Depths: The Psalms Speak for Us Today*, rev. ed. (Philadelphia: Westminster Press, 1983), pp. 76-77.

[21]Dennis Ray Bratcher, "The Theological Message of Habakkuk: A Literary-Rhetorical Analysis" (PhD dissertation, Union Theological Seminary, 1984), p. 294.

[22]Kenneth L. Barker and Waylon Bailey, *Micah, Nahum, Habakkuk, Zephaniah*, NAC 20 (Nashville: Broadman, 1998), p. 269.

adjective "mute" (אִלֵּם, *'illēm*) and noun "idol" (אֱלִיל, *'ĕlîl*) with similar sound (2:18); and anabasis, a figure in which a writing, speech, or discourse ascends step by step, with each step increasing the sense or emphasis of the text (1:5).[23]

The woe (*hôy*) oracles (2:6-20) describe the Babylonian foe and its imminent judgment with a number of gripping metaphors. Perhaps the earlier simile of the eagle (1:8) gives rise to the description of Babylon setting his nest on high in order to escape the clutches of ruin (2:9). The metaphor of "house" (בַּיִת, *bayith*, translated "realm" in 2:9 and "house" in 2:10) portends the dissolution of the Babylonian realm as the stones and beams cry out against the Babylonians' wicked house (2:11). The final woe depicts Babylon as one who gives his neighbor wine in an apparent show of hospitality, but who actually seeks to get his companion drunk so he may look at the companion's nakedness (2:15). The following verse then describes Yahweh's wrath as a cup in Yahweh's right hand which Babylon will drink. The drunken Babylon will then experience the shame he has brought on others. These metaphors, however, are countered by the image of Yahweh as the Divine Warrior.

Chapter 3 uses a theophanic narrative (3:3-7) and a victory psalm (3:8-15) in an epic portrayal of Yahweh as the Divine Warrior. As epic, it focuses on the hero Yahweh who is identified with the archaic or heightened epithets Eloah ("God" in the NIV), the Holy One (3:3), God my Savior (3:18), and Sovereign LORD (3:19). Heightened expression describes formative events Yahweh performed in the nation's history (3:3-15).[24] Yahweh uses a full arsenal to show skill as a soldier. Yahweh's horses and chariots are victorious over the rivers and sea (3:8,15), and Yahweh is skilled with bow, arrow, and spear (3:4,9,11), while marching forth on the battlefield. Yahweh even pierces an opponent's head with the opponent's own spear (3:14). Personification permeates the descriptions of Yahweh's advance and the reaction to it. Plague goes before Yahweh, and Pestilence follows his steps (3:5). Nations tremble (3:6), the tents of Cushan and shelters of Midian are in distress and anguish (3:7), the mountains writhe (3:10), and the sun and moon stand still (3:11). Potent simi-

---

[23]E.W. Bullinger, *Figures of Speech Used in the Bible* (London; New York: Eyre & Spottiswoode; E. & J.B. Young, 1898), p. 429.

[24]*DBI*, p. 357.

les also describe Yahweh's saving power and presence. The knowledge of Yahweh's glory will fill all the earth as the waters cover the seas (2:14). Yahweh's splendor is like the sunrise (3:4). The book concludes with the grand affirmation that the Sovereign Yahweh is the prophet's strength who makes his feet like the feet of a deer and enables him to go on the heights (3:19). The book concludes with juxtaposed images of dread, agricultural failure, deprivation, and victory (3:16-19). These images, like the literary forms and devices preceding them, speak to the readers' emotions and intellect to reinforce the prophetic message of the book.

## THEOLOGY

Habakkuk occupies the eighth position among the twelve Minor Prophets in both the MT and LXX. Paul House divides the Book of the Twelve into three sections. The first, Hosea through Micah, emphasizes covenant and cosmic sin. The second, Nahum through Zephaniah, focuses on covenant and cosmic punishment, and the third, Haggai through Malachi, centers on covenant and cosmic restoration.[25] Like Nahum, its predecessor in the second section, Habakkuk announces the fall of a Mesopotamian power. This proclamation of Babylon's imminent fall, however, arises in the course of announcing the coming judgment upon those of Judah who have violated the covenant. It thus shares with Zephaniah, the third book in the section, a theme of Yahweh's judgment on both the wicked inside and outside the Sinaitic covenant. Nevertheless, judgment is not the final word for Habakkuk. The famous dictum of Habakkuk 2:4 that the righteous will live by faithfulness offers a hope not unlike that found in Zephaniah that the humble who seek righteousness and humility may be sheltered in the day of Yahweh (2:3) and the meek and humble who trust in Yahweh's name will be left in Zion (3:12). Habakkuk also anticipates the postexilic theme of restoration by showing Yahweh willing to subject Judah to punishment in order to receive her back purified.[26]

---

[25]Paul R. House, *The Unity of the Twelve*, JSOTSupp 97, BLS 27 (Sheffield: Almond Press, 1990), p. 72.

[26]Ibid., p. 91.

The theme of Yahweh raising Babylon to judge Judah expands upon earlier texts in the Torah and the Prophets. Deuteronomy 28:49-52 foretells that Yahweh will raise up a nation from the ends of the earth that will swoop down like an eagle to punish sin (Hab 1:6,8). This nation will leave behind the stripped fields and empty stalls that Habakkuk anticipates (Hab 3:17; see also Joel 1:7,12). Isaiah 10 has articulated this theme by identifying Assyria as the rod of Yahweh's anger. Isaiah claims Yahweh will punish the arrogant Assyria after using Assyria to punish Judah. Habakkuk explores Yahweh's similar use of the Babylonians.

Habakkuk gives special nuances to a number of common features in the prophetic tradition. The book is an "oracle" (מַשָּׂא, maśśā') (see comments on 1:1). As a maśśā' it is a prophetic discourse that seeks to explain the manner in which the will of Yahweh will be demonstrated in human affairs.[27] The prophet, however, does not simply announce Yahweh's word; he questions Yahweh's announced intentions (1:12-17). Although the primary role of the prophet is to call Israel or Judah back to covenant fidelity when they stray from the Sinaitic covenant, Habakkuk reverses this by taking Yahweh to task for what seems like negligence in keeping Yahweh's covenant obligations.[28]

Like others in the prophetic tradition, Habakkuk anticipates a day in which Yahweh will call to judgment the unjust society of his day. Nevertheless, more than any other prophet, he gives special attention to the perplexing issues of theodicy, particularly the persistence of injustice among the people of Yahweh and the delay of Yahweh in responding to them. The central issue around which the book of Habakkuk revolves is the problem of affirming Yahweh's just rule in the midst of an unjust world. Habakkuk deals with this issue in a way more directly and forcefully than any other prophet.[29]

This struggle to comprehend the prosperity of the wicked and the suffering of the righteous is one of many elements the book shares with Psalms, Job, and prophetic texts influenced by the

---

[27]William J. Dumbrell, *The Faith of Israel: Its Expression in the Books of the Old Testament* (Grand Rapids: Baker, 1988), p. 217.

[28]David W. Baker, "Habakkuk," in *New Dictionary of Biblical Theology*, ed. by T. Desmond Alexander et al. (Downers Grove, IL: InterVarsity, 2000), p. 253.

[29]Hiebert, "Habakkuk," p. 624.

Psalms. Others include the use of the lament form (see Literary Features), the question "How long?" (Hab 1:2; Ps 4:2; 6:3; 89:46; 90:13; Isa 6:11; Zech 1:12), the call to wait for Yahweh in difficult circumstances (Hab 2:3; Ps 27:14; 33:20; 130:5-6), the establishment of an appointed time for salvation by Yahweh (Hab 2:4; Ps 75:2; 102:13), the glory of Yahweh covering the earth (Hab 2:14; Ps 67:1-2; 72:19; Isa 6:3; 11:9), and Yahweh being one's strength (Hab 3:19; Ps 18:1; 46:1; Isa 12:2). The final chapter uses theophanic language similar to that in other biblical psalms to depict Yahweh as the Divine Warrior who comes to rescue the upright (Judg 5:4-5; Ps 7:10-13; 35:1-3; 74:13-15; 77:16-19; 97:4-5; Nahum 1:4-5).

The New Testament speakers and writers quote two Habakkuk texts. Paul concludes his sermon in Pisidian Antioch with a quotation from Habakkuk 1:5 (Acts 13:41). In the context of the sermon, the words warn against the failure to accept the forgiveness of sins and justification that comes through faith in Jesus, whom God raised from the dead (Acts 13:36-39). However, when the Jews in Pisidian Antioch reject these words of salvation, God does something they would never imagine: God brings salvation to the Gentiles (Acts 13:46-48).

Three prominent citations of Habakkuk 2:4 occur in Romans 1:17, Galatians 3:11, and Hebrews 10:37-38. While the writer of Hebrews uses the passage in a call for perseverance, the two Pauline uses appear in arguments about the means of salvation. One may correctly affirm that the use in Hebrews aligns more closely with the original intent of Habakkuk while Paul's use is more abstract and general.[30] Nevertheless, one need not make too much of this distinction. The Greek noun πίστις (pistis, "faith") in these New Testament texts translates the Hebrew noun אֱמוּנָה (ʾĕmûnāh) whose basic meaning is one of firmness, fidelity, steadfastness, and trust.[31] The element of fidelity is certainly present in Hebrews 10. The Pauline texts, on the other hand, capitalize on the nuance of trust, but within contexts not unlike that of the original oracle of Habakkuk. Just as the prophet and the righteous are called to live by faithfulness or trust in the context of a coming revelation (2:3), Romans 1:17

---

[30]Roberts, *Nahum, Habakkuk, and Zephaniah*, p. 111; Bruce, *Habakkuk*, pp. 860-861.

[31]BDB, p. 53.

affirms "the righteous will live by faith" in an announcement of a revelation of a righteousness from God available through the gospel. Both the Habakkuk and Romans texts precede descriptions of the coming of divine wrath upon the wicked (Hab 2:6-20; Rom 1:18-32). Galatians 3:11 shares with Habakkuk the elements of trust in God and divine revelation. Abraham trusts in God and the announcement that all nations would be blessed through Abraham (Gal 3:6-9). The scene which Paul recalls from Abraham's life in this context is one in which Abraham questions Yahweh's purpose before trusting in Yahweh (Genesis 15). Both Habakkuk and Paul call upon their readers to trust in Yahweh's word and power for salvation rather than upon their own efforts and understandings, and the writer of Hebrews echoes Habakkuk's call for a trust in Yahweh's word and power in anticipation of his final salvation.

## MESSAGE

The book of Habakkuk gives voice to the confusion of the righteous remnant of Judah regarding the outworking of the day of Yahweh.[32] The prophet accuses Yahweh of inaction as he cries out to Yahweh for justice in the midst of a society in which torah appears to have no effect (1:2-4). Yahweh responds that the Babylonians will be used to bring judgment on the wicked (1:5-11). The prophet questions the appropriateness of this "answer" by noting the Babylonians are more wicked than are the wicked in Judah (1:12-17). The remainder of the book highlights the need to trust Yahweh and to wait for salvation from the present distress. The rhetorical purposes of the book are carried primarily by 2:1-5 and 3:16-19.[33] The worshiper of Yahweh must wait in faithfulness for the time Yahweh has appointed for the judgment of the wicked and the deliverance of the righteous. This appointed time may not come as rapidly as the righteous would prefer, and the righteous may suffer in the interim, but Yahweh is to be trusted since deliverance is sure. The anticipation of the coming of Yahweh in power and victory over the nations as in the past (Habakkuk 3) justifies the believer's faithfulness.

---

[32]House, *Unity of the Twelve*, p. 234.
[33]McConville, *Guide to the Prophets*, p. 217.

Yahweh's victory will bring an end to the arrogance of the Babylonians who abuse the power Yahweh grants them (1:5-11; 2:6-20).

Like Job, Habakkuk questions the ways of Yahweh in a form of
literature called a theodicy, a justification or defense of God as
omnipotent, all-loving, and just in the face of evil. Habakkuk's reasons for questioning God differ from those of Job. Whereas Job
maintains his own innocence and asks why the righteous suffer,
Habakkuk questions why the unrighteous appear to go unpunished.
He is not asking why he or his people are suffering, but is instead
asking why judgment does not come. The questioning of God by
Habakkuk, like that in the book of Job and the laments of Psalms,
reminds the believer that Yahweh is not threatened by honest questioning from worshipers.

As is the case with Job, the response of Yahweh to Habakkuk
concerning the question of the suffering of the righteous and the
prospering of the wicked is less a philosophical answer than it is an
issue of survival. The book teaches that the worshipers can trust
Yahweh to judge all sin. Wicked individuals and nations may prosper for a time, but Yahweh will triumph and set things right. This
assurance, however, does not exclude Yahweh's people from enduring the effects of sin for a time. Yahweh, however, will always be a
source of hope and victory.[34] It is in this context that the modern
reader must understand the famous phrase associated with this
book, "the righteous will live by faith[fulness]" (Hab 2:4).

Also like Job, the text moves from the perplexing situation to resolution in theophany. What begins with a question mark ends in an
exclamation point: the answer to Habakkuk's "Why?" is "Who!" His
perplexity is resolved in a new perspective of Yahweh's control.
Habakkuk's vision in chapter 3 of Yahweh as a mighty warrior who
conquers the chaotic powers of Yahweh's and Israel's enemies
reminds the reader that Yahweh is active in international history. As
in the earlier vision of the prophet Nahum, Habakkuk portrays
Yahweh as the sovereign king, mighty warrior, just judge, and protector of Israel.[35] The portrayal of the Babylonians as adept and powerful warriors in chapter 1 heightens the impact of the depiction of
Yahweh as the warrior-king in chapter 3. These two portraits, in turn,

---

[34]Bergen, "Habakkuk: The Man and His Times," p. 11.
[35]Chisholm, *Minor Prophets*, p. 198.

suggest several themes. First, the echoes of the first portrait within the second emphasize the truth that Yahweh often works within the affairs of humanity's history to achieve greater purposes. War with the Babylonians is secondary to the war which Yahweh has launched against the nations and the forces of wickedness. Second, the human instruments that Yahweh might choose to use for divine purposes may be totally unaware of that choosing and may even have objectives at variance with those of Yahweh. The purpose of Yahweh, however, ultimately will be victorious. Third, because Yahweh may choose to use an instrument whose immediate purposes are at variance with divine purposes, it may appear that Yahweh has relinquished control to another or that Yahweh is in alliance with the powers of evil themselves. In spite of this, Yahweh still maintains control and will, in the end, execute divine wrath upon those who vaunt themselves and fail to recognize Yahweh. Finally, the people of Yahweh will experience both deserved and undeserved pain and trial at the hands of those at odds with the purposes and character of Yahweh. No one can deny this pain or its severity. One must look beyond the immediate experience, however, to view the ultimate good purpose of Yahweh, the salvation of people.

Even though one may easily identify the historical enemies of the righteous and Judah in Habakkuk, the book only identifies Babylon explicitly in 1:5. Moreover, the description of the Babylonians in the book contains no particularly concrete notes relating to Babylonian history, but utilizes instead traditional images of strength.[36] This allows the reader to understand the Babylonians of Habakkuk 1 as more than an historical entity. They represent all arrogant parties who deify themselves by their actions. The Babylonians then function within the text as a powerful figure of that which is evil.[37] The series of woe (*hôy*) oracles (2:6-20) continues this general description by using several descriptive phrases applicable to almost any wicked oppressor from any era.[38] For example, the language used in Habakkuk 2:9-12 to condemn the Babylonians is similar to the indictments

---

[36]J.H. Eaton, *Obadiah, Nahum, Habakkuk, and Zephaniah* (London: SCM Press, 1961), p. 90.

[37]Bratcher, "Theological Message of Habakkuk," p. 104.

[38]Donna Stokes Dykes, "Diversity and Unity in Habakkuk" (PhD dissertation, Vanderbilt University, 1976), p. 12.

of Judean leadership in Jeremiah 22:13 and Micah 3:10. Among those evil acts Yahweh condemns are drunkenness, greed, theft, violence, oppression, debauchery, abuse of nature, and idolatry. Yahweh indeed will avenge wickedness and has set a time for judgment. The concept of a fixed time for judgment (Hab 2:3) anticipates a key feature of apocalyptic literature.[39]

While the book begins with an interrogation of Yahweh, it ends with intercession and worship. It speaks of the transformation of doubt and grief through prayer (Hab 1:2-4,12-17; 3:2-19; cf. Ps 73:16-17) within the context of worship (Hab 2:20; 3:19).[40] This context of worship provides the prophet and the reader a new perspective fashioned from a recollection of older revelations of Yahweh.[41]

[39]Southwell, "Habakkuk: Theology of," *NIDOTTE*, 4:690.
[40]Ibid.; Barker and Bailey, *Micah, Nahum, Habakkuk, Zephaniah*, p. 275.
[41]Dumbrell, *Faith of Israel*, p. 220.

# OUTLINE

# SELECTED BIBLIOGRAPHY ON HABAKKUK

Abrego, José María. "Habakkuk." In *The International Bible Commentary: A Catholic and Ecumenical Commentary for the Twenty-First Century*. Edited by William R. Farmer. Collegeville, MN: Liturgical Press, 1998.

Andersen, Francis I. *Habakkuk: A New Translation with Introduction and Commentary*. AB 25. New York: Doubleday, 2001.

Armerding, Carl. "Habakkuk." In *Expositor's Bible Commentary*, vol. 7. Edited by Frank E. Gaebelein. Grand Rapids: Zondervan, 1985.

Baker, David W. *Nahum, Habakkuk, Zephaniah: An Introduction and Commentary*. TOTC 23b. Downers Grove, IL: InterVarsity, 1988.

Barker, Kenneth L., and Waylon Bailey. *Micah, Nahum, Habakkuk, Zephaniah*. NAC. Nashville: Broadman, 1999.

Bergen, Robert. "Habakkuk: The Man and His Times." *BI* 30 (2004): 9-11.

Blue, J. Ronald. "Habakkuk." In *The Bible Knowledge Commentary: An Exposition of the Scriptures*, vol. 1. Edited by John F. Walvoord and Roy B. Zuck. Wheaton, IL: Victor Books, 1983–1985.

Boadt, Lawrence. *Jeremiah 26–52, Habakkuk, Zephaniah, Nahum*. Old Testament Message 10. Wilmington, DE: Michael Glazier, 1982.

Bratcher, Dennis Ray. "The Theological Message of Habakkuk: A Literary-Rhetorical Analysis." PhD dissertation, Virginia: Union Theological Seminary, 1984.

Brownlee, William H. "The Composition of Habakkuk." In *Hommages à André Dupont-Sommer*, pp. 255-275. Paris: Andrien-Maisonneuve, 1971.

Bruce, F.F. "Habakkuk." In *The Minor Prophets: An Exegetical and Expository Commentary*, vol. 2. Edited by Thomas Edward McComiskey. Grand Rapids: Baker, 1993.

Bruckner, James. *Jonah, Nahum, Habakkuk, Zephaniah.* The NIV Application Commentary. Grand Rapids: Zondervan, 2004.

Draper, Charles W. "The Chaldeans." *BI* 30 (2004): 35-40.

Eaton, J.H. "The Origin and Meaning of Habakkuk 3." *ZAW* 76 (1964): 144-171.

Gowen, Donald E. *The Triumph of Faith in Habakkuk.* Atlanta: John Knox, 1976.

Haak, Robert D. *Habakkuk.* VTSupp 44. Leiden: Brill, 1991.

Hahlen, Mark Allen. "The Literary Design of Habakkuk." PhD dissertation, Louisville, KY: The Southern Baptist Theological Seminary, 1992.

Hiebert, Theodore. *God of My Victory: The Ancient Hymn of Habakkuk 3.* HSM 38. Atlanta: Scholars Press, 1986.

_____. "Habakkuk." In *NIB*, vol. 7. Edited by Leander E. Keck. Nashville: Abingdon, 1996.

_____. "The Use of Inclusion in Habakkuk 3." In *Directions in Biblical Hebrew Poetry*, pp. 119-140. Edited by Elaine R. Follis. JSOTSupp 40. Sheffield: University of Sheffield, 1987.

Janzen, J. Gerald. "Eschatological Symbol and Existence in Habakkuk." *CBQ* 44 (1982): 394-414.

Margulis, Baruch. "The Psalm of Habakkuk: A Reconstruction and Interpretation." *ZAW* 82 (1970): 409-442.

Patterson, Richard D. *Nahum, Habakkuk, Zephaniah.* WEC. Chicago: Moody, 1991.

Roberts, J.J.M. *Nahum, Habakkuk, and Zephaniah: A Commentary.* OTL. Louisville, KY: Westminster John Knox, 1991.

Robertson, O. Palmer. *The Books of Nahum, Habakkuk, and Zephaniah.* NICOT. Grand Rapids: Eerdmans, 1994.

Széles, Mária Eszenyei. *Wrath and Mercy: A Commentary on the Books of Habakkuk and Zephaniah.* ITC. Grand Rapids: Eerdmans, 1987.

# HABAKKUK

## I. THE ORACLE OF HABAKKUK (1:1–2:20)

The book contains two major sections: 1:1–2:20 and 3:1-19. The first section, labeled "oracle" (see comments on 1:1 below), consists of a dialogue between the prophet and Yahweh, alternating between prophetic complaint and divine response. Following the title (1:1), the section begins with a prophetic complaint (1:2-4) followed by a divine response (1:5-11). Then a second prophetic complaint (1:12-17) is followed by a second divine response (2:1-20). In a sense the oracle begins with the problematic implications of the rise of Babylon as a world power (1:5-11); that Yahweh has granted such domination to the Babylonians causes the prophet to question whether Yahweh is then responsible for the ensuing injustice associated with Babylon's despotic rule (1:2-4).[1] The second prophetic complaint (1:12-17) resumes the earlier complaint, expressing confidence in the character of Yahweh (1:12) but questioning Yahweh's apparent responsibility for this injustice (1:13-17). The second divine response (2:1-20) addresses the dilemma posed by the prophet, reinterpreting the earlier divine revelation (1:5-11): Yahweh is responsible for the rise of Babylon but not for the injustice associated with their rule. The prophet inquires about Yahweh's response and about the prophet's own reaction (2:1); Yahweh replies that the prideful and arrogant Babylon is now destined to fall (2:2-5) and undergo reproof (2:6-20).

---

[1]Michael H. Floyd, *Minor Prophets: Part 2*, FOTL 22 (Grand Rapids: Eerdmans, 2000), pp. 81-84.

## A. TITLE (1:1)

¹The oracle that Habakkuk the prophet received.

**1:1** The title of the book of Habakkuk is different from the usual prophetic title. Like Nahum 1:1, it lacks a phrase that is typically found among the opening words of a prophetic book: "the word of the LORD" (Jer 1:2; Ezek 1:3; Hos 1:1; Joel 1:1; Jonah 1:1; Micah 1:1; Zeph 1:1; Hag 1:1; Zech 1:1; Mal 1:1). It also lacks the naming of a king, either Hebrew or foreign, who is contemporary with the prophet (Isa 1:1; Jer 1:2-3; Hos 1:1; Amos 1:1; Micah 1:1; Zeph 1:1; Hag 1:1; Zech 1:1). Furthermore, it lacks the listing of the prophet's family (Isa 1:1; Jer 1:1; Ezek 1:3; Hos 1:1; Joel 1:1; Jonah 1:1; Hag 1:1; Zech 1:1), location (Jer 1:1; Ezek 1:1; Amos 1:1; Jonah 1:1; Micah 1:1; Hag 1:1), and date (Jer 1:2; Ezek 1:1; Amos 1:1; Hag 1:1; Zech 1:1). Instead, Habakkuk 1:1 contains the prophet's name with the designation "the prophet" (cf. Ezek 1:3; Amos 1:1; Hag 1:1; Zech 1:1) and describes the work as an **oracle**.

The prophet's name **Habakkuk** may be related to the Hebrew verb meaning "to caress" or "to embrace," or it may derive from an Akkadian word for a garden plant. This represents a fairly common Israelite practice to use plant names in personal names (e.g., Tamar, Elon, Hadassah), and the presence of an Akkadian loan word in seventh-century-B.C. Judah is quite plausible given the Assyrian presence in Palestine since the eighth century B.C.[2] The prophet is mentioned in the second-century-B.C. apocryphal book Bel and the Dragon (vv. 33-39), an expansion of the book of Daniel found in the LXX and Vulgate. In it, Habakkuk is miraculously transported from Judah to Babylon to feed Daniel in the lion's den.

Habakkuk is called a **prophet** (נָבִיא, *nābî'*) here and again in 3:1. This term may derive from a passive participle of a root related to the Akkadian word meaning "to call."[3] The word thus emphasizes the divine calling of one called *nābî'*. Oddly only Habakkuk, Haggai, and Zechariah are also identified as prophets in the verses that open their respective books. The word **received** in the NIV translates the verb חָזָה (*ḥāzah*), generally translated "saw" in other versions (e.g., ESV, KJV, NASB, and NRSV). The word indicates that the prophet

---

[2]Roberts, *Nahum, Habakkuk, and Zephaniah*, p. 86.
[3]*HALOT*, pp. 661-662.

is also a seer (הֹזֶה, *hōzeh*) (2 Sam 24:11; 2 Kgs 17:13; 1 Chr 21:9; 25:5; 29:29; 2 Chr 9:29; 12:15; 19:2; 29:25,30; 33:18; 35:15; Isa 29:10; 30:10; Amos 7:12; Micah 3:7). The related noun "vision" (חָזוֹן, *hāzôn*) elsewhere can refer to specific visionary events or as a general term for any sort of revelatory experience (Isa 1:1; 29:7; Jer 14:14; 23:16; Lam 2:9; Ezek 7:13,26; Dan 1:17; 8:1-2,13,15,17,26; 9:21,24; 10:14; 11:14; Hos 12:10; Obad 1:1; Nah 1:1; Hab 2:2-3). That Habakkuk "sees" may point to the intensity of what Habakkuk has experienced whether audibly or visually.[4]

The word "oracle" (מַשָּׂא, *maśśāʾ*) occurs eighteen times in the prophetic books (the word is translated "prophecy" in the TNIV). It stands at the beginning of individual speeches (e.g., Isa 13:1; 14:28; 15:1; 17:1; 19:1; 21:1; 22:1; 23:1; 30:6; Ezek 12:10; Zech 9:1; 12:1) and entire books (Hab 1:1; Mal 1:1). It can address a specific nation, city, people, or historical circumstance. Generally *maśśāʾ* indicates a particular type of prophetic pronouncement.[5] The oracle answers those in the Israelite community who may doubt or wonder about Yahweh's intended action in a particular historical situation. Specifically, an oracle asserts Yahweh's involvement in the historical situation, clarifies any previous prophecy about the situation, and provides a basis for an appropriate response.

For Habakkuk, the topic of the oracle is the rise of Babylon, and the oracle addresses both the community of the faithful (Habakkuk serves as a representative of the people) and the object of divine action (Babylon). The initial problem is the implications of the rise of Babylon as a world power, causing the prophet to question whether Yahweh is then responsible for the injustice associated with Babylon's abusive rule (1:5-11). This problem, however, is resolved by the assertion that Yahweh is now acting to destroy the power of the Babylonians (2:2-20). This assertion provides the basis for an appropriate response of Habakkuk (and his readers) to wait patiently and expectantly, trusting that Yahweh will soon bring an end to Babylon's domination of Judah (3:1-19).[6]

---

[4]María Eszenyei Széles, *Wrath and Mercy: A Commentary on the Books of Habakkuk and Zephaniah,* ITC (Grand Rapids: Eerdmans, 1987), p. 15.

[5]Richard D. Weis, "Oracle," *ABD,* 5:28-29; Michael H. Floyd, "The מַשָּׂא (*maśśāʾ*) as a Type of Prophetic Book," *JBL* 121 (2002): 401-422.

[6]Floyd, "מַשָּׂא," pp. 413-415.

## B. HABAKKUK'S FIRST COMPLAINT (1:2-4)

²How long, O LORD, must I call for help, / but you do not listen? / Or cry out to you, "Violence!" / but you do not save? / ³Why do you make me look at injustice? / Why do you tolerate wrong? / Destruction and violence are before me; / there is strife, and conflict abounds. / ⁴Therefore the law is paralyzed, / and justice never prevails. / The wicked hem in the righteous, / so that justice is perverted.

Habakkuk 1:2-4 consists of a prophetic complaint in which the prophet voices a complaint as the people's representative. It includes typical elements of the form: invocation ("How long, O LORD"), description of trouble ("Destruction and violence are before me"), and reproach ("you do not listen" and "you do not save"). Absent, however, is a clear petition for help; rather the prophet reproaches Yahweh for a failure to respond to repeated petitions. The prophet accuses Yahweh of failing to respond (1:2) and of being indifferent to evil (1:3); the inaction and action of Yahweh has thus resulted in the paralysis and perversion of justice (1:4). The unit blames Yahweh for the injustice experienced by Habakkuk and his community, but the unit does so to inquire about what Yahweh may do to remedy the situation.

**1:2-3** The lament in 1:2-4 exhibits the accusatory tone of a complaint, since it charges Yahweh with the failure both to hear and to act. Like Job, Habakkuk has experienced things that seem to negate his prior understanding of Yahweh. The phrase **How long**? appears several times in the Old Testament to introduce questions where someone is complaining about the actions of another. Of special note are examples in the Torah where Yahweh shows frustration with Israel (Exod 16:28; Num 14:11,27) and in the Psalms where people inquire of Yahweh about the length of time certain circumstances will persist (Ps 6:3; 13:1; 35:17; 79:5; 82:2; 94:3). Psalms 35:17, 82:2, and 94:3 provide very close parallels to Habakkuk 1:2-4, since the psalmists also ask why Yahweh fails to remedy injustice and wickedness. The prophet is distressed by Yahweh's seeming failure to respond (NIV **listen**) when he cries for help (שִׁוַּע, šāwaʻ). Although the Old Testament portrays Yahweh as one who comes to the aid of those who cry for help (Ps 18:6; 30:2; 72:12), the covenant people also experience times in which Yahweh seems deaf to their calls (Job 30:20; Ps 18:41). The use of forms of the verbs "hear" (שָׁמַע, šāma‘) and **save** (יָשַׁע, yāša‘) present a sharp contrast between the characteristic pattern of the past actions of Yahweh to deliver and Yahweh's present inaction. The appearance of the noun **violence** (חָמָס, ḥāmās) in the second and third verses accentuates this contrast. Noun and verb forms of this root occur sixty-seven times in the MT and indicate extreme wickedness, oppression, and violence.[7]

Verse 3 also extends the censure against Yahweh with the accusation that Yahweh has actively contributed to the speaker's plight. The complaint thus depicts Yahweh as an adversary rather than a savior. The psalmists often employ the interrogative **why**? (לָמָה, lāmmāh) in laments to introduce complaints against Yahweh for his perceived inaction against evil (Ps 10:1; 22:1; 42:9; 43:2; 44:23-24; 74:11; 79:10; 88:14). Here the prophet suggests that Yahweh seems to condone violence and cruelty. The violence described in this verse matches the circumstances of the reign of Jehoiakim (2 Kgs 24:4; Jer 22:17).

In fact, the prophet uses six different terms in verses 2 and 3 to describe the evil committed against the righteous by the wicked: "violence" (חָמָס, ḥāmās), **injustice** (אָוֶן, ’āwen), **wrong** (עָמָל, ’āmāl), **destruction** (שֹׁד, šōd), **strife** (רִיב, rîb), and **conflict** (מָדוֹן, mādôn). The word ḥāmās designates grievous violence and abuse perpetrated on another (Gen 49:5; Judg 9:24; 1 Chr 12:17; Ps 7:16; 11:5; 25:19; 27:12; 35:11; 74:20; 140:1,4,11). In addition to indicating physical violence, it may refer to malicious or false testimony in court (Exod 23:1; Deut 19:16; Ps 27:12; 35:11; 58:2) or socioeconomic injustice (Ezek 28:16; Micah 6:12). The commentary on Habakkuk found among the Dead Sea Scrolls accuses the "Wicked Priest" of working ḥāmās by amassing wealth through plunder and shedding blood (1QpHab VIII,8-12 and IX,5-9). The noun ’āwen, used approximately eighty times in the Old Testament, may come from the same root as אוֹן (’ôn), a word with a basic meaning of power. This, together with the contexts in which ’āwen is found may indicate its denotation

---

[7]For some representative uses, see Gen 6:11,13; Exod 23:1; Deut 19:16; Ps 7:16; 25:19; 27:12; 72:14; Prov 10:11; Amos 3:10; Micah 6:12; the same word appears elsewhere in Hab 1:9 and 2:17.

of an abuse of power that brings harm, trouble, or destruction.[8] It may apply to oppression of the poor (Ps 94:4-7; Isa 10:1; Micah 2:1-2), to physical violence (Hos 6:8), and malicious, abusive, or deceptive speech (Job 11:11; Ps 10:7; 28:3; Prov 6:12; 19:28; Isa 29:20; Zech 10:2). The basic meaning of *'āmāl* is the misery associated with work and toil. Its use here reflects a more focused meaning of trouble caused by wickedness. This meaning arises in several contexts, especially in contexts where it appears in tandem with such words as *'āwen* (Job 15:35; Ps 10:7; Isa 10:1) and *šōd* (Prov 24:2). Denoting devastation and havoc, *šōd* is elsewhere paired with "hunger" (כָּפָן *kāphan*) in Job 5:22 and שֶׁבֶר (*šeber*), a noun referring to brokenness or injury (Lev 24:20; Jer 8:21; Nahum 3:19). The word *šōd* may also denote plunder accumulated by ruthless means (Ezek 45:9; Amos 3:10), and *šōd* is paired elsewhere with *ḥāmās* in Jeremiah 6:7; 20:8; Ezekiel 45:9, and Amos 3:10. Although in Jeremiah 20:8 the pairing signifies the result of judgment, the remaining sets of parallel uses, as here, denote the cause for judgment. Both *rîb* and *madôn* are synonyms for contention that appear in parallel also in Proverbs 17:14 and Jeremiah 15:10. The denotation of *madôn* is fairly uniform; it refers to dissension, dispute, and conflict (Ps 80:6; Prov 6:14; Jer 15:10). Although *rîb* also may simply signify some sort of struggle or strife between parties (Judg 12:2; Ps 18:43; 55:9), it appears in several contexts to describe a lawsuit or legal contention. Of particular note are examples of this judicial use of *rîb* in parallel with *ḥāmās* in Exodus 23:1-3,6 and Deuteronomy 19:16-17. The presence of *ḥāmās* as well as reference to injustice, law, and justice in verses 2 through 4 suggest *rîb* here signifies abuse of the court system by the powerful in Judah.

Thus, the evil that perplexes the prophet is not found in an enemy nation that lacks knowledge of Yahweh but is within the covenant community itself. The theory that the wicked (1:4) are the Assyrians flounders on two accounts. The paralysis of torah (i.e., law) points to a situation within the covenant people of Judah rather than one thrust upon them by Assyria, and the book makes no direct mention of Assyria.[9] The mention of torah's paralysis also rules out identifying the wicked of 1:2-4 with the Babylonians as does the

---

[8] Eugene Carpenter and Michael A. Grisanti, "אָוֶן" *NIDOTTE*, 1:310.
[9] Chisholm, *Minor Prophets*, p. 185.

assertion in 1:6 that the Babylonians would rectify the wrongs described in verses 2-4.

**1:4** The conjunction עַל־כֵּן (*'al-kēn*) appears twice in verse 4, translated first **therefore** and second "so that" (it also appears in vv. 15,16). It states as a fact, rather than by declaration, the results of the actions in the preceding verses.[10] Verse 4 indicates that the vehicles of any expected salvation are inoperative. The law or torah with its promises of blessing for obedience and punishment for disobedience (Deuteronomy 27–28) is numbed and ineffective, like hands rendered useless by cold temperatures. Social **justice** does not **prevail** in the civil and political life of Judean society (cf. Micah 3:11; 7:3). **The wicked** encircle **the righteous** with overpowering dominance and hostile intent.

## C. YAHWEH'S FIRST RESPONSE (1:5-11)

[5]**"Look at the nations and watch— / and be utterly amazed. / For I am going to do something in your days / that you would not believe, / even if you were told. / [6]I am raising up the Babylonians,[a] / that ruthless and impetuous people, / who sweep across the whole earth / to seize dwelling places not their own. / [7]They are a feared and dreaded people; / they are a law to themselves / and promote their own honor. / [8]Their horses are swifter than leopards, / fiercer than wolves at dusk. / Their cavalry gallops headlong; / their horsemen come from afar. / They fly like a vulture swooping to devour; / [9]they all come bent on violence. / Their hordes[b] advance like a desert wind / and gather prisoners like sand. / [10]They deride kings / and scoff at rulers. / They laugh at all fortified cities; / they build earthen ramps and capture them. / [11]Then they sweep past like the wind and go on— / guilty men, whose own strength is their god."**

[a]*6 Or Chaldeans*     [b]*9 The meaning of the Hebrew for this word is uncertain.*

Habakkuk 1:5-11 exhibits the form of a prophetic sentinel report, in which the prophet functions in a manner similar to that

---

[10]BDB, p. 487.

of a sentry. Other examples of prophetic sentinel reports include Isaiah 21:6-10; 52:7-10; Ezekiel 3:17-21; 33:2-9; Nahum 2:1-10; and Habakkuk 2:1. The limits of the unit are marked by the change of address from the previous unit. In verses 2-4, the prophet addresses Yahweh, but here someone (i.e., Yahweh) addresses a group with the plural commands, "Look" and "watch." Likewise, verse 12 returns to the prophet addressing Yahweh. The unit is linked thematically with the previous one with the words "look/watch" (vv. 3,5), "justice" (vv. 4,7), and "violence" (vv. 2-3,9). The unit begins by calling the prophet to attention ("Look" and "watch"), urging the prophet to assume the role of a watchman (v. 5). What will amaze the prophet is the divine commission of Babylon as the dominant world power. The remainder of the unit contains the announcement of Yahweh's intended action of raising up the Babylonians (v. 6) and a description of their brutal conduct in war and of their guilt of self-deification (vv. 7-11). The unit asserts that Yahweh stands behind the rise of Babylon as a world power and invites Habakkuk (and his readers) to wonder about this action and Yahweh's intention for it.

**1:5** The "answer" to Habakkuk's original complaint appears in verses 5-11.[11] Plural imperatives in the verse point to a change of addresses; those who are to **look and watch** are the righteous that the prophet represents in his initial complaint. Significantly, Yahweh does not refute the prophet's assessment of the evil that surrounds him, nor does Yahweh chastise him for voicing his concerns. Implicitly Yahweh agrees that evil surrounds the righteous but does not indicate why Yahweh tolerates it for so long. Instead, Yahweh gives an "answer" with which Habakkuk will once again struggle. Yet Yahweh will use the Babylonians as an instrument to depose the wicked of Judah. Babylon's rise to power is part of Yahweh's intention (v. 6) in spite of the way in which they rule (vv. 7-8) and in spite

---

[11]Lament forms in the prophetic literature differ occasionally from the community and individual songs of lament found in Psalms because prophetic laments often contain an answer to the complaint in some form of divine utterance (e.g., Jer 11:21-23; 12:5-6; 15:19-21). Habakkuk 1:5-11, on the surface, comprises such a reply. The absence of any standard introductory formula at the beginning of the passage heightens its drama by casting it in a form that creates the impression of direct address, according to O. Palmer Robertson, *Nahum, Habakkuk, and Zephaniah*, NICOT (Grand Rapids: Eerdmans, 1994), pp. 136-137.

of their brutal conduct in war (vv. 9-11); neither do they recognize that they serve the purpose of Yahweh, but they are guilty of self-deification (v. 11).

Four imperatives begin verse 5. The first and second imperatives "look" (רְאָה, *rā'āh*) and "watch" (נָבַט, *nābaṭ*) echo the use of the same verbs in verse 3 where the prophet asks why Yahweh forces him to look at injustice and why Yahweh tolerates or "watches" (cf. ESV, NJB, NJPS) wrong. The third and fourth imperatives, **be utterly amazed** in the NIV, translate two different forms of the same Hebrew root (cf. the NRSV's "Be astonished! Be astounded!"); this double imperative construction heightens the degree of the command (cf. Isa 29:9; Zeph 2:1).[12] The imperatives add a sense of urgency to the divine command and prepare for a sense of incredulity about the divine assertion in the next verse. The Hebrew text reads "a deed is doing" (cf. the NRSV's "a work is being done"), but the NIV and other translations (e.g., ESV, KJV, NASB, NET, NLT, NJB), as does the LXX, supply a first person pronoun to indicate Yahweh as the subject: **I am going to do something**. The phrase **in your days** indicates the nearness of the events, perhaps a date during the lifetime of the prophet and his audience, and the content of Yahweh's response suggests a time when Babylon is yet on the rise. A fitting time would be around the Battle of Carchemish in 605 B.C. but before the Babylonians' first incursion into Palestine in 604 B.C. Habakkuk (and his readers) will be in disbelief about Yahweh's intended action. For who among the people of Judah would believe that Yahweh would give them over to the ruthless and arrogant Babylonians?[13]

**1:6** Anticipation grows at the beginning of verse 6 with the use of the exclamatory phrase כִּי־הִנְנִי (*kî-hinnî*, "for behold"), not translated by the NIV (but see ESV, KJV, NASB, NRSV, NJB, and NJPS). The interjection "behold" (הִנֵּה, *hinnēh*) occurs over a thousand times

---

[12]Keil, *Minor Prophets*, p. 58.

[13]Paul concludes his sermon in Pisidian Antioch with a quotation from Habakkuk 1:5 (Acts 13:41). In the context of the sermon the words warn against the failure to accept the forgiveness of sins and justification that comes through faith in Jesus, whom God raised from the dead (Acts 13:36-39). However, when the Jews in Pisidian Antioch reject these words of salvation, God does something they would never imagine: God brings salvation to the Gentiles (Acts 13:46-48).

in the Old Testament and demands attention be paid to what follows. More importantly, it appears as part of a formula (*hinnēh* followed by a participle) that characteristically introduces prophetic speech on behalf of Yahweh, that is, Yahweh now speaks to Habakkuk.[14] The emerging expectation, however, is short-lived, when Yahweh announces the rise of an instrument of judgment, identified here as **the Babylonians** (the Hebrew has "Chaldeans," so reflected by ESV, KJV, NASB, NRSV, NJB, and NJPS).

However, the description of the Babylonians that follows introduces elements that move the reader back toward a context of disorientation. These descriptions of the Babylonians confound the seemingly positive foreshadowing of verse 5. It had seemed Yahweh is about to exercise control in the world and to act in accordance with divine justice. Instead, Yahweh who gazes unmoved at wrong (v. 3) now summons Habakkuk (and the readers) to look among the nations to see an unbelievable work (v. 5) that involves a brutal and self-deifying nation whose existence and manner raises more questions than it answers. Disorientation occurs when the reader sees Yahweh raise up the Babylonians who, in turn, make their own strength their god. In this way, the last line of verse 5 is an irony. A work beyond belief has been promised, but the anticipated salvation oracle is stood on its head.

The term Chaldeans is not applied consistently throughout ancient records. It names the tribes of western Semites in southern Mesopotamia just northwest of the Persian Gulf, the people in Mesopotamian locale who were not ethnic Chaldeans (the Assyrian king Shalmaneser II refers to a number of tribes in the region by that title), and astrologers from Babylonia during the Hellenistic era.[15] Shortly after 2000 B.C., Amorite kings like Hammurabi bring Babylon to prominence as the political seat of southern Mesopotamia. Hittites conquer Babylon around 1595 B.C. but soon withdraw. Into the political vacuum that ensues come the Kassites. Over four centuries, the Kassites help Babylon reach new cultural and international prestige. An Elamite invasion around 1160 B.C., how-

---

[14]Paul Humbert, "La formule hébraïque en *hineni* suivi d'un participle," in *Opuscules d'un hébraïsant*, Mémoires de l'Université de Neuchâtel 26 (Neuchâtel: Secrétariat de l'Université, 1958), pp. 54-59.

[15]E.g., Josephus, *J.W.* 2.112; Draper, "Chaldeans," p. 35.

ever, destroys the Kassite dynasty. A later fourth dynasty comes to power when the Elamites withdraw in the wake of the victory of Nebuchadnezzar I (1124–1103 B.C.).[16] Repeatedly during the seventh and sixth centuries, Chaldean tribal leaders gain control of northern Babylonia only to lose it again to the Assyrians. Supremacy over Assyria is finally won in a series of victories under the kings of the eleventh (or Chaldean) dynasty, Nabopolassar (625–605 B.C.) and Nebuchadnezzar II (605–562 B.C.). Nabopolassar gains control of Babylon by 626 B.C. In 612 B.C., both Calah and Nineveh fall to a coalition of Babylonian, Mede, and Scythian forces, a conquest preceded by the fall of Asshur to the Medes. In 609 B.C., the Babylonians conquer the last major Assyrian stronghold in Haran and then defeat the Egyptians at Carchemish in 605 B.C. The "Chaldeans" in verse 6 are these Neo-Babylonians, who rise to prominence during the reign of Nebuchadnezzar II (605–562 B.C.) and flourish until their defeat in 539 B.C. by Cyrus the Great, king of Persia.

The raising up of the Babylonians in verse 6 may not refer to the time in which Babylon initially exerted itself as an international power in the era, but rather to their appointment by Yahweh as his instrument against the oppressors of 1:2-4 (cf. Isa 10:5-6). Their description as a **ruthless and impetuous people who sweep across the whole earth** would have been somewhat out of place until after the battle of Carchemish (605 B.C.). Before that time, they rarely engage in swift blitzkrieg-like attacks over large distances. After being victorious in Carchemish, however, Nebuchadnezzar pursues the Egyptian army over 150 miles to Hamath. The Babylonians attack with violence (cf. Judg 18:25; 2 Sam 17:8) and speed, taking countries that are **not their own** (cf. to the wording of Yahweh's promise to Israel in Deut 6:10-11).

**1:7** The fierce disposition of the Babylonians is further described with the words **feared** (אָיֹם, 'āyōm) and **dreaded** (נוֹרָא, yārē'). The word 'āyōm connotes the awesome dread aroused by a mighty army; it appears elsewhere only in the metaphorical descriptions of Solomon's beloved who is as "majestic" as an advancing army (S of S 6:4,10). Later Habakkuk uses the word yārē' to express his standing in awe before Yahweh (3:2). By repeating the words "justice" or

---

[16]Ibid., p. 36.

"law" (both translate מִשְׁפָּט, *mišpāṭ*) in the description of the wicked (vv. 3-4) and of the Babylonians (vv. 7,9), Habakkuk both shows the appropriateness of the punishment and introduces the tension that is the subject of the second interchange between the prophet and Yahweh (1:12–2:20). In verse 4, the prophet laments that "justice never goes out" and "justice goes out perverted," whereas verse 7 describes the Babylonians as **a law to themselves** (cf. the NET's "they decide for themselves what is right" and the NJB's "a law and authority to themselves"). Judah has ignored Yahweh's *mišpāṭ*; therefore, Babylon's *mišpāṭ* will be imposed upon Judah.

**1:8** The comparisons of Babylon's **horses to leopards**, **wolves**, and **vultures** accentuate both the swiftness and fierceness of the Babylonian army. The word "vulture" (נֶשֶׁר, *nešer*) is more often translated "eagle" (e.g., ESV, KJV, NASB, NRSV, NLT, and NJB). Of the twenty-six uses of *nešer* in the Hebrew Bible, the NIV translates only three "vulture" (Prov 30:17; Micah 1:16; Hab 1:8). Only one of these, Proverbs 30:17, describes actions that one would clearly associate with a vulture rather than an eagle. In fact, a separate noun is used in two instances (Lev 11:13; Deut 14:12) to distinguish the vulture (פֶּרֶס, *peres*) from the eagle (*nešer*). While the description of the birds **swooping to devour** may favor "vultures" here in verse 8, the image of **com**ing **from afar** in the previous line likely favors "eagles."[17] Nevertheless, the NIV translates *nešer* as "eagle" in Jeremiah's descriptions of the far-reaching Babylonians (Jer 4:13; 48:40; 49:22). By referring to the distant origins of the Babylonians, their swooping like a vulture and their siege techniques (v. 10), the prophet evokes images of the covenant curses described in Deuteronomy 28:49-52.

**1:9** The verse repeats the word "violence" (חָמָס, *ḥāmās*) used earlier in the description of the wicked (vv. 2-3). In verse 3, the prophet laments the violence before him, whereas verse 9 depicts the Babylonians as being **bent on violence** (cf. the NET's "all of them intend to do violence"). The violence which characterizes the situation lamented in verses 2-3 still exists at the hands of those introduced as Yahweh's instruments of justice; they too are guilty of the same violence (2:8,17). The similes of this verse describe the power-

---

[17]Richard D. Patterson, *Nahum, Habakkuk, Zephaniah*, WEC (Chicago: Moody, 1991), p. 151.

less nations who succumb to the Babylonian onslaught. The unstoppable Babylonians advance **like a** scorching **desert wind** from the eastern deserts, and countless **prisoners** (2:5) are caught up in their rush.[18]

**1:10** Verse 10 portrays the arrogances of the Babylonians as they mock other **kings** and **laugh at cities** whose fortifications prove no match for the mighty siege works of the Babylonians. The **build**ing of **earthen ramps** refers to ancient siege practices, in which dirt is piled up against the walls of a city to form a ramp over which attacking soldiers might enter the city over the wall (2 Sam 20:15; 2 Kgs 19:32; Isa 23:13; 29:3; Jer 32:24; 33:4; Ezek 17:17).[19] Ironically, the wicked of Judah who hem in the righteous (v. 4) would themselves be hemmed in by the horrors of siege works (Jer 39:1).[20]

**1:11** The Hebrew of verse 11 is difficult and its proper translation uncertain. The NIV and most other versions (cf. the ESV, NASB, NET, NRSV, and NJB) understand the first half of the verse to be a continuation of the description of the Babylonian armies who arrive and then depart swiftly **like** a strong **wind** and the second half of the verse to be an indictment of the Babylonian's guilt for regarding their **own strength** as if divine. However, at least three alternative readings are proposed. The first reading is reflected in the KJV: "Then shall *his* mind change, and he shall pass over, and offend, *imputing* this his power unto his god." The first line reflects the LXX in suggesting that the king (representing the army of Babylon) repents. The Vulgate implies that the king's spirit is changed and passes from him before he falls. The second reading emends the Hebrew form (אָשֵׁם, *'šm*) by one letter to read as the verb "devastate" (יָשִׂם, *yāśim* from שָׁמַם, *šāmam*) rather than the adjective for **guilty** (אָשֵׁם, *'āšēm*).[21] This reading is supported by the Habakkuk commentary among the Dead Sea Scrolls (1QpHap IV, 9). It suggests that the strength of the Babylonian army continues to devas-

---

[18]Armerding, "Habakkuk," 7:503. On the difficulties in translating this verse, see Patterson, *Nahum, Habakkuk, Zephaniah*, pp. 151-152.

[19]Cf. the description of Sennacherib's defeat of Jerusalem (*ANET*, p. 288). Remnants of the assault ramp used by the Romans to take Masada in A.D. 73–74 are still visible; see Ehud Netzer, "Masada," *NEAEHL*, 3:983-984.

[20]Armerding, "Habakkuk," p. 503.

[21]Robert D. Haak, *Habakkuk*, VTSupp 44 (Leiden: Brill, 1991), pp. 46-47; Keil, *Minor Prophets*, p. 59.

tate new territories for their patron god. The second reading translates the noun רוּחַ (*rûaḥ*) as "spirit" rather than "wind" and then
reads the Hebrew form (*'šm*) as a first person form of the verb "be
astonished" (another possible meaning if the correct root word is
*šāmam* rather than the similar adjective for "guilty" [*'āšam*]). The first
half of the verse reads, "The spirit passed on and departed, and I
was astonished," and thus indicates the ending of the divine answer
which had begun in verse 5. The last half of the verse might read,
"This one [has] his strength as his god." Accordingly, it aligns with
the response that Yahweh anticipates in verse 5 (i.e., "you would not
believe, even if you were told"), heightens the tension for the
prophet and the reader (since the text affirms the blasphemy of
Babylon), and foreshadows the content of the prophet's next complaint in verses 12-17.[22]

## D. HABAKKUK'S SECOND COMPLAINT (1:12-17)

[12]O LORD, are you not from everlasting? / My God, my Holy
One, we will not die. / O LORD, you have appointed them to execute judgment; / O Rock, you have ordained them to punish. /
[13]Your eyes are too pure to look on evil; / you cannot tolerate
wrong. / Why then do you tolerate the treacherous? / Why are you
silent while the wicked / swallow up those more righteous than
themselves? / [14]You have made men like fish in the sea, / like sea
creatures that have no ruler. / [15]The wicked foe pulls all of them
up with hooks, / he catches them in his net, / he gathers them up
in his dragnet; / and so he rejoices and is glad. / [16]Therefore he
sacrifices to his net / and burns incense to his dragnet, / for by
his net he lives in luxury / and enjoys the choicest food. / [17]Is he
to keep on emptying his net, / destroying nations without mercy?

Habakkuk 1:12-17 consists of a prophetic complaint, in which
the prophet voices a complaint as the people's representative. It
includes typical elements of the form: invocation ("O LORD"), affirmation of trust ("we will not die"), description of trouble ("the

---

[22]For this second alternate reading, see Roberts, *Nahum, Habakkuk, and Zephaniah*, pp. 97-100.

wicked swallow up those more righteous than themselves"),
reproach ("why are you silent"), and plea for deliverance ("Is he to
keep on emptying his net destroying nations without mercy?"). The
unit contains an affirmation of Yahweh's moral integrity (v. 12), a
reproach of Yahweh's apparent responsibility for the injustice associated with the rise of Babylon (v. 13), and an extended simile that
describes Babylon's unstoppable conquest of the world (vv. 14-17).
The unit begins in verse 12 with a change of address from the plural commands of verse 5. Now Yahweh is once more addressed by
the prophet in a complaint form connected to Habakkuk's first complaint (vv. 2-4) by several elements. First, the Hebrew text of verse
12 begins with an interrogative particle (הֲ, *hă*), and verse 13 uses the
same interrogative that appears in verse 3, "why" (לָמָּה, *lāmmāh*).
Second, the parallelism of the verbs "look" (רָאָה, *rā'āh*) and "tolerate" (נָבַט, *nābaṭ*) in verse 13 calls to mind the use of these same verbs
in verses 3 and 5. Finally, in both verses 3-4 and 13, this verb pair
precedes a description of the fate of the righteous at the hands of
the wicked. These connections make the second lament an expansion and intensification of the first complaint. In verses 12-17, the
prophet approaches Yahweh on behalf of the people, expressing
their trust in Yahweh but also their questions regarding Yahweh's
responsibility for the injustices of the Babylonian oppression and of
the exploitation seemingly inherent in created order.

**1:12-13** The titles and descriptions applied to Yahweh in verses
12-13 are striking. The appearance of several laudatory remarks
gives the passage a momentary semblance of a confession of trust,
but the remainder of the complaint foils these positive images. First,
verse 12 describes Yahweh as **everlasting**. Elsewhere, biblical writers
use "everlasting" (קֶדֶם, *qedem*) to describe Yahweh's eternality in
contexts that speak of Yahweh's past saving actions, especially
Israel's preservation from Egypt (Deut 33:27; Ps 44:1; 74:12; 77:11;
Micah 7:20). Seemingly Habakkuk reminds Yahweh of the covenant
relationship to Israel. Second, verse 12 identifies Yahweh as **My
God**. The word "God" (אֱלֹהִים, *'ĕlōhîm*) is frequently used as a title
for Yahweh, occurring over 2500 times in the Old Testament. The
title appears in the first verse of Genesis, "In the beginning God created the heavens and the earth," and *'ĕlōhîm* often refers to the
majestic power of Yahweh (Ps 68:32-35), especially in contexts relat-

ing to the creation of the world (Gen 1:1-12,14,16-18,20-21,24-29,31; 2:2-5,7-9,15-16,18-19,21-22), Yahweh's covenant with Abraham (Gen 17:3,7-9,15,18-19,22-23), and Israel's exodus from Egypt (Exod 3:6; 13:17-19; 14:19; 15:2,26). Thus, *'ĕlōhîm* expresses the concept of divine faithfulness to the covenant and divine power in relation to the creation. Nonetheless, verse 13 questions God's concern for the righteous, and verse 14 questions God's concern in the creation of humanity. Third, verse 12 identifies Yahweh as **My Holy One**, an epithet bolstered by verse 13: **Your eyes are too pure to look on evil; you cannot tolerate wrong** (cf. Jer 5:3). The designation is reminiscent of the language with which the divine choice of Israel is described (Deut 7:6-9). These lines of verses 12-13, however, precede the accusatory questions, **Why then do you tolerate the treacherous? Why are you silent while the wicked swallow up those more righteous than themselves?** Fourth, verse 12 calls Yahweh **Rock**, a common title in the Psalms; it implies the reliability, stability, and protective nature of Yahweh (Deut 32:4,15,18; Ps 18:3,32,47; 19:14; 28:1; 31:3; 61:3; 62:3,7,8; 71:3; 73:26; 78:35; 89:27; 92:16; 94:22; 95:1; 144:1). Verses 12-14, however, accuse Yahweh, the Holy God, of not protecting the better interests of the people.

In the second line of verse 12, the NIV follows the MT's reading, **we will not die** (the LXX contains the same reading). Another ancient interpretation reads, "you will not die." The MT may reflect an attempt by later scribes to avoid associating the idea of death with Yahweh in any way. A second-person reading of the second line matches the use of the second person in the remainder of the verse; however, the first-person reading of the line may function as an expression of trust that is a typical element of the complaint genre. While the prophet acknowledges that Yahweh has set the Babylonians for judgment and has **ordained them** for **punish**ing, the two questions of verse 13 identify the instrument of Yahweh's judgment as treacherous and wicked ones who swallow up those more righteous than themselves.

**1:14-17** Habakkuk 1:14-17 consists of an extended simile that describes Babylon's military domination and exploitation. The image of the net occurs in Sumerian art as an image of military power; for example, the Stele of the Vultures depicts the enemies of Eannatum, king of Lagash, caught in a large net held by a Sumerian god.[23] Those who make their own strength their god (v. 11) now are ensnaring Yahweh's people with Yahweh's approval. The prophet portrays people as seeming to exist only for the Babylonians' economic gratification. Worse still, the Babylonians attribute their success to their own military might. These circumstances cause the prophet to wonder if the Babylonians' injustices will go unpunished.

Whereas verse 12 portrays Yahweh as the one who actively set in place the Babylonians for judgment and correction, verse 13 portrays Yahweh as inactive and unmoved while gazing upon the treacherous ones, and as silent while the wicked swallows up the righteous. Verse 14 once again describes Yahweh in more active terms. Here, however, Yahweh is not moving suddenly to vindicate the people. Instead, it appears that Yahweh has merely made humanity **like fish in the sea** and like creeping things[24] which lack a **ruler**. Although humanity is created to rule over the fish and creeping things (Gen 1:26-28), here humanity is reduced to the level of these **creatures**.[25]

The interchange between active and inactive portrayals of Yahweh in verses 12-14 spotlights the dilemma upon which the two laments of the book of Habakkuk focus. Yahweh seems aloof, unaware, uncaring, or impotent in the face of evil. When Yahweh does take action, however, the Holy One and the Rock is portrayed as working that which seems counter to Yahweh's moral character. The bewilderment within the second lament then hardens in verses 15-17, which describe the rapacity of the enemy. The use of fishing vocabulary and images in verse 15 harks back to verse 14 to implicate God as the ultimate author of the woeful situation. Yahweh has made humanity like the fish of the sea, and the **wicked foe** then **pulls up** humanity **with** a **hook, catches them in his net**, and **gathers them up in his dragnet**. The final line of verse 15 also notes the delight with which the enemy does this deed and further calls into question the character of Yahweh who raises up the enemy. Verse 16, moreover, accentuates the incongruity of this scenario, since the

---

[23]*ANEP*, fig. 298.

[24]The Hebrew noun רֶמֶשׂ (*remeś*) essentially means "crawling creature" or "moving creature" (Gen 1:24-26; 6:7,20; 7:14,23; 8:17,19; 9:3; 1 Kgs 4:33; Ps 104:25; 148:10; Ezek 8:10; 38:20; Hos 2:18). This is the only place where the NIV translates it as "sea creature." The parallelism, however, favors the understanding of the noun here to refer to creatures that move about in the sea.

[25]McConville, *Guide to the Prophets*, p. 214.

success of the wicked foe has become an occasion for the worship of the instruments of his conquest. The two words **sacrifice** (זָבַח, zābaḥ) and **burn incense** (קָטַר, qāṭar), when occurring together, connote illegitimate worship (1 Sam 2:15; 1 Kgs 3:3; 11:8; 13:2; 22:43; 2 Kgs 12:3; 14:4; 15:4,35; 16:4; 2 Chr 28:4; Isa 65:3; Hos 4:13; 11:2).[26] The questions in verse 17 bring the complaint to a climax; the verse in Hebrew begins with a causal marker "therefore" (עַל־כֵּן, 'al-kēn), a word which appears also in verses 15 and 16 (the NASB translates the word in all three instances). The three occurrences indicate that Habakkuk's argument builds dramatically to the questions posed in verse 17.[27] The questions, **Is he to keep emptying his net, destroying nations without mercy?** and "O LORD, are you not from everlasting?" in verse 12, bracket the second complaint with temporal references. These questions highlight the dilemma by contrasting an affirmation of Yahweh's eternal nature and a statement about the seemingly endless persecution of the enemy (the temporal adverb is translated in various ways; cf. "keep on," "continually," "always," or "forever" in the ESV, KJV, NASB, NET, and NLT). The query whether the adversary continues to destroy the nations without mercy also upends the expectations of the earlier affirmation, "we will not die" (1:12).

Thus, this section functions to solidify and heighten the tensions already evident in the preceding sections. The first complaint laments the perceived inattention of Yahweh to the wickedness and violence, as torah is numbed and justice goes out distorted. The response contained within verses 5-11 then raises the expectations of a vindication of the righteous with the announcement of the working of an awe-inspiring work. The equating of this work with Yahweh's raising up the Babylonians quickly reverses this anticipation, when the subsequent verses describe the Babylonians in dubious terms. Verses 15-17 echo many of the sentiments regarding the Babylonians found within the prior section (vv. 5-11), but here they appear on the lips of Habakkuk. The section brings to the forefront the issue of theodicy. Habakkuk confronts Yahweh with the incongruity between the traditional understanding of Yahweh's nature and the concern for Yahweh's use of a wicked instrument to avenge

---

[26]Armerding, "Habakkuk," 7:508.

[27]Patterson, *Nahum, Habakkuk, Zephaniah*, pp. 167-168.

injustice. As a result, the second complaint intensifies the desire for a resolution.

## E. YAHWEH'S SECOND RESPONSE (2:1-20)

[1]I will stand at my watch / and station myself on the ramparts; / I will look to see what he will say to me, / and what answer I am to give to this complaint.[a]

[2]Then the LORD replied:

"Write down the revelation / and make it plain on tablets / so that a herald[b] may run with it. / [3]For the revelation awaits an appointed time; / it speaks of the end / and will not prove false. / Though it linger, wait for it; / it[c] will certainly come and will not delay.

[4]"See, he is puffed up; / his desires are not upright— / but the righteous will live by his faith[d]— / [5]indeed, wine betrays him; / he is arrogant and never at rest. / Because he is as greedy as the grave[e] / and like death is never satisfied, / he gathers to himself all the nations / and takes captive all the peoples.

[6]"Will not all of them taunt him with ridicule and scorn, saying,

"'Woe to him who piles up stolen goods / and makes himself wealthy by extortion! / How long must this go on?' / [7]Will not your debtors[f] suddenly arise? / Will they not wake up and make you tremble? / Then you will become their victim. / [8]Because you have plundered many nations, / the peoples who are left will plunder you. / For you have shed man's blood; / you have destroyed lands and cities and everyone in them.

[9]"Woe to him who builds his realm by unjust gain / to set his nest on high, / to escape the clutches of ruin! / [10]You have plotted the ruin of many peoples, / shaming your own house and forfeiting your life. / [11]The stones of the wall will cry out, / and the beams of the woodwork will echo it.

[12]"Woe to him who builds a city with bloodshed / and establishes a town by crime! / [13]Has not the LORD Almighty determined / that the people's labor is only fuel for the fire, / that the nations exhaust themselves for nothing? / [14]For the earth will be filled with the knowledge of the glory of the LORD, / as the waters cover the sea.

[15]"Woe to him who gives drink to his neighbors, / pouring it from the wineskin till they are drunk, / so that he can gaze on their naked bodies. / [16]You will be filled with shame instead of glory. / Now it is your turn! Drink and be exposed[g]! / The cup from the LORD's right hand is coming around to you, / and disgrace will cover your glory. / [17]The violence you have done to Lebanon will overwhelm you, / and your destruction of animals will terrify you. / For you have shed man's blood; / you have destroyed lands and cities and everyone in them.

[18]"Of what value is an idol, since a man has carved it? / Or an image that teaches lies? / For he who makes it trusts in his own creation; / he makes idols that cannot speak. / [19]Woe to him who says to wood, 'Come to life!' / Or to lifeless stone, 'Wake up!' / Can it give guidance? / It is covered with gold and silver; / there is no breath in it. / [20]But the LORD is in his holy temple; / let all the earth be silent before him."

[a]*1 Or and what to answer when I am rebuked*    [b]*2 Or so that whoever reads it*    [c]*3 Or Though he linger, wait for him; / he*    [d]*4 Or faithfulness*    [e]*5 Hebrew Sheol*    [f]*7 Or creditors*    [g]*16 Masoretic Text; Dead Sea Scrolls, Aquila, Vulgate and Syriac (see also Septuagint) and stagger*

Habakkuk 2:1-20 consists of two parts: a prophetic inquiry (2:1) and a divine reply (2:2-5) that includes a series of five "woe" speeches (2:6-20). These two components corroborate the identification of the section as an example of a report of an oracular inquiry; the form describes a prophet's attempt to seek an answer from Yahweh and the divine revelation received in reply to the inquiry.[28] The section begins with the prophet's assertion that he will stand watch for a reply from Yahweh and then determine his response to that reply (v. 1). Then Yahweh answers the prophet, giving directions about the prophet's reception of the divine revelation (v. 2) and stating the contrast between the fate of the greedy and the fate of the righteous (v. 4). The reply of Yahweh (who speaks on behalf of "all of them," i.e., all peoples and nations) continues (v. 6) but in form of a reproof speech[29] against arrogant Babylon. The series of five speeches are characterized as taunt, ridicule, and scorn (vv. 6-8,9-11,12-14,15-

---

[28]Floyd, *Minor Prophets*, pp. 118-120; for other examples of the form, see 1 Sam 14:36-42; 23:6-14; 1 Kgs 22:1-23; 2 Kgs 8:7-15; Jer 21:1-14; Zech 7:2-7.
[29]Ibid., pp. 131-139.

17,18-20). The first four have a similar structure; each consists of a "woe" exclamation in reaction to some negative behavior ("Woe to him who piles up stolen goods"), a rhetorical question or statement indicating the consequences of such behavior ("Will not your debtors suddenly arise?"), and a causal conjunction introducing a statement of the principle of just reversal ("because you have plundered many nations, the peoples who are left will plunder you"). The fifth of the speeches differs from the first four in the order in which the basic elements occur; the rhetorical question and the causal conjunction come first, then the "woe" exclamation. Thus, the fifth woe speech stands as climax to the section. Chapter 2 shows the prophet waiting for an answer from Yahweh and thereby exemplifying the attitude of faithfulness that the divine response commends; furthermore, the section portrays the Babylonians' unjust accumulation of power and wealth as ultimately self-defeating.

**2:1** The first person singular verb forms in verse 1 indicate the beginning of a new section. Following the complaint in 1:12-17, the reader anticipates some form of an oracle of salvation or word of assurance. Once more, however, the text delays this expectation. The reader encounters a soliloquy that serves as a transition from the dialogue of chapter 1 to the divine response of chapter 2 and prepares the reader for some momentous encounter with Yahweh. The prophet asserts that he will reply in accordance with how adequate (or acceptable) he thinks Yahweh's response is. This intensifies the reader's anticipation of an awaited response.[30] The soliloquy, however, does intimate a cautious optimism. The stated intention to take a **stand** upon a rampart signals hope that the awaited time has come. The word translated **ramparts** may refer to the city walls, as is suggested by the role of watchman, or siege works, as it is translated elsewhere (Deut 20:20; Ezek 4:2). A city watchman stands on top of the city walls looking for the approach of danger (Ezek 33:2-6) or the approach of a messenger (2 Sam 18:24-28; Isa 52:7-10); the role of watching for divine communication is one assigned to the Old Testament prophets (Jer 6:17; Ezek 3:16-21; 33:7-9; Hos 9:8). The use of this picture is especially striking in light of its parallel in Isaiah 21:6-10 where the lookout who stands continually day by day

---

[30]J. Gerald Janzen, "Eschatological Symbol and Existence in Habakkuk," *CBQ* 44 (1982): 403.

upon the watchtower is greeted with the message, "Fallen, fallen is Babylon." While the announcement, **I will look to see what he will say to me, and what answer I am to give to this complaint**, retains a measure of an argumentative flavor, it suggests that Yahweh will enter into dialogue with the prophet. This represents an important step forward, since the prophet has accused Yahweh of being silent when the wicked one swallowed up the one more righteous than he (1:13), and has considered Yahweh's response (1:5-11) inadequate.

Whereas the motif of waiting is fairly subtle in chapter 1, it becomes much more overt in 2:1. The first three verbs in the verse exemplify this movement by characterizing the waiting of the prophet as active rather than passive. The first verb appears in the prophet's declaration, **I will stand at my watch**. The verb "stand" (עָמַד, 'āmad) appears several times in the context of standing before Yahweh in an effort to ascertain truth, seek justice, or request divine favor (Gen 18:22-23; 19:27; Num 5:16,18,30; Deut 4:10; 10:8,10; 19:17; 1 Kgs 17:1; 18:15; 2 Kgs 3:14; 5:16; 2 Chr 20:13,17). The second verb **station** (יָצַב, yāṣab) also appears in parallel with "stand" in 2 Chronicles 20:17 (the NIV translates the verb as "take up your positions"). In both passages, it characterizes this stance as one of quiet expectation. That this quiet expectation is not passive is borne out by its use in Exodus 14:13-14 where Moses commands the Israelites to station themselves and to see the deliverance which Yahweh is about to accomplish for them. Yahweh assures them that Yahweh will fight for them and that they need only to be still. Nonetheless, the command of Yahweh in verse 15 that the Israelites march forward indicates that this stillness is hardly a passive state. They are to be still in that they are to act in expectation of Yahweh's deliverance, not in expectation of deliverance through their own power. This verb also appears in contexts where individuals are about to receive a commission (Deut 31:14; Judg 20:2). To station oneself thus implies an expectation that will bear fruit in some sort of action. The prophet will wait, for he expects a revelation. The third verb "look" (צָפָה, ṣāphāh) conveys the idea of seeking a full awareness of a situation. Micah 7:7 illustrates the connotations of expectancy inherent in the word. There the NRSV reads, "But as for me, I will look to the LORD, I will wait for the God of my salvation; My God will hear me."

The NIV (cf. ESV, KJV, NASB, and NET) follows the MT in the last half of the verse: "I will look to see what he will say to me and what answer I am to give to this complaint." Other versions, such as the NRSV (cf. NLT, NJB, and NJPS), reflect an alternative textual tradition found in the Peshitta or Syriac translation, "I will keep watch to see what he will say to me, and what he will answer concerning my complaint." In both readings the prophet looks to what Yahweh will say. While the reading in the NIV draws attention to how the prophet will respond to Yahweh's corrective reply, the reading in the NRSV puts emphasis on how Yahweh will answer the prophet's complaint. Although the reading in the NRSV more suitably parallels the preceding line,[31] the reading reflected in the NIV is more consistent with the prophet's desire to continue, if needed, his complaint to Yahweh.[32] The term "complaint" (תּוֹכַחַת, *tôkaḥath*) generally means argument (Job 13:6; 23:4; Ps 38:14) or correction/ reproof (Ps 39:11; 73:14; Prov 1:23; 3:11; 5:12; 6:23). It comes from the same root of the word translated "punish" (יָכַח, *yākaḥ*) in 1:12 (cf. "reproof" in the ESV and "correct" in the NASB). These two words form an inclusio for the section 1:12–2:1. In the same way that Habakkuk recognizes the Babylonians have been ordained to punish Judah, the prophet expects to receive correction from Yahweh to his complaint.

**2:2** Yahweh answers Habakkuk and commands that the vision be written and confirmed on tablets. The phrasing **Write down the revelation and make it plain** is a hendiadys for "write the vision clearly." Perhaps the prophet envisions a writing of the revelation's content **on tablets** that would be placed in a prominent place such as the temple complex. Isaiah 30:8 recounts a similar command that a revelation be written on a tablet for an everlasting testimony to future generations (cf. Jer 32:8). Such may be the case here, since the written revelation serves as a reliable guarantee ("and will not prove false" in v. 3) of Yahweh's future actions (cf. Isa 8:1-4,16-17; 30:8-11).[33]

---

[31]Francis I. Andersen, *Habakkuk: A New Translation with Introduction and Commentary*, AB 25 (New York: Doubleday, 2001), p. 194; Haak, *Habakkuk*, p. 54; Hiebert, "Habakkuk," p. 639.

[32]Patterson, *Nahum, Habakkuk, Zephaniah*, pp. 162-163; Marvin A. Sweeney, *The Twelve Prophets* (Collegeville, MN: Liturgical Press, 2000), p. 470.

[33]Hiebert, "Habakkuk," p. 641.

The use of the noun "revelation" (חָזוֹן, ḥāzôn) draws the reader back to the superscription (1:1) where the cognate verb "received" (חָזָה, ḥāzāh) appears. This echo helps establish this passage as the rhetorical and hermeneutical center of the book.[34] The word ḥāzāh can refer to the totality of revelation received by and communicated by the prophet (Isa 1:1; Obad 1:1), or it could refer to a more specific means of prophetic revelation (Isa 29:7; Dan 8:1). The word can also refer to something visual, that is, something that is seen by the prophet (Dan 7:1), or to something not visual, that is, an event in which the word of Yahweh is received by the prophet (1 Chr 17:15; Ps 89:19; Prov 29:18).[35] Running with a message suggests its urgency or importance (cf. 2 Sam 18:19-27; 2 Chr 30:6,10; Esth 3:13,15; Jer 23:21; 51:31; Zech 2:4). The NIV marginal reading offers the more literal rendering "whoever reads it" in place of "herald"; however, the word "herald" conveys that Habakkuk is the one commissioned to announce the revelation, since the image of running as a messenger coincides with prophetic action described elsewhere (Jer 23:21).

**2:3** The third verse impresses the reader with the basic character of the revelation: its eschatological nature and its certainty.[36] **The revelation awaits an "appointed time"** (מוֹעֵד, môʿēd), which designates a fixed future time for accomplishing a task. It is used for the end of the term of a woman's pregnancy (Gen 18:14), holy days (Exod 23:15; Lev 23:2,4,37,44; 2 Chr 8:13), a prearranged meeting time (1 Sam 13:8,11; 20:35), and a time for a display of Yahweh's favor (Ps 102:13). The revelation **speaks** to **the end** (קֵץ, qēṣ), a noun which further emphasizes the fixed nature of the appointed time (Gen 8:6; Exod 12:41; Num 13:25; Deut 9:11; 15:1; 31:10; 2 Chr 21:19; Esth 2:12; Isa 23:17). Because the revelation speaks to the end, it requires a permanent record to confirm its reliability beyond the prophet's own day (the fall of Babylon in 539 B.C. almost 70 years after Habakkuk's prophecy).[37]

These words of Yahweh affirm the prophet who stands expectant of what Yahweh will say, but the words also emphasize that the prophet may not see the evidence of Yahweh's action immediately.

---

[34]Janzen, "Eschatological Symbol," p. 396.
[35]Jackie A. Naudé, "חזה," NIDOTTE, 2:59.
[36]Robertson, *Nahum, Habakkuk, and Zephaniah*, p. 170.
[37]Armerding, "Habakkuk," pp. 511-512.

Yahweh promises a vision which will certainly come and which **will not prove false**; however, that vision is for the "appointed time" and speaks of "the end." On the one hand, this emphasizes that the awaited resolution lies yet in the future. On the other hand, the presence of an appointed time assures that it will indeed come. The verb "wait" (חָכָה, *ḥākah*) appears fourteen times in the Old Testament (2 Kgs 7:9; 9:3; Job 3:21; 32:4; Ps 33:20; 106:13; Isa 8:17; 30:18 [2×]; 64:4; Dan 12:12; Hos 6:9; Hab 2:3; Zeph 3:8) with most uses connoting an attitude which combines earnest expectation with confident hope.[38] The summons by Yahweh to wait for the vision which is certainly to come at the appointed time thus fortifies the previous notes of expectation with an added element of hope (cf. Hab 3:16). In verse 3, the reader also encounters a paradox which affects the understanding of passages appearing previously in the book. The statement, **Though it linger, wait for it; it will certainly come and will not delay**, recalls earlier statements involving time. The first complaint (1:2) begins with the question, "How long?" Yahweh announces that a work is working in the prophet's days (1:5). The second complaint begins by ascribing eternity to Yahweh (1:12) and ends by questioning whether the foe would keep destroying nations continually (1:17). The tension between the possibility of the vision lingering and its coming without delay requires the acknowledgement of the present actions of Yahweh which are not readily apparent and the anticipation of the future actions of Yahweh which are ultimately certain.

**2:4-5** Verse 4[39] does not recount the vision itself (vv. 2-3), but rather it portrays two contrasting responses to the vision. The wicked one relies on self rather than Yahweh and does not survive, but the righteous lives by means of faithfulness and is vindicated. The rhetorical structure of these two verses emphasizes the vindication of the righteous by enclosing the solitary line, "But the righteous will live by his faith," within two statements that express the fate of the wicked.[40]

---

[38]Edwin Yamauchi, "חָכָה," *TWOT*, 1:282.

[39]On the difficulties in translating the verse, see J.A. Emerton, "The Textual and Linguistic Problems of Habakkuk II.4-5," *JTS* 18 (1977): 1-18; and Gerald Janzen, "Habakkuk 2:2-4 in the Light of Recent Philological Advances," *HTR* 73 (1980): 53-78.

[40]Lawrence Boadt, *Jeremiah 26–52, Habakkuk, Zephaniah, Nahum* (Wilmington, DE: Michael Glazier, 1982), p. 181.

The first statement (v. 4) about the wicked begins with the interjection **see** (הִנֵּה, *hinnēh*), which demands attention be paid to what follows (elsewhere in Hab 1:6; 2:13,19). The wicked are **arrogant** and desire what is not right. The word **desire** (נֶפֶשׁ, *nepheš*) in the NIV translates a word rendered as "soul" in other versions (e.g., ESV, KJV, NASB); *nepheš* also appears in 2:5 as "greed" and in 2:10 as "life." While *nepheš* is most often translated in the NIV as "life" or "soul," the word may refer to "breath" (Gen 1:30; 1 Kgs 17:22), "throat" (Jer 4:10), "neck" (see Ps 69:1 in the ESV or NRSV), "appetite" (Ps 78:18), "desire" (Prov 13:2), the person who desires (Ps 42:1-2; 63:1; Isa 26:8-9), or the whole person (Exod 21:23; 1 Kgs 19:3; 2 Kgs 1:13); these last two connotations are sometimes translated with a personal pronoun (Ps 143:3; Jer 9:9).[41] The context of verses 4-5 suggests the notion of desire, albeit negative (cf. Isa 5:14), whereas the occurrence of the word in verse 10 connotes the life of the person.

The compound particle (וְאַף כִּי, *wᵉʾaph kî*), which is translated **indeed** in the NIV, begins the second group of statements about the wicked in verse 5. The particle commonly introduces an argument *a fortiori*, that is, from lesser to greater (cf. Deut 31:27; 1 Sam 14:30; 21:5; 23:3; 2 Sam 4:11; 16:11; 2 Kgs 5:13; Prov 11:31; 15:11; 19:7,10; 21:27; Ezek 14:21). The wicked possess an insatiable **greed**, one which is depicted with the images of drunkenness (1 Sam 30:16; Prov 20:1; 31:4-7; Isa 5:11-12,22-23; Amos 6:6; Hab 2:16)[42] and death (Ps 49:14; Prov 30:15-16; Isa 5:14); these images connote the political and military ambitions of the wicked. According to Daniel 5:1-31, the Babylonian empire is overthrown during a time of drunken revelry (cf. Hab 2:16). The description of the counterpart of the righteous in verses 4-5 also connects with previous portrayals of the wicked. In 1:13, the prophet asks why Yahweh tolerates the "treacherous" (cf. NLT and NJB); in 2:5, the same verb, translated "betray,"

---

[41]Bruce K. Waltke, "נֶפֶשׁ," *TWOT*, 2:587-591.

[42]Most versions including the NIV contain the word "wine" (see Andersen, *Habakkuk*, pp. 217-218). However, the commentary on Habakkuk found among the Dead Sea Scrolls (1QpHab) contains the word "wealth" instead of "wine," a reading adopted by the NRSV, NLT, and NJB (see Roberts, *Nahum, Habakkuk, and Zephaniah*, p. 113). The NJPS has still a third option for the word, "defiant" or "presumptuous" (see Patterson, *Nahum, Habakkuk, Zephaniah*, pp. 180-181).

describes the betrayal the wicked experience. The word translated **gather** and **take captive** in verse 5 (אָסַף, *'āsaph*) appears earlier in 1:9, where the Babylonians' "gather prisoners like sand," and in 1:15, where the wicked foe gathers up nations in his dragnet.

The focal assertion of verses 4-5 comprises the positive response to the vision: **But the righteous will live by his faith**. The noun "righteous" (צַדִּיק, *ṣaddîq*) refers to one who conforms to an ethical standard (Gen 6:9; 15:6; Ezek 3:21); accordingly, the "righteous" is one who serves Yahweh (Mal 3:18), obeys the commands of Yahweh (Deut 6:25; Ps 1:1-6; Ezek 18:9; Hos 14:9), remembers the covenant with Yahweh (Isa 51:1-8), cares for the poor and needy (Job 29:12-15; Ps 37:21; Prov 29:7), and lives according to the spirit of Yahweh (Isa 32:15-17; Ezek 36:25-27).[43] Habakkuk's use of *ṣaddîq* may reflect this general meaning of the term, or the prophet may use *ṣaddîq* more specifically to identify those who are mistreated and oppressed by the wicked (cf. 1:4,13), a meaning of the word found elsewhere in the prophetic literature (Isa 29:20-21; Lam 4:13; Ezek 13:22; Amos 2:6-7; 5:12).[44]

Preferred is the NIV marginal reading of "faithfulness" (cf. the TNIV) instead of "faith," since it better represents the basic meaning of אֱמוּנָה (*'ĕmûnāh*); the word generally means "firmness," "reliability," "steadiness," or "loyalty" (e.g., Exod 17:12; 2 Kgs 12:15; 22:7; 2 Chr 19:9; 34:12; Ps 89:2; 119:90; Prov 12:17,22; Isa 59:4; Jer 5:1; 9:3). In fact, this text represents the only time the NIV translates *'ĕmûnāh* as "faith"; most often the NIV renders *'ĕmûnāh* as "faithfulness" (20 of 49×). Furthermore, the text is ambiguous regarding whose faithfulness results in life for the righteous. Even though the NIV reads, "the righteous will live by his faith[fulness]," the context provides at least three options for identifying the antecedent of the pronoun "his." One, "his" may refer to the righteous one just mentioned; this option is assumed by most modern translations, especially those who render the pronoun as "their" (e.g., NLT and NJB). Two, "his" may refer to Yahweh. The LXX reads, "The righteous shall live by my [Yahweh's] faith[fulness]," a reading that makes sense if one understands the passage to affirm that Yahweh sustains the righteous through the present crisis.[45] Three, the third person

---

[43]Harold G. Stigers, "צָדַק," *TWOT*, 2:752-755.

[44]Hiebert, "Habakkuk," p. 631.

[45]Keil, *Minor Prophets*, pp. 402-403.

pronoun may refer to the vision of verses 2-3, thus "its reliability."[46] Nevertheless, the contrast between the proud and the righteous probably indicates that it is the faithfulness of the righteous one rather than Yahweh's faithfulness or the vision's reliability about the end to which the assertion refers.

The structure of the Hebrew text of verse 4 places the verb "will live" in the final climactic position. The righteous will be sustained through the coming invasion (Hab 3:16), but the proud will meet their end. Although powerful now, the wicked foe is in danger, but the righteous possesses true life and security (cf. Ps 73:15-28). The affirmation that the righteous will live by faithfulness is thus a description of how the readers are to live between the present time and the appointed time of the vision's fulfillment.[47] The affirmation that the righteous will live by their faithfulness connects with several earlier passages in Habakkuk. In the first complaint, the prophet asserts that the wicked hem in the righteous (1:4), and in the second complaint, he maintains that the wicked have swallowed up the righteous (1:13). The opening words of the second complaint assert that the supplicants should not die (1:12), while its closing words ask whether the wicked will continue to kill nations (1:17). The affirmation that the righteous will indeed live thus addresses the concerns put forth in these earlier complaints. Habakkuk 2:4 is also cited three times in the New Testament: Romans 1:17, Galatians 3:11, and Hebrews 10:37-38. Of the three, Hebrews 10 uses the text in a way closest to its original context in its call for the reader to persevere with confidence in the face of suffering and persecution and to do the will of God in order to receive the salvation which God has promised.

**2:6** The continuation of the motif of waiting is more subtle in the woe (הוֹי, *hôy*) sayings (vv. 6-20) than in verses 1-5. While no distinct vocabulary of waiting is found, the woes carry forward the expectation that the currently oppressed nations will taunt the arrogant who, at the present, seem immune to punishment. Even if the punishment of the wicked is still future, its certainty is connoted by the woe sayings, which affirm that Yahweh does not overlook the injustice and violence done by those who oppress the righteous. Thereby,

---

[46]Haak, *Habakkuk*, p. 59; Roberts, *Nahum, Habakkuk, Zephaniah*, pp. 111-112.

[47]Roberts, *Nahum, Habakkuk, Zephaniah*, p. 112.

verses 6-20 bring some resolution to earlier tensions within the text. All the nations who have suffered at the hands of the arrogant one will **taunt him with ridicule and scorn**. The word "taunt" actually represents two Hebrew words, "take up" and "taunt" (cf. the ESV and NASB). The verb "take up" (נָשָׂא, nāśśā') here links to the superscription which uses a cognate noun to identify the contents of the book as an "oracle" (מַשָּׂא, maśśā'). The reiteration of "all" links verse 6 with the final lines of verse 5 in which the arrogant gathers all the nations and takes captive to himself all the peoples. This coupling highlights the reversal of the fortunes for the arrogant and all the nations and peoples.

Habakkuk 2:6-20 presents the world's opinion of Babylon in agreement with Yahweh's reply to Habakkuk; the words of the nations (voiced by Yahweh) are described with the words "taunt," "ridicule," and "scorn." The word translated "taunt" (מָשָׁל, māšāl) does not refer to a fixed literary form, but it designates a variety of literary forms that share a basic component of comparison or analogy used in some way to present a paradigm or model.[48] It can refer to a proverb (Prov 25:1; 26:7,9), a parable (Ps 78:2), an allegory (Ezek 17:2), a taunt (Isa 14:4), or a byword indicating ill repute (Ps 44:14; Jer 24:9). When occurring with the verb "lift up," māšāl anticipates some type of reversal in the situation (Num 23:7,18; 24:3,15, 20,21,23; Job 27:1; 29:1; Isa 14:4; Micah 2:4). Here that reversal involves the announced judgment against the Babylonians. The word translated "ridicule" (מְלִיצָה, mᵊlîṣāh) derives from the verb "to scorn" (לִיץ, lîṣ; cf. Isa 28:22; 29:20; Hos 7:5) and refers to a mocking poem; the only other occurrence of mᵊlîṣāh refers to an enigmatic saying requiring wisdom to understand it (Prov 1:6). The word "scorn" (חִידָה, ḥîdāh) refers to a riddle, question, or story whose meaning must be determined by the audience (Judg 14:12-19; 1 Kgs 10:1; 2 Chr 9:1).[49] These three words are drawn from the wisdom genre (see Prov 1:8); all the peoples who have suffered oppression from the Babylonians will use such speech, mysterious and mocking, to ridicule the fall of Babylon.[50]

---

[48]Timothy Polk, "Paradigms, Parables, and Mešālîm: On Reading the Māšāl in Scripture," *CBQ* 45 (1983): 565-566.

[49]Edwin Yamauchi, "חִידָה," *TWOT*, 1:267.

[50]Barker and Bailey, *Micah, Nahum, Habakkuk, Zephaniah*, p. 332.

**2:6-8** The interjection **woe** (הוֹי, *hôy*) begins each of five sayings (vv. 6-8,9-11,12-14,15-18,19-20) that emphasize the imminent doom of the wicked. The word *hôy* is used elsewhere for the cry of mourning heard at funerals (1 Kgs 13:30; Jer 22:18-19; Isa 1:4; Amos 5:16); however, in the present context, these exclamations present an ironic cry of anguish over the sudden reversal of the fortunes of the evil one (cf. the NJB and NJPS).[51] A more literal rendering of the opening line of verse 6 pronounces woe on "one who is heaping up what is not his own." The phrase "not his own" (לֹא לוֹ, *lō' lô*) also appears in 1:6. There Yahweh asserts the rise of the Babylonians who walk the expanses of the earth "to seize dwelling places not his own," but here the piling of things "not his own" contributes to the Babylonians' demise rather than blessing. This reversal thus reduces the tension created by the first divine response (1:5-11). The word **extortion** (עַבְטִיט, *'abṭîṭ*) refers to some item used to secure a loan by a lender; this pledge of payment often coincides with undue or illegal force to enforce the loan or exploitation or enslavement of the poor (2 Kgs 4:1-7; Neh 5:1-13). The NIV marginal reading (cf. the TNIV, NASB, and NRSV) offers "creditors" instead of "debtors" for the difficult Hebrew term נָשַׁךְ (*nāšak*) that deals with interest. The notion of reversal within the passage makes the reading of "debtor" more plausible. Whatever translation is correct, the thrust of the passage is clear: the one who has piled up and extorted will now pay. Historically, the Babylonians paid at the hands of the Medes and the Persians (cf. Isa 13:17-18; Dan 5:28). The question **How long?** that appears in the original complaint (1:2) appears again in 2:6. The former question initiates a series of statements emphasizing Yahweh's nonresponse to the evil surrounding the prophet. Here the question now introduces the rhetorical questions (2:7) that indicate the consequences of the Babylonian accumulation of wealth through extortion: **Will not your debtors suddenly arise? Will they not wake up and make you tremble? Then you will become their victim. Because** the Babylonians **have plundered many nations,** they now may expect those people to **plunder** them.

---

[51]Donald E. Gowen, *The Triumph of Faith in Habakkuk* (Atlanta: John Knox, 1976), pp. 59-62; James G. Williams, "Irony and Lament: Clues to Prophetic Consciousness," *Semeia* 8 (1977): 62-65.

Perhaps the most significant link to an earlier section surfaces in verse 8 with the use of the noun חָמָס (ḥāmās), translated **destroyed** in the NIV and "violence" in other versions (e.g., ESV, KJV, NASB, NRSV, and NJB). This associates the first woe saying with the first complaint, where the prophet cries out "violence" (1:2) and with the first divine response, where the Babylonians are described as coming bent on violence (1:9). The violence characteristic of the wicked in 1:2 and 1:9 will become a basis for the violence the wicked will experience. Other links between the first hôy oracle and that which precedes it help create important developments in the message of the book. The first complaint (1:2-4) had lamented the perceived delay in the manifestation of Yahweh's justice. The second divine response (2:1-5) had acknowledged that Yahweh's retribution of evil and vindication of righteousness are not always visible in the present, but are, nevertheless, existent. In 2:6-8, the reader finds that justice is indeed working and soon will be seen. The deeds of the wicked will bring their own recompense, and the ones who had been oppressed will find vindication. While these developments do represent an advance, they by no means resolve all earlier tensions in the book. The opening lament (1:2-4) rebukes Yahweh for inaction in the face of violence and wickedness. Yahweh's activity in the first response (1:5-11) then seems incongruous with Yahweh's character. While the second response (2:2-5) presents a more positive image of Yahweh's intervention, it is no less enigmatic. Now, while verses 6-8 announce a judgment upon the evil, the verses do not mention Yahweh as an active participant, so the question remains, "Where is Yahweh?"

**2:9-11** The second hôy oracle (vv. 9-11) insists that the efforts of the Babylonians to acquire material security through dishonest means will result in their doom. Elements within the woe saying give it a memorable character. These include alliteration in the Hebrew text (בֹּצֵעַ בֶּצַע, bōṣēaʿ beṣaʿ), which the NIV translates as **him who builds . . . gain**, and repetition of the Hebrew word for "evil" (רַע, raʿ), which highlights the irony of the oppressor's fate ("build his realm by *unjust* [i.e., evil] gain" as opposed **to escape the clutches of ruin** [i.e., evil]). Also notable is the house imagery; the NIV translates the first use of "house" (בַּיִת, bayith) in verse 9 as **realm** (cf. the ESV, NASB, NET, and NRSV), here denoting a physical place as a symbol of exaltation ("on high") and security ("escape the clutches of ruin") in parallel with the metaphor "nest" (see Isa 14:4,13-15;

Obad 3-4). Verse 10 uses "house" figuratively for the family unit,[52] thus denoting the oppressor and his descendants. Since the oppressor has **plotted the ruin of many peoples**, he now brings shame upon his own progeny and endangers his own life (cf. Prov 20:2). Verse 11 personifies building materials that cry out against their builder;[53] the NIV, TNIV, and NRSV translate the singular building components as plurals. This final image of building materials that are normally silent (cf. Exod 15:16) speaking forth vividly portrays the reversal that will soon take place. The verb **cry out** (זָעַק, zāʿaq) echoes its previous use in the opening complaint (1:2) and accentuates this reversal of fortune. The prophet has cried out in his anguish, but now the house of the wicked cries out, a cry that Yahweh will not ignore indefinitely (Hab 3:13).[54]

**2:12-14** The third *hôy* oracle (vv. 12-14) claims that the Babylonian's use of violence and injustice to establish a city will be rendered futile by Yahweh of hosts, the knowledge of whose glory will fill the earth. The third woe saying continues the building motif from the previous *hôy* oracle (vv. 9-11), and, since verse 11 does not reveal the content of the outcry by the stone and beam, one is tempted to read verses 12-14 as a quotation of their words.[55] Micah 3:10 addresses an analogous accusation against the rulers of Jerusalem. The most significant feature of the third saying, however, is the clear portrayal of Yahweh's just action in verses 13 and 14. The previous sayings describe an impersonal justice in which the acts of the wicked result in punishment. The third saying, however, portrays Yahweh as active in the retribution. The presence of the interjection, הִנֵּה (hinnēh), which does not appear in the NIV (cf. the ESV and KJV), and of the divine name, **the LORD Almighty**, further accentuates the role of Yahweh as the impetus behind the reverses suffered by the wicked in the previous woes. "The LORD Almighty" (or as other versions, such as the ESV and NRSV, read, "the LORD of Hosts") is commonly used in the Old Testament to refer to Yahweh as the champion and guardian of the people (see comments on Nahum 2:13). Verse 13 implies that the just punishment for Babylon

---

[52]*HALOT*, p. 125.
[53]Bratcher, "Theological Message of Habakkuk," pp. 182-185.
[54]See Jer 22:13-23 for similar images of the undoing of a "house."
[55]Roberts, *Nahum, Habakkuk, and Zephaniah*, p. 122.

would be the burning of the city, and similarly Jeremiah contains prophecies about the destruction of Babylon by **fire** (Jer 50:32; 51:58).

The concluding words of the third saying contain significant echoes and contrasts of earlier passages. The prophet's initial complaint laments the perceived absence of Yahweh. This is now reversed with the promise of a universal inundation of Yahweh's glory (v. 14). The last word in verse 14, the noun **sea** (ם*י*, *yām*) appears also in 1:14 where Yahweh is portrayed as creating humanity as hapless fish of the sea who fall prey to the oppressor. Now, the sea is part of a positive simile describing the extent to which the **knowledge of** Yahweh's **glory** will fill **the earth** (cf. the similar wording of Isa 11:9). The glory of Yahweh entails the reality of Yahweh's presence and the manifestation of Yahweh's character (Exod 29:43; 40:34-35; 1 Kgs 8:11; 2 Chr 5:14; 7:1-3; Ezek 11:23; 43:4-5). Therefore, the entire earth will acknowledge the reputation for greatness that belongs to Yahweh (Hab 3:3). That the knowledge of Yahweh's glory fills the earth counters the Babylonian claim that Marduk, the god of their city, rules over creation.[56] The phrase **as the waters cover the sea** amplifies both the certainty and the extent of this display. Thus, the first three *hôy* oracles move from a veiled to visible outworking of Yahweh's justice.

**2:15-17** The fourth *hôy* oracle (vv. 15-17) indicts the Babylonians of forcing drunkenness upon their **neighbors** for lewd pleasure and of destroying lands and cities; such violent actions result in shame not glory. This practice of making neighbors **drunk** to expose their **naked**ness likely expresses the sexual abuse of captives of war.[57] Verse 16 focuses on the role Yahweh plays in the demise of the wicked. The previous woe (vv. 12-14) announces Yahweh's involvement in the judgment of the wicked and looks forward to a grand revelation of Yahweh's glory. Verse 16 portrays Yahweh as the one handling a cup whose contents shame the wicked (on the "cup" as a symbol of divine wrath and retribution, see Ps 16:5; Isa 51:17,21-22; Jer 25:15-17; 51:6-8; Lam 4:21). Retribution comes as the one who causes his neighbor to drink wine in order to view his nakedness himself succumbs to drink (cf. Lam 4:21). The NET captures the

---

[56]Sweeney, *The Twelve Prophets*, p. 476.
[57]Andersen, *Habakkuk*, pp. 247-249; Sweeney, *The Twelve Prophets*, p. 477.

graphic wording of the Hebrew text: "Now it is your turn to drink and expose your uncircumcised foreskin!" The one who has gloried in the nakedness, **shame**, and **disgrace** of the conquered nations will experience disgrace **instead of glory**.[58] This exchange of glory for disgrace has special significance in light of the first chapter's portrayal of the Babylonians as self-deifying tyrants (1:11) and of the preceding woe's announcement of the universal knowledge of Yahweh's glory (2:14). Verse 16 affirms, as do verses 9-10, that the actions of the wicked to glorify self will accomplish the opposite.[59]

The words of verse 17 form a powerful conclusion to the fourth *hôy* oracle. The oppressor will now experience violence. The employment of "violence" recalls its earlier uses (1:2,3,9; 2:8) and, in tandem with verse 8, affirms that violence will not go unpunished. The offenses listed in verse 17, the disregard for the creation and for human life, underscore the theme of Yahweh's punitive action against those who have overstepped their bounds. Psalm 104:16 affirms that Yahweh has planted the cedars of Lebanon (on the forests of Lebanon as symbolic of greatness and glory, see Isa 2:12-13; 14:8; 35:2), but the Babylonians have done **violence** against **Lebanon**, evidently by stripping the forest of its trees for the building projects of Nebuchadnezzar.[60] The reason for the judgment, namely the **shed**ding of human **blood**, that concludes this saying (v. 17) appears also at the conclusion of the first woe (v. 8). Its placement here focuses attention on the contrast between the *hôy* oracles that end with the refrain. More so than the first saying, the fourth saying affirms the involvement of Yahweh in the judgment of the wicked.[61] The first saying makes no mention of Yahweh and presents the "debtors" and "the peoples who are left" as the active agents of punishment. The fourth woe, however, presents Yahweh and the cup in Yahweh's right hand as the agents of judgment against Babylon, the enemy of creation and humanity.

**2:18-20** Several factors contribute to the impact of the final saying in the series of five woe oracles. Perhaps the most striking is its

---

[58]Boadt, *Jeremiah 26–52, Habakkuk, Zephaniah, Nahum*, p. 187.

[59]Roberts, *Nahum, Habakkuk, and Zephaniah*, p. 124.

[60]*ANET*, p. 307; on the prohibition against the destruction of trees during a siege, see Deut 20:19-20.

[61]Bratcher, "Theological Message of Habakkuk," p. 197.

structure. It delays the customary "woe" (הוֹי, *hôy*) and instead begins with two rhetorical questions and with a ridicule of idolatry rather than an allusion to Babylonian violence. This deviation from the pattern and the peculiar structure of the fifth woe contribute to the oracle's impact, since the postponement of the *hôy* heightens the tension created by the two rhetorical questions found in verse 18.[62] As with the other woe oracles, this saying includes significant connections with preceding passages within the book. The clustering of various words for idols helps bring to the fore the theme of idolatry introduced previously (1:11,16).[63] Consequently, verses 18-20 highlight the absurdity of placing one's confidence in an **image** which humans have shaped. Not only do **idols teach lies**, but in reality they cannot give revelation at all (cf. Isa 44:9-20; 45:20; 46:7; Jer 10:14; 51:17; Hos 4:12). This stands in contrast with 2:3 where the vision Yahweh is about to give will not prove false. The **idol cannot speak** (2:18) and is **lifeless** (2:19); therefore, the one who carves the idol has no other option than to replicate the image's silence before Yahweh (2:20). The use of the preposition "in" (בְּ, *bᵊ*) in the last line of verse 19 and in the first line of verse 20 contributes to the contrast between ineffectual idols and the effectual presence of Yahweh. "There is no breath in it," no life or spirit at all *in* the midst of the wooden or stone thing overlaid with gold and silver, but "the LORD is *in* his holy temple."[64] The gravity of this contrast is further accented by the interjection "behold" (הִנֵּה, *hinnēh*), a word that is not translated by the NIV and TNIV (cf. the ESV, KJV, NASB, and NRSV).

The mention of Yahweh's presence in the **holy temple** matches others in the Old Testament where the context speaks of Yahweh as the dispenser of justice (Ps 11:4-5; Micah 1:2-4). The theme of the **earth's silence before** Yahweh also has important parallels in

---

[62]For arguments that the MT has transposed verses 18 and 19 or that the oracle is a secondary addition to the original text, see Roberts, *Nahum, Habakkuk, and Zephaniah*, p. 126, and J.M. Powis Smith, William Hayes Ward, and Julius A. Brewer, *A Critical and Exegetical Commentary on Micah, Zephaniah, Nahum, Habakkuk, Obadiah, and Joel*, ICC (Edinburgh: T. & T. Clark, 1911), p. 18.

[63]Bratcher, "Theological Message of Habakkuk," p. 200.

[64]William H. Brownlee, "The Composition of Habakkuk," in *Hommages á André Dupont-Sommer* (Paris: Andrien-Maisonneuve, 1971), p. 272.

Scripture. Zephaniah 1:7 calls for silence in the presence of Yahweh in expectation of the day of Yahweh and the judgment coming with it. Zechariah 2:13 invokes silence from all humanity when Yahweh arises from the holy dwelling in order to avenge Zion. The connotations produced by the concluding words of verses 18-20, therefore fortify the recognition of Yahweh's active involvement in the affairs of humanity and the anticipated vindication of the righteous. The close of chapter 2 contains several key contrasts with the opening of the chapter. Whereas verse 1 portrays the prophet at his post upon a rampart waiting, verse 20 depicts Yahweh in the heavenly temple poised to enact justice (Ps 11:4-7). In 2:1, the prophet prepares himself to give answer to Yahweh when Yahweh responds to his concerns and complaints. However, in 2:20, all the earth remains silent; the time for questions or rebuttals has ended.

## II. THE PRAYER OF HABAKKUK (3:1-19)

The book contains two major sections: 1:1–2:20 and 3:1-19. The second section, labeled "prayer" (see comments on 3:1 below), continues the dialogue between the prophet and Yahweh, even if the divine response is not a word from Yahweh per se, but a depiction of the appearance of Yahweh. It consists of the prophet's prayer (v. 2), the narration of Yahweh's theophany and conquest (vv. 3-15), and the prophet's affirmation of confidence in Yahweh (vv. 16-19b). A superscription (3:1) identifies the entire section as a prayer, and a postscript (v. 19c) gives instructions about its performance. In his prayer, Habakkuk recalls his own fearful reaction to Yahweh's deeds and asks Yahweh to renew this work and to show mercy in Habakkuk's day (v. 2). In the narration, the prophet recounts the theophany of Yahweh, in terms reminiscent of Yahweh's appearance at Sinai (vv. 3-7). Habakkuk also describes the conquest of Yahweh, in terms descriptive of Yahweh as the Divine Warrior who defeats the personified forces of chaos in order to deliver the righteous and to crush the wicked (vv. 8-15). In his affirmation of confidence, Habakkuk expresses his intention to wait for the day of calamity to come upon the Babylonians, in spite of fear and famine, and to rejoice in Yahweh, his Savior and strength (vv. 16-19b). Thus, chapter 3 expresses the prophet's representative and exemplary role for the people: Habakkuk entreats Yahweh for deliverance and remembers the appearance and actions of Yahweh, and he obediently and confidently waits on Yahweh for that deliverance, already begun in the present situation by Yahweh.

The genre or form of chapter 3 has been classified as a song of victory[65] or a prophetic complaint.[66] The identification of the section as a victory hymn or divine warrior hymn notes the hymnic nature of the poem but minimizes the complaint elements in the chapter. The classification of the section as a prophetic complaint emphasizes the unity of the poem as a complaint but does not sufficiently account for the poem's connection with a historical figure (v. 1) and its continued use in a liturgical context (v. 19). Consequently, Michael Floyd has suggested that Habakkuk 3 be understood as a prophetic psalmody script.[67] Such a designation recognizes an overlapping of prophecy and psalmody in the chapter (cf. 1 Chr 16:1-43). The section then is rightly regarded as a poetic composition but with prophetic and liturgical annotations; namely, the superscription links the psalm with a particular historical figure and circumstance and the postscript gives instructions about the psalm's representation in a setting of worship.[68]

Habakkuk 3 is important for the message of the book.[69] Without it, the prophet's complaints in chapter 1 receive no resolution. The

---

[65]W.F. Albright, "The Psalm of Habakkuk," in *Studies in Old Testament Prophecy*, ed. by H.H. Rowley (Edinburgh: T. & T. Clark, 1950), pp. 1-18; Theodore Hiebert, *God of My Victory: The Ancient Hymn of Habakkuk 3*, HSM 38 (Atlanta: Scholars Press, 1986), pp. 81-128.

[66]J.H. Eaton, "The Origin and Meaning of Habakkuk 3," *ZAW* 76 (1964): 159; Baruch Margulis, "The Psalm of Habakkuk: A Reconstruction and Interpretation," *ZAW* 82 (1970): 437-440; Gowen, *Triumph of Faith*, pp. 69-70.

[67]Floyd, *Minor Prophets*, pp. 153-157.

[68]James Washington Watts, "Psalms in Narrative Contexts of the Hebrew Bible" (PhD dissertation, Yale University, 1990), p. 279, observes that psalms found in the Hebrew Bible within narrative contexts invite the reader to join in the celebration of those acts that the narrative describes. Although this theophanic psalm in Habakkuk 3 does not lie within a narrative context, it does perform a similar function in the book, making the words of the prophetic psalm suitable for use in public worship.

[69]Sometimes chapter 3 is thought to be a postexilic addition to the book, in part because the commentary on Habakkuk found among the Dead Sea Scrolls (1QpHab) comments on only chapters 1–2. However, other scrolls found later (MurXII and 8 H9evXIIgr) do include Habakkuk 3.

narration of Yahweh's appearance, coming in power over the earth
and the nations, contrasts with the pretentious power of Babylon
(1:5-11; 2:6-20). Whereas both descriptions of Babylon and Yahweh
engender fear, the depiction shows Yahweh to be superior to the
approaching enemy. Also, the intentions of Babylon and Yahweh differ. The Babylonians come for violence and for gathering captives
like sand (1:9); however, Yahweh comes forth to crush the wicked
and to save the people and the anointed one (3:13). Moreover, in the
chapter's conclusion (3:17-18), the prophet ultimately expresses his
trust in the reliability of Yahweh (cf. 2:2-4).[70] That Habakkuk concludes with a poetic theophany stands in contrast with the book of
Nahum. The book of Nahum begins with a poetic theophany of the
avenging Yahweh who wields awesome power to bring vengeance
upon adversaries and protect those who seek refuge in Yahweh. This
description establishes the norm for the nature and activity of
Yahweh, and the book of Nahum goes on to apply this norm in the
specific case of Nineveh. Therefore, in Nahum little is left to ponder
concerning both the nature of Yahweh and the inevitable outworking of the action of Yahweh. But such is not the case with Habakkuk;
the prophet initially wonders about the inactivity of Yahweh and the
appointment of Babylon to execute judgment, and only later does
Habakkuk 3 clearly depict the victory of Yahweh. While the book of
Nahum moves from the general to the specific, the book of
Habakkuk moves from the specific to the general.[71]

## A. SUPERSCRIPTION (3:1)

[1]**A prayer of Habakkuk the prophet. On** *shigionoth.*[a]
[a]*1* **Probably a literary or musical term**

**3:1** A superscription introduces Habakkuk 3. The word translated **prayer** (תְּפִלָּה, *tᵉphillāh*) is a general word for prayer, which often
indicates intercessory prayer (2 Kgs 19:4; Isa 37:4; Jer 7:16; 11:14)
and appears in the title of several psalms (Ps 17:1; 86:1; 90:1; 102:1;
142:1; cf. 72:20). Habakkuk's name is preceded by a prepositional
prefix that normally indicates authorship (Ps 3:1; 24:1; 25:1; 26:1;

---

[70]Roberts, *Nahum, Habakkuk, and Zephaniah,* p. 149.
[71]Childs, *Introduction to the Old Testament as Scripture,* p. 454.

27:1), that is, the prayer written by **Habakkuk the prophet** (see comments on 1:1 regarding the word "prophet"). The final word of the verse is *Shigionoth*, a Hebrew word (שִׁגְיֹנוֹת, *šigyōnôth*) with a meaning no longer understood. It appears elsewhere only in the singular form in Psalm 7:1. If the word derives from the Akkadian *shigu*, then it may possibly refer to a lament; however, such identification is contested.[72] The word and the preposition preceding it are translated in the LXX "with song" (μετὰ ᾠδῆς, *meta ōdēs*). Efforts to define the word according to its biblical usage, etymology, and translation have not successfully determined the word's meaning. Repeated use of *Selah* in the chapter, perhaps as a liturgical pause (3:3,9,13), may suggest that *Shigionoth* is also a literary or musical term rather than a word descriptive of the psalm's meaning.[73]

## B. PROPHETIC PSALM (3:2-19b)

[2]**LORD, I have heard of your fame; / I stand in awe of your deeds, O LORD.**

**Renew them in our day, / in our time make them known; / in wrath remember mercy.**

[3]**God came from Teman, / the Holy One from Mount Paran. / Selah**[a]

**His glory covered the heavens / and his praise filled the earth. / [4]His splendor was like the sunrise; / rays flashed from his hand, / where his power was hidden. / [5]Plague went before him; / pestilence followed his steps. / [6]He stood, and shook the earth; / he looked, and made the nations tremble. / The ancient mountains crumbled / and the age-old hills collapsed. / His ways are eternal. / [7]I saw the tents of Cushan in distress, / the dwellings of Midian in anguish.**

[8]**Were you angry with the rivers, O LORD ? / Was your wrath against the streams? / Did you rage against the sea / when you rode with your horses / and your victorious chariots? / [9]You uncovered your bow, / you called for many arrows. / Selah / You**

---

[72]Andersen, *Habakkuk*, pp. 271-272.

[73]José María Abrego, "Habakkuk," in *The International Bible Commentary: A Catholic and Ecumenical Commentary for the Twenty-First Century*, ed. by William R. Farmer (Collegeville, MN: Liturgical Press, 1998), p. 1173.

split the earth with rivers; / [10]the mountains saw you and writhed. / Torrents of water swept by; / the deep roared / and lifted its waves on high.

[11]Sun and moon stood still in the heavens / at the glint of your flying arrows, / at the lightning of your flashing spear. / [12]In wrath you strode through the earth / and in anger you threshed the nations. / [13]You came out to deliver your people, / to save your anointed one. / You crushed the leader of the land of wickedness, / you stripped him from head to foot. / Selah / [14]With his own spear you pierced his head / when his warriors stormed out to scatter us, / gloating as though about to devour / the wretched who were in hiding. / [15]You trampled the sea with your horses, / churning the great waters.

[16]I heard and my heart pounded, / my lips quivered at the sound; / decay crept into my bones, / and my legs trembled. / Yet I will wait patiently for the day of calamity / to come on the nation invading us. / [17]Though the fig tree does not bud / and there are no grapes on the vines, / though the olive crop fails / and the fields produce no food, / though there are no sheep in the pen / and no cattle in the stalls, / [18]yet I will rejoice in the LORD, / I will be joyful in God my Savior. / [19]The Sovereign LORD is my strength; / he makes my feet like the feet of a deer, / he enables me to go on the heights.

[a]3 A word of uncertain meaning; possibly a musical term; also in verses 9 and 13

**3:2** Verse 2 returns to the typical cycle in the book of a prophetic complaint followed by a divine response. The prophet has heard of Yahweh's **fame** (שֵׁמַע, šēma‘), a noun used for a general report of news (Isa 23:5), the fame of a particular person (1 Kgs 10:1), or hearsay not involving direct personal encounter (Job 42:5).[74] These reports have filled the prophet with awe (v. 16). By referring to Yahweh's reputation as a basis for requesting the renewal of Yahweh's works, the prophet's prayer reflects a similar movement to the communal laments found in the Psalms (Ps 44:1-7; 77:5-20; 143:5-9). The word **renew** in the NIV translates a form of the verb "to live," which appears earlier in the pronouncement of 2:4, "the righteous

---

[74]Herman Austel, "שֵׁמַע," *TWOT*, 2:939.

will live by faith." The NJB attempts to make this connection overt with its rendering, "Make it live again in our time." The NIV's **in our day** and **in our time** both times translate a Hebrew phrase which literally means, "in the midst of the years" (cf. ESV, KJV, and NASB). The association of years elsewhere in the Old Testament with "appointed times" (Gen 1:14; 17:21; Exod 23:14-15; Neh 10:32-33) may indicate that the reference to years here links this verse with the earlier reference to the "appointed time" in 2:3.[75] One may understand the request "in wrath remember mercy" to be a qualification of the request for the revival of Yahweh's works. The prophet desires a renewal of such divine deeds as the exodus and conquest, but he also recognizes that the coming invasion of the Babylonians is a work of Yahweh. Consequently, he desires that Yahweh temper the coming judgment and hasten the judgment on Babylon anticipated in 2:6-20.

**3:3** Verses 3-7 recount the theophany of Yahweh, in terms reminiscent of Yahweh's appearance at Sinai (see comments on Nahum 1:3 for "theophany"). This epic portrayal of Yahweh's march from the south begins with the word **God**. The divine name translated "God" is not the usual name El or Elohim, but Eloah. This ancient name appears only 57 times in the Old Testament, chiefly in Job (41×). It appears in contexts which portray God as a deliverer (Deut 32:15; Ps 18:31; 50:22; Isa 44:8) and which contrast the impotence of pagan gods with the power of the God of Israel (2 Chr 32:15; Dan 11:37). The archaic nature of the epithet itself also contributes to its effect within the passage. The NIV, ESV, KJV, and NRSV present Yahweh's procession **from Teman** as a past act, but the use of the Hebrew imperfect with the verb "come" favors the present tense translation found in the NASB, NET, NJB, and NJPS. Thus, the visionary experience is described as it happens. This particular use of a third person imperfect form of the verb is the fourth within the book. The first and second (1:8-9) describe the coming Babylonian force. The third use (2:3) promises the vision for the appointed time is certain to come without delay. The coming of Eloah, then, relieves the tension created by the description of the coming Babylonians with the vision of the coming Yahweh. Teman is associated with Edom (Jer 49:7-8,20; Ezek 25:13; Amos 1:12; Obad 9), and Paran

---

[75]Roberts, *Nahum, Habakkuk, and Zephaniah*, p. 150.

refers to a mountain range in the Sinai Peninsula to the south of
Judah (Num 10:12; 13:3,26; 1 Sam 25:1). These places represent
points in the route by which Yahweh leads the covenant nation from
Sinai to Canaan in the exodus. Just as Yahweh has led them into
Canaan and enables them to gain possession of the land, Yahweh
now is seen coming again in judgment. In view of 2:20, the coming
forth from these points in the vicinity of Edom rather than from the
heavenly temple is striking. Yahweh begins this approach not in
heaven, but at specific sites on earth.[76] This affirms that the manifestation of Yahweh's character will not merely be a theoretical
proposition, but will take place in time and space. The title **Holy
One** focuses further attention on a transformation of perspective
which has occurred in the text. It had been used in 1:12 in a somewhat sarcastic manner, but 3:3 uses it positively. A positive, expectant mood has replaced the mood of disappointment and disillu-
sionment within the earlier portions of the text. Verse 3 may allude
to Deuteronomy 33:2 and Judges 5:4-5. The former depicts Yahweh
coming from Sinai, Seir, and **Mount Paran**. The latter depicts the
mountains quaking before the Holy One of Sinai after he has gone
out from Seir and marched forth from Edom. These allusions awak-
en in the reader a hope for Yahweh's renewed action for the people.
Whereas the first half of verse 3 uses an imperfect form of the verb
"come," the second half of the verse uses perfect tense forms. This
change may signify that the present coming of Yahweh springs forth
from the **glory** of God that has already enveloped the universe. The
pairing of the verbs **covered** (כָּסָה, *kāsāh*) and **filled** (מָלֵא, *māle'*)
occurs also in Exodus 40:34-35 where the cloud covers the Tent of
Meeting and fills the tabernacle, and in Isaiah 11:9 and Habakkuk
2:14 where **the earth** is filled with the knowledge of the glory of
Yahweh as the waters cover the sea. The verb *kāsāh* appears by itself
in the statement that the violence done to Lebanon will overwhelm
Babylon (2:17). While it may be impossible to reach a definitive conclusion as to the meaning of *selah*,[77] one must take its presence within

---

[76]Brownlee, "Composition of Habakkuk," p. 273; Robertson, *Nahum,
Habakkuk, and Zephaniah*, p. 221.

[77]Conjectures share an element of emphasis: they posit a pause, a dramatic change, or an act of reflection within the recital. For a concise, yet
thorough summary of theories, see Széles, *Wrath and Mercy*, p. 48.

the canonical text seriously. The rhetorical impact of *selah* after the first two lines of verse 3 may highlight the coming of Yahweh as Divine Warrior.

**3:4** The prophet compares the appearance of Yahweh to the sunrise. The term **splendor** (נֹגַהּ, *nōgāh*) is used elsewhere to describe the radiance of Yahweh's presence (2 Sam 22:13; Ps 18:12,28; Ezek 1:4,28; 10:4). The NIV renders the ordinary word for "light" (אוֹר, *'ôr*) as **sunrise** in verse 4. The noun, however, clearly refers to lightning in at least 7 of its 122 uses (Job 36:30,32; 37:3,11,15; 38:24; Hos 6:5). The mention of **rays** (the Hebrew uses the word "horns") **flashing from his hand**, contextual association with the Sinai theophany (Exod 19:16; 20:18), other theophanic descriptions of Yahweh coming in a thunderstorm (Job 36:27–37:5; 37:15-22; Ps 18:7-15; Ezek 1:4-28), and references to the Lord's arrows (Hab 3:9,11) increase the likelihood that the intended image in verse 4 is lightning rather than sunlight. Moreover, Canaanite and Mesopotamian representations of their gods often appear with lightning as their weapons.[78] This image of wielding lightning implies that Yahweh has emerged from the holy temple (2:20) prepared to strike down the wicked about whom Habakkuk has complained.

**3:5** The entourage of the Divine Warrior Yahweh consists of the vanguard **Plague** (דֶּבֶר, *deber*) and the rearguard **Pestilence** (רֶשֶׁף, *rešeph*), personified terms descriptive of divine punishment. Texts in the Pentateuch depict plague as a weapon used by Yahweh against enemies (Exod 5:3; 9:15; Lev 26:25; Num 14:12), and Jeremiah groups plague together with famine and sword 14 times to depict the destruction Yahweh is bringing on Judah (Jer 14:12; 21:7,9; 27:8,13; 29:17,18; 32:24,36; 34:17; 38:2; 42:17,22; 44:13). Although the NIV translates *rešeph* as pestilence, it translates four of its other six uses with notions of burning or lightning (Job 5:7; Ps 76:3; 78:48; S of S 8:6). It is difficult to determine which meaning is intended here since the idea of burning arose from the association of the noun with the name of the west Semitic god of fever and pestilence.

**3:6** The prophet who has earlier pledged to stand at his watch (2:1) now witnesses Yahweh taking a stand which, in turn, shakes **the earth**. When Yahweh stands, the sun and moon also stand still in the

---

[78]Chisholm, *Minor Prophets*, p. 194; Roberts, *Nahum, Habakkuk, and Zephaniah*, pp. 134, 152-153.

heavens (3:11). When Yahweh looks, **the nations tremble**. The dis-
solving of **mountains** and hills are common features of biblical theophanies (Exod 15:14-16; Judg 5:4-5; Ps 18:7; 46:2; 68:8; 97:4-5; 144:5;
Joel 2:10; Amos 1:2; Micah 1:3-4; Nahum 1:3-5; Zech 14:4-5). The
verb describing the **collapse** of **the age-old hills** (שָׁחַח, šāḥaḥ) elsewhere connotes a humbling that knocks the arrogance out of someone (Job 9:13; Isa 2:9,11,17, 5:15; 25:12; 26:5; 60:14).[79] The hills thus
become an image for what will happen to the arrogant in Judah and
Babylon. The NIV obscures the recurrence of the Hebrew word
translated **ancient** and then **eternal** (עוֹלָם, 'ôlām). This repetition
highlights the security the covenant people of Yahweh possess.
When Yahweh stands on the earth, the "age-old" hills collapse, but
the "eternal" ways of Yahweh remain. The NRSV attempts to render
the recurrence of 'ôlām in English: "The eternal mountains were
shattered; along his ancient pathways the everlasting hills sank low."
While the NIV reads, **His ways are eternal** for the last line of verse
6, the TNIV has "he marches on forever." The NIV contains the
more traditional rendering (cf. the ESV, KJV, and NASB), but the
TNIV follows another translation of the line (cf. NET, NJB, NJPS),
which understands it to depict the travel of Yahweh along the same
route in the southern desert (vv. 3,7) as in the days of Moses and
Deborah (Deut 32:13; 33:2; Judg 5:4).[80]

**3:7** The prophet now sees the nations react in a manner reminiscent of the dread described in the song of Exodus 15. There
Yahweh's deliverance of Israel at the Red Sea causes Philistia, Edom,
and Moab to tremble (Exod 15:14-15), even though Israel's ultimate
objective is Canaan. Here **Cushan** and **Midian** are terrified when
they realize they live in the pathway of Yahweh's advance, even
though the real enemies are the wicked in Judah and Babylon.
Midian and Cushan are located in the southern Transjordan near
Edom. Cushan, the term in parallel with Midian, is an ancient term
that probably goes back to Kushu mentioned in Egyptian texts of ca.
1800 B.C.[81] The mention of it and Midian continue the epic depiction of Yahweh's march into Canaan from the south. The mention

---

[79]Victor Paul Hamilton, "שָׁחַח," *TWOT*, 2:915.
[80]For discussion of the translation options, see Andersen, *Habakkuk*,
pp. 309-310.
[81]Kenneth A. Kitchen, "Midianites," *NBD*, p. 764.

of **tents** and "tent curtains" (cf. the ESV, NASB, NET, and NJB) may denote the tenuous position of the people of Cushan and Midian who live in the way of Yahweh's march. If ancient mountains crumble, what can those who dwell in tents expect? The unit (vv. 3-7) concludes, as it began, with two poetic lines containing two references to geographical locations: Cushan and Midian. The first half of verse 3 has emphasized the real presence of Yahweh by depicting Yahweh's advance with specific geographical settings. The unit's conclusion then emphasizes that one will also see the results of Yahweh's advance within certain geographical settings. This bracketing technique highlights the fusion between the mythical and the historical in Habakkuk 3:3-7.

**3:8** Verses 8-15 describe the conquest of Yahweh, in terms descriptive of Yahweh as the Divine Warrior who defeats the personified forces of chaos in order to deliver the righteous and to crush the wicked. The unit moves from a recital of Yahweh's preparation for the battle to the engagement of the battle. This description, characterized by the predominance of the second person, dramatically conveys the idea that Yahweh has now arrived and is, in some way, present for the speaker.[82] The unit speaks directly to God (v. 3) who is now addressed as Yahweh ("the LORD"). As such, verse 8 begins with rhetorical questions that force reflection on the object of Yahweh's anger. Although the epic depiction of Yahweh's victory over **rivers** and the **sea** may be an adaptation of the Canaanite creation myth in which River and Sea are personified as forces opposed to Baal (Ps 74:12-17; 80:11; 89:9; 89:25; 93:4),[83] it may also allude to Yahweh's demonstration of power in the parting of the Red Sea and the stopping of the Jordan River (Exod 14:15-31; Josh 3:15-17; Ps 66:6; 77:16-19; 78:13; 80:11; 106:9; 114:3-5; 136:13-15). The personification of Yahweh's enemies as sea and river intimates that Yahweh is victorious in both historical and cosmic realms. The depiction of Yahweh as a **victorious chariot** warrior here and other places (2 Kgs 6:17; Ps 68:17, 104:3; Isa 66:15; Jer 4:13) is a natural development from the account of the warrior Yahweh hurling Pharaoh and his chariots into the midst of the Red Sea (Exod 15:1,3-4). Moreover,

---

[82]Eaton, "Origin and Meaning of Habakkuk 3," p. 165.
[83]McConville, *Guide to the Prophets*, p. 215.

the allusion to such paradigmatic events suggests the significance of this anticipated intervention by Yahweh.[84]

**3:9** Verse 9 continues the epic portrayal of Yahweh as the Divine Warrior; now Yahweh commissions or empowers **bow** and **arrows** (cf. Jer 47:6-7)[85] and **splits the earth with rivers**. In theophanic texts, the shooting of arrows often appears as a metaphor for lightning (Ps 18:14; 77:17-18; 144:6; Zech 9:14). Streams of blood flowing from an arrow-punctured body may be the basis for depicting rivers flowing from a torn earth. The verb "split" (בָּקַע, *bāqaʿ*) appears often in association with military action and violence. Several times it describes troops breaking into a city or other area (2 Kgs 25:4; 2 Chr 21:17; Ezek 30:16). When thrown from high places, captives and children are split open upon the rocks below (2 Kgs 8:12; 2 Chr 25:12). Pregnant women are also ripped open (2 Kgs 15:16; Amos 1:13).[86] The rhetorical impact of *Selah* in the middle of the verse may highlight the power of warrior Yahweh to deliver the faithful.[87]

**3:10-11** These two verses depict the reaction of the natural world to the conquest of Yahweh. The **mountains** see Yahweh and tremble, a word associated with the fear and pain of women in childbirth (Isa 13:8; 26:17; Jer 4:31). Likewise, the flooding waters recognize the power of Yahweh (3:9). The word **deep** (תְּהוֹם, *tᵉhôm*) appears in accounts of the creation (Gen 1:2) and the flood (Gen 7:11; 8:2). It commonly refers to the forces of the sea that obey Yahweh (Exod 15:5,8; Isa 51:10; Ezek 26:19; 31:15; Ps 33:7; 77:16; 135:6). The **lift**ing **waves** of the roaring deep signifies the vain attempt of the powers of chaos (i.e., the nations) to conquer the order established by Yahweh (cf. Job 38:8-11; Ps 93:3-4; Jer 5:22). The word "stand" (עָמַד, *ʿāmad*) appears for the third time in the book (2:1, 3:6,11). In 2:1, Habakkuk pledges to stand on his watch to see what Yahweh would say to him. In 3:6, the theophany depicts Yahweh standing and shaking the earth. In 3:11, Yahweh's march, in turn, causes the **sun and moon** to stand **still in the heavens** at the brilliant **flash** of Yahweh's **arrows** and **spear**. This last use possibly alludes to the sun and moon standing still at Gibeon when Joshua defeats the Amorites (Josh 10:12-13).

---

[84]Roberts, *Nahum, Habakkuk, and Zephaniah*, p. 155.

[85]Haak, *Habakkuk*, p. 95.

[86]John N. Oswalt, "בָּקַע," *TWOT*, 1:124.

[87]Barker and Bailey, *Micah, Nahum, Habakkuk, Zephaniah*, p. 367.

**3:12-15** Verses 12-15 portray Yahweh in combat against the nations that threaten Judah. The marching of Yahweh against enemies is cause for the people of Yahweh to celebrate (Judg 5:4; Ps 68:8).[88] That Yahweh **threshes** the **nations in anger** indicates that Yahweh's wrath against the rivers, streams, waters, and sea (v. 8,15) is a likely image for rage against the nations who oppress Judah.[89] On several occasions, the book of Psalms portrays the enemies of Yahweh and the covenant people as the sea or waters (Ps 18:16-17; 74:13-18; 77:13-19; 144:6-7). In verse 13, the double use of the word (יֵשַׁע, yēša'), translated **deliver** and **save**, to affirm Yahweh's deliverance of the people and salvation of the anointed one answers the prophet's question in 1:2, "How long, O LORD, must I call for help . . . but you do not save?" At the most, the salvation of the anointed one probably refers to the deliverance of the Davidic house over against the leader of the wicked land.[90] However, the parallelism of the first half of the verse may indicate that **your anointed one** is equivalent to **your people** (cf. Ps 28:8) rather than some sort of messianic reference. The phrase **the leader of the land of wickedness** in verse 13 may be translated "the head of the house of wickedness" (cf. ESV). This likely alludes to 2:9-11 where the prophet portrays the Babylonians as a house built on unjust gain. Even though suggested by 2:15-16 (cf. 2 Sam 10:4; Isa 20:4), the leader is likely **stripped** not of clothes, but rather of his weapons (Gen 24:20; 2 Chr 24:1; Isa 22:6) or of his life (Ps 141:8).[91] The crushing (מָחַץ, māḥaṣ) of the head is a standard Old Testament image for total conquest (Num 24:17; Judg 5:26; Job 26:12; Ps 68:21). The *Selah* at the end of the verse may accentuate the victory of Yahweh. In verse 14, the picture of Yahweh **pierc**ing the **head** of the wicked **with his own spear** (cf. 2 Sam 17:51) anticipates that Babylon and its allies will fall under the weight of their own wickedness (cf. Hab 2:6-20).[92] Apparently, the prophet sees himself in the midst of the enemy's attack, when he refers to the enemy's attempt to **scatter us** (v. 14). The enemy **warriors storm out**, a word used of a storm actually or metaphorically

[88]Victor Paul Hamilton, "צער," *NIDOTTE*, 3:824.
[89]Chisholm, *Minor Prophets*, p. 195; Roberts, *Nahum, Habakkuk, Zephaniah*, p. 156.
[90]Roberts, *Nahum, Habakkuk, and Zephaniah*, p. 156.
[91]Patterson, *Nahum, Habakkuk, Zephaniah*, p. 253.
[92]Robertson, *Nahum, Habakkuk, and Zephaniah*, p. 240.

(cf. 2 Kgs 6:11; Isa 54:11; Hos 13:3; Jonah 1:11,13; Zech 7:14), and delight in the moment when they are able to murder the defenseless (cf. Ps 10:8-10).[93] Other versions (e.g., the ESV, KJV, NET, NRSV, NJB, and NJPS) translate עָנִי ('ānî) as "poor," instead of the NIV's **wretched** (on 'ānî see comments on Zeph 3:12). The "wretched," or better the "poor," are indeed the righteous, the true people of Yahweh (Hab 1:4,13; 2:4; cf. Isa 54:11). Verse 15 returns to earlier themes in the theophany, especially from verse 8, and likewise to allusions to the exodus from Egypt and the crossing of the Jordan (Exod 15:10; Ps 114:3,5). The epic depiction of Yahweh riding his **horses** over **the sea** and **churning its waters** (cf. Ps 77:19) is a clear indication that Yahweh will destroy Judah's wicked oppressors. As Yahweh has delivered the Israelites out of Egypt, Yahweh will now save the righteous of Judah.[94]

**3:16-19** The final unit (vv. 16-19) returns to the first-person perspective of verse 2 and focuses on the reaction of the prophet to the coming of Yahweh portrayed by the preceding unit (vv. 3-15). It also communicates the final resolution of the book by virtue of its position at the end of the prophetic psalm (ch. 3) and the book itself.[95] This unit forms an inclusio with verse 2 through the use of the divine name Yahweh, the use of the root רגז (rgz), and the use of the verb "I heard" (שָׁמַע, šāma') followed by a description of fear in the life of the prophet.[96] In verse 2 the prophet has asked Yahweh to remember mercy in "wrath" (רֹגֶז, rōgez). After viewing the theophany the prophet describes his reaction to it in verse 16 with a double use of the verb רָגַז (rāgāz, "pounded" and "trembled"). This same verb has been used in verse 7 to describe the anguish of Midian. The prophet's reaction in the final stanza contains three elements: an expression of overwhelming awe (v. 16), an awareness of coming loss (v. 17); and a resolution of trusting joy (vv. 18-19).[97]

**3:16** The verse, no longer part of the theophanic vision, describes the prophet's overwhelming reaction to it with physical responses

[93]Keil, *Minor Prophets*, p. 426.
[94]Patterson, *Nahum, Habakkuk, Zephaniah*, p. 250.
[95]Bratcher, "Theological Message of Habakkuk," p. 133.
[96]Theodore Hiebert, "The Use of Inclusion in Habakkuk 3," in *Directions in Biblical Hebrew Poetry*, ed. by Elaine R. Follis, JSOTSupp 40 (Sheffield: University of Sheffield, 1987), pp. 129-131.
[97]Robertson, *Nahum, Habakkuk, and Zephaniah*, p. 242.

that typically express great fear, anxiety, and mortality: pounding heart (Ps 99:1; Isa 64:2; Jer 33:9; Joel 2:1; Micah 7:17), **quivering lips** (the verb usually describes the effects on the ears; cf. 1 Sam 3:11; 2 Kgs 21:12; Jer 19:3), **decaying bones** (Ps 22:15; 31:10; 102:5; Lam 1:13; Ezek 37:11), and **trembling legs** (Dan 5:6). The NIV and most other versions (e.g., the ESV, NET, NRSV, NLT, and NJB) render verse 16 to say that the prophet waits **for calamity to come upon the invading nation**, but the NASB and the NJPS understand the verse to say that the prophet waits for the invasion to come upon Judah. In either case, the prophet clearly knows that judgment must precede salvation and therefore exhibits the attitude called for in 2:3. The NIV's **wait patiently** translates the Hebrew verb that generally means "to rest" (נוּחַ, *nûaḥ*). The verb denotes the presence of security, an absence of movement, and a settled state in a particular place. When used abstractly, it also connotes the finality of victory and salvation.[98] This rest implies safety and security from one's enemies and from that which might threaten happiness. This response to the theophany goes beyond this in that the prophet vows to rest even while the enemy is invading and before it is vanquished. The earlier descriptions of the enemy have elicited doubt and questioning (1:12-17); now the prophet affirms his confidence in Yahweh, resting in the life of faithfulness (2:4). While the prophet's original question of "How long?" (1:2) lingers, its urgency has lessened. The phrase "day of calamity" or "day of trouble," which occurs fourteen other times in the Old Testament, generally refers to some particular crisis (Gen 35:3; 2 Kgs 19:3; Ps 20:1; 50:15; 77:2; 86:7; Prov 24:10; Isa 37:3; Jer 16:19; Obad 12,14; Nahum 1:7; Zeph 1:15; Zech 10:11). Here the phrase connects with the second divine response in 2:1-5, where Yahweh instructs the prophet to wait for the "appointed time," certain to come and without delay. The vision for the "appointed time" then anticipates the "day of calamity."[99] The confidence displayed in anticipation of the day of calamity corresponds to the assurance that the vision will certainly come in 2:3 and to the declaration in 2:4 that the righteous will live by faithfulness.

**3:17** The prophet anticipates the awful consequences of the coming invasion. This verse uses three couplets, each introduced with

---

[98]Leonard J. Coppes, "נוּחַ," *TWOT*, 2:562.

[99]Bratcher, "Theological Message of Habakkuk," p. 274.

**though** in the NIV and each increasing in severity,[100] to describe the scarcity that would ensue after the invasion of the enemy. The crops and livestock listed here are all part of Yahweh's provision, promised to the people in bountiful harvests if they observe the covenant (Lev 26:3-13; Deut 28:1-14). Nonetheless, verse 17 reflects the covenant curses, resulting from disobedience, of the decimation of crops and livestock (Lev 26:14-45; Deut 28:31-34,49-51). Even in the midst of distressing circumstances (cf. the depiction of Jerusalem's fate in Lam 2:12,20, 4:4,9-10; 5:17-18), Habakkuk is ready to **rejoice in** Yahweh.

**3:18** In verse 18 the thought of scarcity in the wake of an invasion gives rise to a positive statement of confidence. This statement parallels the similar affirmation in verse 16, "Yet I will wait patiently for the day of calamity." Whereas negative circumstances have previously given rise to doubts concerning the covenant loyalties of Yahweh, they now provide an opportunity to rejoice as the prophet waits in hope. The crucial difference is that the prophet now focuses upon Yahweh rather than these negative circumstances. The word order of the first line of the eighteenth verse epitomizes this shift in perspective as the prepositional phrase "in Yahweh" appears before the verb, "will exult"; the Hebrew word order is: "yet I in Yahweh will exult." The title **God my Savior** (or, as in the ESV, KJV, NASB, and NRSV, "the God of my salvation") appears elsewhere in the Old Testament (Ps 18:46; 25:5; 27:9; Micah 7:7). In 3:18 the designation identifies Yahweh as the embodiment of salvation, and the identification of Yahweh as "my strength" in verse 19 exhibits a dramatic reversal of the sentiment of the opening complaint (1:2). In contrast with the misguided joy the wicked experiences in military victory (1:15), the prophet now has joy in God his Savior (v. 18).

**3:19a-b** The prophet acclaims that **the Sovereign LORD** (אֲדֹנָי יהוה, *'ădōnāy YHWH*, generally translated Lord GOD in other versions) **is** his **strength**. Although Yahweh is described elsewhere as someone's strength (Exod 15:2; Neh 8:10; Ps 18:1; 28:7-8; Isa 12:2; Jer 16:19), this is the only instance where the noun חַיִל (*ḥayil*) is used to do so. The basic meaning of the noun *ḥayil* is one of strength; it is used over 100 times with the extended meaning of "army," "host," or

---

[100]Barker and Bailey, *Micah, Nahum, Habakkuk, Zephaniah*, p. 375.

"forces."[101] This unique use here may be a sort of double entendre which contrasts Yahweh as Habakkuk's "army," with the Babylonians who worship their own military strength.[102] Verse 19 reflects Psalm 18:33 in which the psalmist compares himself to **a deer** (cf. 2 Sam 22:34). The verb **enables to go** (דָּרַךְ, *dārak*), sometimes translated "to walk" or "to tread" (cf. the ESV, KJV, NASB, and NRSV) links verse 19 to verse 15 where the same verb is used to describe Yahweh's trampling of the sea. Thus, Yahweh's trampling has enabled the prophet to walk **on the heights** of victory (cf. Deut 32:13; 33:29).

## C. POSTSCRIPT (3:19c)

**For the director of music. On my stringed instruments.**

**3:19c** The words **the director of music** translate a noun of uncertain meaning (מְנַצֵּחַ, *mᵉnaṣṣēaḥ*) that appears in superscriptions in the Psalms fifty-five times (e.g., Ps 4:1; 5:1; 6:1; 8:1; 9:1; 11:1; 12:1). Its use in 2 Chronicles (2:2,18; 34:12-13) suggests the idea of leadership or supervision. The postscript then apparently offers instructions regarding instrumentation for the use of Habakkuk's prophetic psalm in public worship (cf. Ps 54:1; 55:1; 61:1; 67:1). The subscription with its musical terminology complements the superscription and brackets the third chapter of Habakkuk with liturgical language. More importantly, the postscript emphasizes that Habakkuk 3 is more than the personal resolution of the prophet. The assignment of the psalm to the director ensures that it will be celebrated by future generations, drawing each participant into the experience of the prophet[103] and thereby inviting the reader to join in the celebration of the acts of Yahweh that the chapter depicts.

---

[101]Carl Philip Weber, "חיל," *TWOT*, 1:272.

[102]Roberts, *Nahum, Habakkuk, and Zephaniah*, p. 158.

[103]Robertson, *Nahum, Habakkuk, and Zephaniah*, p. 248.

# THE BOOK OF
# ZEPHANIAH

# INTRODUCTION

## AUTHORSHIP

Built from the verb "to hide or shelter" (צָפַן, ṣāphan) and the shortened form of Yahweh (יָ, yāh), the name Zephaniah (צְפַנְיָה, ṣᵉphanyāh) means "Yahweh has hidden" or "Yahweh has sheltered."[1] The prophet shares his name with three others in the Old Testament (2 Kgs 25:18; 1 Chr 6:36; Jer 21:1; 52:24; Zech 6:10). The sacrificial imagery found in the book of Zephaniah (1:7-8; 3:18) may suggest that the prophet be identified with "the second priest" (2 Kgs 25:18; Jer 21:1; 52:24) put to death by the Babylonians along with other officials at Riblah.[2] However, other prophets, known not to be priests, use similar sacrificial imagery (see Amos 4:4-5; Hos 6:6; Micah 6:6-8), and committed worshipers of Yahweh would have been familiar with sacrificial terminology and would have had a concern for temple purity.[3] Zephaniah's genealogy, furthermore, appears to link him with the tribe of Judah (see comments in paragraph below) rather than Levi. Therefore, lacking other prevailing evidence, any identification of Zephaniah as a cultic prophet remains problematic.[4] Rabbinic tradition identifies Zephaniah as a contemporary of Jeremiah and Huldah who both prophesied in the days of Josiah. Whereas Jeremiah preaches in the streets of

---

[1]Although Zephaniah 2:3 mentions the possibility of one being sheltered on the day of Yahweh, a different word for sheltered (סָתַר, sāthar) is used there.

[2]Donald L. Williams, "The Date of Zephaniah," *JBL* 82 (1963): 85.

[3]Frank E. Eakin, Jr., "Zephaniah," in *Hosea–Malachi*, ed. by Clifton J. Allen, BBC 7 (Nashville: Broadman, 1972), p. 279; David W. Baker, *Nahum, Habakkuk, Zephaniah: An Introduction and Commentary*, TOTC 23b (Downers Grove, IL: InterVarsity, 1988), p. 84.

[4]James D. Newsome, Jr., *The Hebrew Prophets* (Atlanta: John Knox, 1984), p. 82.

Jerusalem and Huldah preaches to the women, Zephaniah speaks in synagogues.[5]

Allusions to Jerusalem's geography (1:10-13) and several references to Jerusalem and "the city" (1:4,12; 3:1,7,11,14,16) may indicate that the prophet is a long-time resident, if not a native, of the city. Equally plausible is that a Judahite from outside Jerusalem would be conversant and concerned with the city, but the apparent connection of the prophet with the royal house strengthens the link between Zephaniah and the city. The prophet's genealogy (1:1) extends to four generations. Since the tracing of a genealogy to the fourth generation is unusual (the only other is in Jer 36:14), Zephaniah is likely a descendant of Hezekiah, one of the few good kings of Judah. The king Hezekiah is the only preexilic biblical figure so named. Zephaniah is identified as "the son of Cushi." Since Cush is the biblical name for an area encompassing southern Egypt and northern Sudan and Ethiopia, some conjecture that the name "Cushi" is actually a gentilic noun that indicates the prophet's father and the prophet are Ethiopian, and the longer genealogy is intended to give the prophet greater legitimacy in Judah.[6] The name, however, lacks the definite article. Therefore, it probably does not simply indicate that Zephaniah's father is "the Cushite." Even so, it may retain the memory of a Cushite connection in his family tree. Hezekiah has alliances with Ethiopians and Egyptians (Isa 30; 31; 2 Kgs 18:21; 19:9-10), and it is possible that an alliance has been sealed with a marriage between royal families.[7] A Cushite association with the prophet may explain his references to "Cush" in Zephaniah 2:12 and 3:10.

---

[5]S. 'Olam Rab. 20; Pesiq. R. 26.2

[6]Aage Bentzen, *Introduction to the Old Testament* (Copenhagen: Gad, 1948–1949), 2:153; Marvin A. Sweeney, *Zephaniah: A Commentary*, Hermeneia (Minneapolis: Augsburg Fortress, 2003), p. 49.

[7]For arguments against such a Cushite connection, see Raymond B. Dillard and Tremper Longman III, *An Introduction to the Old Testament* (Grand Rapids: Zondervan, 1994), p. 415; R.K. Harrison, *Introduction to the Old Testament* (Grand Rapids: Eerdmans, 1969), p. 939; and Norman K. Gottwald, *The Hebrew Bible: A Socio-Literary Introduction* (Philadelphia: Fortress, 1985), p. 390.

# HISTORICAL BACKGROUND

The opening verse of the book locates the ministry of Zephaniah "during the reign of Josiah son of Amon king of Judah" (1:1), a period spanning from 640 to 609 B.C. The religious reforms of Josiah's great-grandfather Hezekiah (715–686 B.C.) more than a half century earlier did not result in lasting change. Hezekiah's son Manasseh and grandson Amon reversed them and plunged Judah into a return to Canaanite Baalism. Amon's officials, however, plotted against him, assassinated him, and put his eight-year-old son Josiah on the throne. At age 16, the young king began to seek Yahweh (2 Chr 34:3). This devotion led to two major periods of reform, the first beginning in 628 B.C. (2 Chr 34:3-7), and the second following the discovery of a copy of the Book of the Law within the temple in 622 B.C. (2 Kgs 22:3–23:27; 2 Chr 34:8–35:19). These reforms included a repudiation of Baalism and Mesopotamian astral deities, a desecration and demolition of sites formerly dedicated to the worship of Baal and Asherah, a repair of the temple, a removal of the high places, a centralization of worship in Jerusalem, and an observance of the Passover.

The reforms of Josiah repudiated the previous Assyrian domination of Judah. Assyrian power was diminishing in a period of international turmoil. The death of the Assyrian king Ashurbanipal in 627/626 B.C. hastened the rise to power of the Babylonians. Although the details are somewhat uncertain, the Scythians, a nomadic people from the Asian highlands who infiltrated the Mesopotamian Valley in the eighth century via the Caucasus, may also have contributed to the decline of Assyrian power. A Scythian attack on Assyria in 632 along with Babylonian rebellion made it possible for Josiah to carry out his reforms without fear of Assyrian intervention.[8] Perhaps the Scythians also invaded the eastern Mediterranean coast and Egypt between 630 and 625 B.C. In a disputed account, Herodotus indicates Scythian influence extended down the Palestinian coast as far as Egypt where they were bought off by either Pharaoh Psammetichus I (663–609 B.C.) or Psammetichus II (595–589 B.C.).[9] Josiah died in 609 B.C. at the hands of the

---

[8]Harrison, *Introduction*, p. 940.
[9]Herodotus, *Histories* 1.104-106.

Egyptians in a failed attempt to stop their movements north to join the Assyrians in a battle against the Babylonians. With Josiah's death came Judah's last good chance for lasting repentance and reform.

# DATE

The ministry of Zephaniah is dated during the reign of Josiah (640–609 B.C.); yet, the book's internal evidence narrows that time frame. The foretelling of the fall of Nineveh in 2:13 indicates the book had to have been written prior to 612 B.C. The text condemns the princes and king's sons (1:8) but does not mention the king by name. Because of this, some conclude that Josiah is in the earlier period of his reign during the prophet's ministry,[10] but this is not a necessary conclusion from the data. Princes and king's sons practicing the sins of Zephaniah 1:8-9 could have existed in the middle and later periods of Josiah's reign. Many royal descendants fathered by Manasseh and Amon may have survived through much of Josiah's lifetime, since Josiah died at age 39. Moreover, Jehoahaz, Jehoiakim, and Zedekiah, the three sons of Josiah who later came to the throne of Judah, returned to the pagan practices that characterize Judah's rulers (2 Kgs 23:31-32,36-37; 24:18-20; 2 Chr 36:5-8,11-14).

The text gives no definitive signs that any of the Josianic reforms have already occurred; in fact, the prophet speaks against practices common in the days of Manasseh and Amon. References to the moral and religious conditions of Judah (1:4-6,8-9,12; 3:1-3,7) seem to point to a time before the reforms of 622/621 B.C. that follow the discovery of the Book of the Law (2 Kgs 23:4-7).[11] Second Chronicles 34 indicates the Josianic reforms occurred in stages even prior to the discovery of the book of the law in 622/621 B.C. starting as early as 628/627 B.C. The reference to the remnant of Baal in Zephaniah 1:4, moreover, may point to a date between the two reform movements of 628 and 622 B.C.[12] If that is so, the prophet's

---

[10]E.g., Harrison, *Introduction*, p. 940; J.J.M. Roberts, *Nahum, Habakkuk, and Zephaniah: A Commentary*, OTL (Louisville, KY: Westminster John Knox, 1991), p. 160.

[11]Robert B. Chisholm, Jr., *Interpreting the Minor Prophets* (Grand Rapids: Zondervan, 1990), p. 201.

[12]Marvin A. Sweeney, *Zephaniah: A Commentary*, Hermeneia (Minneapolis:

oracles may have served to encourage Josiah to finish the good work he had begun. A date between the two stages of Josiah's reforms would also accord well with events in the Mesopotamian world. Ashurbanipal has died in 627 B.C., and the Babylonians have declared their independence from Assyria in the following year. Such a time would provide an excellent background for the pronouncement of the fall of Nineveh in 2:13-15. Jeremiah also inaugurates his prophetic ministry at this time, and he condemns some of the same pagan influences spoken against by Zephaniah in his early ministry (Zeph 1:4-5; cf. Jer 2:8; 8:2; 19:5,13).

Alternate theories place the book after Josiah's reforms. At least two scholars point to the unclear identity of the enemy who would be the instrument of the day of Yahweh in order to date Zephaniah in the days of Jehoiakim (609–597 B.C.) rather than Josiah.[13] They allege no clear enemy exists in the days of Josiah, and the judgment oracles could not have arisen until Babylon becomes a threat. In addition to disregarding the book's own superscription, this theory fails to acknowledge the literary and rhetorical effect produced by the lack of a monolithic identification of a human agent of Yahweh's judgment. Throughout the book, the focus remains on Yahweh as the one who brings judgment (1:2-4,8-9,12,17; 2:5,8-9,13; 3:6-9). The text of Zephaniah indeed reflects a period of international uncertainty such as during the days of Josiah. While it is certain that nations will fall, it is uncertain to whom they will be subject. The oracle against Philistia (2:4-7) itself may reflect Josiah's desires to expand Judah's territory.

A more credible alternative locates Zephaniah's ministry and book in the latter days of Josiah's reign. It questions the inference that Zephaniah has preceded the reform movement. Further, it questions the conclusion that the sins decried in the book are an accurate indicator of its date, since a distinction should probably be made between the official reforming activities of Josiah and the

---

Augsburg Fortress, 2003), p. 61, notes the use of the root אסף (*'sp*), with the meaning "harvest" or "ingathering," at key junctures in the book (1:2, 3:8,18) and posits an even more specific setting during a celebration of Sukkoth (i.e., Feast of Ingathering, Feast of Tabernacles) during this time.
[13]Williams, "Date of Zephaniah," pp. 77-88; J P. Hyatt, "The Date and Background of Zephaniah," *JBL* 7 (1949): 25-29.

abuses and sins among the wealthy and general population.[14] Although there are similarities between Zephaniah and Jeremiah, Jeremiah preaches through both the early and later days of Josiah. The phrase "remnant of Baal" (Zeph 1:4) is better understood in reference to a situation after the reforms when their impact has waned.[15] John Calvin notes that Judah is habitually unfaithful *after* the reforms and thereby places the book subsequent to the reforms.[16] Nevertheless, the interim between the two stages of the Josianic reforms best fit Zephaniah's description of Judah's sin and the international situation reflected in the book.

## LITERARY FEATURES

The title of Zephaniah (1:1) contains three parts: the prophetic word formula, an identification of the prophet and his ancestry, and an identification of the historical context of the prophet's ministry. The first of these, the prophetic word formula ("The word of the LORD that came to"), is the typical introductory phrase used among the prophetic books. (Jer 1:2; Ezek 1:3; Hos 1:1; Joel 1:1; Jonah 1:1; Micah 1:1; Hag 1:1; Zeph 1:1; Mal 1:1). The formula asserts the divine origin of the prophecy and names the prophet to whom that word comes.

The book consists of four major sections: Zephaniah 1:1, 1:2–2:3, 2:4–3:7, and 3:8-20. Zephaniah 1:1 contains the book's title and identifies the book's prophet. Zephaniah 1:2–2:3 consists of an announcement of judgment upon Judah and Jerusalem (1:2-6) followed by an exhortation to prepare for the day of Yahweh (1:7-18) and by an exhortation to repent before the day of Yahweh (2:1-3). Zephaniah 2:4–3:7 presents a series of prophecies of punishment against the nations (2:4-15) and a prophetic charge of failure to repent against Jerusalem (3:1-7). These prophecies of punishment and the prophetic charge provide the basis for heeding the commands

[14]Dillard and Longman, *Introduction*, p. 416.
[15]Gordon McConville, *A Guide to the Prophets*, vol. 4, *Exploring the Old Testament* (Downers Grove, IL: InterVarsity, 2002), p. 220.
[16]John Calvin, *Habakkuk–Malachi*, vol. 15, *Calvin's Commentaries*, trans. by John Owen (Grand Rapids: Baker, 1984), p. 186.

of 2:1-3. Zephaniah 3:8-20 consists of two prophetic exhortations: an exhortation to wait for the action of Yahweh (3:8-13) and an exhortation to rejoice at the promise of Yahweh (3:14-20).

Zephaniah contains several prophetic genres or forms. Perhaps the most prominent is the prophecy of punishment. Generally the prophecy of punishment (1:2-6) includes an announcement of punishment (1:2-4) and an accusation of offense (1:5-6). Other examples consist of prophecies against Philistia, Moab, Ammon, Cush, and Assyria (2:4-15); these prophecies against foreign nations are sometimes called oracles against the nations. Also, Zephaniah makes use of prophetic exhortation, a form with command and motive clause (1:7,10; 3:8,14). Specifically, two forms used in Zephaniah are similar in form to the prophecy of punishment and in function to the prophetic exhortation. The call to repentance with motivation for such repentance (2:1-3) expands the development of the accusation. The prophetic charge of failure to repent against Jerusalem (3:1-7) explains the reasons why Yahweh also punishes Jerusalem along with the nations. Such charge, however, becomes the basis for a renewed call to repentance.

The theme that persists throughout Zephaniah is the day of Yahweh (1:7-10,14-17,18; 2:2-3; 3:8,11,16). Zephaniah presents "that day" as an occasion of Yahweh's intervention into human affairs to judge the nations (2:4-15), especially those who are enemies of the Israelites (3:8,18), and to judge the covenant people for their religious idolatry, economic oppression, and rebellious arrogance (1:4-13; 3:1-7,11). However, the day of Yahweh is also an occasion of Yahweh's restoration of the faithful among the covenant people (2:1-3; 3:14-20) and purification of the faithful from among the nations (3:9-10). Zephaniah describes the nature of the day of Yahweh as imminent (1:7,14) and catastrophic (1:15-17); the day demonstrates Yahweh's wrath (1:18–2:3; 3:8) and Yahweh's salvation (2:3; 3:9-20).

Although showing less literary sophistication than some of the other prophets, Zephaniah does contain a number of rhetorical features. These include metaphor (1:7; 3:3,8), simile (1:12,17; 2:2,9), personification (3:14-16), synecdoche (1:16; 2:13; 3:16), paronomasia (i.e., rhyming words in the Hebrew text in 1:2; 2:7; 3:20), and anthropopatheia (i.e., the ascribing of human attributes to God in 1:4; 2:13). Striking examples from the natural order illustrate realities in the social order, for example, "roaring lions" and "evening wolves" (3:3). The prophet directly addresses the shameful nation (2:1-3), the Philistines (2:4-5), the Cushites (2:12), Jerusalem (3:1-7), and the Daughter of Zion/Jerusalem (3:14-17). The prophet also recounts first-person speeches by Yahweh (1:2-6,8-12; 3:6-12,18-20), emphasizing the direct action of Yahweh. Several units use repetition (1:2-3,15-16; 2:1-3; 3:14-15); notably the sevenfold repetition of "day" in 1:15-16 may represent a reversal of creation, an undoing of the seven days of creation in a single day.

## THEOLOGY

The book of Zephaniah is named Σοφονίας (*Sophonias*) in the LXX and *Sophonias* in the Vulgate, and it appears as the ninth book in both their orderings of the Minor Prophets. Paul House characterizes the book as the bottom of a "U-shaped pattern" in the Book of the Twelve, before the ascent in the final three books.[17] As such, it concludes an emphasis upon judgment that begins in Nahum. The sins of all polytheists on earth chronicled in Hosea through Micah will be punished. The remaining three books in the Twelve explain more fully a hope for the future that exists beyond that devastation.[18] Zephaniah represents a transitional work with its descriptions of judgment on all nations complemented by oracles announcing salvation for both Israel and the nations.

The content of the book shows solidarity with the entire canon. Echoes of the Torah include allusions to the Noahic flood (1:2-3), the destruction of Sodom and Gomorrah (2:9), and the Tower of Babel narrative (3:9-10). The reasons for divine wrath and the description of the day of Yahweh (1:4-17) reflect the covenant curses of Deuteronomy 27–28 and are reminiscent of narratives in the Former Prophets. The emphasis on the day of Yahweh also links the book to the texts of the Latter Prophets.[19] The book's special emphasis on humility (2:3) appears frequently in the Kethuvim, that is, the

---

[17]Paul R. House, *The Unity of the Twelve*, JSOTSupp 972; BLS 27 (Sheffield: Almond Press, 1990), p. 151.

[18]Ibid., p. 383.

[19]Ibid., p. 381.

Writings (Ps 9:13; 10:12,17; 25:9; 34:2; 37:11; 147:6; 149:4; Prov 3:34; 14:21; 18:12; 22:4).

Zephaniah built primarily upon the foundation of the eighth-century prophets who preceded him. Of particular influence upon him was the message of judgment in Amos and Hosea and Isaiah's future hope.[20] Like Hosea, he condemns syncretistic false worship, and like Amos he attacks the pride of the powerful who abuse and neglect society's weak and poor (1:9; 3:1-4). He combines Amos's concept of divine judgment as eradication with Hosea's notion of judgment as rehabilitation to speak of a purifying nature of divine judgment. This purifying judgment, in turn, serves to create a future redeemed people of God founded upon a faithful remnant.

Parallel content indicates the substantial influence of Isaiah on Zephaniah. Concepts shared by the books include: Yahweh's outstretched hand (1:4; cf. Isa 5:25; 9:12,17,21; 10:4), the theme of the day of Yahweh (1:7-8,10,14-16,18; 2:1-3; 3:8,11,16,19-20; cf. Isa 2:6-21; 13:6-22), oracles against the nations (2:4,5-15: cf. Isa 13–23), condemnation of Assyria (2:13-15; cf. Isa 10:5-34; 14:24-27), a poor and humble remnant (3:12-13; cf. Isa 1:9; 6:12-13; 7:1-9; 10:20-24), the downfall of haughty and proud (3:11; cf. Isa 2:6-21), and the restoration of Jerusalem pictured as a mother or bride (3:14-20; cf. Isa 3:25–4:1; 61:10; 62:5; 66:13).[21]

Zephaniah shares several themes with his contemporary, Jeremiah. Among these are images of universal destruction (1:3; Jer 4:25-26; 50:3), condemnation of the worship of astral deities (1:5; Jer 8:2), sacrificial language as an image of judgment on Judah (1:7; Jer 46:10), the shame of unrighteous Judah (2:1; 3:5; Jer 3:3; 6:15; 8:12), oracles against Ashkelon, Moab, and Ammon (2:2,9; Jer 47:5; 48:1-47; 49:1-6), the pouring out of Yahweh's anger (3:9; Jer 10:25), the failure of Judah to heed Yahweh's voice (3:2; Jer 7:23-28), and promises of the restoration of Judah's fortunes and Yahweh bringing exiles home (2:7; 3:20; Jer 29:14; 32:44).

Along with the other seventh-century minor prophets, Nahum and Habakkuk, Zephaniah speaks about the justice of Yahweh on an international scale. Yahweh is sovereign over all the nations and may raise a nation to use as an instrument of judgment (Hab 1:6). Still,

---

[20]Eakin, "Zephaniah," p. 275.
[21]Sweeney, *Zephaniah*, p. 16.

no nation may challenge Yahweh's authority (Nahum 1:9-14), and no nation can escape the fire of Yahweh's anger (Zeph 3:8). Yahweh especially loathes the arrogance of the nations (Nahum 2:9; 3:8-13; Hab 1:11; 2:4-5; Zeph 2:10,15), and "Yahweh of Hosts" or "Yahweh of the Armies" (NIV, LORD Almighty) will oppose them (Nahum 2:13; 3:5; Hab 2:13; Zeph 2:9). When Yahweh's judgment comes on the nations, Yahweh's superiority over the nations' gods will be manifest (Nahum 1:14; Hab 2:18-20; Zeph 2:11).[22]

The judgment of the nations is a component of the pervasive theme around which Zephaniah's message revolves: the imminent day of Yahweh. Zephaniah develops the concept of the day of Yahweh more than any other prophet.[23] This concept probably originated in association with the concept of "holy war." The popular understanding of the day of Yahweh in the eighth century was to identify it as a day of destruction and judgment that would come upon the enemies of Yahweh who, by extension, are also Israel's enemies. Also, this day would be a day of vindication and exaltation for Israel and Judah. Amos 5:18-20, however, questions this understanding by announcing that Yahweh will also judge the covenant people in the day of Yahweh. Whereas the portrayal of the day of Yahweh in Amos gives little indication of hope, Zephaniah does so by incorporating the concept of a preserved remnant seen earlier in Isaiah (Isa 1:23-26; 7; 10:20-23).[24] One may account for the comparative absence of hope in Amos by noting his original audience is the northern kingdom. Zephaniah, however, addresses the southern kingdom which is connected to the Davidic dynasty. Significantly, the most hope-laden words of Amos deal with the rebuilding of "David's fallen tent" (Amos 9:11-12).

For Zephaniah, the day of Yahweh will be a day of battle and destruction that will devastate Judah and Jerusalem as well as her neighbors. The judgment of Judah and Jerusalem will purge Yahweh's covenant people and will create the nucleus of a new com-

---

[22]Robert B. Chisholm, Jr., "The Seventh Century Prophets (Nahum, Habakkuk, Zephaniah)," in *A Biblical Theology of the Old Testament*, ed. by Roy B. Zuck, Eugene H. Merrill, and Darrell L. Bock (Chicago: Moody, 1991), pp. 413-416.

[23]McConville, *Guide to the Prophets*, p. 226.

[24]Eakin, "Zephaniah," p. 274.

munity of Yahweh that also will include worshipers of Yahweh from among the nations (3:9-13,20). The day of Yahweh comes then to represent the time when Yahweh's intended order replaces the current state of affairs.

The references to the nearness of the day (1:7,14) and to coming defeats of Judah, Philistia, Moab, Ammon, Cush, and Assyria (1:4-13; 2:4-15) indicate that Zephaniah anticipates the day in the near future. The Babylonian conquests in the ancient Near East during the sixth and early fifth centuries would provide fulfillment for much of what he envisions. Nevertheless, many of its far-ranging pictures of cosmic judgment (1:2-3,18; 3:8) and of salvation (3:9-13) may not be limited to that era. These more eschatological descriptions of the day of Yahweh in Zephaniah may be considered part of the transition in the Old Testament from prophecy to apocalyptic.[25]

The New Testament does not quote Zephaniah, but the Nestle-Aland *Novum Testamentum Graece* (i.e., *Greek New Testament*) lists four allusions: Matthew 13:41 (1:3), Revelation 6:17 (1:14-16), Revelation 16:1 (3:8), and Revelation 14:5 (3:11). These passages share an eschatological perspective. Additional influence on the New Testament writers may be seen in references to the day of the Lord or the day of Christ (Rom 2:16; 1 Cor 1:8; 5:5; 2 Cor 1:14; Phil 1:6,10; 2:16; 1 Thess 5:2; 2 Thess 2:2; 2 Pet 3:10) and additional vocabulary and images of the day of Yahweh (Mark 13:24-25; 1 Cor 15:52; 1 Thess 4:16; Rev 18:2).

## MESSAGE

In many respects, Zephaniah is one grand inclusio, in that it begins and ends with the word of Yahweh (1:1) who has spoken (3:20).[26] Yahweh speaks in several sections where over twenty-five first person singular verbs appear (1:2,3,4,8,9,12,17; 2:5,8; 3:6,7,9, 11,12,18,19,20). These portray Yahweh as both sovereign and active. Zephaniah announces that Yahweh will act decisively in human history to implement aspects of the divine plan. In that day, Yahweh will judge the sin of the people and the nations, be victorious over

---

[25]Newsome, *Hebrew Prophets*, p. 86.
[26]Baker, *Nahum, Habakkuk, Zephaniah*, p. 88.

enemies, and deliver the people. Yahweh must punish the sins of Judah, but this punishment is not simply punitive; it is redemptive. In spite of the onslaught of divine fury, Yahweh's faithfulness and mercy to the remnant will prevail. The divine purpose in choosing Israel will not be frustrated by judgment, but it will be realized in an elect remnant.

The day of Yahweh will bring judgment on the nations, but it also will transform. Two accounts from Genesis supply images and vocabulary for Zephaniah's description of the day of Yahweh. Chapter 1 describes the judgment on the nations by alluding to the Genesis flood narrative to depict the day of Yahweh as an unraveling of creation (Zeph 1:2-3). Vocabulary from the tower of Babel narrative (Genesis 11) then is employed to portray service and worship rendered to Yahweh from among the nations (Zeph 3:9-10). Thus, Yahweh will purify Judah and create a multinational remnant (2:11; 3:9-13).

By purifying Judah and Jerusalem and the lips of the peoples (3:9), Yahweh will demonstrate fidelity to the Abrahamic promise (Gen 12:1-3; 18:18-19) that all the earth will be blessed through Abraham and his descendants.[27] Jerusalem and Zion, where Yahweh's throne will be established, will be honored by the nations (3:14-20). The prophecy thus moves from universal judgment to the universality of salvation. This doctrine of an elect remnant distinguishes between the people of God as a political-ethnic entity and the people of God as a group of believers.[28]

The appropriate response by the people to this is humility and allegiance to Yahweh (2:1-3). The appropriate actions of keeping Yahweh's commands (מִשְׁפָּט, mišpāṭ) and seeking righteousness (צֶדֶק, ṣedeq) themselves flow out of a humble searching after Yahweh (2:3). This call to repentance stands at the rhetorical and thematic center of the book.[29] The majority of the references to the day of Yahweh in the book can be understood in the context of the events

---

[27]William J. Dumbrell, *The Faith of Israel: Its Expression in the Books of the Old Testament* (Grand Rapids: Baker, 1988), p. 225.

[28]Alberto J. Soggin, *Introduction to the Old Testament: From Its Origins to the Closing of the Alexandrian Canon*, trans. by John Bowden (Philadelphia: Westminster, 1980, rev. ed.), p. 281.

[29]Eakin, "Zephaniah," p. 274.

that accompanied an anticipated decline of Assyrian domination in Josiah's day. Zephaniah's proclamation of the coming day then is less a look into the distant future than it is a call for repentance in Judah in the late seventh century B.C.[30] Those who repent and seek Yahweh the King of Israel who is present with Zion and mighty to save (3:15,17) will experience the transformation from judgment to restoration (3:19-20).

---

[30]Marvin A. Sweeney, "Zephaniah: Prophet of His Time — Not the End Time!" *BRev* 20 (2004): 36.

# OUTLINE

# SELECTED BIBLIOGRAPHY ON ZEPHANIAH

Baker, David W. *Nahum, Habakkuk, Zephaniah: An Introduction and Commentary*. TOTC 23b. Downers Grove, IL: InterVarsity, 1988.

_____ . "Zephaniah." In *New Dictionary of Biblical Theology*. Ed. by T. Desmond Alexander, et al. Downers Grove, IL: InterVarsity, 2000.

Ball, Ivan J. *Zephaniah: A Rhetorical Study*. Berkeley: BIBAL, 1988.

Barker, Kenneth L., and Waylon Bailey. *Micah, Nahum, Habakkuk, Zephaniah*. NAC. Nashville; Broadman, 1999.

Berlin, Adele. *Zephaniah: A New Translation with Introduction and Commentary*. AB 25A. New York: Doubleday, 1994.

Bruckner, James. *Jonah, Nahum, Habakkuk, Zephaniah*. The NIV Application Commentary. Grand Rapids: Zondervan, 2004.

Chisholm, Robert B., Jr. "The Seventh Century Prophets (Nahum, Habakkuk, Zephaniah)." In *A Biblical Theology of the Old Testament*. Ed. by Roy B. Zuck, Eugene H. Merrill, and Darrell L. Bock. Chicago: Moody, 1991.

Eakin, Frank E., Jr. "Zephaniah." In *Hosea–Malachi*. Ed. by Clifton J. Allen. BBC 7. Nashville: Broadman, 1972.

House, Paul R. *Zephaniah: A Prophetic Drama*. JSOTSupp 69. Sheffield: Almond, 1988.

Hyatt, J.P. "The Date and Background of Zephaniah." *JBL* 7 (1949): 25-29.

King, Greg A. "The Message of Zephaniah: An Urgent Echo." *AUSS* 34 (1996): 211-222.

Motyer, J. Alec. "Zephaniah." In *The Minor Prophets: An Exegetical and Expository Commentary*, vol. 3. Ed. by Thomas Edward McComiskey. Grand Rapids: Baker, 1998.

Patterson, Richard D. *Nahum, Habakkuk, Zephaniah.* WEC. Chicago: Moody, 1991.

Roberts, J.J.M. *Nahum, Habakkuk, and Zephaniah: A Commentary.* OTL. Louisville, KY: Westminster John Knox, 1991.

Robertson, O. Palmer. *The Books of Nahum, Habakkuk, and Zephaniah.* NICOT. Grand Rapids: Eerdmans, 1994.

Sweeney, Marvin A. *Zephaniah: A Commentary.* Hermeneia. Minneapolis: Augsburg Fortress, 2003.

_____ . "Zephaniah: Prophet of His Time − Not the End Time!" *BRev* 20 (2004): 36-40, 43.

Széles, Mária Eszenyei. *Wrath and Mercy: A Commentary on the Books of Habakkuk and Zephaniah.* ITC. Grand Rapids: Eerdmans, 1987.

Vogels, Walter. "Zephaniah." In *The International Bible Commentary: A Catholic and Ecumenical Commentary for the Twenty-First Century.* Ed. by William R. Farmer. Collegeville, MN: Liturgical Press, 1998.

Williams, Donald L. "The Date of Zephaniah." *JBL* 82 (1963): 77-88.

# ZEPHANIAH

## I. TITLE (1:1)

**¹The word of the LORD that came to Zephaniah son of Cushi, the son of Gedaliah, the son of Amariah, the son of Hezekiah, during the reign of Josiah son of Amon king of Judah:**

**1:1** The title of the book of Zephaniah contains three parts (cf. Hos 1:1; Micah 1:1). One, the message of the book is described as **the word of the LORD**, a common introductory phrase among the prophetic books (Jer 1:2; Ezek 1:3; Hos 1:1; Joel 1:1; Jonah 1:1; Micah 1:1; Hag 1:1; Zech 1:1; Mal 1:1). Two, the identification of the prophet provides information about his pedigree. The name **Zephaniah** means "Yahweh protects" or "Yahweh hides" (cf. Ps 31:20-21). In addition to the prophet, three different men are named Zephaniah in the OT: (1) an ancestor of the prophet Samuel who is an ancestor of Heman, a singer in the temple choir (1 Chr 6:36); (2) a priest, son of Maaseiah and contemporary of Jeremiah (Jer 21:1; 29:25,29; 37:3; 52:24), who is executed by a Babylonian commander (2 Kgs 25:18-21); and (3) the father of a Josiah to whom Zechariah delivers a message regarding the Branch (Zech 6:10,14). Zephaniah's extended genealogy is probably intended to show he is the great-great-grandson of King **Hezekiah** and that his father **Cushi** is indeed an Israelite and not a foreigner. The name of Zephaniah's father, Cushi, has led to the conjecture that Zephaniah is African (either Ethiopian or Egyptian) rather than Israelite (cf. Gen 10:6; 2 Kgs 19:9; Isa 18:1). Two others are named Cushi in the OT: a soldier appointed by Joab to tell David of Absalom's death (2 Sam 18:21-32) and the great-grandfather of Jehudi, a royal court official in service of Jehoiakim, king of Judah (Jer 36:14). In some instances in the OT, Ethiopia, or more precisely Cush/Nubia, is used as a synonym for Egypt (Isa 20:3-5; Ezek 30:4; Nahum 3:9), and this may represent the actual political situation in the seventh century during which Egypt is ruled by the Twenty-fifth (or Cushite) Dynasty (712–663 B.C.) (cf. 2 Kgs 19:9; Isa 18:1,7; Zeph 3:10). Zephaniah's Israelite origins, nevertheless, seem clear since all of the other names in the genealogy, including the prophet's, end with a shortened form of the name of Israel's God, "Yah." The last ancestor mentioned is named Hezekiah, who may be the king of Judah (715–687 B.C.) bearing that name (2 Kings 18–20). Whatever Zephaniah's origin, his genealogy seemingly connects him with foreigners and royalty, two groups to which his message is specifically directed. Three, the final phrase of the first verse places the prophet's ministry within a particular historical context, **the reign of Josiah**, **king of Judah** from 640–609 B.C. (2 Kgs 22:1–23:30). This establishes parameters for the prophet's ministry and helps the reader place Zephaniah's words within a historical context that makes their content intelligible.

## II. ANNOUNCMENT OF THE DAY OF YAHWEH (1:2–2:3)

The first major section of the book consists of an announcement of judgment on Judah and Jerusalem (1:2-6) followed by an exhortation to prepare for the day of Yahweh (1:7-18) and an exhortation to repent before the day of Yahweh (2:1-3). These two prophetic exhortations (1:7–2:3) extend the prophecy of punishment (1:2-6) through the use of first person statements about the intent of Yahweh's actions (1:2-4,8-9,12,17) and the use of third person statements about the effects of Yahweh's actions (1:10,13-16,17-18). Such narrative descriptions of these future events serve as motivations upon which the first exhortation, "Be silent before the Sovereign Lord," is based. The second exhortation directly addresses Judah and Jerusalem as the "shameful nation" and suggests that the future devastation described may be averted for them if the call to repentance is heeded. Zephaniah 1:2-18 reports Yahweh's intent to execute judgment and presents images of the consequences that will fall on the wicked. This disaster Zephaniah calls "the day of the Lord"

(1:7), a motif employed in order to prepare the reader for the exhortation to seek Yahweh in 2:1-3.

## A. ANNOUNCEMENT OF JUDGMENT ON JUDAH (1:2-6)

[2]"I will sweep away everything / from the face of the earth," / declares the LORD. / [3]"I will sweep away both men and animals; / I will sweep away the birds of the air / and the fish of the sea. / The wicked will have only heaps of rubble[a] / when I cut off man from the face of the earth," / declares the LORD. / Against Judah [4]"I will stretch out my hand against Judah / and against all who live in Jerusalem. / I will cut off from this place every remnant of Baal, / the names of the pagan and the idolatrous priests— / [5]those who bow down on the roofs / to worship the starry host, / those who bow down and swear by the LORD / and who also swear by Molech,[b] / [6]those who turn back from following the LORD / and neither seek the LORD nor inquire of him.

[a]3 The meaning of the Hebrew for this line is uncertain.    [b]5 Hebrew *Malcam*, that is, Milcom

Zephaniah 1:2-6 exhibits the typical elements of a prophecy of punishment, including an announcement of punishment (vv. 2-4) and an accusation of offense (vv. 5-6). The unit begins with statements of universal judgment (vv. 2-3) before the charges against Judah (vv. 4-6); thus, the text both catches the interest of its original audience, Judah, and magnifies Judah's guilt. This order is later reversed, when Yahweh's judgment on Judah (vv. 7-13) is described before universal judgment on the nations (vv. 14-18). The oracle formula, "declares the LORD," appears twice in quick succession, and the second occurrence does not make a sharp distinction between the sections of announcement ("I will") and accusation ("those who"), since verse 4 continues the speech of Yahweh. Rather, the oracle formulas heighten the startling indictment of Yahweh against the idolatry of Judah. The unit then announces the intention of Yahweh to bring disaster upon the world and, more specifically, upon Judah for its idolatrous worship.

**1:2-3** The first two words heard by the prophet's audience, translated **I will sweep away**, sound alike in Hebrew (אָסֹף אָסֵף, *'āsōph*

'āsēph). While the two words provide a clear example of assonance, they form an expression difficult to explain.[1] The expression combines two different verb forms (an infinitive with an imperfect), a common way to mark emphasis or intensity, but it does so with two different words ("gather/remove" and "come to an end"), an uncommon variation of this emphatic construction (cf. Jer 8:13). Here the two verbs express complete removal, that is, a complete destruction. Furthermore, the first of these verbs (אָסֹף, 'āsaph), most often translated "gather" in the NIV, frequently occurs in the context of harvest (Exod 23:10; Lev 23:39; 25:3; 25:20; Deut 16:13; 28:38; Ruth 2:7; Job 39:12; Isa 62:9; Jer 40:10). The word may point to an origin of Zephaniah's prophecy during the autumn festival of Ingathering, also known as Sukkot (Exod 23:16; 34:22; Deut 16:13-15; Zech 14:16-19), an association also supported by the sacrifice imagery in the next unit (1:7-9; cf. 2:1-2). Even though the people are celebrating the gathering of the harvest, Yahweh is planning the gathering of the people for judgment.[2]

The language of these verses is also reminiscent of both the Genesis creation account and flood narrative. Specifically, Zephaniah uses the same or similar words for **animals**, **birds**, and **fish**, and plays on the words for **earth** (אֲדָמָה, 'ădāmāh) and **man** (אָדָם, 'ādām), vocabulary found in Genesis 1:20-30.[3] Zephaniah also describes the extent of the impending devastation in language evocative of the Noahic flood. The phrase **the face of the earth** appears in Genesis 6:7 and 7:4, which record Yahweh's intention to destroy every living creature, and in Genesis 7:23, which records the result of that destruction.[4] Such wording here serves to present the opening announcement of judgment, as a kind of undoing of creation. By threatening to **cut off** 'ādām twice, once at the beginning of verse 3 and once at the end of the verse, Zephaniah emphasizes Yahweh's judgment on humanity (the TNIV correctly translates the sense of

---

[1] See Patterson, *Nahum, Habakkuk, Zephaniah*, pp. 300-301.

[2] Sweeney, *Zephaniah*, pp. 61-62.

[3] Adele Berlin, *Zephaniah: A New Translation with Introduction and Commentary*, AB 25A (New York: Doubleday, 1994), pp. 73-74, suggests that the language of Zephaniah 1:3 alludes to Deuteronomy 4:16-18 that prohibits making images of men, women, birds, or fish in order to worship them.

[4] Cf. Deut 6:15; 7:6; and 14:2, where "the face of the earth" occurs in a covenantal context.

'*ādām* as "people"). This interest in the divine judgment of humanity is highlighted in the line about the wicked, a line omitted from the LXX. The ambiguity of the Hebrew wording has led to various renderings, which understand the line in parallel with the object of the previous verb (e.g., the ESV's "and the rubble with the wicked"), in conformity with the other first person statements in the verse (e.g., the NRSV's "I will make the wicked stumble"), in anticipation of the condemnation of idolatry in the following verses (e.g., the NET's "The idolatrous images of these creatures will be destroyed along with evil people" and the TNIV's "and the idols that cause the wicked to stumble"), or in limitation of the complete devastation of humanity to only those who do not seek Yahweh (e.g., the NIV's **the wicked will have only heaps of rubble**).

The double use of the oracle formula, **declares the LORD**, at the conclusion of both verses 2 and 3 lends special significance to the statements phrased in the first person singular (1:2-4). By portraying Yahweh as the powerful creator capable of obliterating all creation, the prophet magnifies the threats against Judah and Jerusalem that follow and heightens the necessity of Josiah's reforms after 622 B.C. (2 Kings 22–23; 2 Chronicles 34).[5] That Judah should fall under judgment along with the nations indicates a failure of the covenant people to fulfill the reason for their election: to be a blessing to all the nations of the world (Gen 12:1-3). Yahweh will rectify this situation, however, by sweeping away all who have perverted his goodness (1:3) and have worshiped false gods (1:4-6).

**1:4** Verse 4 progressively sharpens the focus of Yahweh's judgment **against Judah** (the country) and **Jerusalem** (the capital city) then finally the **remnant of Baal** and particular groups of idolaters. A standard formula for statements of judgment is the image of the stretched out hand. It is prominent in the Exodus plague and Red Sea narratives (Exod 7:19; 8:1,2; 9:22; 10:12,21; 14:16,21,27) and in statements of Yahweh's judgment on the pagan enemies (Isa 14:26-27; Ezek 35:3) and the covenant people (Jer 21:5; Ezek 14:13; 16:27). The promise to **cut off** (כָּרַת, *kārath*) often appears where Yahweh threatens to punish or destroy a group (Lev 17:10; 20:3,5,6; 26:30; 1 Kgs 9:7; 14:10; 21:21; 2 Kgs 9:8; Isa 14:22; Ezek 14:13,17; 21:8; 25:13,16; 29:8; 30:15; 35:7; Amos 1:5,8; 2:3; Micah 5:9,10,11,12;

[5]Sweeney, *Zephaniah*, p. 57.

Nahum 2:14; Zech 9:6,10). In the OT, **this place** frequently names the temple (Deut 12:5,11; 1 Kgs 8:29-30,35; 2 Kgs 18:25; 22:16-20; 2 Chr 6:20-21,26; 7:12,15; Ezek 42:13; Hag 2:9), but within this context, it more likely refers to the territory of Judah and Jerusalem (cf. 2 Chr 34:24-28; Jer 19:3-13; 27:22; 33:10-12; 40:2). "The remnant of Baal" may be a summary title for those listed in the following phrases, that is, pagans and idolaters. Baal usually refers to the Canaanite fertility god Hadad, who has a number of local manifestations. With King Ahab's support Jezebel imports a Phoenician form of Baal worship (1 Kgs 16:30-33) that eventually infiltrates the southern kingdom (2 Kgs 8:16-19; 11:18; 2 Chr 21:6-7; 23:17). Verse 4 probably speaks of this Baal; nevertheless, the Assyrians also had a deity named Bel (Baal). In the context of Assyria's recent control over Judah, the phrase here could refer to the syncretism of the worship of Yahweh and Mesopotamian deities. The phrase "the remnant of Baal" may anticipate the beginning of Josiah's reforms in 622 B.C. or refer to a time after the king's reforms have reduced, though not completely diminished, the influence of Baal. The reading of the LXX, "the names of Baal" rather than "the remnant of Baal," may point to the earlier date. The image of cutting off **the names of the pagans and idolatrous priests**, a term found elsewhere only in 2 Kings 23:5 and Hosea 10:5, may intensify the notion of destruction by implying the lack of future descendants among them to preserve their memory (cf. "remembrance" in the TNIV) or to perpetuate their error (cf. Exod 12:15,19; 30:33; 31:14; 1 Kgs 14:10,14; 21:21; 2 Kgs 9:8).

**1:5-6** The last three lines of the unit (1:2-6) list the types of people Yahweh will destroy: those who worship the stars, those who mix the worship of Yahweh and other gods, and those who do not worship Yahweh at all. **Worship**ing **the starry host** pertains to astral worship broadly practiced among ancient Semites, especially the Assyrians (cf. 2 Kgs 21:3-5; 23:4-5). Such worship is introduced into Judah during the days of Manasseh and Amon, the kings preceding Josiah, but it receives clear condemnation (Deut 7:2-5; 2 Kgs 17:16; 21:1-7; 23:4-5; Jer 19:13). To facilitate an unobstructed view of the stars, worship of astral deities often took place on rooftops (2 Kgs 23:12; Jer 19:13; 32:29). The NIV's **Molech** translates the MT's מַלְכָּם (*malkām*, "their king"), a reading also attested by the LXX. The designation represents the worship of a pagan god alongside Yahweh.

This god should probably be identified as Milcom (cf. ESV, NASB, and NJB), the primary god of the Ammonites (1 Kgs 11:5,33; 2 Kgs 23:13). The name Milcom, in turn, is a distortion of the name Melek (or Melech), the Hebrew word for king (מֶלֶךְ, *melek*); Melek is also itself distorted to Molech (מֹלֶךְ, *mōlek*), which uses the proper Hebrew consonants (*mlk*) but replaces the vowels (two *e*'s) with those (an *ō* and *e*) from the Hebrew noun for "shame" (בֹּשֶׁת, *bōšeth*). Most biblical references to Molech associate him with human sacrifice (Lev 18:21; 20:2-5; 2 Kgs 23:10; Jer 32:35), an act considered the ultimate sacrifice by Israel's neighbors. To **swear by** Yahweh and by Molech is religious syncretism, and this amounts to an outright rejection of Yahweh (Zeph 1:6) in view of the demand for exclusive devotion (Exod 20:3-6).

The mention in verse 6 of those who **neither seek the LORD nor inquire of him** might be a summary statement; however, it might refer to a category of person not mentioned earlier, namely, those who have completely abandoned Yahweh or, at the least, have adopted a practical atheism. Whereas the prophet earlier criticizes those who practice syncretistic worship, this phrase names individuals who turn from (cf. Ps 78:57; 80:18; 129:5; Prov 14:14; Isa 50:5) and do not call upon Yahweh at all. The verbs "to seek" (Deut 4:29; Ps 24:6; 27:8; 105:4; Isa 51:1; Hos 3:3; 5:6,15; Amos 8:12; Zech 8:21,22) and "to inquire" (Deut 4:29; Ps 24:6; 78:34; 105:4; Isa 9:13; 31:1; 55:6; 58:2; 65:10; Jer 10:21; 21:2; 29:13; 37:7; Hos 10:12; Amos 5:4,6) are commonly found in contexts referring to prayer to or inquiry of Yahweh. When they appear together, the words heighten the notion of earnest search (Deut 4:29; 1 Chr 16:11; 2 Chr 20:3-4; 26:5; Ps 24:6; 105:3-4; Jer 29:13). "To seek" appears three more times in Zephaniah 2:3.

## B. EXHORTATION TO PREPARE
## FOR THE DAY OF YAHWEH (1:7-18)

[7]**Be silent before the Sovereign LORD, / for the day of the LORD is near. / The LORD has prepared a sacrifice; / he has consecrated those he has invited. / [8]On the day of the LORD's sacrifice / I will punish the princes / and the king's sons / and all those clad / in foreign clothes. / [9]On that day I will punish / all who avoid step-**

ping on the threshold,[a] / who fill the temple of their gods / with violence and deceit.

[10]"On that day," declares the LORD, / "a cry will go up from the Fish Gate, / wailing from the New Quarter, / and a loud crash from the hills. / [11]Wail, you who live in the market district[b]; / all your merchants will be wiped out, / all who trade with[c] silver will be ruined. / [12]At that time I will search Jerusalem with lamps / and punish those who are complacent, / who are like wine left on its dregs, / who think, 'The LORD will do nothing, / either good or bad.' / [13]Their wealth will be plundered, / their houses demolished. / They will build houses / but not live in them; / they will plant vineyards / but not drink the wine.

[14]"The great day of the LORD is near— / near and coming quickly. / Listen! The cry on the day of the LORD will be bitter, / the shouting of the warrior there.

[15]That day will be a day of wrath, / a day of distress and anguish, / a day of trouble and ruin, / a day of darkness and gloom, / a day of clouds and blackness, / [16]a day of trumpet and battle cry / against the fortified cities / and against the corner towers. / [17]I will bring distress on the people / and they will walk like blind men, / because they have sinned against the LORD. / Their blood will be poured out like dust / and their entrails like filth. / [18]Neither their silver nor their gold / will be able to save them / on the day of the LORD's wrath. / In the fire of his jealousy / the whole world will be consumed, / for he will make a sudden end / of all who live in the earth."

[a]*9* See 1 Samuel 5:5.    [b]*11* Or *the Mortar*    [c]*11* Or *in*

Zephaniah 1:7-18, a prophetic exhortation, extends the prophecy of punishment (vv. 2-6) with a command and motive clause (v. 7) followed by a narrative description of future events (vv. 8-10). This same structure is repeated with a second command and motive clause (v. 10) followed by a double narrative description, one from Judah's perspective (vv. 11-13) and another from a universal perspective (v. 14-18). This double narration mirrors in reverse order the earlier statements of divine judgment on Judah (vv. 4-6) and on all humankind (vv. 2-3). The narration of Yahweh's intended action is advanced by the verb phrase, "it will come about" (וְהָיָה, $w^ehāyāh$), and

the prepositional phrase, "on that day" (בְּיוֹם, *bᵊyôm*). The NIV omits
the verb phrase that occurs four times (vv. 8,10,12,13); but the NASB
translates the four occurrences respectively, "it will come about,"
"there will be," "it shall come about," and "moreover." The prepositional phrase appears in the NIV as "on the day" or "on that day"
(vv. 8,9,10,18). Furthermore, the narration intersperses third person
descriptions (e.g., "The LORD has prepared a sacrifice") with first person speech by Yahweh (e.g., "I will punish the princes"). Thus, the
sequence of command ("Be silent" and "Wail"), motivation ("for,"
but omitted by the NIV in v. 11), and narration ("it shall be" and "I
will punish") follows a similar pattern in both instances (vv. 7-10 and
11-13). The repetition of the full saying, "the day of the LORD is
near," in verse 14 (earlier in v. 7) sets off the following unit (vv. 14-
18) that elaborates on the nature of the day of Yahweh as imminent
and catastrophic. As a whole, Zephaniah 1:7-18 calls for the readers
to prepare in silence and with lament for the unexpected yet
inevitable consequence of their religious idolatry and economic corruption, a consequence Zephaniah calls the day of Yahweh.

**1:7** The interjection, **Be silent**, is used mainly in the prophets
(Amos 6:10; 8:3; Hab 2:20; Zech 2:13; elsewhere in Num 13:30; Judg
3:19; Neh 8:11) and often calls for people to stop speaking or weeping. Here the word demands silence and awe in the presence of **the
Sovereign LORD** (אֲדֹנָי יהוה, *ʾădōnāy YHWH*, generally translated Lord
GOD in other versions) and focuses the reader's attention on the subsequent description of the imminent **day** of Yahweh. This command
is followed by two motive clauses; both are signaled by the Hebrew
word כִּי (*kî*, "for"), but only the first one is translated in the NIV (cf.
NASB and NJPS).

The first of the motive clauses introduces a theme that carries
through to the conclusion of the section in Zephaniah 2:3: the day
of Yahweh is near. The statement is found elsewhere in other
prophetic writings (Isa 13:6; Ezek 30:3; Joel 1:15; 3:14; Obad 1:15)
and later in Zephaniah 1:14, where it begins a unit descriptive of the
imminence, distress, and wrath associated with the day of Yahweh.
In general, the day of Yahweh is understood as an occasion of
Yahweh's intervention in human affairs to judge the nations, especially those who are enemies of the Israelites (Isa 13:9-11; 19:16-17;
27:1; Jer 46:10; Ezek 30:3-4; Joel 3:12-14; Obad 15; Zeph 3:8), and to

restore the faithful among the covenant people (Isa 11:11; 26:1; 27:12-13; Jer 30:7-8; Joel 2:32; 3:16-18; Micah 4:6-7; Zeph 3:14-20). However, like Amos (5:18-20), Zephaniah turns the concept against Judah and Jerusalem by announcing that Yahweh's judgment comes against Judah, who has assimilated pagan worship and rejected Yahweh (Zeph 1:4-6).

The second of the motive clauses characterizes this judgment as Yahweh's preparation of Judah as **a sacrifice**. Customarily Yahweh sacrifices enemies (Isa 34:6; Jer 46:10); this time Judah is the victim for sacrifice. Other accounts of the invitation of people to a sacrifice (1 Sam 9:22-24; 16:1-5; 2 Sam 15:7-12; 1 Kgs 1:5-10,41-53; 2 Kgs 10:18-25) may highlight an irony in this text in which those who have been **consecrated** become those killed in the sacrifice.[6] Another possible reading is that those whom Yahweh has consecrated and invited to the sacrifice are the armies of Judah's enemies or birds and wild animals who feed on the corpses (Ezek 39:17-20).[7] Such sacrificial imagery is also appropriate as bloodshed is involved in both sacrifice and the crimes committed by those being punished (v. 9).

**1:8-9** Zephaniah anticipates the day of Yahweh when Yahweh appears to perform the sacrifice of the royal court and others responsible for social injustices in Judah. This intended action of Yahweh is introduced by two phrases in the Hebrew text, "it will come about" and **on that day**, even though the NIV translates only the second one. With the first of several first person speeches in the section (vv. 8-9,12,17), Yahweh announces the divine intention to punish (**I will punish**). Forms of the verb פָּקַד (*pāqad*, variously translated in the NIV as "punish, count, number, appoint, muster, care") appear five times in Zephaniah (1:8,9,12; 2:7; 3:7). The verb denotes a careful viewing by someone in authority that results in a considerable change in circumstances for the subordinate.[8] It appears in covenant contexts where Yahweh is portrayed as one who protects and enforces the covenant even to the third and fourth generation (Exod 20:5; 34:7; Num 14:18; Deut 5:9). Whereas its use in verses 8-

[6]Mária Eszenyei Széles, *Wrath and Mercy: A Commentary on the Books of Habakkuk and Zephaniah*, ITC (Grand Rapids: Eerdmans, 1987), p. 80.

[7]Roberts, *Nahum, Habakkuk, and Zephaniah*, p. 178.

[8]R. Laird Harris, "פָּקַד," *TWOT*, 2:731; Tyler F. Williams, "פָּקַד," *NIDOTTE*, 3:658.

12 and 3:7 connotes a negative visitation of punishment, 2:7 speaks of a positive care for the remnant.

Furthermore, Yahweh identifies four specific groups and the reasons for their punishment. One is royalty. Yet this criticism of **the princes** (i.e., **the king's sons**) is historically difficult. If the book's background relates to the earlier period of Josiah's reign, the young king would have had no sons of sufficient age to be criticized. The phrase "king's sons" instead may be a title for officials who exercise some authority during Josiah's reign (cf. "officials" in the TNIV). Or, it may refer to the descendants of Manasseh and Amon who are still alive. The LXX uses the more general phrase "the house of the king." In either case, the "king's sons" excludes King Josiah, since he initiates religious reform in Judah. Two are **those who wear foreign clothes**. The worship of Baal sometimes involves special clothing (2 Kgs 10:22), and the same adjective translated "foreign" elsewhere designates foreign gods (Mal 2:11). Thus, the phrase may refer to a kind of religious syncretism. More likely, however, is the reference to Assyrian fashions worn as a sign of submission to and acceptance of Assyrian domination. Three are **those who avoid stepping on the threshold**. The avoidance of stepping on the threshold may have originated among the Philistines (1 Sam 5:5). In antiquity, the threshold is thought to be the abode of demons; to step on the threshold, then, is to allow demons entry.[9] This belief leads to the later Roman practice of carrying a bride across the threshold. Another suggestion takes the image as one of economic injustice that portrays the suddenness with which the oppressor enters the home of their victim.[10] Perhaps such an image is akin to the modern expression of getting one's foot in the door. The prevailing depictions of idolatry in verses 4-5, however, argue for understanding the phrase along religious lines, rather than economic. Four are the violent and deceitful. To the previous charge of idolatry is now added

---

[9]Roberts, *Nahum, Habakkuk, and Zephaniah*, p. 179, cites three difficulties with this view: the verb translated "avoid" generally means to leap or step (cf. 2 Sam 22:30; Ps 18:29; S of S 2:8; Isa 35:6); the word "threshold" commonly describes the temple (Ezek 9:3; 10:4,18; 46:2; 47:1); and the phrase "temple of their gods" is rendered "temple of their Lord" in the LXX, suggesting that the prophet may be describing priests who fill the temple with "violence and deceit."

[10]Chisholm, *Minor Prophets*, p. 205.

immorality, specifically, wealth that is obtained through oppressive means. The LXX identifies the temple as "the house of the Lord God," rather than a pagan temple. If this sense is correct, the indictment indicates that some have violated the Jerusalem temple (cf. 2 Kgs 21:3-8; Jer 7:30; Ezek 8:5-6).

**1:10** Like the preceding verse, the Hebrew text begins with the same two phrases, "it will come about" and **on that day**, but the NIV translates only the second one. Here the phrases and the oracle formula (see comments at v. 2 above on **declares the LORD**) introduce Yahweh's announcement that judgment begins with Jerusalem (vv. 10-13). The locations mentioned — **the Fish Gate**, **the New Quarter**, and **the hills** — are all on the north side of the city, the side most vulnerable to attack. The Fish Gate is a gate along the city's north wall west of the temple mound (2 Chr 33:14; Neh 3:3; 12:39), probably named for its proximity to a fish market (perhaps Neh 13:16). The New Quarter refers to the Second Quarter (cf. ESV, NASB, NRSV) or Mishneh (cf. NJPS), a newer part of the city created when Hezekiah built a defensive wall around the western hills of the city (2 Chr 32:5). During the reign of Josiah, the prophetess Huldah lived there (2 Kgs 22:14). "The hills" probably refers to the hills within the city, namely Moriah (2 Chr 3:1; cf. Gen 22:2), Ophel (2 Kgs 5:24; Micah 4:8), and Zion (2 Sam 5:7; 1 Kgs 8:1). Three words, **cry**, **wail**, and **crash** (a word that often applies to the impending collapse of Judah, cf. Isa 30:13-14; Jer 4:6; 6:1; Lam 2:11,13; 3:47-48), express an increasing anguish that anticipates Yahweh's directive in the next verse.

**1:11** The imperative **wail** calls for the inhabitants of Jerusalem to mourn the disaster that overtakes them. Generally this word is addressed to the nations in anticipation of their destruction (Isa 14:31; 15:2-3,8; 16:7; 23:1,6,14; Jer 48:20,31,39; 49:3; 51:8; Zech 11:2). The word conveys an intense lament (Hos 7:14; Joel 1:5,11,13) or sorrowful repentance (Isa 65:14; Jer 4:8; 47:2; Micah 1:8), occasioned by the approach of the day of Yahweh (Isa 13:6; Ezek 30:2; Amos 8:3). Specifically, the word is addressed to those living **in the market district** and those who do business there. The NIV's "market district" and the NRSV's "Mortar" represent a Hebrew noun not used elsewhere in the OT as a proper noun; in Judges 15:19 the word indicates a bowl-shaped area (cf. Prov 27:22). Its association with commercial activity (i.e., construction and masonry) also points to a location on the west side of the city, probably the Tyropoeon Valley, where the market district developed near the roads leading to the coastal plain. Even though **all your merchants** renders the Hebrew phrase "all the people of Canaan," the phrase probably does not indicate that all the people of Canaan are exterminated. Instead, the trading expertise of the Canaanites provides the appropriate background for correlating the name "Canaan" and the occupation of "merchant" or "trader" (Job 41:6; Prov 31:24; Isa 23:8-9; Ezek 16:29; 17:4; Hos 12:8; Zech 14:21); furthermore, the phrase provides a subtle but clear reminder of Judah's inappropriate religious and economic connection with the Canaanites.[11] The use of **silver** is striking in that the book comes from an era in which the use of currency is gaining acceptance. Coinage is believed to have had its origins in Asia Minor during the seventh century; the Assyrians are frequently credited for establishing a cash basis for trade within their area of influence.[12]

**1:12-13** Again the NIV omits the phrase which introduces both verses 12 and 13 in the Hebrew text, "it will come about" (cf. NASB), but the wording **at that time** (cf. 3:18-19) functions in a way similar to the earlier temporal pronouncements, "on the day of the Lord" (v. 8) and "on that day" (vv. 9-10). Yahweh searches diligently for the unrighteous in **Jerusalem**, for no one can hide from Yahweh (Ps 139:11-12). Proverbs 31:18 uses the image of a **lamp** to portray the diligence of the ideal woman; here the image applies to Yahweh. Whereas Jeremiah 5:1-6 describes Yahweh's futile search for a righteous person within Jerusalem, Zephaniah portrays Yahweh successfully finding the unrighteous, punishing those who are stagnant and untroubled. The verb **complacent** (קָפָא, qāphā') is used in Exodus 15:8 with the meaning of "congealed" and Job 10:10 with the notion of "curdled." Here "complacent" is used in conjunction with "dregs," a word found elsewhere in the Old Testament only three times (Ps 75:8; Isa 25:6; Jer 48:11); the sense of the two words is expressed in the expanded clause in the NIV: **who are like wine left on its dregs**. This figure of wine left on the dregs is evidently proverbial for indifference (cf. Jer 48:11). When wine is allowed to sit too long, a thickening or coagulation occurs in which its heavier solid

[11]Sweeney, *Zephaniah*, p. 92.
[12]John W. Betlyon, "Coinage," *ABD*, 1:1076-1089.

particles settle, leaving dregs at the bottom of the bottle, skin, or cask. This image portrays the apathy and practical atheism of the people who may not have denied the existence of Yahweh on a theoretical level but who have denied Yahweh's activity either for good or bad on a pragmatic level.[13] The NIV's **who think** renders the inference of the Hebrew idiom evident in the NRSV's "who say in their hearts." Verse 13 intimates that the judgments described in the preceding verses come at the hands of foreign nations who plunder Judah's wealth, perhaps attained through dishonest means. The last half of verse 13 has the character of a futility curse in which people are denied the benefits of their labor; thus, the statements, **They will build houses but not live in them; they will plant vineyards but not drink the wine**, may allude to the covenant curses (Deut 28:30,39) and represent a reversal of the blessing of the land promised by Yahweh (Deut 6:10-11; Josh 24:13).

**1:14-18** Verse 14 begins with the same statement as does verse 7: "the day of the LORD is near." However, in verses 14-18 the focus now shifts from a judgment against Judah to a warning for all people. Verse 14 presents the day of Yahweh as an imminent threat. Verses 15-16 highlight the horror of the day with a sevenfold repetition of the word "day" (יוֹם, yôm). This repetition may represent a reversal of creation, an undoing of the seven days of creation in a single day.[14] Verses 17-18 identify the reason for the coming punishment, that is, the people's sin against Yahweh, and describe the inescapable destruction of the day of Yahweh.

**1:14 Near** (קָרוֹב, qārôb) is placed in emphatic position at the beginning of the verse. This adjective is used often elsewhere to speak of imminent peril (Deut 22:2; 32:35; Isa 13:6,22; Jer 48:16) and with "the day" or the **day of the LORD** to speak of coming judgment (Ezek 7:7; 30:3; Joel 1:15; 2:1; 3:14; Obad 15; Zeph 1:7). Ezekiel 30:3 includes, like Zephaniah 1:14-16, a double use of qārôb and an extended description of the day. These two passages contrast with others that portray the nearness of Yahweh, the divine name, and salvation (Ps 34:8; 75:1; 85:9; 145:18; Isa 50:8). Not only is the

---

[13]Baker, *Nahum, Habakkuk, Zephaniah*, p. 98.

[14]Walter Vogels, "Zephaniah," in *The International Bible Commentary: A Catholic and Ecumenical Commentary for the Twenty-First Century*, ed. by William R. Farmer (Collegeville, MN: Liturgical Press, 1998), p. 1177.

day near, it comes **quickly**. Extrabiblical Egyptian, Phoenician, and
Ugaritic sources indicate the adverbial form translated "coming
quickly" by the NIV could be related to some kind of soldier.[15] If this
is true, its use forms a subtle introduction to the military imagery
appearing later in the passage (vv. 14,16). The term translated **the
shouting of the warrior** denotes the battle cry of frenzied soldiers in
Isaiah 42:12 (cf. Zeph 1:16); here it may portray the desperate cry of
the vanquished warrior, whose bitter cry is described in the previous
line. If so, the last two lines of verse 14 represent the intermingling
of victims' cries of terror and warriors' cries of battle. However, the
TNIV seems to suggest that the cry in both lines comes from
Yahweh with its rendering, "the Mighty Warrior shouts his battle
cry." The emotional response to tragic experiences is often represented with a bitter taste (e.g., Gen 27:34; 1 Sam 1:10; 15:32; Job
7:11; 10:1; Jer 2:19; Ezek 27:30-31).

**1:15-16** Verses 15-16 use the sevenfold repetition of **day** to highlight the horror of the day of Yahweh; such repetition may allude to
the creation account (Gen 1:3–2:3). However, the day of Yahweh
brings darkness (cf. Amos 5:18-20) and the end of life on earth
(Zeph 1:17-18). The description of the day also contains a set of five
pairs of nearly synonymous terms. **Darkness, gloom, clouds, blackness, trumpet,** and **battle cry** (15-16) are reminiscent of the tumult
and terror of the Sinai theophany (Exod 19:9,16-19; 20:18-21; Deut
4:11; 5:22). In his temple dedication speech, Solomon notes that
Yahweh dwells in darkness (1 Kgs 8:12; 2 Chr 6:1). Whereas these
texts and others (Judg 5:4; 2 Sam 22:12; Job 22:14; Ps 18:11; 77:17;
97:2) use darkness and cloud imagery to describe Yahweh's presence, Zephaniah now highlights the ironic character of the day of
Yahweh by using the image of darkness to describe Yahweh's judgment rather than protection.[16] Similarly, the trumpet, often associated with the salvation of Yahweh in the Day of Atonement (Lev
25:9), the Feast of Tabernacles (Ps 81:3), and various military victories (Josh 6:4-20; Judg 3:27; 6:34; 7:8-22) is now associated with the
judgment of Yahweh. The final clauses of verse 16 identify the
objects against which this dreadful day would be directed: **the fortified cities** and **corner towers**. Combined with the mention of trum-

---

[15]Baker, *Nahum, Habakkuk, Zephaniah*, p. 99.
[16]Sweeney, *Zephaniah*, p. 100.

pet and battle cry, it makes explicit a militaristic notion that has pre-viously only been covert.

**1:17-18** Yahweh's wrath escalates throughout the entire section; nine times Yahweh says **I will** do something (Zeph 1:2,3[2×],4[2×], 8,9,12,17), and each of these assertions increases the intensity of the condemnation against Judah as a whole.[17] The effects of divine wrath are again expressed in terms of covenant curses (see v. 13; cf. Deut 28:28-29): **they will walk like blind men** (cf. Isa 59:10; Lam 4:14). The TNIV renders the sense of the image: "they will grope about like those who are blind" (cf. NJB). Perhaps the people become blind from the unnatural darkness in verse 15, but certainly their helplessness and distress derives from their sin against Yahweh. The graphic imagery of the loss of **blood** shows the fragile nature of life in that day; blood and internal organs are poured out **like filth** or dung (cf. TNIV), unworthy of attention (2 Kgs 9:37; Jer 9:22). Such imagery, combined with the imagery of consumption by fire in verse 18, resumes the earlier theme of sacrifice first introduced in verse 7. The blood and entrails of those who have been consecrated for sac-rifice are spilled out and consumed by fire. Furthermore, the notice that the whole earth is consumed may reinforce this sacrificial image by likening Judah's defeat to the whole burnt offering.[18] The whole world is consumed in the **fire of** [Yahweh's] **jealousy** (קִנְאָה, *qin'āh*). The word *qin'āh* can refer to Yahweh's zeal or righteous jealousy that does not tolerate rivals (Num 25:11; Deut 29:20). As the jealous God, Yahweh does not stand idly by while other gods capture the attention of the people that belongs rightly only to Yahweh. Yahweh's jealousy is often given as an assurance of a promised deliverance or exaltation of Yahweh's people (2 Kgs 19:31; Isa 9:7; 26:11; 37:32; Ezek 36:5-6; Zech 1:14; 8:2). Zephaniah 3:18 also promises the con-sumption of the whole world with the fire of Yahweh's jealousy. This universal judgment is unavoidable, and deliverance from it cannot be deferred by any human means, including wealth. That humanity seeks salvation from judgment through **silver** and **gold** may refer to their wealth (1:11,13), but it may also refer to idols which are com-monly made from these materials (cf. Isa 2:20; 30:22; Ezek 7:19-20).

---

[17]Paul R. House, *Zephaniah: A Prophetic Drama*, JSOTSupp 69 (Sheffield: Almond, 1988), p. 70.

[18]Sweeney, *Zephaniah*, pp. 77-78.

The practice of cities paying attackers to avoid or lift attacks is common (see 2 Kgs 15:17-20; 18:13-15; 24:8-14). The pronouncement that **the whole world will be consumed** links the opening (vv. 2-3) and the closing of the section (vv. 17-18); together they form an inclusio, that is, a similar idea stated at the beginning and end of a section, on the motif of universal destruction. Still the language of the section is hyperbolic, as is typical for depictions of divine judgment and as is evidenced in the following section that offers instructions for deliverance from the day of Yahweh's wrath.[19]

## C. EXHORTATION TO REPENT
## BEFORE THE DAY OF YAHWEH (2:1-3)

[1]**Gather together, gather together, / O shameful nation, / [2]before the appointed time arrives / and that day sweeps on like chaff, / before the fierce anger of the LORD comes upon you, / before the day of the LORD's wrath comes upon you. / [3]Seek the LORD, all you humble of the land, / you who do what he commands. / Seek righteousness, seek humility; / perhaps you will be sheltered / on the day of the LORD's anger.**

Following the initial announcement of the coming of the day of Yahweh (1:2-18), the prophet then presents a call to repentance (2:1-3) and a motivation for such repentance (cf. Mal 2:1-9,13-17). The section makes evident the paraenetic (i.e., exhortatory) character of the book of Zephaniah, and this section represents its rhetorical center, calling Judah to seek Yahweh and thereby escape the impending wrath of the day of Yahweh.[20] Specifically, the section contains two commands with a description of the potential result for following the commands. The first command, a call to assemble, is directed to the "shameless nation." Their assembly, however, must occur according to certain temporal conditions, namely, before the day of Yahweh's wrath (2:1-2). The second command, a call to seek Yahweh, is addressed to "all you humble of the land." This command is further emphasized in the commands to seek righteousness and to seek

---

[19]Roberts, *Nahum, Habakkuk, and Zephaniah*, p. 185.
[20]Sweeney, *Zephaniah*, p. 50.

humility (2:3). Obeying these commands may result in shelter on the day of Yahweh's anger. In addition, the following announcements of punishments against the nations (vv. 4-15) provide further rationale for obeying these commands. Therefore, the intent of Zephaniah 2:1-3 is to urge Judah to reverse patterns of behavior (that is, religious syncretism, practical atheism, and economic oppression) in order to avert disastrous consequences associated with the day of Yahweh. The repentance of the humble of the land anticipates what is prophesied about the people of the earth (2:11; 3:9).

**2:1** The call to repentance begins with a summons for the people to assemble. With a repetition of the imperative, the prophet makes an earnest appeal for the people to **gather together**. The other six uses of this verb "gather" in the Old Testament refer to the gathering of stubble or sticks. Exodus 5:7-12 use the word in the account of the gathering of straw by the Hebrew slaves to make bricks, and Numbers 15:32-33 use it to describe the actions of a person who desecrates the Sabbath day by gathering wood. The widow of Zarephath gathers sticks in preparation for cooking a meal in 1 Kings 17:10-12. Elsewhere the word does not describe the gathering of people. Its use here may enhance the earlier sacrifice imagery by depicting the people as inherently involved in their own destruction.[21] In essence, the people are gathering together for kindling, an action which readies them for destruction. The people are addressed as a **shameful nation**. The term "nation" (גּוֹי, gôy) usually describes a pagan people (e.g., Exod 34:10; Lev 25:44; Num 14:15; Deut 15:6; 1 Kgs 11:2; 1 Chr 14:17; Isa 11:10). Although it is used elsewhere of Israel itself (e.g., Exod 19:6; Deut 4:6; Isa 1:4; 9:3; 10:6; cf. Zeph 2:9), the term may have been used here to associate the shameful behavior of Judah with the pagan nations.[22] The NIV's "shameful" (כָּסַף, kāsaph) reflects a passive form of the verb (cf. Gen 31:30; Ps 84:3 where the word means to "long for," but here the word is negated, i.e., "not longed for") that may constitute an ironic echo of the word translated "silver" (כֶּסֶף, keseph) in 1:18.[23] The silver of the shameful nation (cf. "without shame" in the NASB, NJB, and NJPS) does not rescue them when Yahweh comes in judgment.

---

[21]Ibid., p. 114.
[22]Baker, *Nahum, Habakkuk, Zephaniah*, p. 102.
[23]Sweeney, *Zephaniah*, p. 115.

**2:2** The assembly of the people must occur before the day of Yahweh. This temporal condition is repeated three times in phrases that begin with the word **before**. The threefold use of "before" (טֶרֶם, *ṭerem*) is paralleled by the threefold use of "seek" (בַּקְּשׁוּ, *bāqaš*) in the next verse; both repetitions express the urgency of the prophet's call. The NIV's **before the appointed time arrives** dulls the Hebrew phrase that may be translated "before the giving birth of the decree" (cf. the TNIV's "before the decree takes place"). The image of **chaff** is used in other passages to express the fragility and suitability for destruction of those whom Yahweh comes to judge (Job 21:18; Ps 1:4; Isa 17:13-14; 29:5-6; Hos 13:1-3). Here it refers to the ease with which the wicked nation is scattered at the coming of the wrath of Yahweh. The appointed or decreed time, of course, refers to the day of Yahweh, which is mentioned in the third of the three "before" phrases.

**2:3** The threefold use of the imperative **seek** (on the meaning of *bāqaš* see 1:6 above) makes the idea of seeking Yahweh more intense, and the parallelism of the verse indicates that seeking Yahweh involves ethical demands. To seek Yahweh means to **seek righteousness** and **humility**. The phrase **all the humble of the land** (v. 3) is a unique phrase in the Hebrew Bible, but Amos 8:4 uses a similar phrase that lacks the adjective "all" and the definite article with the noun "land." Although the prophets usually portray the humble as impoverished victims of the oppression of the unjust (Isa 11:4; 29:19; 32:7; Amos 2:7; 8:4), no such emphasis appears here. The humble are characterized simply as those **who do what** Yahweh **commands**. The Hebrew adjective used as a noun here, "humble" (עָנָו, *'ānāw*), is derived from a verb that indicates the suffering of affliction, either from an outward (Deut 21:14) or inward (Lev 26:29,31; Ps 35:13) source. The adjective stresses the moral and spiritual quality of an absolute dependency on God that issues forth from the self-affliction (or self-denial) of the godly.[24] Such action on the part of the humble is expressed, for example, through fasting and contrition during the observance of the Day of Atonement (Lev 16:29,31). The humble know that Yahweh is their savior (Ps 10:17; 76:9). Notably in Numbers 12:1-3 Moses is described as more humble than anyone on the face of the earth. Although having his authority questioned by Miriam and Aaron and suffering personal attack in that

---

[24]Leonard J. Coppes, "עָנָה," *TWOT*, 2:682.

process, no response by him is recorded. Instead, Yahweh comes to his rescue. As a result, Miriam is stricken with leprosy. Moses responds to that by praying for her healing.[25] The NIV in 3:12 also translates as "humble" (עָנִי, 'ānî), a word usually signifying poverty (Exod 22:25-26; Lev 19:10; 23:22; Deut 15:11; Job 29:12; 34:28; Isa 10:2). Several of its appearances in the Psalms (9:18; 25:16; 34:6; 68:10; 69:29; 74:19) and elsewhere (2 Sam 22:28), however, indicate that it bears, in some contexts, a meaning akin to that of 'ānāw. If these groups spoken of in verse 3 and 3:12 are indeed roughly synonymous, then the admonition for the humble to seek Yahweh (2:3) is complemented by the later assurance that Yahweh will leave within the city the meek and humble who trust in Yahweh's name (3:12). Zephaniah thus identifies the humble with the remnant, that is, the humble are those from among the "shameless nation" who heed the call to assemble and by their obedience to this command of Yahweh show themselves to be humble.[26]

Furthermore, Zephaniah ventures that the humble may escape the destruction of Yahweh's anger coming on the prideful and carefree (2:8,10,15; 3:11). Their protection is depicted with the word "shelter," a word used for Moses' hiding his face from Yahweh in the burning bush (Exod 3:6), for Job's longing to be hidden in the grave until Yahweh's anger has passed (Job 14:13), and for the psalmist's desire for Yahweh to keep him safe in the day of trouble (Ps 27:5). The mention of possible escape on the day of Yahweh's anger here seems to contradict 1:4. But this notion overstates the implication of "all" in 1:4 (cf. Gen 6:5,12-13; 7:19,21), and such a theology of confidence cannot be judged adverse to the prophetic perspective.[27] The reserved nature of **perhaps you will be sheltered on the day of the LORD's anger** highlights that salvation on the day of Yahweh is ultimately an act of God's grace.[28] The LXX eliminates the ambiguity of "perhaps" with the reading: "in order that you may be covered." Nonetheless, the use of "perhaps" has tremendous rhetorical effect (cf. Jer 20:10; 26:3; 36:3,7): if the righteous cannot be certain

---

[25]William J. Dumbrell, "עָנָה," *NIDOTTE*, 3:456.

[26]Floyd, *Minor Prophets*, p. 216.

[27]Eakin, "Zephaniah," p. 282; cf. other texts that offer a hope of escape and restoration for those who seek Yahweh and turn from their evil ways at the onslaught of the day of Yahweh (Amos 5:4-6,14-15; Joel 2:12-17).

[28]Baker, *Nahum, Habakkuk, Zephaniah*, p. 103.

of their deliverance from the day of Yahweh's wrath, how certain is the fate of the wicked.[29]

# III. ANNOUNCEMENT OF JUDGMENT AGAINST THE NATIONS (2:4–3:7)

Following the call to repentance (2:1-3), 2:4–3:7 presents a series of prophecies of punishment against the nations (2:4-15; cf. Amos 1:3–2:16) and a prophetic charge of failure to repent against Jerusalem (3:1-7). Together these descriptions of punishment and the prophetic charge provide the basis for heeding the commands in 2:1-3. Specifically, the prophecies against the surrounding nations are clearly linked in the Hebrew text to the commands by the word "for" (כִּי, *kî*), which is not translated in the NIV (cf. ESV, KJV, NASB, NJB, NRSV). Two woe addresses follow (2:5-15; 3:1-7), each beginning with the particle "woe" (הוֹי, *hôy*), and provide reasons why the "humble of the land" should seek Yahweh, righteousness, and humility. The prophecies of punishment begin with Judah's immediate neighbors (2:4-11) then shift to the ancient Near Eastern centers of power in Egypt and Assyria (2:12-15). The charge against Jerusalem (3:1-7) explains the reasons why Yahweh also punishes Jerusalem along with the nations, but the charge also becomes the basis for a renewed call to repentance, anticipating the following exhortation to wait for Yahweh in 3:8 and the desire of Yahweh to restore the remnant of Israel (3:9-20). Therefore, in 2:4–3:7, the prophet seeks to motivate Judah to heed the call to repentance in 2:1-3 through the announcement of punishment against surrounding nations and the city of Jerusalem.

## A. ANNOUNCEMENT OF JUDGMENT AGAINST PHILISTIA (2:4-7)

**[4]Gaza will be abandoned / and Ashkelon left in ruins. / At midday Ashdod will be emptied / and Ekron uprooted. / [5]Woe to you who live by the sea, / O Kerethite people; / the word of the LORD**

---

[29]Chisholm, *Minor Prophets*, p. 207.

**is against you, / O Canaan, land of the Philistines. / "I will destroy you, / and none will be left." / [6]The land by the sea, where the Kerethites[a] dwell, / will be a place for shepherds and sheep pens. / [7]It will belong to the remnant of the house of Judah; / there they will find pasture. / In the evening they will lie down / in the houses of Ashkelon. / The LORD their God will care for them; / he will restore their fortunes.[b]**

[a]6 The meaning of the Hebrew for this word is uncertain.      [b]7 Or *will bring back their captives*

Zephaniah 2:4-7 presents the first of four prophecies of punishments in the chapter. This prophecy concerns Judah's neighbor to the west, Philistia, and describes the depopulation of its major urban centers (vv. 4-5) and the subsequent restoration of the pastoral viability of the land for Judah (vv. 6-7). Generally prophecy of punishment contains a description of punishment and an accusation which provides reasons for the divine action; here only the announcement of punishment is given. The particle "woe" does not function in verse 5 as a distinct genre marker (see comments on Nahum 3:1 on the woe oracle) but rather evokes the mood of lamentation and connects the prophecies against the nations with the prophecy concerning Jerusalem in 3:1-7, which also begins with the word "woe."[30]

**2:4** The first word of the Hebrew text, generally translated "for" (כִּי, *kî*) but not present in the NIV (cf. ESV, KJV, NASB, NJB, NRSV) makes this verse an integral link between the preceding section (vv. 1-3) and those following (vv. 5-15). Whereas verses 2-3 present theoretical scenarios of the future, verses 4-15 clearly demonstrate Yahweh's intentions to punish the nations that surround Judah: Philistia to the west, Moab and Ammon to the east, Cush to the south, and Assyria to the north. Specifically, verses 4-7 indicate that the doom of the Philistines portends the future of Jerusalem and Judah should the people not follow the prophet's call to seek Yahweh.[31] The four cities listed in verse 4, **Gaza, Ashkelon, Ashdod,** and **Ekron,** represent the whole of Philistia; only Gath of the ancient league of Philistine cities is not mentioned (cf. Josh 13:3; 1 Sam

---

[30]Michael H. Floyd, *Minor Prophets: Part 2*, FOTL 22 (Grand Rapids: Eerdmans, 2000), p. 219.

[31]Sweeney, *Zephaniah*, p. 112.

6:17), but the Assyrian king Sargon II (721–705 B.C.) has already taken Gath in the eleventh year of his reign (ca. 712–711 B.C.). The cities are listed from south to north, which may reflect an invasion against them from the south by the Egyptians. The meaning of **at midday Ashdod will be emptied** is uncertain. It might indicate that the destruction of the city would be swift, with the struggle over by noon, or that a sudden attack would come at midday while the city's inhabitants rested. The descriptions of the demise of the Philistine cities Gaza and Ekron bracket verse 4 with elements of wordplay in the Hebrew text between the names of the cities and the description of their judgment, since Gaza (עַזָּה, *'azzāh*) sounds similar to the word **abandon** (עָזוּב, *'āzāb*) and Ekron (עֶקְרוֹן, *'eqrôn*) sounds similar to the word **uproot** (עָקַר, *'āqar*).

**2:5** The inhabitants of the Philistine cities are now addressed directly with the invective particle **woe** (see comments on Nahum 3:1) and the challenge formula, **the word of the LORD is against you** (see comments on Nahum 2:13), but Zephaniah 2:7 indicates that the prophet's concern is really Judah. The Philistines are described with three expressions. Those **who live by the sea** is a suitable geographical designation for the coastal country. **Kerethite people** (1 Sam 30:14; Ezek 25:16) is a term reflecting their origin from the island of Crete (Deut 2:23; Jer 47:4; Amos 9:7). The geographical name **Canaan** is rarely used in connection with the **Philistines** (even if the Philistines occupy part of the territory of Canaan), but here Canaan may be used to recall previous mentions of merchants or handlers of silver (1:11) and to indicate that Philistia shares the same threat of extinction. The final line of verse 5, **I will destroy you, and none will be left**, emphasizes Yahweh's involvement (the TNIV adds, "He says" before the first person statement) in the judgment of the Philistines.

**2:6** The seacoast of Philistia becomes uninhabited but suitable for the care of sheep. The gist of the verse is clear, even if the translation of it is made difficult by the word כְּרֹת (*kᵊrōth*), which is rendered variously as "Crete" (LXX), "Cheroth" (NJPS), "Kerethites" (NIV), "cottages" (KJV), "caves" (NASB), "pastures" (ESV, NJB, and NRSV), and "wells" (TNIV). Nonetheless, the word undoubtedly makes a play on the word **Kerethites** in verse 5 (which is why the NIV translates it this way in v. 6), since the words in both verses contain the same three consonants. Thus, the place of the Kerethites becomes the location of **shepherds**' wells, if as suggested by the TNIV the word is correctly derived from the word כָּרָה (*kārāh*).[32]

**2:7** Moreover, this prophecy of punishment against Philistia holds a positive purpose for Judah: Yahweh preserves **the remnant of the house of Judah** and restores their prosperity in the eventual return to pastoral life (cf. Jer 23:3; Micah 2:12). "Remnant" refers to the small group of people who remain faithful to Yahweh and survive Yahweh's judgment and thereby become the basis for a renewed people of Yahweh (Deut 4:27; 2 Kgs 19:30-31; Isa 10:20-22; 11:12; 37:31-32; 46:3-4; Jer 31:7; Ezek 9:8; 14:22; Joel 2:32; Hag 1:12-14; Zech 8:11-12). Although the theme of the "remnant" usually occurs in texts that anticipate or reflect back upon the Babylonian exile (e.g., Jer 6:9; 23:3; 31:7; Micah 2:12; 4:7; 5:7-8; Hag 1:14; 2:2; Zech 8:6,11,12), its use here (also in 2:9; 3:13) does not mean that it has been added to the text of Zephaniah after the exile. It is quite plausible that the notion of a remnant would naturally attach to those who have survived the various incursions of Assyria into Judah.[33] In fact, Hezekiah requested that Isaiah pray for such a remnant (2 Kgs 19:4; Isa 37:4). The reference to the remnant links the promise of protection to the preceding section (v. 3) and anticipates the inheritance of land in the following one (v. 9). The word translated **care for** (פָּקַד, *pāqad*) reverses the earlier uses of *pāqad* in 1:8-9 and 12 (cf. 3:7), where it is translated "punish" (see comments on 1:8-9 above). The last phrase in verse 7 may be translated, **he will restore their fortunes**, or as in the NIV text note, "he will bring back their captives." The difficulty results from an uncertainty about whether to read a Hebrew word as "fortunes" (NASB, NET, NIV, NJB, and NRSV) or "captivity" (KJV), a difference of only one vowel. The ancient versions (Greek, Aramaic, Syriac, and Latin) favor the reading "he will restore their captivity" or "he will bring back their captives." The threat that Yahweh would express punishment for the nation's sins through deportation (Deut 28:32,36,49-52,64) and the promise that Yahweh would gather the penitent people from among the nations (Deut 30:1-5) support the likelihood of this reading. The difference between the two translations, however, is slight; "restore their fortunes" is more general, while "restore their captives" is

---

[32]BDB, p. 500; cf. Gen 26:25 and Num 21:18.
[33]Sweeney, *Zephaniah*, p. 140.

more specific. Both communicate the desire of Yahweh to restore Judah after a time of misfortune or punishment.

## B. ANNOUNCEMENT OF JUDGMENT AGAINST MOAB AND AMMON (2:8-11)

[8]"I have heard the insults of Moab / and the taunts of the Ammonites, / who insulted my people / and made threats against their land. / [9]Therefore, as surely as I live," / declares the LORD Almighty, the God of Israel, / "surely Moab will become like Sodom, / the Ammonites like Gomorrah— / a place of weeds and salt pits, / a wasteland forever. / The remnant of my people will plunder them; / the survivors of my nation will inherit their land."
[10]This is what they will get in return for their pride, / for insulting and mocking the people of the LORD Almighty. / [11]The LORD will be awesome to them / when he destroys all the gods of the land. / The nations on every shore will worship him, / every one in its own land.

Zephaniah 2:8-11 presents the second of four prophecies of punishment in the chapter. This prophecy concerns Judah's neighbors to the east, Moab and Ammon. It describes the actions of the "awesome" Yahweh who responds to their aggression against the people of Yahweh (v. 8), accomplishes their complete desolation (vv. 9-10), and defeats all gods of the land (v. 11). This prophecy differs from the previous one in at least four ways. One, it does not address Moab and Ammon directly, as verses 4-7 do with Philistia. Two, it makes a specific accusation against the two nations, namely, their insults and taunts against the people of Yahweh. Three, it grounds the actions of Yahweh in a divine oath (v. 9), instead of introducing the announcement of punishment with the word "woe." Four, it depicts a judgment of desolation (cf. Gen 19:24-25), while the territory of Philistia holds a positive pastoral purpose for Judah.

**2:8 Moab** and Ammon are located east of Judah. Moab's land is bordered on the west by the Dead Sea, on the north by the Arnon River, on the east by the desert, and on the south by Edom. North of Moab is Ammon, bordered on the west by the Jordan River, on the north by the Jabbok River, on the east by the desert, and on the south by the Arnon River. This judgment speech makes specific accusation against Moab and Ammon: they insult and threaten the people of Yahweh.[34] The prophet makes a double use of a pair of verbs in verses 8 and 10, חָרַף (ḥārāph), translated **insulted** and "insulting," and גָּדַל (gādāl), translated "make **threats**" and "mocking." The verb gādāl denotes the self-aggrandizement of the Moabites and Ammonites against Yahweh's people. This first use in verse 8, parallel to an accusation that Moab and Ammon insult the people of Yahweh, describes their actions in political-military terms, that is, they make threats against Judah's land. The second use of gādāl connects their actions with the divine name, "the LORD Almighty" or in other versions "the LORD of Hosts," that is, they mock the people of Yahweh. The only appearances of the divine name "the LORD Almighty" in the book (vv. 9-10) are quite appropriate. The name literally means "Yahweh of the armies" and connotes Yahweh's sovereign power and authority over all armies (e.g., angels, Israel, and the nations) and over all natural forces (e.g., wind, rain, earthquake, and locust). Yahweh is the powerful God of Israel who can rescue the remnant from Moab and Ammon. The verb ḥārāph denotes insult, reviling, derision, or blasphemy. It appears in the account of the taunting of Hezekiah and Judah by the Assyrian king Sennacherib (2 Kgs 19:4,16,22,23; Isa 37:4,17,23,24). A descendant of Hezekiah recalls the punishment of those who insult Yahweh and the people of Yahweh, and he anticipates another such visitation by Yahweh. In the account of David and Goliath, the one who defies the ranks of Israel (1 Sam 17:10,25,26,36) is also seen as defying "the LORD Almighty, the God of the armies of Israel" (1 Sam 17:45).

**2:9** Two rhetorical features in verse 9 signal the certainty of the judgment coming to Moab and Ammon. First, the introductory particle **therefore** typically introduces the announcement of punishment in the judgment speech. Second, a compound oath formula contains the oath **as surely as I live** and the oath formula **declares the LORD Almighty, the God of Israel**. This construction has its nearest parallels in 1 Samuel 2:30 and Isaiah 17:6. Isaiah 17:6, however, lacks the introductory particle "therefore," and neither passage includes the declaration "as surely as I live" or the mention of

---

[34]On the hostility of Moab and Ammon toward Judah, see Judg 11:13; Ezek 25:2-7; and Amos 1:13–2:3.

"armies" (translated "Almighty" in the NIV). The standard oath "as surely as I live" emphasizes the commitment of Yahweh to what the prophet announces. The full designation "the LORD Almighty, the God of Israel" appears elsewhere in the accounts of Yahweh's covenant with David (2 Sam 7:27; 1 Chr 17:24), in calls for Yahweh to save the people (Ps 59:5; Isa 37:16), and in contexts of hope in Jeremiah (e.g., Jer 31:23; 34:14-15). However, the designation primarily occurs in judgment speeches proclaiming the imminent destruction of Judah and of those seeking refuge in Egypt (e.g., Jer 19:3; 35:17; 42:15-18; 44:2-11). Its use here in verse 9 takes its place among other uses where a proclamation of judgment on a gentile nation is linked directly to Israel or Judah's salvation or restoration (Isa 21:8-10; Jer 46:25-28; 50:18-20; 51:33-44). This use of the divine description echoes David's use of the title to designate the one whom Goliath defies and to name the one who gives David victory (1 Sam 17:45).

The similes comparing **Moab** and **Ammon** to **Sodom** and **Gomorrah** (Gen 19:12-29; cf. Amos 4:11) suggest the extent of both their depravity and their impending destruction. It also links their demise with their origins,[35] since the nations of Moab and Ammon originate from the incestuous unions of Lot with his two daughters (Gen 19:30-38). While Lot escapes Sodom and Gomorrah with his daughters, ironically divine judgment now catches up with him. **Weeds** is an image of depopulation and desolation (cf. "briars" in Isa 5:6; 7:23-25), and **salt pits**, a figure of sterility and barrenness. However, just as the remnant of the house of Judah takes possession of the Philistine lands (vv. 6-7), so also the remnant of Yahweh's people, that is, the remnant of Yahweh's nation, inherit the land of Moab and Ammon (v. 9).

**2:10** The judgment saying concludes with a climactic announcement that the destruction of Moab and Ammon is a sign of Yahweh's victory over the gods of the nations and the future worship of Yahweh by the nations. The word translated **pride** (גָּאוֹן, gāʾôn) in the judgment of Ammon and Moab plays a substantial part in Isaiah's depiction of the day of Yahweh. It is used positively in a threefold refrain (where the NIV translates it as "majesty") that speaks of prideful and arrogant men who "will flee from the dread of the

[35]Sweeney, *Zephaniah*, p. 139.

LORD and the splendor of his majesty" (Isa 2:10,19,21). It is used negatively in the description of the day of Yahweh as a day in which Yahweh puts an end to the arrogance of the haughty (Isa 13:11). Moab and Ammon have insulted the people of Yahweh. This verb rendered **insulting** (*ḥārāph*), signifying a treatment with contempt, insult, or reproach, appears earlier in verse 8 where it speaks of their contemptuous treatment of Yahweh's people. Goliath and Sennacherib, king of Assyria, show reproach for Israel and Israel's God before their demise (1 Sam 17:10,25-26,36,45; 2 Kgs 19:4,16,22-23; 2 Chr 32:17; Isa 37:4,17,23-24), and the psalmists beseech Yahweh to take action against those who reproach Yahweh and his people (Ps 42:10; 74:10,18; 89:50-51; 102:8).

**2:11** Verse 11 describes the effects of Yahweh's judgment upon the nations as it relates to their gods. The word **awesome** (יָרֵא, *yārē'*) has the basic meaning in its passive form of "be fearful, cause astonishment, and inspire awe."[36] In the Old Testament, it is a common description for Yahweh and Yahweh's actions (Deut 7:21; 10:17,21; 1 Sam 12:18; Neh 1:5; 4:14; 9:32; Ps 47:2; 68:35; 76:7; 99:3; 106:22; 111:9; 145:6; Isa 64:2; Dan 9:4; Mal 1:14) and even for the day of Yahweh (Joel 2:11,31; Mal 4:5). The defeat of nations like Moab and Ammon demonstrates Yahweh's awesome superiority over foreign gods, that is, Yahweh **destroys** these pagan **gods** by destroying the nations who depend on them. In this way, Yahweh removes the temptation for the people of Yahweh to worship these foreign gods (cf. the earlier denunciation of idolatry in 1:4-6).[37] The expectation of Yahweh's **worship** among the nations after this victory over their gods provides a transition between the prophecy of punishment against Moab and Ammon and the pronouncements against Cush and Assyria. The same God who has power over those nations close to Judah also demonstrates authority over those nations more powerful and farther away. This anticipation of Yahweh's awesome display of power over the gods of the nations is also anticipated in the Psalms (Ps 47:2; 76:12). In contrast to prophetic texts in the so-called "Zion tradition" that picture the worship of Yahweh by the nations as pilgrimages of those peoples to Zion or Jerusalem (Isa 2:2-4; Micah 4:1-5; Zech 14:16-19), Zephaniah pictures this worship occur-

---

[36]BDB, p. 431.
[37]Floyd, *Minor Prophets*, p. 225.

ring in each nation's own territory (cf. Isa 19:19-25; Mal 1:14).[38] The nations are no longer merely the recipients of divine judgment, since Zephaniah 2:11 describes their conversion and thereby possible inclusion in the remnant of Yahweh's people (2:3,7,9); in chapter 3, the promise of salvation to the nations (3:9-10) actually precedes the promise to Israel (3:12-18).[39]

## C. ANNOUNCEMENT OF JUDGMENT AGAINST CUSH (2:12)

[12]**"You too, O Cushites,**[a] / **will be slain by my sword."**

[a]*12 That is, people from the upper Nile region*

Zephaniah 2:12 presents the third of four prophecies of punishments in the chapter. This one mentions briefly Cush, an ancient designation of the territory on the Upper Nile, south of Egypt, sometimes translated Ethiopia in other versions. The prophecy directly addresses the Cushites and describes their punishment by Yahweh's sword. The verse connects with the previous mention of the nations from every shore in verse 11, as the prophet shifts from Judah's immediate neighbors to the powerful nations of Egypt and Assyria. Possibly the prophecy assumes that Yahweh has already punished Egypt, and thus it serves as a transitional unit in anticipation of the prophet's greater concern with Assyria in verses 13-15.

**2:12** Verse 12 begins with the particle **too** which serves both to link the section to the preceding text and to establish it as a new judgment speech against Cush. Although Moses' Midianite wife Zipporah is referred to as a "Cushite" (Num 12:1) and "Cushan" elsewhere parallels "Midian" (Hab 3:7), most uses of the term "Cush" (see comments on Nahum 3:9) in the Old Testament refer to the territory of the upper Nile region (2 Kgs 19:9; Esth 1:1; 8:9; Job 28:19; Ps 87:4; Isa 11:11; 18:1; 20:3-5; 37:9; 43:3; 45:14; Jer 46:9; Ezek 29:10; 30:4,5,9; 38:5; Nahum 3:9). The **sword** is used elsewhere in the Old Testament as a metaphor for physical harm (Zech 11:17),

---

[38]Roberts, *Nahum, Habakkuk, and Zephaniah*, p. 202.

[39]Paul R. House, *Old Testament Theology* (Downers Grove, IL: InterVarsity, 1998), p. 382; Brevard S. Childs, *Introduction to the Old Testament as Scripture* (Philadelphia: Fortress, 1979), pp. 459-460.

death (Amos 9:4), or judgment via war (Jer 14:12-18; 21:7,9; 24:10; Ezek 14:17,21). The image of Yahweh's sword depicts divine judgment upon the disobedient and the enemies of Israel (Deut 32:41; Ps 7:12-13; Isa 31:8; 34:6; 66:16; Jer 12:12; 47:6; Ezek 21:8-17,28-32). The NIV obscures the shift from second to third person in the middle of the verse, which could be rendered: "Also you Cushites, slain by my sword are they." The third person perspective at the end confirms that the initial second person address to Cush is a fictive address actually intended for an audience in Jerusalem or Judah. Although the NIV translates verse 12 as a future event, no verb appears in the verse. Therefore, the verse may possibly refer to a present or past phenomenon. That the **Cushites** have not ruled Egypt since their defeat by the Assyrians in 663 B.C. suggests that the verse represents a past event.[40] Such a reference, moreover, provides a powerful portent for the coming fall of Nineveh and Assyria spoken of in verses 13-15.

## D. ANNOUNCEMENT OF JUDGMENT AGAINST ASSYRIA (2:13-15)

[13]**He will stretch out his hand against the north** / **and destroy Assyria,** / **leaving Nineveh utterly desolate** / **and dry as the desert.** / [14]**Flocks and herds will lie down there,** / **creatures of every kind.** / **The desert owl and the screech owl** / **will roost on her columns.** / **Their calls will echo through the windows,** / **rubble will be in the doorways,** / **the beams of cedar will be exposed.** / [15]**This is the carefree city** / **that lived in safety.** / **She said to herself,** / **"I am, and there is none besides me."** / **What a ruin she has become,** / **a lair for wild beasts!** / **All who pass by her scoff** / **and shake their fists.**

---

[40]Sweeney, *Zephaniah*, p. 146. By equating Cush with Egypt, Eakin, "Zephaniah," p. 285, attempts to connect the origin of the prophecy with Egypt's conquering of Judah and the deportation of Jehoahaz in 609 B.C. (2 Kgs 23:31-34) or with the defeat of Egypt and Assyria by the Babylonians and Medes at Carchemish in 605 B.C., but Roberts, *Nahum, Habakkuk, Zephaniah*, p. 202, finds such specific identifications doubtful.

Zephaniah 2:13-15 presents the fourth of four prophecies of punishment in the chapter. This prophecy concerns the downfall of Assyria and its capital city, Nineveh, whose destruction represents the demise of the entire nation. In contrast to the cities of Philistia (vv. 6-7) which become usable pastureland, Nineveh becomes a desolate wilderness inhabited by wild animals (vv. 13-15). The section offers neither direct accusation against Assyria nor an explicit description of the benefits of such punishment for Judah; instead the prophecy focuses on Yahweh's actions (v. 13) and the effects of Yahweh's actions (v. 14). It ends with a brief taunt (v. 15) that contrasts Nineveh's exaggerated claim about her self-sufficiency with the certainty of her destruction, now expressed as a past event and one which incites the derision of passersby.

**2:13** Verses 13-15 announce the impending destruction of Assyria, whose destruction is the worst of the nations in chapter 2, perhaps because they stand as a real enemy to Judah (suggesting that Zephaniah is written before Nineveh's fall in 612 B.C.). The Arabian Desert to the east of the Levant (i.e., the entire region on the eastern shore of the Mediterranean Sea) makes any direct route to Judah or Israel from Mesopotamia impossible; therefore, the biblical writers typically depict Mesopotamian enemies as coming from the north rather than the east. Furthermore, an invasion from the north is most feared because of Jerusalem's vulnerability from that direction (cf. Jer 1:15). The image of **stretch**ing **out** the **hand** is used prominently to portray judgment in the plague narratives of Exodus (7:19; 8:5; 9:22,23; 10:12,13,21,22; 14:16,21,26,27; 15:12) and in Isaiah (5:25; 9:12,17,21; 10:4; 14:27; 23:11; 31:3). The representation of **Nineveh** as **dry as the desert** reverses typical depictions of the well-watered city that is located on the Tigris River and has a canal running through its center.[41]

**2:14** The city of Nineveh is transformed into an area now inhabited by both domesticated and wild animals. While **flocks and herds** refer to animals in general, especially sheep, cattle, and goats, the identification of the two birds mentioned is somewhat uncertain. Most modern translations identify the קָאַת (qā'ath) as a type of owl (e.g., NIV and NRSV read **desert owl**, and NEB, "horned owl"), but other versions identify it as a seabird, following the Peshitta and

---

[41]Sweeney, *Zephaniah*, p. 152.

Vulgate, and render it as "cormorant" (KJV) or "pelican" (NASB, NJB). Nineveh's geographical location and its dry description in this context, however, make "pelican" an unlikely option. Both the context and the use of the term in other passages also make the LXX translation "chameleon" doubtful. The creature's voice **will echo through the windows**, and Leviticus 11:13-18 and Deuteronomy 14:17 indicate it is an unclean bird of some sort (cf. "jackdaw" in the NJPS). A variety of suggestions attend קִפֹּד (*qippôd*), and no agreement exists even to what class of animal it belongs. Some understand it to be a bird (NIV and NRSV **screech owl** and KJV "bittern"), but others translate it as a mammal such as a "hedgehog" (NASB) or "porcupine" (NJB). While one might naturally associate birds with animals that reside on **columns**, it is also plausible that rodents could live on the ruins of erect or fallen columns. The **beams of cedar** that no doubt lined the inner rooms of important buildings are now **exposed**. This may refer either to exposure to the elements caused by collapsed roofs and walls or to cedar walls that have been stripped of the gold that once overlaid them (cf. 1 Kgs 6:20-22).[42]

**2:15** Verse 15 is a summary that reflects on the downfall of the city and whose time perspective differs from the two preceding verses. Verses 13-14 speak of the city's fall in the future, but verse 15 speaks of it as a past event. The shift in perspective connotes the certainty of what Yahweh has decreed. Nineveh is characterized as a **carefree city** (cf. TNIV's "city of revelry") **that lived in safety**. This noun appears frequently as part of Old Testament blessings and promises of a secure life (Lev 25:18-19; 26:5; Deut 12:10; Jer 23:6; 32:37; 33:16), but the term also often refers to a false security one possesses before a great calamity (cf. Judg 18:7; Isa 47:8; Jer 49:31). The prophet quotes Nineveh's boasts of self-sufficiency with great irony (cf. similar boasts of Babylon in Isa 47:8-10). The last half of verse 15 begins with the exclamation **What** (cf. "How" in the NASB), a particle often used in contexts of extreme shock or disbelief (Judg 16:15; 1 Sam 16:2; 2 Sam 1:19,25,27; 6:9; Ps 73:19; Isa 14:4,12; Jer 2:21; 9:19; 48:39; 50:23; 51:41; Ezek 26:17; Obad 6). Jeremiah 50:23 and 51:41 use similar language to speak of Babylon's end. The reference to **lair for wild beasts** reflects the depiction in the previous

---

[42]Sweeney, *Zephaniah*, p. 154.

verse. The picture of passersby **scoff**ing, hissing, whistling, **shak**ing **their fists**, or making hand gestures is a common Old Testament image of derision (1 Kgs 9:8; Jer 18:16; 19:8; 49:17; 50:13; Lam 2:15; Ezek 27:36). The prophecy of punishment against Assyria may have been placed last in this series to emphasize Yahweh's intention to rescue Judah from the Assyrian menace.

## E. CHARGE OF FAILURE TO REPENT AGAINST JERUSALEM (3:1-7)

[1]**Woe to the city of oppressors, / rebellious and defiled! /** [2]**She obeys no one, / she accepts no correction. / She does not trust in the LORD, / she does not draw near to her God. /** [3]**Her officials are roaring lions, / her rulers are evening wolves, / who leave nothing for the morning. /** [4]**Her prophets are arrogant; / they are treacherous men. / Her priests profane the sanctuary / and do violence to the law. /** [5]**The LORD within her is righteous; / he does no wrong. / Morning by morning he dispenses his justice, / and every new day he does not fail, / yet the unrighteous know no shame.**

[6]**"I have cut off nations; / their strongholds are demolished. / I have left their streets deserted, / with no one passing through. / Their cities are destroyed; / no one will be left—no one at all. /** [7]**I said to the city, / 'Surely you will fear me / and accept correction!' / Then her dwelling would not be cut off, / nor all my punishments come upon her. / But they were still eager / to act corruptly in all they did.**

Zephaniah 3:1-7 consists of a prophetic charge of failure to repent, a form which is similar to a prophecy of punishment but with the accusation more specifically developed (e.g., Jer 15:5-9; 25:1-14). The accusation is generally comprised of two parts: a prophetic claim that certain behavior stands opposed to Yahweh and a prophetic assertion that such behavior has not been reversed.[43] Often the sections are connected by an adversative conjunction (e.g., Amos 4:6-11), here translated in the NIV as "yet" (וְלֹא, *wəlōʾ*) in 3:5 and "but" (אָכֵן, *ʾākēn*) in 3:7. The section begins with the particle

---

[43]Floyd, *Minor Prophets*, p. 637.

"woe" (v. 1), which connects it verbally with the preceding series of prophecies of punishment against the nations (2:5-15). But now the one addressed is the city of Jerusalem, although not specifically identified but here described as "the city of oppressors, rebellious, and defiled." The city has failed to heed the call to repentance and to be true to Yahweh (v. 2), failures which are attributed primarily to a corrupt leadership (vv. 3-4). The justice of Yahweh stands in contrast to the incorrigibility of Jerusalem (v. 5), and Yahweh's punishment of the nations and their cities (v. 6) stands in contrast to Jerusalem's failure to accept correction and eagerness to act corruptly (v. 7). Thus, 3:1-7 explains the reason for the punishment described but serves also as a prophetic exhortation, extending yet another opportunity for repentance and providing the basis for the following exhortation to wait on Yahweh in verse 8.

Chapter 3 begins with the particle "woe," as does 2:5 above, but its opening words do not clearly identify the one against whom it is directed. An ancient reader whose Scripture does not possess the chapter and verse numbers or the section headings that appear in modern Bibles may not have sensed that the words against Nineveh have ended. Zephaniah's audience very well may have used the words of 3:1 to characterize Nineveh as a "city of oppressors, rebellious, and defiled" (cf. Jonah 1:2 and Nahum 3:1). They might also have typified Nineveh as disobedient, accepting of no correction, and lacking trust in Yahweh (Zeph 3:2). The LXX and Peshitta both reflect such an association of the passage with Nineveh. The LXX reads Zephaniah 2:15 as the first verse of chapter 3, and the Peshitta adds, "and he shall say," to the end of 2:15, thus linking the opening of chapter 3 with words spoken against Nineveh. Nevertheless, the last line of verse 2, "she does not draw near to *her* God" (emphasis added), together with references to the priests' profaning of the sanctuary and doing violence to the torah (3:4) make it clear that the prophecy of punishment is directed against Jerusalem. The delay of a clear identification of the prophecy's object lends greater rhetorical power to its accusation of the city and its leaders. Jerusalem's unrighteousness and failure to give heed to Yahweh's instruction has rendered her little better than Nineveh. This rhetorical ploy is akin to Amos 1–2 that also involves the audience in self-condemnation, but it has a different objective. The stinging accusation of

Zephaniah 3:1-4 sets the stage for the prophet's announcement of the transformation Yahweh will bring for his people.[44]

**3:1** In 1:4-9, the first indictment of Judah focuses on the worship of other gods; at this point the indictment focuses on the failures of Jerusalem's corrupt political and religious leadership. Verse 1 makes a general accusation (on "woe" see 2:5 above) against Jerusalem, here characterized as oppressive (no longer a place for justice), **rebellious** (no longer the bride of Yahweh), and **defiled** (no longer consecrated to Yahweh).[45] The word translated **oppressors** appears most frequently as part of the Mosaic legislation for the protection of the resident alien, a requirement based in the experience of slavery in Egypt (Exod 22:21; Lev 19:33; 25:14,17; Deut 23:16; Jer 22:3; Ezek 18:7-16; 22:7,29), but it also occurs elsewhere in description of Jerusalem's corrupt leaders who have turned from Yahweh (Ezek 45:8; 46:18). "Rebellious" translates a word which often describes the failure of Jerusalem and Judah to obey Yahweh's commands (Isa 3:8; 30:9; 63:10; Jer 4:17; 5:23; Ezek 2:5-6; 3:9,26,27; 5:6). The word translated "defiled" also appears in Isaiah 59:3 and Lamentations 4:14 to describe those who have been stained with the blood of their victims.

**3:2** Verses 2-4 expand the general accusation against Jerusalem in the preceding verse, describing in greater detail the sins of the city and her corrupt political and religious leadership. Specifically, Jerusalem refuses to complete four actions: to listen, accept **correction**, **trust in the LORD**, and worship Yahweh **her God**. The word translated **obey** in the NIV is rendered "listen" in other versions (cf. ESV, NJB, and NRSV); the word means to listen with the result of obedience (e.g., Isa 1:19; Micah 5:15; Jer 12:17). In this context, **draw near** refers to the approach of Yahweh in worship, especially regarding the proper presentation of one's offering to Yahweh (Exod 3:5; Lev 4:14; 9:4-10; Num 16:17; 18:15; Deut 5:23,27; cf. Jer 30:21).

**3:3** Four leadership categories are specifically listed in verses 3 and 4, each class corrupted in its own way. First, **official** (שַׂר, śar) is a general word for leader, military commander, prince, or royal official (Num 21:18; Josh 5:14-15; Judg 4:2; 9:22; 1 Sam 17:55; 22:2;

---

[44]Sweeney, *Zephaniah*, p. 162.
[45]Vogels, "Zephaniah," p. 1178.

2 Chr 21:9; 31:8; Isa 10:8; Jer 26:11). The NIV does not translate the expression "within her" (cf. ESV, KJV, NASB, NJPS) that appears here and then in verse 5. This repetition creates a contrast between the officials within Jerusalem and Yahweh who also is within the city. Second, the NIV translates as **rulers** a form of the verb שָׁפַט (*šāphaṭ*), a verb characteristically associated with judgment and justice. Its broadest denotation, however, is with vindication or rescue, and the Old Testament uses it to describe the activities of leaders of Israel (cf. Judg 2:16,17,18,19; 3:10; 10:2-3; 12:7-14; 15:20; 16:31). Thus, while "judges" may be a better translation (cf. ESV, KJV, NASB, NJB, NRSV, NJPS), "ruler" or "leader" is also acceptable. Although the terms "officials" and "rulers" represent secular leaders, significantly the king is not mentioned. The lack of condemnation for a king in the midst of a description of the corruption among Judah's secular and religious leaders probably reflects the prophet's support of the king Josiah (640–609 B.C.) either before his reforms or during their early stages.[46] The rulers or judges act as **evening wolves, who leave nothing for the morning**. This metaphor highlights both the presumption with which the dishonest officials pervert justice in Judah and the helplessness of their victims. The blessings of Jacob on his sons depict Judah as a lion (Gen 49:9; cf. Ps 22:12-21 where the sufferer is threatened by roaring lions) and Dan as a ravenous wolf (Gen 49:27) in order to portray the virtues of courage and strength. Here, however, the prophet uses the images to depict the leaders' perversion of their power to oppress their own countrymen.[47]

**3:4** Third, Zephaniah characterizes the **prophets** as **arrogant** and **treacherous men**, his only recorded accusation of the prophets. The word "arrogant" denotes recklessness (cf. NASB and NRSV) and compulsiveness (Judg 9:4). Elsewhere it describes Reuben's sleeping with Jacob's concubine Bilhah (Gen 49:4), the brigands that assembled around Abimelech (Judg 9:4), and the reckless lies uttered by false prophets (Jer 23:32). These contexts, as in verse 4, involve improper acts of those taking false prerogatives. "Treacherous" translates a common word, signifying deceit, betrayal, and unfaithfulness (Exod 21:8; Judg 9:23; Job 6:15; Ps 59:5; Prov 11:3; Jer 3:7-11,20; Mal 2:10-16). Fourth, Zephaniah charges that **priests profane**

---

[46]Sweeney, *Zephaniah*, p. 159.
[47]Roberts, *Nahum, Habakkuk, and Zephaniah*, p. 213.

**the sanctuary and do violence to the law** (cf. Ezek 22:26). This is especially telling in light of the requirement in Leviticus 10:10 for them to distinguish between the holy and the common, between the unclean and the clean, and to teach the Israelites all the decrees Yahweh has given them through Moses (cf. Jer 2:8; 18:18; Mal 2:7). The word translated "do violence" designates an extreme, sinful violence such as social injustice, murder, or plunder (Gen 49:5; Judg 9:24; Jer 51:46; Hab 1:9; 2:8,17). It appears in the preexilic prophets mainly in contexts speaking of the exploitation of the poor and weak by rich landowners and rulers (e.g., Jer 22:3). The priests do violence to the law or torah. The common translation of the noun תּוֹרָה (tôrāh) as "law" tends to obscure the positive connotations of this word which derives from a causative form of the word "to guide." Modern culture views law as a restricting thing, but its Old Testament uses often signify beneficial and authoritative instruction or guidance (Job 22:22; Prov 1:8; 3:1; 4:2; 6:20,23; 7:2; Isa 1:10; 2:2; 5:24; 8:16,20; 30:9; Jer 8:8; Micah 4:4).

**3:5** The fifth verse constitutes a key shift in theme, since it begins a portrayal of Yahweh's righteousness in contrast to the previous portrayal of Jerusalem's leaders. The statement that **the LORD within her is righteous** anticipates a later affirmation that "the LORD your God is with you" (v. 17) and is the foundation for the promises in the following sections (3:6-13,14-20). Moreover, the use of the phrase "within her" again in verse 5 creates a contrast between the officials within Jerusalem (v. 3) and Yahweh who also is within her. The word group of which "righteous" (צַדִּיק, ṣaddîq) is a member denotes conformity to a standard. When applied to Yahweh as here, the standard is the nature and will of Yahweh.[48] The prophet's use of "righteous" to describe Yahweh in a context preceding the announcement of salvation (vv. 8-20) is reminiscent of the nuanced use of the word group in the Psalms and Isaiah where the righteousness of Yahweh is seen in parallel with the acts of salvation and deliverance (Ps 24:5; 35:24; 40:9-10; 51:14; 65:5; 71:2; 71:15-16; 98:2; Isa 59:9-17; 61:10-11; 62:1-2; 63:1). The description of Yahweh in verse 5 looks forward and backward. It functions as an introduction to the following Yahweh speech in verses 6-13 by showing the legitimacy of punishments he will dispense and the rationale for the salvation he will bestow. For

---

[48]Harold G. Stigers, "צָדֵק," *TWOT*, 2:754.

example, its description of Yahweh as one who **dispenses justice** (מִשְׁפָּט, *mišpāṭ*) **morning by morning** anticipates Yahweh's decision (also *mišpāṭ* but translated "I have decided" in the NIV) to assemble the nations in order to pour out his wrath upon them (v. 8). It looks backward by repeating the word "morning" from verse 3 and, in doing so, shows that Yahweh vindicates those who have been oppressed. Whereas Jerusalem's corrupt leaders leave nothing for the morning, Yahweh dispenses his justice morning by morning (cf. Lam 3:22-23). However, in spite of the clear evidence of Yahweh's righteous actions, the **unrighteous** disregard their own **shame**, that is, they do not perceive their own guilt and are indifferent about Yahweh's judgment of the nations (v. 6).[49]

**3:6** In verses 6-7, Yahweh directly addresses the city. In verse 6, Yahweh recounts the destruction of Judah's enemies, a reminder intended as a warning to Judah. In particular, Yahweh punishes the **nations** (2:4-15) so that Judah would repent (2:1-3) and receive future promises (3:8-20). The noun translated **strongholds** has the basic meaning of "corner" (Exod 27:2; 38:2; 2 Kgs 14:13) or "cornerstone" (Job 38:6). It appears earlier modifying the noun "towers" (1:16); in both occurrences in Zephaniah, described are key points in a defensive wall. Second Chronicles 26:15 uses this noun to designate Jerusalem's "corner defenses." Since a cornerstone is a pivotal structure in a building, the noun comes to denote a leading element or leader (Judg 20:2; 1 Sam 14:38; Isa 19:13; Zech 10:4). The basic meaning of the verb form translated **deserted** by the NIV is "be dried up" (Gen 8:13; Judg 16:7-8; 2 Kgs 19:24; Job 14:11; Ps 106:9; Isa 11:15; 19:5-6; 44:27; 51:10; Nahum 1:4). Its use to describe the disappearance of previously existing waters leads, as here, to a metaphorical sense of destruction, devastation, or disappearance (Judg 16:24; 2 Kgs 19:17; Isa 34:10; 37:18; 42:15; 60:12; Ezek 6:6; Amos 7:9).

Two specific elements link verse 6 to previous proclamations of judgment within the book. One, the phrases **with no one passing through** and **no one will be left—no one at all** recall the images of sweeping destruction in 1:2-3. Two, the verb יָשַׁב (*yāšab*, "to dwell"),

---

[49]A. Cohen, *The Twelve Prophets*, 2nd ed., rev. by A.J. Rosenberg, Soncino Books of the Bible (New York: Soncino, 1994), p. 247.

translated in verse 6 as "be left," links this description of judgment to others in the book where the verb also appears. The first three uses occur in judgment against Jerusalem. Yahweh promises to stretch a hand against those who live in Jerusalem (1:4), commands those who live in the market district to wail (1:11), and declares that those who think Yahweh will do nothing will not dwell in houses they have built (1:13). The fourth use echoes the book's initial theme of the destruction of all who live on the earth (1:18; cf. 1:2-3). The last two uses in the second chapter speak of the elimination of those who dwell in a foreign nation, Kerethites (2:5) and Ninevites (2:15). The words of verse 6 and the words of those earlier passages to which it is linked set the stage for the bewilderment in the prophet's words in verse 7. Should not Jerusalem have been driven to repentance by the previous words of judgment uttered against her and against her enemies?

**3:7** Yahweh continues to address the city in verse 7; the action of Yahweh cutting off the nations is meant to warn Judah, but such warning is to no avail. The word **surely** translates an adverb (אַךְ, *'ak*) that emphasizes the contrast between what follows and what has preceded.[50] Here, it accents the dismay of Yahweh and the prophet who both marvel at Judah's failure to repent in light of Yahweh's previous declarations of judgment. In response to previous actions and words, Yahweh has anticipated that Judah would fear Yahweh. The verb **fear** (יָרֵא, *yārē'*) and its related nouns and adjectives deal with the emotion of fear or dread (Exod 14:13; Deut 1:21; 2:4; 5:5; 1 Sam 7:7), reverence or awe (Exod 14:31; Lev 19:3; 26:2; Ps 112:1), worship (Deut 14:22-23; Josh 22:25; 2 Kgs 17:32-34), or righteous behavior in response to Yahweh's commands (Deut 5:29; 6:2; 31:11-12; Ps 19:7-9). The following phrase, **and accept correction** (i.e., an openness to learn both from experience and from observation), taken together with the descriptions of the wicked in 1:4-6, indicates the "fear" Yahweh has hoped to elicit involves proper worship and behavior. Yahweh's desire for Jerusalem to demonstrate such fear anticipates the later promise of Yahweh's presence with her so that Jerusalem and Zion need never again fear harm (vv. 15-16). That Judah should fear Yahweh is only fitting, for Yahweh is also feared ("be awesome to" in the NIV) by Moab and Ammon "when he

---

[50]BDB, p. 36.

destroys all the gods of the land" (2:11). The desire by Yahweh that the city accept correction mirrors the indictment of the "city of oppressors" that "accepts no correction" (3:2). The noun translated **dwelling place** most often is used to refer to Yahweh's heavenly dwelling place (cf. Deut 26:15; 2 Chr 30:27; Jer 25:30; Zech 2:13) or to Yahweh's dwelling place in the tabernacle or temple (2 Chr 36:15; Ps 26:8). Very rarely does it refer to a place of human habitation, and in those instances, it appears in zoomorphic metaphors of destruction. Nineveh is depicted as a lion's den that is no more (see comments on Nahum 2:11); Jerusalem, towns of Judah, and Babylon are depicted as "haunts" of jackals (Jer 9:11; 10:22; 51:37). The verb **cut off** (כָּרַת, *kārath*) appears four previous times in the book to describe universal destruction (1:3) and the judgment on Jerusalem and Judah (1:4,11). Yahweh's statement about cutting off the nations (3:6) intensifies the expression of Yahweh's longing that Jerusalem's dwelling not be cut off in verse 7. The NIV **my punishments come** translates the verb פָּקַד (*pāqad*), variously translated in the NIV as "punish, count, number, appoint, muster, care" (see comments on 1:8).

Verse 7 ends with the disheartening statement, **But they were still eager to act corruptly in all they did.** This statement begins with an adverb (אָכֵן, *'āken*), translated "but"; it shows an emphatic contrast especially following the verb **I said**, as is the case here.[51] This construction emphasizes the surprising nature of Judah's response. "They were still eager" translates a verb (שָׁכַם, *šākam*) that frequently conveys the idea of early rising. Zephaniah joins his contemporary Jeremiah in using it to connote eagerness or tenacity (see Jer 7:13,25; 11:7; 25:3-4; 26:5; 29:29; 32:33; 35:14, and 44:4 where NIV often translates the word "again and again"). The prophet portrays Yahweh as astonished that Judah not only rejects correction but "gets up early" to sin grievously. In spite of Yahweh's actions, Judah acts corruptly. This description of their behavior links the passage to the Genesis account of the flood. There, the earth is corrupt (Gen 6:11) because all of its people act corruptly (Gen 6:12). Therefore, God decides to corrupt ("destroy" in the NIV) the earth (Gen 6:13,17). This allusion to the Noahic flood, in turn, forms

------

[51]BDB, p. 38.

another link between the present passage and the book's opening
words (1:2-3).

## IV. ANNOUNCEMENT OF SALVATION
## FOR THE REMNANT OF ISRAEL (3:8-20)

The fourth major section of the book consists of two prophetic
exhortations: an exhortation to wait for the action of Yahweh (vv. 8-
13) and an exhortation to rejoice at the promise of Yahweh (vv. 14-
20). The adverb "therefore" marks the beginning of the section and
the speech report formula "says the LORD" marks its ending. Each of
the two units begins with imperatives: "wait" in verse 8 and "sing,
shout, be glad, rejoice" in verse 14. Zephaniah 3:8-20 is addressed to
those identified in the previous unit (vv. 1-7) to persuade the people
of Judah to repent at the prospect of Yahweh reversing the disasters
portrayed earlier in the book and restoring the scattered remnant of
Israel. As a whole, the section emphasizes that Yahweh will gather
first the nations for judgment (v. 8) and then those scattered from
Judah for restoration (v. 18). The verb "gather" (אָסַף, 'āsaph),
appears earlier in the book only in 1:2, where it is translated "sweep
away," so with this word the book has come full circle.

## A. EXHORTATION TO WAIT FOR
## THE ACTION OF YAHWEH (3:8-13)

[8]**Therefore wait for me," declares the LORD, / "for the day I will
stand up to testify.[a] / I have decided to assemble the nations, / to
gather the kingdoms / and to pour out my wrath on them— / all
my fierce anger. / The whole world will be consumed / by the fire
of my jealous anger.**

[9]**"Then will I purify the lips of the peoples, / that all of them
may call on the name of the LORD / and serve him shoulder to
shoulder. / [10]From beyond the rivers of Cush[b] / my worshipers, my
scattered people, / will bring me offerings. / [11]On that day you will
not be put to shame / for all the wrongs you have done to me, /
because I will remove from this city / those who rejoice in their
pride. / Never again will you be haughty / on my holy hill. / [12]But**

I will leave within you / the meek and humble, / who trust in the
name of the LORD. / [13]The remnant of Israel will do no wrong; /
they will speak no lies, / nor will deceit be found in their mouths.
/ They will eat and lie down / and no one will make them afraid."

[a]8 Septuagint and Syriac; Hebrew *will rise up to plunder*     [b]10 That is,
the upper Nile region

Zephaniah 3:8-13 presents the first of two prophetic exhortations
that close the book. The unit is introduced by the adverb "therefore," the command "wait for me," and the oracle formula "declares
the LORD" (v. 8) and provides a supporting motivation for the command in the form of a prophecy of salvation (vv. 9-13). Specifically,
the unit exhorts the people of Judah to wait for the action of
Yahweh and explains what this divine action means for nations of
the world (vv. 8-10) and for the people of Yahweh who trust in
Yahweh (vv. 11-13). The jealous anger (see on 1:18 above) of Yahweh
will consume the whole world, although some among the nations
whose lips are purified will join in the worship of Yahweh. Likewise,
Yahweh will remove the haughty from Jerusalem but leave the remnant of Israel, consisting of the meek and humble who trust in
Yahweh. In this way, 3:8-13 reinforces the earlier exhortation to
repent before the day of Yahweh (2:1-3) but more clearly expresses
the future existence (that is, the remnant will be free of falsehood
and fear) for those who trust in Yahweh.

**3:8** Verse 8 serves as a transition between the indictment of verses 1-7 and the message of restoration and salvation in verses 9-20.[52]
Since the word **therefore** (לָכֵן, *lākēn*) comes after the accusations in
verses 1-7, the reader might expect an announcement of judgment
to follow. The only other use of *lākēn* appears in 2:9, where it precedes the divine declaration of judgment against Moab and Ammon.
However, here it introduces the divine command to wait, the
description of impending judgment against the nations and the
prideful (vv. 8,11), and the more important message of hope that
portrays the reversal of the disasters depicted in the book's opening
sections.[53] The verb **wait** (חָכָה, *ḥākāh*) appears often in contexts

---

[52]Széles, *Wrath and Mercy*, p. 100.
[53]David A. Dorsey, *The Literary Structure of the Old Testament: A Commentary
on Genesis–Malachi* (Grand Rapids: Baker, 1999), p. 313.

where one is living in expectation of Yahweh's deliverance or blessing (Ps 33:20; Isa 8:17; 30:18; 64:4; Hab 2:3). Significantly, the text of Habakkuk follows its call to wait for the timing of Yahweh with a description of Yahweh's judgment on the nations (Hab 2:4-20) and the prophet's statement of trust in Yahweh (Hab 3:1-19). In Zephaniah 3:8, the appearance of a second person masculine plural imperative form (**wait for me**) might cause the reader to note the previous appearance of similar imperatives in 2:1-3 ("gather" and "seek"). The humble remnant of that passage is no doubt the intended recipient of this call to wait for Yahweh.

The text of the NIV (**I will stand up to testify**) reflects the wording of the LXX and Peshitta (the Syriac translation of the Bible), both of which suggest that the purpose for Yahweh's rising is "to testify" rather than "to plunder" (as in the MT). The difference between the readings concerns only one letter, that is, whether the Hebrew word is rightly understood as עֵד (ʿēd) or עַד (ʿad). If the NIV (cf. the NASB and NRSV) is correct to take the term as ʿēd, then the verse uses a legal metaphor to portray Yahweh as testifying against the nations. If, however, the MT and the NIV marginal reading is preferable (cf. the ESV, KJV, NET), then the verse depicts the consumption of the whole world as prey (ʿad appears elsewhere only in Gen 49:27 and Isa 33:23) when Yahweh pours out wrath upon the nations. The context of 3:8 may favor the latter option.[54]

After this notice that Yahweh rises up to plunder, the Hebrew text has three sentences that begin with the particle כִּי (kî); the NIV does not translate the causal particle in any of the three occurrences (cf. "for" in the ESV). The first two describe impending punishments against the nations (v. 8), but the third announces the means by which even the nations will worship Yahweh (v. 9). Yahweh will **assemble** (ʾāsaph) and **gather** (קָבַץ, qābaṣ) **the nations**. These verbs appear in tandem elsewhere in this book (vv. 18-19) and in the Old Testament (Isa 11:12; Ezek 11:17; Micah 2:12; 4:6,11-12) to describe Yahweh's gathering of the remnant. Thus, the announcement here that Yahweh will gather together the nations contains an ironic element of salvation as well as judgment.[55] The coming judgment is here depicted as the consumption of **the whole earth by the fire of**

[54]Sweeney, *Zephaniah*, p. 181.
[55]Ibid.

**[Yahweh's] jealous anger**, an image appearing earlier in Zephaniah (see comments on 1:18 above; cf. also 2:2).

**3:9** While verse 8 refers to the day on which Yahweh consumes the nations with jealous anger, verse 9 speaks of a time (cf. "at that time" in the ESV and NRSV) when Yahweh will convert the nations, an expectation characteristic of the exilic literature (Isa 55:4-5; Micah 4.1-2). No longer do the nations receive merely divine judgment, but surprisingly they too **call on the name of** Yahweh with purified speech. The vocabulary used to describe the purification of the nations' speech is itself telling. The verb translated "turn" or "change" (הָפַךְ, *hāphak*) in some of the other versions (e.g., ESV, KJV, NRSV) denotes a change in the essence of a thing. The account of the signs given to Moses uses it to describe the changing of Moses' staff into a snake (Exod 7:15) and of the Nile's water to blood (Exod 7:17,20). It depicts ferocious upheaval such as the destruction of cities (Gen 19:21,25,29; Lam 4:6; Amos 4:11; Jonah 3:4) or the routing of an enemy (Deut 29:23). The NIV evidently combines the meaning of this verb "I will change" (*hāphak*) and the participle "purified" (that modifies "lip") into the single verb phrase **I will purify**. Thus, the Hebrew text, which is basically "I will change for the people a purified lip," is rendered by the NIV, **I will purify the lips of the peoples** (cf. NLT). The purification of lips stands for the purification (and conversion) of the person (Isa 6:5-7), and this purification of the nations may signal the reversal of the story of Babel (Gen 11:1-9).[56] The word translated "lips" (שָׂפָה, *sāphāh*) also appears in Genesis 11:1,6-7,9 (there translated "language" in the NIV), where it refers to that which Yahweh confused. This language once confused is now recovered through the purification of the lips of the people. With purified speech the nations now call on Yahweh's name rather than on the names of their former gods (cf. Hos 2:17; Zeph 1:4-5) and **serve**, that is, worship (cf. Exod 3:12; 12:31; Deut 6:13; Ps 2:11; Isa 19:21,23; Jer 35:15), Yahweh **shoulder to shoulder**, an image symbolizing unified effort and derived from the yoking together of draft animals (cf. Num 13:23). Here such unity among the nations is based upon the universal recognition of Yahweh.

**3:10** The description of Yahweh's worshipers as **scattered people** provides another parallel with the Babel account (Gen 11:4,8-9)

---

[56]Eakin, "Zephaniah," p. 287; Sweeney, *Zephaniah*, pp. 182-183.

and suggests that foreign nations, rather than merely exiled Israelites, are in view here. Although some uncertainty remains about such an identification, it seems likely for at least four reasons: Cush is named in the verse and Jerusalem is not clearly mentioned until the next verse, the word "peoples" is plural and thus indicates a multinational remnant (the phrase "daughter of" in the Hebrew text, not translated in the NIV but found in the ESV, often denotes the collective inhabitants of a city or land), similar language is used in Psalms 68:29 and 72:10 for the bringing of offerings from the nations, and similar promises are made elsewhere regarding Cush in Isaiah 18:7 and 19:18-25.[57] **Beyond the rivers of Cush** conveys the idea of the most distant regions imaginable (on Cush and its location, see comments at Nahum 3:9 and Zeph 1:1; 2:12 above). The "scattered people" who bring offerings to Yahweh, then, refers to **worshipers** among the nations (cf. 2:11), and these people are the complements of the Daughter of Zion who no longer sorrow over the inability to keep the appointed feasts (3:14,18).[58]

**3:11** From the converted among the nations, the unit (3:8-13) now turns to focus on the removal of the prideful and haughty in Jerusalem and the restoration of the meek and humble. The reference to **that day** recalls earlier references to the "day of Yahweh" (1:7-10,14-16,18; 2:2-3; 3:8). Here (and in 3:16) the phrase indicates a future time following the judgment of the day of Yahweh in which Yahweh's people will realize the scenario the prophet is about to describe in verses 11-20. Furthermore, the middle line of the Hebrew text begins with the words כִּי־אָז (kî-'āz), translated "for then" in most other versions (e.g., ESV, KJV, NASB, NET, NRSV, NJPS). The same two words introduce verse 9, and they generally refer to some future event when followed by an imperfect tense verb (Deut 29:19; Josh 1:8; Job 11:15; 38:21; Jer 22:22). In verse 9 the phrase "for then" anticipates the purification of the lips of the nations; in verse 11 it expects the removal of the prideful from Jerusalem. On that day Jerusalem will no longer be **put to shame** (on "put to shame," see comments on v. 12 below) because those who rejoice in an inordinate sense of their own status and accomplishment will be complete-

[57]House, *Old Testament Theology*, p. 185; Chisholm, *Minor Prophets*, p. 213; and Sweeney, *Zechariah*, p. 185.
[58]Széles, *Wrath and Mercy*, p. 108.

ly removed from the **holy hill**. Old Testament prophetic and poetic texts regularly use the word גָּבַהּ (*gābah*) to describe the haughtiness of men that Yahweh will punish (Ps 131:1; Prov 18:12; Isa 3:16; Jer 13:15; Ezek 16:50; 28:2,5,17; Obad 4), but the writer of Chronicles also describes prominent Davidic kings who succumb to such haughtiness. The pride of Uzziah leads to his downfall when he enters the temple to burn incense to Yahweh (2 Chr 26:16), and Hezekiah becomes proud and does not respond to Yahweh's kindness (2 Chr 32:25). Isaiah describes the day of Yahweh as a day when the arrogant and prideful are destroyed (Isa 2:12,17; 3:16). The adjective עַלִּיז (*'allîz*), translated **rejoice** in the NIV, appears elsewhere six times (Isa 13:3; 22:2; 23:7; 24:8; 32:13; Zeph 2:15), each with a sense of revelry and merriment. The cognate verb translated "exult" appears in verse 14. The contrast between verse 11 and verse 14 highlights the distinction between the arrogance of those who will perish and the humility of the spared remnant in that day.

The significance of the things that will happen "on that day" is magnified by the introduction of second person feminine forms in verses 11-19, which address the personified city of Jerusalem, the place of Yahweh's "holy hill" (Ps 2:6; 24:3; 48:1; Isa 27:13; 56:7; 66:20; Zech 8:3). The NIV adds **this city** to the wording of the verse to clarify the addressee for the modern reader, even though the second singular references continue throughout the verse. The TNIV identifies the addressee as "Jerusalem" but retains one of the second person pronouns in the middle line: "those who revel in your glory." Actually, the Hebrew text of Zephaniah refers to the city by name only four times (1:4,12; 3:14,16) and by the word "city" once (3:1). In this way, the prophet points to a day in which Yahweh will **remove** the arrogant and the prideful from Jerusalem and leave within the city a meek and humble remnant characterized by trust in the name upon which the nations have now also come to call (v. 9).

**3:12** Consequently, there remains a remnant from among Yahweh's covenant people and the nations who are characterized by faith. The imperative of 2:3 is transformed into a promise for **the meek and humble**, who will be saved from the terrible judgment of the day of Yahweh when the arrogant are purged from their midst.[59]

---

[59]Greg A. King, "The Message of Zephaniah: An Urgent Echo," *AUSS* 34 (1996): 216-217.

The term "meek" (עָנִי, ʿānî) typically denotes the poor, needy, or afflicted (e.g., Ps 9:18; 12:5; 22:24; 25:16; 35:10; 37:14; 40:17; 68:10; 70:5; 72:4,12; 74:21; 82:3; 86:1; 109:22; 140:12; Isa 3:14-15; 10:2; 14:32; 26:6; 32:7; 41:17; 49:13; 54:11; 58:7), or it may even describe one wrongfully accused (e.g., Zech 7:10; 11:7,11). Here, however, the word refers to those without economic means or social standing (cf. the "humble" in the ESV, NASB, NET, NRSV, and NJB), and in the context of the book it is basically synonymous with a similar word (עָנָו, ʿānāw) translated "humble" in 2:3 (cf. ʿānî in 2 Sam 22:28; Ps 18:27; Isa 66:2).[60] Likewise, the term "humble" (דַּל, dal) is generally a sociological term for the weak, disenfranchised, and exploited (Gen 41:19; Isa 3:14-15; 10:2,30; Amos 8:6), but at this point it takes on a more theological aura (along with ʿānî) for those who regard themselves as helpless and insignificant in comparison to Yahweh (cf. "lowly" in the ESV, NASB, NRSV, and NJB) and who willingly submit to Yahweh as their sole source of strength (cf. "all you humble of the land, you who do what he commands" in 2:3).[61] The affirmation that those **who trust** (חָסָה, ḥāsāh) in Yahweh's **name** (v. 12) will not be put to shame (בּוֹשׁ, bôš; v. 11) is especially significant in light of the other uses of this pair of verbs in close proximity in the Psalms (25:20; 31:1; 71:1). In those contexts, the psalmist cries out to Yahweh for deliverance so that he will not be put to shame. Here, the prophet indicates such cries among his audience will be heard. Although the theme of trusting in Yahweh is fairly frequent, the notion of trusting in Yahweh's name appears only here. The closest parallel is Psalm 5:11, which speaks of the gladness of those who trust in Yahweh and the joy of those who love Yahweh's name. However, the source of the concept of trusting Yahweh's name may be the influence of Deuteronomy on the Josianic reforms of Zephaniah's day. Deuteronomy frequently refers to the place that Yahweh chooses to put his name (12:5,11,21; 14:23,24; 16:2,6,11; 26:2).[62]

---

[60]On the overlapping connotations of ʿānî and ʿānān, see Clay Alan Ham, *The Coming King and the Rejected Shepherd: Matthew's Reading of Zechariah's Messianic Hope*, NTM 4 (Sheffield: Sheffield Phoenix Press, 2005), pp. 22, 28.

[61]Széles, *Wrath and Mercy*, p. 109; King, "The Message of Zephaniah," p. 217.

[62]Sweeney, *Zephaniah*, p. 190.

**3:13** In this verse appears the fourth reference to "remnant"; it stands as the last in a progression of the "remnant" language in the book. First, "the remnant of Baal" (1:4) will be destroyed in the day of Yahweh. Second, "the remnant of the house of Judah" (2:7) will possess former Philistine land. Third, "the remnant of my people" will plunder Moab and Ammon (2:9). Fourth, **the remnant of Israel** (v. 13) **will do no wrong**, will be free of falsehood, and will dwell securely. As in 2:7 and 2:9, "remnant" (cf. "those who are left" in the ESV and NJB) here refers to the small group of people who remain faithful to Yahweh and survive Yahweh's judgment and thereby become the basis for a renewed people of Yahweh (on "remnant," see 2:7 above; the TNIV moves the phrase "the remnant of Israel" to the previous verse: "The remnant of Israel will trust in the name of the LORD"). The phrase "remnant of Israel" may reflect Josiah's desire to extend Davidic rule over the territory of the former northern kingdom,[63] and Zephaniah's reserving of the title "remnant of Israel" until the end may also anticipate the fulfillment of Yahweh's original purposes for the covenant people as the center of the divine plan for the world.

The descriptions of the remnant of Israel in verse 13 bear marked resemblance to the description in Psalm 15:1-3 of those who may live on Yahweh's holy hill (v. 11).[64] The remnant will do no wrong and speak no lies, a manner of action completely contrary to the former inhabitants of Jerusalem who are rebellious, disobedient, ravenous, arrogant, treacherous, and violent (vv. 1-4). In particular, the character of Yahweh's people will reflect Yahweh's own character. Yahweh does no wrong (v. 5), and neither does the remnant of Israel. Verse 13 concludes the unit (vv. 8-13) with a pastoral metaphor (cf. the addition in the NET, "peacefully like sheep," which makes such imagery overt): the remnant of Israel will not be made afraid as they graze and **lie down** (cf. Hos 2:18; Amos 9:14-15). This image corresponds to the earlier picture in 2:6-7 where the remnant of Judah will find pasture in the land of the Kerethites and will lie down in the houses of Ashkelon. The statement, **no one will make them afraid**, describes a condition of undisturbed security (Lev 26:6; Deut 28:26; Job 11:19; Isa 17:2; Jer 7:33; 30:10; 46:27; Ezek 34:28; 39:26; Micah 4:4; Nahum 2:11).

---

[63]Ibid., p. 191.
[64]Ibid., p. 192.

## B. EXHORTATION TO REJOICE
## AT THE PROMISE OF YAHWEH (3:14-20)

[14]**Sing, O Daughter of Zion;** / **shout aloud, O Israel!** / **Be glad and rejoice with all your heart,** / **O Daughter of Jerusalem!** / [15]**The LORD has taken away your punishment,** / **he has turned back your enemy.** / **The LORD, the King of Israel, is with you;** / **never again will you fear any harm.** / [16]**On that day they will say to Jerusalem,** / **"Do not fear, O Zion;** / **do not let your hands hang limp.** / [17]**The LORD your God is with you,** / **he is mighty to save.** / **He will take great delight in you,** / **he will quiet you with his love,** / **he will rejoice over you with singing."**

[18]**"The sorrows for the appointed feasts** / **I will remove from you;** / **they are a burden and a reproach to you.**[a] / [19]**At that time I will deal** / **with all who oppressed you;** / **I will rescue the lame** / **and gather those who have been scattered.** / **I will give them praise and honor** / **in every land where they were put to shame.** / [20]**At that time I will gather you;** / **at that time I will bring you home.** / **I will give you honor and praise** / **among all the peoples of the earth** / **when I restore your fortunes**[b] / **before your very eyes,"** / **says the LORD.**

*[a]18 Or "I will gather you who mourn for the appointed feasts; / your reproach is a burden to you*     *[b]20 Or I bring back your captives*

Zephaniah 3:14-20 presents the second of two prophetic exhortations that close the book. The unit itself contains two parts: a command to rejoice (vv. 14-17) and a speech of Yahweh (vv. 18-20). First, the command consists of four imperatives ("sing, shout aloud, and be glad and rejoice") directed to Daughter of Zion/Jerusalem (v. 14) and a narrative description of the past and future actions of Yahweh (vv. 15-17). Already Yahweh has taken away punishment and turned back the enemy; on that day the presence of Yahweh, the King of Israel, will overcome fear and bring salvation, and Yahweh will respond with rejoicing at the deliverance of Judah. Second, the first-person speech describes the salvation which Yahweh will bring to the restored remnant (that is, removal of sorrow, rescue from oppression, return from dispersion, reception of honor, and restoration of fortunes) and concludes with the speech report formula "says the LORD" (vv. 18-20). Therefore, the intent of verses 14-

20 is to urge Judah to rejoice because of Yahweh's past actions of deliverance and future intentions for Judah and because of Yahweh's own promise to restore the scattered remnant of Yahweh's people.

In verses 1-7, the prophet presents the reasons for Jerusalem's punishment. He then describes how Yahweh will cause the remnant to be honored among the nations who turn to Yahweh (vv. 8-13). Finally, Yahweh's people are given a series of assurances that Yahweh will indeed cause them to be honored among the peoples of the earth (vv. 14-20). The content and mood of verses 14-20 is akin to that of Amos 9:11-15, Zechariah 14, and Isaiah 40–55, and the unit stands in sharp contrast with the judgment oracles of chapter 1. There the prophet commands Judah to remain silent because of sin (1:7); here he commands the remnant to sing and shout because of salvation. There the judgment of the day of Yahweh reverses the creation of the world (1:2-3), but here the promises of restoration (3:15-20) replace that judgment.[65]

**3:14** Verse 14 uses three titles to name the addressees. The feminine titles of the addressees (**Daughter of Zion** and **Daughter of Jerusalem**) reflect a characteristic ancient depiction of a city as a woman or a deity's bride. Thus, a place is personified as a daughter (cf. the phrase "daughter of my dispersed ones" in v. 10 above). Although used for other cities (Ps 45:12; 137:8; Isa 23:10,12), most commonly the idiom refers to Zion (2 Kgs 19:21; Ps 9:14; Isa 1:8; 10:32; 16:1; 37:22; 52:2; 62:11; Jer 4:31; 6:2,23; Lam 1:6; 2:1,4,8,10, 13,18; 4:22; Micah 1:13; 4:8,10,13; Zech 2:10; 9:9) or Jerusalem (2 Kgs 19:21; Isa 37:22; Lam 2:13,15; Micah 4:8; Zech 9:9). Only five other times do Zion and Jerusalem appear together in the same text (2 Kgs 19:21; Isa 37:22; Lam 2:13; Micah 4:8; Zech 9:9). The first and last titles, "Daughter of Zion" and "Daughter of Jerusalem," in themselves communicate a redemption theme. Jerusalem is earlier referred to in the feminine as rebellious, defiled, and incorrigible; moreover, she fails to draw near to her God (vv. 1-4). Now Yahweh addresses her with feminine titles and verses 14-15 affirm that the one to whom Jerusalem would not draw near is now with her. The middle title, **Israel**, has appeared previously in the book in promises of restoration. The God of Israel promises that the nation will inher-

---

[65]House, *Theology*, p. 383.

it the land of the Moabites and Ammonites (2:9) and that the remnant of Israel will do no wrong (3:13). The addressees are summoned to **sing** and **rejoice** at Yahweh's victory over their enemies and Yahweh's presence among them as king of Israel (v. 15). Isaiah employs the motif of a call to sing (Isa 12:6; 24:14; 35:6; 42:11; 44:23; 49:13; 54:1; 61:7) that is found often in Psalms (Ps 5:11; 32:11; 33:1; 35:27; 67:4; 81:1; 95:1; 98:4,8; 132:9; 149:5).

**3:15** The call to sing in verse 14 is based upon the affirmations of verse 15: Yahweh **has taken away** the **punishment** of Zion and **has turned** away her enemies, Yahweh is king in her midst, and she will not need to fear ever again. These affirmations involve the past, present, and future. Yahweh here is called the **king of Israel**, a title given to no human king in Zephaniah. This characterization is a severe criticism of the failures of the monarchy in Israel and Judah and is reminiscent of Deuteronomy, in which Yahweh is king (Deut 33:5) and human kings take a minor role (Deut 17:14-20).[66] The presence of Israel's king, Yahweh, within her explains how Jerusalem's punishment is taken away and her enemies are turned back and how she will **never again** have to **fear any harm**. To highlight Yahweh's presence is also to imply Yahweh's absence during an earlier time of punishment. Isaiah 8:17 speaks of Yahweh hiding from Judah during the Assyrian invasion, and Ezekiel 8–11 pictures the glory of Yahweh departing the temple and Jerusalem, thus leaving Jerusalem defenseless against the Babylonians.[67]

**3:16** The verse begins with the last of more than twenty references to the day of Yahweh in the book (Zeph 1:7-10,14-17,18; 2:2-3; 3:8,11,16). **On that day** Yahweh will remove the haughty from Jerusalem (v. 11) and remove any reason for Zion, a synonym for Jerusalem, to fear harm (vv. 15-16). The command not to be afraid frequently introduces salvation oracles (2 Kgs 19:6; 2 Chr 20:15; 32:7; Isa 35:4; 37:6; 41:10,13; 54:4; Jer 30:10; 46:27-28). Parallel to this exhortation **not** to **fear** is a call for Zion **not** to **let** their **hands hang limp**. The image of hands hanging limp conveys discouragement and fear (Jer 47:3); it often expresses a need for courage and action in the face of difficulty (2 Sam 4:1; 2 Chr 15:7; Ezra 4:4; Neh 6:9; Isa 13:7; Jer 6:24; 50:43; Ezek 7:17; 21:12). Like the call to sing

---

[66]McConville, *Guide to the Prophets*, p. 199.
[67]Sweeney, *Zephaniah*, p. 199.

in verse 14, these two exhortations are based upon affirmations of the presence of Yahweh within Zion and the assurances of security without fear (vv. 15,17). Yahweh's presence now to save and protect contrasts Yahweh's earlier presence to judge (v. 5).

**3:17** Zion rejoices because of the presence of Yahweh God (cf. Deut 6:15; 7:21), and so too Yahweh rejoices at the deliverance of Zion. The NIV description **he is mighty to save** obscures the more militaristic Hebrew phrase (גִּבּוֹר יוֹשִׁיעַ, *gibbôr yôšî*), which is better translated "the Mighty Warrior who saves" in the TNIV (cf. ESV, NASB, NET, NRSV, NJB, and NJPS). The description of Yahweh as a warrior coincides with the earlier title "king of Israel" (v. 15). In the ancient Near East the king is often a warrior, and Yahweh is portrayed as both king and warrior in Exodus (15:1,3-4,6-7,18). The NIV translates a very difficult Hebrew line, **he will quiet you with his love** (cf. ESV, KJV, NASB, NLT, and NJPS). This translation, however, is problematic. First, there is no pronoun "you" in the Hebrew line. Second, the verb חָרַשׁ (*ḥārāš*) usually has an intransitive meaning; it refers to the state of the subject ("be silent") rather than describing what the subject does to another ("cause to be silent"). Consequently, the MT may be better translated, "he is quiet in his love." This, however, does not seem to make sense within the context of the preceding and following lines. Some translations (e.g., NET, NRSV, and NJB) follow the LXX reading: "he will renew you in his love." Another possibility adopts a second meaning of the Hebrew root *ḥārāš*, meaning "to plow" (Deut 22:10; Judg 14:18; 1 Sam 8:12; 1 Kgs 19:19; Prov 20:4; Jer 26:18; Hos 10:13; Job 4:8; and Ps 129:3). Thus, the sentence may be translated, "he will plow with his love." In the light of Samson's use of the word "plow" (*ḥārāš*) in Judges 14:18, the statement may be a sexual image applied to the renewal of the relationship between the warrior Yahweh and the Daughter of Zion.[68] Such a reading links verse 17 with the prophetic tradition of Israel/Zion as the bride who is reunited to Yahweh (Isaiah 54; Ezekiel 16; Hosea 2) and so may contrast the fate of Jerusalem with that of the Philistine cities portrayed in 2:4.[69] Verse 17 may thereby give further rationale for Zion to have courage by employing the bridegroom-bride metaphor to speak of Yahweh's great love for the

---

[68]Ibid., pp. 193, 203.
[69]Ibid., p. 203.

city. The word for "love" in the verse is אַהֲבָה (*'ahăbāh*), a love not preconditioned by the covenant relationship as is חֶסֶד (*ḥesed*), a word not appearing in Zephaniah. The word *'ahăbāh* most often refers to love between humans (Gen 29:20; 1 Sam 20:17; 2 Sam 1:26; 13:15; Prov 5:19; 10:12; 15:17; 17:9; 27:5; S of S 2:4-5,7; 3:5,10; 5:8; 7:6; 8:4,6-7), but it denotes in a few instances, as here, divine love for the people (Isa 63:9; Jer 31:3; Hos 11:4). Yahweh's delight over Zion reflects the Mosaic promise of Yahweh's delight over the people after their deliverance from exile (Deut 30:9). Indeed, Yahweh sings at the salvation of Zion.

**3:18** In the final three verses of the book, a first-person speech describes the salvation Yahweh will bring to the restored remnant. The speech emphasizes the future actions of Yahweh with the repeated first-singular verbs generally translated **I will**. Yahweh will remove sorrow, rescue the lame, gather those scattered, and give praise and honor. The people who are scattered in judgment (perhaps in the exile, a notion made explicitly in the NASB and implicitly in the NET) cannot celebrate the appointed feasts (cf. Lam 1:4; 2:6-7,22). This **burden** and **reproach** (cf. Joel 2:17,19; Micah 6:16) Yahweh will **remove** from them. No longer will other nations insult (the same Hebrew word as the one translated "reproach" in 3:18) and taunt the people of Yahweh (2:8; cf. Isa 25:8).

The Hebrew of verse 18 is difficult. The NRSV and NJB follow the LXX and disconnect the reference to festival from the reference to sorrow and connect it instead to the preceding image of Yahweh's rejoicing in verse 17. These versions then render the remainder of the verse as a promise to remove reproach and disaster from Jerusalem. Following the MT, the NIV, its alternate reading ("I will gather you who mourn for the appointed feasts; your reproach is a burden to you"), the TNIV ("all who mourn over the lost of your appointed festivals"), and KJV render it as a promise that Yahweh will remove from the faithful the sorrow they feel for being unable to observe the annual appointed feasts (e.g., Passover, Feast of Weeks, and Feast of Tabernacles among others described in Leviticus 23, Numbers 28–29, and Deuteronomy 16). This interpretation may reflect circumstances of Josiah's reforms. One of the highlights of his reformation in 622 B.C. is an observance of the Passover in Jerusalem. This action and the others narrated in 2 Kings 23 (cf.

2 Chronicles 34–35) are partially facilitated by a decrease of Assyrian power and the subsequent loss of control in the western fringes of its empire during the period.

**3:19** The NIV does not translate the first word of the Hebrew text "look" (הִנֵּה, *hinnēh*), which, when followed by a participle, signals some future action (Hos 2:14; Joel 2:19; 4:7; Amos 2:13; 6:11,14; 7:1,4,8; 8:11; 9:9,13; Micah 1:3; 2:3; Hab 1:6; Zech 9:9; 11:16; 12:2; 14:1; Mal 2:3; 3:1; 4:1,5). The phrase **at that time**, which occurs at the beginning of both verses 19 and 20 echoes its earlier use in 1:12 in which Yahweh is portrayed as searching out Jerusalem to punish the complacent. As verse 19 opens, Yahweh is again seen punishing, but this time Yahweh takes action against the oppressors. The description of "that time" quickly changes, however, seeing as Yahweh moves from dealing with wrongdoers to rescuing **the lame**, gathering the **scattered**, and bringing them home. The language of verses 19 and 20 draws upon earlier promises of rescue in Deuteronomy 30:4; Isaiah 11:12; and especially the depiction of the exiled remnant as "lame" and "scattered" in Micah 4:6-7 (cf. Isa 35:5-10). The remnant's return home also results in a transformed reputation. Yahweh **will give them praise and honor**, even in the lands where they have been subjugated and **put to shame**. The word "shame" (בֹּשֶׁת, *bōšeth* and its derivatives) refers to the public disgrace that results from defeat by an enemy (Jer 2:26; Micah 1:11) and particularly such defeat and exile (Ezra 9:6; Isa 1:29; 30:5; Jer 2:36; 9:19; Dan 9:7). The word "honor" (see more in comments on v. 20 below) expresses the connotation of the Hebrew word "name" (שֵׁם, *šēm*), which often stands for reputation or renown (Gen 11:4; 12:2; 2 Sam 8:13; Neh 9:10; Isa 63:12,14; Jer 32:20; Ezek 39:13; Dan 9:15).[70] Thus, Yahweh will restore honor to those who once have been a people of shame (Zeph 2:1; 3:11; cf. Deut 26:19; Jer 13:11).

**3:20** Verse 20 begins with the repetition of the same phrase that opened verse 19 (**at that time**) and repeats two of the statements from the previous verse (**I will gather you** and **I will give you honor and praise**). However, verse 20 makes more explicit (**I will bring you home**) what was more metaphorical in verse 19 ("I will rescue the lame").[71] Also different is the manner in which verse 20 designates

---

[70]*BDB*, p. 1028.
[71]Sweeney, *Zephaniah*, p. 207.

the addressees. In verses 11-19 Jerusalem is addressed with the second-person feminine singular pronoun, but verse 20 switches to second-person masculine plural pronouns, perhaps addressing those scattered among the nations. While the promises of verses 19 and 20 are commonly understood to refer to the return from the Babylonian exile,[72] these promises of gathering need not refer exclusively to that event. The people of Yahweh in Zephaniah's day have also experienced scattering at the hands of the Assyrians.

The final verses of the book indicate that the promise to Abraham will find its ultimate fulfillment. The NIV's "honor" in both verses 19 and 20 translates the Hebrew šēm, which generally means "name." Yahweh has promised to make Abram's name great (Gen 12:2). The giving of a name by Yahweh signified a changed and exalted status for Abram (Gen 17:5), Sarai (Gen 17:15), and Jacob (Gen 32:28). The combination of šēm with "praise" (תְּהִלָּה, tᵉhillāh) in these verses also holds importance, since this passage is opposite to the normal use of the word pair. Whereas they most frequently appear together in contexts where the people praise Yahweh and honor Yahweh's name (1 Chr 16:35; Ps 100:4; 106:47; 145:21), Yahweh here is the one who gives honor and a name to the people. Also significant for this passage is the use of the two words in Deuteronomy 26:16-19. There, Moses reminds Israel of their commitment to follow Yahweh with all their heart and soul and to observe all the commands. In response to that commitment, Yahweh has declared that Israel is a treasured possession and that Yahweh will set them in praise above the nations, giving them fame and honor. Israel would then be a people holy to Yahweh. Here in Zephaniah, a rebellious and apostate Judah has been purified, leaving a meek and humble remnant that trusts in Yahweh and lives in obedience (2:3; 3:12-13). This transformed people are once again treasured by Yahweh and are honored among the nations.

The phrase **restore your fortunes** or "bring back your captives" (see comments on Zeph 2:7 above) appears first in Deuteronomy 30:3 and is used repeatedly to speak of restoration (for Job, Job 42:10; for Egypt, Ezek 29:14; for Moab, Jer 48:47; for Ammon, Jer 49:6; for Elam, Jer 49:39; for Israel or Judah, Ps 14:7; 53:6; Jer 29:14; 30:3,18; 31:23; 32:44; 33:7,11,26). The expression is common in

[72]Chisholm, *Minor Prophets*, p. 214.

Jeremiah for the salvation that follows the exile (Jer 30:3,18; 31:23; 32:44; 33:7,11,26). The phrase **before your very eyes** appears six other times in the OT (Deut 1:30; 4:34; 9:17; 1 Sam 12:16; Jer 29:21; 51:24). It emphasizes the certain occurrence of an event. The phrase combined with the oath **says the LORD** offers assurance that the promise of Yahweh will indeed happen. The book concludes with this speech report formula, "says the LORD." Thus, the message of Zephaniah is depicted from beginning to end as "The word of the LORD" (1:1).

# THE BOOK OF
# HAGGAI

# INTRODUCTION

## AUTHORSHIP

The book's superscription supplies no genealogy for Haggai and identifies him simply as "the prophet." The only other biblical references to the prophet occur in Ezra 5:1 and 6:14. No further information about him appears there aside from his work being associated with that of Zechariah. Haggai is called "the prophet" five times in the book that bears his name (1:1,3,12; 2:1,10) and twice in Ezra (5:1; 6:14).

His name חַגַּי (*ḥaggay*) apparently derives from the word for "festival" or "feast," suggesting that the prophet may have been born during one of the Hebrews' three annual feasts, Passover/Unleavened Bread, Weeks or Pentecost, and Tabernacles or Ingathering. A similar instance may be seen in the case of the name Shabbethai, meaning "born on the Sabbath" (Ezra 10:15).[1] Biblical names related to Haggai's include Haggi, a son of Gad and grandson of Jacob (Gen 46:16; Num 26:15), Haggith, the wife of David and mother of Adonijah (2 Sam 3:4; 1 Kgs 1:11, 2:13; 1 Chr 3:2), and Haggiah, a Levite descendant of Merari (1 Chr 6:30). Evidence from Hebrew seals, Aramaic sources, and Akkadian and Egyptian parallels indicates a relative popularity of the name in the Old Testament world.[2]

The paucity of biographical information about Haggai inside and outside the book leaves several issues in question. Haggai's concern for the reconstruction of the temple raises the issue of whether he is a priest. In 2:11-13, Yahweh Almighty instructs Haggai to ask the priests questions about communicable holiness and defilement. Do these questions indicate the prophet is not a priest and, therefore,

---

[1] R.K. Harrison, *Introduction to the Old Testament* (Grand Rapids: Eerdmans, 1969), p. 944.

[2] Hans-Walter Wolff, *Haggai: A Commentary*, trans. by Margaret Kohl (Minneapolis: Augsburg, 1988), p. 16.

must inquire of the priests?[3] Or, do they reflect a priest asking his fellow priests a question in order to make a point? One should not attempt to use the questions to draw conclusions one way or the other because the cleanliness laws would have been somewhat universally known.[4] They appear in the text as a rhetorical strategy rather than as a source of biographical data. No Jewish tradition clearly links him with tribe of Levi or line of Zadok,[5] but *Lives of the Prophets*, a first-century-A.D. Jewish work, preserves the tradition that Haggai is buried near the tomb of the priests (14:2). Jerome, in his *Commentary on Haggai* (I, 13), maintains that the prophet was of priestly descent. If so, this could explain the attribution of four Psalms in the LXX to him (Psalms 145, 146, 147, and 148 according to the numbering in the LXX). The question, at best, remains debatable.

The age of Haggai at the time of his ministry is also conjecture. The question posed by Haggai in 2:3 may indicate that the prophet is old enough to have seen Solomon's temple. If so, he would be at least seventy years old at the time of his prophecy and may have died shortly after discharging his message.[6] This conclusion, however, is not necessary. If Haggai is of the generation that saw the destruction of Jerusalem and the temple, it is perhaps more plausible to assume he would pose the question, "Who among *us* is left?" as opposed to "Who among *you* is left?"[7] *Lives of the Prophets* states Haggai probably comes to Jerusalem from Babylon as a young man (14:1). Consequently, no unequivocal evidence exists that Haggai is an aged man who has directly experienced the splendor of Solomon's temple. Nor does the listing of Haggai before Zechariah in Ezra 5:1 and 6:14 necessarily indicate that Haggai is the older of the two contemporaries.[8] The dates of the beginnings of their respective ministries (Hag 1:1; Zech 1:1) may account for this ordering.

---

[3]Ibid., p. 17.

[4]J. Alec Motyer, "Haggai," in *The Minor Prophets: An Exegetical and Expository Commentary*, ed. by Thomas Edward McComiskey (Grand Rapids: Baker, 1998), 3:964.

[5]Carroll Stuhlmueller, *Rebuilding with Hope: A Commentary on the Books of Haggai and Zechariah*, ITC (Grand Rapids: Eerdmans, 1988), p. 12.

[6]Raymond B. Dillard and Tremper Longman III, *An Introduction to the Old Testament* (Grand Rapids: Zondervan, 1994), p. 423.

[7]Motyer, "Haggai," p. 964.

[8]Robert L. Alden, "Haggai," in *Expositor's Bible Commentary*, ed. by Frank E. Gaebelein (Grand Rapids: Zondervan, 1985), 7:572.

A final question exists as to whether Haggai is part of the community that returns to Palestine from the exile or part of the group left behind in Judah in 586 B.C. On one hand, Ezra 2 and Nehemiah 7 do not list the prophet among those returning from the exile, thus indicating he is among the people left behind in Judah in 586 B.C.[9] On the other hand, parallels between the thought of Haggai and the exilic prophet Ezekiel (Hag 2:3,7,9//Ezek 1:28; 8:4; 9:3; 10:4,18-19; 11:22-23; 43:2-5; 44:4; Hag 2:21-22//Ezek 37:15-28; 38:17-23; Hag 2:23//Ezek 34:23) suggest that Haggai is among the group of returnees.[10] The Jewish tradition recorded in the pseudepigraphal work *Lives of the Prophets* suggests a median option (14:1): the prophet is taken to Babylon in his youth but then returns before the larger return of the Jews under Sheshbazzar. Although he has experienced the exile, he is resident in the land when the larger contingent of exiled Jews returns.

## HISTORICAL BACKGROUND

The prophets Haggai and Zechariah minister within the first half century of Israel's postexilic era. This era begins as the Medo-Persian Empire supersedes the Babylonian Empire, which has earlier conquered the kingdom of Judah in 586 B.C. and carried a large number of its inhabitants into exile. The Medes and the Persians, the two most significant Aryan peoples, inhabit the Iranian Plateau east of the Tigris River. A prominent leader of the Persians in the seventh century, Achaemenes, establishes the Achaemenid dynasty, but the Medes dominate the Persians until Cyrus ascends to the Persian throne in 550 B.C. Cyrus overthrows the Median king Astyages (550 B.C.) and then conquers Lydia (546 B.C.). The so-called Nabonidus Chronicle and the Cyrus Cylinder both record the peaceful surrender of Babylon in 539 B.C. to Medo-Persian forces led by Cyrus.[11]

In the following year, Cyrus issues an edict that emancipates captive peoples living in the Babylonian exile. This policy, crafted by

---

[9]Wolff, *Haggai*, p. 17.
[10]Stuhlmueller, *Rebuilding with Hope*, p. 12.
[11]*ANET* pp. 305-307, 315-316.

Cyrus for dealing with conquered peoples, differs greatly from that of earlier Near Eastern empires. By allowing captive peoples to return to their homelands and to rebuild destroyed sanctuaries, Cyrus seeks to avoid unnecessary friction with the subjected peoples and to present the new monarchy as the liberator from Babylonian oppression.[12] Comparison of biblical literature, extrabiblical literature, and inscriptions indicate this edict of Cyrus is published in versions specific to each captive people. Second Chronicles 36:23, Ezra 1:2-4, and Ezra 6:2-5 contain recollections of the version published among the Jewish community and provide detailed instructions about the return of the Jews from captivity. The Persians grant the Jews permission to return to their homeland, to rebuild the temple, to offer sacrifice, and to bring back to Jerusalem the gold and silver articles that the Babylonians have taken during the destruction and sacking of the temple in 586 B.C. The Persians also provide financial assistance from the Persian treasury for these enterprises.

Nevertheless, no Jewish return to Palestine *en masse* occurs, in part, because the exiles have followed Jeremiah's instructions (Jeremiah 28–29) and have become economically established in Babylon. Instead, a small group numbering around fifty thousand makes the nine hundred mile journey back to Jerusalem in 538 B.C. (Ezra 2:1-66). This group may include poorer members of the exile community who have little to lose in such a venture,[13] those with a sense of adventure, and those who possess a fervent devotion for the land of the ancestors.

The relationship among those credited with leading the early returnees is less than certain. Ezra 1:5-11 indicates the returnees are led by a prince (נָשִׂיא, *nāśî'*) named Sheshbazzar. Although some identify Sheshbazzar with a son of Jehoiachin named Shenazzar in 1 Chronicles 3:19,[14] such an identification is doubtful. The name Sheshbazzar appears to derive from the name of the Babylonian sun god *šamaš*, whereas Shenazzar derives from that of the moon god

---

[12]J. Alberto Soggin, *Introduction to the Old Testament: From Its Origins to the Closing of the Alexandrian Canon*, trans. by John Bowden, rev. ed. (Philadelphia: Westminster, 1980), p. 322.

[13]Alden, "Haggai," p. 571.

[14]Norman K. Gottwald, *The Hebrew Bible: A Socio-Literary Introduction* (Philadelphia: Fortress, 1985), p. 430; Eugene H. Merrill, *Haggai, Zechariah, Malachi*, WEC (Chicago: Moody, 1994), pp. 7-8.

*šin.*[15] Ezra 5:14 later designates Sheshbazzar as Judah's governor (פֶּחָה, *peḥah*). On the other hand, Ezra 2:1-2 does not list Sheshbazzar among the leaders of those who return to Jerusalem and Judah, and portions of the Ezra narrative portray Zerubbabel and Joshua the priest as the community's leaders (2:2; 3:2,8; 4:2,3; 5:2).[16] Nevertheless, Ezra never calls Zerubbabel the "governor" as does Haggai (1:1,14; 2:2,21).

Zerubbabel's name apparently comes from a Babylonian name (*zēr bābili*) that means "offshoot of Babylon."[17] As such, it probably indicates he is born in the exile. Joshua, like Zerubbabel, probably belongs to the group which comes to Judah from Babylon. His father Jehozadak is deported by Nebuchadnezzar (1 Chr 6:15), and his grandfather, Seraiah, is taken captive in 587 B.C. and executed in Riblah (2 Kgs 25:18,21). The majority of the texts giving Zerubbabel's lineage identify him as the son of Shealtiel (Ezra 3:2,8; 5:2; Hag 1:1,12,14; 2:2,23) who, in turn, is the son of the deported king of Judah, Jehoiachin (2 Kgs 24:8-17; 1 Chr 3:17). The MT of 1 Chronicles 3:17-19, however, identifies Zerubbabel as a grandson of Jehoiachin through another of Jehoiachin's sons, Pedaiah. Nonetheless, the LXX of 1 Chronicles 3:17 indicates that Zerubbabel is the son of Shealtiel instead of Pedaiah. These differing genealogical notes may be coordinated if Shealtiel, the eldest son of Jehoiachin, has become the legal father of Zerubbabel through levirate marriage after Zerubbabel's natural father, Pedaiah, dies (see Deut 25:5-10).[18]

Several explanations have been offered for the relationship between Sheshbazzar and Zerubbabel. One, the names Sheshbazzar and Zerubbabel refer to the same person who is identified by both a Hebrew and Babylonian name.[19] Josephus seems to concur with this

---

[15]Keith Schoville, *Ezra–Nehemiah*, College Press NIV Commentary (Joplin, MO: College Press, 2001), p. 45; Derek Kidner, *Ezra and Nehemiah: An Introduction and Commentary*, TOTC 11 (Downers Grove, IL: InterVarsity, 1979), pp. 139-142; Phyllis A. Bird, "Sun," *HBD*, p. 1073.

[16]The Hebrew text of Haggai and Zechariah spells the name of the high priest Jehoshua (English translation "Joshua"), not the shorter Jeshua as in Ezra and Nehemiah. Joshua is used here throughout.

[17]Bryan E. Beyer, "Zerubbabel," *ABD*, 6:1084-1086.

[18]Wolff, *Haggai*, p. 38.

[19]James E. Smith, *The Books of History* (Joplin, MO: College Press, 1995), p. 673.

identification,[20] but the Apocrypha distinguishes between the two (1 Esd 6:18). Two, Sheshbazzar is the Persian appointed official given special oversight over the initial return and temple reconstruction, whereas Zerubbabel is an unofficial, popular leader who leads under Sheshbazzar's auspices.[21] Three, Sheshbazzar, who may or may not have been a member of the Judean royal family, acts as an interim governor entrusted by the Persians with circumscribed duties during the early resettlement period. His authority then gives way to Zerubbabel, a prince from the Davidic house, and Joshua the high priest.[22] Four, the meanings of the titles "prince" (nāśî') and "governor" (peḥāh) are somewhat fluid. The derivation of the noun nāśî' from the verb meaning "to lift up" (נָשָׂא, nāśā') may indicate a notion of being elected or selected for a special purpose.[23] Elsewhere in the Old Testament, nāśî' refers to tribal leaders or captains (Exod 16:22; Num 1:16,44; 1 Chr 2:10; 2 Chr 1:2) as well as to members of the royal house (1 Kgs 11:34; Ezek 34:24; 37:25). The noun translated governor (פֶּחָה, peḥāh) is a general term designating a representative of a foreign ruler with some level of authority over a group. Thus, "prince" (nāśî') is appropriately applied to Sheshbazzar, and "governor" (peḥāh), to both to Sheshbazzar and Zerubbabel.

References to the laying of the temple foundations provide further complications. Ezra 3:7-10, Haggai 1:12-14, and Zechariah 4:9 all suggest that Zerubbabel lays the foundations of the new temple; Ezra 5:14-16, however, indicates Sheshbazzar does. Notably, Sheshbazzar is mentioned in the context of Persian royal communications and edicts, and Zerubbabel, in contexts concerning the theological implications of the rebuilding of the temple.[24] While the work of Sheshbazzar is overtly connected with Persian interests in the initial steps of restoration, both Zerubbabel and Joshua are linked with Jewish interests in the restoration of the temple. Moreover, the verb

---

[20]Josephus, *Antiquities* 11.13.

[21]Kidner, *Ezra and Nehemiah*, pp. 139-142.

[22]Gottwald, *Hebrew Bible*, p. 430; Merrill, *Haggai, Zechariah, Malachi*, pp. 7-8.

[23]E.A. Speiser, *Genesis*, AB 1 (Garden City, NY: Doubleday, 1964), p. 170; F. Charles Fensham, *Ezra and Nehemiah*, NICOT (Grand Rapids: Eerdmans, 1954), p. 46.

[24]William J. Dumbrell, *The Faith of Israel: Its Expression in the Books of the Old Testament* (Grand Rapids: Baker, 1988), p. 226.

יָסַד (*yāsad*) may refer to the initial laying of the foundation and to the progressive stages in building operations (Ezra 3:6,10; 5:16; Hag 2:18; Zech 4:9). The word *yāsad* may denote the laying of a foundation (Isa 28:16), the construction of the larger foundation walls (1 Kgs 5:17; 7:10), or the restoration of the temple (2 Chr 24:4,27).[25] Thus, the accounts may refer to the differing official roles that Sheshbazzar and Zerubbabel play at different stages of the second temple's construction.

Ezra 3–4 recounts early attempts to rebuild the temple. Joshua and Zerubbabel rebuild the altar for burnt offerings and begin offering on it by the first day of the seventh month (September–October) of 537 B.C. (3:1-6). After celebrating the Feast of Tabernacles (3:4), they begin reconstruction of the temple in the second month of the second year of the return (April–May 536) (3:8). Hostility and opposition from the neighboring peoples of the land causes the work to cease by 536 B.C. Since the temple mound is, at that time, the northeast fortification of the city, its rebuilding is easily misinterpreted as an attempt to reconstruct the city's defenses. This political opposition, together with economic hardships linked to inflation, drought, and crop failure (Hag 1:6,9,11), make the task too daunting for the small community of the return.[26] Work does not recommence for sixteen years.

Events in the larger Persian Empire during this period of inactivity contribute to an environment conducive for the resumption of the work. After establishing the Medo-Persian Empire, Cyrus dies fighting in the area of modern-day Afghanistan around 530 B.C. His son Cambyses succeeds him, and Cambyses consolidates his hold on the empire by assassinating his brother Bardiya. The highlight of the eight-year reign of Cambyses is a conquest of Egypt in the first Persian military campaign to the west. The march of Cambyses' army through Palestine toward Egypt may diminish the already limited resources of the community and contribute to the poverty described by Haggai.[27] Cambyses dies suddenly on his return from

[25]W.H. Schmidt, "יָסַד," *TLOT*, 2:547.

[26]Soggin, *Introduction*, p. 323.

[27]Joyce G. Baldwin, *Haggai, Zechariah, Malachi: An Introduction and Commentary*, TOTC 24 (Downers Grove, IL: InterVarsity, 1972), p. 16; Alden, "Haggai," p. 571.

Egypt in 522 B.C. A struggle for power ensues from which a general of Cambyses, Darius, arises. The early years of Darius's reign are marked by outbreaks of resistance and revolts led by a certain Gaumâta who pretends to be Bardiya, the deceased brother of Cambyses. Gaumâta's revolt is crushed by the end of September 522 B.C., and Darius consolidates power by his second year (520 B.C.).[28] After establishing the peace of the empire, Darius resumes the benevolent policies of Cyrus. He encourages local rule, supports and codifies local laws and customs, and rebuilds sanctuaries that then serve as administrative centers.[29]

Ezra 5–6 indicates that in 520 B.C. Haggai and Zechariah deliver a series of messages to stir the people to begin again work on the temple. Haggai and Zechariah stress that a full national renewal is not possible until the temple is rebuilt. The return of the people to the land, the reconstruction of the temple, and the reaffirmation of the Davidic covenant are interlocking pieces of Yahweh's plan.[30]

Tattenai, the governor of the Persian satrapy *Bābili ebi nāri* ("Babylon beyond the River," translated "Trans-Euphrates" in the NIV), then conspires with an official named Shether-Bozenai and others to block the building of the Jews' temple. They claim that the Jews are incorrect in their assertion that Cyrus the Great has authorized the rebuilding of the temple. Nevertheless, a search of the royal archives in Ecbatana proves Cyrus has indeed authorized it, and Darius orders Tattenai and Shether-Bozenai to interfere no longer (Ezra 5:1–6:11). No doubt the desire of Darius to establish Judah as a buffer against Egypt at the western fringe of the empire contributes to the support for temple rebuilding he expresses in Ezra 6:3-12.[31] Through the encouragement of Haggai and Zechariah and under the leadership of Zerubbabel and Joshua, the Jews complete the second temple (Ezra 6:15) on the third day of the month of Adar in the sixth year of Darius (March 12, 516 B.C.), some three and a half years after they begin building again.

---

[28]For arguments on identifying the second year of Darius as 520 B.C., see Wolff, *Haggai*, pp. 74-76.

[29]Stuhlmueller, *Rebuilding with Hope*, p. 13.

[30]Paul R. House, *Old Testament Theology* (Downers Grove, IL: InterVarsity, 1998), p. 383.

[31]Gottwald, *Hebrew Bible*, p. 430.

Haggai's prophecy reflects the early upheavals in Darius's reign as well as the relative stability after the elimination of Gaumâta. In the light of promises spoken by earlier prophets of restoration following judgment, the early unrest perhaps triggers new hopes for a great transformation of Judah. The peace that follows in 520 B.C. then provides the political scenario that facilitates the Jews' reconstruction of the temple and the reestablishment of clear lines of religious and secular authority.[32]

During his reign of thirty-six years, Darius expands the empire from India in the east to Greece in the west and reorganizes it into twenty regions called satrapies which are further subdivided into provinces. Judah is in the satrapy *Bābili ebi nāri* ("Babylon beyond the River," translated "Trans-Euphrates" in the NIV) that includes Syria and Palestine. What is uncertain is whether, from the start, Judah has the status of a separate province[33] or whether it falls under the authority of the province of Samaria until at least the time of Nehemiah.[34] An argument for Judah being a province independent of Samaria is the discovery of coins in some Israelite cities with the Persian name of the area, *Yehud*, inscribed on them. This suggests the Persians have granted a degree of local authority.[35] The established use of the phrase "governor of Judah" within the book also indicates Judah is an independent province at this time.[36] Whatever the case, the leadership within the Jewish community is divided between the high priest and the governor.

Zerubbabel drops from the biblical record after the completion of the temple. Theories that the prophetic messages of Haggai and Zechariah lead him to rebel against Darius go beyond the historical data, as do those theories that allege he is deposed by Persian authorities who fear rebellion among the Jews.[37] The memorandum issued

---

32]Stuhlmueller, *Rebuilding with Hope*, p. 13.

[33]Merrill, *Haggai, Zechariah, Malachi*, p. 7; Stuhlmueller, *Rebuilding with Hope*, p. 13.

[34]Motyer, "Haggai," p. 966.

[35]Lawrence Boadt, *Reading the Old Testament: An Introduction* (New York: Paulist, 1984), p. 433; Wolff, *Haggai*, p. 39.

[36]Gottwald, *Hebrew Bible*, p. 429.

[37]For a discussion of various theories, see Richard A. Taylor and E. Ray Clendenen, *Haggai, Malachi*, NAC (Nashville: Broadman & Holman, 2004), p. 199, Andrew E. Hill and John H. Walton, *A Survey of the Old Testament* (Grand Rapids: Zondervan, 1991), p. 411, and comments on Haggai 2:23 below.

by Darius to Tattenai (Ezra 6:1-12) gives no indication that Darius suspects the Jews of any sedition or that Zerubbabel is considered a traitor.[38] Although Zerubbabel disappears from official records, the temple becomes the focal point of Jewish life.

## DATE

The book indicates the precise dates for the four major oracles delivered by the prophet within the book (1:1; 2:1,10,20) and for the positive response to the first oracle (1:15). These dates and their modern equivalents are:

First oracle (1:1-11): 1st day, 6th month, 2nd year of Darius = August 29, 520 B.C.

Response to the first oracle (1:12-15): 24th day, 6th month, 2nd year of Darius = September 21, 520 B.C.

Second oracle (2:1-9): 21st day, 7th month = October 17, 520 B.C.

Third oracle (2:10-19): 24th day, 9th month, 2nd year of Darius = December 18, 520 B.C.

Fourth oracle (2:20-23): 24th day, 9th month = December 18, 520 B.C.

Thus, the prophet's recorded ministry extends a little less than four months. Zechariah's recorded ministry begins in the eighth month of Darius's second year (Zech 1:1), sometime between Haggai's second and third oracles (2:1-9; 2:10-19).

Such extensive dating of oracles and events appears also in the earlier book of Ezekiel (1:1-2; 8:1; 20:1; 24:1; 26:1; 29:1,17; 30:20; 31:1; 32:1,17; 33:21; 40:1), in the contemporary Zechariah (1:1,7; 7:1), and in the later books Ezra (1:1; 3:1,6,8; 4:24; 6:15; 8:31; 10:9,17) and Nehemiah (1:1; 2:1; 5:14; 6:15; 7:73–8:2; 9:1; 13:6). This phenomenon reflects the annalistic style of history writing practiced by the Neo-Babylonians and Persians, and the dating of these oracles in reference to a Persian king places Haggai's work in an international context.[39]

---

[38]Baldwin, *Haggai, Zechariah, Malachi*, p. 17.

[39]David L. Petersen, *Haggai and Zechariah 1–8: A Commentary*, OTL (Philadelphia: Westminster Press, 1984), p. 43; Merrill, *Haggai, Zechariah, Malachi*, pp. 4-5.

The book is likely completed sometime between the issue of Haggai's challenges and the completion of the temple in 516 B.C.[40] The simple description of Haggai as "the prophet" suggests that the book appears in its present form at a time near enough the events to make unnecessary any further description.[41]

## LITERARY FEATURES

Hans Walter Wolff characterizes Haggai as "one of the most minor of the minor prophets, indeed one of the most despised. . . . And yet this little book is a model of effective proclamation."[42] This statement reflects the notion in Old Testament studies that, in spite of the success of his prophetic mission, the craft of Haggai exhibits stylistic clumsiness and little literary art.[43] Such a characterization is unfair. Though the book may not possess the elegance of a work like Isaiah, it does possess a literary distinctiveness and art worthy of appreciation.

Whether one should categorize the book as prose or poetry is uncertain. A comparison of standard Hebrew Bibles demonstrates this; the older *BHK* prints Haggai as prose, but the newer *BHS* does so as poetry. Any determination is further complicated for lack of a clear distinction between the categories of biblical prose and poetry, and those in the biblical world may not have distinguished between the two.[44] Instead, the biblical literature exists on a continuum from loosely parallel structures characterized as prose to more heightened forms of rhetoric classified as poetry.[45] Nevertheless, the Hebrew text of Haggai does not contain the short "lines" one might expect in poetry, but it does have a sort of parallelism and height-

---

[40]David R. Hildebrand, "Temple Ritual: A Paradigm for Moral Holiness in Haggai II 10-19," *VT* 39 (1989): 154-168; Hill and Walton, *Survey*, p. 410.

[41]Motyer, "Haggai," p. 973.

[42]Wolff, *Haggai*, p. 11.

[43]Harrison, *Introduction*, p. 947; Pfeiffer *Introduction to the Old Testament* (New York: Harper and Brothers, 1941), p. 603; Soggin, *Introduction*, p. 326.

[44]James Kugel, *The Idea of Biblical Poetry* (Baltimore: Johns Hopkins University Press, 1998), pp. 59-95, comes close to concluding that no real distinction exists between biblical prose and poetry.

[45]See Robert Alter, *The Art of Biblical Poetry* (New York: Basic Books, 1985), pp. 4-11.

ened imagery, features often associated with biblical poetry.[46] Consequently, the book may be described as using an elevated prose, the quality of which distinguishes it within the prophetic literature.

Even though its multiple messenger and oracular formulas (1:2,5,7,8,9,13; 2:4,6,7,8,9,11,17,23), its prophetic word formulas (1:1,3; 2:1,10,20), and prophetic reports (1:12-15) give the book a third person perspective, sentences of direct address predominate the book. For example, fourteen imperative verbs (1:5,7,8; 2:2,4,11, 15,18,21), four second person verbs (1:6,8,9; 2:5), and fourteen second person pronouns (1:4,9,13; 2:3,4,6,14,21,23) appear in the book. Moreover, an aura of confrontation arises from the rhetorical questions that appear in all but the final oracle (1:4,9; 2:3,12-13,19).

Strategic repetition of key phrases also characterizes Haggai's style. The admonition to "give careful thought to your ways" appears in 1:5 and 7, and "give careful thought" appears in 2:15 and 18. The command "Be strong" is issued three times in 2:4, once each to Zerubbabel, Joshua, and all the people of the land. The listing of Zerubbabel, Joshua, and the remnant of the people itself appears three times (1:12,14; 2:2). Yahweh twice states, "I will shake the heavens and the earth" (2:6,21), and twice affirms, "I am with you" (1:13; 2:4). The prophet freely uses messenger and oracular formulas beyond the introduction and closing of oracles (2:4,7,9,14,23). He also shows an affinity for the divine name "the LORD Almighty," using it fourteen times.

The prophet strengthens his message with allusions to earlier texts. The description of scant harvests after planting appears also in Deuteronomy 28:38-40, Hosea 4:10, and Micah 6:15. The depiction of the results of drought in 1:11 is reminiscent of Hosea 2:9. The curse for disobedience, "I struck all the work of your hands with blight, mildew and hail, yet you did not turn to me," is similar to Deuteronomy 28:22. The admonition to "be strong," given to Zerubbabel, Joshua the high priest, and to all the people of the land because Yahweh would be with them (2:4), is comparable to the thrice repeated command to Joshua the son of Nun to "be strong" and the accompanying assurances of Yahweh's presence with him (Josh 1:5-6,7,9).

---

[46]Alter, *Art of Biblical Poetry*, pp. 10-11; Leland Ryken, *Words of Delight: A Literary Introduction to the Bible*, 2nd ed. (Grand Rapids: Baker, 1992), p. 159; Alden, "Haggai," pp. 573-574; Harrison, *Introduction*, p. 947.

Subtle, yet powerful images intensify the prophet's message. Pictures of the finished houses of the Israelites contrast with that of the house of Yahweh in ruin (1:4). The question addressed to the priests (2:11-14) uses images of cultic defilement and consecration to communicate the necessity for the community to rebuild the temple and to maintain holiness. The temple remains in ruin, like a corpse in their midst, defiling the entire community. The impurity of the people of Yahweh affects all their work and worship. A sort of antithetical parallelism in 1:6 portrays the economic frustrations of the community, and word pictures of decimated grain heaps and wine vats (2:16) as well as fruitless vines and fig trees (2:19) contrast with Yahweh's promise of blessing (2:19). The image of the signet ring (2:23) conveys the special role the family of David still has in the plans of Yahweh.

The imagery of Haggai also contributes to the development of apocalyptic literature in the postexilic books. Haggai, along with Zechariah and Malachi,[47] represents a transitional form between standard eschatological material and a more developed apocalyptic literature that focuses on that which lies beyond the end after a dissolution of earthly structures.[48]

## THEOLOGY

The book of Haggai is named Ἀγγαῖος (*Aggaios*) in the LXX and Aggaeus in the Vulgate. It appears as the tenth book within the Book of the Twelve or the Minor Prophets. Paul House characterizes the book as the beginning of an ascent within a "U-shaped pattern" in the Book of the Twelve.[49] The ascent in Haggai, Zechariah, and Malachi echoes the theme in Ezekiel of a brighter future beyond

[47]Accepted here is a preexilic rather than a postexilic date for the book of Joel. For discussion of this issue, see Harrison, *Introduction*, pp. 876-880; Dillard and Longman, *Introduction*, pp. 363-367; James Smith, *The Minor Prophets* (Joplin, MO: College Press, 1994), p. 35; Gleason L. Archer, Jr., *A Survey of Old Testament Introduction* (Chicago: Moody Press, 1964), pp. 311-315.

[48]Stuhlmueller, *Rebuilding with Hope*, p. 10.

[49]Paul R. House, *The Unity of the Twelve*, JSOTSupp 97, BLS 27 (Sheffield: Almond Press, 1990), p. 151.

judgment in which the presence of Yahweh in the midst of the remnant community transforms the judgment of the exile into glory.[50]

Haggai centers the promise of a bright future for Yahweh's people in their completion of the temple. The Old Testament literature indicates Israel's esteem for the temple by using such designations as Yahweh's "resting place" (Ps 132:14) and the "place the LORD your God will choose as a dwelling for his Name" (Deut 11:9). The temple represents Yahweh's presence in harmony with the people (Ps 132:13-14; 1 Kgs 6:13).[51] The promise of Yahweh's presence among the people goes back to the covenant statement of Leviticus 26:11-12, "I will put my dwelling place among you, and I will not abhor you. I will walk among you and be your God, and you will be my people." The Pentateuch also characterizes the tabernacle as a representation of Yahweh's presence or dwelling among Israel (Exod 25:8; 29:44-46). The later temple is accorded a similar significance (1 Kgs 8:13,20,29; Ps 101:7). Haggai resembles the earlier prophet Ezekiel and his contemporary Zechariah by making the temple a focal point of the presence of Yahweh, the reality of Yahweh's covenant with Judah, and the sign of Yahweh's renewed desire to bless them (Ezek 37:26-28; 43:1-5; Hag 1:13; 2:4; Zech 2:5,10-11,13; 8:3). These concerns lead to the admonitions by Haggai to Zerubbabel the governor, Joshua the high priest, and the community to "be strong" (2:4). These admonitions also reflect the challenge by David to Solomon to complete the first temple (1 Chr 28:10,20).

Not only do the temple, and the tabernacle before it, signify the divine presence among the people, they also represent the kingship of Yahweh over the people. Yahweh designates it as the "place of my throne and the place for the soles of my feet" (Ezek 43:7). Temples in Israel's ancient near eastern context are considered the dwelling place or palace of the deity.[52] Haggai 2:15 and 2:18 highlight this connection between the temple and Yahweh's kingship by using the noun הֵיכָל (hêkāl), a noun that normally refers to the Old Testament temple (1 Kgs 7:21,50; 2 Kgs 18:16; 23:4; Ezra 3:6,10; 4:1; Neh 6:10-

---

[50]House, *Old Testament Theology*, p. 347.

[51]J. McKeown, "Haggai," *NDBT*, p. 257.

[52]Carol L. Meyers and Eric M. Meyers, *Haggai, Zechariah 1–8*, AB 25B (New York: Doubleday, 1987), pp. 52-53; *HALOT*, pp. 244-245.

11; Isa 6:1; Jer 7:4; Ezek 8:16), but one that may refer instead to a palace (1 Kgs 21:1; 2 Kgs 20:18; Ps 45:8,15; 144:12; Isa 13:22; 39:7; Dan 1:4; Hos 8:14; Nahum 2:6). The reconstructed temple, therefore, is an especially poignant reminder that Yahweh is king over Israel, even though no human monarch reigns in Jerusalem. Prosperity and peace will result if Yahweh is present as king in Judah (2 Sam 23:2-5; Ps 96:10-13; 132:11-18; Hag 2:19).

The rebuilding of the temple has eschatological importance. Micah 3:12, 4:1-4, and Isaiah 2:2-4 indicate a sequence of destruction, a time of desolation, the reestablishment of Yahweh's house, and then the "latter days" of the messianic age.[53] Several factors suggest that Haggai holds a similar notion: the rebuilt temple is a condition for the eschatological messianic age. One, the eschatological texts of Ezekiel 38:19-23 and Zechariah 14:13-14 use language similar to that in 2:6-9 to describe the judgment and destruction visited upon the nations and a collection of wealth from the nations that occurs in the context of a reestablished house of Yahweh (Ezekiel 40–43; Zech 14:20-21). Two, the prophet uses the eschatological language "I will shake the heavens and the earth" to speak of both the results of the rebuilt house of Yahweh (2:6-9) and of Yahweh taking Zerubbabel as signet ring (2:23). Three, the promise of the glory of Yahweh filling the house (2:7) reflects the eschatological visions of Ezekiel 43:1-5 and 44:4. Four, the day the foundation of the temple is laid becomes the day from which one may mark the blessing of Yahweh (2:15-19).

The rebuilt temple testifies to the dynamics of covenant. Ezekiel anticipates a day in which the land will be purified, a new temple is built, and all the tribes live in peace and order under the leadership of a prince and high priest (Ezekiel 40–48). Haggai follows in that tradition, calling for both the rebuilding of the temple under the leadership of Zerubbabel and Joshua (1:7-8; 2:4) and a quest for holiness (2:10-14). Like Ezekiel and the entire line of prophetic voices back to Amos, Haggai affirms that a temple without covenant fidelity has no power to bring Yahweh's blessing to the people.[54] Conversely, the rebuilding of the temple is an act of faith, repre-

---

[53]Baldwin, *Haggai, Zechariah, Malachi*, p. 20.
[54]Boadt, *Reading the Old Testament*, p. 439.

senting the hope of the community that, despite the exile, the old covenant promises still stand.[55]

The text of Haggai uses "Yahweh" fourteen times and "Yahweh their God" two times to refer to the God whose presence the temple signifies and who blesses the postexilic community. Present also is the specialized description צְבָאוֹת יהוה (*YHWH ṣᵉbā'ôth*) rendered in the NIV as "LORD Almighty" and in other English translations as "the Lord of Hosts" (ESV, KJV, NASB, NRSV, NJPS), "Yahweh Sabaoth" (NJB), or "sovereign Lord" (NET). This title appears fourteen times in the book (Hag 1:2,5,7,9,14; 2:4,6-9,11,23) and more than 260 times in the Old Testament (e.g., 1 Sam 1:3; 17:45; Ps 24:10; Isa 1:9; Jer 2:19; Hos 12:5; Amos 3:13; Micah 4:4; Hab 2:13; Zeph 2:9). Its use as a title for Yahweh may relate to the appearance of "the commander of the army [צָבָא, *ṣābā'*] of the LORD" in Joshua 5:13-15. The noun *ṣābā'* refers to an army; consequently, the title designates Yahweh as God of War or God of the Armies. By using this prominent name, Haggai indicates that the great God of Israel, who is sovereign over nations and history, is willing to be active in Israel's postexilic story.[56]

Of particular import for Haggai is the use of the name "LORD Almighty" in earlier texts narrating the transportation of the ark of the covenant to Jerusalem by David (2 Sam 6:2,17-18) and in the account of Yahweh's covenant with David. Nathan's announcement of that covenant is prefaced by the messenger formula "This is what the LORD Almighty says" (2 Sam 7:8), a messenger formula that appears five times in Haggai (1:2,5,7; 2:6,11). Furthermore, the name LORD Almighty appears in the context of statements ensuring David an enduring dynasty (2 Sam 7:26-27). The involvement of the Davidic heir Zerubbabel in the reconstruction of the temple once more involves the Davidic house with a signification of the presence of Yahweh within Jerusalem.

As the God of the Armies, the LORD Almighty is at work in the world. The political circumstances of the era dictate that the dates of the oracles within the book must be given in reference to Persian kings, but Yahweh has charge of them. This chronological cross-referencing also places the prophet's message about the work of

[55]Baldwin, *Haggai, Zechariah, Malachi*, p. 21.
[56]McKeown, "Haggai," *NDBT*, p. 257.

Yahweh in an international context. Yahweh is not a tribal god but the global God.[57] He will shake the nations so that their wealth comes into Jerusalem (2:6-9).

The book's prevailing theme, the necessity of the postexilic community rebuilding the temple, joins with the foundational theme of the continuance of Yahweh's promise to David. The covenant oracle to David (2 Samuel 7) begins a prominent link of the Davidic house to Yahweh's house within prophetic messianic expectation. Even though David wants to build a house for Yahweh, Yahweh promises to build him a house (2 Sam 7:5,11). Likewise, the book of Haggai focuses attention on the Davidic house in the context of temple construction. The temple building activities of Zerubbabel link him to David, and this connection between the house of David and a restored temple parallels elements within the message of restoration announced in Ezekiel 40–48.[58]

The book begins and ends with references to Zerubbabel, the governor of Judah (1:1; 2:20-23). These descriptions of Zerubbabel as both Yahweh's "servant" and "chosen" one (2:23) give him a similar status to that afforded David (2 Sam 3:18; 6:21; 7:5,8,26; 1 Kgs 8:16) and also connect the concluding oracle with Isaiah 42:1 and 52:13, where the titles appear with messianic overtones. Moreover, the title "signet ring" attributed to Zerubbabel in 2:23 is applied elsewhere to the Davidic king in Jeremiah 22:24. The promise about Zerubbabel is set "on that day," a day beyond the time of the original audience but one that reassures the remnant that Yahweh has indeed preserved David's line. Although Zerubbabel is himself not the coming king, his existence ensures the possibility of a future messianic son of David.[59] The prophet clearly understands that Yahweh has not forgotten the promises, and the eschatological people of the Yahweh Almighty arise from the tiny, impoverished community of postexilic Israel.[60]

The repetition of the phrases "Give careful thought to your ways" (1:5,7), "Give careful thought" (2:15,18), and "from this day

---

[57]Merrill, *Haggai, Zechariah, Malachi*, p. 5; Petersen, *Haggai and Zechariah 1–8*, p. 43.

[58]Dumbrell, *Faith of Israel*, p. 229.

[59]House, *Old Testament Theology*, p. 386.

[60]Dumbrell, *Faith of Israel*, p. 229.

on" (2:15,18,19) beckon the community to consider the connections between obedience and blessing and between disobedience and curse (1:3-6,7-11; 2:15-19). The failure of the community to honor Yahweh has led to covenant curses like those spoken of in Deuteronomy 28:15-24 and 38-42. Second Kings 17:7-23 and 2 Chronicles 36:15-16 cite failure to heed the prophetic word as a reason for the fall of the northern and southern kingdoms. Nevertheless, the pre-exilic prophets anticipate a righteous and obedient remnant that will arise from among Israel (Isa 10:20-21; Jer 23:1-4; 50:20; Amos 5:14-15; Micah 4:7; 5:7-8; Zeph 3:13). By applying the term "remnant" to those living in Jerusalem (1:12,14), Haggai links the postexilic community with these promises. The obedience of the remnant is prerequisite for the community to experience the benefits of the promises of Yahweh. Significantly, the final two oracles (2:10-19,20-23), delivered on the same day, conjoin the Mosaic theme of the blessing of obedience with the messianic hope.

In spite of his audience's claims that they are too poor to build the temple, Haggai asserts that they are poor *because* they have not rebuilt it. He highlights this through a play on words (1:4,11): because "this house remains a ruin" (חָרֵב, ḥārēb), the LORD Almighty has "called for a drought" (חֹרֶב, ḥōreb). Exodus 25:8 and 29:44-46 link the willingness of Israel to construct the tabernacle to Yahweh's promise to dwell with Israel. In the same way, the faithful response of Judah to the commands "Go up into the mountains and bring down timber and build the house" (1:8) and "Be strong, all you people of the land, . . . and work" (2:4) is a condition for Yahweh's presence among Judah (1:8; 2:15-19).

Haggai enjoys a distinction among the prophets of seeing the immediate result of his faithful preaching. The people respond to the commands and promises in a way uncharacteristic of their predecessors. They repent when their ancestors have not, and this generation responds like a true remnant. Therefore, the Davidic and Mosaic blessings remain in effect, and the temple represents both the honoring of Yahweh by Israel[61] and the continued blessing of Israel by Yahweh.

---

[61]House, *Old Testament Theology*, p. 386.

# MESSAGE

With only thirty-eight verses, Haggai is the shortest book of the Old Testament outside of Obadiah. Nevertheless, its content, which builds upon significant preexilic themes, does not lack substantial theology. Haggai exhibits the greatest focus among the prophetic writers as he remains fixed on a specific objective,[62] driven by a double impulse. One, he chastises the community for their failure to complete the rebuilding of the temple. This failure, in turn, has led to their adverse circumstances (1:4-6,9-11). Two, he reassures the people by promising manifestations of Yahweh's glorious presence should they put their hands to the work (1:8).[63] Moreover, the renewed presence of Yahweh among the people will result in a renewal of the Davidic promise.[64]

The command of 1:8, "'Go up into the mountains and bring down timber and build the house, so that I may take pleasure in it and be honored,' says the LORD" captures the prophet's central message. This passion for the temple seems odd or out of place to new covenant believers whose thought has been influenced by the words of Stephen, "The Most High does not live in houses made by men" (Acts 7:48), and by the words of Paul, "Don't you know that you yourselves are God's temple and that God's Spirit lives in you? (1 Cor 3:17) and "In him you too are being built together to become a dwelling in which God lives by his Spirit" (Eph 2:22). Reading back into the Old Testament this new covenant emphasis leads to an unfortunate undervaluing or denigration of Haggai's focus.[65]

As the Holy Spirit signifies the presence of Yahweh within the contemporary believer (Eph 2:22), so does the temple, and the tabernacle before it, signify Yahweh's presence among the people. Indeed, the temple and tabernacle represent the kingship of Yahweh over the people. Inasmuch as a temple represents the palace of the deity (see "Theology" above), the reconstructed temple reminds the postexilic community that Yahweh still is king over Israel even in the

---

[62]Merrill, *Haggai, Zechariah, Malachi*, p. 16.

[63]Wolff, *Haggai*, p. 22.

[64]Stuhlmueller, *Rebuilding with Hope*, p. 16.

[65]See, for example, James D. Newsome, Jr., *The Hebrew Prophets* (Atlanta: John Knox, 1984), p. 162.

absence of a human monarch in Jerusalem. Furthermore, if Yahweh abides among Judah as king, then prosperity and peace attend Yahweh's people (2 Sam 23:2-5; Ps 96:10-13; 132:11-18; Hag 2:19).

The rebuilding of the temple following the return of the Jews to Palestine restores honor to the name of Yahweh among the nations. After the nations have profaned the temple in the conquest of Jerusalem (586 B.C.), they no doubt infer the superiority of their gods over Yahweh. They do not realize that Yahweh has earlier withdrawn the divine glory from the temple (Ezekiel 10). Thus, Yahweh's honor is bound up in the temple, and its reconstruction brings honor to Yahweh not only in the eyes of Israel, but also in the eyes of the nations. The promise that the desired things (wealth) of the nations will come into the temple (2:7) reflects the practice of tribute being brought to a great king.

The community may devote itself to the task of building the temple with the assurance that the Davidic heir Zerubbabel represents the renewal of the covenant Yahweh made with David (2 Samuel 7; 1 Chronicles 17). He is the servant, the chosen one, and the signet ring of Yahweh (2:20-23) who represents Yahweh's continuing commitment to Israel. The messianic and eschatological promises of the earlier prophets remain. Zerubbabel does not himself become the anticipated king, but Zerubbabel stands at the center of the messianic line. The Davidic lineage from two of David's sons, Solomon and Nathan, comes together in Zerubbabel, the father of Abiud and Rhesa, who are ancestors of Joseph and Mary respectively (1 Chr 3:5,19; Matt 1:6,13-16; Luke 3:23,27,31). Whether the earlier promise of the coming of "the desired of all the nations" to fill Yahweh's house with glory (2:7) is a direct messianic promise is debatable (see comments on 2:7). Nevertheless, the New Testament clearly takes up the theme of the glorious presence of Yahweh among the people to describe the incarnation of Jesus Christ. "The Word became flesh and made his dwelling (i.e., "tabernacled") among us. We have seen his glory, the glory of the One and Only" (John 1:14). "The Son is the radiance of God's glory and the exact representation of his being" (Heb 1:3).

Haggai challenges the early postexilic community of Judah to look beyond their meager resources and difficult circumstances in order to believe daringly the ancient promises of Yahweh. The rebuilding of the temple in the hope of Yahweh's presence among them and of eschatological messianic blessing requires an act of faith. The community must not fear. They must be strong and give careful thought to the power of Yahweh Almighty whose glory will fill the temple in but a little while (2:4-7). The writer of Hebrews later uses the only New Testament quotation from Haggai to call his readers to the same strength, courage, and faith required of Haggai's audience. If Yahweh Almighty will once more shake the heavens and the earth (Hag 2:6) so that only Christ's unshakable kingdom remains, should not participants in the new covenant be faithful (Heb 12:25-27)?

# OUTLINE

# SELECTED BIBLIOGRAPHY
# ON HAGGAI

Alden, Robert L. "Haggai." In *Expositor's Bible Commentary*, vol. 7. Ed. by Frank E. Gaebelein. Grand Rapids: Zondervan, 1985.

Baldwin, Joyce G. *Haggai, Zechariah, Malachi: An Introduction and Commentary*. TOTC 24. Downers Grove, IL: InterVarsity, 1972.

Bedford, Peter Ross. "Discerning the Time: Haggai, Zechariah and the 'Delay' in the Rebuilding of the Jerusalem Temple." In *The Pitcher Is Broken*, pp. 71-94. Ed. by Stephen W. Holloway and Lowell K. Handy. JSOTSupp 190. Sheffield: Sheffield Academic Press, 1995.

Boda, Mark J. "Haggai: Master Rhetorician." *TynBul* 51 (2000): 295-304.

_____ . *Haggai, Zechariah*. The NIV Application Commentary. Grand Rapids: Zondervan, 2004.

_____ . "Majoring in Minors: Recent Research in Haggai and Zechariah." *Currents in Biblical Research* 2 (2003): 33-68.

Clines, David J.A., "Haggai's Temple, Constructed, Deconstructed, and Reconstructed." *Scandinavian Journal of the Old Testament* 7 (1993): 51-77.

Coggins, Richard J. *Haggai, Zechariah, Malachi*. Old Testament Guides. Sheffield: Sheffield Academic Press, 1987.

Floyd, Michael H. "The Nature of the Narrative and the Evidence of Redaction in Haggai." *VT* 45 (1995): 470-490.

Hildebrand, David R. "Temple Ritual: A Paradigm for Moral Holiness in Haggai 2:10-19." *VT* 39 (1989): 154-168.

Kessler, John. "Building the Second Temple: Questions of Time, Text, and History in Haggai 1.1-15." *JSOT* 27 (2002): 243-256.

March, W. Eugene. "Haggai." In *NIB*, vol. 7. Ed. by Leander E. Keck. Nashville: Abingdon, 1996.

Mason, Rex A. *The Books of Haggai, Zechariah, and Malachi*. CBC. Cambridge: Cambridge University Press, 1977.

_____. "The Purpose of the 'Editorial Framework' of the Book of Haggai." *VT* 27 (1977): 413-421.

Merrill, Eugene H. *Haggai, Zechariah, Malachi*. WEC. Chicago: Moody, 1994.

Meyers, Carol L., and Eric M. Meyers. *Haggai, Zechariah 1-8*. AB 25B. New York: Doubleday, 1987.

Motyer, J. Alec. "Haggai." In *The Minor Prophets: An Exegetical and Expository Commentary*, vol. 3. Ed. by Thomas Edward McComiskey. Grand Rapids: Baker, 1998.

Petersen, David L. *Haggai and Zechariah 1-8: A Commentary*. OTL. Philadelphia: Westminster Press, 1984.

Redditt, Paul Lewis. *Haggai, Zechariah and Malachi*. New Century Bible. Grand Rapids: Eerdmans, 1995.

Stuhlmueller, Carroll. *Rebuilding with Hope: A Commentary on the Books of Haggai and Zechariah*. ITC. Grand Rapids: Eerdmans, 1988.

Taylor, Richard A., and E. Ray Clendenen. *Haggai, Malachi*. NAC. Nashville: Broadman & Holman, 2004.

Tollington, Janet E. *Tradition and Innovation in Haggai and Zechariah 1-8*. JSOTSupp 150. Sheffield: Sheffield Academic Press, 1993.

Vera, José Loza. "Haggai." In *The International Bible Commentary: A Catholic and Ecumenical Commentary for the Twenty-First Century*. Ed. by William R. Farmer. Collegeville, MN: Liturgical Press, 1998.

Verhoef, Pieter A. *The Books of Haggai and Malachi*. NICOT. Grand Rapids: Eerdmans, 1987.

_____. "Notes on the Dates in the Book of Haggai." In *Text and Context: Old Testament and Semitic Studies for F.C. Fensham*, pp. 259-267. Ed. by Walter Classen. JSOTSupp 48. Sheffield: Sheffield Academic Press, 1988.

Wolff, Hans-Walter. *Haggai: A Commentary*. Trans. by Margaret Kohl. Minneapolis: Augsburg, 1988.

# HAGGAI

## I. NARRATION OF THE PROPHECY ABOUT REBUILDING THE TEMPLE (1:1-15)

Haggai 1:1-15 describes how Haggai persuades the people to change their perspective on the proper time for building the temple and reports the positive response of the people who begin to build the temple under the leadership of Zerubbabel and Joshua. As such, the section contains two parts: a prophetic disputation (vv. 1-11) and a prophetic report (vv. 12-15). The genre of prophetic disputation serves as a kind of public debate to counter popular opinions; the disputation does not record an actual exchange between debaters, but it reflects such an exchange (cf. Isa 40:27-31; Jer 7:1-15; 8:8-9; 26:1-7; Ezek 11:14-21; Micah 2:6-11).[1] Thus, verse 2 briefly summarizes the popular attitude about building the temple, and verses 3-11 argue against such a notion, hoping to disabuse the people of the opinion that it is not yet time to build the temple. To reverse this popular attitude, Haggai asks the people a rhetorical question about living in their houses already built while Yahweh's house remains in ruin (vv. 3-4), directs them to consider the present circumstances of economic failure (vv. 5-6), directs them to consider building a house for Yahweh (vv. 7-8), and explains the theological reason for the economic failure: Yahweh's house remains in ruin (vv. 9-11). The genre of prophetic report is used by the narrator to bring to light the involvement of Yahweh in a past event (cf. Mal 3:13–4:6).[2] Haggai 1:12-15 shows how the course of action urged by Haggai begins. The people heed the voice of Yahweh and the message of the prophet (v. 12), and Haggai gives the people a message of encouragement:

---

[1]Michael H. Floyd, *Minor Prophets: Part 2*, FOTL 22 (Grand Rapids: Eerdmans, 2000), p. 638.

[2]Ibid., p. 642.

Yahweh is present with them (v. 13). Yahweh stirs the spirits of Zerubbabel and Joshua, and the people begin work on the temple under their leadership (vv. 14-15).

Both of these forms, prophetic disputation and prophetic report, suit the larger genre of the book as a whole, which is prophetic history, a form which contains a narrative for which a prophetic message is central. In chapter 1, the narration identifies the time of the prophet's disputation (v. 1) and of the people's response (v. 15) and comprises both messages from the prophet (1:3,13) and observations from the narrator about Yahweh's involvement in the sequence of events (vv. 12,14). Therefore, verses 1-11 show Haggai's arguments (economic and theological) to be persuasive in countering the popular opinion about delaying work on the temple, and verses 12-15 recount the removal of the people's fear, following their acceptance of Haggai's argument, and the removal of any opposition to the project, such that rebuilding can begin under the leadership of Zerubbabel and Joshua.

## A. PROPHETIC DISPUTATION ABOUT
## THE TIME TO REBUILD (1:1-11)

[1]In the second year of King Darius, on the first day of the sixth month, the word of the LORD came through the prophet Haggai to Zerubbabel son of Shealtiel, governor of Judah, and to Joshua[a] son of Jehozadak, the high priest:

[2]This is what the LORD Almighty says: "These people say, 'The time has not yet come for the LORD's house to be built.'"

[3]Then the word of the LORD came through the prophet Haggai: [4]"Is it a time for you yourselves to be living in your paneled houses, while this house remains a ruin?"

[5]Now this is what the LORD Almighty says: "Give careful thought to your ways. [6]You have planted much, but have harvested little. You eat, but never have enough. You drink, but never have your fill. You put on clothes, but are not warm. You earn wages, only to put them in a purse with holes in it."

[7]This is what the LORD Almighty says: "Give careful thought to your ways. [8]Go up into the mountains and bring down timber and build the house, so that I may take pleasure in it and be honored,"

says the LORD. ⁹"You expected much, but see, it turned out to be little. What you brought home, I blew away. Why?" declares the LORD Almighty. "Because of my house, which remains a ruin, while each of you is busy with his own house. ¹⁰Therefore, because of you the heavens have withheld their dew and the earth its crops. ¹¹I called for a drought on the fields and the mountains, on the grain, the new wine, the oil and whatever the ground produces, on men and cattle, and on the labor of your hands."

ᵃ1 A variant of *Jeshua*; here and elsewhere in Haggai

**1:1** Haggai 1:1 indicates the date, origin, and recipients of Haggai's first prophetic message. The **first day of the sixth month** in the **second year of King Darius** corresponds to August 29, 520 B.C. The first day of the month is the first day of the new moon in the lunar calendar. Evidently it is observed, in some way, as a holy day with burnt offerings, drink offerings, and grain offerings and with the sounding of trumpets (Num 10:10; 28:11-15; Ezra 3:5; Ps 81:3; Isa 1:13-14; 66:23; Hos 2:11; Amos 8:5). This level of precision given to dating a prophecy by a specific day is found elsewhere only in Zechariah (1:7; 7:1) and Ezekiel (1:1; 8:1; 20:1-2; 24:1; 26:1; 29:1; 29:17; 30:20; 31:1; 32:1,17; 33:21; 40:1). The appearance of precise dates throughout the book emphasizes that the rebuilding of the temple is not humanly inspired, but is rather a divine work.[3] Darius the Great is son of Hystaspes and rules Persia as its third emperor (522–486 B.C.), following Cyrus (559–530 B.C.) and Cambyses (530–522 B.C.); he is not to be confused with Darius the Mede mentioned in Daniel (9:1; 11:1). Darius is responsible for the Behistun inscription, an account of his accession to power, successes in war, and suppressions of rebellion. Carved into the side of a cliff located in the Kermanshah Province of Iran, the inscription is written in Old Persian, Elamite, and Babylonian and thus has provided the means for deciphering cuneiform script.

The prophetic word formula, **The word of the LORD came through the prophet Haggai**, introduces the prophetic revelation of the entire book. In 1:3 and 2:1, the same formula introduces the report of specific prophecies. In each instance, the formula focuses

---

[3]Pieter A. Verhoef, *The Books of Haggai and Malachi*, NICOT (Grand Rapids: Eerdmans, 1987), p. 48.

on the prophet as the intermediary of the divine word. The Hebrew text states that the word of Yahweh comes "by the hand" (בְּיַד, bᵊyad) of Haggai. This rare idiom is found only four times among the prophetic books (Hag 1:1,3; 2:1; Mal 1:1); however, it occurs frequently in the Pentateuch in reference to Moses (Exod 9:35; 35:29; Lev 8:36; 10:11; Num 4:37,45,49; 10:13; 15:23; 27:23; 36:13). The more common expression, "the word of the LORD came to" (אֶל, 'el) Haggai, appears in Haggai 2:10,20. Like Habakkuk and Zechariah, Haggai is identified only by the description, "the prophet" (נָבִיא, nābî'; cf. Ezra 5:1; 6:14). This term may derive from a passive participle of a root related to the Akkadian word meaning "to call."[4] The word thus emphasizes the divine calling of one called nābî'. Haggai's name (חַגַּי, ḥaggāy) may come from the Hebrew noun for "festival" or "feast" and might indicate that he has been born on a feast day. Other Old Testament names derived from the חַג (ḥag) stem include Haggi (Gen 46:16; Num 26:15), Haggith (2 Sam 3:4), and Haggiah (1 Chr 6:30).

Although ultimately directed at the remnant of the people (v. 12), the word of Yahweh comes through Haggai **to Zerubbabel . . . and Joshua,** the civic and religious leaders of the restored Jewish community. Zerubbabel's name apparently comes from a Babylonian name (zēr bābili) that means "offshoot of Babylon."[5] As such, it probably indicates he is born in the exile and thus demonstrates a degree of assimilation into Babylonian culture during the exile. He is not to be identified with Sheshbazzar (Ezra 1:8; 5:14-15) who, according to the Aramaic annals of Ezra 5:14-16, begins the initial rebuilding of the temple.[6] Even though Josephus seems to identify Sheshbazzar as Zerubbabel,[7] the Apocrypha distinguishes between the two (1 Esdras 6:18). Rather, Zerubbabel is the **son of Shealtiel** and so it seems the grandson of the last Davidic king Jehoiachin, who himself is deported to Babylon (2 Kgs 24:8-17). However, while the MT of 1 Chronicles 3:17-19 identifies Shealtiel as son of Jehoiachin, the text indicates that Zerubbabel is one of the sons of Pedaiah, another of Jehoiachin's sons. The LXX of 1 Chronicles 3:19 (as does

---

[4]*HALOT*, pp. 661-662.
[5]Beyer, "Zerubbabel," *ABD*, 6:1084-1086.
[6]Stuhlmueller, *Rebuilding with Hope*, p. 19.
[7]Josephus, *Ant.* 11.13.

Hag 1:1 and Ezra 3:2; 5:2) says rather that he is son of Shealtiel instead of Pedaiah. The genealogical note of Haggai 1:1 may be coordinated with MT of 1 Chronicles 3:19, if Shealtiel, the eldest son of Jehoiachin, has become the legal father of Zerubbabel through levirate marriage after Zerubbabel's natural father, Pedaiah, dies (see Deut 25:5-10).[8] Both the exiled Jews and the Babylonians recognize Jehoiachin as the legitimate king of Judah (2 Kgs 24:8), and so Zerubbabel probably represents a logical choice by the Persians for the administrative responsibilities of governor. The term **governor** (פֶּחָה, *peḥāh*), an Akkadian loan word, is a reminder that Zerubbabel serves by appointment of a Persian king. The term suggests an office but perhaps not something as precise as "governor." It may simply convey the general jurisdiction over the Persian province **of Judah** or perhaps Samaria including Judah (cf. Ezra 4:10,17).[9] Joshua **the high priest**, **son of Jehozadak**, is known as Jeshua son of Jozadak in Ezra and Nehemiah (Ezra 2:2; 3:2,8-9; 5:2; Neh 7:7; 12:1). Perhaps he is the grandson of the chief priest Seraiah whom the Babylonians execute shortly after the destruction of Jerusalem (2 Kgs 25:18-21) and the son of Jehozadak who is taken into exile (1 Chr 6:15). Zechariah 3:1-10 portrays the cleansing of Joshua and the removal of the guilt of sin, and Zechariah 6:10-15 identifies him as a royal figure who builds the temple.

**1:2** Verse 2 cites a popularly held opinion about the time in which the temple should be built, introducing this citation with the messenger formula, **This is what the LORD Almighty says**. The formula indicates that Haggai communicates a message to his readers from Yahweh, who in this verse is designated for the first of fourteen times as "the LORD Almighty" (1:2,5,7,9,14; 2:4,6-9,11,23). The Hebrew phrase (יְהוָה צְבָאוֹת, *YHWH ṣᵉbā'ôth*) is also rendered in other English translations as "the LORD of Hosts" (ESV, KJV, NASB, NRSV, NJPS), "Yahweh Sabaoth" (NJB), or "sovereign LORD" (NET), and the NIV's translation captures a nuance similar to the LXX rendering, "almighty Lord" (κύριος παντοκράτωρ, *kyrios pantokratōr*).[10]

---

[8] Wolff, *Haggai*, p. 38.

[9] Merrill, *Haggai, Zechariah, Malachi*, p. 20.

[10] For a discussion on the etymology and significance of the name "the LORD of Hosts," see Baldwin, *Haggai, Zechariah, Malachi*, pp. 44-45, and A.S. van der Woude, "צָבָא," *TLOT*, pp. 1044-1046.

The name YHWH ṣᵊbā'ôth appears more than 260 times in the Old Testament (e.g., 1 Sam 1:3; 17:45; Ps 24:10; Isa 1:9; Jer 2:19; Hos 12:5; Amos 3:13; Micah 4:4; Hab 2:13; Zeph 2:9), at least 90 of these occur in the postexilic prophets (e.g., Hag 1:2; Zech 1:3; Mal 1:4).[11] Its use as a title for Yahweh may relate to the appearance of "the commander of the army [צְבָא, ṣābā'] of the LORD" in Joshua 5:13-15. The noun ṣābā' refers to an army organized for war or warfare in general; consequently, the title designates Yahweh as God of War or God of the Armies. The designation portrays Yahweh as sovereign not only over creation but over nations and history. Furthermore, in Haggai's postexilic context, the name draws attention to the kingship of Yahweh, the presence of Yahweh,[12] and the expectation that Yahweh would restore the Davidic monarchy. The appearance of the name suits the present verse, since the house of Yahweh signals the presence of Yahweh among the people. The failure of the community to rebuild the temple may imply their ambivalence about the presence of Yahweh among them.[13]

The phrase **these people** makes a distinction between the leaders Joshua and Zerubbabel and the community as a whole and may contain a notion of disapproval or rejection (cf. Isa 6:9-10; 8:6; 28:11,14; Jer 4:11; Zech 8:11). Here quoted by Yahweh and disputed by the prophet, the statement, **The time has not yet come for the LORD's house to be built**, records the claim of the people regarding the proper time to build the temple.[14] The Hebrew nouns "time"

---

[11]A longer form of the expression adds "God" (אֱלֹהִים, 'ĕlōhîm), "the LORD God of Hosts," either as YHWH 'ĕlōhîm ṣᵊbā'ôth (Ps 59:5; 80:4,7,14,19; 84:8) or as YHWH 'ĕlōhê ṣᵊbā'ôth (2 Sam 5:10; 1 Kgs 19:10,14; Ps 89:8; Jer 5:14; 15:16; 35:17; 38:17; 44:7; Amos 4:13; 5:14,15,16,27; 6:8).

[12]This notion of divine presence is emphasized in the early association of the ancient name for Yahweh with the Ark of the Covenant. In 1 Samuel 4:4, the ark is called "the ark of the covenant of the LORD of Hosts, who is enthroned between the cherubim" (cf. 2 Sam 6:2). The use of the name "the LORD of Hosts" in the postexilic context highlights the promise of Yahweh's renewed presence with the people.

[13]Motyer, "Haggai," p. 974.

[14]Haggai makes no mention of a possible earlier attempt to lay the foundation of the second temple in 536 B.C. but aborted due to opposition from neighboring peoples (Ezra 3:8-13; 4:1-5,24; 5:16). For possible (political, economic, and theological) reasons why the people are hesitant to build the temple, see Taylor and Clendenen, *Haggai, Malachi*, pp. 119-120.

(עֵת, 'ēth) and "house" (בַּיִת, bayith) both appear three times in verses 2 and 4. Haggai uses this repetition to voice a stirring indictment on the people. The text could be rendered, "This people have said, "The *time* has not come — the *time* for the *house* of Yahweh to be built. . . . Is it a *time* for you yourselves to live in your paneled *houses*, but this *house* is desolate?" The use of the word "house" also allows for a significant wordplay (Hag 1:2,4,8-9,14; 2:3,7,9). With it Haggai highlights the contrast between the people's interest in their own residences rather than in the place of Yahweh's residence; they are concerned about the wrong house.[15] Furthermore, the portrayal of the temple as a "house" focuses upon it as a divine dwelling place.[16] To leave Yahweh's house in disrepair is to disrespect Yahweh who dwells there.

**1:3-4** Haggai 1:3 repeats the prophetic word formula found in verse 1, characterizing Haggai as the mediator of the divine word. In response to the people's claim about the proper time for rebuilding the temple (v. 2), Haggai asks the people about their having already built houses for themselves (v. 4). In particular, the phrase **for you yourselves** (לָכֶם אַתֶּם, lākem 'attem) intimates that the people are committed to their own interests rather than those of Yahweh. The description of houses as **paneled**, in other contexts, suggests royal dwellings, with cedar paneling (see 1 Kgs 6:9; 7:3,7; Jer 22:14-15). Still here "paneled" is likely better understood as "roofed," since the Hebrew verb סָפַן (sāphan) generally means "to cover." Rather than accusing the people of possessing extravagant and luxurious houses, Haggai simply implies that the people's homes are roofed in, completely built, and inhabitable and that Yahweh's house is nowhere near completion, unfit for Yahweh as a dwelling place.[17] The word **ruin** (חָרֵב, ḥārēb) elsewhere describes the sacking of Solomon's temple in 586 B.C. (Neh 2:3,17; Jer 33:10; Ezek 36:35-38). Here it may signify that the temple remains in a state of physical destruction (cf. Neh 2:17) or in an uninhabitable condition (cf. Jer 33:10-12). Certainly the use of ḥārēb contrasts the people's interest in their own houses even though Yahweh's **house** remains in "ruin" (v. 9) and

---

[15]Ibid., p. 116.

[16]Meyers and Meyers, *Haggai, Zechariah 1–8*, pp. 21-22.

[17]Rex A. Mason, *The Books of Haggai, Zechariah, and Malachi*, CBC (Cambridge: Cambridge University Press, 1977), p. 16.

anticipates the later description of food shortages with the same root (חֹרֶב, ḥōreb translated "drought" in the NIV (v. 11).

**1:5-6** Verse 5 begins with the emphatic adverb **now** (עַתָּה, ʿattāh), which also appears three times in chapter 2 (vv. 3,4,15), and the messenger formula (1:2,7; 2:6), **this is what the LORD Almighty says**, indicating that Haggai delivers a message from Yahweh. The adverb and messenger formula introduces another unit of the disputation speech (vv. 2-11); here the prophet issues a command for the people to consider carefully their current situation and offers a statement and examples regarding the economic problems they presently experience. The command **Give careful thought** (שִׂימוּ לְבַבְכֶם, śîmû lᵉbabkem), with the literal meaning "set to your hearts," is used five times in Haggai (1:5,7; 2:15,18[2×]). The last one of these adds the particle of entreaty or exhortation (נָא, nāʾ), which is generally not translated in the NIV and other English translations (although often is rendered "now" in the NASB). The idiom demands serious reflection such that the people might discern the connection between their economic difficulties and their negligence of Yahweh's house (vv. 6,9-11). Verse 6 presents a contrasting statement that typifies the futility of the people's effort to garner sufficient produce from the land, **You have planted much, but have harvested little.** Following this are four examples: they **eat but** are not satisfied, they **drink but** are not filled, they wear **clothes but are not warm**, and they **earn wages** but lose monetary assets.[18] With the specific wording of these futility curses, the prophet has invoked the language reminiscent of the covenant curses in Deuteronomy (Deut 28:15-19,23-24,38-40,45; cf. Lev 26:18-20)[19] and thus indicates the underlying cause for the present economic failure, the neglect of building a house for Yahweh (v. 9).

**1:7-8** This unit begins with the messenger formula, **This is what the LORD Almighty says**, and ends with the oracle formula, **says the LORD**. The combination of the two formulas specifies that what is said between them comes from Yahweh; furthermore, only this unit

---

[18]The wording of the NIV, "You earn wages, only to put them in a purse with holes in it," reflects the frequent practice in the ancient world of workers who carry their wages in a small pouch suspended from a waist cord. The metaphor may indicate inflationary circumstances in which income is available, but their wages do not cover entirely their expenses.

[19]Wolff, *Haggai*, p. 44.

(vv. 7-8) in the larger section (vv. 1-11) is so defined, suggesting that
it is the counter thesis to the disputation: now is the time to build
the house.[20] Again, the idiom, **Give careful thought to your ways**
(v. 6), demands that the people give serious consideration of their
circumstances, but this time specific instructions follow: **Go up into
the mountains and bring down timber and build the house.** The
Hebrew noun translated "mountains" (הַר, *har*) in the NIV is singular, not plural. This may mean that the prophet is calling the people
to go up to "the mountain," that is, the temple mount. The people
should go there in order to build the temple rather than to go merely in search of wood.[21] Otherwise, the specific location of these
mountains is unknown, although different types of wood are available at the time from the Judean hills (cf. Neh 8:15), the high country near Hebron, and the mountainous regions of Carmel and
Lebanon. Since Cyrus king of Persia has earlier authorized the pro-
curement of cedar (Ezra 3:7), the present need for timber may indicate that the community has already used up the cedar for building
their own houses. More likely, however, is that the wood spoken of
here is not the cedar provided by Cyrus but rather timber of various
types to be used as scaffolding and non-ornate elements of the
building.[22]

The purpose for building the temple is **so that** Yahweh might
take delight in it and the presence of Yahweh might enter the temple. The verb **take pleasure** or "be pleased" (רָצָה, *rāṣāh*) occurs frequently in Leviticus in contexts speaking of the acceptance or nonac-
ceptance of cultic offerings (1:4; 7:18; 19:7; 22:23,25,27). Furthermore, the use of the verb "honored" (כָּבֵד, *kābēd*), translated in other
versions as "glorified" (e.g., ESV, KJV, NASB, NJB, and NJPS),
implies a special endowment of Yahweh's glorious presence and an
acknowledgment of that presence. The appearance of Yahweh's

---

[20]Marvin A. Sweeney, *The Twelve Prophets*, BerOl: Studies in Hebrew
Narrative and Poetry (Collegeville, MN: Liturgical Press, 2000), p. 538;
David A. Dorsey, *The Literary Structure of the Old Testament: A Commentary on
Genesis–Malachi* (Grand Rapids: Baker, 1999), p. 316.

[21]Sweeney, *Twelve Prophets*, p. 538; against this notion is C.F. Keil, *Minor
Prophets*, in *Biblical Commentary on the Old Testament*, by C.F. Keil and R.
Delitzsch, trans. by James Martin, reprint (Grand Rapids: Eerdmans, 1988),
10:476.

[22]Meyers and Meyers, *Haggai, Zechariah 1–8*, p. 28; Wolff, *Haggai*, p. 45.

glory is associated with Sinai (Exod 24:16-18; 34:29-35), the tabernacle (Num 14:10), the ark (1 Sam 4:21-22), and Solomon's temple (Ps 24:7-10; Isa 6:3; Ezek 11:23). The subsequent desecration of Solomon's temple causes the glory of Yahweh to leave it (Ezek 10:18-19; 11:23), but its reconstruction might allow for the presence of Yahweh to inhabit the temple again (Hag 2:7,9; Zech 2:5,10-11).[23] The particular verb form (Niphal) translated **be honored** in the NIV can have a passive (as in most English translations) or reflexive (as in the NJB, "I shall manifest my glory there") meaning. If it is read as reflexive ("I will allow myself to be honored"), it may emphasize that Yahweh attains glory through the people's obedience to Yahweh's own command to rebuild the temple (see Exod 14:4,17-18; Lev 10:3; Isa 26:15; 66:5; Ezek 28:22; 39:13).[24]

**1:9** Verse 9 presents an argument similar to that in verse 6; here the statement contrasts the people's expectation with their actual return. Their efforts to provide for themselves have yielded very little. However, verse 9 goes beyond verse 6 by offering a reason for the poor harvest. Yahweh has deprived the people of ample harvest (cf. Amos 4:6-10; Micah 6:13-15), a role highlighted in the phrase **I blew away**. The word translated **brought** (בוֹא, *bô'*) appears three times in verses 6-9: "harvest" (v. 6), "bring" (v. 8), and "brought" (v. 9). The first and third refer to the people's actions with no avail: they plant much, but harvest little, and what they bring home, Yahweh blows away. The second use of the word names the action that pleases Yahweh: bring timber to build the temple. That Yahweh blows away their harvest calls to mind the image of a threshing floor, which in some instances are the very places where temples are built (2 Sam 24:18-25; 1 Chr 21:18–22:1).[25] More pointedly, the rhetorical question **Why?** and the oracle formula, **declares the LORD Almighty** (1:9,13; 2:4[3×],8,9,14,17,23[3×]), introduce the cause of the present economic failure. Yahweh's **house . . . remains** in **ruin**, but the people remain **busy with** their **own house**s. Other versions (e.g., KJV, NASB, NRSV, and NJPS) translate the Hebrew word (רוּץ, *rûṣ*) rendered "busy" in the NIV as "run" or "hurry off." The figurative sense of the word signifies the people's quick pursuit of selfish interests

[23]Merrill, *Haggai, Zechariah, Malachi*, p. 27.
[24]BDB, p. 457; Wolff, *Haggai*, p. 46.
[25]Sweeney, *Twelve Prophets*, p. 539.

(cf. Prov 1:16; Isa 59:7), in this case regarding their own houses rather than Yahweh's.

**1:10** The verse begins with the emphatic phrase, **therefore because of you** (עַל־כֵּן עֲלֵיכֶם, *'al-kēn 'ălêkem*), highlighting the people's guilt in contrast with the references to Yahweh's role in verses 9 and 11.[26] Also, the phrase "because of you" is further accentuated by its position before the verb in the Hebrew text and its similar sound with the phrase *'al-kēn*, translated "therefore." Several verses previous (2,3,5,7,8, and 9) each contain a formulaic phrase announcing the divine origin of a statement ("This is what the LORD Almighty says," "declares the LORD Almighty," and "says the LORD"), but verse 10 begins with *'al-kēn*, an expression used to signal, by way of fact, a concluding statement or resulting action.[27] The withholding of **dew** and **crops** results from the people's failure to rebuild the temple. Here **the heavens** and **the earth** are personified, implying that they do Yahweh's bidding and are also appalled at the people's disobedience (cf. Jer 2:12-13). The absence of dew, an essential source of moisture during the dry summer months, reveals the reversal of blessing, that is, the curse for disobedience (Gen 27:39; 2 Sam 1:21; 1 Kgs 17:1; Hag 1:10).[28] Conversely, the presence of dew points to divine blessings (Gen 27:28; Deut 33:13; Job 38:28; Prov 3:19-20; Hos 14:5; Zech 8:12). In the same manner, a poor harvest of crops reflects divine judgment (Lev 26:18-20; Deut 28:15,38-40; Isa 5:10; 17:10-11; Jer 8:13; 12:13; Hag 1:6), while reaping a good harvest signals blessing from Yahweh (Gen 26:12; Lev 25:18-22; 26:3,5-10).

**1:11** While heaven and earth appear as the visible factors that contribute to drought and crop failure (v. 10), Yahweh here claims to be their initial and invisible cause. Yahweh has called on the forces of nature to serve as agents of divine wrath (cf. 2 Kgs 8:1; Ps 105:16; Isa 17:13; Ezek 32:5-6; 33:28). Drought is here, as in other texts, a sign of Yahweh's displeasure (Deut 11:17; 28:22-24; 2 Sam 1:21; 1 Kgs 17:1; Ps 107:33-34; Isa 5:6-13; Jer 2:2-3; 14:1-6; 50:38; Ezek 22:23-24; Amos 4:7). The word **drought** (חֹרֶב, *ḥōreb*) is a word-play on the earlier references to "ruin" (חָרֵב, *ḥārēb*) in verses 4 and 9. The use of this wordplay emphasizes how appropriate the pun-

---

[26]Ibid., p. 538.
[27]BDB, p. 487; Dorsey, *Literary Structure*, p. 315.
[28]*DBI*, p. 207.

ishment is for the transgression;[29] the condition of their fields ("drought") is like that of the temple ("ruin"). **Grain, new wine, and oil** are three staple crops of Palestine (Deut 7:13; 11:14; 12:17; 14:23; 18:4; 28:51; Hos 2:8,22), and they are often mentioned in contexts of blessing or cursing (Gen 27:28; Deut 7:13; 8:7-8; 11:13-14; 32:13; Ps 4:7; Jer 31:12; Joel 1:10; 2:18-24; 3:18; Hos 2:8; Amos 9:13-14). The drought affects not only the produce of the land but also people and livestock, rendering all agricultural efforts ineffectual (cf. Deut 28:33). The **labor** (יְגִיעַ, $y^egîa'$) of the **hands** refers to work one does until tired and exhausted (Josh 24:13; Isa 49:4).[30] Its use here is appropriate in a context where verse 6 speaks of the community's frustration with poor returns on their efforts.

## B. PROPHETIC REPORT ABOUT THE PEOPLE'S RESPONSE (1:12-15)

[12]**Then Zerubbabel son of Shealtiel, Joshua son of Jehozadak, the high priest, and the whole remnant of the people obeyed the voice of the LORD their God and the message of the prophet Haggai, because the LORD their God had sent him. And the people feared the LORD.**

[13]**Then Haggai, the LORD's messenger, gave this message of the LORD to the people: "I am with you," declares the LORD.** [14]**So the LORD stirred up the spirit of Zerubbabel son of Shealtiel, governor of Judah, and the spirit of Joshua son of Jehozadak, the high priest, and the spirit of the whole remnant of the people. They came and began to work on the house of the LORD Almighty, their God,** [15]**on the twenty-fourth day of the sixth month in the second year of King Darius.**

Haggai 1:12-15 comprises a prophetic report, showing how the course of action urged by Haggai begins. The people heed the voice of Yahweh and the message of the prophet (v. 12), and Haggai gives the people a message of encouragement: Yahweh is present with

---

[29]Robert B. Chisholm, Jr., *Interpreting the Minor Prophets* (Grand Rapids: Zondervan, 1990), p. 221.
[30]Ralph H. Alexander, "יְגִיעַ," *TWOT*, p. 362.

them (v. 13). Yahweh stirs the spirits of Zerubbabel and Joshua, and the people begin work on the temple under their leadership (vv. 14-15). What is more, this section advances the theological concept of "remnant" (שְׁאֵרִית, *šᵊʾērîth*), a term that appears six times in the post-exilic prophets (Hag 1:12,14; 2:2; Zech 8:6,11,12). The concept of remnant receives its greatest articulation in the eighth-century prophets Amos, Micah, and Isaiah. For example, in Amos the concept refers to three groups: an historical remnant surviving some catastrophe (1:8; cf. Isa 37:4), a faithful remnant possessing genuine spirituality and faith in Yahweh (5:15; cf. Isa 10:20-22), and an eschatological remnant receiving the everlasting kingdom after the restoration of "David's fallen tent" (9:11-12; cf. Micah 4:1-7).[31] In the exilic period, Jeremiah predominantly chooses to use forms of the word "remove" (גָּלָה, *gālāh*), most often translated "carry into exile" in the NIV, to reference those who go into exile (e.g., Jer 1:3; 13:19; 20:4; 27:20; 29:1,4,7,14) rather than *šᵊʾērîth*. For him, *šᵊʾērîth* is a negative term that denotes those left behind in Jerusalem by the Babylonian conquerors (e.g., Jer 24:8; 40:11; cf. Neh 1:2-3) and connotes insignificance or total destruction (e.g., Jer 6:9; 8:3; 11:23; 44:12). Ezekiel, however, employs the positive denotations and connotations of *šᵊʾērîth* (e.g., Ezek 6:8; 11:13).[32] The postexilic prophets identify the remnant with the small community of Jews who have survived and returned from exile (Hag 1:12,14; 2:2-3; Zech 8:6).[33]

**1:12** The verse lists the full names of **Zerubbabel** and **Joshua**, as in 1:1, presumably to verify with certainty their compliance to Yahweh's directives (1:6); likewise, **Haggai** is identified, as in 1:1, by name and title, evidently for the same reason.[34] Included with them is **the whole remnant of the people**. The use of "remnant" in Haggai is significant in two ways (see comments on "remnant" under the previous introductory paragraph). First, the term is used only after members of the community and their leaders are obedient to the voice of Yahweh (so too Yahweh is now called **their God** in verses 12 and 14).[35] Second, the term may not apply to the entire commu-

---

[31]Sang Hoon Park, "שְׁאֵרִית," *NIDOTTE*, 4:15-16.
[32]Ibid., 4:16.
[33]Stuhlmueller, *Rebuilding with Hope*, p. 22.
[34]Sweeney, *Twelve Prophets*, p. 540.
[35]Ralph L. Smith, *Micah–Malachi*, WBC 32 (Waco: Word, 1984), pp. 154-155.

nity that returns from Babylon,[36] for only the leadership and "the whole remnant *of the people*" respond. Since the term "this people" appears earlier in verse 2, one may suppose that the "remnant" here refers to only part of the community who responds in obedience (cf. Zeph 3:11-20). If this is true, the rhetorical strategy in Haggai 2:10-14 does not merely encourage sustained obedience by those who respond in chapter 1 but calls to faith those who remain disobedient. Zerubbabel, Joshua, and the remnant respond with obedience and fear. The word translated **obey** (שָׁמַע, *šāma'*) has the basic meaning to "hear" (see Deut 6:4; Ps 44:1); by extension the word means to "pay attention" (so rendered in Hag 1:12 by the NJB and NJPS) or to "obey," that is, to listen and do (see Exod 24:7; 1 Sam 12:14; Neh 9:16; Isa 42:24).[37] This is especially so when *šāma'* is followed by the word **voice**, as in this verse (cf. Gen 3:17; Exod 19:5; Deut 4:30; 13:4,18; 1 Sam 8:7; Jer 3:13,25; 7:23,28; Dan 9:10; Zech 6:15). The phrase **feared the LORD** describes a reverent and obedient response in the presence of Yahweh. The reference in verse 14 shows that the people's response is more than cultic; it entails the action of coming and working on the temple.

**1:13 Haggai** now called a **messenger** (מַלְאָךְ, *mal'āk*) speaks a **message** (מַלְאָכוּת, *mal'ākûth*) from Yahweh. The word *mal'āk* appears elsewhere as a title for prophets (2 Chr 36:15-16; Isa 42:19; 44:26; cf. the name "Malachi" in Mal 1:1) and for priests (Mal 2:7), but more often refers to an "angel" (Gen 19:12-17; 24:40; Exod 23:20; Num 20:16; 1 Kgs 13:18; Ps 91:11; Zech 1:9,13; 5:5; 6:4-5). The appearance of supernatural messengers often engenders fear and requires reassurance (Gen 21:17; Judg 6:12; 2 Kgs 1:15; Ps 34:7; cf. Matt 1:20; 28:5; Luke 1:12-13,30; 2:10). So too the appearance of Haggai as "messenger" coincides with the people's fear, and his message brings them the reassurance of Yahweh's presence and the indication of their success ("I am with you" is repeated in Hag 2:4; cf. Gen 26:3; Isa 43:5). The message **I am with you** is enclosed within references to the divine name, **this message of the LORD** and **declares the LORD**, both of which imply Yahweh's presence to save. The assurance of Yahweh's presence normally uses the preposition "with" (עִם, *'im*) and the second person singular suffix. The form

---

[36] Wolff, *Haggai*, pp. 51-52; Keil, *Minor Prophets*, pp. 478-479.
[37] Hermann J. Austel, "שָׁמַע," *TWOT*, p. 938.

here, however, uses "beside" (אֵת, 'eth) with the second person plural suffix, a form that appears only here, Haggai 2:4, and Jeremiah 42:11. The nuance here is probably "I am at your side."

**1:14** Verse 14 states that Yahweh stirs up the spirits of **Zerub-babel**, **Joshua**, and **the whole remnant** such that they come and begin to work on the temple for their God. Just as verse 12 lists the full names to indicate complete compliance, so does this verse. The expression "to stir up the spirit" generally depicts Yahweh's motiva-tion of people to assume a particular action (1 Chr 5:26; 2 Chr 21:16; 36:22; Jer 51:1,11). More significant for this context, however, are the accounts in 2 Chronicles 36:22-23, where Yahweh prompts Cyrus, and in Ezra 1:5, where Yahweh moves the hearts of the fam-ily heads of Judah and Benjamin as well as the priests and Levites to go up and build the house of Yahweh in Jerusalem (cf. Exod. 35:29; 36:2). Here the phrase also attests to Yahweh's sovereignty, even if it follows the people's obedience to the voice of Yahweh. Therefore, in verse 14, the action of the people in coming to **work on the house of the LORD Almighty** reverses their resistant declaration in verse 2, "The time has not yet come for the LORD's house to be built." The word "work" may denote various vocations (Exod 31:3; 35:2; Deut 5:13; Esth 3:9; Prov 24:27), but it also refers specifically to work on the tabernacle (Exod 35:21; 36:1) and the temple (1 Kgs 5:16).[38]

**1:15** The first half of verse 15 states that work begins on the tem-ple **on the twenty-fourth day of the sixth month**, that is, September 21, 520 B.C. Thus, the work begins on the temple some 23 days after Haggai's original prophecy (1:1-11); perhaps the delay in beginning the work takes place to prepare for the enterprise[39] or to accommo-date for the harvest.[40] At least two translations (NRSV and TNIV) take the last half of verse 15, **in the second year of King Darius**, with the following verse that begins chapter 2. If so, then Haggai 1:15b–2:1 is formulated in a manner similar to Haggai 1:1 and 2:10, listing the day, month, and year in King Darius's reign. Thus, the first part of verse 15 assigns a date to the people's response of beginning work on the temple, and the last part of verse 15 provides the date for the narration of prophecy about the promised glory of the new

[38]Sweeney, *Twelve Prophets*, p. 542.
[39]Ibid.
[40]Merrill, *Haggai, Zechariah, Malachi*, p. 32.

temple (2:1-9).[41] If the traditional versification is correct, the mention of the second year of King Darius in verse 14 may form an inclusio with the earlier reference to Darius (1:1) and may also serve as the year for both 1:12-15 and 2:1-9.[42]

## II. NARRATION OF THE PROPHECY ABOUT THE PROMISED GLORY OF THE NEW TEMPLE (2:1-9)

[1]**On the twenty-first day of the seventh month, the word of the LORD came through the prophet Haggai:** [2]**"Speak to Zerubbabel son of Shealtiel, governor of Judah, to Joshua son of Jehozadak, the high priest, and to the remnant of the people. Ask them,** [3]**'Who of you is left who saw this house in its former glory? How does it look to you now? Does it not seem to you like nothing?** [4]**But now be strong, O Zerubbabel,' declares the LORD. 'Be strong, O Joshua son of Jehozadak, the high priest. Be strong, all you people of the land,' declares the LORD, 'and work. For I am with you,' declares the LORD Almighty.** [5]**'This is what I covenanted with you when you came out of Egypt. And my Spirit remains among you. Do not fear.'**

[6]**"This is what the LORD Almighty says: 'In a little while I will once more shake the heavens and the earth, the sea and the dry land.** [7]**I will shake all nations, and the desired of all nations will come, and I will fill this house with glory,' says the LORD Almighty.** [8]**'The silver is mine and the gold is mine,' declares the LORD Almighty.** [9]**'The glory of this present house will be greater than the glory of the former house,' says the LORD Almighty. 'And in this place I will grant peace,' declares the LORD Almighty."**

Haggai 2:1-9 contains a narration of Haggai's prophecy about the promised glory of the new temple. In general, the section is part of the sequence of episodes in the larger story of the book, and thus its genre is rightly understood as prophetic history, a form which contains a narrative for which a prophetic message is central. Nonetheless, the section also consists of several other prophetic forms: a

---

[41]Petersen, *Haggai and Zechariah 1–8*, p. 62; R. Smith, *Micah–Malachi*, p. 155; Taylor and Clendenen, *Haggai, Malachi*, pp. 145-146.

[42]Meyers and Meyers, *Haggai, Zechariah 1–8*, pp. 36-37; Merrill, *Haggai, Zechariah, Malachi*, p. 29; Verhoef, *Books of Haggai and Malachi*, p. 89.

report of prophetic revelation, a commission to prophesy, and a prophetic exhortation.[43] One, it describes the prophet's reception of the word from Yahweh more so than the prophet's communication of that message to his hearers (v. 1-3). Two, it records an authoritative charge to the prophet, including specific instructions about the message and its recipients (v. 2). Three, it includes commands with supporting rationale (vv. 4-9). A date formula and a prophetic word formula (v. 1) precede directions for Haggai about delivering the prophecy, its content, and its recipients (v. 2). The prophetic message begins with a series of rhetorical questions (v. 3) followed by a series of exhortations (vv. 4-9). These exhortations include the command to be strong (because Yahweh is with them and Yahweh's Spirit remains among them) and the admonition not to be afraid (because Yahweh will shake the nations and Yahweh's new house will possess a greater glory). Therefore, Haggai 2:1-9 seeks to encourage the work of rebuilding the temple that has already begun by countering any declining morale (perhaps from previously experienced economic difficulties or from an unfavorable comparison with the previous temple structure) with assurances from Yahweh about the temple's future glory.

**2:1** Haggai 2:1 indicates the date and origin of Haggai's second prophetic message. The **twenty-first day of the seventh month** corresponds to October 17, 520 B.C., some seven weeks since Haggai's first prophetic message (1:1-11) and nearly a month since work has begun on the temple (1:12-15). The seventh month is the month in which the Feast of Tabernacles is observed, beginning on the fifteenth day and ending on the twenty-first day (Exod 34:22; Lev 23:33-43; Num 29:12-39; Deut 16:13-15). Tabernacles (also known as Booths or Ingathering) is one of the three great annual festivals, celebrating harvest at the close of the agricultural year, recalling Yahweh's provision during the wilderness wanderings, and apparently renewing the Mosaic covenant. Even though the agricultural conditions described in Haggai 1:11 no doubt make the festival's observance less joyous, the timing of the prophetic message is significant in that Solomon also has dedicated the first temple in the seventh month (1 Kgs 8:2; 2 Chr 7:8-10). Since the efforts at reconstruction of the future temple seem insignificant in comparison to

---

[43]Floyd, *Minor Prophets*, pp. 282-285.

the glory of the former temple (Hag 2:3; cf. Ezra 3:12-13), Yahweh, **through Haggai** (regarding the prophetic word formula see comments on 1:1 above), encourages the people about the glory of the future temple (vv. 4-9) on the last day of the festival during which the first temple has been dedicated.

**2:2-3** These verses begin the report of prophetic revelation, in which Yahweh commissions Haggai to deliver a prophecy and gives instructions regarding its recipients and its contents. Yahweh instructs Haggai to **speak to** the same audience as the previous prophecy (1:12): **Zerubbabel, Joshua,** and **the remnant of the people.** Specifically, Yahweh directs Haggai to **ask them** a series of three questions to challenge their perceptions about the reconstruction of the temple (v. 3).[44] The phrase "its former glory" recalls the splendor of Solomon's temple (1 Kings 6), destroyed when Jerusalem fell to the Babylonians in 586 B.C. (2 Kgs 25:9-17), and the fuller description **this house in its former glory** may suggest that Zerubbabel's temple is regarded as a continuation of Solomon's. However, the Decree of Cyrus prescribes that the rebuilt temple be ninety feet long and ninety feet wide (Ezra 6:3), a size which would exceed the dimensions of Solomon's temple (1 Kgs 6:2). Thus the present disappointment may regard the lack of materials thought suitable for the structure and the lack of the sacred objects, like the Ark of the Covenant, needed to fill it. Here the word "glory" (כָּבוֹד, *kābôd*) simply refers to the grandeur or magnificence of the temple building (cf. 2 Chr 32:27; Ps 49:16-17) rather than to the entry of Yahweh's glory into it (cf. Exod 40:34-35; 1 Kgs 8:11).[45] The adverb **now** (עַתָּה, *'attāh*) appears at the end of its clause, thus admitting and emphasizing the lack of glory the new structure appears to have.[46] Although it is not stated here, perhaps some of the older members of the community have taken part in the original attempt to rebuild in 536 B.C. (Ezra 3:8-13), and the reaction expressed by **seem to you like nothing** is comparable to that of those who have earlier completed the foundation of the temple (Ezra 3:12-13). Verse 3 then asks a series of questions answered by verses 6-9, which also use some of the same words from verse 3: former, house, and glory.

---

[44]Wolff, *Haggai*, p. 77.
[45]Ibid.
[46]Motyer, "Haggai," p. 987.

**2:4** Exhortations to be strong and courageous are often grounded in Yahweh's promise of success (Deut 31:6; Josh 1:6-9; Judg 7:9-15; 2 Chr 32:7).[47] For example, the command to "be strong" prefaces words of encouragement for those going to war (Deut 31:6-7; Josh 10:25; 2 Sam 10:12; Josh 1:9; 2 Chr 19:11; 32:7). The threefold repetition of **be strong** recalls the challenge of Moses and Yahweh to Joshua in preparation for the conquest of Canaan (Deut 31:6-7; Josh 1:6,7,9,18) and the encouragement of David to Solomon in preparation for building the temple, an encouragement also paired with the command to **work** (1 Chr 28:10,20). The inference then is that Yahweh, who helps Solomon build the former temple, now enables **Zerubbabel, Joshua,** and **the people** to construct the present temple. In contrast to other references in the book (Hag 1:1,14; 2:2,21), Zerubbabel is not addressed as "governor of Judah," a title suggesting that his authority derives from the Persian king.[48] Rather, Zerubbabel like Joshua and all the people of the land are encouraged and empowered by Yahweh, as is evidenced in the threefold repetition of the oracle formula. Two shorter formulas, **declares the LORD,** precede the longer formula, **declares the LORD Almighty**. Whereas the shorter formulas punctuate calls for Zerubbabel, Joshua, and the people of the land to be strong, the longer underscores the climactic affirmation, **for I am with you**. The presence of the LORD Almighty (that is, the LORD of Hosts) provides both motivation and strength for the work to which the people are called. Elsewhere, the term "the people of the land" has different connotations.[49] In preexilic times, the phrase refers to the upper class consisting of landowning citizens and political leaders (2 Kgs 11:14-15; 21:24; 23:30). Ezra 4:4 uses the expression "the people of the land" (עַם־הָאָרֶץ, 'am-hā'āreṣ), translated "peoples around them" in the NIV, in reference to enemies of "the people of Judah" (עַם־יְהוּדָה, 'am-yᵉhûdāh) who oppose earlier efforts to rebuild the temple (Ezra 4:1-5; cf. Neh 10:28,30). However, here the designation **all you people of the land**, as in Zechariah 7:5, probably refers to the whole

---

[47]*DBI*, p. 176.

[48]Wolff, *Haggai*, p. 78.

[49]On the general use of the phrase in the Old Testament, see E.W. Nicholson, "The Meaning of the Expression עַם הָאָרֶץ in the Old Testament," *JSS* 10 (1965): 59-66.

postexilic community and denotes the same group as does "all the remnant of the people" in Haggai 1:12-14 and 2:2 (see comments on 1:12 above).[50] In Haggai the people of the land are indeed the supporters of the temple rebuilding project, the very ones whom Haggai holds responsible for the work of rebuilding.[51] Thus, the designation "the people of the land," perhaps drawing on the connotation of its preexilic usage, may serve Yahweh's attempts to turn away the attention of the people from their sense of inadequacy (Hag 2:3) with Yahweh's reassurance of competency (vv. 4-5). The commands to "be strong" and to "work" are followed by a motivation clause that is introduced by the conjunction "for" (כִּי, *kî*). The leaders and the people should work because Yahweh supports their efforts and assures the success of their effort. Yahweh promises to be present with them ("For I am with you"), an assertion further reinforced by the oracle formula ending the verse ("declares the LORD Almighty").

**2:5** The first part of 2:5, **This is what I covenanted with you when you came out of Egypt**, is absent from LXX and is considered an editorial gloss by the NJB and NEB. If the wording actually represents a later scribal addition to the MT, it may have originated from a marginal reference to Exodus 29:45-46, a passage ending the section on the consecration of the priests.[52] This explanation, however, accounts only for the reference to the exodus from Egypt and the dwelling of Yahweh among the people but not the making of the covenant. More likely, the wording reflects the confirmation of the covenant (Exod 24:8) and its renewal (Exod 34:10,27; cf. Deut 29:1); in particular, these passages use both the words "word" (דָּבָר, *dābār*), presumably translated "what" in the NIV, and "make a covenant" (כָּרַת, *kārāth*).[53] Notably the latter of these two episodes follows the golden calf rebellion (Exodus 32–33), which itself interrupts the description of the tabernacle's construction (Exodus 25–40). Moreover, the mention of the Spirit's presence in the second part of 2:5 (**And my Spirit remains** [עָמַד, *'āmad*] **among you**), which is similar to the earlier assurance "I am with you" (Hag 2:4), may also recall

---

[50]Motyer, "Haggai," p. 987; Taylor and Clendenen, *Haggai, Malachi*, p. 153.

[51]Meyers and Meyers, *Haggai, Zechariah 1–8*, p. 51.

[52]Baldwin, *Haggai, Zechariah, Malachi*, p. 47.

[53]Other passages use the same vocabulary, namely, "make a covenant" (*kārāth*), "came" (יָצָא, *yāṣā'*), and "Egypt" (Deut 29:25; 1 Kgs 8:9,21; 2 Chr 5:10; Jer 31:32; 34:13).

other portrayals of the presence of Yahweh during the exodus as the Spirit of Yahweh (Neh 9:20,30; Isa 63:10-14),[54] whose presence is said to "stand" or "stay" (*'āmad*) at the entrance of the tent of meeting in a pillar of cloud (Exod 33:9-10; cf. Exod 13:21-22).[55] Now Haggai reminds the people rebuilding the temple that the Spirit of Yahweh is present with them just as Yahweh has been present with their ancestors, with whom Yahweh made the covenant after bringing them out of Egypt, when they build the tabernacle. These allusions to the exodus, covenant, tabernacle, and divine presence form the basis for the apocalyptic language in verses 6-9.[56] In spite of fears experienced in earlier stages of the temple's reconstruction (cf. Ezra 3:3; 4:4-5),[57] Haggai admonishes the people **not** to **fear** because Yahweh will cause a cosmic upheaval that will bring a greater glory to the present temple (Hag 2:6-9).

**2:6** Verse 6 actually begins with the causal conjunction "for" (כִּי, *kî*) not translated by the NIV (cf. the ESV, NRSV, and NJB). Thus verses 6-9 give rationale for the admonition not to be afraid in verse 5. Five formulas, which introduce or conclude divine speech, appear in the next unit (vv. 6-9). The first is a messenger formula, **This is what the LORD Almighty says**, which marks the beginning of the unit containing four alternating oracle formulas: "says the LORD Almighty" (vv. 7,9) and "declares the LORD Almighty" (vv. 8,9). The proliferation of these formulas with the name "the LORD Almighty" (or "the LORD of Hosts") is fitting in this unit which exhibits many themes relating to the supremacy of Yahweh, who is victorious over creation (v. 6) and over the nations (v. 7), the very source of the covenant people's prosperity (vv. 7-8) and of the glory that fills the temple (vv. 8-9). The phrase, rendered in the NIV as **in a little while . . . once more**, reads in the Hebrew text something like, "yet one,

---

[54]Mark J. Boda, *Haggai, Zechariah,* The NIV Application Commentary (Grand Rapids: Zondervan, 2004), pp. 122-123.

[55]Mason, *Books of Haggai, Zechariah, and Malachi,* p. 20; Verhoef, *Books of Haggai and Malachi,* p. 100. This use of the word "stand" (עָמַד, *'āmad*) may also represent an ironic reversal of a dominant cultic use of the concept of standing before Yahweh. Whereas the Levites (Deut 10:8-10), the priests (Ezek 44:15), and the assembly of Israel (Lev 9:5; Deut 4:10) are called to stand before Yahweh, Yahweh now stands in their midst.

[56]Merrill, *Haggai, Zechariah, Malachi,* p. 39.

[57]The command not to fear appears frequently in Isaiah in oracles of redemption and future glory (40:9; 41:10-14; 43:1,5; 44:2; 54:4).

little is it." A similar phrase appears elsewhere in eschatological passages (Ps 37:10; Isa 10:25; Jer 51:33; Hos 1:4). The LXX alters the phrase slightly to "yet once more" (ἔτι ἅπαξ, *eti hapax*), a reading emphasized in Hebrews 12:26-28 where the writer envisions the final shaking of the created order such that only Christ's unshakable kingdom remains. The phrase in Haggai anticipates the promise of Yahweh's action in **shak**ing **the heavens and the earth**. The words "in a little while" emphasize the promise's imminent and certain fulfillment,[58] while the words "once more" may allude to the precedent of Yahweh's previous activity, perhaps, in view of other allusions in verses 4-5 to exodus traditions, the "shaking" of Mount Sinai at Yahweh's appearance (cf. Exod 19:16-19).[59] Grammatically, the Hebrew text uses the emphatic pronoun **I** to stress that it is Yahweh who acts, and the participle "shaking" suggests that Yahweh is acting at present. The exceptional action of Yahweh, here described as a kind of cosmic cataclysm, signifies a change in favor for Haggai and his readers (cf. Isa 51:6). The word "shake" (רָעַשׁ, *rāʿaš*), appearing later in 2:21, evokes the images of the crossing of the Red Sea (Ps 77:18), the shaking of Mount Sinai (Ps 68:8), and also the imagery of the Divine Warrior (Judg 5:4). Its use, nevertheless, does not demand that the prophet anticipates actual geological upheaval or international turmoil, since the word is used metaphorically elsewhere (e.g., 2 Sam 22:8; Ps 18:7; 46:3; Isa 24:18; Joel 2:10; 3:16; Nahum 1:5). Furthermore, the particular form of *rāʿaš* used here (*hiphil* stem) is rare and usually occurs in contexts of historical rather than meteorological upheaval (e.g., Ps 60:4; Isa 14:16; Ezek 31:16).[60] Thus, the verse uses theophanic imagery to express the far-reaching implications of the reconstruction of the temple, which affect all creation ("the heavens and the earth"; cf. Hag 1:10) and all the earth (**the sea and the dry land**).

**2:7** This cataclysmic shaking affects not only the heavens and the earth but also the **nations**, moving from creation to the realm of human affairs (on the word "shake" see 2:6 above). Such imagery, reminiscent of the theophanic tradition in which the appearing of Yahweh is accompanied by universal shaking (Exod 19:18; Judg 5:4-

---

[58]Wolff, *Haggai*, p. 81.
[59]Boda, *Haggai, Zechariah*, p. 123.
[60]Wolff, *Haggai*, p. 81.

5; Ps 18:7-15), serves here to encourage the disheartened builders of Yahweh's house.[61] Although **the desired of all nations** has been traditionally understood as a messianic reference (cf. the Vulgate, KJV, and NKJV),[62] such a reading seems unlikely in the context of verses 7-8 which envision the wealth (i.e., silver and gold) of the nations coming to the temple. The translation of the word "desired" (חֶמְדַּה, *ḥemdāh*) is somewhat problematic. It appears in a singular form in the Hebrew text but is translated by a plural form in the LXX, likely because the LXX takes the Hebrew form with a plural vocalization (i.e., the LXX reads the consonants as if pointed with plural vowels).[63] Several modern versions also translate the word with the plural word "treasures" (e.g., the ESV, NLT, and NJB; cf. "precious things" in the NJPS), a rendering which may express well the sense of the Hebrew word if it is correctly understood to represent a collective notion (cf. "wealth" in the NASB).[64] Nonetheless, by declining to translate *ḥemdāh* as a plural noun, the NIV may (wrongly?) intimate a messianic understanding of the word.[65] Occurring some sixteen times in the MT (1 Sam 9:20; 2 Chr 21:20; 32:27; 36:10; Ps 106:24; Isa 2:16; Jer 3:19; 12:10; 25:34; Ezek 26:12; Dan 11:8,37; Hos 13:15; Nahum 2:9; Hag 2:7; Zech 7:14), the word *ḥemdāh* generally refers to inanimate items of particular value (e.g., ships, houses, fields, and other treasured objects). The reference to silver and gold in verse 8 points to a similar understanding of "desire" as "treasures" in the present context[66] and may depict a return of the treasures once taken from the temple (2 Kgs 25:13-17). If so, the bringing of "the riches of the nations" in Isaiah 60:5-9 may present a similar parallel (cf. Zech 14:14; Rev 21:26). Perhaps Haggai here echoes the exodus motif of the Israelites' spoiling of the Egyptians (Exod 3:21-22; 11:2-3; 12:35-36) in order to gain materials for tabernacle

---

[61]Ibid., p. 85.

[62]The wording "Dear Desire of every nation" in Charles Wesley's hymn, entitled "Come, Thou Long Expected Jesus," suggests a messianic reading of verse 7, although the NT never quotes Hag 2:7 as a messianic prophecy.

[63]*HALOT*, p. 326; GKC, §145e.

[64]*IBHS*, §7.2.1.

[65]Herbert Wolf, "'The Desire of All Nations' in Haggai 2:7; Messianic or Not?" *JETS* 19 (1976): 97-102, argues that the word "desire" is deliberately ambiguous and thus allows for both a material and messianic reference.

[66]Boda, *Haggai, Zechariah*, pp. 124-125; Taylor and Clendenen, *Haggai, Zechariah*, pp. 160-165; Verhoef, *Books of Haggai and Malachi*, p. 104.

construction (Exod 25:1-8; 35:21-29). Certainly the tribute of the
nations is a primary source in furnishing the temple of Solomon
(2 Sam 8:7-11; 1 Kgs 7:51) and the temple of Zerubbabel (Ezra 6:8-
12; 7:12-26; cf. 2 Macc 3:3). Such gifts are appropriate in view of
Yahweh's sovereignty over all nations (2 Chr 20:6; Ps 2:8; 7:8; 22:28;
47:8; 82:8; 99:1; Jer 10:7) and Yahweh's promise to bless all nations
through Abraham and Israel (Gen 12:3; 18:18; 22:18; 26:4; Exod
19:5-6; Ruth 1:16; cf. Gal 3:8).[67] The coming of the nation's treasures
provides the means by which Yahweh will **fill** the restored temple
**with glory** (כָּבוֹד, *kābôd*), a word in the present context (also vv. 3,9)
that refers to the grandeur or magnificence of the temple building
(cf. 2 Chr 32:27; Ps 49:16-17).[68] However, both Ezekiel and Zechariah
associate "glory" with the resplendent presence of Yahweh in the
sanctuary (Ezek 1:28; 8:4; 9:3; 10:4,18-19; 11:22-23; 43:2,4-5; 44:4;
Zech 2:5,8). In so doing, they reflect earlier Pentateuch texts that
refer to the glory of the divine presence (Exod 29:42-43; 40:34-35;
Lev 9:5-6,23). Thus, Haggai here may use a wordplay alluding to the
filling of the temple with Yahweh's glory, evidenced by the enhance-
ment of the temple with material glory.[69] Concluding with a messenger formula, verse 7 thus indicates that these promises to shake
the nations and to fill the temple with glory originate from **the LORD
Almighty**.

**2:8** Verse 8 specifies the wealth of the nations that comes to the
house of Yahweh. The listing of **silver** before **gold** reflects the economic standards of the period in which the value of silver as currency is greater than that of gold; only during a later period (after 500
B.C.) does gold replace silver as the more valuable commodity.[70] Both
silver and gold are used to provide for the construction of Solomon's
temple (1 Kgs 7:51; 1 Chr 29:2,7). The double use of the possessive
phrase "to me" (לִי, *lî*), translated **mine** in the NIV, emphasizes
Yahweh's exclusive right to the wealth of the nations;[71] the appearance of these two phrases before the words "silver" and "gold" in the

---

[67]Verhoef, *Books of Haggai and Malachi*, p. 103.

[68]Petersen, *Haggai and Zechariah 1–8*, p. 68; Verhoef, *Books of Haggai and
Malachi*, p. 104.

[69]Mason, *Books of Haggai, Zechariah, and Malachi*, p. 21; Boda, *Haggai,
Zechariah*, pp. 125-126.

[70]Meyers and Meyers, *Haggai, Zechariah 1–8*, pp. 54, 348.

[71]Wolff, *Haggai*, p. 82.

Hebrew text is reflected in the rendering of the NJB, "Mine is the silver, mine the gold!" Ezra 6:8-12 records how an order from Darius provided monies for the temple reconstruction from the revenues of the royal treasury of the province of Trans-Euphrates. Perhaps this decree arrives soon after Haggai speaks these words.[72] Yahweh's absolute claim to possess the wealth of the nations (cf. Job 41:11; Ps 24:1-2; 50:10-12) counters the meager means of those building the temple, since they have recently suffered through drought and famine (1:6,9-11). More important than the monetary gifts of Darius, Haggai and his readers receive such reassurance directly from the LORD of Hosts (**declares the LORD Almighty**).

**2:9** Verse 9 describes two results of Yahweh's action in shaking all creation ("the heavens and the earth") and all nations: this present house will have a **greater** glory than **the former house**, and Yahweh will grant peace to this place. Both of these results complete the rationale or motivation (see comments on the conjunction "for" under 2:6 above) that supports the earlier prohibition, "do not fear" (2:5). The first result is supported by the formula **says the LORD Almighty**, and the second result, by the formula **declares the LORD Almighty**. Both of these formulas emphasize that the one promising such results is indeed the LORD Almighty (or the LORD of Hosts). If aid comes from Persia as Darius promises (Ezra 6:8-12), the fulfillment of the divine promise about the greater **glory of this present house** may occur at the completion of Zerubbabel's temple. Or, the promise may be fulfilled with the enlargement and embellishment of Zerubbabel's temple by Herod the Great (cf. Mark 13:1; Luke 21:5; John 2:20).[73] The depiction of the treasures of the nations filling the house of Yahweh (2:7-8), furthermore, may intimate that the nations will join the Jews in the worship of Yahweh at the temple, thereby making its glory greater (cf. Isa 2:2-4; 27:13; 57:13; 60:3-5; 66:20; Zech 14:16-21).[74] However, interpretations that identify the fulfillment of the promise of greater splendor in the divine habitation of Yahweh (Hag 2:4-5)[75] or in the physical presence of Jesus (John 2:2)[76] are

---

[72]Baldwin, *Haggai, Zechariah, Malachi*, p. 48.

[73]Ibid., p. 48; Cohen, *Twelve Prophets*, p. 261.

[74]Meyers and Meyers, *Haggai, Zechariah 1–8*, p. 54.

[75]E.g., Merrill, *Haggai, Zechariah, Malachi*, p. 41.

[76]E.g., Motyer, "Haggai," p. 991; Verhoef, *Books of Haggai and Malachi*, p. 109.

bound to an incorrect contextual reading of "glory" and an incorrect
messianic reading of "desired" in verse 7 (see comments on 2:7
above). Elsewhere Haggai refers to the temple as "house" (1:2,8,9,14;
2:3,7,9) or "temple" (2:15,18). In the context of verse 9, **this place** is
synonymous with "this present house," a synonym for the temple (cf.
1 Kgs 8:29-30; 2 Chr 6:20-21,38,40; 7:12).[77] In other comparable contexts, the word "place" (מָקוֹם, *māqôm*) refers to Jerusalem as the place
chosen by Yahweh (Deut 12:5; 2 Kgs 22:16-20; Jer 7:3,7,20). The use
of "this place" may recall Yahweh's selection of a place of worship to
establish the divine name (Deut 12:5-26; 14:23-25; 15:20; 16:2-16;
17:8,10; 18:6; 26:2; 31:11), Solomon's designation of the temple as a
place for Yahweh's name (1 Kgs 8:29-30,35; 2 Chr 6:20-21,26,40), and
more importantly Yahweh's promise to attend to the prayers of the
people offered in "this place" (2 Chr 7:12,15). The **grant**ing of **peace**
(שָׁלוֹם, *šālôm*) brings to an end the curse of drought and unproductive
labor (Hag 1:6,9-11). The word *šālôm* is generally rendered "peace"
(e.g., ESV, KJV, NASB, NET, and NJB), but some versions (e.g.,
NRSV and NJPS) translate the word as "prosperity," a sense recalling
these earlier economic difficulties. Moreover, *šālôm* denotes the
eschatological blessings of the covenant relationship between
Yahweh and Israel (cf. Jer 14:13; Ezek 34:25-26; 37:26); such blessings
also extend to the nations (cf. Zech 9:10).[78]

## III. NARRATION OF THE PROPHECY ABOUT DIVINE BLESSINGS FOR A DEFILED PEOPLE (2:10-19)

[10]On the twenty-fourth day of the ninth month, in the second
year of Darius, the word of the LORD came to the prophet Haggai:
[11]"This is what the LORD Almighty says: 'Ask the priests what the
law says: [12]If a person carries consecrated meat in the fold of his
garment, and that fold touches some bread or stew, some wine, oil
or other food, does it become consecrated?'"

The priests answered, "No."

[13]Then Haggai said, "If a person defiled by contact with a dead
body touches one of these things, does it become defiled?"

---

[77]Boda, *Haggai, Zechariah*, p. 127; Wolff, *Haggai*, p. 83.
[78]Verhoef, *Books of Haggai and Malachi*, p. 107.

"Yes," the priests replied, "it becomes defiled."

[14]Then Haggai said, "'So it is with this people and this nation in my sight,' declares the LORD. 'Whatever they do and whatever they offer there is defiled.

[15]"'Now give careful thought to this from this day on[a] —consider how things were before one stone was laid on another in the LORD's temple. [16]When anyone came to a heap of twenty measures, there were only ten. When anyone went to a wine vat to draw fifty measures, there were only twenty. [17]I struck all the work of your hands with blight, mildew and hail, yet you did not turn to me,' declares the LORD. [18]'From this day on, from this twenty-fourth day of the ninth month, give careful thought to the day when the foundation of the LORD's temple was laid. Give careful thought: [19]Is there yet any seed left in the barn? Until now, the vine and the fig tree, the pomegranate and the olive tree have not borne fruit.

"'From this day on I will bless you.'"

[a]15 Or to the days past

Haggai 2:10-19 contains a narration of the prophecy about divine blessings for a defiled people. The section continues the general sequence of episodes in the larger story of the book, and thus its genre is rightly understood as prophetic history, a form which contains a narrative for which a prophetic message is central. Even so, the section also consists of two other prophetic forms: a report of a prophetic symbolic action (cf. Jer 13:1-11; Hos 1:2-9; 3:1-5; Zech 6:9-15; 11:4-17) and a prophetic exhortation.[79] One, it describes the prophet's actions as a symbolic dramatization of the prophet's message (vv. 11-13), consisting of a commission to act (v. 11), a report of compliance (vv. 12-13), and an interpretation of the action's significance (vv. 14-19). Two, it includes commands with supporting rationale, here not introduced with the typical causal conjunction "for" but drawn from the analogy of the symbolic action of consulting the priest (vv. 15-19). A date formula and a prophetic word formula (v. 10) precede the command for Haggai to request a priestly ruling from the law (v. 11) about the transfer of holiness from consecrated meat to some other food (v. 12) and of defilement from a dead body to a person (v. 13). Following the inquiries of Haggai and the

---

[79]Floyd, *Minor Prophets*, pp. 294-295; Wolff, *Haggai*, p. 89.

responses of the priests, Haggai compares the present condition of the people to the priests' statements about ritual purity (v. 14) and instructs them to consider their experience of agricultural productivity before and since the building of the temple has resumed (vv. 15-19). Therefore, verses 10-19 seek to encourage the continuation of rebuilding the temple structure (since only the presence of a completed temple, not merely an altar to offer sacrifices, may properly purify the people), by reminding the people of the curse upon their previous agricultural endeavors and by assuring the people of the divine blessing soon to come.

**2:10** Haggai 2:10 indicates the date and origin of Haggai's third prophetic message. **The twenty-fourth day of the ninth month in the second year of Darius** corresponds to December 18, 520 B.C.[80] The date, itself holding no special significance, comes two months and three days since Haggai's second prophetic message (v. 1-10), three months since work began on the temple (1:15), and three months and twenty-three days since Haggai's first prophetic message (1:1-11). The prophetic word formula, **the word of the LORD came to the prophet Haggai**, is similar to the one found earlier (1:1,3; 2:1; but cf. 2:20), except that the word of the LORD is said to come "to" Haggai rather than "through" him (see comments on 1:1 above). The difference in wording is slight, but it may emphasize Haggai's reception of the divine word rather than his role as the one who delivers that word.

**2:11** Verse 11 begins with the messenger formula, **This is what the LORD Almighty says** (on the title "the LORD Almighty," see comments on 1:2 above). The formula here legitimizes Haggai's inquiry of the priests.[81] Yahweh thus commissions Haggai to request a ruling from **the priests** about **what the law says**. Such a priestly decision or "ruling" (so translated in the NASB, NRSV, NJB, and NJPS) is here called "law" (תּוֹרָה, *tôrāh*), a characteristic type of speech for priests just as is "counsel" (עֵצָה, *'ēṣāh*) for wisdom teachers and "word"

---

[80]Zechariah begins to prophesy a few weeks earlier "in the eighth month of the second year of Darius" (Zech 1:1). Like Haggai, he calls the people to return to Yahweh so that Yahweh may return to them with blessing (Zech 1:3).

[81]Sweeney, *Twelve Prophets*, p. 547.

(דָּבָר, *dābār*) for prophets (Deut 17:11; Mal 2:7; cf. Jer 18:18; Ezek 7:26; Hos 4:6; Zech 7:2-4).[82]

**2:12-13** Yahweh instructs Haggai to inquire of the priests for an official ruling regarding ritual purity. The inquiry concerns two specific questions about the transmission of holiness and defilement. The rhetorical construction of the two scenarios is similar; each begins with the hypothetical particle "if," followed by a complicating factor (in the first instance signaled by the word "and") and then by an appeal for a ruling (indicated by the interrogative particle, not translated with an English word per se but expressed by the concluding question mark).[83] The first scenario concerns the transfer of holiness from sacrificial meat. That is, **if a person carries** home some of the holy **meat** (cf. Jer 11:15) from a fellowship offering (Lev 7:11-21) **in the fold of his garment and that** portion of the garment **touches some** other foodstuff, **does** this other foodstuff also **become** holy? In reply, **the priests answer, "No."** The priestly tradition in Leviticus 6:26-27 (cf. Exod 29:21,37) assumes that the consecrated meat makes the fold of the garment holy, but evidently such holiness cannot be transferred from a consecrated object indirectly to a third person or object.[84] The second scenario concerns the transfer of defilement from a dead body. That is, **if a person** becomes **defiled** from **contact with a** corpse and the defiled person **touches** the same foodstuff, **does it become defiled?** In reply, **the priests** answer affirmatively by repeating the main verb in the question, **"It becomes defiled."** Ritual impurity results from contact with a corpse (Lev 22:4-6; Num 5:2; 6:6-7; 9:6; 19:11-13,22), and it can be transferred, unlike holiness, even to a third level.

**2:14** In verses 12-13, the priests provide an official ruling regarding the transfer of purity and impurity; in verse 14, **Haggai** applies this ruling to the present condition of the people before Yahweh. This analogy between the ruling of the priests and the status of the

---

[82]Wolff, *Haggai*, p. 90; see Erin M. Meyers, "The Use of *Tôrâ* in Haggai 2:11 and the Role of the Prophet in the Restoration Community," in *The Word of the Lord Shall Go Forth: Essays in Honor of David Noel Freedman in Celebration of His Sixtieth Birthday*, ed. by Carol L. Meyers and M. O'Connor (Winona Lake, IN: Eisenbrauns, 1983), pp. 69-76.

[83]Michael Fishbane, *Biblical Interpretation in Ancient Israel* (Oxford: Clarendon, 1985) p. 307.

[84]Ibid., p. 297;. Hildebrand, "Temple Ritual," p. 161.

people is made overt with the threefold repetition of the comparative particle **so** (כֵּן, *kēn*). The NASB renders all three occurrences:
"'So is this people. And so is this nation before Me,' declares the
LORD, 'and so is every work of their hands; and what they offer there
is unclean.'" The expression **this people** (הָעָם־הַזֶּה, *hā'ām-hazzeh*),
also found in 1:2, refers elsewhere, except for Isaiah 23:13, to the
people of Yahweh (e.g., Isa 6:9-10; 8:6,11,12; 9:16; Jer 4:10-11;
5:14,23; Zech 8:6,11-12).[85] The word "nation" (גּוֹי, *gôy*) generally
refers to non-Israelite nations (e.g., Exod 34:24; Lev 18:24), but the
expression **this nation** (הַגּוֹי הַזֶּה, *haggôy hazzeh*) refers to the people
of Yahweh (Exod 33:12-13; Judg 2:20; 2 Kgs 6:18; cf. Jer 5:9,29; 7:28;
9:9). Even though these two expressions regularly refer to Yahweh's
own people; they often carry overtones of reproach and rejection
(cf. Jer 6:19,21; 14:10-11).[86] A striking parallel that combines the
phrase "this nation" with the noun "people" appears in Moses' plea
for Israel: "Remember that this nation is your people" (Exod 33:13).
Notably this incident of the golden calf has likely influenced the
wording of Haggai 2:4-5. Just as the guilty party is named with corresponding expressions ("this people" and "the nation"), the indictment against them is expressed with a certain parallelism (**whatever
they do and whatever they offer there**). The first of these may refer
to the work on the temple site,[87] the produce of their agricultural
efforts (cf. Hag 1:6,10-11; 2:15-18),[88] or, like the second one, the
offering of sacrifices on the altar.[89] The word "offer" (קָרַב, *qārab*) is
common in the OT for the presentation of sacrificial offerings (e.g.,

---

[85]Other commentators (e.g., Wolff, *Haggai*, pp. 92-94) identify "this people" as the Samaritan community who prevent the original attempt to
rebuild the temple (Ezra 4:1-5). If so, Haggai 2:12-14 may intimate that the
impurity of Samaritans would defile the Judean community but the holiness
of the Judean community could not make the Samaritans holy. Nonetheless,
the notion that "this people" refers to the Samaritans ignores the earlier use
of the expression for the Judean community (1:2) and the apparent omission
of any reference to the Samaritans in the book (Brevard S. Childs, *Introduction to the Old Testament as Scripture* [Philadelphia: Fortress, 1979], p. 468).

[86]Aelred Cody, "When Is the Chosen People Called a *gôy*," *VT* 14 (1964):
2; Herbert G. May, "'This People' and 'This Nation' in Haggai," *VT* 18
(1968): 193.

[87]Verhoef, *Books of Haggai and Malachi*, p. 120.

[88]Petersen, *Haggai, Zechariah 1–8*, p. 83.

[89]Boda, *Haggai, Zechariah*, p. 146.

Lev 1:2-3,5,10,13-15; Num 5:25; 6:14,16),[90] and the adverb "there" probably points to the altar of the unfinished temple building (cf. Ezra 2:68–3:13). The impurity of the people of Yahweh affects all their work and worship. Moreover, the temple remains in ruin, like a corpse in their midst, defiling the entire community.[91]

**2:15** The transitional word **now** (וְעַתָּה, *wᵉ'attāh*) links verse 15-19 with verses 10-14[92] and initiates an appeal for the people to consider their past (**before one stone was laid on another**) and future (**from this day on**) circumstances. The word "now" has both a temporal (at the present time) and inferential (based on the previous statement) sense, although the latter may be primary here (cf. 1:5; 2:4).[93] The command to **give careful thought** (see comments on 1:5 above) in this verse anticipates its two uses in verse 18. It demands serious reflection such that the people might discern the connection between what they have experienced, in particular their economic difficulties (vv. 16-17) caused by their present impurity (vv. 11-14), and the blessings anticipated by the short promise of verse 19: "from the day I will bless you." The phrase "from this day on" is problematic because of the word translated "on" (מַעַל, *ma'al*) in the NIV. It generally refers to spatial directions (i.e., "above" as in Exod 20:4; Deut 4:39; Isa 45:8), chronological sequences (i.e., a certain age or "more" as in Exod 30:14; Lev 27:7; Num 1:3), or comparative degrees (i.e., "higher" and "more" in Deut 28:43 and 2 Chr 17:12). At issue is whether *ma'al*, here and in verse 18, refers to the past or the future. For example, the NJPS renders the first reference in

---

[90]Leonard J. Coppes, "קָרַב," *TWOT*, p. 812.

[91]Baldwin, *Haggai, Zechariah, Malachi*, p. 51; Fishbane, *Biblical Interpretation*, p. 298.

[92]The relationship between 2:15-19 and 10-14 is disputed by those who (e.g., Johann Wilhelm Rothstein, *Juden und Samaritaner: Die grundlegende Scheidung von Judentum und Heidentum*, BWANT 3 [Leipzig: Hinrichs, 1908]: 53-73; and Wolff, *Haggai*, pp. 59-60) have suggested that 15-19 belongs after 1:15a and that 10-14 is not directed at the prophet's own community but the Samaritans whom the prophet calls "this people" in verse 14. On the chronological and contextual problems relating to this proposal, see May, "'This People' and 'This Nation' in Haggai," pp. 190-197; and Taylor and Clendenen, *Haggai, Malachi*, pp. 61-63. Furthermore, the Minor Prophets scroll found in the caves of Murabba'at provides early and substantial support for the text of Haggai in the MT and in its present order.

[93]BDB, pp. 773-774.

verse 15 as "from this day backward" and the second reference in verse 18 as "from this day forward" (cf. the NIV's marginal reading and the NET's "on the recent past" for v. 15).[94] However, most versions (e.g., the ESV, NRSV, NLT, and NJB) take *ma'al* as referring to the future in both verses 15 and 18, coinciding with its temporal use elsewhere (1 Sam 16:13; 30:25) and anticipating the promised blessing in verse 19.[95] The wording in the NIV, **consider how things were**, does not represent wording from the Hebrew text (though it may reflect the LXX's "How were you?" that begins v. 16), but it serves to signal a change in temporal perspective from the consideration of future blessings ("from this day on") and of past curses ("before"). The section probably implies the beginning of the masonry work ("one stone was laid on another") on the foundation of the temple and perhaps the ceremony during which the first stone is placed (cf. Zech 4:6-10).[96] In either case, this occasion provides the opportunity for the people to consider their past economic difficulties and sinful impurity (1:6,10-11; 2:16-17) and the future anticipation of divine blessings (v. 19).

**2:16-17** With language similar to that of Haggai 1:6, verse 16 describes a yield well below expectation; the harvest of grain and grapes is not even half of what has been expected. The word **heap** refers to a pile of harvested grain (Ruth 3:7; Neh 13:15; S of S 7:2), and the word **measures** in this context seems to suggest a certain liquid measure;[97] it occurs once elsewhere as "winepress" in Isaiah 63:3. Likewise, the description of the reason for the unmet expectations in verse 17 reflects language from 1:10-11; Yahweh has **struck** the produce of their agricultural efforts **with blight, mildew, and hail**. That Yahweh strikes the people with these disasters is further emphasized by the oracle formula that concludes the verse (**declares the LORD**). The nearly identical phrases "whatever they do" and **all the work of your hands** in verses 14 and 17 link the two parts of the

---

[94]In support of these renderings, see Keil, *Minor Prophets*, pp. 206-207; and Meyers and Meyers, *Haggai, Zechariah 1–8*, pp. 48, 58-59, 63.

[95]*HALOT*, p. 613; Verhoef, *Books of Haggai and Malachi*, p. 122.

[96]Boda, *Haggai, Zechariah*, p. 147. Here a different word is used for "temple" (הֵיכָל, *hêkāl*), although it appears to be interchangeable with "house" (בַּיִת, *bayith*) that occurs more commonly in Haggai (1:2,4,8,9,14; 2:3,7,9).

[97]Cohen, *Twelve Prophets*, p. 263; for a discussion of other possible meanings, see Taylor and Clendenen, *Haggai, Malachi*, p. 184.

section (2:10-14,15-19), and in the context of the covenant curses that follow refer to the agricultural endeavors of the people. The poor harvest results from their disobedience. Blight and mildew, although commonly paired (Deut 28:22; 1 Kgs 8:37; 2 Chr 6:28; Amos 4:9), designate quite different agricultural disasters. Blight refers to the scorching of crops that results from the dry easterly winds (cf. Gen 41:6; Hos 13:15), and mildew refers to a fungus that results from damp westerly winds. Hail denotes precipitation in the form of ice pellets and usually causes severe damage to plants; accordingly, it serves as a symbol for destruction and judgment (Exod 9:18-34; 10:5-15; Ps 18:12-13; 78:47-48; 105:32; 148:8; Isa 28:2,17; Ezek 13:11). In spite of these agricultural disasters, the people persist in their disobedience to Yahweh. The NIV (along with other English translations) adds a verb to the last phrase, **yet they do not turn to me**. This rendering may be influenced by the wording of Amos 4:9, which also speaks of Yahweh's sending of blight and mildew in order to encourage the people to return to Yahweh. Evidently the people take care only for their needs and bring no offering for Yahweh, for they cannot properly worship Yahweh so long as the temple remains unfinished.[98]

**2:18-19** Now that the rebuilding of the temple has begun, verses 18-19 contain Yahweh's promise of blessing. Verse 18 parallels verse 15 but with a different time perspective. Both call on the people to give careful thought to the day when the laying of the foundation of the temple begins. Verse 15 asks the people to consider the time before construction has begun, but verse 18 asks the people to consider **from this day on**, that is, **from** the **twenty-fourth day of the ninth month** (December 18, 520 B.C.) **when the foundation of the . . . temple** is **laid**. The time reference here (same as v. 10) relates to the day on which the people resume work on the temple, after a sixteen-year lapse, rather than the time when the foundation is first laid in 536 B.C. (cf. Ezra 3:8-13; 5:16).[99] Furthermore, the significance placed upon "this day" (2:15,18,19) may suggest the occurrence of a second ceremony for laying (or repairing)[100] the foundation stone (cf.

---

[98]Sweeney, *Twelve Prophets*, p. 552.

[99]Cohen, *Minor Prophets*, p. 263.

[100]Cf. the noun form "restoration" (יְסוֹד, $y^{e}s\hat{o}d$) of the verb "laid" (יָסַד, $y\bar{a}sad$) occurring in 2 Chr 24:27. See A. Gelston, "The Foundations of the Second Temple," *VT* 16 (1966): 232-235.

Zech 4:9; 8:9-10).[101] In verse 19, Haggai calls the people to consider the low stock of seed and the lack of crops. The productivity of a seed, its absence and its presence, indicates judgment or blessing (cf. Lev 26:16; Num 24:7; Ezek 17:5; Zech 8:12).[102] **Vine, fig, pomegranate**, and **olive** are agricultural staples for the Palestinian economy (Num 13:23; Deut 8:7-8); they are used for food, drink, fuel, and dye. Haggai asks two questions about these agricultural frustrations, but whether Haggai intends a negative or positive answer to these questions is uncertain. If a negative response is implied (that is, no **seed** is **in the barn**), agricultural conditions remain bleak; the barns are empty, and the community has little or no reserve grain.[103] If a positive response is implied (that is, the seed already planted will produce great quantities), agricultural futures are promising; the seed lies germinating in the field, and Yahweh promises a bumper crop.[104] In either case, the people must await the harvest for which Yahweh gives them assurance. Because the people have demonstrated obedience by laying the foundation of the temple, Yahweh will remove the covenant curses due to their disobedience and renew the productivity of the land (cf. Deut 30:1-3). The founding of the house marks a turning point; the people pass from the experience of divine hostility (2:17) to divine blessing (2:19). Yahweh's promise to **bless** them is thus seen against the negative assertion in verse 17 ("you did not turn to me").

## IV. NARRATION OF THE PROPHECY ABOUT YAHWEH'S PROMISE TO ZERUBBABEL (2:20-23)

[20]The word of the LORD came to Haggai a second time on the twenty-fourth day of the month: [21]"Tell Zerubbabel governor of Judah that I will shake the heavens and the earth. [22]I will overturn royal thrones and shatter the power of the foreign kingdoms. I will

[101]Chisholm, *Minor Prophets*, p. 225; Verhoef, *Books of Haggai and Malachi*, p. 167.

[102]*DBI*, pp. 770, 772.

[103]Boda, *Haggai, Zechariah*, pp. 149-150; Taylor and Clendenen, *Haggai, Malachi*, pp. 189-190.

[104]David J. Clark, "Problems in Haggai 2.15-19," *BT* 34 (1983): 436-439; Sweeney, *Twelve Prophets*, p. 553.

**overthrow chariots and their drivers; horses and their riders will
fall, each by the sword of his brother.**

[23]"'On that day,' declares the LORD Almighty, 'I will take you,
my servant Zerubbabel son of Shealtiel,' declares the LORD, 'and I
will make you like my signet ring, for I have chosen you,' declares
the LORD Almighty."**

Haggai 2:20-23 contains a narration of the prophecy about
Yahweh's promise to Zerubbabel. The section occurs as the climactic
episode in the larger story of the book, whose predominant genre is
prophetic history, a form that contains a narrative for which a
prophetic message is central. Also, the section itself consists of several other prophetic forms, most conspicuously a report of a prophetic
revelation but also a commission to prophesy and a prophetic promise.[105] First, it describes the prophet's personal reception (rather than
public communication) of a message from Yahweh, including the
command to speak to Zerubbabel (v. 21) and the speech Haggai
should say to Zerubbabel (vv. 22-23). Second, it records an authoritative charge to the prophet, including specific instructions about the
message (vv. 21-22) and the political leader to whom it is addressed
(v. 23). Third, it contains statements of Yahweh's commitment to act
on behalf of Zerubbabel; these statements are expressed as first person speech of Yahweh ("I will take you . . . and I will make you like
my signet ring"). A prophetic word formula and a date citation (v. 20)
precede a speech from Yahweh (vv. 21-23). The section reports that
Yahweh commissions Haggai to prophesy about Yahweh's actions
that will eventually legitimize Zerubbabel's status as a divinely chosen
signet ring. Therefore, Haggai 2:20-23 provides a final encouragement for the rebuilding of the temple with Yahweh's promise to
Zerubbabel, signifying something similar to a Davidic king who represents the authority of Yahweh in this world.

**2:20** Haggai 2:20 indicates the origin and date of Haggai's fourth
prophetic message. The prophetic word formula, **the word of the
LORD came to Haggai,** is similar to the one found earlier (1:1,3; 2:10)
except that like the formula in verse 10 it says that the word of Yahweh
comes "to" Haggai rather than "through" him. The slight difference
emphasizes Haggai's reception of the divine word rather than his role

---

[105]Floyd, *Minor Prophets*, pp. 299-300.

as the one who delivers that word. The date formula identifies only the day of the prophetic message (**the twenty-fourth day**), but the ordinal number translated **a second time** resumes the date information from verse 10, that is, it takes place on the same day as the previous message, December 18, 520 B.C. Thus, the focus of Haggai 2:20-23 shifts from rebuilding the temple to the selection of Zerubbabel as leader, from human disobedience to the divine guarantee of blessing.

**2:21** Verse 21 records an authoritative charge to the prophet to speak to **Zerubbabel**, who is generally addressed throughout the book with the title **governor of Judah** (1:1,14; 2:2,21). The typical patronym "son of Shealtiel" (1:1,12,14; 2:2) is here omitted (cf. 2:4), although it appears later in verse 23 (the LXX adds "son of Shealtiel" in v. 21). Verse 21 also begins the description of a sequence of actions (vv. 21-23) that are all Yahweh's doing. No human authority acts on Zerubbabel's behalf, nor are any great military exploits of Zerubbabel anticipated. Rather, Haggai connects the selection of Zerubbabel (v. 23) with cataclysmic changes affecting all creation like those described in verses 6-7 (see comments on vv. 6-7 above), except now these cosmic disruptions lead to the subjugation of the nations (v. 22). If verses 6-7 focus on the result of Yahweh's intervention, then verses 21-23 depict the actions associated with that intervention.[106] The **shak**ing or quaking (רָעַשׁ, *rā'aš*) of **the earth** is also associated with the deliverance of David (Ps 18:7; 2 Sam 22:8). The theophanic imagery here expresses the far-reaching implications of Yahweh's selection of Zerubbabel. Although Zerubbabel who is from the Davidic line is only a Persian governor of a small community, Yahweh intends more for that community and for Zerubbabel as the following verses show.

**2:22** The statements in verse 22 may express the expectation of an imminent overthrow of the Persian Empire;[107] nonetheless, they do so with language drawn from traditions of Israel's past. These images of conquest derive mainly from the defeat of the Egyptians and the Midianites. The verbs **overturn** and **overthrow** both translate הָפַךְ (*hāphak*), a verb used for divine intervention in human affairs that results in dramatic change. For example, the word is used with reference to the Egyptian plagues (Exod 7:15,17,20; 10:19)

---

[106]Boda, *Haggai, Zechariah*, p. 161.
[107]Sweeney, *Twelve Prophets*, p. 553.

but also to the destruction of Sodom and Gomorrah (Gen 19:21,25,29; Deut 29:23; Amos 4:11). The mention of **chariots**, **horses**, and **riders** is reminiscent of the overwhelming of the pharaoh's army in the Red Sea (Exod 15:1,4,19,21) and the rout of Sisera (Judg 4:14-16). The word *hāphak* (there translated "tumbling" and "turned" in the NIV) and the phrase **each by the sword of his brother** (cf. the TNIV's "comrade") evoke the plight of Midian's army (Judg 7:13,22). Also, similar to Haggai 2:22 is Ezekiel's description of the defeat of Gog (Ezek 38:17-23; cf. Zech 14:1-3). The comparison is particularly striking in view of the preceding symbolic action (Ezek 37:15-28) that features themes prominent in Haggai: the return from exile (37:21), the cleansing from disobedience (37:23), the appointment of a Davidic ruler (37:24), the rebuilding of the temple (37:26-28), and the covenant of peace (37:26). Whereas the shaking of the nations in Haggai 2:7 results in the nations bringing tribute into the temple, here it results in their defeat, signified by the word **fall** (יָרַד, *yārād*), a common euphemism for death (Exod 15:5; Isa 34:7; Jer 48:15; Lam 1:9; Ezek 30:6; cf. the rendering of Hag 2:21 in *Targum Jonathan*, "they will be killed"). Such defeat of **foreign kingdoms** (cf. "the kingdoms of the nations" in the ESV, NRSV, and NJPS) reverses the covenant curses listed previously in Haggai (1:6,10-11; 2:16-18) and ultimately fulfills Yahweh's earlier promise to give Israel a place of honor above the nations (Deut 26:19; 28:1).

**2:23** Three oracle formulas in verse 23 draw attention to Yahweh as the one who chooses Zerubbabel as signet ring. The first and third of these formulas use the divine name **the LORD Almighty**, or as found in other versions, the "LORD of Hosts" (see comments on 1:2 above). The title complements the preceding verses (21-22) that depict Yahweh as the one who overturns thrones, shatters kingdoms, and overthrows chariots and horses. Each element of the promise to Zerubbabel is then confirmed by Yahweh. The phrase **on that day** occurs more than two hundred times in the OT, almost half of which occur in the prophets where it is used most often in Isaiah (54×), Jeremiah (10×), Ezekiel (13×), and Zechariah (22×). In the prophetic books, "on that day" typically emphasizes some decisive action of Yahweh (e.g., Isa 2:11-20; 3:7,18; Jer 25:33; Amos 8:3,9; 9:11; Hos 2:18,21; Zech 13:2; 14:4), and the phrase may be linked to the eschatological time referred to as the "day of Yahweh" (see comments on Zeph 1:7). Verse 23 omits the official title for **Zerubbabel**, since "governor," a title he holds by appointment from the Persian king, would be inappropriate after the overthrow of nations in the previous verse. Rather, Zerubbabel is called **my servant** and **son of Shealtiel**. The title "servant" is applied to Abraham (Gen 26:24), Isaac (Gen 24:14), Jacob (Isa 43:10), Moses (Num 12:7-8), Joshua (Josh 24:29), Caleb (Num 14:24), Job (Job 1:8), David (2 Sam 7:5-8), Hezekiah (2 Chr 32:16), Isaiah (Isa 20:3), and the servant of Yahweh (Isa 42:1; 49:6; 52:13). The designation is particularly associated with Davidic kings (2 Sam 3:18; 7:5,8; 1 Kgs 11:32-36; 1 Chr 17:4; 2 Chr 32:16; Ps 78:70; 89:3; 132:10; Ezek 34:23). In addition, the patronym "son of Shealtiel" underscores Zerubbabel's genealogical connection with the line of David (1 Chr 3:19).

Two divine actions will legitimize Zerubbabel's new status: Yahweh takes him and makes him like a signet ring. First, the verb **take** (לָקַח, *lāqaḥ*) appears frequently in contexts of election or special selection (Exod 6:7; Deut 4:20, 34; Josh 24:3). Elsewhere it announces interventions that bring about a change of individual status or function (Gen 24:7; 2 Kgs 2:3; Amos 7:15), especially with regard to the appointment of Davidic kings (2 Sam 7:8; 2 Kgs 11:37; 14:21; 23:30). Second, the verb **make** (שׂים, *śûm*) with the comparative preposition "like" connotes the idea of "making into something" (cf. Gen 13:16; 1 Sam 8:1; 1 Kgs 19:2; Hos 2:3); the expression to make **like** a **signet ring** speaks of Zerubbabel's appointment as the representative of Yahweh for the restoration community.[108] The signet contains the seal of a king, worn as a ring on the finger (Gen 41:42; Esth 3:10; 8:2) or on a cord around the neck (Gen 38:18,25); it is used to put the official seal on a royal document (1 Kgs 21:8; Esth 8:8,10).[109] The promise to Zerubbabel here constitutes a reversal of the curse placed on Jehoiachin (Jer 22:24-30) which seemingly terminates the Davidic covenant. Two generations removed from Jehoiachin (1 Chr 3:17) and cleansed by the suffering of exile (Ezra 2:2), Zerubbabel is designated as Yahweh's signet ring, the guarantor of the temple's completion (cf. Zech 4:6-7) and of the promises associated with the building of the temple.[110]

---

[108]Wolff, *Haggai*, p. 105.

[109]See Bonnie Magness-Gardiner, "Seals, Mesopotamian," *ABD*, 5:1062-1064. Seals are also used in the ancient Near East to authenticate a piece of legal business and to make it binding (Jer 32:9-15).

[110]Wolff, *Haggai*, p. 10.

The appointment of Zerubbabel as Yahweh's signet ring comes because of Yahweh's sovereign choice (**for I have chosen you**). The verb "choose" (בָּחַר, *bāḥar*) is specifically associated with the choice of David as ruler (1 Sam 16:8-10; 1 Kgs 8:16; 1 Chr 28:4-5; 29:1; 2 Chr 6:5-6) and of the Davidic dynasty (1 Sam 10:24; 2 Sam 6:21).[111] The use of the terms "chosen" and "my servant" (v. 23) have direct messianic connotations elsewhere in the OT (e.g., Isa 41:9; 42:1; 43:10; 44:1-2; 50:10; 52:13; 53:11). To identify a descendant of David with this messianic language is not unusual (e.g., Ezek 34:23). In a similar context, Zechariah (3:8; 6:12) designates Zerubbabel as "the Branch," a messianic term used of a Davidic king in Isaiah (11:1) and Jeremiah (23:5-6; 33:14-16). Thus, the language of the section shows that Haggai likely sees Zerubbabel as a messianic figure, one who represents a hope for political independence under a restored Davidic dynasty[112] and one who, like the Davidic monarchy, represents Yahweh the heavenly king on the earth.[113]

In the time of Haggai, the prophetic message about Zerubbabel accomplishes its purpose, the completion of the temple.[114] For this, Zerubbabel is remembered, along with Joshua, in the apocryphal book Sirach: "How shall we magnify Zerubbabel? He was like a signet ring on the right hand, and so was Jeshua son of Jozadak; in their days they built the house and raised a temple holy to the Lord, destined for everlasting glory" (49:11-12, NRSV). Nevertheless, the history of the period provides no evidence as to what becomes of Zerubbabel. Theories that the prophetic messages of Haggai and Zechariah lead him to rebel against Darius go beyond the historical data, as do those theories that allege he is deposed by Persian authorities who fear rebellion among the Jews.[115] Evidence to the contrary may exist in the form of a seal from the postexilic era that bears the name of Shelomith, a name identical to the name of the daughter of

---

[111]Janet E. Tollington, *Tradition and Innovation in Haggai and Zechariah 1-8*, JSOTSupp 150 (Sheffield: JSOT Press, 1993), pp. 137-144; Meyers and Meyers, *Haggai, Zechariah 1-8*, p. 70.

[112]Mason, *Books of Haggai, Zechariah, and Malachi*, p. 25; Sweeney, *Twelve Prophets*, p. 555.

[113]Boda, *Haggai, Zechariah*, p. 165; Floyd, *Minor Prophets*, p. 298.

[114]Meyers and Meyers, *Haggai, Zechariah 1-8*, p. 84.

[115]For a discussion of various theories, see Taylor and Clendenen, *Haggai, Malachi*, p. 199.

Zerubbabel (1 Chr 3:19). The seal designates a certain Shelomith as the אָמָה (*'amah*) of Elnathan, the governor of Yehud from ca. 510–490 B.C. While the meaning of *'amah* is uncertain, the word may be related to the word for mother (אֵם, *'ēm*) and thus designate a woman of nobility with political prominence, such as a queen mother (cf. the use of *'ēm* in 1 Kgs 1:11; 2:13,19-20; 2 Chr 22:2-3) or an official's wife. If the Shelomith of the seal is the daughter of Zerubbabel, he likely continues as governor beyond the completion of the temple in a manner that warrants the continued prominence of his family. Perhaps Zerubbabel's successor Elnathan marries Zerubbabel's daughter or, at the least, elevates Zerubbabel's daughter to a prominent position in the government in order to maintain the link between the governor's office and the Davidic line.[116]

Whether Zerubbabel continues as governor and his family is involved in later Judean politics, his significance exceeds the prophet's apparent expectations. The language associated with the Davidic covenant applied to Zerubbabel (see discussion above) suggests that Zerubbabel represents the renewal of the Davidic covenant and its hopes. Just as Ezekiel uses the name of David to represent Judah's coming deliverer and king (Ezek 34:23-25), the person of Zerubbabel prefigures a coming eschatological figure.[117] Moreover, Zerubbabel stands at the center of the messianic line, since the Davidic lineage from two of David's sons, Solomon and Nathan, comes together in Zerubbabel, the father of Abiud and Rhesa, who are ancestors of Joseph and Mary respectively (1 Chr 3:5,19; Matt 1:6,13-16; Luke 3:23,27,31).

---

[116]Meyers and Meyers, *Haggai, Zechariah 1–8*, pp. 9, 12-13; Nahman Avigad, *Bullae and Seals from a Post-Exilic Judean Archive*, Qedem 4, Monographs of the Hebrew University Institute of Archeology (Jerusalem: Hebrew University of Jerusalem Institute of Archaeology, 1976), pp. 12-13; Erin M. Meyers, "The Shelomith Seal and Aspects of the Judean Restoration: Some Additional Reconsiderations," *ErIsr* 18 (1985): 33-38.

[117]Taylor and Clendenen, *Haggai, Malachi*, pp. 199-200.

# THE BOOK OF
# ZECHARIAH

# INTRODUCTION

## AUTHORSHIP

Ezra twice mentions the prophet Zechariah in conjunction with Haggai (Ezra 5:1; 6:14). Together, in 520 B.C., they encourage the postexilic community to renew the reconstruction of the temple that has remained dormant for more than fifteen years. The prophet's name (זְכַרְיָה, z³karyāh) means "Yahweh remembers," and some thirty individuals in the Old Testament bear it. The book of Zechariah identifies the prophet as the son of Berechiah son of Iddo (Zech 1:1,7); both Ezra and Nehemiah present Zechariah simply as the son of Iddo, a priest who returns to Palestine in 538 B.C. under Zerubbabel (Ezra 5:1; 6:14; Neh 12:4,16). Perhaps the prophet's father Berechiah dies early in Zechariah's life, and Zechariah is then raised by his grandfather.[1] More likely, the author of Ezra–Nehemiah uses the term "son" to denote a descendant and wants to associate Zechariah with a more famous figure in his family line.[2] Such an omission of members in a genealogical record is not uncommon (cf. 1 Kgs 19:16 with 2 Kgs 9:2,14). The invocation of Iddo's name may also be an attempt to link Zechariah with an earlier Iddo who prophesies in the days of Rehoboam (930–913 B.C.).[3]

Zechariah is the head of a priestly family in the days of Joiakim (Neh 12:16), the high priest who holds office between Joshua son of Jehozadak (Hag 1:1,12; 2:2,4; Zech 3:1,3,4,6,8,9; 6:11) and Eliashib (Neh 3:1), the high priest in the days of Nehemiah (ca. 445 B.C.). Probably Zechariah is a young man when he begins his prophetic

---

[1]Eugene H. Merrill, *Haggai, Zechariah, Malachi*, WEC (Chicago: Moody, 1994), p. 94.

[2]Joyce G. Baldwin, *Haggai, Zechariah, Malachi: An Introduction and Commentary*, TOTC 24 (Downers Grove, IL: InterVarsity, 1972), p. 88.

[3]Clinton R. Gill, *The Minor Prophets: A Study of Micah through Malachi*, Bible Study Textbook Series (Joplin, MO: College Press, 1971), p. 263.

ministry in 520 B.C., and his prophetic and priestly ministries extend into the following decades. Similar to the priest-prophets Jeremiah (Jer 1:1) and Ezekiel (Ezek 1:3), Zechariah's priestly lineage leaves its mark on the content of his writing, particularly, his knowledge of Mosaic law (Zech 7:8-10; 8:14-17), fasting (8:18-19), priestly attire (3:1-5; 14:20), and articles from the temple (4:2-3; 14:20-21).

The dated messages within the text of Haggai and Zechariah indicate the last two oracles of Haggai (2:10-19,20-23) are delivered in the ninth month of the second year of Darius king of Persia (Dec. 520 B.C.), and the first oracle of Zechariah (1:1-6) occurs in the eighth month of the same year (Oct./Nov. 520 B.C.). So the prophetic ministry of Zechariah overlaps that of Haggai by one month. The last explicitly dated oracle in Zechariah (7:1) is delivered on the fourth day of the month Kislev in the fourth year of Darius (December 7, 518 B.C.). Therefore, the historical background for at least the earlier part of Zechariah (1–8) is parallel to that of Haggai, and Zechariah continues Haggai's insistence on the completion of the temple. The latter half of the book (9–14) likely reflects a period following the completion of the temple in 516/515 B.C. (see Date below).

Three superscriptions or headings appear in chapters 1–8 (1:1; 1:7; 7:1-3). These headings, attached to two oracles (1:2-6; 7:4–8:23) and a series of visions (1:8–6:15), identify Zechariah as their author. No such authorial identification accompanies the headings of the two oracles in the second half of the book (chapters 9–11 and 12–14). At least from the time of the seventeenth-century scholar Joseph Mede (A.D. 1586–1638),[4] chapters 9–14 have been assigned to a different author than Zechariah son of Berechiah. Noting that Matthew 27:9-10 attributes to Jeremiah words that bear remarkable similarity to Zechariah 11:12-13,[5] Mede then postulates that chapters 9–11 are not originally written by Zechariah but instead are a separate, preexilic collection of prophecy by Jeremiah that Jewish scribes

---

[4]Cited in H.G. Mitchell, *A Critical and Exegetical Commentary on Haggai, Zechariah, Malachi, and Jonah*, ICC (Edinburgh: T&T Clark, 1912), p. 232, and Baldwin, *Haggai, Zechariah, Malachi*, p. 63.

[5]Jerome, *Comm. Matt.* 4.27.10, claims to have read an apocryphal edition of the book of Jeremiah in which this quotation from Matthew appeared word for word. For an English translation of the passage from Jerome, see Manlio Simonetti, ed., *Matthew 14–28*, ACCS Ib (Downers Grove, IL: InterVarsity, 2002), p. 275.

have mistakenly added to Zechariah 1-8.[6] Critical scholarship has since considered these chapters to be anonymous appendices later attached to Zechariah 1-8, either by one author (9-14)[7] or two separate authors (9-11 and 12-14).[8]

Indeed, marked differences, including temporal viewpoint, genre, vocabulary, and personal names, do exist between Zechariah 1-8 and 9-14. Whereas chapters 1-8 focus upon the rebuilding of the temple and other immediate concerns of the early postexilic community, chapters 9-14 envision an occasion involving the eschatological day of Yahweh. While 1-8 contains reports of prophetic visions and of prophetic revelation, 9-14 consists of two poetic oracles that incorporate prophecies of punishment and of salvation. Specific vocabulary and syntactical constructions that occur in 1-8 do not resurface in 9-14. Personal names and dates are absent from 9-14, even though they occur frequently in 1-8 (e.g., 1:1,7; 3:1,3,4,6,8; 4:6,7,9,10; 6:10,11,14; 7:1,2). For example, Joshua and Zerubbabel, the two leaders of the community named frequently in the first half of the book (3:1,3,4,6,8,9; 4:6,7,9,10; 6:11) do not appear at all in the second. Instead, chapters 9-14 use the metaphor of shepherds for leaders in the community (10:2,3; 11:3,5,8,9,15,16,17; 13:7).

Once the literary separation of Zechariah 9-14 from 1-8 is accepted, critical scholarship then further removes the possibility of Zechariah son of Berechiah authoring chapters 9-14 by dating these oracles from the late Persian (500 B.C.), early Greek (330 B.C.), and

[6]Mede, however, is evidently unaware of the apparent Jewish literary practice of citing the name of the more notable prophet when combining elements from more than one text. See Gleason L. Archer and G.C. Chirichigno, *Old Testament Quotations in the New Testament: A Complete Survey* (Chicago: Moody, 1983), p. 163; cf. Mark 1:2, which is attributed to Isaiah, even though the citation consists mainly of Mal 3:1 rather than Isa 40:3. On composite citations in ancient Jewish literature, see Joseph A. Fitzmyer, "'4Q Testimonia' and the New Testament," in idem., *Essays on the Semitic Background of the New Testament* (London: Geoffrey Chapman, 1971), pp. 59-89.

[7]Otto Eissfeldt, *The Old Testament: An Introduction*, trans. by Peter R. Ackroyd (New York: Harper & Row, 1965), pp. 435-440; Rex Mason, "The Relation of Zech 9-14 to Proto-Zechariah," *ZAW* 88 (1976): 227-238; Mitchell, *Haggai, Zechariah, Malachi, and Jonah*, p. 250.

[8]Brevard S. Childs, *Introduction to the Old Testament as Scripture* (Philadelphia: Fortress, 1979), pp. 475-476, 479-480; David L. Petersen, *Zechariah 9-14 and Malachi: A Commentary*, OTL (Louisville, KY: Westminster/John Knox, 1995), pp. 24-26.

even the Maccabean (135 B.C.) periods.[9] Among the chief arguments for a late date are the notion that the anticipated conflict
between Israel and Greece (9:13) reflects the fourth-century movements of Alexander the Great or the second-century hostilities
between the Maccabeans and Seleucids,[10] the increasing prominence
of eschatological and apocalyptic language in chapters 9–14 that is
considered characteristic of later literature,[11] and the divergent content in the two halves of the book (1–8 and 9–14).

Notwithstanding these literary and historical issues, the supposition that Zechariah the son of Berechiah is the author of both
Zechariah 1–8 and 9–14 remains possible for several reasons. The
mention of certain historical and national descriptions, such as
Assyria, Egypt, Ephraim, and Greece, do not provide definitive evidence for an accurate dating of the book and therefore cannot elim-
inate the possibility that Zechariah son of Berechiah uses such portrayals. Neither the mention of Ephraim with Judah/Jerusalem
(9:10-13) nor the naming of Assyria and Egypt (10:10) demands a
preexilic date. An exilic or postexilic author could draw upon the
language of earlier texts to communicate such a message. Indeed,
both Jeremiah (30:3-4; 31:6,27,31; 33:14) and Ezekiel (37:16) speak
of a reunification of Israel/Ephraim and Judah after the fall of the
northern kingdom in 722/21 B.C. Furthermore, the concern for the
reunion of Ephraim and Judah represented in 9:13 and 10:6-7 is
understandable in the early postexilic period when the territories of
the former northern and southern kingdoms lie in the two different
imperial provinces of Samaria and Yehud (Judah).[12] Likewise, Zechariah may use the language of Isaiah (11:11-16) and Hosea (11:11) by
presenting Assyria and Egypt as images for the enemies of God's
people, even though they have ceased to be an extensive threat by
the sixth century B.C.[13] Nor does allusion to the Greeks require a
late postexilic date since Assyrian inscriptions by Sargon II (722–705

---

[9]Eissfeldt, *Old Testament*, p. 436.

[10]Matthias Delcor, "Les allusions à Alexandre le Grand dans Zach 9.1-8,"
*VT* 1 (1951): 123-124; Joseph Blenkinsopp, *A History of Prophecy in Israel*, rev.
ed. (Louisville, KY: Westminster/John Knox Press, 1996), p. 231.

[11]Childs, *Introduction to the Old Testament*, p. 481.

[12]Mark J. Boda, *Haggai, Zechariah*, The NIV Application Commentary
(Grand Rapids: Zondervan, 2004), p. 31.

[13]Robert B. Chisholm, Jr., *Interpreting the Minor Prophets* (Grand Rapids:
Zondervan, 1990), pp. 232-233.

B.C.) and Sennacherib (705–681 B.C.) indicate Greek traders and mercenaries are already active in the ancient Near East.[14] Such activity anticipates a growing role of the Greeks in the region in the time of Zechariah.

The notion that varying genres and diverse topics signal multiple authors suffers from the errant assumption that any single author may write with only one style on a limited set of topics. Given the longstanding canonical testimony that chapters 9–14 belong with 1–8, only a radical difference in content and style would suggest different authors. The increased apocalyptic perspective of the second half is consistent with the transition in subject matter from the historical conditions readily recognized by the original audience to the eschatological future involving individuals whose names are not yet known. Moreover, apocalyptic tendencies surface in chapters 1–8 (see Literary Features), as does a degree of eschatological language (2:11; 3:10; 8:23). The various motifs within the content of the book, however, complement one another, and significant similarities exist between the two halves of the book. One may indeed read chapters 9–14 as a development of the literary and theological themes of 1–8. The salvation of Jerusalem is a focus of both halves (1:12-16; 9:9-10; 12; 14), as are the return of the exiles (8:7; 10:9-12), the cleansing from sin (3:1-9; 5:1-11; 12:10–13:2), and the salvation of the nations (2:18,20-23; 9:10; 14:16-19). Both halves of the book refer to a promise of fertility (8:12; 14:6,8), a renewal of the covenant (8:8; 13:9), the outpouring of Yahweh's Spirit (4:6; 12:10), and the coming of a triumphant but humble messianic figure (3:8; 4:6; 9:9-10).[15]

The two halves of the book begin and end with similar themes. Both begin with the potential or anticipated coming of Yahweh or a divine representative to Jerusalem (1:1-6; 9:1-8) and conclude with the coming of the nations to Jerusalem to seek after or to worship Yahweh (8:20-23; 14:16-21).[16] Additional themes common both to

---

[14]Raymond B. Dillard and Tremper Longman, III, *An Introduction to the Old Testament* (Grand Rapids: Zondervan, 1994), p. 431.

[15]Childs, *Introduction to the Old Testament*, pp. 482-483; Gordon McConville, *A Guide to the Prophets*, Exploring the Old Testament (Downers Grove, IL: InterVarsity, 2002), 4:244; Ralph L. Smith, *Micah–Malachi*, WBC 32 (Waco: Word, 1984), p. 242.

[16]William J. Dumbrell, *The Faith of Israel: Its Expression in the Books of the Old Testament* (Grand Rapids: Baker, 1988), p. 230.

1–8 and 9–14 include: Yahweh's intervention among the nations (1:15; 2:12,15; 6:8; 8:7; 9:1-7,13; 10:9-10; 11:10; 12:1-4,9; 14:3,13-15) and on behalf of Jerusalem (1:14-17; 2:2-4,16; 8:3-4,8; 12:1-3,8; 14:4-5,10), the security of Jerusalem (2:9; 14:11), a cleansing from sin (3:4-5,9; 12:10–13:1), a coming king (6:11-12; 9:9), the establishment of divinely appointed leadership (7:2-3; 10:1-3; 11:4-5,8), and the inclusion of the Gentiles among the people of Yahweh (2:15; 6:15; 8:22; 9:7; 14:16).[17] Thus, chapters 9–14 reflect various themes, hopes, and concerns found in 1–8 and bring them to a satisfying conclusion.

Both sections contain similar vocabulary, characteristic phrases, and literary devices. For example, the appellation "Daughter of Zion" appears in 2:10 and 9:9. An identical phrase (מֵעֹבֵר וּמִשָּׁב, mē'ōbēr ûmiššāb) occurs nowhere else in the Hebrew Old Testament but appears in 7:14 and 9:8 (translated by the NIV "could come or go" in 7:14 and "marauding" in 9:8). Both halves of the book exhibit a fondness for the vocative: Zion (2:7; 9:13), Daughter of Zion (2:10; 9:9), Daughter of Jerusalem (9:9), Daughter of Babylon (2:7), Satan (3:2), mighty mountain (4:7), house of Judah and house of Israel (8:13), prisoners of hope (9:12), Greece (9:13), Lebanon (11:1), pine tree, cypress, or juniper (11:2), oaks of Bashan (11:2), and sword (13:7). Lamarche observes a chiastic structure that unites chapters 9–14,[18] and Baldwin argues for the presence of chiasm in 1–8.[19] Consequently, reasons relating to history, genre, theme, and language support the conclusion that Zechariah son of Berechiah is author of the entire book.

## HISTORICAL BACKGROUND

The background of the first eight chapters of Zechariah resembles that of the book of Haggai. Zechariah works alongside Haggai (Ezra 5:1; 6:14) within the first half century of Israel's postexilic era, beginning in 539 B.C. with the surrender of Babylon to Medo-

---

[17]Thomas Edward McComiskey, "Zechariah," in *The Minor Prophets: An Exegetical and Expository Commentary*, ed. by Thomas Edward McComiskey (Grand Rapids: Baker, 1998), 3:1017.

[18]Paul Lamarche, *Zacharie IX–XIV: Structure litteraire et messianisme* (Ebib; Paris: J. Gabalda, 1961), pp. 112-133.

[19]Baldwin, *Haggai, Zechariah, Malachi*, pp. 74-81, 85-86.

Persian forces led by Cyrus.[20] In the following year, Cyrus issues an edict that emancipates captive peoples living in the Babylonian exile. This policy crafted by Cyrus for dealing with conquered peoples differs greatly from that of earlier Near Eastern empires. By allowing captive peoples to return to their homelands and to rebuild destroyed sanctuaries, Cyrus seeks to avoid unnecessary friction with the subjected peoples and to present the new monarchy as the liberator from Babylonian oppression.[21] Comparison of biblical literature, extrabiblical literature, and inscriptions indicate this edict of Cyrus is published in versions specific to each captive people. Second Chronicles 36:23, Ezra 1:2-4, and Ezra 6:2-5 contain recollections of the version published among the Jewish community and provide detailed instructions about the return of the Jews from captivity. The Persians grant the Jews permission to return to their homeland, to rebuild the temple, to offer sacrifice, and to bring back to Jerusalem the gold and silver articles that the Babylonians have taken during the destruction and sacking of the temple in 586 B.C. The Persians also provide financial assistance from the Persian treasury for these enterprises.

Nevertheless, no Jewish return to Palestine *en masse* occurs, in part, because the exiles have followed Jeremiah's instructions (Jer 28–29) and have become economically established in Babylon. Instead, a small group numbering around fifty thousand makes the nine hundred mile journey back to Jerusalem in 538 B.C. (Ezra 2:1-66). This group may include poorer members of the exile community who have little to lose in such a venture,[22] those with a sense of adventure, and those who possess a fervent devotion for the land of the ancestors.

The relationship among those credited with leading the early returnees is less than certain. Ezra indicates the returnees are led by a Sheshbazzar, who is designated prince (נָשִׂיא, *nāśî'*) in 1:8 and governor (פֶּחָה, *peḥāh*) in 5:14, but Haggai and Zechariah do not men-

---

[20]*ANET*, pp. 305-307, 315-316; on the rise of the Medo-Persian Empire, see Haggai Introduction: Historical Background, pp. 251-252.

[21]J. Alberto. Soggin, *Introduction to the Old Testament: From Its Origins to the Closing of the Alexandrian Canon*, trans. by John Bowden, rev. ed. (Philadelphia: Westminster, 1980), p. 322.

[22]Robert L. Alden, "Haggai," in *Expositor's Bible Commentary*, ed. by Frank E. Gaebelein (Grand Rapids: Zondervan, 1985), p. 571.

tion Sheshbazzar. Haggai instead identifies Zerubbabel as the governor (Hag 1:1,14; 2:2,21). Both Ezra and Zechariah speak of Zerubbabel, but neither overtly identifies him as the governor (Ezra 3:2,8; 4:2,3; 5:2; Zech 4:6,7,9,10).[23]

Ezra 3–4 recounts early attempts to rebuild the temple. Joshua and Zerubbabel rebuild the altar for burnt offerings and begin offering on it by the first day of the seventh month (September–October) of 537 B.C. (3:1-6). After celebrating the Feast of Tabernacles (3:4), they begin reconstruction of the temple in the second month of the second year of the return (April–May 536) (3:8). Hostility and opposition from the neighboring peoples of the land cause the work to cease by 536 B.C. Since the temple mound is, at that time, the northeast fortification of the city, its rebuilding is easily misinterpreted as an attempt to reconstruct the city's defenses. This political opposition, together with economic hardships linked to inflation, drought, and crop failure (Haggai 1:6,9,11), make the task too daunting for the small community of the return.[24] Work does not recommence for sixteen years.

Events in the larger Persian Empire during this period of inactivity contribute to an environment conducive for the resumption of the work. Cambyses, the son of Cyrus, succeeds the emperor when Cyrus dies in battle around 530 B.C. Cambyses consolidates his hold on the empire by assassinating his brother Bardiya and begins an eight-year reign highlighted by the first Persian military campaign to the west. En route to his conquest of Egypt, the army of Cambyses marches through Palestine, an act no doubt contributing to the poverty described in Haggai 1:6 and Zechariah 8:10.[25] Cambyses dies suddenly on his return from Egypt in 522 B.C. A struggle for power ensues from which a general of Cambyses, Darius, arises, but the early years of his reign are marked by outbreaks of resistance and revolt which must be squelched, the most prominent of these being led in Babylon by Nidintu-Bel (Nebuchadnezzar III). The many allusions to Babylon within Zechariah (1:15,19,21; 2:6,7; 5:11; 6:8,10) reflect the continuing relevance that Babylon plays in the prophet's

---

[23]On the possible explanations of the relationship between Sheshbazzar and Zerubbabel, see Haggai Introduction: Historical Background, pp. 253-254.
[24]Soggin, *Introduction*, p. 323.
[25]Alden, "Haggai," p. 571; Baldwin, *Haggai, Zechariah, Malachi*, p. 16.

era.[26] Darius consolidates power by his second year (520 B.C.),[27] and after establishing the peace of the empire, resumes the benevolent policies of Cyrus. He encourages local rule, supports and codifies local laws and customs, and rebuilds sanctuaries that then serve as administrative centers.[28]

Ezra 5–6 indicates that in 520 B.C. the prophets Haggai and Zechariah deliver a series of messages to stir the people to begin again work on the temple as a crucial step for full national renewal. The return of the people to the land, the reconstruction of the temple, and the reaffirmation of the Davidic covenant are interlocking pieces of Yahweh's plan.[29] Whereas Haggai emphasizes the reconstruction of the temple as a sign and source of Yahweh's blessing, Zechariah emphasizes the role of repentance and renewal within the covenant community as a means to that end.[30] Moreover, Zechariah lays greater emphasis upon the enduring ramifications of rebuilding the temple beyond his age and that of his audience.[31]

Work recommences, but officials in the Persian satrapy of *Bābili ebi nāri* ("Babylon beyond the River," translated "Trans-Euphrates" in the NIV) then conspire to block the building of the Jews' temple. They claim that the Jews are incorrect in their assertion that Cyrus the Great has authorized the rebuilding of the temple. Nevertheless, a search of the royal archives in Ecbatana proves Cyrus has indeed authorized it, and Darius orders interference to cease (Ezra 6:1-11). No doubt the desire of Darius to establish Judah as a buffer against Egypt at the western fringe of the empire contributes to the support for temple rebuilding he expresses in Ezra 6:3-12.[32] Under the leadership of Zerubbabel and Joshua, the Jews complete the second temple (Ezra 6:15) on the third day of the month of Adar in the sixth

---

[26]Boda, *Haggai, Zechariah*, pp. 27-28.

[27]McComiskey, "Zechariah," p. 1005; for arguments on identifying the second year of Darius as 520 B.C., see Hans-Walter Wolff, *Haggai: A Commentary*, trans. by Margaret Kohl (Minneapolis: Augsburg, 1988), pp. 74-76.

[28]Carroll Stuhlmueller, *Rebuilding with Hope: A Commentary on the Books of Haggai and Zechariah*, ITC (Grand Rapids: Eerdmans, 1988), p. 13.

[29]Paul R. House, *Old Testament Theology* (Downers Grove, IL: InterVarsity, 1998), p. 383.

[30]Merrill, *Haggai, Zechariah, Malachi*, p. 62.

[31]Ibid., p. 71.

[32]Norman K. Gottwald, *The Hebrew Bible: A Socio-Literary Introduction* (Philadelphia: Fortress, 1985), p. 430.

year of Darius (March 12, 516 B.C.), some three and a half years after they begin building again.

Zechariah 1–8 reflects the relative stability that follows the early upheavals of Darius's reign. The early unrest no doubt encourages hope for the fulfillment of promises of restoration spoken by earlier prophets, but the peace that then follows in 520 B.C. sends conflicting signals. The peace provides a political scenario in which the Jews' may reconstruct the temple and reestablish clear lines of religious and secular authority under the governor and high priest,[33] but the Persians are still in firm control of the region.

Persian records indicate Darius conducts a campaign against Egypt in the winter of 519–518 B.C. Possibly the last dated oracle in Zechariah (7:1–8:23) is occasioned by reflection on what has happened in Palestine during this western campaign.[34] The close of Darius's reign, as its beginning, demands the emperor direct his attention against rebellions and enemies on the western fringe of the empire. With the help of the Athenians, the Ionian cities of Asia Minor and Cyprus seek to repel Persian authority in 499 B.C. A Persian campaign against Athens in 492 B.C. has success in Thrace and Macedonia, but then fails when a storm wrecks the Persian fleet off Mount Athos in the northern Aegean Sea. The Greeks later rout Persia in the battle of Marathon (490 B.C.). This defeat likely leads the Persians to take aggressive actions to preempt rebellion on the more vulnerable western fringe of the empire. The description of foreign aggression against Jerusalem in Zechariah 12 and 14 may reflect the experience of such political and military suppression. Darius dies in 486 B.C., and his son Xerxes[35] succeeds him. Xerxes' early military successes include the defeat of the Spartans at the Pass of Thermopylae and an occupation of Athens in 480 B.C. Nevertheless, the Greeks turn the tide in a monumental naval battle at Salamis and, in 479 B.C., the Persians suffer successive losses to the Greeks at Plataea and Mycale. All hopes for a western expansion of the Persian Empire now die.[36]

The escalation in international turmoil, the multiplication of military garrisons in major cities along strategic routes of Palestine, and

---

[33]Stuhlmueller, *Rebuilding with Hope*, p. 13.
[34]Merrill, *Haggai, Zechariah, Malachi*, p. 63.
[35]The ESV, KJV, NASB, and NRSV use his Hebrew name Ahasuerus.
[36]R.E. Hayden, "Xerxes," *ISBE*, 4:1161.

the precarious political situation of postexilic Israel in the closing years of Darius and early years of Xerxes provide a plausible backdrop for the undated portions of Zechariah (chs. 9–14). The content of the latter half of the book, especially oracles concerning Israel's false shepherds and the repudiation of Yahweh's appointed leaders (10:1-3; 11:1-3,4-17; 13:7-9), also suggest a present or coming crisis of leadership within the postexilic community itself. Though Zechariah retains Jerusalem and the Davidic house as a focus of hope, grave concerns about the leadership of the nation remain.[37] The text of Malachi indicates these concerns come to fruition in a lax and apostate priesthood.

## DATE

The date of Zechariah is intrinsically linked with the issue of authorship. If the unitary authorship of the book can be maintained (see Author above), then a date in the early postexilic era follows. More specific dating for the ministry and book of Zechariah is provided by a series of dates given in the text of Haggai and Zechariah. Zechariah's recorded ministry begins in the eighth month of Darius's second year (1:1) (Oct./Nov. 520 B.C.). Haggai's second oracle (Hag 2:1-9) occurs on the twenty-first day of the seventh month of the second year of Darius (October 17, 520 B.C.), and his third and fourth oracles (Hag 2:10-19,20-23) are both delivered on the twenty-fourth day of the ninth month of the same year (December 18, 520 B.C.). Thus the ministry of Zechariah overlaps that of Haggai by at least one month.

Dates for two other oracles are given in Zechariah. The prophet's series of night visions (1:7–6:15) are dated on the twenty-fourth day of the eleventh month of Darius's second year (February 15, 519 B.C.), and the prophetic report in 7:1 is dated the fourth day of the ninth month in the fourth year of Darius (December 7, 518 B.C.). Some uncertainty exists regarding the date in 7:1, whether it designates the occasion for the entirety of chapters 7–14 or only chapters 7–8. Most likely, the length of chapters 7–14 taken with the new headings in 9:1 and 12:1 argue for the latter, that is, only chapters

---

[37]Boda, *Haggai, Zechariah*, pp. 44-45.

7–8 occur on the fourth day of the ninth month of the fourth year of Darius. Persian records indicate that Darius conducts a campaign against Egypt in the winter of 519–18 B.C. Possibly the last dated prophetic report in Zechariah (7:1–8:23) is occasioned by reflection on what has happened in Palestine during this western campaign.[38]

The content and language of the latter half of the book of Zechariah likely reflect a period following, but not far removed from, the completion of the temple in 516 B.C. The description of foreign aggression against Jerusalem in Zechariah 12 and 14 may reflect the escalation in international turmoil within the region and the multiplication of Persian military garrisons in major cities and along strategic routes of Palestine. The precarious political situation of postexilic Israel accompanies a series of Persian defeats at the hand of the Greeks at the turn of the fifth century in the closing years of Darius and the early years of Xerxes (see Historical Background above).

Analysis of grammatical and syntactical characteristics of the Hebrew found in Zechariah 9–14 indicates that its composition is between 515–475 B.C.,[39] not long after the prophet delivers the oracles of chapters 1–8. Some among those who accept multiple authorship of the book even argue that the latter half of the book originates from the early postexilic period during the lifetime of the sixth-century prophet or shortly thereafter by those who see themselves in his "tradition."[40] Thus, plausibly the prophet continues his prophetic and writing ministry over a period of four decades from 520 to 480 B.C.

---

[38]Merrill, *Haggai, Zechariah, Malachi*, p. 63.

[39]McComiskey, "Zechariah," pp. 1014-1015; Andrew E. Hill, "Dating Second Zechariah: A Linguistic Reexamination," *HAR* 6 (1982): 105-134; Andrew E. Hill, *Malachi*, AB 25D (New York: Doubleday, 1998), pp. 395-400.

[40]Albert Wolters, "Zechariah, Book of," in *Dictionary for Theological Interpretation of the Bible*, ed. by Kevin J. Vanhoozer (Grand Rapids: Baker, 2005), p. 863; see Carol L. Meyers and Eric M. Meyers, *Zechariah 9–14*, AB 25C (New York: Doubleday, 1993), pp. 15-26; Petersen, *Zechariah 9–14 and Malachi*, pp. 9-23; Marvin A. Sweeney, *The Twelve Prophets*, BerOl: Studies in Hebrew Narrative and Poetry (Collegeville, MN: Liturgical Press, 2000), p. 565.

## LITERARY FEATURES

Similar to Jeremiah and Ezekiel, his priest-prophet predecessors, Zechariah mixes prose and poetry to communicate his message. Chapters 1–8 primarily contain prose reports of prophetic visions and prophetic revelation. Poetry appears in 9:1–11:3 before a prose report of prophetic symbolic action in 11:4-16. With only the exception of two short poetic oracles in 11:17 and 13:7-9, the remainder of the book is prose. The two halves of the book (1–8 and 9–14) begin and end with similar themes. Both start with the anticipated coming of Yahweh or a divine representative to Jerusalem (1:1-6; 9:1-8) and then conclude with the coming of the nations to Jerusalem to seek after or to worship Yahweh (8:20-23; 14:16-21).[41]

Zechariah 1–8 consists primarily of eight reports of prophetic visions (1:7–6:14), and Zechariah 9–14, of two prophetic oracles called *maśśā'* (see on 9:1–11:17 below). More specifically, 1:1-6 contains a report of the reception of "the word of the LORD" by the prophet. Zechariah 1:7–6:15 reports eight prophetic visions (1:7–6:8) and a symbolic crowning of Joshua (6:9-15). Chapters 7 and 8 contain a question from community leaders regarding fasting and the reply of Yahweh; the chapters give way to prophetic exhortation (e.g., 7:9-10) and less often prophetic historical exemplum (e.g., 7:11-14). The first prophetic oracle (9:1–11:17) contains a prophecy of punishment against foreign nations (9:1-8), a prophetic call to rejoicing (9:9-10), prophetic exhortation (9:11–10:12), a prophetic sentinel report (11:1-3), and a report of prophetic symbolic action (11:4-17). The second prophetic oracle (12:1–14:21) includes a prophecy of punishment against foreign nations (12:1–13:6) and two prophecies of salvation (13:7-9 and 14:1-21), regarding the exaltation of Yahweh as king of the earth, worshiped by Judah and the nations.

The prophet makes extensive use of figures of speech. Various similes relate to the present or future condition of Israel and Judah. The fathers have made their hearts as hard as flint (7:12), so then the nation suffers defeat and disgrace. But Yahweh transforms their humble state giving them power, dignity, and prominence among the nations. Yahweh bends Judah as a bow (9:13) and makes Judah

---

[41]Dumbrell, *Faith of Israel*, p. 230; House, *Old Testament Theology*, p. 387.

like a warrior's sword (9:13) and a proud horse in battle (10:3). The feeblest among Jerusalem are like David, and the house of David is like God, like the Angel of Yahweh going before them (12:8). Yahweh makes the leaders of Judah like a firepot in a woodpile, like a flaming torch among sheaves (12:6). Though the people wander like sheep (10:2), Yahweh saves them "on that day as the flock of his people" (9:16). When Yahweh pours out a spirit of grace and supplication on the house of David and the inhabitants of Jerusalem, they look on the one they have pierced and mourn as one who grieves for a firstborn son. This weeping is like the weeping of Hadad Rimmon (see comments on 12:10-11). Precious metals and gems provide the material for three of the similes describing the future status of Israel/Judah. Israel sparkles in Yahweh's land like jewels in a crown (9:16), and Yahweh refines the remnant like silver and tests them like gold (13:9).

An array of metaphors appears throughout. At the opening of the book, the nations are at rest (1:11). They have lifted their horns against the land of Judah so that no one could raise his head (1:21). Nevertheless, their destruction is assured because Yahweh promises to be a wall of fire around about Jerusalem (2:5), protecting the city, "the apple of his eye" (2:8). The protection of Yahweh Seba'oth ("the LORD Almighty") results in growth and blessing for Jerusalem. The measuring line is stretched out over Jerusalem (1:16) as Yahweh gathers those exiles who have been scattered to the four winds of heaven (2:6). Those who have been scattered abroad return, passing through the sea of trouble (10:11). Yahweh strengthens them as they walk in Yahweh's name (10:12). The coming blessing and security of Yahweh's people is depicted as someone inviting a neighbor to come sit under a vine and fig tree (3:10). In the face of aggression from the nations, Yahweh makes Jerusalem into a cup that sends the surrounding peoples reeling, and into an immovable rock that causes those who attempt to lift it to injure themselves (12:2-3). Metaphorical depiction of the leaders of the redeemed community is potent. Joshua is a burning stick snatched from the fire (3:2). His continued standing is contingent upon his walking in the ways of Yahweh (3:7). The prophet twice speaks of a coming one who is named the Branch (3:8; 6:12). Joshua and Zerubbabel are envisaged as "sons of oil" in 4:14 (see comments on 3:8; 4:14; 6:12).

The most pervasive metaphor in the book, however, is that of the shepherd and the sheep. A failure in Israel's leadership results in a people who wander like sheep lacking a shepherd (10:2) or who suffer at the hands of negligent or malicious shepherds (11:5,15-17). An angered Yahweh takes action against these shepherds (10:3; 11:3,8), since the flock rejects faithful shepherding (11:8-9). In the end, Yahweh's shepherd is stricken, causing the sheep to scatter. A remnant of the flock, however, remains; they are later purified and made into the people of Yahweh (13:7-9).

The book of Zechariah includes several instances of apostrophe, a rhetorical addressing of a person, usually absent, or a personified thing. Calling upon or unto these entities often engenders enthusiasm and urgency for the content of the message. Zion and those who dwell among the daughter of Babylon (2:7; 9:13) are called to escape. The Daughter of Zion (2:10) is called to rejoice because Yahweh is coming to live among her. Yahweh promises to transform the house of Judah and the house of Israel (8:13), translated simply "Judah" and "Israel" in NIV, from objects of cursing to blessing. In 9:12, Yahweh announces the intention to restore double to the prisoners of hope. At other times, the enemies or obstacles of Israel are delivered messages of doom intended to inspire hope in the audience. The mighty mountain is "called down" and informed it becomes a plain in the presence of Zerubbabel (4:7). Greece (9:13) is notified that Yahweh has stirred up the sons of Zion and wields them like a warrior's sword against her sons. Lebanon is called to open her doors so that fire may destroy her cedars. The pine trees, junipers, or cedars (see comments on 11:2) as well as the oaks of Bashan are then summoned to wail (11:2-3). The final apostrophe in the book is especially ominous for it calls on the sword to strike Yahweh's shepherd (13:7). This tragic event, nonetheless, results in the refining of Yahweh's people (13:8-9).

Other figures of speech include personification and metonymy. Two personifications occur in chapter 5. Verses 3-4 speak of the covenant curse entering a house to destroy it completely, and verses 6-7 depict wickedness as a woman being sent off to Babylon. Elsewhere, personifications portray larger groups of people. The inhabitants of Jerusalem are personified as the "daughter of Zion" and the "daughter of Jerusalem" (9:9), and the inhabitants of Babylon, as the "daughter of Babylon" (2:7). Frequent metonymy, a figure of speech consisting of the use of the name of one thing for something with which it is associated, occurs. A stretched out measuring line (1:16) represents reconstruction and growth of the city. Horns (1:18), chariots, war horses, and a battle bow (9:10; 10:4) depict military power. The four winds of heaven (2:6) stand for the totality of the ancient Near East into which Israel has been scattered. In 10:10, Egypt and Assyria signify those lands of captivity, whereas Gilead and Lebanon represent Israel's homeland in Palestine. The sword suggests trouble (11:17), and the cornerstone and tent peg (10:4) imply stability and security.

Zechariah is a visionary who utilizes images, ancient and powerful, to communicate his message. The changing of clothes (3:1-5) and a fountain (13:1) are frequent Old Testament images for spiritual cleansing (Ps 36:9; 68:26; Isa 61:10; Jer 2:13; 17:13). "Horns" (2:18-21; cf. 1 Sam 2:1,10; 2 Sam 22:3; Ps 18:2; 75:10; Ezek 29:21; Dan 7:7,8,11,20,21,24) represent nations or kings. The first and last of the night visions (1:7-17; 6:1-8) depict divine sovereignty and omniscience with reference to horses of various colors that go about the whole world. Equine imagery also appears in images of salvation and transformation (9:10; 10:3-5) and of eschatological judgment and redemption (12:4; 14:15,20). One of the most memorable images of the book, the donkey, provides a symbol of humility and peace as well as royalty (9:9). Dominating chapters 9–14 are the images of shepherd and sheep. Perhaps most notable among these is 13:7, "Strike the shepherd and the sheep will be scattered," a passage quoted in Matthew 26:31 and Mark 14:27.

Most prominently, however, "the book shimmers with apocalyptic hues."[42] The English word "apocalyptic" derives from the Greek verb ἀποκαλύπτω (apokalyptō), meaning "to uncover, disclose, or reveal," from which also originates the Greek title of the book of Revelation, apokalypsis. The adjective "apocalyptic" designates a large body of canonical and noncanonical Jewish and Christian writings, the majority of which are written during the intertestamental and New Testament periods (ca. 200 B.C.–A.D. 100), although earlier Old Testament texts, such as Isaiah 24:1–27:13, Daniel 7–12,[43]

---

[42]"Zechariah, Book of," *DBI*, p. 978.

[43]This assumes, of course, an exilic date for Daniel. See various Old

and Zechariah, may be classified as apocalyptic or proto-apocalyptic. Reconstructing the historical origin of apocalyptic literature is problematic, since information for the period in which most of it develops is limited.[44] Even though it is often characterized as a body of literature arising from marginalized groups in crisis, evidence for this is scant. Equally plausible is that the literature arises from visionary groups.[45] One may safely surmise, however, that it originates in a time during which the faithful seek to develop a philosophy of history that incorporates and transcends the disconcerting events happening around them.[46]

Attempts to distinguish between standard prophetic literature and apocalyptic literature often characterize prophetic eschatology as "this-worldly," since it depicts developments from within the flow of history, and apocalyptic eschatology as "other-worldly," since it envisions improvements only from outside of human history. For example, prophetic eschatology envisions the hope for a messiah arising out of the line of David within historical events, while apocalyptic eschatology looks forward to a salvation from beyond history, inaugurated by a cosmic upheaval that terminates history and introduces a new type of existence.[47] The righteous prevail, when the current earthly historical existence is eclipsed by a transcendent kingdom established by Yahweh or the messiah.[48]

This distinction is a problematic oversimplification in that it does not recognize the difference between biblical and nonbiblical apocalyptic literature. Canonical apocalyptic[49] themes stand in contrast with those of noncanonical apocalyptic literature, such as Jewish

---

Testament introductions (e.g., Dillard and Longman, *An Introduction to the Old Testament*) for a discussion of the date and authorship of Daniel.

[44]John N. Oswalt, "Recent Studies in Old Testament Apocalyptic," in *The Face of Old Testament Studies: A Survey of Contemporary Approaches*, eds. by David W. Baker and Bill T. Arnold (Grand Rapids: Baker, 1999), p. 371.

[45]Ibid., p. 373.

[46]Ibid., p. 370.

[47]William J. Dumbrell, "Apocalyptic Literature," *NIDOTTE*, 4:395.

[48]George Eldon Ladd, "Why Not Prophetic-Apocalyptic?" *JBL* 77 (1956): 193.

[49]To emphasize the link between prophetic literature and biblical apocalyptic, Ladd (ibid.) designates canonical apocalyptic literature as "prophetic-apocalyptic" and noncanonical apocalyptic works as "nonprophetic apocalyptic."

pseudepigraphic works (e.g., 1 and 2 Enoch, 4 Ezra, 2 and 3 Baruch, Jubilees, and the Apocalypse of Abraham). Noncanonical apocalyptic is quite pessimistic about the present age. Yahweh is seen as aloof and no longer active in redemption (e.g., 1 En 89:51-77), acting only in the coming of the messianic era. Although biblical apocalyptic indeed recognizes the present evil, it insists that Yahweh is still involved in present events that are precursors to coming eschatological consummation. With the exception of 1 Enoch 92–105, noncanonical apocalyptic also deemphasizes ethics. Biblical apocalyptic literature, however, does not disregard ethics, since prophetic eschatology is itself ethically oriented.[50]

The genre of apocalyptic literature itself has been characterized as "a genre of revelatory literature with a narrative framework, in which a revelation is mediated by an otherworldly being to a human recipient, disclosing a transcendent reality which is both temporal, insofar as it envisages eschatological salvation, and spatial insofar as it involves another, supernatural world."[51] Elements of this description or their close equivalents are clearly present in Zechariah. Though the second half of the book (9–14) lacks a plot line with a beginning, middle, and end, the night visions of the first half (1:7–6:8) are narrated in a natural progression, and the dating of its oracles (1:1,7; 7:1) give the book an historical framework. An angel accompanies and dialogues with the prophet throughout the night visions (1:8,9,11,12,14,19; 2:3; 3:1,3,4,5,6; 4:1,4,11; 5:5,10; 6:4,5). Even though the realities disclosed to the prophet in the first half of the book are temporally oriented, they are no less eschatologically oriented than those in the second. Nor is the first half of the book less transcendent and supernatural.[52]

To list other characteristics of apocalyptic is daunting; indeed most of the literature commonly labeled "apocalyptic" fails to include one or more elements of the defining criteria often suggested. Consequently, it may be more helpful to speak of an apocalyptic aura that encompasses literary genre, ideas, and motifs as well as the

---

[50]Ibid., pp. 198-199; Oswalt, "Recent Studies," p. 389.

[51]John J. Collins, "Introduction: Towards the Morphology of a Genre," *Semeia* 14 (1979): 9.

[52]See, for example, the use of the formulas "in that day" and "in those days" in 2:11, 3:10, and 8:23, the vision of Joshua's cleansing in 3:1-10, and visions of chapters 5 and 6.

dominant eschatological framework described above.[53] The content usually appears within narrative reports of revelatory experiences involving the mediation of angels or journeys into the celestial realms. These revelations portend the breaking into the present evil age of divine salvation;[54] such glimpses beyond this world make clear the continued authority and reign of Yahweh.[55] The unforgettable and often surreal visions of ultimate reality provide hope for the audience whose troubling circumstances are now placed in a cosmic and suprahistorical perspective. Because the realities to which the apocalyptic writer points break into this world from the heavenly sphere and are timeless and universal, the writer's language, by necessity, becomes more symbolic and nonliteral.[56]

Apocalyptic imagery is bold, graphic, surreal, and otherworldly, involving depictions of heightened terror and blessedness.[57] Often it is dialectical with sharp categories of good and evil.[58] Leading motifs of apocalyptic present in Zechariah include the following: symbolism involving animals (1:8-21; 6:1-8) and numbers (1:18,20; 2:5; 3:9; 4:2-3,10-12,14; 5:9; 6:1,5; 11:7; 14:4), summons to righteousness and faithfulness (7:9-10), cataclysmic changes of the earth's physical features (14:4,6-8,10), divine deliverance and vindication of Jerusalem and Judah (9:8,14; 12:1-9; 14:1-15), divine provision, that is both abundant and secure, (3:10; 8:3-5,12; 9:8,10,17; 14:11), and divine presence within a purified community (1:16; 8:3; 14:20-21).

## THEOLOGY

The book of Zechariah (זְכַרְיָה, z⁰karyāh), named Ζαχαρίας (zacharias) in the LXX, is the eleventh book within the Book of the Twelve or the Minor Prophets. Occupying the penultimate location in the Book of the Twelve, Zechariah develops further the story of

---

[53]Oswalt, "Recent Studies," p. 371.

[54]Kevin Hall, "Apocalyptic Literature," *BI* 31 (Summer 2005): 8.

[55]"Apocalypse, Genre of," *DBI* p. 35.

[56]Dumbrell, "Apocalyptic Literature," p. 395; Hall, "Apocalyptic Literature," pp. 9-10.

[57]"Apocalyptic Visions of the Future," *DBI*, p. 37; Frederick Murphy, "Introduction to Apocalyptic," *NIB*, ed. by Leander E. Keck (Nashville: Abingdon, 1996), 7:7.

[58]"Apocalyptic Visions of the Future," *DBI*, p. 37.

judgment to salvation traced throughout this prophetic collection.[59] This ascent toward salvation reiterates the theme in Ezekiel of a brighter future beyond judgment in which the presence of Yahweh in the midst of the remnant community transforms the judgment of the exile into glory.[60]

Zechariah prophesies near the completion of the Old Testament period. Therefore, the book, deeply rooted in what precedes it in the history of revelation, bears an abundance of allusions to earlier canonical writings.[61] Like the remainder of the prophetic writings, Zechariah is grounded in themes from the Pentateuch. The book places Judah in a setting similar to that of Deuteronomy in which Israel stands before the promised land. Zechariah now transforms the traditions of blessings in the promised land into a message of hope for Judah and for the nations.[62] The future blessings of Israel require faithfulness to Yahweh whose promise makes possible the blessings.

Several themes from the Torah create this metaphoric setting, particularly, the promise of covenant, the demand for justice, and the language of cult. The covenant promise of Yahweh's dwelling with Israel as their God, especially signified in the tabernacle (Exod 13:21-22; 14:19-24; 25:8; 29:45-46; 40:34-35; Lev 26:12), surfaces in Zechariah (1:16; 2:10; 8:3; 8:8-9; 14:5). The zeal or jealousy of Yahweh to protect this relationship (Exod 20:5; 34:14; Deut 5:9) is also articulated in Zechariah (1:13-15; 8:2). Yahweh promises to redeem Judah (Zech 10:8) just as Yahweh has redeemed Israel from Egypt (Deut 7:8; 9:26; 13:5; 15:15; 24:18). Therefore, they must remember Yahweh's past actions on their behalf (Zech 10:9; cf. Deut 5:15; 7:18; 8:2,18; 9:7; 15:15; 16:3,12; 24:18,22; 32:7) and walk in ways of Yahweh (Zech 3:7; 10:12; cf. Deut 8:6; 10:12; 11:22; 19:9; 26:17; 28:9; 30:16). Prominent among the notion of walking in the ways of Yahweh is the demand for justice and compassion, especially in

---

[59]McConville, *Guide to the Prophets*, p. 254.

[60]House, *Old Testament Theology*, p. 347.

[61]Rex A. Mason, "The Use of Earlier Biblical Material in Zechariah 9–14: A Study in Inner Biblical Exegesis," in *Bringing Out the Treasure: Inner Biblical Allusion in Zechariah 9–14*, ed. by Mark J. Boda and Michael H. Floyd, JSOTSupp 370 (Sheffield: Sheffield Academic Press, 2003), pp. 1-203; Wolters, "Zechariah, Book of," p. 863.

[62]McConville, *Guide to the Prophets*, p. 255.

regards to the poor, the alien, the fatherless, and the widow (Zech 7:8-10; cf. Exod 22:22; Lev 6:2-3; 19:12-13,33; Deut 10:18; 14:29; 16:11-12,14; 24:10,12,14,17,19-21), and the demand for truthfulness (Zech 5:3-4; 7:9; 8:3,17,19; cf. Exod 20:16; 23:1,7; Lev 19:11; Deut 5:20; 19:15-18). Not to walk in the ways of Yahweh invites covenant curse (Zech 5:3; 8:13; cf. Lev 26:11-39; Deut 11:26-28; 28:15-68; 29:25-28; 30:17-20), and restoring the relationship with Yahweh requires repentance from the community (Zech 1:4-6; 7:11; cf. Lev 26:40-45; Deut 4:30-31; 30:1-10). In addition, certain foundational ideas within Zechariah rely heavily on cultic language and concepts. Especially important is priestly (Zech 3:1-5; cf. Exod 28:1-14,36), sacrificial (Zech 4:12; 14:20-21; cf. Exod 25:6; 27:20-21; 29:7; 30:25,31; 39:38; 40:9; Lev 8:2,10,12), and tabernacle/temple (Zech 3:6-7; 4:1-3; cf. Exod 25:31-40; 27:9; 38:9; 39:40) language.

Zechariah also stands within the tradition of the earlier prophets (1:4; 7:7,12),[63] applying their message to new circumstances. Several instances demonstrate the prophet's awareness of these earlier prophetic works, especially, Isaiah, Jeremiah, and Ezekiel. The shepherd and sheep images so central to Zechariah (10:2-3; 11:3,5,8-9,15-17; 13:7-9) appear frequently in Isaiah (5:17; 40:11; 53:6-7; 56:11; 61:5), Jeremiah (3:15; 10:21; 12:10; 17:16; 22:22; 23:1-4; 25:34-36; 31:10-12; 50:6; 51:23), and Ezekiel (34:2-17,20-23,31; 37:24). The enemies that have afflicted Israel and Judah have come from the north (Zech 2:6; cf. Isa 14:31; Jer 1:13-14; 4:6; 6:1,22; 10:22; 13:20; 25:9), and from the north Yahweh gathers the people (Zech 2:6; cf. Isa 43:6; 49:12; Jer 3:12; 16:15; 23:8; 31:8; 46:10). A remnant from among the nations also comes to acknowledge Yahweh as divine king (Zech 2:11; 8:20-23; 14:16; cf. Isa 1:24-31; 2:2-4; 26:16–27:6; 45:14; 60:3; 65:13-16; Jer 30:7-11; 32:36-44; Ezek 20:33-44). Other messianic imagery, especially from the Servant Songs of Isaiah (42:1-4; 49:1-6; 50:4-9; 52:13–53:12), anticipates the use of the titles "my servant, the Branch" (Zech 3:8) and "the Branch" (Zech 6:12) and the depiction of a coming Davidic king (Zech 9:9-10) who will bring blessing to Israel (Isa 9:6-7; 11:1; 32:1; Jer 23:5; 33:15; Ezek 17:22; 34:23-24; 37:22-24). Isaiah (6:5; 24:23; 41:21; 43:15; 44:6) and Jeremiah (8:19; 10:7,10; 46:18; 48:15; 51:57) also provide the backdrop for Zechariah's portrayal of

---

[63]House, *Old Testament Theology*, p. 387; Wolters, "Zechariah, Book of," p. 863.

Yahweh as the king of Israel and of the world (14:9,17). The covenant promise of Yahweh's dwelling with Israel as their God, also found within the Torah (see above), figures prominently in Jeremiah (7:23; 11:4; 24:7; 30:22; 31:1,33; 32:38) and Ezekiel (11:20; 37:23), and its appearance in these two prophetic works no doubt contributes to its use in Zechariah (1:16; 2:10; 8:3; 14:5).

The book of Isaiah makes special contribution to several concepts in the book of Zechariah. The glorious presence of Yahweh as a wall of fire about Jerusalem is founded upon both memories of the exodus (Exod 14:15-25) and images in Isaiah 4:5-6. The leveling of mountains (Isa 40:4; 41:15; 45:2) portrays Yahweh's power to remove obstacles and hindrances to divine purposes (Zech 4:7). The transformation of Jerusalem and the temple mount result in The City of Truth and The Holy Mountain (Zech 8:3; cf. Isa 2:1-4; 11:9; 27:13; 56:7; 57:13; 65:11,25; 66:20). The people are called not to fear but to let their hands be strong (Zech 8:13; cf. Isa 35:3-4). Yahweh promises to shield the people of Judah (Zech 9:14-15), just as Yahweh has shielded Hezekiah and Jerusalem from the Assyrians (Isa 31:5; 37:35; 38:6). Yahweh answers the people who call in times of need (Zech 10:6-7; cf. Isa 30:19; 41:17; 49:8; 58:9; 65:24). Freedom for prisoners is proclaimed as a result of the ministry of Yahweh's servant (Isa 42:6-7; 49:8-9) and the coming of the appointed king (Zech 9:10-11).

Likewise, themes from Jeremiah also are evident in the text of Zechariah. The call to repentance in the introductory oracle of Zechariah (1:4-6) reiterates the recurring summons of Jeremiah (3:14; 4:1; 18:11; 25:5; 35:15), and the recounting of the ancestors' refusal to listen (Zech 7:11-14) resounds similar indictments in Jeremiah's temple sermon (Jer 7:13,26-28). Israel has experienced the seventy-year exile that Jeremiah has prophesied (Jer 25:11-12; 29:10-14; Zech 1:12). Yet, in spite of Israel's past failure, Yahweh even now promises restoration and transformation (Zech 8:13; cf. Jer 31:27-28,31-32; 33:3-8,10-11,16). The advent of the Branch (Zech 3:8; 6:12; cf. Jer 23:5-6; 33:15;) results in salvation, security, forgiveness, and righteousness (Zech 3:9-10; 6:13; cf. Jer 23:1-4; 33:8,15-18).

Zechariah, furthermore, uses several images especially prominent in Ezekiel. The measuring of Jerusalem (Zech 2:2) is reminiscent of Ezekiel's vision of a man measuring the temple, its courts, and its altar (Ezek 40:1–43:17). Ezekiel provides background for

Zechariah's depiction of the return of Yahweh's presence to Jerusalem (Zech 1:16; 2:10; 8:3; 8:8-9; 14:3-5). The vision of Ezekiel 8–11 shows the glory of Yahweh departing the temple and Jerusalem. Now, the less-than-spectacular beginnings of the resettlement and rebuilding of Jerusalem in Zechariah's day call into question the promise that the glory of Yahweh dwells among Israel in Jerusalem and in the temple (Ezek 37:27; 43:1-5). Nevertheless, the glory of Yahweh does again reside in Jerusalem (Zech 2:5; 8:3; cf. Ezek 39:21; 43:2,4,5; 44:4), when Yahweh acts according to divine zeal for Jerusalem and on account of the holy name of Yahweh (Zech 8:3; cf. Ezek 5:13; 36:6; 39:25).

The prophetic ministries of Zechariah and Haggai overlap by at least one month (see Date and Historical Background above). Not surprisingly, the controlling ideas of Haggai and Zechariah reinforce and complement one another. For Haggai, the community demonstrates its repentance by rebuilding the temple (1:7-8). For Zechariah, repentance also includes social justice (7:1–8:32). Both Haggai and Zechariah long for a return of Yahweh's glorious presence with Israel. Haggai 1:8 summarizes this desire in the words, "'Go up into the mountains and bring down timber and build the house, so that I may take pleasure in it and be honored,' says the LORD." Zechariah summarizes this desire in 1:3, "This is what the LORD Almighty says: 'Return to me,' declares the LORD Almighty, 'and I will return to you,' says the LORD Almighty." Although the content of the books is generally complementary, subtle differences do exist between Haggai and Zechariah. Haggai exhorts the people to restart the construction of the temple (Haggai 1), while Zechariah encourages them, along with their leaders, to complete the task (Zechariah 4).[64] Although Haggai looks briefly beyond the immediate circumstances of the community to a coming day of glory (Hag 2:6-9,20-23), Zechariah paints a more extensive portrait of that day and of the role of the nations within it.

In many ways, those Jews who return to Palestine after the Decree of Cyrus and those Jews who remain among the Diaspora find themselves caught between the prospects of the promises given by the earlier prophets and of their present circumstances. The different perspectives of the two halves of the book substantiate this

[64]Selman, "Zechariah: Theology of," *NIDOTTE*, 4:1303-1307.

tension between the "now" and the "not yet." Zechariah 1–8 clearly speaks to the context of 520–518 B.C., and Zechariah 9–14 points forward to realities beyond the completion of the Jerusalem temple. By providing a vision of the final victory of Yahweh, the "not yet" of chapters 9–14 encourages the postexilic community to action in the "now."[65] Nonetheless, the two halves of the book begin and end with similar themes. Both begin with the anticipated coming of Yahweh or a divine representative to Jerusalem (1:1-6; 9:1-8) and then conclude with the coming of the nations to Jerusalem to seek after or to worship Yahweh (8:20-23; 14:16-21).[66]

Zechariah does not dwell on the earlier failures of the nation but focuses on the present and future obligations of the community as the people of Yahweh. Zechariah insists that the temple be the top priority of the community; just as the theophany at Sinai (Exodus 19) precedes the giving of the law (Exodus 20), the architectural theophany of the completed temple precedes the full restoration of the covenant embodied in the Torah.[67] Though the temple is the center of attention in chapters 1–8, it is nearly absent from 9–14. Nevertheless, its presence is implied at the book's conclusion, when the survivors of the nations come to Jerusalem for the Feast of the Tabernacles (14:16-21). The temple now serves its ultimate purpose as a sign of the presence of Yahweh among the people.

However, before the presence of Yahweh may be communicated to the world, the people are cleansed through the outpouring of Yahweh's Spirit (12:10; 13:1-3), the guarantor of the promises of Yahweh (4:6).[68] Repentance leads to covenant renewal (1:1-6); the people turn toward Yahweh (1:4,6), and Yahweh to them (1:16; 8:3). This, moreover, leads to the return of the exiles to Jerusalem (10:9,10) and the restoration of blessing to Judah (9:12). Genuine repentance (1:3-6; 7:4-7) and obedience (6:15), especially in the form of social justice (7:8-10; 8:16-17), precede these promised blessings. Attendant with these concerns is the need for the priesthood (3:1-7) and the land (5:1-4; 13:1-6) to be cleansed from defilement. Between

---

[65]I.M. Duguid, "Zechariah," *NDBT*, p. 258; McConville, *Guide to the Prophets*, p. 252.
[66]Dumbrell, *Faith of Israel*, p. 230.
[67]Selman, "Zechariah: Theology of," 4:1304.
[68]Ibid., 4:1306.

two main depictions of final conflict and victory (12:1-9; 14:1-21) is a section portraying Jerusalem as a penitent mourner, now cleansed from sin (12:10–13:9). This arrangement emphasizes that only a purified remnant benefits from the climactic victory of Yahweh (14:2,16).[69]

The return of the exiles to Palestine has initiated a new era in which Yahweh fulfills earlier promises of Israel's restoration. The mention of the coming Branch (Isa 11:1; Jer 23:5-6; 33:15) expands the promises of a restored Davidic throne by associating the Branch with the high priest as well as the Davidic prince (Zech 3:8-9; 6:11-15). Renewed temple worship (1:16; 4:8-10) includes the nations who recognize the sovereignty of Yahweh (2:11; 8:20-23; 14:16). Nevertheless, these events do not come automatically, nor does the entire nation experience them. Only the faithful followers, who are purified by Yahweh (13:8-9), realize these promised blessings.

Zechariah envisions the glory of Yahweh, which has departed the temple and Jerusalem (Ezekiel 8–11), once more residing in a reconstructed temple (Zech 1:16; 8:7-9). Furthermore, Yahweh is a wall of fire about the city and its glory within (2:5). Thus, Jerusalem as a whole becomes what the temple is: the residence of Yahweh's glory. The descriptions of the pervasive holiness of Jerusalem in 14:20-21 complement this image as Israel now exhibits the holiness befitting the dwelling of Yahweh with them (Lev 11:44-45). The people's commitment to rebuild the temple (Zech 8:9) and to live as Yahweh's holy people precedes the habitation of the glory of Yahweh.[70] Significantly, the book makes no overt mention of the completion of the temple that no doubt occurs within the prophet's ministry. Perhaps its absence, at the time of the book's writing, suggests that the spiritual renewal of the community stands just as incomplete as the temple once stood (Zech 4:9).[71]

A coming messianic figure, variously portrayed as the Branch (Zech 3:8; 6:12), the Daughter of Jerusalem's coming king (9:9-10), the shepherd of Yahweh (13:7), and the one who is pierced (12:10), initiates future blessings for the community. Zechariah links the anticipation of this figure to the present time by offering Joshua as

---

[69]McConville, *Guide to the Prophets*, p. 242.

[70]Dumbrell, *Faith of Israel*, p. 231.

[71]Boda, *Haggai, Zechariah*, p. 45; McConville, *Guide to the Prophets*, p. 251.

a sign of that coming one (3:8-9; 6:9-15),[72] much as Haggai presents Zerubbabel as a sign of the coming Branch (Hag 2:20-23). In the meantime, the people of Yahweh suffer from inadequate, defiled, or unfaithful leadership (Zech 3:1-10; 4:1-14; 10:1-12). This false and unfaithful leadership of Israel results in drought rather than fertility, which Torah promises in return for covenant faithfulness (Lev 26:3-12; Deut 28:8-12). The nation is not without fault for they reject the leadership of Yahweh's true shepherd (9:16; 10:3; 13:7), thus their actions bring devastation rather than blessing upon themselves (11:4-17; 12:10; 13:7-8; 14:1-2).[73]

Though Israel must suffer now with inadequate leaders, the one who pledges to be a wall of fire about Jerusalem (2:5) prevails, and Jerusalem is lifted to a place of prominence towering over the remaining land and remains secure (14:10). The portrayal of Jerusalem as the sanctified center of a new creation and the royal city from which Yahweh reigns anticipates the images of Revelation 21–22.[74] One is remiss, however, for failing to notice the pervasive tone of conflict throughout the book. Travail for Yahweh's people precedes Yahweh's victory. This struggle exists on a celestial level: "the Satan" accuses Joshua the high priest (3:1). It exists also on the terrestrial level: the "four horns" represent the past enemies of the people of Yahweh (1:18-19), the "mighty mountain" confronting Zerubbabel (4:7) stands for opposition, and future gatherings of the nations around Jerusalem fight against it, plunder it, and terrorize its inhabitants (12:3; 14:2). Enemies also arise from within (11:4-16). Even though this struggle is not to be unexpected or ignored by Yahweh's people, neither is it the last word. Yahweh has stood by the people and continues to do so. Yahweh rebukes Satan (3:2), and the mountain before Zerubbabel is leveled (4:7). Yahweh protects the people (2:5), "the apple of his eye" (2:8), intervening on behalf of the people and defeating those who gather against them (9:8; 12:2-4; 14:3-5). The victory of Yahweh, however, is demonstrated most clearly in the cleansing of the people (5:1-11; 13:1-6) and in the drawing of the nations into the people of Yahweh (2:11; 8:20-23;

---

[72]Duguid, "Zechariah," *DNBT*, p. 259.
[73]Chisholm, *Minor Prophets*, p. 274.
[74]Dumbrell, *Faith of Israel*, pp. 235-236.

14:16-19), who repeat the affirmation made by Abimelech to Abraham, "God is with you" (Gen 21:22).[75]

The influence of the book of Zechariah extends beyond the literature of the Old Testament. For example, the Dead Sea Scrolls may develop, to some extent, the expectation of two messiahs, one from the royal line and another from of priestly descent (e.g., 1QS IX, 11; 1QSa II, 11–22), from Zechariah (e.g., 3:8-9; 4:14; 6:9-15).[76] Several direct quotations from Zechariah occur in the New Testament, and many of these within the passion narratives.[77] The account of Jesus' entry into Jerusalem (Matt 21:5; John 12:15) quotes Zechariah 9:9, the accounts of Judas's betrayal (Matt 26:14-16; 27:3-10) use Zechariah 11:12-13, the prediction of the disciples' desertion after Jesus' arrest (Matt 26:31; Mark 14:27) cites Zechariah 13:7, and the description of the corpse of Jesus (John 19:37) refers to Zechariah 12:10. Other New Testament texts allude to texts within

---

[75]Dumbrell, *Faith of Israel* p. 233; Duguid, "Zechariah," pp. 259-260.

[76]See James H. Charlesworth, et al. (eds.), *The Messiah: Developments in Earliest Judaism and Christianity*, First Princeton Symposium on Judaism and Christian Origins (Minneapolis: Fortress Press, 1992); Craig A. Evans, "Qumran's Messiah: How Important Is He?" in *Religion in the Dead Sea Scrolls*, ed. by John J. Collins and Robert A. Kugler (Grand Rapids: Eerdmans, 2000), pp. 135-149.

[77]Mark C. Black, "The Rejected and Slain Messiah Who Is Coming with His Angels: The Messianic Exegesis of Zechariah 9–14 in the Passion Narratives" (PhD dissertation, Emory University, 1990); F.F. Bruce, "The Book of Zechariah and the Passion Narratives," *BJRL* 43 (1960–61): 336-353; idem, *New Testament Development of Old Testament Themes* (Grand Rapids: Eerdmans, 1968), pp. 100-114; C.H. Dodd, *According to the Scriptures: The Sub-Structure of New Testament Theology* (London: Nisbet, 1952), pp. 64-67; Ian M. Duguid, "Messianic Themes in Zechariah 9–14," in *The Lord's Anointed: Interpretation of Old Testament Messianic Texts*, ed. by Philip E. Satterthwaite, Richard S. Hess, and Gordon J. Wenham (Grand Rapids: Baker Book House, 1995), pp. 265-280; R.T. France, *Jesus and the Old Testament: His Application of Old Testament Passages to Himself and His Mission* (London: Tyndale, 1971), pp. 103-110; Craig A. Evans, "Jesus and Zechariah's Messianic Hope," in *Authenticating the Activities of Jesus*, NTTS 28, ed. by Bruce Chilton and Craig A. Evans (Leiden: E.J. Brill, 1999), pp. 373-388; Clay Alan Ham, *The Coming King and the Rejected Shepherd: Matthew's Reading of Zechariah's Messianic Hope*, NTM 4 (Sheffield: Sheffield Phoenix Press, 2005), pp. 12-13; Barnabas Lindars, *New Testament Apologetic: The Doctrinal Significance of the Old Testament Quotations* (Philadelphia: Westminster Press, 1961), pp. 10-34; Douglas J. Moo, *The Old Testament in the Gospel Passion Narratives* (Sheffield: Almond Press, 1983), pp. 173-224.

Zechariah. In particular, Matthew 24:30-36 reflects an eschatological (rather than messianic) use of material from Zechariah, describing the reaction of universal mourning at the coming of the Son of Man (Zech 12:10-14), the universal regathering of the elect (Zech 2:6), and the lack of knowledge regarding the chronological arrival of the day of Yahweh (Zech 14:7).[78]

The New Testament writers affirm that the "not yet" of the prophets has arrived in the person of Jesus Christ, and the "last days" have broken into history (Acts 2:16-17). Nevertheless, the New Testament still testifies that much of the "not yet" in Zechariah remains "not yet." Indeed, many of the images of Zechariah reappear in Revelation. Among them are horses (Zech 1:8; 6:2,6-7; 10:3; 12:4; 14:15, 20; Rev 6:2,4-5,8; 9:7,9,17,19; 18:13; 19:11,14,18-19,21), the use of the numbers two, four, and seven (Zech 1:18,20; 2:5; 3:9; 4:2-3,10-12,14; 5:9; 6:1,5; 11:7; 14:4; Rev 1:4,11-12,16,20; 2:1; 3:1; 4:5-6,8; 5:6,8,14; 6:1,6; 7:1-2,11; 8:2,6; 9:12-15; 10:3-4; 11:4,10; 12:3,14; 13:1,11; 14:3; 15:1,6-8; 16:1; 17:1,3,7,9,10-11; 19:20; 20:8; 21:9), the question "how long?" (Zech 1:12; Rev 6:10), the measuring of the city (Zech 2:1; Rev 11:1-2; 21:15-16), seven eyes (Zech 3:9; Rev 5:6), the lampstand (Zech 4:2-3; Rev 1:20), the two olive trees and two lampstands (Zech 4:14; Rev 11:4), and a woman representing evil (Zech 5:5-11; Rev 17:1-18). The statement from the heavenly throne in Revelation 21:3, "Now the dwelling of God is with men, and he will live with them. They will be his people, and God himself will be with them and be their God," is analogous to Yahweh's statement in Zechariah 2:11 and looks forward to the day of Yahweh's final victory and to the new Jerusalem distinguished by its holiness (Zech 14:16-21; Rev 21:1-27).[79]

## MESSAGE

Along with his contemporary Haggai, Zechariah comes to prominence nearly two decades after Judah's exile during days of frustrated anticipation. The nation has paid the price for their ancestors' unfaithfulness to the covenant, the forced exile in Babylon. In keep-

---

[78]Ham, *Coming King*, pp. 94-98.
[79]Duguid, "Zechariah," p. 260.

ing with promises of earlier prophets, power in the region has now shifted from the Babylonians to the Medo-Persian Empire, and the Decree of Cyrus has provided the opportunity for those Hebrews who desire to return home and rebuild the temple of Yahweh in Jerusalem. Nevertheless, the groups that have made their way back to Palestine from Mesopotamia are relatively small; life in the homeland has been difficult, crops have been paltry, and the temple reconstruction begun in 538 B.C. has ground to a halt. The diminished city and the incomplete temple symbolize the status of the glorious promises for the future that the preexilic and exilic prophets have proclaimed: the fulfillment of these promises has begun, but their accomplishment seems in doubt, causing the people to ask, where is the glory of Yahweh and the temple? (cf. Hag 2:3).

Zechariah responds by calling upon the postexilic community to remain faithful. They must trust Yahweh to fulfill these promises in time. In many respects, postexilic Jews living in Palestine and those who elect to remain among the Diaspora find themselves caught between the prospects of the promises given by the earlier prophets and the realities of their own contemporary circumstances. Much like believers in the New Testament and later, they find themselves between the past and the future, looking back upon initial salvation and forward to ultimate and final salvation.[80] The two halves of Zechariah address this tension of the "now" and the "not yet," since chapters 1–8 speak to the context of 520–518 B.C. and chapters 9–14 point forward to realities beyond the completion of the Jerusalem temple. By providing a vision of the final victory of Yahweh, the prophet encourages the postexilic community to action in "the now."[81]

While awaiting the fulfillment of these promises, Israel must repent of past wrongs (1:2-6) and then remain faithful to the covenant. For Zechariah, the community demonstrates its repentance by rebuilding the temple (1:16; 8:9) and by acting responsibly and compassionately toward the disadvantaged in the community (chs. 7–8). The return of Yahweh's glorious presence to Jerusalem and Israel is contingent on their repentance. This message is summarized in 1:3, "This is what the LORD Almighty says: 'Return to me,'

---

[80]McConville, *Guide to the Prophets*, p. 253.
[81]Duguid, "Zechariah," p. 258; McConville, *Guide to the Prophets*, p. 252.

declares the LORD Almighty, 'and I will return to you,' says the LORD Almighty." Zechariah portrays the ensuing outcome of their repentance and obedience to encourage the people of Judah to complete the task of rebuilding the temple. Once more does Yahweh promise to dwell in Jerusalem in the reconstructed temple (1:16; 2:10-11; 8:3,7-9; 14:5). The pictures of the pervasive holiness of Jerusalem in 14:20-21 complement this image; Israel now exhibits the holiness befitting the dwelling of Yahweh with them (cf. Lev 11:44-45). The coming messianic figure, portrayed as the Branch (3:8; 6:12), the daughter of Jerusalem's coming king (9:9-10), the shepherd of Yahweh (13:7), and the one who is pierced (12:10), initiates future blessings for the community. These blessings, however, are not restricted to Israel alone. A company from the nations (2:11; 8:20-23; 14:16-19) joins a remnant from Israel (13:7-9) to constitute the new people of Yahweh who recognize Yahweh Seba'oth ("the LORD Almighty") as king of the whole earth (14:9,16-17).

Zechariah shares with the remainder of biblical apocalyptic the expectation that Yahweh breaks into history, bringing salvation (and judgment), from beyond (see Literary Features above). This, however, does not lead to despair in the present age. Events in this age have meaning; they contribute to the coming of Yahweh's intervention. Therefore, the work of Zerubbabel and the people in constructing the temple and the priestly ministry of Joshua have long-term significance.[82] Zechariah calls the faithful to persevere and to live faithfully even if, at present, such action does not appear to be rewarded. Although the frustration of their earthly existence is very real, another reality exists.[83] The supernatural reality and purposes of the King, the LORD Almighty (14:17), summon the readers to live as the people of Yahweh within and often in spite of their historical circumstances.

---

[82]Oswalt, "Recent Studies," pp. 374-378, 389.
[83]Ibid., 390.

# OUTLINE

# SELECTED BIBLIOGRAPHY
# ON ZECHARIAH

Andiñach, Pablo R. "Zechariah." In *The International Bible Commentary: A Catholic and Ecumenical Commentary for the Twenty-First Century*. Ed. by William R. Farmer. Collegeville, MN: Liturgical Press, 1998.

Baldwin, Joyce G. *Haggai, Zechariah, Malachi: An Introduction and Commentary*. TOTC 24. Downers Grove, IL: InterVarsity, 1982.

Boda, Mark J. *Haggai, Zechariah*. The NIV Application Commentary. Grand Rapids: Zondervan, 2004.

_____ . "Majoring in Minors: Recent Research in Haggai and Zechariah." *Currents in Biblical Research* 2 (2003): 33-68.

Boda, Mark J., and Michael H. Floyd, eds. *Bringing Out the Treasure: Inner Biblical Allusion in Zechariah 9–14*. JSOTSupp 370. Sheffield: Sheffield Academic Press, 2003.

Bruce, F.F. "The Book of Zechariah and the Passion Narratives." *BJRL* 43 (1960–61): 336-353.

Coggins, Richard J. *Haggai, Zechariah, Malachi*. Old Testament Guides. Sheffield: Sheffield Academic Press, 1987.

Cunliffe-Jones, Hubert. *A Word for Our Time? Zechariah 9–14, the New Testament and Today*. London: Athlone, 1973.

Duguid, Ian M. "Messianic Themes in Zechariah 9–14." In *The Lord's Anointed: Interpretation of Old Testament Messianic Texts*. Pp. 265-280. Ed. by Philip E. Satterthwaite, Richard S. Hess, and Gordon J. Wenham. Grand Rapids: Baker, 1995.

Hahlen, Mark A. "The Background and Use of Equine Imagery in Zechariah." *Stone-Campbell Journal* 3 (2000): 243-260.

Ham, Clay Alan. *The Coming King and the Rejected Shepherd: Matthew's Reading of Zechariah's Messianic Hope*. New Testament Monographs 4. Sheffield: Sheffield Phoenix Press, 2005.

Kline, Meredith G. "The Structure of the Book of Zechariah." *JETS* 34 (1991): 179-193.

Larkin, Katrina J.A. *The Eschatology of Second Zechariah: A Study of the Formation of a Mantological Wisdom Anthology.* Contributions to Biblical Exegesis and Theology 6. Kampen: Kok Pharos, 1994.

Leske, Adrian M. "Context and Meaning of Zechariah 9:9." *CBQ* 62 (2000): 663-678.

Mason, Rex A. *The Books of Haggai, Zechariah, and Malachi.* CBC. Cambridge: Cambridge University Press, 1977.

————. "The Relation of Zech 9–14 to Proto-Zechariah." *ZAW* 88 (1976): 227-239.

————. "The Use of Earlier Biblical Material in Zechariah 9–14: A Study in Inner Biblical Exegesis." In *Bringing Out the Treasure: Inner Biblical Allusion in Zechariah 9–14.* Pp. 1-208. Ed. by Mark J. Boda and Michael H. Floyd. JSOTSupp 370. Sheffield: Sheffield Academic Press, 2003.

McComiskey, Thomas Edward. "Zechariah." In *The Minor Prophets: An Exegetical and Expository Commentary.* Vol. 3. Ed. by Thomas Edward McComiskey. Grand Rapids: Baker, 1998.

Merrill, Eugene H. *Haggai, Zechariah, Malachi.* WEC. Chicago: Moody, 1994.

Meyers, Carol L., and Eric M. Meyers. *Haggai, Zechariah 1–8.* AB 25B. New York: Doubleday, 1987.

————. *Zechariah 9–14.* AB 25C. New York: Doubleday, 1993.

Ollenburger, Ben C. "The Book of Zechariah." In *NIB.* Vol. 7. Ed. by Leander E. Keck. Nashville: Abingdon, 1996.

Petersen, David L. *Haggai and Zechariah 1–9: A Commentary.* OTL. Philadelphia: Westminster, 1984.

————. *Zechariah 9–14 and Malachi: A Commentary.* OTL. Louisville, KY: Westminster/John Knox, 1995.

Redditt, Paul Lewis. *Haggai, Zechariah and Malachi.* NCB. Grand Rapids: Eerdmans, 1995.

————. "The Two Shepherds in Zechariah 11:4-17." *CBQ* 55 (1993): 676-686.

Stuhlmueller, Carroll. *Rebuilding with Hope: A Commentary on the*

*Books of Haggai and Zechariah*. ITC. Grand Rapids: Eerdmans, 1988.

Thomson, J.G. "The Shepherd-Ruler Concept in the Old Testament and Its Application in the New Testament." *SJT* 8 (1955): 406-418.

Tollington, Janet E. *Tradition and Innovation in Haggai and Zechariah 1–8*. JSOTSupp 150. Sheffield: Sheffield Academic Press, 1993.

Tuckett, Christopher M., ed. *The Book of Zechariah and Its Influence*. Burlington, VT: Ashgate, 2003.

# ZECHARIAH

## I. REPORT OF THE PROPHETIC WORD
## GIVEN TO ZECHARIAH (1:1-6)

[1]In the eighth month of the second year of Darius, the word of the LORD came to the prophet Zechariah son of Berekiah, the son of Iddo:
[2]"The LORD was very angry with your forefathers. [3]Therefore tell the people: This is what the LORD Almighty says: 'Return to me,' declares the LORD Almighty, 'and I will return to you,' says the LORD Almighty. [4]Do not be like your forefathers, to whom the earlier prophets proclaimed: This is what the LORD Almighty says: 'Turn from your evil ways and your evil practices.' But they would not listen or pay attention to me, declares the LORD. [5]Where are your forefathers now? And the prophets, do they live forever? [6]But did not my words and my decrees, which I commanded my servants the prophets, overtake your forefathers?

"Then they repented and said, 'The LORD Almighty has done to us what our ways and practices deserve, just as he determined to do.'"

Zechariah 1:1-6 contains a report of a prophetic revelation given to Zechariah. This particular prophetic genre, which describes a prophet's private reception of the "word of the LORD," generally contains two parts: a prophetic word formula (v. 1) and a quotation of the message received (vv. 2-6).[1] Like other similar reports (e.g., Jer 34:8-22; Ezek 14:1-11) this one includes information about the date of the revelation and mentions specific historical circumstances. The message itself reminds the people of Yahweh's anger with their pre-

---

[1]Michael H. Floyd, *Minor Prophets: Part 2*, FOTL 22 (Grand Rapids: Eerdmans, 2000), p. 646.

exilic ancestors who did not heed the warnings of earlier prophets and thus experienced divine judgment. Therefore, Zechariah 1:1-6 attempts to convince the present generation of people not to repeat the failures of previous generations so that they may experience divine blessing by returning to Yahweh. Rhetorically, this opening provides a preface that, together with a longer sermon of comparable content in chapters 7–8, brackets the visions that extend from 1:7 through 6:8.

**1:1** Similar to the opening verse of Haggai, the first prophetic message in Zechariah is also dated during **the second year** (520 B.C.) **of Darius** the Great (522–486 B.C.), son of Hystaspes. This pronouncement takes place **in the eighth month** (late October to late November), but no day is identified as in Haggai. The reason for omission of the day in this initial date is unclear, since the day is specified elsewhere in the book (1:7; 7:1). Perhaps this omission is a device to link the book of Haggai with Zechariah.[2] The last two prophetic messages of Haggai are both delivered on the twenty-fourth day of the ninth month (December 18, 520 B.C.), so the public ministry of Zechariah overlaps that of Haggai by approximately one month. Moreover, Zechariah delivers his first prophetic message, introduced by the common phrase **the word of the LORD** (Jer 1:2; Ezek 1:3; Hos 1:1; Joel 1:1; Jonah 1:1; Micah 1:1; Hag 1:1; Mal 1:1), within one or two months after the people of Judah respond to Haggai's message and resume temple construction in the sixth month (Hag 1:15). By this time, Darius has already suppressed rebellion in the Persian Empire, a situation indicated in the report of the heavenly riders who find "the whole world at rest and in peace" (Zech 1:11).

**Zechariah** is the **son of Berechiah**, who is **the son of Iddo**. Elsewhere Zechariah's name appears only in Ezra (5:1; 6:14) and Nehemiah (12:16). These passages indicate the prophet's kinship to Iddo, but do not mention Berechiah. It is possible that Berechiah dies young, and Zechariah is reared by his grandfather. Zechariah then accompanies his grandfather from the Babylonian exile and succeeds him in the office of priest (Neh 12:16).[3] A simpler explanation is that, while the opening verse of Zechariah names both father and grand-

---

[2]Carol L. Meyers and Eric M. Meyers, *Haggai, Zechariah 1–8*, AB 25B (New York: Doubleday, 1987), pp. 90-91.

[3]Merrill, *Haggai, Zechariah, Malachi*, p. 94.

father, Ezra and Nehemiah choose only to mention the better-known grandfather.[4] A comparison of 1 Kings 19:16 with 2 Kings 9:2 and 14 shows such an omission of a name is not unusual. The invocation of Iddo's name may also be an attempt to link Zechariah with an earlier Iddo who prophesies in the days of Rehoboam (930–913 B.C.).[5] Jesus cites the slaying of a Zechariah the son of Berechiah between the temple and the altar together with the slaying of Abel (Gen 4:1-8) to define the scope of the innocent blood for which the Jews are guilty (Matt 23:35).[6] There, however, is no extant Jewish tradition to confirm the prophet meets such a death.[7] The execution of another prophet, Zechariah the son of Jehoiada the priest, in the courtyard of the temple is recorded in 2 Chronicles 24:17-20.

**1:2-3** Zechariah's message begins with a statement of Yahweh's attitude toward the people's past failures, highlighted by four references to their **forefathers** (TNIV, "ancestors") (1:2,4,5,6). The words **very angry** translate the Hebrew verb "to be angry" (קָצַף, *qāṣaph*) with its cognate noun "anger" (קֶצֶף, *qāṣeph*) as its object, a construction that strengthens the description.[8] In contrast with the common adage that God hates sin but loves the sinner, the verse indicates that the anger of Yahweh is directed at **the people** and not sin in general.[9] Nonetheless, the stress on these failures from the past implies that an opportunity for a different outcome exists for the present generation. What follows (**therefore**) is a plea to "return" or "turn" (KJV, NET, NJPS) to Yahweh. The word "turn" (שׁוּב, *šûb*) often occurs in a covenant context (e.g., Deut 4:30-31; 30:1-10; 1 Kgs 8:33; Isa 44:22; 55:7; 59:20; Jer 3:14; 4:1; 8:5).[10] Such an association

[4]Baldwin, *Haggai, Zechariah, Malachi*, p. 88.
[5]Gill, *The Minor Prophets*, p. 263.
[6]The Lucan account of Jesus' statement omits Berechiah's name (Luke 11:51). On the allusion to Zechariah in the Matthean text, see Ham, *Coming King*, pp. 92-93.
[7]A first-century-A.D. pseudepigraphal collection of folk stories and legends about prophetic characters, "The Lives of the Prophets," contains the tradition that Zechariah becomes ill and dies in his old age and that he is buried beside Haggai. See Charles Cutler Torrey, *The Lives of the Prophets*, JBL Monograph Series 1 (Philadelphia: Society of Biblical Literature and Exegesis, 1946).
[8]GKC, p. 367.
[9]Baldwin, *Haggai, Zechariah, Malachi*, p. 90.
[10]William L. Holladay, *The Root Šûbh in the Old Testament with Particular Reference to Its Usages in Covenant Contexts* (Leiden: Brill, 1958).

is corroborated in this context by the use of "word" and "statute" in verse 6, words commonly associated with the covenant stipulations made with Israel at Sinai (e.g., Exod 19:7; 20:1; Deut 5:1; 6:1). The prophet does not specify what specific repentance is required, although later sections describe the need for social justice (Zech 7:8-10; 8:16-19). More pointedly, the plea calls the people to return to Yahweh personally ("return to me") rather than to an abstract law or an obedient way of life. If they do, Yahweh promises to return to them also (cf. Mal 3:7). The divine name **the LORD Almighty** (יהוה צְבָאוֹת, *YHWH ṣᵊbā'ôth*), translated as "the LORD of Hosts" (ESV, KJV, NASB) or "Yahweh Sabaoth" (NJB), occurs in three messenger formulas in verse 3 (regarding this divine name, see comments on Nahum 2:13, Zeph 2:9, and Hag 1:2). This striking repetition of *YHWH ṣᵊbā'ôth* underscores the focal message of the section, **Return to me . . . and I will return to you.** The appeal and promise within this verse are complemented by the promise of Zechariah 8:3, where the prophet speaks of the mountain of Yahweh Almighty becoming the Holy Mountain when Yahweh returns to Zion and dwells in Jerusalem.

**1:4-6** Verse 4 reviews what has occurred in the past when those called to turn by **the earlier prophets** do not. Their ancestors demonstrate rebellion and disloyalty in the failure to turn from their **evil ways** and **evil practices**. The pairing of **listen** (שָׁמַע, *šāma'*) and **pay attention** (קָשַׁב, *qāšab*) occurs some twenty-six times to denote the paying of fervent attention to the words of another (e.g., 1 Sam 15:22; Job 13:6; Ps 17:1; Isa 49:1; Jer 18:19). Verse 4 may allude to a similar call by Jeremiah for his audience to turn from their evil ways (18:11; 25:5; 35:15).[11] Verses 5 and 6 pose three consecutive rhetorical questions emphasizing the judgment of Yahweh on the people's ancestors. The recent memory of the exile makes unnecessary any detailed explanation of this judgment. Even though their ancestors have perished and the ministry of the earlier prophets has ended,[12]

---

[11]Baldwin, *Haggai, Zechariah, Malachi*, p. 90.

[12]The noun "forever" (עוֹלָם, *'ôlām*) designates a remote time or an indefinite continuance of time extending into either the past (Deut 32:7; Job 22:15; Ps 24:7,9; Isa 58:12) or the future (Lev 25:32; Deut 15:17; 1 Sam 1:22; Ps 45:2; Isa 55:3; Ezek 37:24-25). When used, as here, with the preposition "to" (לְ, *lᵊ*), it refers to the continuance of the entity (i.e., the earlier prophets) described in the context, according to McComiskey, "Zechariah,"

the words of Yahweh remain. Indeed, Yahweh's words and decrees have overtaken their ancestors. Deuteronomy 28 uses the verb **overtake** (נָשַׂג, *nāśag*) twice to describe covenant curses overtaking the Hebrews should they be unfaithful in the covenant (28:15,45). Some ambiguity exists regarding the antecedent of the pronoun "they" in the statement **Then they repented**. If "they" refers to the **forefathers**, it appears to contradict verse 4. More likely "they" refers to the response of Zechariah's contemporaries to the prophet's message, "Return to me and I will return to you," and it resumes the narrative beginning in verse 1. A similar structure of prophecy and positive response occurs in Haggai 1:1-15. What is more, the connection of the ministries of Haggai and Zechariah in Ezra 5:1 and 6:14 suggests that Haggai's earlier calls to begin anew the construction of the temple play a role in the repentance described in Zechariah 1:6. Such an association also helps to identify the otherwise vague sin for which Zechariah's audience must repent. They must devote themselves to completing the temple, "the material, symbolic representation of God's presence and sovereignty."[13] In this obedience, the postexilic community separates themselves from their ancestors who did not listen to the same prophetic call to repentance.

## II. REPORTS OF EIGHT PROPHETIC VISIONS (1:7–6:8)

Zechariah 1:7–6:8 reports a series of eight prophetic visions: heavenly riders among the myrtle trees (1:7-17), four horns scattered by four craftsmen (1:18-21), a man measuring Jerusalem (2:1-13), clean garments for the high priest (3:1-10), a gold lampstand and two olive trees (4:1-14), a flying scroll (5:1-4), a woman in a basket (5:5-11), and four chariots (6:1-8). These reports focus on the reception of a vision that is primarily visual not verbal; they report what the prophet sees in an extraordinary experience but one also filled with significant meaning.[14] The visions themselves contain things ordinary (2:1-2) or bizarre (5:1-2), figures human (3:1) or

---

3:1030; Allan A. MacRae, "עוֹלָם," *TWOT*, 2:672; Anthony Tomasino, "עוֹלָם," *NIDOTTE*, 3:346-347.

[13]Meyers and Meyers, *Haggai, Zechariah 1–8*, pp. 96-97.

[14]Floyd, *Minor Prophets*, p. 644.

superhuman (1:20-21), locations earthly (2:1) or heavenly (5:9), and events natural (3:5) or supernatural (6:1-8). In each case, the vision is interpreted by an angelic being (1:9,11-14,19; 2:3; 3:6; 4:1,4-5; 5:5,10; 6:4-5). Generally the prophetic vision reports consist of three elements: an introductory statement about what the prophet has seen ("then I looked up"), a transitional statement ("and behold"),[15] and a description of the prophetic revelation. For example, the report of the flying scroll (5:1-4) exhibits all three elements: "I looked" (v. 1), "and there" (v. 1), and "I see a flying scroll" (v. 2), the sight of which is then interpreted (vv. 3-4). Zechariah 1:7–6:8, therefore, attempts to persuade the people to finish the project of rebuilding the temple with a series of prophetic vision reports that depict the significance of a completed temple for Jerusalem.

## A. HEAVENLY RIDERS AMONG THE MYRTLE TREES (1:7-17)

[7]**On the twenty-fourth day of the eleventh month, the month of Shebat, in the second year of Darius, the word of the LORD came to the prophet Zechariah son of Berekiah, the son of Iddo.**

[8]**During the night I had a vision—and there before me was a man riding a red horse! He was standing among the myrtle trees in a ravine. Behind him were red, brown and white horses.**

[9]**I asked, "What are these, my lord?"**

**The angel who was talking with me answered, "I will show you what they are."**

[10]**Then the man standing among the myrtle trees explained, "They are the ones the LORD has sent to go throughout the earth."**

[11]**And they reported to the angel of the LORD, who was standing among the myrtle trees, "We have gone throughout the earth and found the whole world at rest and in peace."**

[12]**Then the angel of the LORD said, "LORD Almighty, how long will you withhold mercy from Jerusalem and from the towns of Judah, which you have been angry with these seventy years?"** [13]**So**

---

[15]Unfortunately, the NIV does not translate the Hebrew word הִנֵּה (*hinnēh*), typically translated "behold" in the NASB, even though *hinnēh* appears in each of the prophetic vision reports (Zech 1:8,11,18; 2:1,3,9-10; 3:8-9; 4:2; 5:1,7; 6:1).

the LORD spoke kind and comforting words to the angel who
talked with me.

[14]Then the angel who was speaking to me said, "Proclaim this
word: This is what the LORD Almighty says: 'I am very jealous for
Jerusalem and Zion, [15]but I am very angry with the nations that feel
secure. I was only a little angry, but they added to the calamity.'

[16]"Therefore, this is what the LORD says: 'I will return to
Jerusalem with mercy, and there my house will be rebuilt. And the
measuring line will be stretched out over Jerusalem,' declares the
LORD Almighty.

[17]"Proclaim further: This is what the LORD Almighty says: 'My
towns will again overflow with prosperity, and the LORD will again
comfort Zion and choose Jerusalem.'"

**1:7** Zechariah 1:7-17 constitutes the first of the prophet's night
visions that extend from 1:8 to 6:15. The lack of additional chronological notations beyond this verse suggests that the visions may
have been received in one night.[16] This particular vision emphasizes
the devotion of Yahweh for the people of Judah. Yahweh Seba'oth
("the LORD Almighty"), who is cognizant of the world situation and
of Judah's place within it, will act on behalf of Judah. Verse 7 serves
as an introduction for all of the prophetic visions that follow in this
book. Zechariah sees these visions **on the twenty-fourth day . . . of
the month of Shebat in the second year of Darius** or February 15,
519 B.C., a time approximately three months after the initial call of
Zechariah (1:1), five months after construction had begun on the
second temple (Hag 1:15), and two months after Haggai's last
prophetic message (2:20-23). That these visions are dated according
to a Persian king indicates the distressing situation of the Jews, who
have failed to turn from their evil ways (Zech 1:4-6).[17] The specific
occasion of these visions may anticipate the approaching confirmation of Zerubbabel (Hag 2:23; cf. Zech 4:1-14).[18]

**1:8** The words **I had a vision** denote the means by which the revelation is conveyed to Zechariah. The phrase translates the verb רָאָה

---

[16]Boda, *Haggai, Zechariah*, p. 193.

[17]Mark A. Hahlen, "The Background and Use of Equine Imagery in
Zechariah," *Stone-Campbell Journal* 3 (2000): 250.

[18]Herbert G. May, "A Key to the Interpretation of Zechariah's Visions,"
*JBL* 57 (1938): 173-184.

(*rā'āh*), which has the basic meaning "to see," rather than the nouns usually used for "vision" (חָזוֹן, *ḥāzôn* or מַרְאֶה, *mar'eh*). The omission of this normal vocabulary in the **night** visions may originate from a desire to portray the prophet as being intellectually alert and not merely dreaming (cf. 4:1).[19]

In the vision, Zechariah sees **a man** mounted on **a red horse . . . among the myrtle trees in a ravine** in front of other **horses** grouped according to their colors: **red, brown, and white.** Several factors indicate the man mounted on the red horse may be identified with the angel of Yahweh in verse 11. One, the man addresses Zechariah (v. 10), but elsewhere in the visions only angels address human beings (e.g., 1:14; 2:4; 3:6). Two, both the mounted man and the angel of Yahweh stand among the myrtle trees (1:8,10-11). Three, the position of the rider ahead of the others implies his command over them (v. 8), an authority also implied by their report to the angel of Yahweh (v. 11).[20] The myrtle (הֲדַס, *hădas*) is an evergreen shrub that bears dark green leaves, white flowers, and berries yielding aromatic oil.[21] The myrtle is connected with the Feast of Tabernacles (Neh 8:14-15), a feast whose celebration appears in the book's conclusion (Zech 14:16-19), and it appears in Isaianic images announcing the eschatological age of salvation (Isa 41:19; 55:13). The phrase "in a ravine" may symbolize, as it does elsewhere, the distress of Yahweh's people (Ps 88:6; cf. Zech 10:11).[22] The symbolic significance of these horses comes not from their colors, since no attention is drawn to these colors beyond their naming.[23] However, the riders with their horses may have evoked notions of either the Persian cavalry or couriers. The context favors the latter since the horses carry messengers who report to the angel of Yahweh that

---

[19]Baldwin, *Haggai, Zechariah, Malachi*, p. 94. The term *ḥāzôn* does appear in Zech 13:4 but in a negative context. There, the prophet anticipates a day in which every prophet is ashamed of his vision.

[20]Chisholm, *Minor Prophets*, p. 238; McComiskey, "Zechariah," p. 1038; Ben C. Ollenburger, "The Book of Zechariah," in *NIB*, ed. by Leander E. Keck (Nashville: Abingdon, 1996), 7:751.

[21]Roland K. Harrison, "Myrtle," *ISBE*, 7:257.

[22]Rex A. Mason, *The Books of Haggai, Zechariah, and Malachi*, CBC (Cambridge: Cambridge University Press, 1977), p. 37.

[23]On the specific coloring of the horses, particularly the ones described as "brown" in the NIV, see Hahlen, "Equine Imagery," p. 250.

they find the whole world at rest and in peace (1:11). Such imagery reminds the original audience of the Persian authority over them, but more importantly it reassures them of Yahweh's knowledge of world affairs and ability to communicate effectively through the prophet.[24]

**1:9-11** Zechariah asks about what he has seen. The stereotypical phrase **the angel who was talking with me** appears throughout the night vision in reference to the one who acts as Zechariah's interpreter (1:9,13-14,19; 2:3; 4:1,4-5; 5:5,10; 6:4).[25] However, here it appears that both Zechariah and the angel hear the answer to Zechariah's question from **the man standing among the myrtle trees** who is later identified as the angel of Yahweh (1:11-12). Yahweh has sent these horses **throughout the earth**. The verb translated in the NIV **go** (הָלַךְ, *hālak*) normally means "walk" (KJV, NET), but sometimes it connotes the exercise of dominion or authority (Gen 13:17; Ezek 28:14; Job 1:7; 2:2-3), an idea intimated in those versions that translate the word "patrol" (ESV, NASB, NRSV, NJB). The final night vision also describes horses who have been commissioned to patrol the earth (Zech 6:7). The other riders report that they have **found the whole world at rest and in peace**. The conquests of Persia have left their empire secure, but the Jews still remain under their domination (v. 12) and have not yet seen evidence of the earth-shaking and kingdom-shattering events prophesied by Haggai (2:21-22).[26] Still, this peace (שָׁקַט, *šāphaṭ*) may bring to the nations a false security (Zech 1:15), as is sometimes conveyed in the word (cf. Jer 48:11; Ezek 16:49).

**1:12** The **angel of** Yahweh asks Yahweh Seba'oth (**the LORD Almighty**) **how long** divine **mercy** will be withheld from **Jerusalem** and **Judah** while the world remains in peace. Earlier Jeremiah has predicted that Judah would experience seventy years of exile after which Yahweh would return them to the land (25:11-12; 29:10-14). The question in this verse intimates that Yahweh's anger remains beyond the **seventy years** and thus may indicate that the prophet's community does not consider the mere return of the exiles following

---

[24]Ibid., p. 251; Meyers and Meyers, *Haggai, Zechariah 1–8*, p. 128.

[25]See David J. Clark, "The Case of the Vanishing Angel," *BT* 33 (1982): 214-215.

[26]Mason, *Haggai, Zechariah, and Malachi*, p. 37.

the decree of Cyrus to be the fulfillment of Jeremiah's prophecy, if the temple and towns of Judah still need to be rebuilt.[27] Because of the militaristic associations of the divine name Yahweh Seba'oth (see comments on 1:3 above), the angel of Yahweh makes an implicit call for Yahweh to act as the divine warrior and commander to bring to an end the peaceful state of the nations.[28]

**1:13-15** Yahweh responds with **comforting words** to the angelic interpreter, who then commands Zechariah to speak to the people. Yahweh speaks **kind** words, indicating that the time is near for the end of judgment against Judah. The title Yahweh Seba'oth (**the LORD Almighty**) appears in the messenger formula that introduces the proclamation beginning in verse 14. Here it supports the reassurance that the angel speaks to the prophet: Yahweh will take vengeance on the nations for their violations against Judah. Now, Yahweh's anger falls on the **nations** who **feel secure** (שַׁאֲנָן, *šaʾănān*). This verb may have the positive connotation of undisturbed peace (Isa 32:18; 33:20), but it is also connected with complacency (Job 12:5; Isa 32:9; Amos 6:1), arrogance (Ps 123:4), and insolence (2 Kgs 19:28; Isa 37:29). The nations receive greater punishment because they have **added to** Israel's **calamity** when acting as agents of Yahweh's punishment on the sinful people (cf. Isa 10:5; 47:6; Jer 25:9).[29]

The first appearances of the title **Zion** in Zechariah occur in verses 14-17, a text that focuses on Yahweh's covenant zeal or jealousy (see comments on Nahum 1:2). The first appearance of Zion in the Old Testament occurs in the narrative of David's conquest of Jerusalem; in 2 Samuel 5:7 Zion refers to the Jebusite fortress, thereafter known as the "city of David" (cf. 1 Chr 11:5). After the Ark of the Covenant is transferred "from the city of David (that is Zion)" (1 Kgs 8:1; 2 Chr 5:2) to the temple, the entire city of Jerusalem including the temple mount is called Zion. Following the construction of

---

[27]Baldwin, *Haggai, Zechariah, Malachi*, p. 97; Boda, *Haggai, Zechariah*, pp. 197-198; Chisholm, *Minor Prophets*, p. 238; McComiskey, "Zechariah," p. 1039; Meyers and Meyers, *Haggai, Zechariah 1–8*, pp. 117-118. On the symbolic use of "seventy" as a characteristic period of divine anger against a city, see E. Lipiński, "Recherches sur le livre de Zacharie," *VT* 20 (1970): 38-39 (cf. the fate of Tyre in Isa 23:15-17).

[28]David L. Petersen, *Haggai and Zechariah 1–8: A Commentary*, OTL (Philadelphia: Westminster Press, 1984), p. 146.

[29]Baldwin, *Haggai, Zechariah, Malachi*, p. 100.

Solomon's temple, the temple mount of Zion becomes "the geographical and architectural equivalent of a theophany,"[30] a concrete representation of the promises of Yahweh becoming reality. In the later writings of the Old Testament, the topographical use of Zion gives way to a theological use. Zion can stand for the people of Yahweh (Isa 46:13; 51:16; 59:20; Jer 14:19; Zech 2:7), and Zion draws attention to the eschatological Jerusalem as the dwelling place of Yahweh (Ps 74:2; 76:2; Isa 8:18; Joel 3:17-21). Furthermore, Zion represents an image that affirms the kingship of Yahweh and connotes the prerogative of Yahweh to protect the people.[31] Particularly in poetic texts, Zion appears with some frequency as a parallel term to the city of Jerusalem (Ps 51:18; 102:21; 135:21; 147:12; Isa 2:3; 30:19; 33:20; 37:32; 40:9; 41:27; 62:1; Jer 26:18; 51:35; Amos 1:2; Zeph 3:14). Various concepts common among these Zion texts also surface in Zechariah. Yahweh, who is designated by the divine title Yahweh Seba'oth (v. 14), expresses anger and assures victory over the nations (v. 15; cf. Ps 46:6; 48:4-7; 76:3,5-6). Yahweh promises to return to Jerusalem with mercy (v. 16), a pledge connoting the dwelling of Yahweh there (cf. Ps 48:1-3; 76:2). Yahweh returns to Zion/Jerusalem, resulting in its prosperity (vv. 16-17; cf. Ps 46:4) and demonstrating its election by Yahweh (v. 17; cf. 1 Kgs 8:16; Ps 78:68-70; Zech 2:12; 3:2). The use of the covenant language of jealousy (vv. 14-15; Exod 20:5; 34:14; Deut 5:9; Zech 8:2) then reinforces these elements of the Zion tradition.

**1:16-17** Because Yahweh is jealous for Jerusalem and Zion (cf. 8:2), Yahweh promises to **return to Jerusalem with mercy**, to rebuild the temple and the city, to make the **towns . . . overflow with prosperity**, to **comfort** the inhabitants of **Zion**, and to **choose** the inhabitants of **Jerusalem** (cf. 2:12; 3:2). The statement **I will return** is in the Hebrew perfect tense which connotes completed action. Although it may refer to a promised future act (as in LXX, NASB, NIV) so certain that it may be regarded as good as done,[32] it may instead refer to

[30]Jon D. Levenson, "Zion Traditions," *ABD*, 6:1099.
[31]Ben C. Ollenburger, *Zion, the City of the Great King: A Theological Symbol of the Jerusalem Cult*, JSOTSupp 41 (Sheffield: Sheffield Academic Press, 1987), p. 19.
[32]*IBHS*, p. 490; Ronald J. Williams, *Hebrew Syntax: An Outline*, 2nd ed. (Toronto: University of Toronto Press, 1976), pp. 29-30.

an act already accomplished (ESV, NET, NRSV, NJB).[33] The latter reading is more appropriate here since the prophet may envision that Yahweh has responded to the turning (or repentance) of the people (v. 6) by empowering them to proceed with rebuilding the temple. The promise also reflects the visions of Ezekiel 10 and 43 in which the glory of Yahweh departs and then returns to Jerusalem.[34] The turning of Yahweh to Jerusalem with compassion seems to result from the people meeting a covenant obligation: they have listened to Haggai's appeal (1:8) to begin again the reconstruction of the temple. Because the people of Jerusalem have kept covenant and started rebuilding the temple, Yahweh will bless them. The fourfold repetition in verse 17 of the adverb "again" (עוֹד, *'ôd*), translated only three times in the NIV (cf. NASB) as **further** and **again** (2×), highlights both the renewal of the blessing and its abundance. Yahweh promises a renewal of prosperity, comfort, and election, promises reminiscent of the days of David and Solomon.[35] In doing so, the promises answer the question of verse 12. The name Yahweh Seba'oth (**the LORD Almighty**), with its militaristic connotations and connections with the temple, appear in the messenger formula to further support the certitude of these promises.

## B. FOUR HORNS SCATTERED BY FOUR CRAFTSMEN (1:18-21)

[18]Then I looked up—and there before me were four horns! [19]I asked the angel who was speaking to me, "What are these?"

He answered me, "These are the horns that scattered Judah, Israel and Jerusalem."

[20]Then the LORD showed me four craftsmen. [21]I asked, "What are these coming to do?"

He answered, "These are the horns that scattered Judah so that no one could raise his head, but the craftsmen have come to terrify them and throw down these horns of the nations who lifted up their horns against the land of Judah to scatter its people."

---

[33]*IBHS*, pp. 486-487; Williams, *Hebrew Syntax*, pp. 29-30.
[34]Mason, *Haggai, Zechariah, and Malachi*, p. 38.
[35]Boda, *Haggai, Zechariah*, p. 201.

**1:18-19** Zechariah 1:18-21[36] recounts the prophet's second night vision, one which promises punishment on those nations that have abused Judah. Immediately noticeable in this vision is the use of the number four (vv. 18,20). First the prophet sees **four horns**, and **the angel** explains that the horns have **scattered Judah, Israel and Jerusalem**. Because horns or antlers give animals a regal appearance and provide them a means for defense or aggression, the horn becomes a common image of regality, prestige, authority, military power, and strength (Deut 33:17; 1 Sam 2:10; Ps 18:2; 75:10; 89:17; 92:10; 112:9; Jer 48:25; Ezek 29:21; Daniel 7-8; Micah 4:13).[37] Thus, some equate the horns with the major world powers of the ancient near east (cf. "these horns of the nations" in v. 21), namely, Assyria, Egypt, Babylon, and Medo-Persia, or with the successive world empires in the visions of Daniel (Dan 2:31-45; 7:1-27).[38] The apocalyptic nature of the night visions, however, argues for a conceptual reading of the image rather than one that demands exact historical identifications.[39] The association of the number four with the notion of completeness[40] may suggest a representation of all the nations who have used their military might to scatter the people of Yahweh[41] or a representation of the four points of the compass from which defeat comes for Jerusalem and Judah in 586 B.C., in particular, Babylon and Judah's neighbors, Ammon, Moab, Edom, and Philistia.[42] Why "Judah, Israel, Jerusalem" are listed in that particular order is unclear. Perhaps "Israel," an honorable name for the nations subsisting in Judah, fosters a sense of national identity and heritage,[43] or the multiple titles portray the whole people of Yahweh scattered in exile.[44]

**1:20-21** Second, the prophet sees **four craftsmen** who come to **terrify** the four horns and **throw** them **down**. The coming of crafts-

---

[36]Zechariah 1:18-21 in the English text corresponds to 2:1-4 in the Hebrew text.

[37]*DBI*, p. 400.

[38]Chisholm, *Minor Prophets*, p. 240; Merrill, *Haggai, Zechariah, Malachi*, p. 110.

[39]McComiskey, "Zechariah," p. 1047.

[40]*DBI*, pp. 307-308.

[41]Merrill, *Haggai, Zechariah, Malachi*, p. 111.

[42]Boda, *Haggai, Zechariah*, p. 213; Chisholm, *Minor Prophets*, p. 240.

[43]Keil, *Minor Prophets*, p. 519; McComiskey, "Zechariah," pp. 1047-1048.

[44]Baldwin, *Haggai, Zechariah, Malachi*, p. 104.

men to undo the horns is surprising given the natural association of horns with animals, unless the horns are made of iron (cf. Micah 4:13). The plural noun חָרָשִׁים (ḥārāšîm) derives from a root meaning "to engrave" or "to cut." From this, translators have traditionally translated the word "craftsmen"; other renderings include "blacksmiths" (NET, NRSV),[45] "carpenters" (KJV), or "ploughmen."[46] The craftsmen destroy the horns and possibly reverse the scattering that the horns of the nations have done to the people of Yahweh (cf. Isa 54:16-17; Ezek 21:31). The nations which previously seem robust like the power of an animal's horns are instead predisposed to destruction.[47] If the four horns represent specific nations, the craftsmen would refer to the empires who overthrew those nations. If the four horns represent Babylon and its allies, then the four craftsmen would refer to the Persian Empire. Since the number four commonly denotes completeness, it may simply indicate that the craftsmen are strong enough to drive away all four horns;[48] all the nations that have persecuted Judah are thoroughly vanquished.

## C. A MAN MEASURING JERUSALEM (2:1-13)

[1]Then I looked up—and there before me was a man with a measuring line in his hand! [2]I asked, "Where are you going?"

He answered me, "To measure Jerusalem, to find out how wide and how long it is."

[3]Then the angel who was speaking to me left, and another angel came to meet him [4]and said to him: "Run, tell that young man, 'Jerusalem will be a city without walls because of the great number of men and livestock in it. [5]And I myself will be a wall of fire around it,' declares the LORD, 'and I will be its glory within.'

[6]"Come! Come! Flee from the land of the north," declares the LORD, "for I have scattered you to the four winds of heaven," declares the LORD.

[7]"Come, O Zion! Escape, you who live in the Daughter of

---

[45]*HALOT*, p. 358; cf. 1 Sam 13:19.

[46]Mark J. Boda, "Terrifying the Horns: Persia and Babylon in Zechariah 1:7–6:15," *CBQ* 67 (2005): 25; cf. Deut 22:10; 1 Kgs 19:19.

[47]Petersen, *Haggai and Zechariah 1–8*, pp. 165-166.

[48]Boda, *Haggai, Zechariah*, p. 216.

Babylon!" [8]For this is what the LORD Almighty says: "After he has honored me and has sent me against the nations that have plundered you—for whoever touches you touches the apple of his eye— [9]I will surely raise my hand against them so that their slaves will plunder them.[a] Then you will know that the LORD Almighty has sent me.

[10]"Shout and be glad, O Daughter of Zion. For I am coming, and I will live among you," declares the LORD. [11]"Many nations will be joined with the LORD in that day and will become my people. I will live among you and you will know that the LORD Almighty has sent me to you. [12]The LORD will inherit Judah as his portion in the holy land and will again choose Jerusalem. [13]Be still before the LORD, all mankind, because he has roused himself from his holy dwelling."

[a]*8,9* Or says *after . . . eye:* [9]*"I . . . plunder them."*

**2:1-2** Zechariah 2:1-13[49] contains the prophet's third night vision. The vision itself (vv. 1-5) and Yahweh's responses following it (vv. 6-13) anticipate the blessing of Yahweh's presence not only in the postexilic Jerusalem but also among the nations who join with Yahweh. Verse 1 introduces a new character into the visions: an unidentified surveyor. Notably, this surveyor engages the prophet in conversation. Zechariah notices that the man is carrying **a measuring line** (חֶבֶל מִדָּה, *ḥebel middāh*). Even though the same word is not used for the measuring line stretched over Jerusalem in 1:16 (קָו, *qan*), the reader naturally associates the two (cf. Ezek 40:3-4). In Zechariah 1:16 the measuring line anticipates the rebuilding of the city; in 2:2 the line is used **to measure** the present boundaries of the city in preparation for the future restoration of the city beyond these limits. City sizes are not usually given in terms of length and breadth in the Old Testament, and the only instances of the measuring of a city's width and length are here and in Ezekiel 40–48.[50]

**2:3-5** The interpreting **angel** that has been with Zechariah through the other two visions leaves and meets **another angel** with urgent (indicated in the double imperative **run, tell**) information for a **young man** (perhaps Zechariah or the surveyor?). The message

---

[49]Zech 2:1-13 in the English text corresponds to 2:5-17 in the Hebrew text.
[50]Petersen, *Haggai and Zechariah 1–8*, pp. 168-169.

from the other angel indicates that **Jerusalem will be a city without walls**. The phrase "a city without walls" translates a noun (פְּרָזוֹת, *p⁰rāzôth*) that designates unfortified towns or villages without protective walls (Deut 3:5; 1 Sam 6:18; Esth 9:6-19; Ezek 38:11). The angel explains that Jerusalem will be a city without walls since its population (both people and domestic animals) will overflow beyond the boundary of the city's walls. This assurance of growth may anticipate the return of Jews to the city in the days of Ezra (458 B.C.) and Nehemiah (445 B.C.) (Ezra 7–8; Nehemiah 2). After these resettlements, the city's population approximates 50,000 (Neh 7:66-69), a number that could have exceeded the abilities of any provisional walls constructed for protection during the period (see Nehemiah's complaint in Neh 1:3).[51] However, by the time of Nehemiah's governorship, the city has still not experienced substantial growth, and Nehemiah does construct physical walls around the city. Nevertheless, the city itself does not need the conventional protection of walls since Yahweh promises to provide the city's ultimate security. Even if the image of a **wall of fire** is unique in the Old Testament, the language of fire and of divine glory clearly reminds the reader of how Yahweh's presence guarded their ancestors and resided in the tabernacle during the exodus and wilderness wanderings (Exod 13:21-22; 14:19-24; 40:34-35; Num 14:10; 16:19,42; Deut 5:24). Isaiah 4:5-6 has a similar picture in which Yahweh creates over Mount Zion and those assembled there a cloud of smoke by day and a glow of flaming fire by night.

**2:6-7** These verses begin a new section in the chapter in which a series of prophetic sayings explicate the significance of the vision in verses 1-5. The audience changes from Zechariah to the Jews in Jerusalem and Judah and those exiles still in Babylon (1:7), and the speaker may no longer be the interpreting angel but rather Zechariah himself (1:9).[52] The NIV opens verse 6 by translating as **"Come! Come!"** a double use of הוֹי (*hôy*), an interjection normally associated with laments or promises of impending judgment (e.g., 1 Kgs 13:30; Jer 22:18; 34:5; Nahum 3:1; Hab 2:9,12,19; Zeph 2:5; 3:1). Here, the interjections draw the attention of Judah and the exiles to the impending judgment on the nations and their need to escape so

---

[51]Merrill, *Haggai, Zechariah, Malachi*, pp. 116-117.
[52]Baldwin, *Haggai, Zechariah, Haggai*, p. 107.

that they do not suffer along with those being judged (cf. the NRSV's "Up! Up!" and the NASB's "Ho there!"). The same interjection appears at the beginning of verse 7 for much the same effect. **The land of the north** designates the direction from which Israel's Mesopotamian enemies, Assyria and Babylon, have come (Jer 1:14; 4:6; 6:1; Zeph 2:13). Although Assyria and Babylon have already fallen to the Medo-Persians in 539 B.C., rebellion against the Persians becomes more commonplace in the land of Babylon after the death of Cambyses, the son of Cyrus, in 522 B.C. While the Jews have experienced favor at the hand of the Persians in the early days of the empire, they then become more susceptible to danger in Babylon. Because of this, Assyria and especially Babylon remain images of opposition and danger for the people of Yahweh.[53] The use of **the four winds of heaven** indicates a universal scope (Jer 49:36; Ezek 37:9; Dan 8:8; 11:4) as does the notion of the four corners of the earth (Ezek 7:2; Rev 7:1; 20:8). In verse 7 the prophet uses **Zion** as the name of a group rather than a place, commanding Zion to **escape** from those countries in which they dwell. The urgency indicates judgment is coming, and all those who remain in the exiled nations will be subject to it.[54]

**2:8-9** Verse 8 presents some difficulty in translating the clause that contains the noun "glory" (כָּבוֹד, *kābôd*). The Hebrew wording reads something like the NASB: "after glory he has sent me against the nations." Inexplicably the NIV reads the noun *kābôd* as a third person verb (**he has honored**). Other versions (e.g., KJV, NASB, NET) understand "glory" as the object for which Yahweh sends the messenger to the nations.[55] The TNIV translates the noun "glory" as a divine name and the subject of the verb "has sent" to render the clause, "After the Glorious One has sent me unto the nations" (cf. NJB). Similar uses of the noun *kābôd* as a divine title appear in three texts that speak of Israel or Judah exchanging "their glory" for idols or pagan deities (Ps 106:20; Jer 2:11; Hos 4:7) and in one text where Yahweh is identified as "the glory of Israel" (Micah 1:15). The context of verse 8 further supports reading *kābôd* as a divine title. Verse

---

[53]Mark J. Boda, "Terrifying the Horns," pp. 35-41.
[54]Baldwin, *Haggai, Zechariah, Malachi*, p. 108.
[55]See Ezek 39:21-24 for an instance of Yahweh gaining glory when the judgment of the nations results in their proper knowledge of Yahweh.

5 has already identified Yahweh as the glory within Jerusalem, and verses 9 and 11 clearly identify as such the subject of the same verb, **the LORD Almighty has sent me.**[56]

Zion is called **the apple** (or "pupil" as in the NJPS) of Yahweh's **eye**, a most important yet vulnerable entity. This image also is used for Yahweh's care of Israel during the exodus (Deut 32:10). Just as the eye is sensitive to touch, Yahweh is sensitive to that which threatens the people of Yahweh and takes their mistreatment as an affront.[57] Therefore, Zion may proceed with the construction of the temple assured of Yahweh's care, protection, and vindication. The language of **rais**ing or shaking (ESV, KJV) the **hand** in verse 9 intimates the idea that Yahweh can easily bring down judgment on the nations who have plundered the people of Yahweh. The raising of Yahweh's hand against the nations so that they are plundered by the people is reminiscent of their Hebrew forebears plundering the Egyptians at the exodus (Exod 12:36; cf. Ezek 39:10). As a result, the people realize the divine commission of Zechariah. Like Moses, Zechariah is validated through the faithfulness of Yahweh rather than through his own efforts (Exod 3:12; Num 16:28-30). The phrase "then you will know that the LORD Almighty has sent me" (vv. 9,11) appears also in 4:9 and 6:15. Its repeated use need not indicate that the contemporaries of Zechariah doubted him; it appears rather as a vindication formula, reinforcing the impact of the prophetic word by announcing that the prophet is sent with authoritative words from Yahweh.[58] The two uses of the vindication formula in this chapter strengthen the announcement of judgment upon the nations (v. 9) and the promise that nations are to be included in the people of Yahweh (v. 11).

**2:10** This section (vv. 10-13) begins with two imperatives, **shout** and **be glad.** This verb pair (רָנַן, *rānan* and שָׂמַח, *śāmaḥ*) appears in passages that celebrate the righteous rule, gracious acts, and protection of Yahweh (Ps 5:11; 32:11; 35:27; 67:4; 90:14; 92:4; Zeph 3:14),

---

[56]The references to glory evidence the influence of Ezekiel on Zechariah. The phrase "glory of the LORD" or the "glory of God" appears fifteen times in Ezekiel (1:28; 3:12,23; 8:4; 9:3; 10:4,18,19; 11:22,23; 39:21; 43:2,4,5; 44:4). Yahweh displays glory among the nations by inflicting punishment upon them (Ezek 39:21).

[57]Boda, *Haggai, Zechariah*, p. 236; McComiskey, "Zechariah," p. 1061.

[58]Boda, *Haggai, Zechariah*, p. 235.

and the combination of words constitutes an appropriate response to the community's deliverance from captivity.[59] **Daughter of Zion** is a poetic personification of the city of Jerusalem and its inhabitants and occurs twenty-six times in the Old Testament (2 Kgs 19:21; Ps 9:14; Isa 1:8; 10:32; 16:1; 37:22; 52:2; 62:11; Jer 4:31; 6:2,23; Lam 1:6; 2:1,4,8,10,13,18; 4:22; Micah 1:13; 4:8,10,13; Zeph 3:14; Zech 2:10; 9:9).[60] The designation "Daughter of Zion" appears in verse 10 as an intentional contrast with the "Daughter of Babylon" in verse 7; because Yahweh promises to **live among** the Daughter of Zion, she must flee from the Daughter of Babylon. Yahweh has spoken earlier of turning toward Jerusalem (1:16). Now Yahweh promises to live among the Daughter of Zion. This promise repeated in verses 10 and 11 uses the same verb (שָׁכַן, *šākan*) that appears in promises that Yahweh would indwell the tabernacle and Solomon's temple (Exod 25:8; 29:45-46; 40:35; 1 Kgs 6:13; 8:12; 1 Chr 23:25) and in prophetic promises of restored harmony between Israel and Yahweh (Ezek 43:7,9; Joel 3:17). This promise of Yahweh's future dwelling in Zion recurs in Zechariah 8:3.

**2:11-12** Significantly, the oracle anticipates the nations' future worship of Yahweh, a promise solemnized both by the second promise of Yahweh's indwelling and by a third use of Yahweh Seba'oth (**the LORD Almighty**) in the chapter (vv. 7,9,11). Yahweh's ultimate purpose is not the obliteration of the nations nor an imperial Israel but rather "the inclusion of the nations among God's covenant people," an outcome that Martin Luther characterizes as a miracle second to none.[61] The pledge that **many nations . . . will become my peop**le together with promises that Yahweh will dwell among them recalls the covenant formula "They will be my people, and I will be their God" (Lev 26:12; Jer 24:7; 32:38; Ezek 11:20; 37:23), a formula elsewhere applied only to Israel or Judah. Just as Exodus 19:6 describes Israel as a royal priesthood from among the nations, verse 12 describes Judah as Yahweh's special heritage. Whereas Yahweh grants the tribes Israel's ancestral allotments or portions (חֵלֶק, *ḥēleq*)

---

[59]Ibid., p. 237.

[60]"Daughter of Jerusalem" appears seven times (2 Kgs 19:21; Isa 37:22; Lam 2:13,15; Micah 4:8; Zeph 3:14; Zech 9:9).

[61]Martin Luther, *Lectures on the Minor Prophets*, vol. 20 of *Luther's Works* (St. Louis: Concordia, 1973), 3:210.

in Canaan (Josh 18:5-6; 19:9; Ezek 45:7; 48:8,21), Yahweh **inherits Judah** (Deut 32:9).

**2:13** The interjection **be still** (הַס, *has*) occurs elsewhere in oracles of coming judgment that include temple or sacrificial imagery (Hab 2:20; Zeph 1:7). Here it denotes the appropriate human response to the coming of Yahweh who **has roused himself from his holy dwelling.** The verb "rouse" (עוּר, *'ûr*) frequently appears in petitions for Yahweh to come to the aid of the worshiper (Ps 7:6; 35:23; 44:23; 59:4; 80:2; Isa 51:9). Significant for this context also are instances in which Yahweh stirs up the spirit of Cyrus king of Persia (2 Chr 36:22; Ezra 1:1), the nations to vanquish Babylon (Jer 50:9; 51:1-2,11), and the spirit of those who return to Palestine under Sheshbazzar (Ezra 1:5), and Zerubbabel, Joshua, and the remnant of the people to work on the temple (Hag 1:14). The earlier promises that Yahweh comes to dwell among the Daughter of Zion (vv. 10,11) and that Yahweh claims Judah as a portion in the holy land (v. 12) links the holy dwelling place of Yahweh with the earthly Zion/Jerusalem, an intersection that is a significant element within the Zion tradition of the Old Testament[62] and within the development of the tradition in the New Testament (Heb 12:22-24).

## D. CLEAN GARMENTS FOR THE HIGH PRIEST (3:1-10)

[1]**Then he showed me Joshua**[a] **the high priest standing before the angel of the LORD, and Satan**[b] **standing at his right side to accuse him.** [2]**The LORD said to Satan, "The LORD rebuke you, Satan! The LORD, who has chosen Jerusalem, rebuke you! Is not this man a burning stick snatched from the fire?"**

[3]**Now Joshua was dressed in filthy clothes as he stood before the angel.** [4]**The angel said to those who were standing before him, "Take off his filthy clothes."**

**Then he said to Joshua, "See, I have taken away your sin, and I will put rich garments on you."**

---

[62]Thomas Renz, "The Use of the Zion Tradition in the Book of Ezekiel," in *Zion, City of Our God,* ed. by Richard S. Hess and Gordon J. Wenham (Grand Rapids: Eerdmans, 1999), pp. 78-80; Levenson, "Zion Traditions," *ABD,* 6:1099.

⁵Then I said, "Put a clean turban on his head." So they put a clean turban on his head and clothed him, while the angel of the LORD stood by.

⁶The angel of the LORD gave this charge to Joshua: ⁷"This is what the LORD Almighty says: 'If you will walk in my ways and keep my requirements, then you will govern my house and have charge of my courts, and I will give you a place among these standing here.

⁸"'Listen, O high priest Joshua and your associates seated before you, who are men symbolic of things to come: I am going to bring my servant, the Branch. ⁹See, the stone I have set in front of Joshua! There are seven eyesᶜ on that one stone, and I will engrave an inscription on it,' says the LORD Almighty, 'and I will remove the sin of this land in a single day.

¹⁰"'In that day each of you will invite his neighbor to sit under his vine and fig tree,' declares the LORD Almighty."

ᵃ1 A variant of *Jeshua*; here and elsewhere in Zechariah     ᵇ1 *Satan* means *accuser*.     ᶜ9 Or *facets*

**3:1** The fourth (3:1-10) and fifth (4:1-14) visions are unique among the night visions in that they alone contain identifiable characters: Joshua and Zerubbabel. The vision itself (3:1-5) and Yahweh's charge to Joshua following it (3:6-10) portray the cleansing of **Joshua as high priest**, an action symbolic of the coming purification of the people by the messiah. The third chapter opens with the prophet seeing a vision of **Satan** accusing the high priest Joshua in the presence of the angel of Yahweh. This Joshua is the son of Jehozadak, mentioned also in Haggai 1:1. The name appears in its Aramaic equivalent, Jeshua, in Ezra and Nehemiah (Ezra 2:2; 3:2,8; 4:3; 5:2; 10:18; Neh 7:7; 12:1,7,10,26). Conceivably Joshua is also the grandfather of the high priest contemporary with Nehemiah (ca. 445 B.C.) (Neh 12:10). The title "high priest" is attributed in the historical books to Jehoiada (2 Kgs 12:7-10) and Hilkiah (2 Kgs 22:4,8; 23:4) who, like Joshua, are associated with temple repair.[63] The Hebrew term "Satan" (הַשָּׂטָן, *haśśāṭān*) with the definite article (cf. the NLT's "the Accuser, Satan" and the NJPS's "the Accuser") suggests it is used here more as a title or role (i.e., "the adversary") than as a per-

_____
[63]Ollenburger, "Zechariah," p. 764.

sonal name.[64] Similar is the description of the accuser in Job (1:6-9,12; 2:1-4,6-7). The only use of *śāṭān* as a personal name is in 1 Chronicles 21:1.

**3:2** Yahweh twice announces a rebuke of Satan. The verb **rebuke** (גָּעַר, *gā'ar*) refers to Yahweh's powerful rebuke that dries up the Red Sea (Ps 106:9; Nahum 1:4) and of Yahweh's rebuke of the arrogant (Ps 119:21). Its use in Malachi 2:3 practically reverses its use here, since there Yahweh threatens to rebuke the descendants of the priests and to spread refuse on the faces of the priests. The concept of the choice of Jerusalem continues in this vision (see 1:17; 2:8,11-12). Yahweh has chosen Jerusalem, and Joshua is **a burning stick snatched from the fire**. This image implies that Yahweh also has chosen Joshua, the priestly representative of Judah, and that Yahweh has delivered the people from exile. Amos 4:11 uses the "brand plucked from the fire" as an image of God's rescue from punishment, and the exodus is depicted with the similar metaphor of escape from an iron furnace (Deut 4:20; 1 Kgs 8:51; Jer 11:4; cf. Exod 18:8-10).

**3:3-4 Joshua** the priest is **dressed in filthy clothes**, but **the angel** commands those standing nearby to remove the soiled clothes and promises that Joshua will instead be clothed in **rich garments**. The significance of the filth of Joshua's clothes is uncertain. Perhaps his clothes are dirty because he is mourning as a sign of repentance;[65] however, the word used to describe these stains on Joshua's clothes is related to a word used elsewhere for "excrement" (Deut 23:13; Ezek 4:12). With his garments thus fouled, the priest is disqualified from service. Verse 2 mentions that Joshua is snatched from the fire, indicating that the priest has been rescued from the state described here. The angel instructs those standing near Joshua, probably members of the priestly company (v. 8), to remove the priest's **filthy clothes**. Then the angel addresses Joshua directly, declaring that his sins **have** been **taken away** and that he will receive rich garments. The noun translated "rich garments" (cf. the TNIV's "fine garments")

---

[64]Mason, *Haggai, Zechariah, and Malachi*, p. 50; the noun *śāṭān* does not always refer to the devil. It refers to human adversaries in 1 Sam 29:4; 2 Sam 19:22; 1 Kgs 5:18; 11:4,23,25. McComiskey, "Zechariah," p. 1069, allows that such a use of the term may be represented here.

[65]Baldwin, *Haggai, Zechariah, Malachi*, p. 114.

appears elsewhere only in Isaiah 3:22 for special garments worn at festive occasions. Here the instructions concerning Joshua's clothes represent the removing of the sin that previously stained him and the people of Yahweh whom he represents (Zech 3:9; cf. Isa 64:6). Similar in character to the investiture of priests (Lev 8:1-9), the wording intimates that the reinstatement of Joshua as high priest following the shame of exile requires an act of divine installation.[66]

**3:5** Zechariah interjects himself into the vision (**Then I said**), urging that **a clean turban** be placed on Joshua's **head**. The reader might naturally associate the turban in this vision with the priestly turban plate in Exodus 28 that reads "Holy to Yahweh" (Exod 28:36). If so, this change in Joshua's attire communicates the cleansing of Joshua, the priestly line, and the nation from their past defilement (Zech 3:9) and the restoration of Joshua to the high priestly function. Even so, two notable dissimilarities exist between Zechariah 3 and Exodus 28. One, the prophet singles out the turban from among several notable items of priestly garb which could have been mentioned: ephod, breastplate, robe, tunic, and sash. Two, even though built on the same root, the noun for "turban" (צָנִיף, ṣānîph) here is not identical to the one in the description of the priestly vestments in Exodus 28:36-39 (מִצְנֶפֶת, miṣnepheth). Furthermore, Mesopotamian temple building practices may indicate a significance of the turban beyond this message of cleansing and restoration. The builder of a Mesopotamian temple (usually a monarch who acts also as a priest) wears a ritually clean garment as he uses a remnant brick or stone from the former temple to lay the foundation of the new temple.[67] A Babylonian stele portrays the seventh-century Assyrian emperor Ashurbanipal carrying such a foundation brick. As he does so, the king is wearing a special turban.[68] In this case, Zechariah 3 presents Joshua being prepared for his role in the renewed temple reconstruction as he is given new garments and, more specifically, a clean turban.[69]

---

[66]Mason, *Haggai, Zechariah, Malachi*, p. 50.

[67]Baruch Halpern, "The Ritual Background of Zechariah's Temple Song," *CBQ* 40 (1978): 171.

[68]Ibid., p. 173.

[69]Ezra 3 indicates that Judah's remnant community actually lays the foundation of the second temple sixteen years earlier in 536 B.C. Under Persian authority the Aaronic priesthood and the Davidic house govern Judah coop-

**3:6-7** Following the vision of clean garments for Joshua, the angel of Yahweh delivers a **charge** from Yahweh Seba'oth (**the Lord Almighty**) **to Joshua** regarding the privileges granted to him as high priest. The militaristic associations of the name Yahweh Seba'oth and its connections with the temple and the Ark of the Covenant make significant its appearances in chapter 3 (see comments on Nahum 2:13; 3:5; Zeph 2:8; and Haggai: Theology). It appears in the messenger formula prefacing the promise of Joshua's future role in the temple (v. 7) and in oracular formulas solemnizing the proclamations of the stone set before Joshua and the removal of the land's sin (v. 9) and of the coming peace (v. 10). The **angel of the Lord** charges Joshua with two conditions, the fulfillment of which lead to three results. If Joshua **will walk in** Yahweh's **ways** (cf. the TNIV's "walk in obedience to me") and **keep** Yahweh's **requirements, then** he **will govern** Yahweh's **house, have charge of** Yahweh's **courts**, and will be given **a place among** those **standing** there. The command to walk (הָלַךְ, *hālak*) in the ways (דֶּרֶךְ, *derek*) of Yahweh appears frequently in Deuteronomy (8:6; 10:12; 11:22; 19:9; 26:17; 28:9; 30:16), and the notion of keeping or carrying out (שָׁמַר, *šāmar*) the requirements or service (מִשְׁמֶרֶת, *mišmereth*) of Yahweh appears in several texts speaking of the priestly responsibilities for the care of the sanctuary, altar, and tabernacle/temple of Yahweh. These texts involve the historical temple of Yahweh (Lev 22:9; Num 3:32; 18:4-5; 1 Chr 23:32) and the visionary temple of Ezekiel (44:8,14,15,16; 48:11). The two phrases appear together elsewhere only in 1 Kings 2:3 where David commands Solomon to walk in the ways of Yahweh and to keep Yahweh's requirements so that Solomon might prosper in all that he does. The statement **you will govern my house** hints at the increasingly important role the high priest and temple would play in the postexilic community in the absence of a monarchy.[70] A repetition of the

---

eratively. Therefore, both Zerubbabel and Joshua participate. The singing of the sons of Asaph and the mixture of shouts of joy and sounds of weeping that occur (Ezra 3:10-13) reflect other elements of the Mesopotamian temple foundation ceremonies. Nevertheless, the sixteen-year interruption in construction that follows may later have necessitated a variation of the ceremony to mark the resumption of building.

[70]Merrill, *Haggai, Zechariah, Malachi*, p. 135; Baldwin, *Haggai, Zechariah, Malachi*, p. 115.

verb *šāmar* highlights the connection between Joshua's obedience and his reward. If Joshua will "keep" Yahweh's requirements, he will be granted to "have charge" of the courts of Yahweh. "Courts" (חָצֵר, *ḥāṣēr*) usually refers to the courts of the tabernacle (Exod 27:9; 38:9; 39:40; Lev 6:16; Num 3:26) or the temple (1 Kgs 6:36; 7:12; Jer 36:10; Ezek 8:16; 10:4). Its use for palace courts (1 Kgs 7:8-9,12; 2 Kgs 20:4; Esth 4:11) is relevant here also because the temple is considered the palace or royal residence of the deity.

**3:8** The attention of **Joshua** and of his priestly **associates** evidently **seated before** him is summoned by the use of the verb **listen** (שְׁמַע, *šāmaʿ*). The **high priest** and his colleagues now serve a prophetic function as they are symbols (NASB, NET, NIV, TNIV) or signs (ESV, NPJS) of divine blessings to come.[71] The noun "sign" (מוֹפֵת, *môphēth*) is applied to the priestly prophet Ezekiel whose actions stand for future events (Ezek 12:6,11; 24:24; cf. Isa 8:18). The phrase "for behold" (כִּי־הִנְנִי, *kî-hinnî*) absent in the NIV (see NASB) emphasizes the certainty of Yahweh's promise to **bring** the **servant, the Branch** (cf. the phrase's use in Isa 65:17,18; Jer 30:10; 46:27). Both of these descriptions, "my servant" (Isa 42:1; 49:6; 52:13) and "the Branch" (Isa 4:2; 11:1; Jer 23:5; 33:15), are significant messianic titles in the Old Testament. Here, however, is the only place where the two titles are conjoined. Since Judah remains a province under Persian rule during the early postexilic period, direct references to a future Davidic monarch are thus cast in terms such as these to avoid the notions of political power and independence (cf. Zech 4:6-10; 6:12; 9:9).[72] Such texts do, however, present "the people's faith in the mysterious arrival of a new David."[73]

**3:9-10** A **stone** is **set in front of Joshua**. This stone is said to have **seven eyes**, and Yahweh Seba'oth (**the LORD Almighty**) pledges to **engrave an inscription on it**. Both the literary context of chapter 4 and the cultural context of Mesopotamian temple rebuilding processes clarify the nature and significance of the stone with its seven eyes. Various textual features suggest a close connection

---

[71]Mason, *Books of Haggai, Zechariah, and Malachi*, p. 51. McComiskey, "Zechariah," p. 1078, rightly cautions against identifying Joshua or anyone in his company as the Branch since the group is identified as the sign of the coming Branch.

[72]Meyers and Meyers, *Zechariah 9–14*, p. 124.

[73]Stuhlmueller, *Rebuilding with Hope*, p. 124.

between the stones described in chapters 3 and 4. In 3:9, Yahweh
sets a stone before Joshua; in 4:7, Zerubbabel brings out a stone.
Each of the community's two authority figures is thus linked with a
stone. Furthermore, the stone of 3:9 has seven "eyes" on it, and a
second reference to these seven eyes in 4:10 occurs after the appearance of the stone of 4:7 (see comments on 4:10 below). The text may
also reflect the Mesopotamian practice of inlaying foundation
stones or tablets with gems.[74] If so, these seven inlaid stones would
look like eyes and doubtless signify divine omniscience and universal dominion, a theme seen already in 1:10-11 and later in 4:10. In
addition to its seven eyes, the stone of verse 9 will have an inscription engraved by Yahweh. Like an artist signing a completed work,
this image offers reassurance of a temple completed to the very last
detail.[75] Thus, the stone which is set before Joshua is likely a building stone whose placement would mark the completion of the building of the temple.[76] This inscribed stone bears seven inlaid gems or
"eyes" representing divine omniscience and divine approval of the
temple reconstruction.[77] The formula "says the LORD Almighty"
appears at the end of verses 9 and 10 (also in 5:4; 8:11; 13:2,7), and
it affirms the notion of the restoration of the temple and the return
of Yahweh's presence to it.[78]

[74]McComiskey, "Zechariah," p. 1079; John H. Walton, Victor H.
Matthews, Mark W. Chavalas, *The IVP Bible Background Commentary: Old
Testament* (Downers Grove, IL: InterVarsity, 2000), pp. 800-801.

[75]A. Cohen, *The Twelve Prophets*, 2nd ed., rev. by A.J. Rosenberg, Soncino
Books of the Bible (New York: Soncino, 1994), p. 283. While the text does
not indicate directly what this inscription is, the concentration of vocabulary
for sight in 3:9 and 4:2 may imply that the inscription in the stone set before
Joshua in the prophet's vision is the lampstand in the next vision (4:1-14).
Two uses of the demonstrative particle "behold" (הִנֵּה, *hinnēh*) appear in 3:9
(the NASB translates both particles; the NIV translates as "see" only the first
one). The prophet is called to "see" the stone set before Joshua in 3:9 and is
then asked what he sees (רָאָה, *rā'āh*) in 4:2, to which the prophet answers
with a second use of *rā'āh* and another use of *hinnēh* introducing a description of his vision of the lampstand. The proximity of the call to see and the
description of what is seen may indicate that the lampstand is the inscription
that Zechariah sees, according to Halpern, "Ritual Background," p. 177.

[76]Meyers and Meyers, *Haggai, Zechariah 1–8*, pp. 207-208.

[77]McComiskey, "Zechariah," p. 1079.

[78]Tryggve N.D. Mettinger, *The Dethronement of Sabaoth: Studies in the Shem
and Kabod Theologies*, trans. by Frederick H. Cryer; ConBOT 18 (Uppsala:
CWK Gleerup, 1982), pp. 80-115.

The **sin of** the **land** will be removed **in a single day**; here land stands for the people, and the removal of sin explains the symbolic act of verse 4. The prophet later writes of a day in which a spirit of grace and supplication is poured out on the house of David and the inhabitants of Jerusalem and a day in which a fountain is opened to cleanse them from sin and impurity (12:10; 13:1), even though a different word for "sin" is used in these verses. Jeremiah 33:8 links the cleansing and forgiveness of sin with the coming of the righteous Davidic Branch (33:15), an enduring priesthood (33:17-18), and Judah and Jerusalem dwelling in safety (33:16). The image of one inviting a **neighbor** to fellowship under a **vine and fig tree** represents peace and security (1 Kgs 4:25; 2 Kgs 18:31; Isa 36:16; Micah 4:4). Its use here recalls the ideal conditions of Solomon's reign, which the phrase first describes in 1 Kings 4:25, and reflects the hopes for the return of such conditions (cf. Jer 23:5-6; 33:15-16). The day in which the sin of the land is removed and the day of peace and security come when Yahweh's servant, the Branch, comes. Until then, Joshua, his associates, and the stone set before Joshua stand for the certain arrival of that promised day.

## E. A GOLD LAMPSTAND AND TWO OLIVE TREES (4:1-14)

[1]Then the angel who talked with me returned and wakened me, as a man is wakened from his sleep. [2]He asked me, "What do you see?"

I answered, "I see a solid gold lampstand with a bowl at the top and seven lights on it, with seven channels to the lights. [3]Also there are two olive trees by it, one on the right of the bowl and the other on its left."

[4]I asked the angel who talked with me, "What are these, my lord?"

[5]He answered, "Do you not know what these are?"

"No, my lord," I replied.

[6]So he said to me, "This is the word of the LORD to Zerubbabel: 'Not by might nor by power, but by my Spirit,' says the LORD Almighty.

[7]"What[a] are you, O mighty mountain? Before Zerubbabel you will become level ground. Then he will bring out the capstone to shouts of 'God bless it! God bless it!'"

⁸Then the word of the LORD came to me: ⁹"The hands of Zerubbabel have laid the foundation of this temple; his hands will also complete it. Then you will know that the LORD Almighty has sent me to you.

¹⁰"Who despises the day of small things? Men will rejoice when they see the plumb line in the hand of Zerubbabel.

"(These seven are the eyes of the LORD, which range throughout the earth.)"

¹¹Then I asked the angel, "What are these two olive trees on the right and the left of the lampstand?"

¹²Again I asked him, "What are these two olive branches beside the two gold pipes that pour out golden oil?"

¹³He replied, "Do you not know what these are?"

"No, my lord," I said.

¹⁴So he said, "These are the two who are anointed toᵇ serve the Lord of all the earth."

ᵃ7 Or *Who*    ᵇ14 Or *two who bring oil and*

**4:1** Zechariah 4:1-14 contains the prophet's fifth night vision. The chapter, which contains the vision itself (vv. 1-5), a series of oracles given to Zechariah (vv. 6-10), and a resumption of the vision's explanation (vv. 11-14), depicts the divine resources through which the rebuilding of the temple is accomplished. Most versions (e.g., ESV, NET, NIV, NRSV, NJPS) imply that the prophet has been sleeping by translating the verb עוּר (*'ûr*) with forms of "wake." However, *'ûr* primarily designates an inciting or rousing to action (Deut 32:11; 2 Sam 23:8; 1 Chr 5:26; 11:11,20; 2 Chr 21:16; 36:22; Ezra 1:1,5; Job 3:8; 8:6; Ps 72:16; Prov 10:12; Isa 13:7; 41:25; 45:13; Hag 1:14; Zech 2:13; 9:13), rather than a literal awakening from sleep. Moreover, the use of the same verb in the comparison **as a man is awakened from his sleep** indicates that a rousing to "a higher state of prophetic receptivity" is intended rather than a physical awakening.[79] Such an elevation of consciousness is fitting if 4:1 begins a new section within the night visions (see Introduction above).

**4:2-3** The angel asks Zechariah what he sees (**What do you see?**), a question typical for reports of a prophetic vision (cf. Jer 1:11,13; 24:3; Amos 7:8; 8:2; Zech 5:2). Zechariah then describes **a solid gold**

---

[79]McComiskey, "Zechariah," p. 1082.

**lampstand**, the exact appearance of which is not known, and **two olive trees** on either side of it. The lamp appears to be in a form known in the postexilic period (cf. 1 Macc 1:21). While some understand this to be a menorah (e.g., NET), it is unlikely that the model is the modern menorah.[80] The lampstand described here also differs from that described in Exodus 25:31-40. It consists of a stand **with a bowl at** its **top with seven lights**, perhaps around the edge of the bowl. Each of the seven lamps then bears seven spouts (i.e., pipes through which oil is poured)[81] or lips (i.e., the place where the wick is placed).[82] The NIV adopts the former idea with **channels**. Two olive trees stand on either side of the bowl upon the lampstand. Similar is a pair of pillars standing to the left and to the right of the entrance in Solomon's temple (1 Kgs 7:41-42). Atop these pillars are capitals or "bowls" (גֻּלָּה, gullāh), as is the case here. These two olive trees figure into the vision as providing an unlimited supply of oil to the lamps.

**4:4-5** It is unclear whether the question **"What are these, my lord?"** refers to the olive trees, the lamp, or both. If the question is about the trees, then the angel delays his answer until verse 14.[83] If, however, the question is about the lamp, then the angel begins to answer that question here.[84] If not one or the other, the plural "these" indicates the prophet is asking about both components of the vision.[85] The angel's question, **"Do you not know what these are?"** is not intended to highlight the ignorance of Zechariah so much as to make clear his need for supernatural insight to understand what he is seeing. Rhetorically, it also serves as a device to heighten the expectation of the answer by delaying it.[86]

---

[80]For more detailed discussion on the possible design and appearance of the lampstand described here, see Baldwin, *Haggai, Zechariah, Malachi*, pp. 119-120; R. North, "Zechariah's Seven-Spout Lampstand," *Bib* 51 (1970): 183-206; Meyers and Meyers, *Haggai, Zechariah 1–8*, pp. 227-234, 264-265, 273-277; and Petersen, *Haggai and Zechariah 1–8*, pp. 216-224.

[81]BDB, p. 427; Paul R. Gilchrist, "צָק," *TWOT*, 1:395.

[82]Lawrence E. Toombs, "Lampstand," *IDB*, 3:64-66; Baldwin, *Haggai, Zechariah, Malachi*, pp. 119-120.

[83]Baldwin, *Haggai, Zechariah, Malachi*, p. 120; McComiskey, "Zechariah," p. 1085.

[84]Merrill, *Haggai, Zechariah, Malachi*, p. 149.

[85]Boda, *Haggai, Zechariah*, p. 273.

[86]Ibid.

**4:6** The angel does not appear to answer Zechariah's question but instead delivers a message encouraging Zerubbabel to complete the rebuilding of the temple. The word rendered **might** (חַיִל, *ḥayil*) by the NIV denotes power that may be demonstrated in physical strength or ability (Ps 18:32; 59:11; Prov 31:3; Eccl 10:10; Zech 9:4), wealth (Gen 34:29; 2 Kgs 15:20; Job 31:25; Ezek 28:4-5; Zech 14:14), or an army (Exod 14:14,17; 1 Kgs 20:1; Ps 33:16; 136:15; Ezek 17:17). The gnomic character of the affirmation in this verse does not preclude any of these senses of the word. Paired with "might" is **power** (כֹּחַ, *kōaḥ*), a noun with basically the same meaning. The same word pair appears in Deuteronomy 8:17-18 where Moses warns Israel not to think that they are able to produce wealth in the land of Canaan through their own abilities; instead, Yahweh enables them to produce wealth. Psalm 33:16 also uses the same pair of words to affirm that a king's army and a warrior's strength are unable to deliver; rather, only Yahweh can deliver (Ps 33:18-19). Likewise, Zechariah 4:6 asserts that human strength cannot accomplish the rebuilding of the temple, but its completion comes only through the Spirit of Yahweh. The oracular formula **says the LORD Almighty** further highlights the contrast between human and divine strength. Zechariah's contemporary Haggai emphasizes the message of Yahweh's presence and power to succeed in the reconstruction of the temple with the words, "My Spirit remains among you. Do not fear" (2:5).

**4:7** Because strength to complete the temple comes from the Spirit of Yahweh (v. 6), obstacles vanish before **Zerubbabel** (v. 7). Isaiah uses the imagery of mountains to represent obstacles (Isa 22:5; 40:4; 41:15; 45:2; cf. Ezra 4:1-5,24), and here the **mighty mountain** likely represents any obstacle, including those despising the day of small things in verse 10, that Yahweh levels before Zerubbabel as he seeks to rebuild the temple.[87] Most modern English translations understand the Hebrew phrase "the stone of the head" (הָאֶבֶן הָרֹאשָׁה, *hā'eben hārō'šāh*) as a **capstone** (NET, NIV) or top stone (ESV, NASB, NRSV) that completes a building (cf. NLT "final stone").

Another possibility connects the stone with the Akkadian term *libittu mahritu*, meaning "the former stone" or "the first stone." This

[87]Baldwin, *Haggai, Zechariah, Malachi*, p. 121; Merrill, *Haggai, Zechariah, Malachi*, p. 160.

"former stone" is a remnant stone set aside from the rubble of the former temple for reuse in the new temple's foundation.[88] Assyrian and Babylonian royal inscriptions record a king's participation in the rebuilding project by placing this remnant brick or stone from the former temple in laying the foundation for the new temple.[89] This practice may provide some precedent for Zerubbabel's actions in following the divine command given through Haggai (Hag 1:7-8) to begin again the rebuilding of the temple; as the Davidic governor appointed by the Persians, he fulfills a role usually performed by a monarch. However, if such a retrieved foundation stone is used in the second temple, it certainly would have been laid sixteen years earlier during the first failed attempt at temple reconstruction begun in 536 B.C. Indeed, verses 7-10 seem more directed toward the temple's completion rather than its beginning, and the stone to be brought out appears to be a finishing rather than a founding stone.[90]

Both verses 7 and 10 refer to a joyous response to an action of Zerubbabel involving a stone. One might then expect the "capstone" (hā'eben hārō'šāh) to parallel the enigmatic "plumb line" (הָאֶבֶן הַבְּדִיל, hā'eben habbᵊdîl in verse 10. The stone of verse 7 may very well be the object in the hand of Zerubbabel in verse 10, if this object is a tin tablet placed within the walls of the temple to commemorate its completion (see on v. 10 below). The cry **"God bless it! God bless it!"** (NIV) is more literally "Grace! Grace! to it" (ESV, NASB, NRSV). It is uncertain whether it represents a desire for Yahweh's favor to dwell upon it (ESV, NASB, NIV, NRSV), an affirmation that Yahweh's grace resides on the community because of the completion of the temple (as in the NET, "Grace! Grace! Because of this"), or an admiration of its beauty (as in the NPJS, "Beautiful! Beautiful!"). Regardless, these cries, taken together with the pronouncement of the preceding verse, affirm that the community does not celebrate its own accomplishments but rather the power of Yahweh's Spirit evidenced among them.[91]

---

[88]Meyers and Meyers, *Haggai, Zechariah 1–8*, p. 247; Petersen, *Haggai and Zechariah 1–8*, pp. 240-241.

[89]Antti Laato, "Zachariah 4,6b-10a and the Akkadian Royal Building Inscriptions," *ZAW* 106 (1994): 53-62.

[90]Baldwin, *Haggai, Zechariah, Malachi*, p. 121; McComiskey, "Zechariah," p. 1088; Merrill, *Haggai, Zechariah, Malachi*, p. 161.

[91]McComiskey, "Zechariah," p. 1088.

**4:8-9** Verses 8 and 9 affirm that **Zerubbabel**, who has **laid the foundation of** the **temple, will** certainly **complete** the temple, and its completion will further vindicate the prophet's authority (cf. Zech 2:9,11; 6:15). A vindication formula (**then you will know that the LORD Almighty has sent me to you**) closes the oracle as it did in 2:9 and 2:11.[92]

**4:10** The question, **"Who despises the day of small things?"** reflects the thoughts of some in the community who consider the temple reconstruction project insignificant (Hag 2:3) or who question the possibility of its completion. Such doubts turn to joy **when they see the plumb line in** Zerubbabel's **hand** as evidence of the work moving forward toward completion. A reading of "tin stone" (NET)[93] instead of "plumb line" (ESV, NIV) may anticipate Zerubbabel placing an inscription on the temple (possibly to mark its completion), a common practice in the reconstruction of fallen temples in Mesopotamia.[94] The parenthetical statement in the NIV may refer to the "seven eyes" in the previous vision (3:9).[95] Here the number **seven**, which indicates completion or perfection, portrays Yahweh's presence in the temple, control throughout the whole earth, and support for the rebuilding efforts (cf. 2 Chr 16:9).

---

[92]McComiskey, ibid., understands the vindication formula to refer to the angel rather than the prophet.

[93]The meaning of הָאֶבֶן הַבְּדִיל (hā'eben hābbᵉdîl) translated "plumb line" by NIV in verse 10 is debated. Even though the phrase hā'eben hābbᵉdîl means "the stone of separation" or "the separate stone," the traditional translations "plumb line" (ESV, NASB, NIV) and "plummet" (NRSV) offer no apparent connection with that concept. The translation "tin tablet" is more plausible for the following reasons: tins or alloys are "separated" from a precious metal; other uses of hābbᵉdîl in the Old Testament seem to refer to metal rather than a tool (Num 31:22; Isa 1:25; Ezek 22:18; 22:20; 27:12); tin or alloy deposits are used in the foundations or walls of Mesopotamian temples; and the use of a plumb line in verse 10 seems peculiar since the order of events in verses 8-10 implies the temple has been completed in verse 10. See Richard S. Ellis, *Foundation Deposits in Ancient Mesopotamia* (New Haven, CT: Yale UP, 1968), pp. 103-104.

[94]David L. Petersen, "Zerubbabel and Jerusalem Temple Reconstruction," *CBQ* 36 (1974): 370-371; Halpern, "Ritual Background," pp. 171-173.

[95]The TNIV renders the verse ("Who dares despise the day of small things, since the seven eyes of the Lord that range throughout the earth will rejoice when they see the chosen capstone in the hand of Zerubbabel?") such that the eyes of Yahweh, rather than those who belittle the temple reconstruction, rejoice at the efforts of Zerubbabel.

**4:11-13** Zechariah again asks about the trees; he first poses a broad question about the identity of the **two olive trees** and then a more specific question. The second question focuses on **two olive branches**. The second question also mentions something new: the presence of two **pipes** that seem to supply the lamp with the oil from the trees. The **golden oil** may not describe the physical color of the oil so much as its value.[96] The angel asks Zechariah if he knows **what these** (olive trees or branches?) **are**, to which Zechariah says he does not know.

**4:14** The angel then explains that these **two are** those **anointed to serve the Lord of all the earth**. Instead of the word (מָשִׁיחַ, *māšîaḥ*) normally translated "anointed (one)" (Ps 2:2; 18:50; 20:6; 28:8; 84:9; 89:38,51; 105:15; 132:10,17; Isa 45:1) or the word (שֶׁמֶן, *šemen*) frequently used for anointing oil (Exod 25:6; 29:7; 30:25,31; 39:38; 40:9; Lev 8:2,10,12), the word "anointed" here translates the Hebrew phrase "sons of oil" (בְנֵי־הַיִּצְהָר, *bᵊnê-hayyiṣhar*). The noun *yiṣhar* frequently occurs in parallel with "new wine" in images of prosperity and fertility.[97] The use of the phrase "sons of oil" (*bᵊnê-hayyiṣhar*) rather than the word for anointing oil (*šemen*) may emphasize the source of the oil rather than its end use. Furthermore, anointing signifies selection and empowerment for tasks. Although Elijah is commanded to anoint Elisha (1 Kgs 19:16),[98] the Old Testament indicates only a regular practice of anointing priests (Exod 28:41; 29:29; 30:30; Lev 8:10; Num 3:3) and kings (1 Sam 9:16; 15:17; 16:3,6; 2 Sam 5:3; 2 Chr 23:11). Consequently, the two olive trees identified here as the two "sons of oil" who stand before the Lord of all the earth are likely Joshua and Zerubbabel, given their prominence in chapters 3 and 4.[99] Joshua and Zerubbabel, therefore, serve as representatives of these religious and political offices, so anointed as

---

[96]Merrill, *Haggai, Zechariah, Malachi*, p. 155.

[97]E.g., Num 18:12; Deut 7:13; 11:14; 12:17; 14:23; 18:4; 28:51; 2 Chr 31:5; 32:28; Neh 5:11; 10:37,39; 13:5,12; Jer 31:12; Hos 2:8,22; Joel 1:10; 2:19,24; Hag 1:11.

[98]First Kings 19 reports Yahweh's instructions to Elijah to anoint Elisha, but the subsequent narrative only implies the actual event.

[99]Baldwin, *Haggai, Zechariah, Malachi*, p. 124; Cohen, *Twelve Prophets*, p. 286; Merrill, *Haggai, Zechariah, Malachi*, p. 150. However, Boda, *Haggai, Zechariah*, pp. 274-276, argues that the "sons of oil" who stand before Yahweh are the prophets.

high priest and civil governor whose authority to govern comes not from some earthly master like Darius but from God who is the Lord (אָדוֹן, *'ădôn* rather than יהוה, *YHWH*) of all the earth (cf. Josh 3:11,13; Ps 97:5; Micah 4:13; Zech 6:5).[100]

## F. A FLYING SCROLL (5:1-4)

[1]I looked again—and there before me was a flying scroll!
[2]He asked me, "What do you see?"
I answered, "I see a flying scroll, thirty feet long and fifteen feet wide.[a]"

[3]And he said to me, "This is the curse that is going out over the whole land; for according to what it says on one side, every thief will be banished, and according to what it says on the other, everyone who swears falsely will be banished. [4]The LORD Almighty declares, 'I will send it out, and it will enter the house of the thief and the house of him who swears falsely by my name. It will remain in his house and destroy it, both its timbers and its stones.'"

[a]*2* Hebrew *twenty cubits long and ten cubits wide* (about 9 meters long and 4.5 meters wide)

**5:1-2** Zechariah 5:1-4 contains the prophet's sixth night vision. The vision (vv. 1-2), followed by a brief explanation (v. 3) and single oracle (v. 4), concerns the importance of purity within the community. Zechariah sees **flying** through the air a **scroll**,[101] **thirty feet** (20 cubits) **long and fifteen feet** (10 cubits) **wide**. These unusually large dimensions indicate that the scroll may not have been unrolled when the prophet initially sees it, since a scroll would typically be ten times as long as it is wide instead of only twice as long as is the case here. Consequently, the "width" of the scroll may actually denote its thickness when rolled. A scroll of such surreal thickness would depict a monumental amount of information and the profound significance of that contained on the scroll.[102]

---

[100]Mason, *Haggai, Zechariah, and Malachi*, p. 48.
[101]The LXX reads "sickle" (δρέπανον, *drepanon*) instead of "scroll."
[102]Boda, *Haggai, Zechariah*, p. 293; Merrill, *Haggai, Zechariah, Malachi*, p. 166. Some (e.g., Meyers and Meyers, *Haggai, Zechariah 1–8*, p. 280) sug-

**5:3** The unidentified speaker in verse 3 equates the scroll with the **curse** (אָלָה, 'ālāh), a technical term referring to the sanctions for violating covenant (Deut 29:20-21). The phrase **over the whole land** may refer to limited regions (Deut 11:25; 1 Sam 30:16; 2 Sam 18:8) or the entire earth (Gen 1:29; 7:3; 8:9; 11:4,8,9). Its use within the night visions reflects the latter connotation (Zech 1:11; 4:14; 6:5). Thus, the prophet may address the entire Jewish community, rather than merely the province of Judah, regarding the purity required of them. While the scroll only mentions two items of covenant law, those two parts, corresponding to the third and eighth commandments (Exod 20:7,15; Lev 19:12; Deut 5:11,19), encompass its entirety. One part focuses on the interpersonal aspect (**every thief will be banished**), while the other focuses on the obligation to Yahweh (**everyone who swears falsely will be banished**).[103] If the commandments alluded to in verses 3 and 4 represent the whole of the Ten Commandments and covenant law, then the curses may very well represent the entire body of curses associated with the covenant (see Leviticus 26 and Deuteronomy 28).[104]

**5:4** The oracular formula **the LORD Almighty says** adds solemnity to the content that follows. The nearest antecedent to the pronoun **it** is the curse rather than the scroll. As a result, the verse carries the sense: Yahweh sends out the curse that enters and remains in **the house of** the one **who swears falsely by** Yahweh's **name** (cf. Zech 8:17), destroying the house completely. The verb (לִין, lîn) translated **remain** by the NIV designates an overnight stay, lodging, or encampment (Gen 19:2; 24:23 25; 28:11; 31:54; 32:11; Exod 34:25; Deut 21:23; Josh 3:1; 6:11). The imagery thus connotes a rapid, even unexpected, realization of the curse's effects. The phrase **both its timbers and stones** connotes the total destruction of both the perjurer's house and the perjurer; indeed, the curse finds him even where he thinks himself secure.

---

gest the measurements of the scroll are intended to be associated with measurements of the porch of Solomon's temple (1 Kgs 6:3) or of the cherubim shadowing the ark of the covenant (1 Kgs 6:24-27), but this is unlikely, so say Baldwin, *Haggai, Zechariah, Malachi*, p. 126; Boda, *Haggai, Zechariah*, p. 293; Ollenburger, "Zechariah," p. 774.

[103]Merrill, *Haggai, Zechariah, Malachi*, p. 168.

[104]Chisholm, *Minor Prophets*, p. 250.

## G. A WOMAN IN A BASKET (5:5-11)

⁵Then the angel who was speaking to me came forward and said to me, "Look up and see what this is that is appearing."

⁶I asked, "What is it?"

He replied, "It is a measuring basket.ᵃ" And he added, "This is the iniquityᵇ of the people throughout the land."

⁷Then the cover of lead was raised, and there in the basket sat a woman! ⁸He said, "This is wickedness," and he pushed her back into the basket and pushed the lead cover down over its mouth.

⁹Then I looked up—and there before me were two women, with the wind in their wings! They had wings like those of a stork, and they lifted up the basket between heaven and earth.

¹⁰"Where are they taking the basket?" I asked the angel who was speaking to me.

¹¹He replied, "To the country of Babyloniaᶜ to build a house for it. When it is ready, the basket will be set there in its place."

ᵃ6 Hebrew *an ephah*; also in verses 7-11      ᵇ6 Or *appearance*
ᶜ11 Hebrew *Shinar*

Zechariah 5:5-11 contains the prophet's seventh night vision. Presented in three parts, the section alternates between the vision (vv. 5,7,9) and its explanation (vv. 6,8,10-11). Both visions in chapter 5 deal with the theme of purity in the community. The first of the two (vv. 1-4) asserts that the judgment of divine curse comes upon those who break covenant; the second (vv. 5-11) communicates the intent of Yahweh to purge the community of wickedness.

**5:5-6** The messenger, evidently the same interpreting **angel** who has accompanied the prophet throughout the previous visions, directs Zechariah to **look** at another object. **A measuring basket** (אֵיפָה, *'êphāh*), a word merely transliterated "ephah" in some versions (e.g., KJV, NASB), is a common household container used for measuring solids or liquids with a capacity of about five gallons or two-thirds bushel (see Ruth 2:17; 1 Sam 1:24). Within this vision, *'êphāh* does not represent an exact use of the term, since a standard ephah measure could likely not hold a woman (see v. 7).[105]

The angel adds that the measuring basket **is the iniquity of the people throughout the land.** Most versions, including the ESV, NIV,

---

[105]O.R. Sellers, "Ephah," *IDB* 2:107.

and NRSV, follow the LXX and Syriac reading "their iniquity" (עֲוֹנָם, '*āwōnām*) instead of the MT reading "their eye" (עֵינָם, '*ênām*), a translation found in the NET and NJPS and reflected in the NASB's "appearance" (cf. Num 11:7; 1 Sam 16:7). Support for the LXX reading assumes that the MT represents a substitution of letter *yod* (י) for the letter *waw* (ו), a fairly common phenomenon in the copying of ancient manuscripts.[106] However, the alteration could have occurred the other way, substituting *waw* for *yod*. If so, the phrase "their appearance throughout the land" may refer to the depiction of wickedness in the images that follow in verses 7-9.[107] Significant also is the identification in verse 8 of the vision as "wickedness" (רִשְׁעָה, *riš'āh*) rather than "iniquity" ('*āwōn*). The noun "eye" frequently appears in Zechariah (2:8; 3:9; 4:10; 9:1; 11:17; 12:4; 14:12), whereas "iniquity" appears only in 3:4 and 9.

**5:7-8** The NIV softens the translation of the interjection "behold" (הִנֵּה, *hinnēh*), a common feature in the reports of Zechariah's visions (Zech 1:8,11,18; 2:1,3,9-10; 3:8-9; 4:2; 5:1,7; 6:1), with the word **then**. The prophet sees a thing made of **lead** on top of the basket. This noun translated **cover** (כִּכָּר, *kikkār*) may refer to a circular loaf of bread (Judg 8:5; 1 Chr 16:3; Prov 6:26; Jer 37:21), a circular territory or district (Gen 13:10; 19:25; 1 Kgs 7:46; Neh 3:22; 12:28), or a round weight (Exod 25:39; 37:24; 38:27; 1 Kgs 20:39; 2 Kgs 23:33). The KJV translates *kikkār* according to its typical weight, one "talent" or about seventy-five pounds (cf. 2 Sam 12:30; 1 Kgs 10:10). Its use here suggests that it depicts a heavy lead cover for the basket. This lead cover is **raised**, revealing **a woman** sitting **in the basket**. The woman seen may be understood as a full-size human only if the '*ēphāh* is a general term for a basket (see comments on 5:6 above). If, however, '*ēphāh* is the standard measure, then the woman may be a figurine or image of a woman[108] or the image of a pagan goddess[109] such as the Queen of Heaven (Jer 7:10-18; 44:1-27), Ashtoreth (1 Kgs 11:5-7), or the Asherah (1 Kgs 18:19; 2 Kgs 23:7). The angel identi-

---

[106]Baldwin, *Haggai, Zechariah, Malachi*, p. 128; Merrill, *Haggai, Zechariah, Malachi*, p. 172; Boda, *Haggai, Zechariah*, pp. 305-306.

[107]McComiskey, "Zechariah," p. 1101; Ollenburger, "Zechariah," p. 778; Meyers and Meyers, *Haggai, Zechariah*, pp. 293, 298.

[108]Ollenburger, "Zechariah," p. 777.

[109]Boda, *Haggai, Zechariah*, p. 306; Meyers and Meyers, *Haggai, Zechariah 1-8*, p. 301.

fies the woman in the basket as **wickedness** (רִשְׁעָה, *riš'āh*), the anti-
thesis of righteousness (Deut 9:4,5; Prov 11:5; 13:6; Ezek 18:20;
33:12). Those who do wickedness arrogantly challenge God (Mal
3:15) and rebel against Yahweh's decrees and laws (Ezek 5:6). In the
context of the previous vision (5:1-4), the wickedness here may be
associated with that perpetrated by the covenant breakers in 5:3-4.[110]
The angel pushes (שָׁלַךְ, *šālak*) the woman identified as wickedness
into the basket and then pushes (also *šālak*) **the lead cover down over**
the **mouth** of the basket. The forceful placement of the woman (cf.
"rammed" in the NJB and "thrust" in the NRSV) and of the leaden
cover suggests the necessity and the finality of her confinement.[111]

**5:9-11** Zechariah then sees **two women** with wings lift **up the bas-**
**ket between heaven and earth**. The women have **the wind** or spirit
(רוּחַ, *rûaḥ*) **in their wings**. Reading *rûaḥ* as "spirit" infers that wickedness is being removed at Yahweh's doing.[112] The two women have
**wings like . . . stork**s, one of the unclean birds listed in Leviticus
11:19 and Deuteronomy 14:18. The unclean cargo is thus carried
away by women associated with uncleanness. The prophet asks the
angel about the ultimate destination of the basket. Whereas the NIV
and NET use **Babylonia** to identify the place the angel identifies, the
ESV, KJV, NASB, and NRSV reflect the Hebrew name used, Shinar
(שִׁנְעָר, *šin'ār*). Genesis 10:10 identifies Shinar as the ancient region in
which the cities of Babylon, Erech, and Akkad are situated; here also
the tower of Babel is built (Gen 11:1-4). Since this land becomes a
symbol for human resistance against the will, righteousness, and rule
of God,[113] it is not surprising that Isaiah 11:11 includes it in the list of
lands from which Yahweh promises to summon the remnant. Such
ancient associations of the place name Shinar with evil likely explain
the writer's selection of it, as opposed to the later names Babylon or
Babylonia. Furthermore, the stork is appropriate for this representation of the removal of wickedness to Babylon, since the Hebrews

[110]On the syntactical links between the two visions (5:1-4 and 5:5-11), see
McComiskey, "Zechariah," p. 1101.
[111]Baldwin, *Haggai, Zechariah, Malachi*, p. 129; McComiskey, "Zechariah,"
p. 1101; Merrill, *Haggai, Zechariah, Malachi*, p. 174.
[112]Baldwin, *Haggai, Zechariah, Malachi*, p. 129; Boda, *Haggai, Zechariah*,
p. 307; Merrill, *Haggai, Zechariah, Malachi*, p. 175.
[113]Baldwin, *Haggai, Zechariah, Malachi*, p. 129; Merrill, *Haggai, Zechariah,
Malachi*, pp. 176-178.

would observe storks migrating north (Jer 8:7), the direction taken to Babylon, the recent place of Judah's exile.[114]

The woman in the basket serves as a foil for the power and effective presence of the living God of Israel.[115] Yahweh has promised to dwell among Israel (Zech 1:16; 2:10-13). Yahweh's house will be rebuilt through the power of Yahweh's empowering Spirit working in Zerubbabel (1:16; 4:6-9). In contrast to Yahweh's return, wickedness is being sent away; when its **house** or temple (בַּיִת, *bayith*) is prepared for **the basket** (5:10-11), it **will be set there in its place**. This noun translated "place" (מְכוֹנָה, *mᵉkōnāh*) often refers to the base for a holy object in a sanctuary (cf. 1 Kgs 7:27-43; Ezra 3:3; Jer 27:19; 52:17,20). Yahweh, however, has brought back the covenant people from Babylon, and Yahweh has promised to live among them (2:10-13) in the house or temple (*bayith*) built by Zerubbabel (4:9).

## H. FOUR CHARIOTS (6:1-8)

[1]I looked up again—and there before me were four chariots coming out from between two mountains—mountains of bronze! [2]The first chariot had red horses, the second black, [3]the third white, and the fourth dappled—all of them powerful. [4]I asked the angel who was speaking to me, "What are these, my lord?"

[5]The angel answered me, "These are the four spirits[a] of heaven, going out from standing in the presence of the Lord of the whole world. [6]The one with the black horses is going toward the north country, the one with the white horses toward the west,[b] and the one with the dappled horses toward the south."

[7]When the powerful horses went out, they were straining to go throughout the earth. And he said, "Go throughout the earth!" So they went throughout the earth.

[8]Then he called to me, "Look, those going toward the north country have given my Spirit[c] rest in the land of the north."

[a]5 Or *winds*    [b]6 Or *horses after them*    [c]8 Or *spirit*

---

[114]Boda, *Haggai, Zechariah*, p. 307.

[115]Michael H. Floyd, "The Evil in the Ephah: Reading Zechariah 5:5-11 in Its Literary Context," *CBQ* 58 (1996): 51-68. A comparison of this passage

Zechariah 6:1-8 contains the prophet's eighth night vision. Presented in two parts, the section alternates between the vision (vv. 1-3,7) and its explanation (vv. 4-6,8). This eighth and final vision corresponds to the first vision (1:7-17).[116] Whereas the first vision portrays Yahweh Seba'oth ("the Lord Almighty") as cognizant of the world situation and of Judah's place within it, the final vision portrays Yahweh Seba'oth as now acting on behalf of Judah and giving them rest from their enemies.

**6:1** Zechariah looks **up again** and sees **four chariots coming out from between two mountains . . . of bronze**. The increased use of the verb "come out" or "go out" (אָצָ֫י, *yāṣā'*) in the seventh and eighth visions (5:3,4,5[2×],6,9; 6:1,5,6[3×],7,8) seems to indicate an "intensely heightened sense of activity" that reaches its climax in the final vision.[117] Yahweh is elsewhere associated with chariots (2 Kgs 6:17; Ps 68:17; Isa 66:15; and Hab 3:8), especially where the chariots represent divine forces bringing about Yahweh's purposes among the nations. Both Israel and the Canaanites share the use of mountain imagery for the residence of God (Ps 3:4; 15:1; 24:3; 48:1-4; 68:16; Isa 14:13; Jer 31:23; Ezek 20:40; 40:2; Dan 2:35),[118] and such a connotation is likely intended here. While the identification of the two bronze mountains is disputed, they may represent the two bronze pillars, Jachin and Boaz, at the entrance of the temple, Yahweh's palace (1 Kgs 7:13-22)[119] and may anticipate the split of the Mount of Olives in Zechariah 14:4. The use of bronze in their description may connote invincibility and impregnability (Isa 45:2; Jer 1:18; 6:28; 15:12,20).

**6:2-3** Horses of various colors, likely corresponding to a natural range of colors among horses, distinguish the four chariots.[120] The

---

with Daniel 1:2 further highlights this contrast. In the days of Jehoiakim king of Judah, Nebuchadnezzar king of Babylon carries away articles from the house of Yahweh in Jerusalem and deposits them in the treasure house of his god.

[116]On the similarities between the first and eighth vision, see Hahlen, "Equine Imagery," pp. 252-254.

[117]Merrill, *Haggai, Zechariah, Malachi*, p. 182.

[118]See Richard J. Clifford, *The Cosmic Mountain in Canaan and the Old Testament*, HSM 4 (Cambridge: Harvard University Press, 1972).

[119]Mason, *Haggai, Zechariah, Malachi*, pp. 59-60; Ollenburger, "Zechariah," p. 783; Sweeney, *The Twelve Prophets*, p. 624.

[120]On the specific coloring of the horses, particularly the ones described

military connotations of these horse-drawn chariots are readily evident, since they serve ancient war machines. The appearance of four chariots, reminiscent of the points of the compass, makes them a fitting symbol of Yahweh's initiative in the world situation on behalf of Judah.

**6:4-5** The angel answers Zechariah's inquiry about the vision, telling him that **these** horses **are the four spirits of heaven**. Some translations (e.g., NASB, NET, NIV, and TNIV) render (רוּחַ, *rûaḥ*) as spirits, whereas others (e.g., ESV, NRSV, NJB, NJPS, and NIV marginal note) render *rûaḥ* as the winds of heaven. Even though the singular noun *rûaḥ* appears in verse 8 in reference to Yahweh's Spirit, the plural form of the noun *rûaḥ* is used elsewhere with the number four ("four winds of heaven") to connote universality (Jer 49:36; Dan 8:8; 11:4; Zech 2:6; cf. 1 Chr 9:24; Ezek 37:9). Such a reading is appropriate to this context. The image of winds suggests the swiftness and strength with which Yahweh, the **Lord of the whole** earth (see comments on 4:14 above), acts on behalf of Judah and throughout the world.[121] These winds go out over the whole earth after presenting themselves before Yahweh and thus demonstrate Yahweh's universal dominion, regardless of whether the world's inhabitants acknowledge him.

**6:6** Verse 6 depicts the movements of three chariots, each led by different color horses: **the black horses** to **the north**, **the white horses** to **the west**, and **the dappled horses** to **the south**. No mention is made of the red horses or a chariot that travels to the east.[122] Perhaps, no chariot is needed for this region, since elsewhere Yahweh is portrayed as the sun rising in the east (Deut 33:1-2; Judg 5:4-5; Ps

---

as "dappled" in the NIV, see Hahlen, "Equine Imagery," p. 252. Although these horses provide some background for the horses in Revelation 6:2-8, one should not read their described tasks in Revelation back into the eighth vision in Zechariah.

[121]Boda, *Haggai, Zechariah*, p. 320; Meyers and Meyers, *Haggai, Zechariah 1–8*, pp. 322-323.

[122]Nonetheless, at least one version (NEB) emends the text to include all four horses: "The chariot with the black horses is going to the land of the north, that with the white to the far west, that with the dappled to the south, and that with the roan to the land of the east." Such an omission may be evidenced by the awkward beginning of the verse, since it begins with the relative particle "which" (אֲשֶׁר, *ʾăšer*).

104; Hab 3:3),[123] or the red horse is not sent out, since this vision is similar to the first one in which the red horse belongs to the commander (Zech 1:8). Of the three directions depicted, the movement of the black horses to the north is emphasized; these horses are named first and again in verse 8. North is a place with ominous connotations for the Hebrews (Jer 1:14; 4:6; 6:22; Ezek 1:4). From there, the enemies of Israel and Judah have entered the land (Jer 10:22), and to the north is the land of the exile (Jer 3:18; 6:22; 16:15; 23:8). Although other nations besides Babylon may be included in the designation "the north" (Isa 41:25; Jer 1:15; 46:10; 50:9), Babylon is surely the focus here. The Hebrew text indicates that the white horses go "after them," that is, after the black horses (see the NIV marginal note, ESV, KJV, NASB, NET, and NJB). An alternative reading, produced from a slight textual emendation that adds one consonant, depicts the white horses going "after the sea" or "toward the west" (see the NIV, NRSV, and NJPS). If the reading "after them" is correct, then the text portrays only movement north and south, the black and white horses to the north and the dappled horses to the south. The reference to the south then focuses attention on Egypt, the frequent enemy and disappointing ally of Israel and Judah (1 Kgs 14:25; 2 Kgs 18:21; 2 Chr 36:3; Isa 30:2-7; 36:6-9; Jer 2:36).[124]

**6:7-8** These **powerful horses** (see v. 3) are impatient **to go throughout the earth**. The prophet relates the angel's command for them to go and the horses' compliance to the angel's command. The image corresponds to the mission of the horses in Zechariah 1:7-17 and reflects the ancient Persian practice of using riders for purposes of communication throughout the empire.[125] The horses then serve as instruments of Yahweh, the Lord of the earth, showing that nothing happens apart from Yahweh's knowledge and authority. The angel calls out (זָעַק, zā'aq) to the prophet. Used mainly to designate a cry for help (Exod 2:23; Judg 3:9,15; 6:6-7; 1 Sam 12:8; 2 Chr 18:31; Job 35:9; Jer 11:11; Hab 1:2), its connotations with desperation lead to its use as a summons (Judg 4:10,13; 2 Sam 20:4-5) and thus indicates the importance of the message which follows in this verse. The angel's close association with Yahweh is signaled by the angel's use of **my**

---

[123]Sweeney, *The Twelve Prophets*, pp. 626-627.
[124]McComiskey, "Zechariah," p. 1109.
[125]Sweeney, *The Twelve Prophets*, p. 627.

**Spirit**. Through the angel, Yahweh declares victory over the people of the **north** (see on 6:6 above), and in so doing, also implies victory over all those who oppose Yahweh. With the victory over the north, Yahweh's Spirit now rests. Israel's freedom from war and adversity is often described as rest (Deut 12:10; 25:19; Josh 1:15; 23:1; 2 Sam 7:1; 7:11; 1 Kgs 5:4; 1 Chr 23:25; 2 Chr 20:30). On occasion, *rûaḥ* may denote one's anger, wrath, resentment, or rage (Judg 8:3; 2 Chr 21:16; Job 15:13; Prov 16:32; 29:11; Eccl 10:4), so the resting of Yahweh's Spirit (*rûaḥ*) may be understood as an appeasement or the relenting of Yahweh's wrath (see NASB; cf. Ezek 5:13; 16:42; 24:13).[126] Yahweh has used the four winds (*rûaḥ*) to enact judgment (Jer 49:36-37) against those who have earlier been used as instruments of punishment against the people of Judah. Now Yahweh's Spirit (*rûaḥ*) is at rest. This series of eight visions (1:7–6:8) is now concluded. The picture of Yahweh's Spirit at rest gives the people of Judah encouragement to continue their work of reconstruction without fear of outside interference.[127] The former conflicts and tragedies associated with the land of the north have been resolved. The Persian policies that have subjugated Babylon and liberated the exiles manifest the sovereignty of Yahweh.[128]

## III. REPORT OF THE SYMBOLIC CROWNING OF JOSHUA AS HIGH PRIEST (6:9-15)

**[9]The word of the LORD came to me: [10]"Take silver and gold from the exiles Heldai, Tobijah and Jedaiah, who have arrived from Babylon. Go the same day to the house of Josiah son of Zephaniah. [11]Take the silver and gold and make a crown, and set it on the head of the high priest, Joshua son of Jehozadak. [12]Tell him this is what the LORD Almighty says: 'Here is the man whose name is the Branch, and he will branch out from his place and build the temple of the LORD. [13]It is he who will build the temple of the LORD, and he will be clothed with majesty and will sit and rule on his throne. And he will be a priest on his throne. And there will be**

---

[126]Cohen, *Twelve Prophets*, p. 292.
[127]Boda, *Haggai, Zechariah*, p. 324; McComiskey, "Zechariah," p. 1110.
[128]Meyers and Meyers, *Haggai, Zechariah 1–8*, p. 331.

**harmony between the two.' ¹⁴The crown will be given to Heldai,ᵃ Tobijah, Jedaiah and Henᵇ son of Zephaniah as a memorial in the temple of the LORD. ¹⁵Those who are far away will come and help to build the temple of the LORD, and you will know that the LORD Almighty has sent me to you. This will happen if you diligently obey the LORD your God."**

ᵃ*14* Syriac; Hebrew *Helem*      ᵇ*14* Or *and the gracious one, the*

Zechariah 6:9-15 contains a report of the symbolic crowning of Joshua as high priest. A prophetic symbolic action vividly conveys an abstract message through some physical activity, whether the action is implied or performed (e.g., Isa 20:1-6; Jer 13:1-11; 19:1-13; 27:1–28:17; 32:6-15; Ezek 4:1-17; 5:1-12; 12:1-25; 24:15-27; Hos 1–3; Hag 2:11-19; Zech 11:4-17). In essence, it provides a visible word in parallel to the spoken word and sets in motion the promises or events portrayed.¹²⁹ This symbolic dramatization typically consists of a commission to act, a report of compliance and an interpretation of the action's significance. Here only the first (vv. 9-13) and third (vv. 14-15) elements appear to be evidenced. Yahweh instructs the prophet to enact a dramatic symbol, the crowning of Joshua the priest. Joshua is the object of a coronation-like ceremony that antici-pates the coming of the messianic Branch who acts as priest and king and builds Yahweh's palace-temple. This act connects closely with the content of the preceding night visions (1:7–6:8) that set forth the ulti-mate demise of Zion's enemies and the glorious future of the people of Yahweh. Therefore, Zechariah 6:9-15 portrays the significance of the completed temple for Judah and its leadership.

**6:9-11** A prophetic word formula (**The word of the LORD came to me**) begins verse 9 and introduces the prophet's report that fol-lows. It focuses on the prophet's reception of this divine message, rather than communication of revelation to recipients per se. In Exodus 25:2-3, the verb **take** (לְקַח, *lākaḥ*) refers to an offering of gold, silver, other precious metals, and fabrics received for the con-struction of the tabernacle; in 2 Kings 25:15 it refers to the seizure of the gold and silver censers and sprinkling bowls from the temple by the Babylonian imperial guard. The object of the verb "take" is

---

¹²⁹J.A. Thompson, *Jeremiah*, NICOT (Grand Rapids: Eerdmans, 1980), pp. 71, 76.

unexpressed in the Hebrew text. The NIV and NRSV supply as the verb's object **silver and gold** from verse 11, while the NASB conveys a similar idea with "offering." Other versions (e.g., ESV, KJV, and NET), however, regard as the verb's object the trio **Heldai, Tobijah, and Jedaiah**; Zechariah should take them **from** among **the exiles . . . who have arrived from Babylon . . . to the house of Josiah son of Zephaniah**. Once there, the prophet is to construct **a crown** (ESV, NASB, NET, NIV, and NRSV) or crowns (KJV) from gold and silver. Since no other explanation for the source of **the silver and gold** exists in the context, the NIV and NRSV are probably correct in understanding that the prophet should take (NIV) or collect (NRSV) silver and gold from the trio of exiles. The noun "exiles" (גּוֹלָה, *gôlāh*) refers elsewhere as a collective for all the exiles (Jer 28:6; 29:4,20,31; Ezek 1:1; 3:11,15; 11:24; Nahum 3:10). In Zechariah it appears here and in 14:2 as the only explicit distinction Zechariah makes among groups in the population of the postexilic community. Apparently the trio has recently returned to Palestine since the mention of their arrival from Babylon would be otherwise unnecessary.[130] They also may have prospered in Babylon and are thus able to supply silver and gold to the prophet. Although the names Tobijah and Jedaiah appear elsewhere in the postexilic period (Ezra 2:36,60; Neh 2:10, 19; 7:39,62; 11:10; 12:6-7,19,21), none of those occurrences involve the same men mentioned here. Only Joshua is explicitly mentioned elsewhere in the biblical text (see on 3:1 above). Possibly Josiah is a descendant of Zephaniah who serves as the priest next in rank to Seraiah, the grandfather of Joshua (2 Kgs 25:18; 1 Chr 6:14-15), at the time of the fall of Jerusalem (586 B.C.). Both Zephaniah and Seraiah are executed by Nebuchadnezzar (2 Kgs 25:18-21).

The act of crowning **Joshua** thus signals an undoing of the shame of that event and the initiation of Yahweh's glorious future plans for the priesthood. This coronation of Joshua leads the reader to recall the investiture of Joshua in 3:4-5 where he receives a clean turban. The Hebrew noun translated "crown" (עֲטָרוֹת, *ʿăṭārôth*) here and in verse 14 is actually a plural form (see the KJV and NJPS). Since it appears with a singular verb in verse 14, it may refer to a composite crown probably fashioned from a band of gold interwov-

---

[130]McComiskey, "Zechariah," p. 1112.

en with a band of silver.[131] Also possible is that two crowns are to be constructed. One is to be placed on Joshua's head (v. 11) and another to be placed in the temple (v. 14).[132] If so, the construction of two separate crowns reminds the community of Yahweh's promise to Jeremiah to continue the royal line of David and the priestly line of Levi (Jer 33:17-18). Even though the term for crown here usually appears in the Old Testament for the crown of a monarch (2 Sam 12:30; 1 Chr 20:2; S of S 3:11; Ps 21:1-3; Ezek 21:26) and not the priestly crown, it does appear in contexts other than those referring to the crown of a monarch (Esth 8:15; Prov 4:9; 12:4; 14:24; Isa 28:5; Ezek 16:12). These nonmonarchical contexts speak of heightened glory and reputation for the wearer; therefore, the image here no doubt anticipates a day of increased priestly prestige as the community's divinely appointed leaders.

**6:12-13** Last in the series of instructions given to Zechariah (take, go, take, make, and set) is the instruction to tell Joshua the message given him by Yahweh (**this is what the LORD Almighty says**). The statement itself introduces one called **the Branch** (**Here is the man**) and emphasizes the Branch's role, particularly in regard to building the temple (**he will branch out from this place and build the temple of the LORD**). The phrase translated, "Here is the man," in the NIV (אִישׁ־הִנֵּה, *hinnēh-'îš*) means rather "Behold a man" as in the NASB (cf. NJPS). This construction elsewhere introduces the appearance of one new to a scene being narrated (Josh 5:13; Judg 7:13; 19:16; 1 Sam 9:6,17; 2 Sam 1:1; 1 Kgs 13:1; 20:39; Ezek 40:3; Dan 10:5; Zech 1:8). Since the presence of Joshua is already noted (Zech 6:11), the prophet probably does not intend the reader to attach the title Branch to Joshua; moreover, the Davidic connections of the title elsewhere (Isa 11:1; Jer 23:5; 33:15) also argue against identifying Joshua, a levitical priest, with the Branch.[133] The statement calls to mind content of Zechariah 3. Whereas 3:8 promises the coming of the Branch, 6:12 implies his presence. Verses 13 and 14 indicate that the Branch **will build the temple**, a task connected with Zerubbabel in 4:6-10.

---

[131]Ibid., pp. 1112-1113.

[132]Boda, *Haggai, Zechariah*, pp. 338, 342; Meyers and Meyers, *Haggai, Zechariah 1–8*, p. 350; Ollenburger, "Zechariah," p. 787.

[133]Boda, *Haggai, Zechariah*, p. 339; McComiskey, "Zechariah," p. 1113; Sweeney, *The Twelve Prophets*, p. 631.

Nonetheless, the Branch in 3:8 and 6:12 is not identified directly as Zerubbabel, and his name may be omitted here in order to emphasize the importance of the priestly line as an assurance (or, in the wording of v. 15, a reminder) of the coming messianic ruler.[134] The Branch will build the temple (הֵיכָל, *hêkāl*) of Yahweh. This is the first use of *hêkāl* in the book; previous references to the temple have used "house" (בַּיִת, *bayith*) (1:16; 3:7; 4:9). Two other phrases describe this royal figure: **clothed with majesty** (cf. 1 Chr 29:25; Ps 21:5; 45:4; Jer 22:18; Dan 11:21) and **sit and rule on his throne** (cf. Deut 17:18; 2 Sam 3:10; 7:16; 1 Kgs 2:45; 8:20; Isa 9:7).

The NIV and NASB imply that the Branch is also **a priest on his throne**. However, other versions (e.g., ESV, NET, NRSV, NJB, and NJPS) distinguish the Branch from the one sitting on the throne as priest. The latter understanding is more likely, since the closing line of verse 13, **there will be harmony between the two**, implies the existence of an individual other than the Branch. Also, the word used here for the throne (כִּסֵּא, *kissē'*) of the Branch and of the priest most often, but not exclusively, denotes the throne of a king. Especially significant for the present context is the use of *kissē'* to designate the seat of the priest Eli near Yahweh's *ḥêkāl* (1 Sam 1:9) and the seat of one providing counsel to the king (1 Kgs 2:19). The word "harmony" renders a Hebrew phrase "counsel of peace" (see the ESV's rendering "the counsel of peace shall be between them both"); therefore, the text appears to envision a high priest who advises the king or to assume (or anticipate) the existence of two authority figures, the Davidic king and the high priest (cf. 1 Chr 29:22).[135]

**6:14** In the end the crown does not rest on Joshua's head.[136] Instead, it is placed **in the temple**, where it serves **as a memorial** (KJV, NET, NIV, NRSV) or reminder (ESV, NASB). The word "memorial"

---

[134]Mason, *Haggai, Zechariah, and Malachi,* p. 63.

[135]Sweeney, *The Twelve Prophets,* p. 632. Although the original readers would naturally associate the words of this oracle with Zerubbabel and Joshua, the royal and priestly ideals represented by those two figures are ultimately expressed by Jesus Christ who indeed conjoins the office of king (Matt 27:11; Mark 15:2; Luke 23:3; John 1:49; 12:13,15; 18:37; Rev 17:14; 19:16) with that of priest (Heb 2:17; 3:1; 4:14-15; 5:1-6; 6:20; 7:26; 8:1-4; 9:11, 25; 10:21). Jesus Christ, the eschatological Branch, builds the ultimate temple of Yahweh, the church (1 Cor 3:17; 6:19; 2 Cor 6:16; Eph 2:21).

[136]Ollenburger, "Zechariah," p. 787; Meyers and Meyers, *Haggai, Zechariah 1–8,* pp. 362-363.

(זִכָּרוֹן, *zikkārôn*) typically refers to a remembrance of some great event, such as Passover (Exod 12:14) or the crossing of the Jordan River (Josh 4:7); it may be that the crowns are equated to the stones of remembrance for the sons of Israel in the high priest's ephod (Exod 28:12,29; 39:7).[137] In the temple, this memorial is visible only to priests. It certainly reassures the priests of Yahweh's gracious intent for them. It may also serve as a warning to any in the priesthood who might seek to wrest high priestly authority from Joshua or secular leadership from Zerubbabel.[138] A similar memorial appears in Numbers 17 where the staff of Aaron that budded is deposited before Yahweh in the tabernacle as a sign to those who rebel against the priests whom Yahweh has appointed (Num 17:10). In the MT, the listing of those to whom the crown is given begins with "Helem." The NIV, however, renders the first name **Heldai**, which appears earlier in verse 10, and Helem may very well be a variant name for that individual.[139] Since the **son of Zephaniah** in verse 10 is Josiah, **Hen** (חֵן, *ḥēn*), meaning "grace," may be an honorific title or nickname for Josiah who is considered to be gracious.

**6:15** The passage concludes with a promise that **those who are far away will come and help to build the temple**. No further description of this group is given. It may refer to later groups of exiles returning with Ezra and Nehemiah (the Hebrew word is used to designate exiled Hebrews in Dan 9:7).[140] It may also be that the promise recalls the oracle of 2:11, in which many nations are joined to Yahweh, and anticipates the one of 8:20-23, in which many peoples and powerful nations come to Jerusalem to seek Yahweh.[141] The vindication formula **you will know that the LORD Almighty has sent me to you** also connects verse 15 to these similar promises, since the same formula appears in 2:11 and the name Yahweh Seba'oth ("the LORD Almighty") appears four times in 8:20-23. The section closes with the conditional statement, **if you diligently obey the LORD your**

[137]Sweeney, *The Twelve Prophets*, pp. 633-634.
[138]Ollenburger, "Zechariah," p. 788.
[139]Another man named Heldai during the days of David (1 Chr 27:15) is known by the variant names "Heled" (1 Chr 11:30) and "Heleb" (2 Sam 23:29).
[140]Boda, *Haggai, Zechariah*, pp. 337, 342; Meyers and Meyers, *Haggai, Zechariah 1–8*, pp. 364-365.
[141]Ollenburger, "Zechariah," p. 788.

**God**. The NIV "diligently obey" translates a phrase combining an infinitive form of the verb "hear" (שָׁמֹעַ, *šāmaʿ*) with an imperfect form of the same verb, a construction that intensifies the action of the verb[142] and here connotes conviction in obedience. The magnificent promises in the preceding verses are contingent on Israel's diligent obedience to Yahweh, an obedience enjoined upon Israel's ancestors with the same or nearly identical verbal and syntactical construction (Exod 15:26; 19:5; 23:22; Deut 15:5; 28:1-2) but an obedience which they have failed to render (Josh 5:6; Judg 2:2; 2 Kgs 18:12).

## IV. REPORT OF A QUESTION REGARDING FASTING AND THE REPLY OF YAHWEH (7:1–8:23)

Zechariah 7:1–8:23 contains the report of a question regarding fasting and the reply of Yahweh. The section begins with a report of an oracular inquiry; this form describes an attempt to seek an answer from Yahweh and the divine revelation received in response to the inquiry.[143] Here the inquiry appears in 7:2-3, and the reply, in 7:4-7. Nonetheless, the oracular inquiry (7:2-7) gives way to other kinds of material, more correctly characterized as a report of a prophetic revelation (7:8–8:23).[144] This particular prophetic genre (see on Zech 1:1-6 above) describes a prophet's private reception of the "word of the LORD" and generally contains two parts: a prophetic word formula and a quotation of the message received. Indeed, from 7:8 through 8:23 a prophetic word formula ("the word of the LORD came to Zechariah" or "this is what the LORD Almighty says") introduces eleven relatively self-contained units (7:8-14; 8:1-2,3,4-5,6,7-8,9-13,14-17,18-19,20-22,23). Most often, these units also consist of prophetic exhortation (7:9-10) and less often include a prophetic historical exemplum (7:11-14).[145] Therefore, Zechariah 7:1–8:23 shows how Zechariah answers a question regarding fasting, a response that also elicits ongoing support for the temple's reconstruction, and renewed commitment to the religious and ethical demands of Yahweh.

---

[142]*IBHS*, pp. 585-587; GKC, p. 342.

[143]For other examples of the form, see 1 Sam 14:36-42; 23:6-14; 1 Kgs 22:1-23; 2 Kgs 8:7-15; Jer 21:1-14; Hab 2:1-5.

[144]Floyd, *Minor Prophets*, p. 416.

[145]Ibid., p. 426.

¹In the fourth year of King Darius, the word of the LORD came to Zechariah on the fourth day of the ninth month, the month of Kislev. ²The people of Bethel had sent Sharezer and Regem-Melech, together with their men, to entreat the LORD ³by asking the priests of the house of the LORD Almighty and the prophets, "Should I mourn and fast in the fifth month, as I have done for so many years?"

⁴Then the word of the LORD Almighty came to me: ⁵"Ask all the people of the land and the priests, 'When you fasted and mourned in the fifth and seventh months for the past seventy years, was it really for me that you fasted? ⁶And when you were eating and drinking, were you not just feasting for yourselves? ⁷Are these not the words the LORD proclaimed through the earlier prophets when Jerusalem and its surrounding towns were at rest and prosperous, and the Negev and the western foothills were settled?'"

⁸And the word of the LORD came again to Zechariah: ⁹"This is what the LORD Almighty says: 'Administer true justice; show mercy and compassion to one another. ¹⁰Do not oppress the widow or the fatherless, the alien or the poor. In your hearts do not think evil of each other.'

¹¹"But they refused to pay attention; stubbornly they turned their backs and stopped up their ears. ¹²They made their hearts as hard as flint and would not listen to the law or to the words that the LORD Almighty had sent by his Spirit through the earlier prophets. So the LORD Almighty was very angry.

¹³"When I called, they did not listen; so when they called, I would not listen,' says the LORD Almighty. ¹⁴"I scattered them with a whirlwind among all the nations, where they were strangers. The land was left so desolate behind them that no one could come or go. This is how they made the pleasant land desolate.'"

**7:1 In the fourth year of King Darius** (518 B.C.), **the word of the LORD** comes **to Zechariah**. More precisely, Zechariah receives this prophetic revelation from Yahweh **on the fourth day of the ninth month, the month of Kislev** or December 7, 518 B.C. Thus, the prophetic word (likely Zechariah 7–8) comes to Zechariah nearly two years after the final prophetic messages delivered by Haggai (2:10-23) and some twenty-two months after the initial visions given to him (1:7–6:8).[146]

---

[146]Although Kislev, the ninth month, also appears in Neh 1:1, perhaps the

**7:2** A delegation from **Bethel** arrives asking the priests and prophets a question about the propriety of maintaining the observance of various fasts. The response to their inquiry constitutes chapters 7 and 8, even if the specific topic of fasting is addressed only in 7:4-7 and 8:18-19. That such a delegation travels to Jerusalem with their particular inquiry may reflect conditions in the empire at the time. While Darius solidifies his control over the empire, he chooses to work through the existing institutions within the satrapies and provinces of the empire. He promotes existing legitimate authorities and local law codes that do not conflict with the empire's objectives.[147] Not surprisingly, questions about proper religious observance are thus addressed to recognized authorities in Jerusalem.

The Hebrew in verse 2 does not allow for certain identification of the party sending the delegation.[148] Although most English translations understand Bethel, a town twelve miles north of Jerusalem, to have sent a group of messengers headed by **Sharezer and Regem-Melech** (e.g., ESV, NASB, NET, NIV, NRSV, and NJB), the name Bethel may be read as part of the name of the one who sent the delegation (Bethel-Sharezer) led by Regem-melech (e.g., the NJPS which reads, "when Bethel-sharezer and Regem-melech and his men sent to entreat the favor of the LORD"). Another possibility regards Sharezer, Regem-Melech, and **their men**, not as those sent but rather as those sending the messengers (i.e., Bethel, that is Sharezer, Regem-melech, and their men, sent to entreat the LORD). The sign of the direct object that usually appears before the object of the verb "sent" (שָׁלַח, šālaḥ) does not appear before Sharezer and Regem-melech; its absence may support this third option.[149]

**7:3** This group of messengers from Bethel is sent to Zechariah to inquire whether the exilic practice of observing the anniversary of

---

most significant reference to the ninth month for this context, according to Meyers and Meyers, *Haggai, Zechariah 1–8*, p. 381, is the memory of a fast in the fourth year of Jehoiakim king of Judah (605 B.C.) in the wake of Nebuchadnezzar's conquest of Ashkelon and march toward Egypt (Jer 36:9). At this time, Jeremiah writes the words of Yahweh's judgment upon Judah on a scroll that his scribe Baruch reads in the temple grounds.

[147]Meyers and Meyers, *Haggai, Zechariah 1–8*, p. 380.

[148]On the difficulties concerning the reading of proper names in verse 2, see Meyers and Meyers, *Haggai, Zechariah 1–8*, pp. 382-384, and Sweeney, *The Twelve Prophets*, pp. 637-638.

[149]McComiskey, "Zechariah," p. 1124.

the temple's destruction should continue in the light of the nearly completed temple reconstruction. The prophets of the preexilic era often found it necessary to stand against a corrupt priesthood (Isa 24:2; Jer 1:18; 20:1; Ezek 22:26; Zeph 3:4), but the **priests . . . and prophets** are here seen acting together to consider the question from Bethel. The prophetic figures Jeremiah and Ezekiel are themselves priests or have priestly connections, and the postexilic prophets Haggai, Zechariah, and Malachi each address priestly and temple concerns.[150] Although translated **fast** by the NIV in verse 3, the verb נָזַר (nāzar) appears only four other times in the OT (Lev 15:31; 22:2; Ezek 14:7; Hos 9:10). In each case, the idea is the consecration of self rather than the abstaining from food. Only in verse 5 does it become clear that fasting (צוֹם, ṣûm) is intended here. The fast **in the fifth month** may have been an annual observance marking the destruction of Solomon's temple on August 14, 586 B.C., nearly seventy years earlier (cf. 2 Kgs 25:8-9). The approaching completion of the temple elicits their question about the propriety of further observance of the fast. That the delegation describes their period of performance as **for so many years** may reflect a notion of weariness. The prophet seizes upon this attitude in the response which follows.[151]

This group sent from Bethel to entreat Yahweh anticipates the many peoples and powerful nations who come to Jerusalem to entreat Yahweh at the close of the section (8:22). Thus, chapter 7 opens with the record of a group of Jews coming to entreat Yahweh, and chapter 8 closes with a group of foreigners coming to Jerusalem to entreat Yahweh. Bethel has long been a center for worship rival to Jerusalem. Under Jeroboam I, it was an early center of aberrant worship in the northern kingdom (1 Kgs 13:25-33). After the Assyrians conquered the northern kingdom (722/21 B.C.), they sent to Bethel a priest who had been exiled from Samaria. This priest instructed those from various nations whom the Assyrians had displaced there how to worship Yahweh. This, nevertheless, perpetuated the syncretism that already had been present (2 Kgs 17:24-33). The destruction of the high place at Bethel in 622 B.C. by Josiah

---

[150]Meyers and Meyers, *Haggai, Zechariah 1–8*, pp. 383, 385.
[151]McComiskey, "Zechariah," p. 1125.

(2 Kgs 23:15-20) leads to the present acknowledgment by Bethel of the priesthood and the Jerusalem temple.[152]

**7:4-7** The prophet counters these messengers with two oracles which each feature a messenger formula bearing the name **the LORD Almighty** (Yahweh Seba'oth) (vv. 4-7,8-14).[153] Neither oracle, however, is a direct answer to the question. The first oracle asks its own set of questions that examine the legitimacy of the "fasting" that has occurred during the exile. The second reviews the sins of former generations who have not heeded prophetic calls to justice and compassion.[154]

Through a series of three rhetorical questions, Yahweh denounces the ineffectual fasts of the people. These rhetorical questions do not answer the delegation's question about fasting per se, but they do anticipate the following prophetic oracles (7:8–8:23) that call the people to proper moral and social action in view of the rebuilding of the temple. The first question asks whether the people have actually fasted and mourned on Yahweh's behalf during the last seventy years when the temple lay in ruins. This question names two specific fasts. The fast **in the fifth** month (mentioned in the delega-

---

[152]Meyers and Meyers, *Haggai, Zechariah 1–8*, p. 398.

[153]The first of four instances of the messenger formula "the word of the LORD Almighty came to me" in chapters 7 and 8 appears in verse 4. These messenger formulas (7:4,8; 8:1,18) divide the two chapters into four parts, but they do more than merely establish boundaries between one oracle and another. Actually, Zechariah 7 and 8 contain the greatest concentration of the name "the LORD Almighty" (Yahweh Seba'oth) and of messenger formulas in Zechariah (7:1,4,8,9,13; 8:1,2,3,4,6[2×],7,9,11,14[2×],18,19,20,23). The significance of this concentration may be more than numeric. Meredith G. Kline, "The Structure of the Book of Zechariah," *JETS* 34 (1991): 179-180, has identified chapters 7 and 8 as the introduction to the second half of the book that itself follows the primary hinge of the book in 6:9-15. A concentration of the divine name "the LORD Almighty" (Yahweh Seba'oth), especially in the context of these messenger formulas, at a pivotal point in the book would point to the name's significant role. The messenger formulas persistently remind the reader of Yahweh's presence and power. In a postexilic political situation, says Pieter A. Verhoef, *The Books of Haggai and Malachi*, NICOT (Grand Rapids: Eerdmans, 1987), pp. 52-53, the word of the emperor of Persia dictates the law for the Jewish community, but the Jews answer to a higher law from a higher potentate, a ruler to whom even the Persians must answer, the LORD Almighty.

[154]Mark J. Boda, "From Fasts to Feasts: The Literary Function of Zechariah 7–8," *CBQ* 65 (2003): 394-395.

tion's original question in 7:3) commemorates the destruction of the first temple and other important buildings in Jerusalem (2 Kgs 25:8-10). The fast in the **seventh month** commemorates the assassination of Gedaliah (582/581 B.C.), the governor left in Judah by appointment of Nebuchadnezzar (2 Kgs 25:25; Jer 40:13-14; 41:1). The time period of **seventy years** (see 1:12 above) is a round number, since strictly speaking a full seventy years have not passed since the fall of Jerusalem until 516 B.C. Zechariah receives this prophetic revelation from Yahweh on December 7, 518 B.C. (7:1). The second question asks whether the people have merely eaten for themselves. Implied here is the notion that, if **eating and drinking** have no impact on Yahweh, then neither does fasting alone.[155] The community has fasted for themselves just as they have feasted to themselves. Thus, in their fasting they have lamented their own personal loss and political humiliation rather than grieving over their own sin and abuse of the covenant relationship with Yahweh. The third question asks the people to recall the words of Yahweh communicated through earlier prophets during a time when Jerusalem and the surrounding regions of Judah are settled. The question may point to the preexilic prophets who questioned the practice of sacrifice devoid of moral and social righteousness (e.g., Isa 1:10-17; Jer 7:21-29; Amos 5:1-27; Micah 6:6-8). The prophet thus recalls a period during the time of the earlier prophets when **Jerusalem and its surrounding towns were at rest**. Earlier times of deceptive peace in Israel's history (Jer 6:14; 8:11; Ezek 13:10,16) have, in reality, been times calling for repentance. Present in this memory may be a warning against complacency for Zechariah's audience which also lives in relative peace (1:11). The term **Negev** is a transliteration of the Hebrew word for "south," referring to the southern region of Judah, from Gaza past Beersheba toward the Dead Sea. The **western foothills** refers to the Shephelah, a range of hills in western Judah between the coastal plain of Palestine and the central mountains in Judah.

**7:8-10** Verse 8 contains a prophetic word formula (**And the word of the LORD came again to Zechariah**), and verse 9 begins with a messenger formula (**This is what the Lord Almighty says**). Both formulas indicate that the material following comes from Yahweh.

---

[155]Sweeney, *The Twelve Prophets*, p. 641.

What Zechariah says here, however, replicates the messages of earlier prophets, perhaps those mentioned previously in verse 7. Verses
9 and 10 consist of two commands and two prohibitions, each of
which stresses a primary concern for the socially marginalized.[156]
The first command (**administer true justice**) calls for proper justice
in the law court (cf. Jer 5:28; 21:12; 22:3,15; and 42:5) and is repeated later in Zechariah 8:16.[157] The second command (**show mercy
and compassion to one another**) combines the two words "mercy"
(חֶסֶד, ḥesed) and "compassion" (רַחֲמִים, raḥămîm). Together they
form a hendiadys (i.e., one concept communicated through two
words), "compassionate love" that complements and tempers the
prior call for true justice.[158] The negative injunctions in verse 10 represent demonstrations of compassionate love, which replicates the
compassion that accompanies Yahweh's return to Jerusalem in 1:16.

The first prohibition (**do not oppress the widow or the fatherless, the alien or the poor**) forbids the exploitation of those who
cannot defend their own rights. This verb "oppress" (עָשַׁק, ʿāšaq) can
have the notion of depriving or wronging. It describes failing to pay
wages to a hired worker (Lev 19:13; Deut 24:14), cheating someone
(Lev 6:2; 1 Sam 12:3-4), or depriving the disadvantaged of security
or the resources they once possessed (Lev 6:4; Ps 119:122; Ezek
22:29; Hos 12:7). The obligation not to oppress the widow or fatherless appears repeatedly in the Law and Prophets (Exod 22:22; Deut
10:18; 24:6,10,12,17; Isa 1:17; Jer 21:12; 22:3; 49:11; Ezek 18:5-
9,12).[159] Significant for this context, however, is Jeremiah 7:5-6.
There, Jeremiah accuses Judah of using the temple as an amulet of
sorts to ward away enemies when, in reality, the people of Judah are
guilty of oppressing the widow, orphan, and alien, an oppression
that desecrates the temple and renders trust in it deceptive. Because

---

[156]Ollenburger, "Zechariah," p. 793.

[157]For comments on the word "administer" (שָׁפַט, šāphaṭ), see on Zeph 3:3
above; for "justice" (מִשְׁפָּט, mišpāṭ), see Mal 4:4 below.

[158]Meyers and Meyers, *Haggai, Zechariah 1–8*, p. 399. The two words (ḥesed
and raḥămîm) appear together also in Ps 77:8-9; 103:4; Jer 16:5; and Hos
2:19.

[159]Although the ordering of widow and fatherless occurs only here and in
Exod 22:21, the pair is found frequently in reverse order (Deut 10:18; 14:29;
16:11,14; 24:17,19,20,21; 26:12-13; Isa 1:17,23; 9:17; 10:2; Jer 49:11; Ezek
22:7).

the Israelites and their ancestors have once been aliens in a land not their own, they are to show kindness to aliens ("foreigners" in the TNIV) among them (Exod 23:9; Lev 19:33; 24:22; Deut 1:16; 24:17; Ezek 22:29). The pair "alien" (גֵּר, *gēr*) and "poor" (עָנִי, *'ānî*) is found in Leviticus 19:10 and 23:22 (for comments on *'ānî*, see on Zeph 3:12 above). Normally, *'ānî* is paired with a synonym such as "afflicted" (אֶבְיוֹן, *'ebyôn*; e.g., Deut 15:11; 24:14; Job 24:14; Ps 9:18; 12:5; 35:10; 37:14; Prov 31:9; 31:20; Isa 32:7; Jer 22:16; Ezek 16:49; 18:12; 22:29; Amos 8:4). "Alien" (*gēr*), however, appears seventeen other times in the OT with "widow and fatherless" (Deut 10:18; 14:29; 16:11,14; 24:17,19,20,21; 26:12,13; 27:19; Ps 94:6; 146:9; Jer 7:6; 22:3; Ezek 22:7; Mal 3:5). Nevertheless, *gēr* and *'ānî* appear together only here and in Leviticus 19:10 and 23:22. This rare combination may reflect a concern for those who lack property and who work as day laborers within the community. Whereas "alien" (*gēr*) refers to an ethnic "outsider," "poor" (*'ānî*) designates an ethnic "insider"; both groups struggle to provide for self and family. Deuteronomy 24:14 forbids the oppression of a hired laborer whether the worker be a fellow Israelite or a non-Hebrew living within Israelite territory. The second prohibition (**in your hearts do not think evil of each other**) forbids even the thought of harming another person; the same phrase appears in 8:16 (translated as "devise evil") and is connected with the prohibition against false accusations.[160] The recollection of these words of the earlier prophets (Zech 7:7-10), taken together with the exhortations in 8:16-17, reminds the postexilic community of the true purpose of fasting: it should signify the repentance of the community desiring a future life of faithfulness to the covenant with Yahweh.[161]

**7:11-14** Verses 11-14 describe the results of the ancestors' failure to respond to Yahweh's message spoken through the earlier prophets. This description reflects elements present in Jeremiah's temple sermon in which the prophet recalls the work of earlier prophets (Jer 7:25) through which Yahweh called to his people (Jer 7:13) and to which the ancestors would not listen (Jer 7:13, 26-28). Judah stubbornly refused to repent, so Yahweh refused to help Judah, and the land became desolate (Jer 7:16, 20, 33). The divine

---

[160]Baldwin, *Haggai, Zechariah, Malachi*, p. 146.
[161]Boda, "From Fasts to Feasts," p. 399.

name **the LORD Almighty** (Yahweh Seba'oth) appears three times in
the verses 11-13, a threefold use reminiscent of Zechariah 1:3. In the
earlier text, Yahweh Seba'oth calls the community to return to
Yahweh; here, the text highlights the consequences of failure to
heed the prophetic word. After a summary statement (**they refused
to pay attention**), verses 11 and 12 portray the disobedience of the
ancestors with a series of figures of speech using body parts. They
do not give their shoulder (כָּתֵף, *kāthēph*) (which the NIV renders
**turned their backs**), their ears (אֹזֶן, *'ōzen*) are dulled from hearing
(NIV **stopped up their ears**), and they set **their hearts** (לֵב, *lēb*) **as
hard as flint** (cf. "adamant" in the KJV, NRSV, NJB, and NJPS). The
ancestors' refusal to listen is highlighted by a repetition of the verb
"hear" (שָׁמַע, *šāma'*) in verses 11-13, translated in the NIV: "stopped
up their ears," **so they could not hear, they . . . would not listen**,
and **I would not listen**. The ancestors have not listened to the law or
to the words of the LORD Almighty **sent by** Yahweh's **Spirit through
the earlier prophets**. The pairing of **law** (תּוֹרָה, *tôrāh*) and **words**
(דְּבָרִים, *dᵊbārîm*) here may represent two categories of authoritative
revelation, the text of the Pentateuch and the nearly complete collection of prophetic writings or *Nevi'im*.[162]

This failure to listen to the prophetic word results in great wrath
from Yahweh. As with other words referring to Yahweh's anger or
wrath, *qeseph* must not be understood as a despotic rage. It rather
refers to Yahweh's actions to restrain evil, to correct a sinner, or to
punish a recalcitrant evildoer, thus protecting the holiness of
Yahweh and the objects of divine love.[163] The phrase "great wrath"
(קֶצֶף גָּדוֹל, *qeseph gādôl*), translated **very angry** in the NIV, appears
four other times to describe the actions of Yahweh (Deut 29:28; Jer
21:5; 32:37; Zech 1:15). In Deuteronomy 29:28, Moses warns Israel
about the calamity directed at those who break covenant with
Yahweh. In Jeremiah 21:5, Yahweh vows to fight against Judah and
her king Zedekiah with great wrath in order to bring about the
Babylonian conquest of Judah. In Jeremiah 32:37, Yahweh promises
the restoration of the people after banishing them among the
nations in great wrath. In Zechariah 1:15, Yahweh expresses great

[162]Meyers and Meyers, *Haggai, Zechariah 1–8*, p. 402.
[163]Gerard Van Gronigen, "קֶצֶף," *TWOT*, 2:808.

wrath toward those nations who have added to Israel's calamity when acting as agents of Yahweh's punishment.

Because the ancestors have refused to hear Yahweh's call, Yahweh refuses to hear the ancestors' calls of distress (cf. Isa 66:4; Jer 7:13; Ezek 8:18). Both the verbs "call" and "listen" in the first line of verse 13 are perfect tense, denoting completed action, but the two verbs in the second line of verse 13 are imperfect tense, denoting an action viewed as incomplete (or even yet future). Most English translations translate all these forms as past tense, but the NET retains the distinction ("just as I cried out, but they would not obey, so they will cry out, but I will not listen"). This distinction brings forward the judgment upon the ancestors as a warning for Zechariah's audience.[164]

Yahweh has **scattered** as a whirlwind the former generations **among all the nations**. The image of a whirlwind depicts the divine punishment of people (e.g., Isa 54:11; Hos 13:3); later in Zechariah a similar image portrays the divine protection of Ephraim and Jerusalem (9:14).[165] The imperfect tense continues into verse 14, perhaps emphasizing the ongoing experience of exile experienced by the majority of Jews at the time. The phrase **where they were strangers** translates the wording in the MT that is more exactly, "whom they had not known" (cf. Jer 9:16; 14:18; 16:13; 22:28). As a result of the repercussions of the Babylonian conquest, the land of Judah has been **left desolate** (שָׁמֵם, šāmēm) and thus lacks security (**no one could come or go**). The ancestors are faulted for their role in making desolate (cf. 2 Chr 36:21) "the land of desire" (אֶרֶץ חֶמְדָּה, 'ereṣ ḥemdāh), a phrase appearing also in Psalm 106:24 and Jeremiah 3:19. The word ḥemdāh generally refers to inanimate items of particular value, for example, land (Ps 106:24; Jer 3:19) or treasures (2 Chr 32:27; Nahum 2:9; Hag 2:7). Jeremiah 12:10, as here, speaks of the transformation of a **pleasant land** into a desolation.[166]

**¹Again the word of the LORD Almighty came to me. ²This is what the LORD Almighty says: "I am very jealous for Zion; I am burning with jealousy for her."**

---

[164]Meyers and Meyers, *Haggai, Zechariah 1–8*, p. 404.

[165]Sweeney, *The Twelve Prophets*, p. 645.

[166]J. Barton Payne, "חָמַד," *TWOT*, 1:295; David Tulley, "חָמַד," *NIDOTTE*, 2:167-169.

[3]This is what the LORD says: "I will return to Zion and dwell in Jerusalem. Then Jerusalem will be called the City of Truth, and the mountain of the LORD Almighty will be called the Holy Mountain."

[4]This is what the LORD Almighty says: "Once again men and women of ripe old age will sit in the streets of Jerusalem, each with cane in hand because of his age. [5]The city streets will be filled with boys and girls playing there."

[6]This is what the LORD Almighty says: "It may seem marvelous to the remnant of this people at that time, but will it seem marvelous to me?" declares the LORD Almighty.

[7]This is what the LORD Almighty says: "I will save my people from the countries of the east and the west. [8]I will bring them back to live in Jerusalem; they will be my people, and I will be faithful and righteous to them as their God."

[9]This is what the LORD Almighty says: "You who now hear these words spoken by the prophets who were there when the foundation was laid for the house of the LORD Almighty, let your hands be strong so that the temple may be built. [10]Before that time there were no wages for man or beast. No one could go about his business safely because of his enemy, for I had turned every man against his neighbor. [11]But now I will not deal with the remnant of this people as I did in the past," declares the LORD Almighty.

[12]"The seed will grow well, the vine will yield its fruit, the ground will produce its crops, and the heavens will drop their dew. I will give all these things as an inheritance to the remnant of this people. [13]As you have been an object of cursing among the nations, O Judah and Israel, so will I save you, and you will be a blessing. Do not be afraid, but let your hands be strong."

[14]This is what the LORD Almighty says: "Just as I had determined to bring disaster upon you and showed no pity when your fathers angered me," says the LORD Almighty, [15]"so now I have determined to do good again to Jerusalem and Judah. Do not be afraid. [16]These are the things you are to do: Speak the truth to each other, and render true and sound judgment in your courts; [17]do not plot evil against your neighbor, and do not love to swear falsely. I hate all this," declares the LORD.

[18]Again the word of the LORD Almighty came to me. [19]This is what the LORD Almighty says: "The fasts of the fourth, fifth, sev-

enth and tenth months will become joyful and glad occasions and happy festivals for Judah. Therefore love truth and peace."

²⁰This is what the LORD Almighty says: "Many peoples and the inhabitants of many cities will yet come, ²¹and the inhabitants of one city will go to another and say, 'Let us go at once to entreat the LORD and seek the LORD Almighty. I myself am going.' ²²And many peoples and powerful nations will come to Jerusalem to seek the LORD Almighty and to entreat him."

²³This is what the LORD Almighty says: "In those days ten men from all languages and nations will take firm hold of one Jew by the hem of his robe and say, 'Let us go with you, because we have heard that God is with you.'"

**8:1** Chapter 8 is divided into two large sections, each of which begins with the prophetic word formula **the word of the LORD Almighty came** (וַיְהִי דְּבַר יהוה צְבָאוֹת, *wayᵊhî dᵊbar YHWH ṣᵊbā'ôth*) in verses 1 and 18. The first section (vv. 2-17) consists of seven oracles (vv. 2,3,4-5,6,7-8,9-13,14-17), each beginning with the messenger formula "This is what the Lord Almighty says" (כֹּה אָמַר יהוה צְבָאוֹת, *kōh 'āmar YHWH ṣᵊbā'ôth*). Only in the second of these oracles (v. 3) does the divine name *YHWH* appear without the full name *YHWH ṣᵊbā'ôth*. The second section (vv. 18-23) contains three oracles (vv. 19,20-22,23), which also begin with the messenger formula "This is what the LORD Almighty says" (*kōh 'āmar YHWH ṣᵊbā'ôth*). Two other messenger formulas occur at the end of oracles or within them: "says the Lord Almighty" (נְאֻם יהוה צְבָאוֹת, *nᵊ'um YHWH ṣᵊbā'ôth*) (8:6,11) and "declares the Lord Almighty" (אָמַר יהוה צְבָאוֹת, *'āmar YHWH ṣᵊbā'ôth*) (8:14). The first of these two is sometimes called an oracle formula; the second, a speech report formula. Noteworthy is the density of the use of the divine name "the LORD Almighty" (*YHWH ṣᵊbā'ôth*) in the chapter. Of the thirty-six times the name appears in the book, fifteen occur in chapter 8. The frequency of the name highlights the power and sufficiency of Yahweh to accomplish in the future what otherwise is humanly impossible.

**8:2** The use of the name **Zion** in this first oracle (v. 2) and in verse 3 reflects a similar use in 1:14-17, where the language of covenant describes Yahweh's jealousy for Zion and the divine name **the LORD Almighty** (Yahweh Seba'oth) underscores Yahweh's pledge to restore the relationship with Jerusalem and Judah. By using Zion, the prophet assures the postexilic community whose existence has been tenuous.[167] **I am very jealous** translates a Hebrew structure that features a verb with a cognate noun object; the reading in the NRSV illustrates the construction: "I am jealous for Zion with great jealousy." The NIV expresses the construction by adding the word "very" to the verb, "I am very jealous." This same construction using forms of the verb "be jealous" (קָנָה, qānāh) occurs more than eighty times to denote a strong desire by the subject for some quality or possession that leads the subject to act. Divine jealousy, then, may result in Yahweh's righteous judgment against those who violate the law (Num 25:11; Deut 29:19-20; Ezek 5:13; 8:3; 16:38; 36:6; 38:9; Zeph 1:18; 3:8), but it may also affect good and salvation for those Yahweh loves (Isa 9:7; 42:13; Ezek 39:25; Joel 2:18).[168] Here it provides the basis for Yahweh's promise to restore Zion and Jerusalem in the following verses.

**8:3** The messenger formula introducing the second oracle (v. 3) omits "Almighty" (Seba'oth) from the divine name. This omission occurs elsewhere in Zechariah only in 1:16, a passage with many parallels to the present text. First, both oracles begin with the statement about the return of Yahweh to a place (Jerusalem in 1:16 and Zion in 8:3). Second, both mention Jerusalem twice. Third, each speaks of the temple, either directly ("my house" in 1:16) or metaphorically (Holy Mountain in 8:3).[169] Fourth, each uses both the divine names Yahweh Seba'oth and Yahweh once. Verse 3 reiterates the earlier assurances from Yahweh's return to Zion and dwelling in Jerusalem (cf. Lev 26:12-13). The ordering of Zion then Jerusalem in verse 3 may be intended as a reversal of the ordering in 1:14-16 (Jerusalem then Zion). Here and in 1:14-16, Yahweh makes a proclamation ("I am very jealous for Zion") and a promise (**I will return to Zion and dwell in Jerusalem**) (cf. 2:10-11). In the Old Testament, God or Yahweh is the subject of the verb "dwell" (שָׁכַן, šākan) some forty-three times with the connotation of an immanent, gracious presence (Exod 24:16; 25:8; Deut 12:11; Ps 74:2; 85:9; 135:21; Ezek 43:1-9).[170]

[167]Merrill, *Haggai, Zechariah, Malachi*, p. 220.
[168]Leonard J. Coppes, "קָנָא," *TWOT*, 2:802; H.G.L. Peels, "קָנָא," *NIDOTTE*, 3:938-939.
[169]Meyers and Meyers, *Haggai, Zechariah 1–8*, p. 412.
[170]Victor P. Hamilton, "שָׁכַן," *TWOT*, 2:935; Gerald H. Wilson, "שָׁכַן," *NIDOTTE*, 4:111-113.

After Yahweh comes to dwell in **Jerusalem**, the city **will be called the City of Truth**. The noun "truth" (אֱמֶת, *'emeth*) appears six times in Zechariah, all in chapters 7 and 8 (7:9; 8:3,8,16[2×],19). "Truth" (*'emeth*) and its cognates have a semantic range of truth, firmness, certainty, security, or faithfulness. Yahweh is described as a God of *'emeth* (Ps 31:5; Jer 10:10) who acts in faithfulness (Gen 24:27; Ps 61:7), and whose actions on behalf of the people result in their peace and security (Isa 39:8; Jer 33:6).[171] Moreover, the city's new name reflects the character of the God whose people they are (Zech 8:8). The notion of Zion as the holy mountain is extensive in the Psalms (43:3; 48:1; 87:1; 99:9). Particularly noteworthy is Psalm 48:1-2 where Zion is likened to Mount Zaphon, the high mountain of Canaanite mythology that serves as an entrance to heaven. There, Mount Zion also is twice affirmed as the city of Yahweh, the Great King. These themes certainly are implicit in verse 3. Zechariah is not alone in speaking of **the Holy Mountain**. It appears earlier seven times in Isaiah (11:9; 27:13; 56:7; 57:13; 65:11,25; 66:20), twice in Ezekiel (20:40; 43:12), and once in Daniel (11:45). The references to **the mountain of the LORD Almighty** and the "Holy Mountain" also are reminiscent of Psalm 2:6, where the messianic king reigns on Yahweh's "holy hill" of Zion, and of the visions in Isaiah 2 and Micah 4, where the eschatological "mountain of the LORD's temple" is established in Zion. Holiness designates separation from the common and profane. The temple mount has lost its holy status as the Babylonian armies have profaned it (Ezek 7:24; 23:39; 25:3) and reduced it to a pile of rubble. The renaming of that mount as the Holy Mountain now signals its renewed holy status.[172] Later chapter 8 offers another reason for the temple mount being known as the Holy Mountain: it will become a center for worship not only for Israel, but also for many peoples and powerful nations (Zech 8:20-22).[173]

**8:4-5** The third oracle (vv. 4-5) offers a vision of Zion's future. The blessedness of the coming days is portrayed with complementary pictures of the aged and youth living securely in a tranquil setting (cf. Isa 65:20). The advanced age of the elderly **men and women**

---

[171]Jack B. Scott, "אמן," *TWOT*, 1:52-53.

[172]McComiskey, "Zechariah," p. 1138.

[173]Merrill, *Haggai, Zechariah, Malachi*, p. 222; Chisholm, *Minor Prophets*, p. 257.

is underscored by the image of them sitting **each with cane in hand**. The imagery of both the elderly and children at leisure depicts socioeconomic conditions such that the community no longer needs the contributions of labor normally demanded even of the aged and relatively young in the culture. The imagery, moreover, thoroughly overturns the representation of the fall of Jerusalem in Lamentations 2:21, "Young and old lie together in the dust of the streets." Zechariah expands the image by explicitly referring to both genders and by speaking of "open places" or "public squares" (רְחֹב, rᵉḥōb) rather than the **streets** (חוּץ, ḥûṣ). The ḥûṣ are rarely what the contemporary reader thinks of as residential streets. The root refers simply to the "outside," and often represents the patchwork network of pathways between houses and buildings. Though the NIV translates rᵉḥōb as "streets," an open area or public square is probably in view here. The threefold repetition of the noun in verses 4 and 5 (the NIV translates the final use in v. 5 **there**) further enhances the image of stability and prosperity. Not many cities in Palestine would have multiple squares or open places.[174] The participle translated **playing** is actually a form of שָׂחַק (śāḥaq), a verb often denoting laughter (Job 5:22; 39:7,18,22; 41:29; Ps 2:4; 37:13; 52:6; 59:8; Prov 1:26; 31:25; Eccl 3:4; Lam 1:7; Hab 1:10). A variant of the verb (צָחַק, ṣāḥaq) appears in the Genesis narratives recounting the laughter of Abraham and Sarah upon hearing that they would have a child (17:17; 18:12,13,15).

**8:6** The fourth oracle (v. 6) offers encouragement to the community by reaffirming Yahweh's power.[175] The message of this oracle receives special prominence by virtue of the oracle's central position in the first section of seven oracles and by being bracketed between the formulaic statements **This is what the LORD Almighty says** and **declares the LORD Almighty**. The oracle asserts that the future of Zion **may seem marvelous to the** community (cf. the NET's "difficult in the opinion of the small community"), but it will not seem difficult to the LORD Almighty (Yahweh Seba'oth). The title **remnant of this people** appears three times in Zechariah (vv. 6,11,12). Its near parallel, "the remnant of the people" appears in Haggai

---

[174]James D. Price, "חוּץ," *NIDOTTE* 2:52-53; Meyers and Meyers, *Haggai, Zechariah 1–8*, pp. 415-416; William White, "רחב," *TWOT*, 2:841.
[175]Meyers and Meyers, *Haggai, Zechariah 1–8*, p. 429.

(1:12,14; 2:2). By referring to the people in this way, Zechariah reinforces the message of a coming change from adverse circumstances.[176] The verb "seem marvelous" (פָּלֵא, pālā') is used to speak of
the wonders (e.g., plagues) Yahweh performs among the Egyptians
(Exod 3:20) and the amazing parting of the Jordan River allowing
Israel to pass through on dry ground (Josh 3:5). The laughter in the
preceding verse (see comments on 8:5 above) taken together with the
affirmation that nothing is too difficult or marvelous (pālā') for
Yahweh in this verse recalls the account of Sarah's laughter upon
learning that she would bear a child (Gen 18:12-15). When she laughs
upon hearing the news, Abraham is rebuked with the question "Is
anything too hard for the LORD?" (Gen 18:14). Variations of this
question occur in Jeremiah 32:17 and 27. If the omnipotent God of
Israel could not be deterred from fulfilling the promise to Abraham,
neither will the LORD Almighty be thwarted from bringing about the
divine purposes for the remnant community.

**8:7-8** The fifth oracle (vv. 7-8) is an eschatological promise that
Yahweh will gather the people from the nations and bring them to
Jerusalem where they will be the people of Yahweh. The oracle
reflects the earlier summons for those in exile to escape (2:6). The
Hebrew construction, translated **I will save** in the NIV, consists of a
form of the particle "behold" (הִנֵּה, hinnēh; see comments on 1:7–6:8
above) followed by a participle form of the verb "to save." This construction indicates what is on the verge of happening, a sense
expressed in the NET ("I am about to save my people"). Yahweh will
bring those dispersed among foreign countries (Zech 2:6; 7:14) to live
in Jerusalem, where indeed Yahweh has chosen to dwell. The wording
of the NASB ("They shall be my people and I will be their God, in
truth and righteousness") reflects more closely the word order in the
MT, placing the phrase "in truth and righteousness" after the affirmation "They shall be my people and I will be their God." In so doing
(see also ESV, KJV, NET, NRSV, NJB), this rendering leaves uninter-
rupted what is surely intended to be an allusion to the covenant formula (Exod 19:5; 29:45; Lev 26:12) to which Jeremiah frequently
refers (Jer 7:23; 11:4; 24:7; 30:22; 31:1; 31:33).[177] The concluding

---

[176]Ollenburger, "Zechariah," p. 795.

[177]The New Testament also uses this language to describe both the present reality of the new covenant relationship (2 Cor 6:16; Heb 8:10) and the
future dwelling of God with people in the New Jerusalem (Rev 21:3).

phrase in the MT ("in truth and righteousness") describes the manner in which Yahweh acts on behalf of the people; Yahweh will, in faithfulness and righteousness (cf. Isa 48:1), be their God (אֱלֹהִים, *'ĕlōhîm*), a divine name that emphasizes divine transcendence and sovereignty more so than the more personal name Yahweh.

**8:9-13** In the sixth oracle (vv. 9-13), Yahweh encourages the people to persevere in the rebuilding of the temple (v. 9) with the expectation that Yahweh will bless the remnant of this people (vv. 12-13) in contrast to the calamity experienced in the past (vv. 10-11). This basic intent of the oracle is seen in the command **let your hands be strong**, which both introduces (v. 9) and concludes (v. 13) the oracle.[178] The KJV preserves the similar idiom in Ezra 4:4, there relating to the discouragement present among those working on the temple ("Then the people of the land weakened the hands of the people of Judah, and troubled them in building"). Here it indicates the courage needed to see the rebuilding of the temple through to completion.[179] The **words spoken by the prophets** to those present when the foundation of the temple was laid provides the basis for this encouragement; however, Ezra 3 mentions no such prophets present when work on the temple began. For this reason, at least one version follows the reading in the LXX "since the day" (e.g., the NJB reads, "Take heart, you who today hear these promises uttered by the prophets since the day when the foundations of the Temple of Yahweh Sabaoth were laid, that the sanctuary would indeed be rebuilt"). Further complicating the matter is the uncertainty about whether the time **when the foundation was laid for the house of the LORD Almighty** refers to the initial stages of temple reconstruction in 536 B.C. (Ezra 3:8-13) or to the renewal of the construction prompted by Haggai and Zechariah in 520 B.C. (Hag 1:1-4,14-15). Verse 10 describes a situation similar to that depicted by Haggai before the resumption of work in 520 B.C. (Hag 1:5-11), and it may be then that Zechariah refers to the words of Haggai (1:6-11; 2:15-19) who likewise employs the verb "be strong" (Hab 2:4).[180]

---

[178]Sweeney, *The Twelve Prophets*, p. 649.

[179]Baldwin, *Haggai, Zechariah, Malachi*, p. 151. Verse 9 uses the two most common names for the temple, the house of Yahweh (בֵּית יהוה, *bayith YHWH*) and the temple or palace (חֵיכָל, *hêkāl*) (see Haggai: Theology).

[180]Baldwin, *Haggai, Zechariah, Malachi*, p. 151. It is plausible that a second laying of foundation may have occurred in 520 B.C. or that the text here

The rationale (the NIV omits the causal conjunction "for" [כִּי, *kî*] that begins the verse) for persevering with rebuilding the temple is stated negatively in verse 10 and positively in verses 11-13. According to verse 10, before beginning the reconstruction of the temple, desperate conditions existed: deficiency of wages (cf. Hag 1:5-6), interference of hostile enemies (Ezra 4:1-5), and antagonism among the people (**I had turned every man against his neighbor**). Verse 11 begins with the temporal adverb **now** (עַתָּה, *'attāh*), which, when combined with the conjunction "and," has an emphatic use and signals a significant contrast. In the prophets, the adverb *'attāh* often introduces the imminent actions of Yahweh either in blessing or in curse (e.g., Isa 33:10; 43:19).[181] Here that action concerns **the remnant of this people** on whose behalf **the LORD Almighty** (Yahweh Seba'oth) will begin a new period of blessing. At the beginning of verse 12, the NIV omits the causal conjunction (כִּי, *kî*) that expresses the effect of this promised blessing, portrayed here primarily in terms of agricultural abundance. Verse 12 employs an interesting variation on the standard image of the land as an inheritance (e.g., Deut 3:28; 12:10; 19:3; 31:7; Josh 1:6) by also presenting Yahweh's pledge to provide good or blessed seed (cf. "a sowing of peace" in the ESV with **the seed will grow well** in the NIV), fruitful vines, abundant crops, and plentiful precipitation as the inheritance (נָחַל, *nāḥal*) given to the remnant. Especially significant is the image of **the vine** to represent not only prosperity but also peace (1 Kgs 4:25; Isa 36:16; Micah 4:4; Zech 3:10). This combination of peace and prosperity is consistent with the image's context. The sowing of peace and its results contrasts the absence of peace and blessing in verse 10 (the word "peace" is there translated as **safely** in the NIV). The phrase **remnant of this people** in verse 12 repeats the language of verse 11 and indicates the significance of the statements in between.[182]

Verse 13 contrasts the prior condition of the people with their promised experience of deliverance and blessing. The unfaithfulness of Israel has resulted in her becoming **an object of cursing**

---

may refer to various stages in the building process rather than solely to the setting of the building's foundation (see comments on Haggai: Historical Background and Haggai 2:18-19).

[181]Allan Harman, "Particles," *NIDOTTE*, 4:1031.

[182]Sweeney, *The Twelve Prophets*, p. 651.

(קְלָלָה, qᵉlālāh), a common motif in Deuteronomy and Jeremiah (Deut 11:26-28; 29:25-28; 30:17-20; Jer 24:9; 25:18; 26:6; 42:18; 44:8; 44:22). The NIV renders simply as **Judah and Israel** the fuller phrase in the original "house of Judah and house of Israel" (see ESV, NASB, NRSV, NJPS). The reunion of the house of Israel with the house of Judah is an element of Jeremiah's prophetic hope (31:27,31; 33:14) in contrast with his indictments of both houses for their unfaithfulness (5:11; 11:10,17; 13:11), even though Jeremiah characteristically places Israel first in his ordering of the two (Israel and Judah). Unlike Jeremiah, Zechariah does not doubt the priority of Judah over Israel.[183] Instead, Yahweh **will save** Judah and Israel (see on 8:7 above) and they will be a blessing. This promise of transformation (from curse to blessing) concludes with **and you will be a blessing**, a phrase reminiscent of the promise to Abraham in Genesis 12:2. The command **Do not be afraid, but let your hands be strong** is reminiscent of the charge in Isaiah to "strengthen the feeble hands, steady the knees that give way; say to those with fearful hearts, 'Be strong, do not fear'" (Isa 35:3-4) and reverses the judgment represented in the rhetorical question asked of Judah by Yahweh, "Will your courage endure or your hands be strong in the day I deal with you?" (Ezek 22:14). Its presence here connects with the opening of the oracle in verse 9 and forms a bracket around the longest oracle in the chapter. The oracle's interior provides motivation for the essential exhortation to the postexilic community, "Let your hands be strong."

**8:14-17** The seventh oracle (vv. 14-17) is similar to the preceding oracle (vv. 9-13), in that Yahweh contrasts the past punishments of Israel with a present determination to do good to Jerusalem and Judah (vv. 14-15). Likewise, this oracle concludes with the command **do not to be afraid** (v. 15) and several other exhortations regarding social justice (vv. 16-17). To be sure, the seventh oracle follows logically from the sixth, since it begins with the causal conjunction "for" (כִּי, kî) omitted in the NIV (see ESV, NASB, NET, NRSV, NJB, and NPJS). In the past, the determination or resolve (זָמַם, zāmam) of **the LORD Almighty** (Yahweh Seba'oth) has resulted in **disaster upon** the ancestors who **angered** Yahweh (see also 1:2,6; cf. Lam 2:17); now Yahweh is equally resolved **to do good . . . to Jerusalem and Judah**.

---

[183]Baldwin, *Haggai, Zechariah, Malachi*, p. 153.

A double use of messenger formulas in verse 14 highlights this divine resolve. This determination to bless stands in contrast with the more frequent use of the verb (*zāmam*) for God's determination to punish.[184] Yahweh's resolve to do good both to Jerusalem and Judah provides an answer to the angel's question in 1:12 as to how long the LORD Almighty (Yahweh Seba'oth) would withhold mercy from Jerusalem and the towns of Judah. Since Yahweh's anger has given way to the restoration, the people of Jerusalem and Judah need have no fear (8:13).

The seventh oracle uses a cluster of imperatives in verses 16 and 17 to call the remnant to practice judicial honesty while the temple is rebuilt (cf. 7:9-10).[185] These commands, like those of 7:9-10, align with earlier prophetic texts (7:7) to demand "the moral action necessary to reconstitute holiness within the community as the Temple is rebuilt."[186] These two verses contain a general introduction (**These are the things you are to do**), two positive commands (**speak the truth** and **render true and sound judgment**), two prohibitions (**do not plot evil** and **do not love to swear falsely**), and a conclusion that provides the basis and source for these exhortations (**I hate all this, declares the LORD**). The two positive commands call for personal honesty and civil justice, reflecting truth and resulting in peace (cf. the ESV's "judgments that are true and make for peace"). The prohibitions of verse 18 reflect earlier proscriptions against devising evil against others (Ps 10:2; 52:2; 140:2; 140:4; Micah 2:1) and swearing or dealing falsely with others (Exod 20:16; 23:7; Lev 6:3; 19:12).

**8:18-19** Verse 18 begins the second section of the chapter (vv. 18-23) with the prophetic word formula **the word of the LORD Almighty came to me** (וַיְהִי דְּבַר יהוה צְבָאוֹת אֵלָי, *wayᵉhî dᵉbar YHWH ṣᵉbā'ôth 'ēlay*). This second section consists of three oracles (vv. 19,20-22,23), each beginning with the messenger formula **This is what the Lord Almighty says** (כֹּה אָמַר יהוה צְבָאוֹת, *kōh 'āmar YHWH ṣᵉbā'ôth*). This second set of three oracles reinforces emphases in the Zion tradition (see on 1:13-15 above), especially the universal reign and conquest of Yahweh (8:20-22) and the nations' worship of Yahweh (v. 23).

---

[184]Ollenburger, "Zechariah," p. 797; Petersen, *Haggai and Zechariah 1–8*, p. 309.

[185]Meyers and Meyers, *Haggai, Zechariah 1–8*, p. 431.

[186]Sweeney, *The Twelve Prophets*, p. 652.

The eighth oracle (v. 19) names two fasts already mentioned in 7:5; to these are added fasts in the **fourth** and tenth months. The **tenth month** fast commemorates the beginning of the siege of Jerusalem by the Babylonians on January 15, 588 B.C. (2 Kgs 25:1), and the observance in the fourth month remembers the breach of the city walls around July 18, 586 B.C. (Jer 39:2-5). Only now does the prophet specifically address the initial question by those of Bethel (7:3). The response, however, is not a simple "yes" or "no" answer that the group probably expects. The prophet has recognized that the question essentially asks whether the community's present is unalterably conditioned by its past. Although their past informs their present, they live in the present in light of their hopes for the future.[187] If the people observe Yahweh's commands, then Yahweh will bless them and cause the pain associated with the fasts to cease.[188] Instead, the fasts are to be transformed into times of joy (שָׂשׂוֹן, śāśôn), a term denoting happiness, delight, and enthusiasm.[189] The former somber fasts will be **occasions** for **glad**ness (שִׂמְחָה, śimḥāh), a noun used earlier in 2:10 in a call for Israel to be glad in response to Yahweh's promised coming to live among them. Meaningful for the use of śimḥāh here are other times in which Israel's festival times are described as days or appointed times of gladness (Num 10:10; Deut 12:7; 14:26; 16:11; 26:11; 27:7; Esth 9:17-18).[190] The word śimḥāh is paired with śāśôn in Jeremiah four times (Jer 7:34; 16:9; 25:10; 33:11). The first three uses speak of joy transformed to gloom and despair in the Babylonian conquest. The final use, on the contrary, anticipates a day when sorrow gives way to joy and gladness. Jeremiah 33:11 and the pairing in the present passage replicate the instances in Isaiah where the verbs are linked to speak of the elation which will accompany the restoration of the remnant community (Isa 35:10; 51:3,11).[191]

The command to **love truth** (אֱמֶת, 'emeth) **and peace** (שָׁלוֹם, šālôm) recalls the injunctions of verse 16 and may allude to Jeremiah's promise of postexilic peace and security given to Judah (33:6). The noun

---

[187]Ollenburger, "Zechariah," p. 800.
[188]McComiskey, "Zechariah," p. 1154.
[189]Gary G. Cohen, "שׂושׂ, שׂישׂ," *TWOT*, 2:873.
[190]Michael A. Grisanti, "שׂמח," *NIDOTTE*, 3:1252; Bruce K. Waltke, "שָׂמַח," *TWOT*, 2:879.
[191]Michael A. Grisanti, "שׂושׂ," *NIDOTTE*, 3:1225.

*'emeth* appears six times in Zechariah. It first appears in 7:9 in the command to administer true judgment. In this chapter, Jerusalem is to be the City of Truth (v. 3), Yahweh promises to dwell among the people as their true (or faithful) God, and the people are command-ed to speak (v. 16) and love (v. 18) the truth. Also appearing six times in the book is *šālôm* (6:13; 8:10,12,16,19; 9:10). Its four uses in chap-ter 8 address the situation that now gives rise to those events spoken of in the chapter's final oracle (v. 23): with truth and peace estab-lished in Judah, the nations now recognize Yahweh.[192]

**8:20-22** In the ninth oracle (vv. 20-22), the name **the LORD Almighty** (Yahweh Seba'oth) appears three times. This threefold use further emphasizes the description of many cities and nations coming to Jerusalem to seek and entreat Yahweh Seba'oth. The active involve-ment of the **inhabitants of many cities** to consult with one another in preparation for their search for Yahweh adds to the aura of Yahweh's earlier promise that "Many nations will be joined with the LORD in that day and will become my people" (2:11) and recalls the eschato-logical searching of the nations in Isaiah 2:2 and Micah 4:2. This promise, however, must be seen in the light of the earlier calls to covenant behavior (Zech 7:9-10; 8:16-17,19). Moses has earlier noted the connection between the covenant obedience of Israel and the attraction of the nations to Yahweh (Deut 4:5-8). The pilgrimage of the nations to Jerusalem **to entreat** Yahweh Seba'oth is foreshadowed by the group from Bethel (7:1-2). Since the people of Bethel are for-mer idolaters (1 Kgs 12:25-33) and the town itself is a settlement of foreigners brought from Assyria (2 Kgs 17:24-41), the example of their inquiry to entreat Yahweh (Zech 7:2-3) is apropos.[193] The verb **seek** (בָּקַשׁ, *bāqaš*) often refers to seeking or inquiring of Yahweh in prayer (Exod 33:7; Zeph 1:6); this is demonstrated by its pairing with "entreat" (חָלָה, *ḥālak*), a verb designating the seeking of Yahweh's favor through a prayer for mercy or help in a time of danger.[194] The pair is used both in verses 21 and 22 with their ordering reversed, thus creating a chiasm in which their combined subjects (i.e., peoples, inhabitants of cities, powerful nations) form an inclusive set.[195]

---

[192]Meyers and Meyers, *Haggai, Zechariah 1–8*, p. 435.
[193]Sweeney, *The Twelve Prophets*, p. 655.
[194]Carl Philip Weber, "חָלָה," *TWOT*, 1:287.
[195]Meyers and Meyers, *Haggai, Zechariah 1–8*, p. 439.

**8:23** The tenth oracle of the chapter (v. 23) concludes the series of oracles with an image of **ten men from all languages and nations** clinging to the **hem of** the **robe** of **one Jew** and pleading that he allow them to **go with** him into the company of God. The Hebrew reads, "all of the tongues of the nations," and perhaps the wording evokes confusion of language in the story of the tower of Babel (Gen 11:1-9; cf. Isa 66:18). Since the number ten often connotes completeness (e.g., Gen 31:7,41; Lev 26:26; Num 14:22; 1 Sam 1:8), its use here probably represents all of humanity outside of Judah. Or, if the number refers to the tenth of the remnant in Isaiah 6:13 that remains after the people are destroyed, then the one Jew may represent Judah as the tenth of the remnant that leads the nations (i.e., the nine-tenths) to recognize Yahweh.[196] The remnant of the people is now a vehicle of blessing for the nations (8:13) through whom the nations have access to Yahweh.[197] The depiction of the longing of the nations for Israel's God is paralleled within the book (14:16-21) and Isaiah (45:14,24; 60:14). The intensity of their desire is indicated in the word **take firm hold** (חָזַק, *ḥāzāq*), a word used elsewhere for Moses taking hold of the snake (Exod 4:4) and for David seizing a lion by its beard (1 Sam 17:35). Clutching a robe may depict an image for an attempted reconciliation (1 Sam 15:27) or merely an act of desperation (Isa 4:1).[198] The ten men of the nations hear **that God** (*'ĕlôhîm*) **is with** the Jews (cf. Isa 7:14). This divine name (*'ĕlôhîm*) appears but three times in Zechariah (6:15; 8:8,23) in contrast with more than one hundred uses of Yahweh (*YHWH*). The choice of *'ĕlôhîm* here represents the perspective of the nations, for *'ĕlôhîm* is the generic and universal term for deity.[199] The nations come seeking after the God of Israel; like Israel, the nations come to know *'ĕlôhîm* as Yahweh when they enter into covenant relationship with Yahweh.

---

[196]Sweeney, *The Twelve Prophets*, p. 656.

[197]The image's fulfillment is seen in the establishment and growth of the church (Matt 28:19; Acts 2:5-11; 9:15; 13:47; 28:28; Rom 1:5; Eph 3:6). That the nations (Gentiles) come to Jerusalem through the assistance of the Jews is an element not foreign to Paul's analogy of the tree and the wild olive branches in Rom 11:13-24.

[198]*DBI*, p. 979.

[199]Meyers and Meyers, *Haggai, Zechariah 1–8*, p. 442.

# V. THE FIRST ORACLE (9:1–11:17)

Both Zechariah 9:1 and 12:1 begin with the word "oracle" (מַשָּׂא, *maśśā'*), which generally indicates a particular type of prophetic pronouncement.[200] Here *maśśā'* (translated "prophecy" in the TNIV) describes the relationship between Zechariah 9–14 and the preceding material in Zechariah 1–8. Thus, these two sections (Zechariah 9–11 and 12–14) function as a reinterpretation of Zechariah 1–8 and its major themes — the intervention of Yahweh among the nations and on behalf of Jerusalem, the reestablishment of divinely appointed leadership, and the inclusion of the Gentiles among the people of Yahweh — to the events of a later time.[201] Specifically, these oracles clarify the continuing validity of the previous prophecy of Zechariah 1–8 and reiterate the intended actions of Yahweh (e.g., Yahweh's disposal of leadership who misrules the people) and the appropriate response of the people (e.g., the people's escape from Jerusalem before its destruction in order to participate in its later purification). Both oracles also incorporate other types of prophetic material. The first *maśśā'* (Zechariah 9–11) contains a prophecy of punishment against foreign nations (9:1-8; cf. Zeph 2:4–3:7), a prophetic call to rejoicing (9:9-10; cf. Zech 3:14-17), prophetic exhortation (9:11–10:12), a prophetic sentinel report (11:1-3; cf. Nahum 2:1-10), and a report of prophetic symbolic action (11:4-17; cf. Zech 6:9-15). The second *maśśā'* (Zechariah 12–14) consists of a prophecy of punishment against foreign nations (12:1–13:6) and two prophecies of salvation (13:7-9 and 14:1-21). Therefore, Zechariah 9–14 shows that Yahweh is transforming the leadership that oppresses the people and the situations that threaten their existence, by depicting the demise of Judah's present leadership, the purification of the people through their present experiences, and the divine intervention that results in the universal recognition of Yahweh.

---

[200]Richard D. Weis, "Oracle," *ABD*, 5:28-29; Michael H. Floyd, "The מַשָּׂא," pp. 401-422.

[201]Floyd, *Minor Prophets*, pp. 450-451; McComiskey, "Zechariah," p. 1017.

## A. PROPHECY OF PUNISHMENT
## AGAINST ISRAEL'S ENEMIES (9:1-8)

### An Oracle

[1]The word of the LORD is against the land of Hadrach / and will rest upon Damascus— / for the eyes of men and all the tribes of Israel / are on the LORD—[a] / [2]and upon Hamath too, which borders on it, / and upon Tyre and Sidon, though they are very skillful. / [3]Tyre has built herself a stronghold; / she has heaped up silver like dust, / and gold like the dirt of the streets. / [4]But the Lord will take away her possessions / and destroy her power on the sea, / and she will be consumed by fire. / [5]Ashkelon will see it and fear; / Gaza will writhe in agony, / and Ekron too, for her hope will wither. / Gaza will lose her king / and Ashkelon will be deserted. / [6]Foreigners will occupy Ashdod, / and I will cut off the pride of the Philistines. / [7]I will take the blood from their mouths, / the forbidden food from between their teeth. / Those who are left will belong to our God / and become leaders in Judah, / and Ekron will be like the Jebusites. / [8]But I will defend my house / against marauding forces. / Never again will an oppressor overrun my people, / for now I am keeping watch.

[a]1 Or Damascus. / For the eye of the LORD is on all mankind, / as well as on the tribes of Israel,

Chapter 9 begins with a prophecy of punishment against foreign nations (for comments on this prophetic form, see Zeph 2:4–3:7 above). This judgment speech is directed against the traditional enemies of Israel, including the Arameans, Phoenicians, and Philistines (vv. 1-8), and it anticipates the coming of the king to Jerusalem (vv. 9-10) and the involvement of Yahweh on behalf of Judah (9:11–10:12). Verses 1-8 portray the victorious north to south march of Yahweh from Syria through Phoenicia and Philistia, ending at the temple in Jerusalem. These verses, however, do not describe any historical battles per se; they use common language and localities to depict the deliverance of the people by Yahweh.[202] The extent of the conquest

---

[202]Paul D. Hanson, *Dawn of Apocalyptic*, rev. ed. (Philadelphia: Fortress, 1979), pp. 316-320. Delcor, "Les allusions," pp. 110-124, suggests that itinerary of locations in 9:1-8 reflects the fourth-century-B.C. conquests of

depicted equals those promised in the Pentateuch (Gen 15:18) and those approximated in the empires of David and Solomon (1 Kgs 4:24).

**9:1** A superscription consisting of the term **oracle** (מַשָּׂא, *maśśā'*) followed by the introductory phrase **the word of the Lord** appears also in Zechariah 12:1 and Malachi 1:1, a combination unique to these three texts (see Nahum 1:1, Hab 1:1, and Mal 1:1 on *maśśā'*). Despite this similarity, the three passages differ. Malachi 1:1 identifies Israel as the subject of the oracle and Malachi as its recipient. Neither Zechariah 9:1 nor 12:1 identifies a subject or recipient for the oracle. The present text describes the word of Yahweh as **against** (בְּ, *bᵉ*) **the land of Hadrach**, whereas 12:1 states that the oracle is concerning (עַל, *'al*) Israel. The name "Hadrach" appears only here in the Old Testament; it referred a northern region in Aram stretching from Aleppo in the north to Damascus in the south. Although Aramaic and Assyrian inscriptions make mention of the place, none date after 698 B.C. Possibly this northern point at the beginning of Yahweh's procession is known by a different name at the time of the writing of this oracle,[203] but the prophet uses a more ancient name to create a paradigmatic portrayal of all enemies of Yahweh. The NIV indicates that the word of Yahweh **will** also **rest upon Damascus** (cf. ESV, NASB, and NJB). The use of the term *maśśā'* in connection with Damascus is reminiscent of Isaiah 17:1-7, an oracle that speaks of the destruction of both Damascus and Ephraim. Just as Isaiah 17:7 promises a day in which people "will look to their Maker and turn their eyes to the Holy One of Israel," Zechariah 9:1 states that **the eyes of men and all the tribes of Israel are on the Lord.**[204] This affirmation is significant when one compares prominent uses of the phrase "all the tribes of Israel" with the content of chapter 9. Yahweh promises to defend the temple (v. 8) in "the city the Lord had chosen out of all the tribes of Israel in which to put his Name" (1 Kgs 14:21; cf. 1 Kgs 11:23; 2 Kgs 21:7; 2 Chr 12:13; 33:7). The promise to Zion (for discussion of "Zion," see 1:13-15 above) of a coming king (v. 9) is certainly based in the memo-

Aram and Palestine by Alexander the Great. Against this notion, see Sweeney, *The Twelve Prophets*, pp. 661-664.

[203]Ollenburger, "Zechariah," p. 804.

[204]See McComiskey, "Zechariah," p. 1160, for a proposal that the Hebrew text of verse 1 should be translated "the Lord has an eye on mankind," a reading adopted by ESV.

ry and covenant with David, the one whom all the tribes of Israel assembled to anoint king (2 Sam 5:1) and who then conquered the Jebusite fortress of Zion through the power of the LORD Almighty (2 Sam 5:6-10).

**9:2-4 Hamath** (modern Hama) was an important Syrian city and Persian province that shared a border with Damascus (see Num 13:21; Josh 13:5; Judg 3:3; Amos 6:2); **Tyre and Sidon** (see Jer 25:22; 27:3; 47:4; Ezek. 27:8; Joel 3:4), the chief cities of Phoenicia, are designated as **skillful** (cf. "wise" in ESV, NASB, NRSV, and NJPS), likely because of their successes in commerce and construction (see Ezek 27). A play on words occurs in verse 3: **Tyre** (צוֹר, *ṣôr*) builds **herself a stronghold** (מָצוֹר, *māṣôr*). In 2 Chronicles 8:5 and 11:5, the term *māṣôr* designates a city capable of withstanding siege. By the postexilic period, the impregnability of Tyre becomes almost axiomatic. Located on an island, isolated from invaders, and with access to supplies by sea, Tyre survives for five years against the Assyrians until 622 B.C. and for thirteen years before the Babylonians withdrew in 572 B.C. Alexander the Great subdues it in seven months by building a causeway to the island in 332 B.C.[205] **Silver** and **gold** (Ps 68:13; Prov 3:14; 8:10; 16:16) allude to Tyre's prosperous commerce, but the phrase **dirt of the streets** appears elsewhere as a metaphor for military defeat (2 Sam 22:43; Ps 18:42; Micah 7:10; Zech 10:5) and thereby portends the devastation described in verse 4. The NIV translates as "but" the exclamatory particle "behold" (הִנֵּה, *hinnēh*), whose presence heightens the attention given to the following statement about the destruction of Tyre. If the NIV, ESV, and KJV are correct in translating the noun חַיִל (*ḥayil*) as "power" rather than "wealth" as in the NASB and NRSV, then the references to the city's defenses, "stronghold" (v. 3) and "power" (v. 4), surround allusions to its wealth, "silver, "gold," and **possessions**. The destruction of Tyre's **power on the sea** presupposes its existence as an island fortress.[206] Ezekiel 26 also speaks of the destruction of Tyre, later accomplished by Alexander the Great.

**9:5-7** Verses 5 through 7 describe the defeat of four Philistine cities, Ashkelon, Gaza, Ekron, and Ashdod, who hear the news of Tyre's destruction. The other member of the ancient Philistine pen-

---

[205]Quintus Curtius Rufus, *History of Alexander* 4.4.10-21.
[206]Sweeney, *Twelve Prophets*, p. 659.

tapolis, Gath, is omitted, perhaps because Uzziah conquers it but does not rebuild there as he does for Ashdod (2 Chr 26:6).[207] Three of the four cities listed here receive special notice by being mentioned twice. **Ashkelon see**s the demise of Tyre **and fears**; it is also **deserted**. **Gaza writhe**s **in agony** and **loses her king**. **Ekron**'s **hope withers**, and **Ekron** becomes **like the Jebusites**, who are old inhabitants of Jerusalem. This promise that "Ekron will be like the Jebusites" may reflect other texts testifying to the continuing existence of the Jebusites among the Israelites as a group absorbed into the community (1 Kgs 9:20; 1 Chr 21:15,18,28; 2 Chr 8:7). The NIV translates the noun מַמְזֵר (*mamzēr*) as **foreigners** in identifying those that **will occupy Ashdod**. Its appearance elsewhere in Deuteronomy 23:3 for one of illegitimate birth accentuates the indignity that Philistia suffers.[208] In the middle of verse 7, the point of view shifts from third to first person, expressing the intended actions of Yahweh. This first person speech continues through verse 13. Yahweh **cut**s **off** ("put an end to" in the TNIV) **the pride of the Philistines** (cf. Isa 13:11,19; 16:6), removes their repulsive religious rituals, and makes them part of the remnant of Yahweh's people. The statement **I will take away the blood from their mouths, the forbidden food from between their teeth** is an expression referring to some type of forbidden religious practice such as eating meat with the blood still in it, or eating unclean or forbidden foods.[209] The noun "forbidden food" (שִׁקּוּץ, *šiqqûṣ*) refers to vile and abominable acts or objects that repulse Yahweh (Deut 29:17; 1 Kgs 11:5,7; 2 Kgs 23:13; Jer 13:27; 32:34; Ezek 5:11; 11:21). The word **leader** (TNIV has "clans," as does the ESV, NET, NRSV, and NJPS) describes rank within the families or clans of Edom (Gen 36:15-43; Exod 15:15; 1 Chr 1:51-54) and of Judah (Zech 12:5-6);[210] here the word suggests that the remnant of the Philistines belonging to Yahweh assume the same status and privileges as families native to **Judah**.[211]

[207]McComiskey, "Zechariah," p. 1161.

[208]Compare "mongrel race" in the NASB and "mongrel people" in the NET, NRSV, and TNIV.

[209]On the possibility of dogs having some cultic significance for the Philistines, see Paula Wapnish and Brian Hesse, "Pampered Pooches or Plain Pariahs? The Ashkelon Dog Burials," *BA* 56 (1993): 55-80.

[210]Jack B. Scott, "אַלּוּף," *TWOT*, p. 48.

[211]Cohen, *The Twelve Prophets*, p. 305.

**9:8** Yahweh pledges to **defend** the temple **against marauding forces** and not to allow **an oppressor** to **overrun** the **people** (cf. Zech 7:14). The verb rendered "defend" by NIV (חָנָה, *ḥānan*) is better translated "encamp at" (ESV, KJV, NRSV, TNIV) or "camp around" (NASB). Notable for this context, *ḥānan* elsewhere describes the siege of the Babylonians against Judah (2 Kgs 25:1; Jer 52:4), the prophetic summons for archers to encamp around Babylon (Jer 50:29), and the psalmist's affirmation that the angel of Yahweh encamps around those who fear Yahweh (Ps 34:7). Even though some have understood **my house** to refer to Yahweh's people spoken of later in the verse,[212] the phrase, when spoken by Yahweh, elsewhere refers to the temple (1 Chr 17:14; 28:6; Ps 101:7; Isa 56:7; Jer 12:7; Ezek 23:39; Hag 1:9; Zech 1:16; 3:7). In contrast with the description of the eyes of people and all the tribes of Israel on Yahweh in verse 1, verse 8 contains Yahweh's promise **for now I am keeping watch**. This promise is not surprising for Yahweh's eyes range throughout the earth (Zech 4:10).[213]

## B. CALL TO REJOICE AT THE COMING KING (9:9-10)

[9]**Rejoice greatly, O Daughter of Zion! / Shout, Daughter of Jerusalem! / See, your king[a] comes to you, / righteous and having salvation, / gentle and riding on a donkey, / on a colt, the foal of a donkey. / [10]I will take away the chariots from Ephraim / and the war-horses from Jerusalem, / and the battle bow will be broken. / He will proclaim peace to the nations. / His rule will extend from sea to sea / and from the River[b] to the ends of the earth.[c]**

[a]*9 Or King*  [b]*10 That is, the Euphrates*  [c]*10 Or the end of the land*

**9:9** Zechariah 9:9-10 comprises a prophetic call to rejoicing, in which the people of **Zion/Jerusalem** are addressed collectively as a personified **daughter** (see comments on Zech 2:10) and urged to **rejoice** (see comments on Zeph 3:14-17) at the entrance of the **king**.[214]

---

[212]E.g., McComiskey, "Zechariah," p. 1163.
[213]On the adverb "now" (עַתָּה, *'attāh*), see comments on Nahum 1:13 and Zech 8:11.
[214]On the citation of Zech 9:9 in Matt 21:5, see Ham, *Coming King*, pp. 20-47.

Rejoicing and shouting in celebration of Yahweh's kingship is a prominent theme in the Psalms (Psalms 47, 96, 98), and the use of "see" (הִנֵּה, *hinnēh*) underscores the significance of the following announcement of the king's procession. This announcement of the coming of a king for the Jews stands out in an historical context when priests and governors appointed by the Persians govern those who have returned to the land. It is also prominent within a literary context that speaks of Gaza losing her king (Zech 9:5). Even though the nations are vanquished (vv. 1-7), Israel's deliverance comes through her king.[215] Zechariah's expectation of a coming is no doubt founded on Ezekiel's promise of a future Davidic king (Ezek 34:23-24; 37:22-24), the anticipated Branch of Isaiah (Isa 11:1) and of Jeremiah (Jer 23:5; 33:14-22), and the rekindled hopes associated with the Davidic house, evidenced in Haggai (Hag 2:20-23) and Zechariah (Zech 3:8; 6:12). The possessive pronoun **your** recognizes the one coming as king of Jerusalem, but the specific identity of the king is some future Davidic monarch (cf. Zech 3:8; 4:6-10; 6:12) or Yahweh (cf. Zech 2:10; 14:9-21).[216]

Following the announcement of the king's entrance into Jerusalem is a description of the king's character. Three words describe the king: **righteous**, **having salvation**, and **gentle**. "Righteous" (צַדִּיק, *ṣaddîq*) may depict the king as the rightful heir to the Davidic throne (cf. Jer 23:5; 33:15),[217] a sense adopted in the NET's rendering "legitimate," or express the vindication of the king by Yahweh (cf. Isa 50:7-9; 53:11-12).[218] "Having salvation" translates a passive participle form of the verb "to save" (יָשַׁע, *yāša'*); this rare form appears in only one other Old Testament text, Psalm 33:16: "No king is saved by the size of his army; no warrior escapes by his great strength." The parallel with Zechariah 9:9 is striking, since both texts emphasize the deliverance of the king apart from military means and subvert any military expectations associated with the "war-horse" (v. 10).[219] "Humble" (עָנִי, *'ānî*) may portray

---

[215]Hahlen, "Equine Imagery," p. 255.

[216]For a discussion of other options ranging from Alexander the Great to the faithful people of Yahweh who are collectively recipients of the Davidic covenant, see Ham, *Coming King*, pp. 25-26, and Adrian Leske, "Context and Meaning of Zechariah 9.9," *CBQ* 62 (2000): 663-678.

[217]Meyers and Meyers, *Zechariah 9–14*, pp. 125-156.

[218]BDB, p. 843.

[219]Hahlen, "Equine Imagery," pp. 255-256.

the king as one wrongfully afflicted (cf. Zech 7:10; 11:7,11) or one who is lowly (see TNIV),[220] even if this nuance of the word 'ānî is not widely attested in the Old Testament (see 2 Sam 22:28; Ps 18:27; Isa 66:2; and Zeph 3:12).[221]

The manner of the king's arrival also underscores his humility. The extended description of the **donkey** (חֲמוֹר, ḥămôr) as **a colt, the foal of a donkey** more narrowly describes the king's mount; the king rides on a particular kind of donkey, a young male donkey, perhaps still unbroken. The donkey is a royal mount in both the premonarchical and early monarchical periods (Judg 5:10; 10:4; 12:14; 2 Sam 16:1-2; 1 Kgs 1:33). Evidence from Ur and Mari indicates the donkey is the royal mount *par excellence* in ancient Near East from the second millennium B.C.[222] The association of the donkey with the promised ruler from Judah (Gen 49:11) and with David (2 Sam 16:1-2) suggests it as an appropriate image for the legitimate Davidic heir.[223] The choice of a donkey rather than a horse to portray the coming of the king also subverts militaristic notions. The horses and chariots that belong to Israel, Persia, or any other nation cannot secure for them the kingdom of Yahweh. This truth resonates with the earlier affirmation that the success of Joshua and Zerubbabel comes not from human power or might (Zech 4:6).

**9:10** Verse 10 uses three poetic lines to describe Yahweh's disarmament of the people: **I will take away the chariots from Ephraim / and the war-horses from Jerusalem / and the battle bow will be broken.** The outer lines of these three begin with forms of the verb "cut off" (כָּרַת, kārath), a common Hebrew metaphor for destruction translated "take away" and "be broken" in the NIV. The mention of Ephraim and Jerusalem, representatives of the northern and southern kingdoms, signals the future reunification of the people of Yahweh (cf. Ezek 37:16-20). The rule of the king who **proclaims peace to the nations will extend from sea to sea and from the River to the ends of the earth.** The extent of this rule alludes to the prom-

---

[220]Stuhlmueller, *Rebuilding with Hope*, p. 125.

[221]The notion of humility or lowliness is more often expressed with the word עָנָו ('ānāw); on the orthographic and semantic confusion between 'ānî and 'ānāw, see Ham, *Coming King*, p. 22.

[222]E. Lipiński, "Recherches sur le livre de Zacharie," *VT* 20 (1970): 50-53.

[223]Meyers and Meyers, *Zechariah 9–14*, pp. 130-131; Hahlen, "Equine Imagery," p. 255.

ises of Genesis 49:10 that the one to whom the scepter belongs receives "the obedience of the nations" and of Psalm 72:8-11 that kings and nations bow down to and serve the Davidic king. The phrase "the River" is a frequent Old Testament reference to the Euphrates (Num 22:5; Josh 24:2-3,14-15; 2 Sam 10:16; 1 Kgs 4:21,24; 1 Chr 19:16; 2 Chr 9:26; Ps 72:8; 80:11; Isa 7:20; 8:7; Jer 2:18). Here the designation associates the geographic description with the boundaries of Solomon's kingdom that included all the kingdoms west of the Euphrates, from Tiphsah, a city on the Euphrates, to Gaza. During Solomon's rule, his kingdom enjoyed peace on all sides (1 Kgs 4:24). The promise in verse 10 thus evokes memories of this past national glory to engender hope for a future restoration and glorification.[224]

## C. EXHORTATION AND RESTORATION FOR JUDAH (9:11–10:12)

[11]**As for you, because of the blood of my covenant with you, / I will free your prisoners from the waterless pit. / [12]Return to your fortress, O prisoners of hope; / even now I announce that I will restore twice as much to you. / [13]I will bend Judah as I bend my bow / and fill it with Ephraim. / I will rouse your sons, O Zion, / against your sons, O Greece, / and make you like a warrior's sword.**

[14]**Then the LORD will appear over them; / his arrow will flash like lightning. / The Sovereign LORD will sound the trumpet; / he will march in the storms of the south, / [15]and the LORD Almighty will shield them. / They will destroy / and overcome with slingstones. / They will drink and roar as with wine; / they will be full like a bowl / used for sprinkling[a] the corners of the altar. / [16]The LORD their God will save them on that day / as the flock of his people. / They will sparkle in his land / like jewels in a crown. / [17]How attractive and beautiful they will be! / Grain will make the young men thrive, / and new wine the young women.**

[a]15 Or *bowl, / like*

---

[224]Ollenburger, "Zechariah," p. 807.

**9:11** The prophetic form of Zechariah 9:11–10:12 may be classified as prophetic exhortation; specifically two commands, "Return to your fortress" (9:12) and "Ask the LORD for rain" (10:1), are followed by two sections of material (9:12-17 and 10:2-12) that describe the involvement of Yahweh on behalf of Judah and thus provide the rationale for these commands. The beginning phrase in verse 11, **as for you**, links what follows to the address to Zion begun in verse 9, and the causal phrase, **because of the blood of my covenant with you**, expresses the reason for Yahweh's favorable actions toward Judah: Yahweh frees the Babylonian exiles because of the covenant made by blood sacrifice in Exodus 24:8.[225] The assurance that Yahweh **frees** the **prisoners** reiterates notions from several Old Testament texts. The prisoners no doubt refers to those still in exile in Babylon (see Ps 107:10; Lam 3:34). The verb to "free" (שָׁלַח, *šālaḥ*) is used frequently in Exodus to speak of the deliverance of the Hebrews (3:20; 4:21,23; 5:1,2; 6:1,11; 7:2,14,16; 8:1,2,20), and the conjoining of covenant and freedom for prisoners is a theme found within the servant songs of Isaiah (42:6-7; 49:8-9). The **waterless pit**, moreover, is reminiscent of the holding of both Joseph and Jeremiah (Gen 37:24; 39:20-22; Jer 38:6-9).[226] The links between this text and the story of Joseph who rises to great heights within a non-Hebrew realm would certainly give hope to those in the postexilic community controlled by Persia.[227]

**9:12-13** Although verses 9-10 promise peace, verses 12-13 promise war. The seeming contradiction is explained in verse 12 where Yahweh announces the intention to **restore** double to Zion, perhaps

---

[225]Petersen, *Zechariah 9–14 and Malachi*, p. 60; Meyers and Meyers, *Zechariah 9–14*, p. 139. The Targumim (i.e., Aramaic interpretative translations of the Hebrew Bible) confirm such identification. *Leviticus Rabbah* 6.5 (on Lev. 5.1) reads, "God said to them: *As for thee also, because of the blood of thy covenant* (Zech. IX, 11), i.e. because you remembered that blood of [the covenant at] Sinai," and *Lev. Rab.* 19.6 (on Lev. 15.25), "as it is said, *As for thee also, because of the blood of thy covenant I send forth thy prisoners out of the pit* (Zech. IX, 11) [which means], You have remembered the blood of Sinai." Reference to the blood of the covenant with Zion may also recall Ezekiel 16:61-63 in which Yahweh's establishment of covenant with Jerusalem results in a renewed relationship with a penitent Judah. On the allusion to Zech 9:11 in Matt 26:28, see Ham, *Coming King*, pp. 100-101.

[226]Ollenburger, "Zechariah," p. 810.

[227]Boda, *Haggai, Zechariah*, p. 419.

to compensate for past disgrace (cf. Isa 61:7). The reference to **prisoners of hope** may draw on other texts that assert hope in the future deliverance of Yahweh (e.g., Jer 31:17; Hos 2:15). Yahweh **bends Judah as** a **bow and fills it with Ephraim**. This image of a unified nation appears earlier Zechariah 8:13 (see also Jeremiah 31 and Ezekiel 34 and 37). The weapons listed are not properly understood as warring instruments but as imagery similar to that applied to the Servant in Isaiah 49:3; it signifies that Yahweh controls the affairs of Judah like an adept **warrior**. The name **Greece** (יָוָן, *yāwān* in the Hebrew text; cf. Dan 8:21; 10:20; 11:2) has led to the supposition of a late date for the book of Zechariah, either following the aftermath of Alexander the Great's Syro-Palestinian conquests in the fourth century B.C. or reflecting the conflict between the Maccabees and the Seleucids in the second century B.C. This reasoning, however, is unwarranted, since another (possibly earlier) prophetic text also mentions the Greeks (Joel 3:6), and the Jews may have known about the efforts of Darius I to conquer Greece, a growing threat to Persian dominance, in the early fifth century B.C.[228]

**9:14-15** Present in verse 14 is the traditional theophanic language used to depict Yahweh as the divine warrior (Exod 24:17; Deut 33:2; Judg 5:4-5; 2 Sam 22:8-16; Ps 29:3-8; 68; Hab 3). These depictions liken the march of Yahweh to an approaching storm. **Lightning** constitutes the **arrow** of Yahweh, and thunder is **the trumpet**.[229] Although Yahweh has previously scattered the people with a whirlwind (Zech 7:14), Yahweh now **marches in the storms of the south** to rescue the people (9:14). The people of Israel are **shield**ed (גָּנַן, *gānan*) by Yahweh Almighty who assures them victory. Six of the eight uses of the verb *gānan* are associated with Yahweh's deliverance of Jerusalem from the Assyrian siege in the days of Hezekiah (2 Kgs 19:34; 20:6; Isa 31:5[2×]; 37:35; 38:6).[230] The use of *gānan* thus connects the deliverance of the community foretold here (cf. Zech 12:7) with the miraculous deliverance from the Assyrians. The reference to **slingstones** may possibly allude to David's victory over the giant Goliath (1 Sam 17:40,50). Two other images in verse 15 depict victory. First is the **drink**ing of **wine** in victorious celebra-

---

[228]Cohen, *The Twelve Prophets*, p. 307; Ollenburger, "Zechariah," p. 810.
[229]Boda, *Haggai, Zechariah*, p. 421.
[230]James E. Smith, "גָּנַן," *TWOT*, 1:168.

tion. Jeremiah employs the verb translated here as **roar** to describe the shouts of those who rise up against their oppressors (Jer 50:42; 51:55). Second is sacrificial **bowl**s filled with blood (Exod 27:2-3; 38:2-3; Num 4:13-14; 7:13,19; 1 Kgs 7:40,45,50; 2 Kgs 12:13; 25:15; Neh 7:70; Jer 52:18-19; Zech 14:20), a common imagery for battle (e.g., Deut 32:42; Isa 34:1-8).[231] The latter image, which includes **sprinkling** on **the corners of the altar**, may refer to Yahweh's previously mentioned impetus for delivering the people, "because of the blood of my covenant with you" (Zech 9:11; cf. Exod 24:1-8).[232]

**9:16-17** The metaphors change in verse 16 to sheep and jewels, portraying Yahweh's high regard for the people. The phrase **on that day**, occurring earlier in 2:11 and 3:10, appears frequently in the remainder of the book (11:11; 12:3,4,6,8,9,11; 13:1,2,4; 14:4,6,8,9,13,20). In the present context, it likely refers to what in other prophetic books is called "the day of Yahweh," a day in which Yahweh judges the nations and restores the faithful among the covenant people (see discussion on Zeph 1:7). Verse 16 clearly focuses on the actions and priority of Yahweh who **saves the people**, **the flock** (cf. the primarily negative use of the image in Zech 10:2; 11:4,7,11,17; 13:7) and the crown of Yahweh. The people of Yahweh **sparkle in** the **land** belonging to Yahweh (2 Chr 7:20; Isa 14:25; Jer 2:7; 16:18; Ezek 36:20; 38:16; Joel 1:6; 2:18; 3:2) **like jewels in a crown**. The word used here for "crown" (נֵזֶר, *nēzer*) is not the one (עֲטָרָה, *'ăṭārāh*) used in Zechariah 6:11. Built on the same root as "Nazirite," the noun denotes the adornment of one who has been set apart for a purpose, e.g., as a priest (Exod 29:6; 39:20; Lev 8:9) or a king (2 Sam 1:10; 2 Kgs 11:12; 2 Chr 23:11; Ps 89:39; 132:18; Prov 27:24).[233] The use of this noun highlights the reaffirmation of Judah within covenant (Zech 9:11). Verse 17 depicts the prosperity of the restored community, especially in the flourishing of **young men** and **women**. In Isaiah 33:17, "beauty" (יֹפִי, *yŏphî*) refers to the future king; here **attractive and beautiful** represents a renewal of the land, now strong and full

---

[231]Boda, *Haggai, Zechariah*, p. 422.
[232]Sweeney, *The Twelve Prophets*, p. 667. On the image of blood as wine, see *DBI*, p. 101; cf. Gen 49:11. The imagery in verse 15 is similar to that in Num 23:23-24, where God causes the people to be like a lion that devours its prey and drinks the blood of its victims.
[233]Thomas E. McComiskey, "נֵזֶר," *TWOT*, 2:567-568.

of vitality, ready to hold a new generation.[234] **Grain** and **new wine** are stock images of abundance, life, and peace; Moses describes Israel as a people who, having been saved by Yahweh, dwell in a land of grain and new wine (Deut 33:28-29).

[1]Ask the LORD for rain in the springtime; / it is the LORD who makes the storm clouds. / He gives showers of rain to men, / and plants of the field to everyone. / [2]The idols speak deceit, / diviners see visions that lie; / they tell dreams that are false, / they give comfort in vain. / Therefore the people wander like sheep / oppressed for lack of a shepherd.

[3]"My anger burns against the shepherds, / and I will punish the leaders; / for the LORD Almighty will care / for his flock, the house of Judah, / and make them like a proud horse in battle.

[4]From Judah will come the cornerstone, / from him the tent peg, / from him the battle bow, / from him every ruler. / [5]Together they[a] will be like mighty men / trampling the muddy streets in battle. / Because the LORD is with them, / they will fight and overthrow the horsemen.

[6]"I will strengthen the house of Judah / and save the house of Joseph. / I will restore them / because I have compassion on them. / They will be as though / I had not rejected them, / for I am the LORD their God / and I will answer them. / [7]The Ephraimites will become like mighty men, / and their hearts will be glad as with wine. / Their children will see it and be joyful; / their hearts will rejoice in the LORD. / [8]I will signal for them / and gather them in. / Surely I will redeem them; / they will be as numerous as before. / [9]Though I scatter them among the peoples, / yet in distant lands they will remember me. / They and their children will survive, / and they will return. / [10]I will bring them back from Egypt / and gather them from Assyria. / I will bring them to Gilead and Lebanon, / and there will not be room enough for them. / [11]They will pass through the sea of trouble; / the surging sea will be subdued / and all the depths of the Nile will dry up. / Assyria's pride will be brought down / and Egypt's scepter will pass away. / [12]I will strengthen them in the LORD / and in his name they will walk," / declares the LORD.

[a]5 Or *ruler, all of them together.* / [5]*They*

---

[234]Boda, *Haggai, Zechariah*, p. 422.

**10:1** Three elements comprise Zechariah 10:1-2: the exhortation to ask Yahweh for rain, the reason for the exhortation (i.e., Yahweh, not idols or diviners, gives rain), and the result of inquiring from false prophets (i.e., the people lack for a "shepherd"). The people are commanded to **ask for rain** from Yahweh. This rain no doubt represents the wider experience of divine blessings and intrinsically links this verse to the earlier promise of grain and new wine in 9:17.[235] The spring rains (מַלְקוֹשׁ, *malqôš*) spoken of here are the latter rains that occur during March and April before harvest; they complement the "former rains" of October and November (Deut 11:14; Jer 5:24). The "latter rains" sometimes appear as an eschatological image for a future pouring out of divine blessing (Hos 6:3; Joel 2:21-25). The imagery of rain is significant to the agricultural society of the Israelites, who, unlike other nations who rely on rivers, depend on Yahweh to bless the land with rain (Deut 11:10-12). The agricultural blessings Israel desires derive from Yahweh **who makes the storm clouds**. The noun חֲזִיז (*ḥăzîz*) rendered "storm clouds" by the NIV is related to the Hebrew root signifying strength. As such, it may refer to violent storms, but its use (cf. Job 28:26; 38:25) does not preclude the notion of beneficial rains.[236]

**10:2** The NIV omits the opening conjunction (כִּי, *kî*), translated "for" in most other versions (e.g., ESV, NASB, NET, NRSV, and NJPS). The second verse thus gives the rationale for the prophet's exhortation to entreat Yahweh for rain (cf. Jer 14:22): the community is seeking help from powerless and deceptive sources (Deut 18:10,14; 1 Sam 15:23) that have disappointed them in the past (1 Sam 12:8; 2 Kgs 17:17). This is especially evident in Israel's struggle with Baalism that gives rise to the battle between Yahweh and Baal in the Elijah narratives. Yahweh proves superiority over Baal by withholding rain from the land and then sending rain upon the entreaty of Elijah (1 Kings 17–18). Specifically, three sources of deceptive inquiry are mentioned. **The idols** that **speak deceit** ("speak deceitfully" in the TNIV) are the teraphim (תְּרָפִים, *tᵉrāphîm*),[237] house-

---

[235]Baldwin, *Haggai, Zechariah, Malachi*, p. 170.

[236]Merrill, *Haggai, Zechariah, Malachi*, p. 268.

[237]Gen 31:19,34-35; Judg 17:5; 18:14,17-18,20; 1 Sam 15:23; 19:13,16; 2 Kgs 23:24; Ezek 21:21; Hos 3:4. On the translation of *tᵉrāphîm* as idols, see *HALOT*, p. 1796.

hold gods thought to draw power from the spirit world[238] or from the worship of ancestors.[239] Divination, known in the ancient Near East and Israel,[240] generally involves the inspection and interpretation of the state of an animal's internal organs (Ezek 21:21). Dreaming, another common means of receiving supernatural information, is inappropriate, unless the dreams come from Yahweh. Zechariah condemns dreaming here (cf. Deut 13:2-6; Jer 23:27-32; 27:9; 29:8) along with other methods of inquiry from false prophecy that produce nothing of value.[241]

The conjunction "therefore" (עַל־כֵּן, 'al-kēn) states as a fact the results of the preceding actions.[242] Because the people have relied upon these deceitful sources, they have gone astray like **wander**ing **sheep**, searching for deity by inappropriate means and thus accepting inappropriate leadership.[243] The shift to sheep imagery allows the prophet to address the political and spiritual leadership among the people (see also Zech 9:16; 11:3-17; 13:7). The depiction of kings as shepherds of the people is common in the ancient Near Eastern literature outside the biblical material.[244] Jeremiah regularly uses the imagery of shepherds for kings (2:8; 3:15; 10:21; 23:1-2; 50:6), and Ezekiel employs the image of straying sheep regarding Judah's unfaithfulness caused by a lack of leadership (34:2-15,23-24). Psalm 78:70-72 explicitly links David's work as a sheepherder to his role as the shepherd of Israel (cf. 2 Sam 5:2). The use of the image here may depict the past and present leadership in Israel or the actions of foreign kings.[245] While the Old Testament literature normally employs the image to speak of Israelite leaders, Jeremiah occasionally employs it for foreigners (Jer 12:10-11; 49:19; 50:44); both Isaiah and Ezekiel use the image of rams (see discussion of "leaders" in verse 3 below) to depict international rulers and kings (Isa 14:9;

---

[238]Baldwin, *Haggai, Zechariah, Malachi*, p. 171.
[239]Meyers and Meyers, *Zechariah 9-14*, pp. 184-187.
[240]*HALOT*, p. 1115.
[241]Sweeney, *The Twelve Prophets*, p. 670.
[242]BDB, p. 487; see also Hab 1:4[2×],15,16; Hag 1:10.
[243]Petersen, *Zechariah 9–14*, p. 72.
[244]See *ANET*, p. 164; Jeremias, "ποιμήν," *TDNT*, 6:486-87; Baldwin, *Haggai, Zechariah, Malachi*, p. 171; and Bruce, *New Testament Development of Old Testament Themes*, p. 100, for examples from Assyria, Babylonia, Canaan, Egypt, and Sumeria.
[245]Ollenburger, "Zechariah," p. 814.

Ezek 39:18). This second reading would alleviate the tension between the statement in verse 2 that the people lack a shepherd and
the expression of Yahweh's anger against shepherds in verse 3. This
would also seem appropriate in light of the positive portrayal of
Zerubbabel in Haggai 1–2 and Zechariah 4. Nevertheless, the imagery
excludes neither option, and the contextual focus is upon Yahweh's
provision of legitimate and effective leadership from within the
house of Judah[246] rather than upon a clear identification of those
who have failed or oppressed Israel. Not only do the people wander
**for lack of a shepherd**, they are **oppressed** (עָנָה, 'ānāh) and suffer at
the hands of these unfit leaders. The phrase "oppressed for lack of
a shepherd" is similar to the recurring biblical dictum "like sheep
without a shepherd" (Num 27:17; 1 Kgs 22:17; 2 Chr 18:16; Ezek
34:5; cf. Matt 9:36).

**10:3** The first half of verse 3 is written in first person, thus high-
lighting the anger and determination of Yahweh against an irresponsible leadership. The NIV renders as **leaders** the noun עַתּוּד
('attûd). Of its twenty-nine appearances in the Old Testament, the
NIV translates it "male goat" fifteen times and "goat" twelve times.
Its extended meaning of "leader" (Isa 14:9) derives from the ancient
practice of shepherds mixing male goats into the sheep flock to help
guide the sheep (Jer 50:8); thus, male goat complements shepherd
in an unfavorable pastoral metaphor.[247] Verse 3 contrasts the disposition of Yahweh toward the leaders of the people and toward the
people themselves with the double use of the verb פָּקַד (pāqad),
translated **punish** and **care for** (see Zech 11:16) in the NIV. The
word denotes an intervention by someone in authority that results
in a considerable change in circumstances for the subordinate.[248]
Here the intervention of Yahweh in the life of the leaders is negative
("punish"), but is positive ("care for") in the circumstances of **the
house of Judah**: Yahweh Almighty cares for the flock by removing
those that lead them poorly (cf. Ezek 34:17).[249] A fascinating transformation of imagery occurs in the second half of verse 3; the focus

---

[246]Meyers and Meyers, *Zechariah 9-14*, pp. 198-202.
[247]*HALOT*, p. 902; Boda, *Haggai, Zechariah*, p. 440; Baldwin, *Haggai,
Zechariah, Malachi*, p. 172.
[248]Victor P. Hamilton, "פָּקַד," *TWOT*, 2:731; Tyler F. Williams, "פקד,"
*NIDOTTE*, 3:658. See the discussion of *pāqad* at Zeph 1:8-9.
[249]Mason, *Books of Haggai, Zechariah, Malachi*, p. 99.

shifts from pastoral to militaristic imagery, depicting the empowerment of a new leadership for the people. After reprimanding the
negligent **shepherds** and announcing the intent to care for Judah,
Yahweh vows to set or direct (שׂוּם, *śûm*) the flock of people to be **like
a proud horse in battle**. Both the horse and the battle bow previously banished from Ephraim and Judah in 9:10 are now reintro-
duced in 10:3-4; Judah itself becomes Yahweh's horse and the battle
bow comes out from Yahweh. Once empowered by Yahweh, the
people are now able to overthrow the horsemen (v. 5). Judah is no
longer terrified by horses or disappointed by them, for Judah is
Yahweh's horse.[250]

**10:4** The Hebrew text of verse 4 does not contain the name of
**Judah** (as in the NIV); instead, the phrase **from him** appears four
times (see the ESV). The third person singular pronouns most likely
refer to Yahweh, as it does in verse 3,[251] although the NASB, NRSV,
and NJPS understand the pronoun to refer to Judah (which they
render "them"). A series of four figurative terms depict strong leadership. The word **cornerstone** (פִּנָּה, *pinnāh*) may refer to the corner
of a house (Job 1:19), altar (Exod 27:2; 38:2), tower (Zeph 1:16; 3:6),
street (Prov 7:8), or gate (2 Kgs 14:13; 2 Chr 25:23; Jer 31:38,40;
Zech 14:10), but here *pinnāh* occurs as a metaphor for a leader or
ruler (Judg 20:2; 1 Sam 14:38; Ps 118:22;[252] Isa 19:13). The peg (יָתֵד,
*yāthēd*) is either a **tent peg** or a peg in a wall on which things are
hung. The imagery denotes something sturdy (Ezra 9:8; Isa 22:23;
33:20; Ezek 15:3) and thus complements the image of the cornerstone in the previous line. That Isaiah applies the term to Eliakim,
to whom has been entrusted the keys to the house of David (Isa
22:20-25), may intimate messianic overtones to the image. The **battle bow** links this text to Zechariah 9:13 where Yahweh bends Judah
as a bow; however, here bow, a symbol for royal and military power,
refers to one who comes from Judah. The word used for **ruler** here
is curious (cf. "oppressor" in the KJV), since נֹגֵשׂ (*nāgaś*) typically
describes the actions of oppressive tyrants (e.g., Zech 9:8). At this
point, it appears in a good sense for "commander" (NRSV) or
"leader" (NJB), as in Isa 60:17.

---

[250]Hahlen, "Equine Imagery," p. 257.
[251]Boda, *Haggai, Zechariah*, p. 441.
[252]On the New Testament use of the image of the cornerstone, see Luke
20:17, Eph 2:20, and 1 Pet 2:6.

**10:5** Verse 5 compares the people to warriors who **trample the muddy streets in battle**. The treading of enemies (cf. the TNIV's "trampling their enemy into the mud of the streets") is a common image in the Old Testament (Ps 44:5; 60:12; 108:13; Isa 14:25; 63:6). Because Yahweh is with Judah, they have a decisive victory. The verb translated **overthrow** is a causative form of a verb (יָבֵשׁ, *yābēš*) that normally denotes a drying up or withering (10:11; 11:17). The **mighty men** of Judah cause **the horsemen** or cavalry, the strongest of the opposing soldiers, to be put to shame (9:5; 13:4; see the ESV, NRSV, NJPS, and TNIV), since the foot soldiers of Judah defeat the enemy cavalry.

**10:6-7** As in verse 3, the use of first person returns and continues through verse 12. This extended speech communicates the personal investment of Yahweh in the transformation of the people, an investment that exceeds even the determination to punish the shepherds and leaders of verse 3. The vocabulary of the first two lines of verse 6 contributes to the strong militaristic overtones of the verse.[253] The assurance that Yahweh **strengthen**s (גָּבַר, *gābar*) **the house of Judah** uses the same root (גבר, *gbr*) as in verse 5 to speak of Judah becoming "mighty men" (גִּבּוֹר, *gibbôr*). The word *gābar* is often used in reference to strength in battle (Exod 17:11; 2 Sam 1:23; 11:23; Isa 42:13; Lam 1:16), and the verb **save** (יָשַׁע, *yāsa‘*) frequently speaks of preservation in battle (Deut 20:4; Judg 3:9; 6:36-37; 7:7; 1 Sam 14:23; Isa 49:25; Hos 1:7). The "house of Judah" and **the house of Joseph** stand for the southern and northern kingdoms. This instance of the infrequent use of "Joseph" for Israel (2 Sam 19:20; Ps 78:67; 80:1; 81:5; Ezek 37:16; Amos 5:6,15; 6:6) likely hearkens back to the exodus and deliverance imagery surrounding the Joseph narrative alluded to in Zechariah 9:11. The remnant of those northern tribes that go into exile when Samaria falls to the Assyrians in 722 B.C. are restored in accordance with earlier prophecies (Isa 11:11-16; Jer 3:11-18; 31:1-22; Ezek 37:15-22).[254] The promise that Yahweh **restore**s the people because of divine **compassion** (cf. Jer 33:26) may recall the tradition in Hosea that reverses the denial of compassion depicted through the symbolic naming of Hosea's daughter Lo Ruhamah

---

[253]Merrill, *Haggai, Zechariah, Malachi*, p. 274.
[254]Boda, *Haggai, Zechariah*, p. 443.

(Hos 1:6–2:1). The promise that Yahweh answers Israel in time of need appears repeatedly in Isaiah (Isa 30:19; 41:17; 49:8; 58:9; 65:24). This reassurance expects the end of Yahweh's rejection (cf. Lam 2:7; 3:17,31) of the exiles and reverses Yahweh's earlier refusal to listen (Zech 7:13; cf. 13:9). The imagery in verse 7, similar to that in verse 5, connects with the depiction of 9:13 and 15. Not only does Judah **become like mighty men**, but so too does **Ephraim**. Moreover, like Judah, the restoration of Ephraim results in **glad**ness and joy, responses represented with images of **wine** (Ps 104:15) and the remembrance of youth. Because the northern kingdom has gone into captivity before Judah, Ephraim may appear here alone in order to emphasize the total scope of the coming restoration.[255]

**10:8** Yahweh announces the intention to gather and redeem the people in a second exodus. The **signal** (שָׁרַק, šāraq) that Yahweh makes to **gather** the people is some kind of audible noise (Job 27:23; Isa 7:18; Ezek 27:36), perhaps similar to a whistle (cf. ESV, NJB, and NJPS) used to attract the attention of sheep (Judg 5:16). Isaiah also portrays Yahweh making this sound to initiate a return of the people from exile (Isa 5:26). Upon their return, Yahweh once again makes them great and increases their numbers. The verb **redeem** (פָּדָה, pādāh) refers to a transferal of ownership from one to another by means of a payment of some sort.[256] It occurs several times in Deuteronomy in recollection of the deliverance of Israel from Egypt (7:8; 9:26; 13:5; 15:15; 24:18) and thus lays the foundation for a motif of a second exodus and entry into the land through the remainder of the chapter. The exodus event has become a paradigm for all events in which Yahweh intercedes on behalf of Israel. Because of this, Isaiah refers to the restoration of the exilic people as a second exodus (Isa 40:3-5; 43:1-7,14-21; 48:20-22; 51:9-11). Haggai, too, uses this imagery (Hag 2:4-5). Zechariah here shares in that well-established tradition by viewing the eschatological deliverance of Israel in terms of a new or second exodus (see Zech 10:11).[257] The phrase **they will be as numerous as before** reflects the promises to Abraham concerning his descendants (Gen 16:10; 17:2; 22:17; Josh 24:3), the account of the multiplication of Israel in Egypt (Exod

---

[255]McComiskey, "Zechariah," p. 1181.
[256]William B. Coker, "פָּדָה," TWOT, 2:716.
[257]Mason, "The Use of Earlier Biblical Material," p. 87.

1:10,12), and the words of Jacob to Joseph, the father of Ephraim (Gen 48:4). Most significant for this passage is Yahweh's promise made through Jeremiah, "I myself will gather the remnant of my flock out of all the countries where I have driven them and will bring them back to their pasture, where they will be fruitful and increase in number" (23:3; cf. Ezek 36:11).

**10:9** While the NIV (cf. ESV, NASB, and NRSV) translates זָרַע (zāraʿ) with **scatter**, the KJV, NET, and NJPS better reflect the verb's basic meaning, the action of sowing seed in the fields (Gen 26:12; Isa 37:30).[258] The notion of sowing expresses the negative experience of the exile connoted by scattering yet also intimates future hope in a way not suggested by "scatter." Israel has been scattered, that is, sown in hopes of a future harvest.[259] **In distant lands** (see 10:10-11), the people **remember** Yahweh. The verb "remember" (זָכַר, zākar) conveys an active reflection upon the past to create appreciation, commitment, and action (Exod 20:8; Josh 1:13; Esth 9:28; Ps 103:18).[260] In Deuteronomy the word "remember" repeatedly appears in commands for the people to recall Yahweh's acts of deliverance (5:15; 7:18; 8:2,18; 9:7,27; 15:15; 16:3,12; 24:18,22; 32:7). Here the original readers may note an allusion to the meaning of Zechariah's name, "Yahweh remembers." As in verse 7, **their children** are mentioned along with the Ephraimites, for they too experience the blessings missed during the exile.[261] The word **survive** probably should be understood according to the sense of coming to life (cf. "sprout forth" in the NET).[262] First, the reading retains the metaphor of sowing in the first half of the verse. Second, the exilic prophet Ezekiel portrays the exiles as dead (Ezek 33:11-12; 37). Only after remembering Yahweh can Israel once again live as the people of Yahweh and enjoy complete **return** and restoration.[263]

---

[258]Walter C. Kaiser, Jr. "זָרַע," *TWOT*, 1:252.

[259]Meyers and Meyers, *Zechariah 9–14*, p. 216; The concessive and contrastive conjunctions "though" and "yet" in the NIV have no clear Hebrew equivalents; instead, the Hebrew text uses only the simple conjunction "and" (see KJV).

[260]Leslie C. Allen, "זָכַר," *NIDOTTE*, 1:1101-1106.

[261]Meyers and Meyers, *Zechariah 9–14*, p. 219.

[262]The NJB reflects the LXX rendering of the verse, "they will instruct their children and then return."

[263]Merrill, *Haggai, Zechariah, Malachi*, p. 277.

**10:10** Yahweh pledges to **bring** the people **back from Egypt** and **Assyria to Gilead and Lebanon**. Egypt and Assyria represent all nations south and north of Israel. The mention of these traditional enemies of the former northern and southern kingdoms evokes memories of slavery and exile and reverses earlier prophetic oracles in which Egypt and Assyria serve as images of judgment (Isa 7:18; Hos 9:3; 11:5). The two countries also appear together in other texts that speak of the reconstitution of the people of Yahweh after they have been punished in the exile (Isa 11:11,16; 27:13; Hos 11:11; Micah 7:12).[264] Gilead is a hilly, wooded region east of the Jordan River extending from the Arnon to the Yarmuk rivers and bisected by the Jabbok.[265] It becomes the territory of Reuben, Gad, and half the tribe of Manasseh following Israel's victories over the Amorite kings east of the Jordan (Num 21:21-35; 32; Deut 3:12-13). Lebanon, on the other hand, is to the north and northwest of Canaan and is never occupied by Israel.[266] These lands, not originally part of the land of Canaan promised to the Hebrews, are frequent images of fertility and abundance (1 Chr 6:80; S of S 4:1,15; 6:5; Isa 29:17; Jer 22:6; Ezek 31:6; Micah 7:14; Nahum 1:4) and are here images of Yahweh's future blessing. Yahweh brings Israel into these lands, since they have occupied available space in their current province and in the territory occupied by the preexilic kingdoms; consequently, the lands of Gilead and Lebanon have been annexed for the overflow of people.[267] More importantly, the occupation of Gilead and Lebanon represents a reversal of the judgment depicted in Jeremiah 22:6: the beauty and fertility of Judah is such that it can be described as that of Gilead and Lebanon.[268]

**10:11** Verse 11 continues the description of the people's return to the land in language reminiscent of the exodus. Still, the translations reflect this uncertainty regarding the imagery's significance. The NIV and NRSV render the opening line as portraying the return of the Israelites **pass**ing **through** a **sea of trouble**. The ESV, KJV,

---

[264]Additionally, Isaiah boldly portrays the offering of salvation in which Egypt and Assyria share (19:23-25).
[265]Michael D. Coogan, "Gilead," *HBD*, p. 348; K.A. Kitchen, "Gilead," *NBD*, p. 412.
[266]K.A. Kitchen and A.K. Cragg, "Lebanon," *NBD*, pp. 680-681.
[267]Boda, *Haggai, Zechariah*, p. 446.
[268]Mason, "The Use of Earlier Biblical Material in Zechariah 9-14," p. 89.

NASB, and NET, however, render the line by depicting Yahweh, the hero in the epic, as the one who subdues the sea of distress by passing through it.[269] Yahweh **subdues the surging sea** and dries up **the depths of the Nile**. Verse 11 closes as verse 10 begins with mention of Assyria and Egypt, particularly the downfall of **Assyria's pride** (cf. Isa 2:6-21; 10:5-34) and the removal of **Egypt's scepter** (cf. Isa 10:24-27).

**10:12** The promise **I will strengthen them** contains the fourth use in the chapter of the root (גבר, *gbr*) dealing with strength (10:5,6,7,12). The image of strength is here directly linked to Yahweh (**in the LORD**) and thus complements the opening of this chapter that exhorts the community to entreat Yahweh.[270] The idiom of walking (cf. the TNIV's "live securely") about (הלך, *hālak*) occurs frequently in Zechariah for the exercise of dominion (1:10,11; 6:7[3×]) or for obedience to Yahweh (3:7); both concepts are present in this context. The formula **declares the LORD** underscores the divine origin of these words and marks the end of the unit (i.e., chapter 10).

## D. REPORT OF THE REJECTION OF THE SHEPHERD (11:1-17)

### 1. Reinforcing the Warnings (11:1-3)

¹**Open your doors, O Lebanon, / so that fire may devour your cedars! / ²Wail, O pine tree, for the cedar has fallen; / the stately trees are ruined! / Wail, oaks of Bashan; / the dense forest has been cut down! / ³Listen to the wail of the shepherds; / their rich pastures are destroyed! / Listen to the roar of the lions; / the lush thicket of the Jordan is ruined!**

Scholars cannot agree whether 11:1-3 concludes the previous section (10:1-12)[271] or introduces the following section (11:4-17).[272]

---

[269]Petersen, *Zechariah 9–14 and Malachi*, p. 70; Meyers and Meyers, *Zechariah 9–14*, p. 224.

[270]Meyers and Meyers, *Zechariah 9–14*, p. 227.

[271]Baldwin, *Haggai, Zechariah, Malachi*, p. 177; Cohen, *The Twelve Prophets*, p. 313; Mason, "The Use of Earlier Biblical Material in Zechariah 9–14," pp. 89-90.

[272]Meyers and Meyers, *Zechariah 9–14*, p. 238; Sweeney, *The Twelve Prophets*, p. 676.

Structurally, 10:12 ends with a formula ("declares the LORD") that typically ends a unit, and 11:1-2 begins with a combination of imperatives and vocatives ("Open your doors, O Lebanon . . . Wail, O pine tree . . . Wail, oaks of Bashan") that often marks the beginning of a unit (see Zech 3:8; 9:9; 13:7).[273] Conceptually, 11:1-3, linked with 10:10-11 by the words "Lebanon," "brought down/cut down" (יָרַד, yārād), and "pride/thickets" (גָּאוֹן, gā'ôn), enforces the warning of judgment against the enemies of Yahweh and serves as the negative counterpart to Yahweh's deliverance of the people (10:3-12). More importantly, the word "shepherd" (10:2-3; 11:4-5,7-9,15-16) also connects 11:1-3 with both the preceding and following units, suggesting that 11:1-3 functions as a bridge between the two units that depict Yahweh's dissatisfaction with bad leadership (10:2-3; 11:4-14) and its replacement with a more threatening figure (11:15-17).

**11:1-2** In a metaphorical call to mourn, Yahweh utters a progression of imperatives, **Open** and **Wail**, the last of which is repeated. "Wail" (יָלַל, yālal) is often a feature in pronouncements of prophetic judgment (e.g., Isa 13:6; 14:31; 23:1,6,14; Jer 4:8; 48:20; Ezek 30:2), making likely that the poem warns of coming events. In verse 3, the repeated noun "sound" (קוֹל, qôl), which the NIV renders "listen to" (cf. the ESV and NJB), functions similarly to the three imperatives. The **doors** or gates of a city function as protective boundaries against external threats. Here the ironic image of opening the doors allows for the unabated entry of the enemy, portrayed as a devastating forest **fire**.[274] The trees of **Lebanon**, which 10:10 identifies as the place to which Yahweh brings the scattered people, and of Bashan are commanded to wail. The **pine tree** (בְּרוֹשׁ, bərôš)[275] of Lebanon wails for the **stately** cedars have **fallen** and **are ruined**. Likewise, the **oaks of Bashan**, the mountainous region east of the

---

[273]David J. Clark and Howard Hatton, *A Handbook on Zechariah*, UBS Handbook Series (New York: United Bible Societies, 2002), p. 277.

[274]Cohen, *The Twelve Prophets*, p. 313.

[275]The ESV, NASB, and NRSV translate *bərôš* as "cypress," the KJV and NET, as "fir," and the NJB and TNIV, as "juniper." Evidently, the *bərôš* is an evergreen common in Palestine and Lebanon in ancient times. Their size and versatility of use indicate the species of tree may be the Aleppo pine or Phoenician juniper, according to Earl S. Kalland, "בְּרוֹשׁ," *TWOT*, 1:135; Larry L. Walker, "בְּרוֹשׁ/בְּרוֹת," *NIDOTTE*, 1:740-741; cf. Meyers and Meyers, *Zechariah 9–14*, p. 243, who identify the tree as "cypress."

Sea of Galilee known for its fertile plateau with pastures and trees
(Deut 32:14; Ps 22:12; 68:15; Ezek 27:6; 39:18), mourn the **cut**ting
**down** of the **dense forest**.

**11:3** In verse 3, the imagery shifts from trees to **shepherds** and
**lions** and suggests that the trees may represent the leaders who
oppress the people of Judah. All three metaphors, trees (2 Kgs 14:9;
Isa 10:33-34; 14:8; Ezek 17:3-4; 31:3-18; Dan 4:10,23), shepherd (see
on 10:2 above), and lion (Jer 50:44; Ezek 19:5-9; Nahum 2:12),[276] are
applied to kings and rulers elsewhere. Perhaps, the naming of three
types of trees—pine, cedar, and oak—may be linked to the three shepherds mentioned in 11:8. Thus, the poem depicts the destruction of
those who mislead Israel. The verb שָׁדַד (*šādad*), translated **ruined**
and **destroyed** in the NIV, appears three times in 11:2-3 to describe
the ruin and destruction of these leaders whose arrogance is noted
in the stately cedars and oaks (Isa 2:13), the **rich** (a word from the
same Hebrew root as "stately" in verse 2) **pastures**, and the "pride
of Jordan" (see KJV, NASB, and NJB), a phrase referring to the **lush**
vegetation that once existed on the banks of the lower **Jordan** River
(cf. Jer 12:5; 49:9; 50:44) and a word (גָּאוֹן, *gā'ôn*) that links this verse
with 10:11.

## 2. A Commission for Zechariah (11:4-17)

⁴This is what the LORD my God says: "Pasture the flock marked
for slaughter. ⁵Their buyers slaughter them and go unpunished.
Those who sell them say, 'Praise the LORD, I am rich!' Their own
shepherds do not spare them. ⁶For I will no longer have pity on the
people of the land," declares the LORD. "I will hand everyone over
to his neighbor and his king. They will oppress the land, and I will
not rescue them from their hands."

⁷So I pastured the flock marked for slaughter, particularly the
oppressed of the flock. Then I took two staffs and called one Favor
and the other Union, and I pastured the flock. ⁸In one month I got
rid of the three shepherds.

---

[276]Lions were fairly common in Canaan in Old Testament times, according to G.S. Cansdace, "Animals of the Bible," *NBD*, p. 42, and Ilse U.
Köhler-Rollefson, "Lion," *HBD*, p. 564. Jeremiah speaks of lions emerging
from the thickets of Jordan (49:19; 50:44).

The flock detested me, and I grew weary of them [9]and said, "I will not be your shepherd. Let the dying die, and the perishing perish. Let those who are left eat one another's flesh."

[10]Then I took my staff called Favor and broke it, revoking the covenant I had made with all the nations. [11]It was revoked on that day, and so the afflicted of the flock who were watching me knew it was the word of the LORD.

[12]I told them, "If you think it best, give me my pay; but if not, keep it." So they paid me thirty pieces of silver.

[13]And the LORD said to me, "Throw it to the potter"-the handsome price at which they priced me! So I took the thirty pieces of silver and threw them into the house of the LORD to the potter.

[14]Then I broke my second staff called Union, breaking the brotherhood between Judah and Israel.

[15]Then the LORD said to me, "Take again the equipment of a foolish shepherd. [16]For I am going to raise up a shepherd over the land who will not care for the lost, or seek the young, or heal the injured, or feed the healthy, but will eat the meat of the choice sheep, tearing off their hoofs.

[17]"Woe to the worthless shepherd, / who deserts the flock! / May the sword strike his arm and his right eye! / May his arm be completely withered, / his right eye totally blinded!"

Zechariah 11:4-17, one of the more enigmatic passages in the Old Testament, consists of a symbolic prophetic action.[277] This genre, found earlier in 6:9-15, describes a symbolic prophetic action that conveys an abstract message through some physical activity, whether the action is implied or performed (see also Isa 20:1-6; Jer 13:1-11; 19:1-13; 27:1–28:17; 32:6-15; Ezek 4:1-17; 5:1-12; 12:2-5; 24:5-27). This symbolic dramatization contains the commission for Zechariah to act and its rationale (Zech 11:4-6), the execution of the commission (11:7-14), and a second commission that serves as an interpretation of the action's significance (11:15-17). Whereas chapters 9 and 10 announce a positive future for the people, chapter 11

[277]Sweeney, *Twelve Prophets*, p. 681; Meyers and Meyers, *Zechariah 9–14*, p. 299; for alternative identifications, see Boda, *Haggai, Zechariah*, p. 461, and Petersen, *Zechariah 9–14 and Malachi*, pp. 88-89.

explains why that future is necessary: irresponsible leaders have neg-atively affected the community (cf. 10:2-3).[278]

**11:4-5** Yahweh commands the prophet to act as shepherd (רְעֵה, *rā'āh*) for the postexilic community depicted as **the flock marked for slaughter** (cf. Ps 44:11,22). Yahweh is identified as **my God**, a title emphasizing the intimate relationship between Yahweh and the prophet[279] and anticipating the affirmation "Yahweh is my God" uttered by those that survive the refining fire in 13:9. The shepherd metaphor appears frequently in the chapter (11:4-5,7-9,15-16; see on Zech 9:16 and 10:2 above) and has figured prominently in Jeremiah and Ezekiel (see especially, Jer 23:1-8 and Ezek 34:1-31). Outside of verse 7, only Jeremiah (7:32; 12:3; 19:6) uses the word "slaughter" (הֲרֵגָה, *hărēgāh*); on two occasions (7:32; 19:6), *hărēgāh* is connected with the destruction of wicked within the community. Here ruthless rulers have brought the people to ruin. The expression **their buyers** designates foreign authorities to whom the Jewish leaders "sold" their subjects for personal gain.[280] The leaders of the people (**those who sell them**) have looked to their own interests (**Praise the LORD, I am rich!**), thereby failing to shepherd the people correctly and leaving the people vulnerable to abuse from "buyers."

**11:6** Verse 6 clarifies the meaning of the image regarding the slaughter of the flock: **the people** experience oppression from **neighbors and** their **king** without any deliverance from Yahweh. This explanation from Yahweh appears in first person speech: **I will no longer have pity . . . I will hand everyone over . . . and I will not rescue them.** The NIV omits the interjection "behold" (הִנֵּה, *hinnēh*) that follows the oracle formula (**declares the LORD**); the word *hinnēh* (see on 9:9 above), appearing here and in 9:16, typically calls atten-tion to an action about to be announced. The lack of divine pity indicates that Yahweh holds responsible to some degree both the people (at least those who reject the prophet) and the leaders, a notion found also in verse 8.[281] The flock experiences oppression from local circles ("neighbor") and from the ruling class ("kings").

---

[278]Meyers and Meyers, *Zechariah 9–14*, pp. 301-303.

[279]Boda, *Haggai, Zechariah*, p. 462.

[280]Baldwin, *Haggai, Zechariah, Malachi*, p. 180.

[281]Mason, "The Use of Earlier Biblical Material in Zechariah 9–14," pp. 100-101.

The word **oppress** (cf. the TNIV's "devastate") expresses the impli-cation of the word "strike" (cf. "smite" in the KJV and NASB) or "beat" (cf. "break to bits" in the NJPS). Here the image depicts the conflict between people that leads to their destroying one other (cf. Deut 1:44; 2 Chr 15:6).[282] Such social injustice and anarchy within the early Persian period is indicated earlier in Zechariah 7:8-10, 8:10, and 8:16-17, and these concerns persist into the time of Nehemiah (5:1,15).[283]

**11:7** Beginning in verse 7, the prophet describes his actions in response to the commission from Yahweh (vv. 4-6). The first person pronoun refers to Zechariah, who acts as a shepherd for the **flock marked for slaughter** on behalf of the sheep merchants. The NIV translates the MT as **the oppressed of the flock** in verse 7 and "the afflicted of the flock" in verse 11. The NRSV, however, reads "sheep merchants" (cf. ESV and NJB) following the LXX which combines the two words present in the MT into one word. The reading "sheep merchants" is preferred since the LXX reading makes better sense in the context of chapter 11: the sheep merchants, then, are the "buyers" mentioned in verse 5 and those who pay the prophet thir-ty pieces of silver in verses 11-13.[284] Then the prophet describes his naming of **two staffs**. The first staff, translated **Favor** by ESV, NASB, NIV, and NRSV, refers to the blessing, stability, and peace the com-munity has enjoyed within its covenant with Yahweh (cf. v. 10; Ps 90:17). Verse 14 indicates the second staff, translated **Union** by the ESV, NASB, and NIV, refers to the relationship between Israel and Judah. This action of naming the two staffs is reminiscent of Ezekiel 37:15-28 in which that prophet writes names on two sticks, "Belonging to Judah" and "Belonging to Joseph." The joining of the two sticks in Ezekiel depicts the reuniting of the two kingdoms, but the breaking of the two staffs in Zechariah (vv. 10-11,14) apparently reverses the symbolic action in Ezekiel.[285]

---

[282]Elsewhere the image of "beating" conveys the scenario of world peace (Isa 2:4; Micah 4:3).

[283]Boda, *Haggai, Zechariah,* p. 463; Ollenburger, "Zechariah," p. 821.

[284]For a detailed argument for "sheep merchants," see Thomas J. Finley, "The Sheep Merchants of Zechariah 11," *GTJ* 3 (1982): 51-65.

[285]Mason, "The Use of Earlier Biblical Material in Zechariah 9–14," pp. 105-107. On the contrasts between Ezekiel 37 and Zechariah 11, see Katrina J.A. Larkin, *The Eschatology of Second Zechariah: A Study of the*

**11:8-9** In verse 8, the prophet describes the dismissal **of three shepherds**, the hostility of **the flock**, and the resignation of the prophet as **shepherd**. **One month** refers to a short period of instability rather than an actual period of around thirty days. The number three often implies completeness or totality and thus may implicate all those who misuse their positions of leadership.[286] Like the trees in verses 1-2, the three shepherds may represent a general group rather than specific individuals.[287] Although most who attempt to identify the three shepherds propose certain priests or kings,[288] several factors suggest that these three shepherds represent false prophets.[289] First, 10:3 associates the lack of a shepherd with the efforts of the people to seek guidance through the methods of false prophecy (e.g., teraphim, divination, and dreaming). Second, the shepherds are described as "foolish" and "worthless" (11:15,17), vocabulary used elsewhere for false prophets whose words lead to sinful behavior (Jer 4:22; 14:14; Hos 9:7). Third, the oracular formulas, "the LORD my God says" (v. 4) and "the LORD said to me" (vv. 13,15), and the affirmation that the prophet's actions reflect the word of Yahweh (v. 11) demonstrate a concern for a true prophet who speaks the word of Yahweh. In this way, chapter 11 depicts Zechariah as the true prophet, commanded by Yahweh to shepherd the people. As a result, the people **detest** the prophet who decides to quit acting as shepherd for the people and thus abandons the people to the consequences of their rejection of him: the people destroy one another (cf. v. 6). This self-destruction within the community recalls the description of social injustice in verse 6.

**11:10-11** When the prophet abandons his role as shepherd, he breaks the **staff called Favor**, an act signifying the removal of the blessings of the Mosaic covenant evidenced in Judah's exile. In this sense, the breaking of the staff provides a retrospective explanation of the community's present situation in view of their past.[290] The

---

*Formation of a Mantological Wisdom Anthology,* CBET 6 (Kampen: Kok Pharos, 1994), pp. 118-123.

[286]Meyers and Meyers, *Zechariah 9–14*, p. 265; "Three, Third," *DBI*, pp. 866-867.

[287]For summaries of proposed identifications made in the history of interpretation, see Baldwin, *Haggai, Zechariah, Malachi*, pp. 181-183.

[288]E.g., Sweeney, *The Twelve Prophets*, p. 680.

[289]Meyers and Meyers, *Zechariah 9–14*, p. 265.

[290]Ibid, p. 303.

prophet speaks with the **I** of Yahweh, implying that the shepherd acts with divine authority,[291] since only Yahweh can repudiate **the covenant** (cf. Lev 26:44; Judg 2:1).[292] No covenant with **all the nations** or "all the peoples" (see ESV, NASB, NRSV, NJB, and NJPS) is attested within the Old Testament, although "peoples" does on occasion refer to various groups that comprise Israel (Gen 27:29; 48:4; 49:10; 1 Kgs 22:28; Isa 3:13; cf. Zech 8:12).[293] Even though the time designation **on that day** simply identifies the time of the revocation with that of the breaking of the staff, the phrase often appears in eschatological contexts (e.g., Zech 2:11; 3:10; 9:16; 12:3,4,6,8,9,11; 13:1,2,4; 14:4,8,9,13,20,21) and thus accentuates the gravity of the situation.[294] The sheep merchants (see on verse 7 above), watching the prophet, recognize that the breaking of the first staff illustrates the will of Yahweh.

**11:12** The prophet requests a wage for his service over the flock, using language that requires the sheep merchants to offer a qualitative assessment of his work as shepherd. The phrase translated **if you think it best** expresses a familiar idiom (rendered more literally in the NASB, "if it is good in your sight") for someone's approval or disapproval (see Gen 16:6; 20:15; Josh 9:25; Judg 10:15; 19:24; 1 Sam 1:23; 11:10; 14:36,40; 2 Sam 15:26; 19:38; 24:22; 2 Kgs 10:5; Esth 8:5,8; Jer 26:14; 40:4) or for Yahweh's judgment of an event or behavior (see Deut 6:18; 12:28; 1 Sam 3:18; 2 Sam 10:12; 2 Kgs 20:3; 1 Chr 19:13; 2 Chr 14:2; Mal 2:17). The sheep merchants weigh out a severance pay of **thirty pieces of silver**.[295] The word **paid** in the NIV renders a phrase meaning "weighed out the wages." The verb "weigh" (שָׁקַל, šāqal) generally refers to the weighing out of silver for purchases (Gen 23:16; Isa 46:6; Jer 32:9-10) or for penalties (Exod 22:17; 1 Kgs 20:39). This practice of weighing out silver continues into the postexilic period, even though the Persians introduce the use of stamped coinage.[296] The noun "wages for work" (שָׂכָר,

---

[291]F. Horst, *Die zwölf kleinen Propheten: Nahum bis Maleachi*, HAT 14 (Tübingen: J.C.B. Mohr, 1964), pp. 251-252.

[292]Mason, "The Use of Earlier Biblical Material in Zechariah 9–14," p. 108.

[293]Meyers and Meyers, *Zechariah 9–14*, pp. 270-271.

[294]Petersen, *Zechariah 9–14 and Malachi*, p. 96.

[295]On the citation of Zech 11:12-13 in Matt 27:9-10, see Ham, *Coming King*, pp. 47-69.

[296]Baldwin, *Haggai, Zechariah, Malachi*, p. 184.

*śākār*)²⁹⁷ is a cognate of the verb form שָׂכַר (*śākar*) used in Judges 18:4 for the payment of a priest-prophet.

The MT text designates the wage itself as "thirty of silver," but the presence of the verb *šāqal* implies the shekel is in view (i.e., "thirty shekels of silver" as in the NRSV). However, the relative value of this amount is uncertain. Both biblical and nonbiblical data indicate that the amount is substantial or, at the least, appropriate for the shepherd's wage.²⁹⁸ Exodus 21:32 demands as restitution thirty shekels of silver for the death of a Hebrew slave. The *Code of Hammurabi* 206-208²⁹⁹ requires a payment of approximately twenty-five shekels of silver for causing the accidental death of a member of the aristocracy and seventeen shekels of silver for causing the death of a commoner. Nehemiah 5:15 represents forty shekels of silver as a burdensome tax. Nevertheless, other extrabiblical data suggests that the ambiguity of a cuneiform sign of a Sumerian number meaning either "thirty" or "half" gives rise to "thirty pieces of silver" becoming an idiomatic expression of a trivial amount in other ancient Near Eastern languages,³⁰⁰ an assessment confirmed by the shepherd's comment in verse 13.³⁰¹ Both the request and payment are ironic, since the breaking of the staff, understood as the word of Yahweh (v. 11), advocates Zechariah as a true prophet, and true prophets do not receive payment for their prophecies (cf. 1 Kgs 22:1-18; Amos 7:12-13).

**11:13** A parenthetical statement in verse 13 also describes the shepherd's wage; the NIV translates as **the handsome price** a phrase meaning something like "magnificence of honor." The phrase's sarcasm draws attention to the inadequate value the sheep merchants have placed on the shepherd's actions. The ironic sense of the "handsome price" is supported by both the flock's regard for the shepherd ("they detested me" in v. 8) and the shepherd's refusal to accept the silver. Yahweh directs the prophet to **throw** the thirty

---

²⁹⁷*HALOT*, p. 1331; *śākār* appears elsewhere in Zechariah only in 8:10.

²⁹⁸Baldwin, *Haggai, Zechariah, Malachi*, p. 184; Sweeney, *Twelve Prophets*, p. 681; and Meyers and Meyers, *Zechariah 9–14*, pp. 275-276.

²⁹⁹*ANET*, p. 175.

³⁰⁰Erica Reiner, "Thirty Pieces of Silver," *JAOS* 88 (1968): 189-190.

³⁰¹Keil, *Minor Prophets*, p. 368; Petersen, *Zechariah 9–14*, p. 97, and Lipiński, "Recherches sur le livre de Zacharie," pp. 53-55, understand the amount as a trifling amount.

pieces of silver **to the potter**. The throwing (שָׁלַךְ, *šālak*) of the silver **into the house of** Yahweh indicates the shepherd's contempt for the payment and also conveys the notion of divine judgment.[302] Like Deuteronomy 9:17-21, where Moses throws down the two tablets of the covenant in order to represent the breaking of covenant and the resultant judgment of Yahweh, the actions of the shepherd represent the annulment of Yahweh's covenant with Judah.

According to the MT, the prophet throws the silver to the potter (יוֹצֵר, *yôṣēr*). However, the Peshitta and Aramaic Targum read "treasury" (אוֹצָר, *'ôṣār*), a reading replicated in several modern translations including the NRSV ("Throw it into the treasury").[303] Matthew 27:5-6 seems to support this second reading as it portrays the chief priests' refusal to put into the treasury the money that Judas casts into the temple. Still the natural reading of verse 13 remains preferable: the silver is thrown to the potter, who is in the temple. The potter's presence in the temple, moreover, may be explained by the need for new earthen vessels used in sacrificial rituals (e.g., Lev 6:28). Rabbinic tradition (*b. Yoma* 21a and *b. Zebah* 96a) also describes the disposal of broken shards used in sacrificial rituals within the temple. The prophet goes to the temple so that his actions may be done in both the presence of the people and of Yahweh. Since the potter's presence is associated with brokenness and rejection,[304] that the shepherd throws the silver to the potter represents the rejection of Yahweh by the sheep merchants (and perhaps Yahweh's rejection of them).[305]

---

[302]Robert B. Chisholm, "שָׁלַךְ," *NIDOTTE*, 4:127; see Josh 10:11; Neh 9:11; Ps 51:11; 102:10; Amos 4:3; Jonah 2:3.

[303]Charles C. Torrey, "The Foundry of the Second Temple at Jerusalem," *JBL* 55 (1936): 256-257, and Otto Eissfeldt, "Eine Einschmelzstelle am Tempel zu Jerusalem," in idem., *Kleine Schriften*, ed. by Rudolf Sellheim and Fritz Maass (Tübingen: J.C.B. Mohr [Paul Siebeck], 1962–79), pp. 107-109, argue that *yôṣēr* should be understood as a technical term for "founder," one who melts down gifts of gold and silver given to the temple, according to the Persian practice described in Herodotus (*Hist.* 3.96). *HALOT*, p. 429, lists "caster (who melts down metal vessels and tools into ingots)" as one of the meanings for *yôṣēr*; so too W.H. Schmidt, "צר," in *TLOT*, 2:566, and the NJB follows this alternative proposal: "Throw it to the smelter."

[304]Merrill, *Haggai, Zechariah, Malachi*, pp. 298-299; James L. Kelso, *The Ceramic Vocabulary of the Old Testament*, BASORSupp 5-6 (New Haven, CT: American Schools of Oriental Research, 1948), p. 9.

[305]Ham, *Coming King*, pp. 56-57.

**11:14** Then the prophet breaks his **second staff called Union**, representing the national division **between Israel and Judah**. Their relationship is described by the word **brotherhood** (or "family bond" in the TNIV), a term that appears nowhere else in the Old Testament. The breaking of the second staff reverses Ezekiel's tying together two sticks (Ezekiel 37) and indicates a delay in the reunification of the northern and southern kingdoms anticipated in Zechariah 9 and 10.[306]

**11:15-16** Yahweh then instructs the prophet, **"Take again the equipment of a foolish shepherd,"** and explains the reason for such action. Although the particular equipment is not listed, the symbolic actions reported in verses 10 and 14 may suggest that the broken staffs comprise the equipment of a foolish shepherd.[307] More important is the shepherd's description as "foolish" (אֱוִלִי, 'ĕwilî), a characterization that implies a moral corruption and deficiency (Ps 107:17), a contempt for wisdom and discipline (Prov 1:7), a refusal to make amends for evil (Prov 14:9), and a disregard for Yahweh's law (Hos 4:6), fear (Prov 1:7), and counsel (Prov 12:15; 15:5).[308] By this symbolic action, Yahweh states the intention to raise up another shepherd. The NIV omits the interjection "behold" (הִנֵּה, hinnēh) that calls special attention to the action about to be announced (cf. v. 6). Both Jeremiah 23:4 and Ezekiel 34:23 announce the same intention of Yahweh **to raise up a shepherd**. Jeremiah states that the sheep no longer need to be frightened or lost. Ezekiel identifies this shepherd as Yahweh's servant David. However, this hope is dashed as Yahweh informs the prophet that the coming shepherd does not **care for** (פָּקַד, pāqad; see on 10:3, where the word is translated "punish") **the lost**, **young**, and **injured** among the flock. Instead, this shepherd's actions, likened to that of a wild animal tearing apart its prey, undo the strong of the flock. He does not **feed the healthy** sheep, but he devours all the available **meat** from the fat or **choice** members of the flock, even meat from the **hoofs**. This behavior contradicts that of the good shepherd of verse 7 who protects the vulnerable; it is also worse than that of the negligent shepherds of verse

---

[306]Mason, "The Use of Earlier Biblical Material in Zechariah 9–14," pp. 105-107.

[307]Petersen, *Zechariah 9–14 and Malachi*, p. 98.

[308]Boda, *Haggai, Zechariah*, p. 466; Louis Goldberg, "אֱוִיל," *TWOT*, 1:19.

5. Those shepherds have failed to protect the flock; this shepherd is consuming his own flock as do the "shepherds of Israel" described in Ezekiel 34:3-4.[309]

**11:17** Verse 17 is a woe oracle exhibiting the standard form of a woe oracle: the interjection **woe** (הוֹי, *hôy*) is followed by an identification of the recipient of Yahweh's wrath and a description of their reprehensible behavior (e.g., Isa 5:11-14,18-19,20,21,22-25; 10:1-3; 28:1-4; 29:1-4,15; 31:1-5; Amos 5:18-20; 6:1-7; Micah 2:1-5; Hab 2:6-17; Zeph 2:5-7). The interjection *hôy* emphasizes the imminent demise of **the worthless shepherd**. It is used five times in Habakkuk (2:6,9,12,15,19) to initiate judgment speeches on the wicked and elsewhere for the cry of mourning heard at funerals (1 Kgs 13:30; Jer 22:18-19; Isa 1:4; Amos 5:16). The worthless shepherd **deserts the flock** and so is deserving of punishment that makes protection of the flock impossible, the striking of the **arm and** the **right eye** with **the sword** (cf. Ezek 30:21-22; Zech 13:7). This woe oracle complements 11:1-3, another poetic passage that also announces destruction of shepherds.[310]

## VI. THE SECOND ORACLE (12:1–14:21)

Like Zechariah 9:1, 12:1 begins with the word "oracle" (מַשָּׂא, *maśśā'*), translated "prophecy" in the TNIV. The designation *maśśā'* generally indicates a particular type of prophetic pronouncement (see on 9:1 above),[311] and here it describes the relationship between Zechariah 12–14 and the preceding material in Zechariah 1–8 and 9–11. The oracles of 9–11 and 12–14 affirm the continuing validity of the previous prophecy of Zechariah 1–8 to the situation they address. Specifically, they reiterate the intended actions of Yahweh (e.g., Yahweh's disposal of leaders who misrule the people) and the appropriate response of the people (e.g., their escape from Jerusalem before its destruction in order to participate in its later purification). In addition, Zechariah 12–14 restates much of 9–11,

---

[309]Boda, *Haggai, Zechariah*, p. 466.
[310]Meyers and Meyers, *Zechariah 9–14*, p. 304.
[311]Richard D. Weis, "Oracle," *ABD*, 5:28-29; Floyd, "The מַשָּׂא (*maśśā'*) as a Type of Prophetic Book," pp. 401-422.

doing so with greater intensity, indicated in part by the increased use of the phrase "on that day" that appears sixteen times in the three chapters. Moreover, 12–14 advances beyond the impasse of the worthless shepherd in 11:15-17 that threatens the hopes of restoration in 9–10.[312] Zechariah 12:2–13:6 recounts the fulfillment of 9:1–11:17, including both the deliverance of Judah in 9:1–10:12 and the crisis of leadership in 11:1-17. Similar to 11:15-17, 13:7-9 envisions Yahweh raising up and then deposing a tyrannical leader. Chapter 14 envisions the outcome of what 9:1–11:7 anticipates: the end of international conflict, the end of foreign domination, the end of oppressive leadership, and the restoration of Yahweh's people. Furthermore, 14:1-21 portrays the ordeal by which Jerusalem is destroyed then restored, following the pattern of exile and restoration in Zechariah 1–8. The second *maśśā'* (Zechariah 12–14) also incorporates other types of prophetic material, specifically a prophecy of punishment against foreign nations (12:1–13:6) and two prophecies of salvation (13:7-9 and 14:1-21). Therefore, Zechariah 9–14 shows that Yahweh is transforming the leadership that oppresses the people and the situations that threaten their existence, by depicting the demise of Judah's present leadership, the purification of the people through their present experiences, and the divine intervention that results in the universal recognition of Yahweh.

## A. PROPHECY AGAINST JERUSALEM'S ENEMIES (12:1–13:9)

### An Oracle

[1]This is the word of the LORD concerning Israel. The LORD, who stretches out the heavens, who lays the foundation of the earth, and who forms the spirit of man within him, declares: [2]"I am going to make Jerusalem a cup that sends all the surrounding peoples reeling. Judah will be besieged as well as Jerusalem. [3]On that day, when all the nations of the earth are gathered against her, I will make Jerusalem an immovable rock for all the nations. All who try to move it will injure themselves. [4]On that day I will strike every horse with panic and its rider with madness," declares the LORD. "I will keep a watchful eye over the house of Judah, but I will blind

---

[312]Floyd, *Minor Prophets*, pp. 505-508.

all the horses of the nations. ⁵Then the leaders of Judah will say in their hearts, 'The people of Jerusalem are strong, because the LORD Almighty is their God.'

⁶"On that day I will make the leaders of Judah like a firepot in a woodpile, like a flaming torch among sheaves. They will consume right and left all the surrounding peoples, but Jerusalem will remain intact in her place.

⁷"The LORD will save the dwellings of Judah first, so that the honor of the house of David and of Jerusalem's inhabitants may not be greater than that of Judah. ⁸On that day the LORD will shield those who live in Jerusalem, so that the feeblest among them will be like David, and the house of David will be like God, like the Angel of the LORD going before them. ⁹On that day I will set out to destroy all the nations that attack Jerusalem.

¹⁰"And I will pour out on the house of David and the inhabitants of Jerusalem a spiritᵃ of grace and supplication. They will look onᵇ me, the one they have pierced, and they will mourn for him as one mourns for an only child, and grieve bitterly for him as one grieves for a firstborn son. ¹¹On that day the weeping in Jerusalem will be great, like the weeping of Hadad Rimmon in the plain of Megiddo. ¹²The land will mourn, each clan by itself, with their wives by themselves: the clan of the house of David and their wives, the clan of the house of Nathan and their wives, ¹³the clan of the house of Levi and their wives, the clan of Shimei and their wives, ¹⁴and all the rest of the clans and their wives.

ᵃ12:10 Or the Spirit　　ᵇ10 Or to

**12:1** A superscription consisting of the term **oracle** (מַשָּׂא, maśśā') followed by the introductory phrase **the word of the LORD** appears also in Zechariah 9:1 and Malachi 1:1, a combination unique to these three texts (see Nahum 1:1, Hab 1:1, and Mal 1:1 on maśśā'). Despite this similarity, the three passages differ. Malachi 1:1 identifies Israel as the subject of the oracle and Malachi as its recipient. Neither Zechariah 9:1 nor 12:1 identifies a subject or recipient for the oracle. Zechariah 9:1 describes the word of Yahweh as "against" (בְּ, bᵉ) the land of Hadrach; the present text states that the oracle is **concerning** (עַל, 'al) **Israel**, a designation which, given the following focus on Jerusalem and Judah, must here refer to the whole people of Yahweh rather than the tribes of the former northern kingdom.

The opening of the oracle consists of a hymnic identification of Yahweh who makes the declaration that follows. It uses three participles to describe Yahweh as the one **who stretches out the heavens, who lays the foundation of the earth, and who forms the spirit of man within him.** The presence of participles implies that Yahweh has a continuing creative ability. These are not simply past acts done by Yahweh but something now being accomplished.[313] The first two actions are frequent descriptions of Yahweh's creative power (Job 9:8; 38:4; Ps 18:9; 102:25; 104:2,5; 144:5; Prov 3:19; Isa 40:22; 42:5; 44:24; 45:12; 48:13; 51:13,16; Jer 10:12; 51:15). Especially significant for the context here is the appearance of both phrases in Isaiah 51:13-16, a passage that precedes an oracle with a theme similar to the present passage. Jerusalem, drunk from the cup of God's wrath, no longer has to drink from it, since Yahweh takes that cup from her hands and gives it to her tormenters who walked over her. The third phrase ("who forms the spirit in human beings" in the TNIV) alludes to the imparting of the breath of life to humans during the creation (Gen 2:7). Its appropriateness here anticipates verse 10 in which Yahweh pours out a spirit of grace and supplication on the house of David and the inhabitants of Jerusalem. The three phrases of the hymn speak the cosmic and personal creative powers of Yahweh, and together they remind the recipient of Yahweh's power to bring about what follows and benevolent concern in doing so.

**12:2-3** Verse 2 begins with the interjection "behold" (הִנֵּה, *hinnēh*), not translated in the NIV. It underlines the significance of the statement it introduces. Of the sixty-three appearances of it in the Minor Prophets, twenty-three occur in Zechariah. In general, the word either makes vivid a visionary element (Zech 1:8,11,18; 2:1,3; 4:2; 5:1,7,9; 6:1,12) or introduces a future prediction (2:9,10; 3:8,9; 8:7; 9:4,9; 11:6,16; 12:2; 14:1). A series of promises cast as first person statements by Yahweh throughout the section speak of the future empowerment of Jerusalem and Judah (12:3,4[3×],6,9-10; 13:2[2×]). The theme of war victory begun in chapters 9–10 is now localized in Jerusalem, no doubt in anticipation of the return of the exiles spoken of earlier (2:3-7; 8:4-8).[314] Yahweh makes **Jerusalem a**

---

[313]Ollenburger, "Zechariah," p. 824.
[314]Baldwin, *Haggai, Zechariah, Malachi*, p. 187.

**cup that sends all the surrounding** nations **reeling.**[315] The cup imagery in this context reverses the common Old Testament depiction of Yahweh's overpowering judgment as a cup that the wicked of Israel or Judah are forced to drink (Ps 75:8; Isa 51:17,22; Jer 25:15,17,28; 51:7; Ezek 23:31-33; Hab 2:16). Here, Jerusalem is the cup which the nations must imbibe. Significant nuances of the cup imagery play out in verse 3. Just as the intoxicated individual ironically initiates his or her own humiliation, the nations also begin their humiliation by gathering against Jerusalem and Judah and seeking to capture (**move**) her. The nations, like the drunken person, begin their activity with confidence, but eventually are overcome.[316] The nations drink the cup when they lay siege to Jerusalem and Judah but experience Yahweh's action on behalf of the people **on that day** (Zech 12:3-4,6,8-9,11; 13:1-2,4; 14:1,5-9,13,20-21), a phrase properly understood as the Old Testament's "day of the LORD" (see comments on Zeph 1:7). Yahweh makes Jerusalem an **immovable rock** (NIV) or a "heavy stone" (see ESV, NASB, NRSV; cf. "burdensome stone" in the KJV and "heavy burden" in the NET).[317] Although the Assyrians and Babylonians have been able to deport large segments of the populations of Israel and Judah, Yahweh promises that now the people are so "heavy" (i.e., strong and substantial) that no enemy nation is able to move them. Those who attempt to do so **injure themselves**. The vocabulary and syntax of the verse indicates the injury is a bloody gash. The only other uses of the verb "injure" (שָׂרַט, *śāraṭ*) and its cognates outside of this verse (Lev 19:28; 21:5)

---

[315]Ollenburger, "Zechariah," p. 826, and Petersen, *Zechariah 9–14 and Malachi*, p. 111, note that the noun used here for "cup" (סַף, *saph*) is not normally used in contexts that use the cup metaphor. In view of the following image of Jerusalem as an immovable stone, they suggest that a second homophonic root meaning "threshold" (see also NEB) is in play here (see such uses in Judg 19:27; 1 Kgs 14:17; 2 Chr 3:17). Arguing against this theory, however, are the multiple Old Testament uses of *saph* for basins or bowls (Exod 12:22; 2 Sam 17:28; 1 Kgs 7:50; 2 Kgs 12:13; Jer 52:19) and the image of reeling (רַעַל, *ra'al*) here and in Isa 51:17, a verse that also speaks of the cup (כּוֹס, *kōs*) of Yahweh's wrath. The similarities between verse 2 and Isaiah 51 argue for understanding *saph* and *kōs* as simple synonyms, according to Meyers and Meyers, *Zechariah 9–14*, p. 313.

[316]*DBI*, p. 186.

[317]The prophet has already made extensive use of stone imagery (3:9; 4:7,10; 5:8).

denote a cutting, and the verbal construction found here, an expression combining two different verb forms (an infinitive with an imperfect), is a common way to mark emphasis or intensity.[318]

**12:4** Yahweh promises to **strike** (נָכָה, *nākah*) **every horse with panic** (תִּמָּהוֹן, *timmāhôn*) **and its rider with madness** (שִׁגָּעוֹן, *šiggā'ôn*); such language is reminiscent of Yahweh's victory over Pharaoh (Exod 15:1,19,21). In addition, Yahweh promises to **keep a watchful eye over Judah** yet, in a touch of irony, strike the eyes of the nation's **horses** with **blind**ness (עִוָּרוֹן, *'iwwārôn*). Deuteronomy 28:28 is the only other text in the Old Testament where these three maladies, panic, madness, and blindness (rhyming words in Hebrew), and the verb "strike" (*nākah*) appear together. In Deuteronomy, these judgments are pronounced upon those in the covenant community who break covenant;[319] now they are turned against Judah's enemies.[320]

**12:5 Then the leaders of Judah** recognize that the power of Yahweh Almighty who humbles the horse and its rider (cf. Zech 10:5) strengthens **the people of Jerusalem**. The distinction between Judah and Jerusalem in verses 5 and 7 may indicate either a present rivalry or potential rivalry between the inhabitants of Jerusalem, including the priesthood and Davidic house, and those in the outlying areas of Judah.[321] The NIV and NET translate the Hebrew noun אַלּוּף ('*allûph*) as "leaders" (cf. "governors" in the KJV), but the ESV, NASB, NRSV, and TNIV render it "clans." The contexts in which its twelve preexilic uses occur (Gen 36:15,16,17,18,19,21,29,30,40,43; Exod 15:15) make it difficult to ascertain whether '*allûph*, like its related noun אֶלֶף ('*eleph*), refers to a clan within a nation or to the leader or chief of a large unit. Its postexilic uses outside of Zechariah (1 Chr 1:51,54), however, indicate "chief" or "leader" is in view here as in Zechariah 9:7 and 12:6. Nevertheless, it is probably significant that the prophet has chosen a term that links the leader intrinsically to the family group. Just as the elders represent the

[318]Boda, *Haggai, Zechariah*, p. 483; Petersen, *Zechariah 9–14 and Malachi*, p. 112; *IBHS*, pp. 585-586; GKC, p. 342.

[319]Meyers and Meyers, *Zechariah 9–14*, p. 319; Petersen, *Zechariah 9–14 and Malachi*, p. 114; Harry F. van Rooy, "תמה," *NIDOTTE*, 4:302; Ronald F. Youngblood, "תִּמָּהוֹן," *TWOT*, 2:972.

[320]Hahlen, "Equine Imagery," pp. 257-258.

[321]Ollenburger, "Zechariah," p. 826.

tribes of Israel on several occasions (see Exod 3:16; 12:21; 19:7; Deut 5:23; 31:28; Josh 7:6; 24:1; 2 Sam 5:3), so now the "leaders" or "chiefs" represent the whole of Judah.[322]

**12:6** Verse 6 offers two images for the destruction that **the leaders of Judah** inflict on the surrounding peoples, that is, the same group Yahweh sends reeling in verse 2 with the cup of Jerusalem. The leaders are **like a firepot** or a blazing pot (see ESV and NRSV) **in a woodpile**. The significance of this image is self-evident, but its magnitude may be greater than the translations connote. Even though the noun עֵץ ('ēṣ) may mean "wood," that meaning is an extension of its basic meaning "tree."[323] If the plural form of the noun indicates the author refers to trees rather than to pieces of wood,[324] then this image provides a true parallel to the second, **a flaming torch among sheaves**. The first image communicates destruction among forests (cf. Judg 9:15; Ezek 20:47; Joel 1:19) and the second destruction among cultivated crops and cut stalks of grain (Amos 2:13; Micah 4:12; Jer 9:22).[325] The image of a flaming torch among the sheaves is reminiscent of the Judges 15 narrative in which Samson ties a torch between the tails of one hundred and fifty pairs of foxes and releases them into the fields, vineyards, and olive groves of the Philistines. The conclusion of verse 6 is somewhat difficult to translate though its basic intent is clear: Judah vanquishes the nations, but **Jerusalem** remains. At the center of the problem is a seemingly redundant use of "Jerusalem" which NIV renders **in her place**. Other translations make explicit an understanding that the first reference to Jerusalem denotes the inhabitants of the city while the second reference denotes the geographical location: "Then the people of Jerusalem will settle once more in their place, the city of Jerusalem" (NET; cf. ESV, NASB, and NRSV). The text may thus communicate that, with Yahweh's assistance, both a restored city and people endure any coming troubles, a significant message for a people nearly destroyed and whose city has been razed.

**12:7** While the context (12:5-8) indicates that hopes still center in

---

[322]Petersen, *Zechariah 9–14 and Malachi*, pp. 108, 114.

[323]Ronald B. Allen, "עֵץ," *TWOT*, 2:688-689; Meyers and Meyers, *Zechariah 9–14*, p, 325; The NIV translates 'ēṣ "wood" 100× and "tree" or "trees" 130×.

[324]Petersen, *Zechariah 9–14 and Malachi*, pp. 105, 116.

[325]Meyers and Meyers, *Zechariah 9–14*, p. 325.

the house of David[326] and that Jerusalem once again gains prominence "on that day," Yahweh intends to grant victory to the people **of Judah first**. The statement suggests a kind of democratization in which Jerusalem and the Davidic rulers do not enjoy undue priority over the remainder of the people of Judah.[327] The concern for the poor and those not enjoying privilege is borne out by the use of the word **dwellings** (אֹהֶל, *'ōhel*; cf. "tents" in the ESV, NASB, and NRSV) to describe Judah's habitations in contrast with "house" (בַּיִת, *bayith*) in the phrase **house of David**. The affirmation that Yahweh saves the tents of Judah first also guards against any aggrandizement of the house of David and Jerusalem's residents. Verse 7 asserts that the **honor** (תִּפְאֶרֶת, *tiph'ereth*) of the house of David and of the **inhabitants of Jerusalem** does not exceed **that of Judah**, but this is not a diminution of Jerusalem and the Davidic house so much as an exaltation of Judah (cf. Jer 33:9). The word *tiph'ereth* frequently refers to the splendor and glory of Yahweh (e.g., 1 Chr 29:11; Ps 71:8; 78:16; 89:17; 96:6; Isa 63:15), and Yahweh imparts *tiph'ereth* to Israel (Isa 28:5; 46:13; 60:19) so that Israel may be exalted above the nations (Deut 26:19).[328]

**12:8-9** Just as Yahweh saves the tents of Judah in verse 7, Yahweh also **shields those who live in Jerusalem**. Six of the eight uses of the verb "shield" (גָּנַן, *gānan*; cf. "defend" in the NASB and NET) in the Old Testament are associated with the deliverance of Jerusalem from the Assyrian siege in the days of Hezekiah when Yahweh promises to save the city for the sake of Yahweh and of David (2 Kgs 19:34; 20:6; Isa 31:5[2×]; 37:35; 38:6).[329] The use of *gānan* thus associates the deliverance of the community with the miraculous deliverance from the Assyrians (cf. 9:15). Verse 8 concludes with a set of complimentary comparisons that underscores the impregnability of Jerusalem.[330] **The feeblest among them** are **like**ned to **David**. This comparison to a legendary hero in Hebrew history signals that Yahweh's protection results in a transformation from weakness to

---

[326]See Petersen, *Zechariah 9–14 and Malachi*, pp. 117-118, for arguments that "house of David" is used in chapters 12 and 13 only to refer to the inhabitants of Jerusalem rather than to the Davidic line.

[327]Baldwin, *Haggai, Zechariah, Malachi*, p. 189.

[328]Victor P. Hamilton, "פָּאַר," *TWOT*, 2:713-714; C. John Collins, "פאר," *NIDOTTE*, 3:572-574.

[329]James E. Smith, "גָּנַן," *TWOT*, 1:168.

[330]McComiskey, "Zechariah," p. 1212.

strength not unlike that seen in Zechariah 10:3. This first comparison then gives rise to the daring comparison, **the house of David
will be like God** (cf. Exod 7:1). Appearing alone, this comparison
would seem blasphemous (cf. Gen 3:5), but it is tempered and clar-
ified by the expansion, **like the angel of** Yahweh **going before them**
(cf. 1 Sam 29:9; 2 Sam 14:17,20; 19:27). Thus, the comparison does
not confer divinity on the house of David but rather an exalted position and responsibility as Yahweh's representative among the fortified people of Yahweh. Verse 9 serves both as a summation of the
preceding section and a transition to the next. Yahweh has **determine**d **to destroy all the nations that attack Jerusalem** (12:2-8), but
the following verses (12:10–13:6) discuss the necessary changes within Yahweh's people that make this possible.[331]

**12:10** In verse 10, Yahweh promises to **pour out on** the people **a
spirit of grace and supplication**, an action that results in their
repentance (12:10-14) and cleansing (13:1). These verses stand in
sharp contrast with the preceding unit (12:1-9); the jubilation of victory is now tempered by mourning for one who has been killed in
the city.[332] Neither the divine name nor a pronoun referring to
Yahweh links the spirit (רוּחַ, *rûaḥ*) poured out here with Yahweh, as
in 4:6, 6:8, and 7:12. Still, the theme of the pouring out (שָׁפַךְ,
*šāphak*) of Yahweh's Spirit (*rûaḥ*), occurring elsewhere in Joel 2:28-
29 and Ezekiel 39:29, supports such an identification here as well.
Two nouns of the same Hebrew root describe Yahweh's Spirit as
one of "grace" (חֵן, *ḥēn*) and "supplication" (תַּחֲנוּן, *taḥănûn*). The first
word, *ḥēn*, refers to an earnest positive response to someone in need
by the one who possesses what the other needs.[333] The other word,
*taḥănûn* (cf. "pleas for mercy" in the ESV and "prayer" in the NJB),
complements this by denoting a cry for *ḥēn* (e.g., 2 Chr 6:21; Ps 28:6;
130:2; Prov 18:23; Jer 31:9; Dan 9:3). The Spirit of Yahweh grants
favor to the people that enables them to respond in repentance,[334]
when **they look on the one** whom **they have pierced**. The word
"pierced" (נָכָה, *nākāh*) does not necessarily indicate a fatal blow[335]

---

[331]Boda, *Haggai, Zechariah*, p. 484.

[332]Baldwin, *Haggai, Zechariah, Malachi*, p. 190.

[333]Edwin Yamauchi, "חָנַן," *TWOT*, 1:302-304.

[334]Boda, *Haggai, Zechariah*, p. 485.

[335]E.g., Gen 37:21; Exod 21:12; Josh 10:26; 2 Sam 1:15; Ps 78:51; Isa 37:36;
Jer 40:15; cf. esp. Deut 20:13; Josh 11:11-12,14; Jer 21:7, which also use the

but can, as it possibly does here, refer to a nonfatal blow (Exod 21:18; Neh 13:25; Isa 10:24; 58:4; Jer 37:15; Hos 6:1; Zech 13:6).

Various proposals have attempted to identify the one pierced as the shepherd struck in 13:7-9, the Suffering Servant of Isaiah 53, the slain king Josiah of Judah (2 Kgs 23:28-30; 2 Chr 35:20-27), Zerubbabel, Judas Maccabeus, Onias III, and others.[336] John 19:37 explicitly identifies Jesus with the one pierced in Zechariah 12:10, and the text in John contains several contextual similarities with Zechariah 12:10, namely, pouring out the spirit, looking, piercing, and the inhabitants of Jerusalem (cf. also Zech 13:1 with John 7:38 and 19:34). Nonetheless, Zechariah does not identify clearly the pierced one with any of these suggestions but rather portrays the piercing of Yahweh. Most versions (e.g., ESV, KJV, NASB, NET, NIV, and NJB) reflect the MT and LXX reading, "they will look on me whom they have pierced," that identifies the one pierced with the first person pronoun **me**. The previous context indicates this pierced one is Yahweh.[337] The NRSV eliminates this stunning image, adopting an amended reading that lacks textual witness, and rendering the clause, "when they look on the one whom they have pierced." Even if the quotation of this text in John 19:37 ("They will look on the one they have pierced") seems, at first glance, to support the third person reading, this modification of Zechariah 12:10 in the fourth Gospel likely reflects the way in which the New Testament writers quote an Old Testament text freely to demonstrate the fulfillment of prophecy in Jesus. Therefore, John 19:37 should not be used to establish the original wording of Zechariah 12:10.

The piercing of Yahweh results in the mourning of those who view the one pierced. Three similes show the severity of this mourning (12:10-11). The modern reader readily understands the first two: **as one mourns for an only child** (cf. Jer 6:26; Amos 8:10) and **as one grieves for a firstborn son**. Only two individuals in the Old Testa-

---

word in relation to "sword." Often Yahweh is its subject (Gen 8:21; Exod 3:20; 12:12; Deut 28:22,27-28; 2 Sam 6:7; 2 Kgs 6:18; Isa 5:25; 53:4; Jer 21:6; Ezek 7:9; Zech 9:4; 12:4).

[336]See Larkin, *The Eschatology of Second Zechariah*, pp. 161-165; Mason, "The Use of Earlier Biblical Material in Zechariah 9–14," pp. 159-164; Petersen, *Zechariah 9–14 and Malachi*, pp. 120-121.

[337]Boda, *Haggai, Zechariah*, p. 488; McComiskey, "Zechariah," p. 1214; Meyers and Meyers, *Zechariah 9–14*, p. 337.

ment are identified explicitly as only children, Isaac (Gen 22:2) and Jephthah's daughter (Judg 11:34), both in the context of intended sacrifice. The Hebrew term "firstborn" (בְּכוֹר, *bᵉkôr*), usually translated in the LXX by πρωτότοκος (*prōtotokos*), takes on messianic overtones in the Greek New Testament (Luke 2:7; Rom 8:29; Col 1:15,18; Heb 1:6; 12:23; Rev 1:5). The death of an only child or of a firstborn son is especially regretful, since it causes peril to the future of a family.[338]

**12:11** The third simile (see 12:10 for the first two) is more distant culturally: **like the weeping of Hadad Rimmon in the plain of Megiddo**. Hadad is the Aramean storm god, known in the Ras Shamra Tablets as Baal. The personal names Hadad (Gen 36:35; 1 Kgs 11:14-22), Hadadezer (2 Sam 8:3-12; 1 Kgs 11:23-25), and Ben-Hadad (1 Kgs 15:20; 20; 2 Kings 8) among Edomites and Arameans reflect his worship. Second Kings 5:18 likewise indicates that Rimmon, possibly a god of thunder, is a god worshiped among the Arameans. Uncertain is whether the weeping of Hadad Rimmon refers to a place of weeping in the plain of Megiddo or to weeping itself on behalf of a god known alternately as Hadad or Rimmon. If a place is intended, then it may refer to an act of mourning commemorating the death of Josiah (609 B.C.) at the hands of the Egyptians in the plain of Megiddo (2 Kgs 23:29; 2 Chr 35:22).[339] If it refers to a cultic act, it may indicate a practice not unlike the weeping for the Babylonian goddess Tammuz denounced in Ezekiel 8:14. Ancient Canaanite mythology evidenced in the Ras Shamra tablets depicts Hadad bewailing the death of a son slain by Mot, the god of the underworld.[340] The prophet's censure of idolatry later in the passage (13:2) does not necessitate a rejection of the latter option. The text is making comparisons to describe the depth of mourning and is not advocating the practice described.

**12:12-14** Verses 12-14 indicate that the whole land will mourn over the one they have pierced.[341] The nine uses of **clan** (מִשְׁפָּחָה,

---

[338]Boda, *Haggai, Zechariah*, p. 486.

[339]McComiskey, "Zechariah," p. 1215; Meyers and Meyers, *Zechariah 9–14*, pp. 343-344; Petersen, *Zechariah 9–14 and Malachi*, p. 122.

[340]Baldwin, *Haggai, Zechariah, Malachi*, p. 192.

[341]Matthew 24:30 alludes to 12:10-14 to describe the universal mourning that occurs when the Son of Man comes and, to a lesser degree, implicitly portrays Jesus with the one pierced. See Ham, *Coming King*, 94-96.

*mišpāḥāh*) and the fivefold repetition of **wives** (אִשָּׁה, *'išāh*) in these
three verses (the constraints of translation from Hebrew to English
make it difficult to discern the presence of these words in every
case) creates a picture of the entire society through redundancy and
the inclusion of both genders.[342] The term *mišpāḥāh* bears a wider
sense than usually connoted by the English term "family." More
often, *mišpāḥāh* refers to a circle of relatives with strong blood ties,
which is also a subdivision of a larger tribe or nation.[343] Though the
Spirit Yahweh has poured out causes all clans to mourn, the royal
and priestly families are emphasized. By the postexilic period, the
focus of the Davidic line had passed from the Solomonic branch to
the branch descending from David's son **Nathan** (2 Sam 5:14).[344] The
clan of **Shimei** descends from **Levi** through Gershom (Exod 6:16-17;
Num 3:17-18; 1 Chr 6:17) rather than through Kohath as does the
Zadokite line of priesthood (1 Chr 6:1-15). For reasons unknown,
the clan of Shimei apparently becomes prominent in the postexilic
era. Just as **David** and Nathan represent the political leadership of
the community, Levi and Shimei represent the religious leadership.
Referring to both clans highlights the universal lamenting that
occurs over the pierced one.

[1]**"On that day a fountain will be opened to the house of David
and the inhabitants of Jerusalem, to cleanse them from sin and
impurity.**

[2]**"On that day, I will banish the names of the idols from the
land, and they will be remembered no more," declares the LORD
Almighty. "I will remove both the prophets and the spirit of impurity from the land. [3]And if anyone still prophesies, his father and
mother, to whom he was born, will say to him, 'You must die,
because you have told lies in the LORD's name.' When he prophesies, his own parents will stab him.**

---

[342]Petersen, *Zechariah 9–14 and Malachi*, pp. 122-123.

[343]Hermann J. Austel, "שׁפח," *TWOT*, 2:947.

[344]Zerubbabel is from the family of Nathan, and Luke indicates Mary also
descends through that line (3:23-31). Matthew, on the other hand, traces the
ancestry of Jesus through Solomon (Matt 1:6-16), apparently in an attempt
to identify Joseph with the messianic Davidic line. The "official" ancestry of
Jesus thus is presented through Solomon, but his "physical" ancestry,
through Nathan.

⁴"On that day every prophet will be ashamed of his prophetic vision. He will not put on a prophet's garment of hair in order to deceive. ⁵He will say, 'I am not a prophet. I am a farmer; the land has been my livelihood since my youth.ᵃ' ⁶If someone asks him, 'What are these wounds on your body?ᵇ' he will answer, 'The wounds I was given at the house of my friends.'

⁷"Awake, O sword, against my shepherd, / against the man who is close to me!" / declares the LORD Almighty. / "Strike the shepherd, / and the sheep will be scattered, / and I will turn my hand against the little ones. / ⁸In the whole land," declares the LORD, / "two-thirds will be struck down and perish; / yet one-third will be left in it. / ⁹This third I will bring into the fire; / I will refine them like silver / and test them like gold. / They will call on my name / and I will answer them; / I will say, 'They are my people,' / and they will say, 'The LORD is our God.'"

ᵃ5 Or *farmer; a man sold me in my youth*    ᵇ6 Or *wounds between your hands*

**13:1** Verses 1-6 indict both the royal and prophetic leadership in postexilic Judah, focusing primarily on the removal of false prophecy. Verse 1 portrays the cleansing **from sin and impurity** (cf. Zech 3:4, 9) through **a fountain** (מָקוֹר, *māqôr*) **opened** up **to the house of David and the inhabitants of Jerusalem** "on that day" (13:1,2,4). That this promised fountain effects cleansing from sin and impurity associates it with ritual cleansing depicted in the Law (e.g., Lev 1:9,13; 6:28; 8:6; 11:25; 13:6; 14:5,8,50; 22:6). "Sin" (חַטָּאת, *ḥaṭṭā'th*) is the principle term for human misconduct in the Old Testament (e.g., Gen 18:20; 50:17; Exod 34:9; 2 Sam 12:13), and "impurity" (נִדָּה, *niddāh*) refers to ritual and sexual impurity (e.g., Lev 20:21; 2 Chr 29:5; Ezra 9:11; Ezek 7:20).[345] The image of a fountain evokes thoughts of fresh and invigorating water. Jeremiah uses *māqôr* to portray Yahweh as a fountain or spring of living water that has been forsaken by Judah (2:13; 17:13). The gravity of this image cannot be overemphasized, for this fountain cleanses even those who have pierced Yahweh.

**13:2** Verse 2 suggests that the piercing or rejection of Yahweh has occurred through the idolatry of the people.[346] It does so by

---

[345]*HALOT*, pp. 306, 673.
[346]Boda, *Haggai, Zechariah*, p. 490.

interpreting the content of verse 1 from the perspective of Ezekiel 36:25-26, which associates the impurity (*niddāh*) of Judah with idolatry and which pictures Yahweh sprinkling Judah with water in order to cleanse them.[347] Other images within the book of the removal of impurity, uncleanness, and sin from the community include the giving of new garments to Joshua (3:1-5), the flying scroll (5:1-4), and the ephah (5:5-11). **The names of the idols** are **banish**ed or "cut off" (cf. ESV, NASB, and NJB) **from the land**. To be cut off from the land is a standard curse in the Old Testament (Josh 7:9; 1 Sam 28:9; Ps 34:16; 37:9,22,34; 109:15; Prov 2:22; Jer 11:19). Verse 8 later speaks of two-thirds of the inhabitants of the land being cut off ("struck down" in the NIV). Cutting off the names of the idols means that the people can no longer ascribe existence, personality, and power to mere crafted images.[348] Later, Zechariah 14:9 asserts that "on that day" the name of Yahweh is the only name. Three passages in the law of Moses form the backdrop for the declaration that the idols **will be remembered no more**. The verb "remember" (זָכַר, *zākar*) appears in the injunction to honor Yahweh by offering sacrifices (Exod 20:24), in the prohibition against invoking the name of other gods in prayer (Exod 23:13), and in the call to remember Yahweh as the one who gives the Hebrews the ability to produce wealth (Deut 8:18). The formula **declares the LORD Almighty** (see Zech 3:9,10; 5:4; 8:11; 13:7; cf. 1:3,16; 8:6 with the verb "says") is fitting in a context in which Yahweh intends to take action against other deities and those who represent them. The removal of **the prophets and the spirit of impurity** (טֻמְאָה, *ṭum'āh*, a term used elsewhere in association with idolatry; e.g., Ezek 36:25) makes clear that these prophets themselves are agents of illicit gods. If false prophets are to be included among the false shepherds spoken of there, then this present passage also echoes concerns in 10:1-3 (see 11:8-9 above). The removal of the spirit of impurity complements the earlier pouring out of a spirit of grace and supplication (12:10).

**13:3** Deuteronomy 18:20-22 (cf. 13:6-11) calls for death by stoning as punishment for prophesying falsely or leading Israel to worship gods other than Yahweh. Here the **parents** of false prophets are

---

[347]Mason, "The Use of Earlier Biblical Material in Zechariah 9–14," p. 163.

[348]Baldwin, *Haggai, Zechariah, Malachi*, p. 195; McComiskey, "Zechariah," p. 1220.

simply putting in effect the death penalty required in the Old Testament. They execute their child by **stab**bing or piercing **him** through (דָּקַר, *dāqar*), the same action done to the one pierced in 12:10. In so doing, the parents demonstrate the repentance of the people. The people who have pierced Yahweh through their idolatry now show their remorse, cleansing the land of idolatry by piercing the false prophets. Their act of piercing, moreover, counters idolatry much as does the piercing enacted by Aaron's grandson Phinehas against Zimri who led Israel in participating with the Midianites in idolatrous fertility cult behavior.[349]

**13:4-6** Verses 4-6 demonstrate how false prophecy associated with idolatry is eradicated from Israel. These actions are so effective that prophets associated with an illicit god seek to avoid detection, the depiction of which draws on earlier traditions. First, false prophets no longer don a **garment of hair in order to deceive** (כָּחַשׁ, *kāḥaš*); this may be an ironic allusion to the deception of Isaac by Jacob and Rebekah, when a hairy garment is an instrument of camouflage (Gen 25:25; 27:16).[350] The prophet's hairy garment (אַדֶּרֶת שֵׂעָר, *'addereth šē'ār*) is the rough clothing worn by Elijah (1 Kgs 19:13), Elisha (1 Kgs 19:19; 2 Kgs 2:14), and John the Baptist in the New Testament era (Matt 3:4). Because the noun *'addereth* is related to a word group with connotations of majesty (cf. Zech 11:3, where the "glory" [*'addereth*] of the shepherds is destroyed),[351] the simple garment of the prophet may still suggest dignity. Second, false prophets claim they are **not prophet**s but **farmers**. This statement hearkens back to the earlier affirmation by Amos to Amaziah, the priest of Bethel, "I was neither a prophet nor a prophet's son, but I was a shepherd, and I also took care of sycamore-fig trees. But the LORD took me from tending the flock and said to me, 'Go, prophesy to my people Israel'" (Amos 7:14-15). Amos seeks to dissociate himself from the false prophets of the northern kingdom by noting his agricultural endeavors that precede his call by Yahweh to prophesy to the kingdom. Here, the false prophets also claim they are farmers rather than prophets. For Amos the claim adds credibility to his message; for the false prophets here it emphasizes their lack of cred-

---

[349]Boda, *Haggai, Zechariah*, pp. 491-492.
[350]Petersen, *Zechariah 9–14 and Malachi*, p. 127.
[351]Leonard J. Coppes, "אדר," *TWOT*, 1:13.

ibility.[352] Furthermore, their claim alludes to Cain as a "worker of the ground" (Gen 4:2, ESV), thus reinforcing their portrayal as worthy of punishment. Third, false prophets attempt to conceal their injuries. The explanation given for the wounds may allude to verse 3 in which parents of the false prophet stab them when they prophesy lies. Such an explanation by the prophet (**The wounds I was given at the house of my friends**) is not only unlikely, it bears sinister irony. The NIV translates as "friends" an intensive participle of the verb "love" (אָהַב, *'āhab*). Such a use, however, usually connotes a lover (e.g., Gen 29:18) rather than a friend and is used at times to speak of spiritual adultery (Jer 22:20,22; Ezek 16:33,36,37; Hos 2:5,7,10,12-13).[353] This word coupled with "house" may indicate that these injuries are the flagellation wounds of prophets who participate in rites in the house (temple?) of a pagan god (Lev 19:28; Deut 14:1; 1 Kgs 18:28; Jer 16:6; 47:5).[354]

**13:7-9** The poem in 13:7-9 resumes the shepherd motif seen earlier in 9:16, 10:2-3, and 11:3-17. Even though this poem shares some features with 11:3-17 (e.g., shepherd imagery and covenant language), 13:7-9 differs in genre, poetic meter, and its application of the shepherd and sword imagery.[355] The use of imperative verbs ("Awake" and "Strike") and a vocative ("O sword") in 13:7, the presence of shepherd and sheep imagery, and the absence of the phrase "on that day," characteristic in the remainder of the chapters 12–14 (12:3,4,6,8,9,11; 13:1,2,4; 14:4,8,9,13,20,21), set this unit off as unique from 12:1–13:6 and 14:1-21. Yet, verses 7-9 develop further the theme of crisis in leadership found in 12:1–13:6 and introduce the theme of a remnant taken up in 14:2. The passage speaks of the

---

[352]Sweeney, *The Twelve Prophets*, p. 694.

[353]BDB, p. 13; P.J.J.S. Els, "אהב," *NIDOTTE*, 1:289-290.

[354]Boda, *Haggai, Zechariah*, p. 493; Meyers and Meyers, *Zechariah 9–14*, pp. 383-384.

[355]Hanson, *Dawn of Apocalyptic*, pp. 338-338, understands 13:7-9 as a poetic fragment originally connected with 11:4-17, and the NEB follows this transposition of the text, printing 13:7-9 after 11:4-17. Stephen L. Cook, "The Metamorphosis of a Shepherd: The Tradition History of Zechariah 11.17 + 13.7-9," *CBQ* 55 (1993): 455-456; Lamarche, *Zacharie IX–XIV*, pp. 108-109; Magne Sæbø, *Sacharja 9–14: Untersuchungen von Text und Form*, WMANT 34 (Neukirchen-Vluyn: Neukirchener Verlag, 1969), pp. 276-277; and R.L. Smith, *Micah–Malachi*, p. 218, argue for the canonical position of Zech 13:7-9.

probable death of a good shepherd that then leaves the flock without a leader to undergo "severe testing and loss, which result in
deeper assurance of their identity as the Lord's people."[356]

**13:7** In verse 7, Yahweh summons the **sword against** the **shepherd**.[357] For emphasis, the noun "sword" appears first in the Hebrew
sentence. The sword appears elsewhere as a metaphor for physical
harm (Zech 11:17), death (Amos 9.4), or divine judgment through
war (Jer 14:12-18; 21:7,9; 24:10; Ezek 14:17,21). Most commonly, the
image of Yahweh's sword connotes judgment upon the disobedient
and the enemies of Israel (Deut 32:41; Isa 31:8; 34:6; 66:16; Jer
12:12; 47:6; Ezek 21:8-17,28-32), but the present passage uses it as an
instrument of divine judgment against the shepherd of Yahweh.[358]
The designation **my shepherd** does not indicate an ordinary leader,
for both the Persian monarch Cyrus (Isa 44:28) and Yahweh (Ps
23:1) are elsewhere called "my shepherd." However, the one identified here is likely not the worthless shepherd of Zechariah 11:15-17,
since Yahweh calls him **the man who is close to me**. Zechariah 13:7-
9 shares similarities with two other texts (Jer 23:1-6 and Ezek 34:1-
31), particularly the concept of the scattering of the sheep. Both
Jeremiah 23:5 and Ezekiel 34:23-24 use monarchical and messianic
terms to represent the shepherd placed over the sheep by Yahweh.

---

[356]Baldwin, *Haggai, Zechariah, Malachi*, p. 197.

[357]Both Matthew 26:31 and Mark 14:27 explicitly quote Zech 13:7 in the
context of Jesus predicting the dispersion of the disciples at his crucifixion
and his reassurance that he would nevertheless go ahead of them into
Galilee after he has risen. The citation of 13:7 in Matt 26:31-35 explains
Jesus' prediction about the desertion of the disciples. Just as the striking of
the shepherd in Zechariah occasions a scattering of the sheep, the arrest of
Jesus occasions the flight of his disciples. Matthew cites Zech 13:7 to establish that, although the desertion of the disciples is tragic and irresponsible,
it still falls within the plan of God, so says D.A. Carson, "Matthew," in
*Expositor's Bible Commentary*, ed. by Frank E. Gaebelein (Grand Rapids: Zon-
dervan, 1984), 8:540. Nonetheless, after predicting the disciples' defection,
Jesus goes on to promise their restoration when he goes ahead of them into
Galilee following his resurrection (Matt 26:32). This promise reflects the
content of Zech 13:8-9, in which a remnant is purified through testing to
become the restored people of Yahweh, asserts W.D. Davies and Dale C.
Allison, Jr, *The Gospel according to Saint Matthew*, ICC (Edinburgh: T. & T.
Clark, 1988–97), 3:486, and David H. Johnson, "Shepherd, Sheep," *DJG*,
p. 752.

[358]Ham, *Coming King*, p. 72.

This may suggest then that a royal ruler is also indicated by "shepherd" here.[359] The first occurrence of an oracle formula (**declares the LORD Almighty**) in the unit (see 13:8 for the other) underscores the divine authority of the prophetic word: Yahweh calls for the sword to strike the shepherd, an act probably implying execution. Similar wording occurs in Jeremiah 21:7 to describe the violent death of King Zedekiah and the inhabitants of Jerusalem. Also comparable is the fourth servant song of Isaiah, in which God strikes the Suffering Servant (Isa 53:4) and the Servant is crushed according to the will of Yahweh (53:10). Nonetheless, Zechariah differs from Isaiah by not affirming the innocence of the shepherd (compared to the Servant) and by indicting both the royal and prophetic leadership in the preceding context (vv. 1-6).[360]

The striking of the shepherd results in the scattering of the sheep. **Sheep** (צֹאן, *ṣōʾn*) is a frequent metaphor for the people of Israel or Judah (2 Sam 24:17; 1 Chr 17:7; 21:17; 2 Chr 18:16; Ps 74:1; 77:20; 78:52; 95:7; 100:3; Isa 53:6; Jer 23:1-3; 50:6; Ezek 34; Micah 2:12; 7:14; Zech 9:16). The verb **scattered** (פּוּץ, *pûṣ*) appears numerous times to describe their exile (Deut 28:64; 30:3; Isa 11:12; Jer 9:16; Ezek 11:17; 12:15; 20:34,41; 22:15). Significant for this context is the use of *pûṣ* in Jeremiah 10:21 and 23:1-2, where the negligence of Judah's shepherds leads to the scattering of the sheep, and in Ezekiel 34:5-6,12, where the sheep are scattered because they lack a shepherd. The text focuses on the judgment of Yahweh against both the shepherd and the people, for Yahweh not only acts to cause the death of the shepherd but also to scatter the flock.[361] The concluding words of the verse, **I will turn my hand against the little ones**, reiterate this dual judgment. Jeremiah uses the title "the little ones" twice in the expanded expression "the little ones of the flock" (49:20; 50:45). This title in 13:7 may refer to the same group desig-

---

[359]Earlier texts, such as 1 Kgs 22:17, use "shepherd" as a figure for "king." The Targum on Zechariah clearly identifies the shepherd as the king and for this reason replaces "man" with "prince": "O sword, *be revealed* against *the king* and against the *prince his* companion *who is his equal, who is like him*, says the Lord of hosts; slay the *king* and the *princes* shall be scattered and I will bring back *a mighty stroke* upon the *underlings*."

[360]Ham, *Coming King*, p. 73.

[361]Meyers and Meyers, *Zechariah 9–14*, p. 388; Petersen, *Zechariah 9–14*, pp. 130-131.

nated "the flock marked for slaughter" in 11:4-7. The language of
Yahweh turning a hand against some group appears in Isaiah 1:25
where Yahweh also promises to purge the dross from Judah and to
remove their impurities. This theme of refinement appears in chapter 13 with the images of a fountain that cleanses from sin and impurity (vv. 1-2) and of refining and testing of silver and gold (v. 9). In
spite of this, the following verses indicate that a remnant of the little ones survives and, when refined, constitutes the people of
Yahweh (vv. 8-9).[362]

**13:8** Verse 8 portrays the destruction throughout the land so
that **two-thirds** of the people **perish**. This division of the land into
thirds reflects the symbolic action depicted in Ezekiel 5, where the
prophet cuts his hair and divides it into thirds.[363] He burns a third
inside the model of the city of Jerusalem he has drawn to represent
those who die from plague or famine in the besieged city. He strikes
a third with the sword outside the model to represent those who fall
by the sword outside the city. The final third is scattered in the wind
to represent those who go into exile. Here, two-thirds are **struck
down and perish**, and **one-third** remains. That the final third here
is **left in it** rather than is scattered reflects the more positive postexilic context in which Israel has returned.[364] The second occurrence of the oracle formula (**declares the LORD**) in the unit (vv. 7-9)
intensifies the divine authority of the prophetic word: the destruction of two-thirds and the purification of one-third happen within
the will of Yahweh.

**13:9** Verse 9 expresses Yahweh's intention to bring the remaining
**third into the fire**, refining **them like silver and test**ing **them like
gold**. The act of purification complements that found in verse 1. The
process of removing the dross and impurities from precious metals
by subjecting the ore to great heat is a common image in the Psalms
and prophetic literature for purification from sin (Ps 17:3; 26:2;
66:10; Isa 1:25; Jer 6:27-30; 9:7; Ezek 22:18-22; Mal 3:2-4). Here that
image is quite appropriate, for Yahweh is seeking to remove all
wickedness from the people in order that Yahweh may dwell with

---

[362]Ham, *Coming King*, p. 74.
[363]Mason, "The Use of Earlier Biblical Material in Zechariah 9–14," pp.
126-128.
[364]Petersen, *Zechariah 9–14 and Malachi*, p. 131.

them and they can endure the holy presence.[365] This intent is borne out by the remainder of verse 9, where a montage of covenant language (cf. Lev 26:12; Deut 26:17-18), in the form of reciprocal statements by Yahweh and the people, depicts the restored relationship between Yahweh and the people as a result of Yahweh's actions against the shepherd. The refined community now **calls on** Yahweh's **name** (1 Chr 16:8; 2 Chr 7:14; Ps 80:18; 99:5; 116:4,13,17; Isa 12:4; Lam 3:55; Joel 2:32; Zeph 3:9) instead of remembering the names of the idols (13:2). Chapter 14 indeed looks to the day when the name of Yahweh is the only name (14:9). When they call upon the name of Yahweh, Yahweh **answers them**. The collection of the three words "call" (קָרָא, *qārā'*), "name" (שֵׁם, *šēm*), and "answer" (עָנָה, *'ānāh*) occurs outside of verse 9 in only two instances in the Old Testament. In 1 Kings 18:24-26, Elijah challenges the prophets of Baal to call upon the name of their gods while he calls on the name of Yahweh. By answering with fire, either Baal or Yahweh is established as the true deity. Although prophets of Baal call on the name of Baal, they receive no answer. Psalm 99:6 affirms that Moses, Aaron, and Samuel are among those who call on the name of Yahweh, who answers them when they call. In Zechariah 13:9, Yahweh asserts, **"They are my people,"** and the people testify, **"The LORD is our God."** Thus Yahweh establishes once again with the people the covenant relationship articulated in the Torah and in covenant declarations found throughout the prophetic literature (Jer 24:7; 31:33; 32:38; Ezek 11:20; 14:11; 37:23; Hos 1:9; 2:23; Zech 8:8).[366] The covenant language with which the passage ends is significant given the passage's beginning; through the slaying the shepherd, Yahweh has effected a redefinition and refinement of the people.[367]

## B. PROPHECY CONCERNING THE VICTORY
## AND WORSHIP OF JERUSALEM'S KING (14:1-21)

[1]**A day of the LORD is coming when your plunder will be divided among you.**

---

[365]John E. Hartley, "צָרַף," *TWOT*, 2:777-778.
[366]Meyers and Meyers, *Zechariah 9–14*, p. 397.
[367]Petersen, *Zechariah 9–14 and Malachi*, p. 132.

²I will gather all the nations to Jerusalem to fight against it; the city will be captured, the houses ransacked, and the women raped. Half of the city will go into exile, but the rest of the people will not be taken from the city.

³Then the LORD will go out and fight against those nations, as he fights in the day of battle. ⁴On that day his feet will stand on the Mount of Olives, east of Jerusalem, and the Mount of Olives will be split in two from east to west, forming a great valley, with half of the mountain moving north and half moving south. ⁵You will flee by my mountain valley, for it will extend to Azel. You will flee as you fled from the earthquakeª in the days of Uzziah king of Judah. Then the LORD my God will come, and all the holy ones with him.

⁶On that day there will be no light, no cold or frost. ⁷It will be a unique day, without daytime or nighttime—a day known to the LORD. When evening comes, there will be light.

⁸On that day living water will flow out from Jerusalem, half to the eastern seaᵇ and half to the western sea,ᶜ in summer and in winter.

⁹The LORD will be king over the whole earth. On that day there will be one LORD, and his name the only name.

¹⁰The whole land, from Geba to Rimmon, south of Jerusalem, will become like the Arabah. But Jerusalem will be raised up and remain in its place, from the Benjamin Gate to the site of the First Gate, to the Corner Gate, and from the Tower of Hananel to the royal winepresses. ¹¹It will be inhabited; never again will it be destroyed. Jerusalem will be secure.

¹²This is the plague with which the LORD will strike all the nations that fought against Jerusalem: Their flesh will rot while they are still standing on their feet, their eyes will rot in their sockets, and their tongues will rot in their mouths. ¹³On that day men will be stricken by the LORD with great panic. Each man will seize the hand of another, and they will attack each other. ¹⁴Judah too will fight at Jerusalem. The wealth of all the surrounding nations will be collected—great quantities of gold and silver and clothing. ¹⁵A similar plague will strike the horses and mules, the camels and donkeys, and all the animals in those camps.

¹⁶Then the survivors from all the nations that have attacked Jerusalem will go up year after year to worship the King, the LORD

**Almighty, and to celebrate the Feast of Tabernacles. [17]If any of the peoples of the earth do not go up to Jerusalem to worship the King, the LORD Almighty, they will have no rain. [18]If the Egyptian people do not go up and take part, they will have no rain. The LORD[d] will bring on them the plague he inflicts on the nations that do not go up to celebrate the Feast of Tabernacles. [19]This will be the punishment of Egypt and the punishment of all the nations that do not go up to celebrate the Feast of Tabernacles.**

**[20]On that day HOLY TO THE LORD will be inscribed on the bells of the horses, and the cooking pots in the LORD's house will be like the sacred bowls in front of the altar. [21]Every pot in Jerusalem and Judah will be holy to the LORD Almighty, and all who come to sacrifice will take some of the pots and cook in them. And on that day there will no longer be a Canaanite[e] in the house of the LORD Almighty.**

[a]5 Or [5]*My mountain valley will be blocked and will extend to Azel. It will be blocked as it was blocked because of the earthquake*     [b]8 **That is, the Dead Sea**     [c]8 **That is, the Mediterranean**     [d]18 **Or** *part, then the Lord*     [e]21 **Or** *merchant*

Zechariah 14:1-21 contains a prophecy of salvation (see on Zeph 3:14-20 above), a genre evidenced in the preceding unit (13:7-9). The section consists of an announcement of salvation in 14:1-5 ("a day of the LORD is coming") and an elaboration of the eventual outcome "on that day" in 14:6-21. Instead of a first-person speech of Yahweh (cf. 13:7-9), the chapter offers a narrative description of the coming day of Yahweh in four episodes (14:1-5,6-7,8-12,13-21); the last three each begin with the phrase translated in the KJV "and it shall come to pass in that day" (וְהָיָה בַיּוֹם, *wĕhāyāh bayyôm*), which includes an eschatological phrase oft repeated in Zechariah 9–14, "on that day" (9:16; 11:11; 12:3-4,6,8-9,11; 13:1-2,4; 14:4,6,8-9,13,20-21). Regarding their subject matter, these four episodes narrate the devastation and rescue of Jerusalem (vv. 1-5), the beginning of a new creation (vv. 6-7), the restoration of Jerusalem as the center of Yahweh's universal reign (vv. 8-12), and the universal worship of Yahweh as king (vv. 13-21). Within the final oracle in Zechariah (12–14), chapter 14 shares with 12:1-9 the theme of the nations waging war against Jerusalem but with significant differences. No royal figure appears in chapter 14; neither does any shepherd (10:2-3; 11:3-5,7-9,15-16; 13:7), prophet (8:9; 13:2,4-6), priests (3:1,8; 6:11,13;

7:3,5), or any other human leader (3:8; 4:6-7,9-10; 6:12; 12:7-8,10,12; 13:1). Chapter 14 has an unmatched universal perspective compared to the rest of the book (e.g., 12:11-14 speaks of the clans of the land of Israel, but 14:17 speaks of the clans of the earth). Moreover, chapter 14 vividly presents Yahweh as king (vv. 9,16,17), more so than any previous section in the book (cf. 2:13; 4:14; 6:5,7; 8:20-23; 9:10). Therefore, Zechariah 14 challenges the reader to consider the eventual destruction of Jerusalem as part of Yahweh's larger purpose and to act accordingly, assured that the victorious intervention of Yahweh results ultimately in the universal worship of Yahweh as king.

**14:1** The interjection "behold" (הִנֵּה, *hinnēh*), not translated in the NIV (cf. ESV and NRSV) introduces the last section of Zechariah 12–14; the Hebrew word underlines the significance of the statement it introduces. Other versions (e.g., the ESV, NASB, and NRSV) translate better the opening line of the chapter, "Behold, a day is coming for the LORD" than the NIV's, **A day of the LORD is coming**. The Hebrew wording emphasizes Yahweh, since the divine name follows the preposition "for," rather than the "coming" of the day. Neither does the verse use the standard phrase translated "day of Yahweh" (see on Zeph 1:7-8 above). Nevertheless, the context here shares several features present in other Old Testament texts depicting the day of Yahweh. In that day, divine judgment comes on the sinful people, but Yahweh purifies a remnant and delivers them from the enemies of Yahweh represented by the nations round about. That remnant is exalted among the nations who also come to acknowledge Yahweh as Lord of the earth (see, e.g., Isa 1:24-31; 2:2-4; 4:2-6; 26:16–27:6; 33:13-24; 59:1–60:22; 65:13-25; Jer 30:7-11; 32:36-44; Ezek 20:33-44; Dan 12:1; Joel 1:15–2:11; Amos 5:18-21; 9:8-15). Preexilic prophets see the day of Yahweh as imminent (cf. Isa 13:6; Joel 1:15; 2:1; 3:14; Obad 1:15; Zeph 1:7,14). From the postexilic perspective, the events of the destruction of Jerusalem and the exile represent the initiation of that eschatological day, already begun but now unfolding; in addition, this perspective embraces a retrospective portrayal of events yet future in eschatological language evocative of past events (e.g., v. 5).[368] The second half of verse 1 (**your plunder will be divided among you**) anticipates the destruction of

---

[368]Meyers and Meyers, *Zechariah 9–14*, p. 409.

Jerusalem depicted in verse 2 and likely draws on the earlier defeat of Jerusalem by the Babylonians in the sixth century (2 Kings 25; 2 Chronicles 36). This statement serves as a poignant reversal of Zechariah 2:8-9, but 14:4 later portrays the return of the wealth of the nations to Jerusalem.

**14:2** A first person statement expresses Yahweh's intent to **gather all the nations to Jerusalem to fight against it** (cf. Ezek 38:7-9; 39:2; Joel 3:2). The word "gather" (אָסַף, *'āsaph*) can refer to the collection of people for fighting (Judg 11:20; 1 Sam 17:1; 2 Sam 10:17; 12:29) and imply the destruction of those gathered (1 Sam 15:6; Hab 1:9,14; 2:5; Zeph 1:2; 3:8). Most often *'āsaph* occurs in the context of harvest (Exod 23:10; Lev 23:39; 25:3; 25:20; Deut 16:13; 28:38; Ruth 2:7; Job 39:12; Isa 62:9; Jer 40:10) and thus may prepare the reader for the mention of the Feast of Tabernacles (14:16-19), the autumn festival of Ingathering, also known as Sukkot (Exod 23:16; 34:22; Deut 16:13-15).[369] The phrase "all the nations" (כָּל־הַגּוֹיִם, *kāl-haggôyim*) appears three times in this chapter (14:2,16,19; cf. 7:14; 12:9). A similar phrase, "all the peoples" כָּל־הָעַמִּים (*kāl-hā'ammîm*), also translated by the NIV "all the nations," is found in verse 12. The use of these two phrases highlights the universal scope of Yahweh's power and rule as well as the radical change in the status of the nations depicted in the chapter.[370] The city suffers a crushing defeat when Yahweh gathers the nations against Jerusalem; it is **captured, the houses ransacked, and the women raped** (cf. Isa 13:16 and Lam 5:11 for rape as an image for the aftermath of conquest). These last two verbs (ransack and rape) also appear in Isaiah 13:16 to describe the devastation of Babylon at the hands of the Persians. The division of the people into two halves, one going **into exile** and the other being spared, does not conflict with 13:8-9 in which the city's inhabitants are divided in thirds, with two-thirds dying and the remaining one-third left to be refined. Chapter 14 merely emphasizes the outcome for those who survive: half go into exile and half stay.[371] The

---

[369]Sweeney, *The Twelve Prophets*, p. 698.

[370]Meyers and Meyers, *Zechariah 9–14*, p. 413. Gill, *Minor Prophets*, p. 366, asserts that verse 2 does not present a prediction of the Roman conquest of Jerusalem (A.D. 70) since the following verses certainly do not fit that era and an invasion by Rome does not constitute one by all the nations.

[371]Meyers and Meyers, *Zechariah 9–14*, p. 415.

treatment is reminiscent of Judah in 586 B.C., when those who survive the Babylonian siege either are removed to Mesopotamia or stay in the land (2 Kgs 25:11-12; Jer 39:9-10). The assurance that the rest of the people are not taken away from the city translates the biblical idiom for curse: they are not cut off from the city (Josh 7:9; 1 Sam 28:9; Ps 34:16; 37:9,22,34; 109:15; Prov 2:22; Jer 11:19). Earlier, Zechariah 13:8 notes that two-thirds of the inhabitants of the land are cut off, which the NIV translates "struck down."

**14:3-4** Yahweh intervenes, fighting **in the day of battle against those nations** that threaten Jerusalem. The statement uses traditional military language for Yahweh's fighting on behalf of the city (cf. Judg 5:4; 2 Sam 5:24; 2 Chr 20:17; Isa 42:13); the background for the image here may be that of Yahweh's defeat of the Egyptians at the crossing of the Red Sea (Exod 14:13-14).[372] On that day Yahweh **stands on the Mount of Olives**, a mile long ridge of four summits running parallel to the Kidron Valley **east of Jerusalem**. Its highest ridge rises some 2,500 feet, more than 290 feet higher than the temple mount. Only here does the title "Mount of Olives" appear in the Old Testament. A similar description, "the ascent of the Olives," is used in 2 Samuel 15:30, when David, his household, and his officials leave Jerusalem to escape from Absalom by ascending the Mount of Olives.[373] The anthropomorphism concerning the **feet** of Yahweh (cf. Isa 60:13; Ezek 43:7) standing on the Mount of Olives obviously continues the notion of military victory evidenced in verse 3. The same Yahweh who has promised to give the Hebrews every place in Canaan where their feet trod (Josh 1:3) now makes a clear claim of ownership of the land. Ezekiel portrays Yahweh as being so angered by Judah's sin that Yahweh departs leaving the city defenseless (Ezekiel 10–11). The Mount of Olives is the last stop in the vicinity

---

[372]Baldwin, *Haggai, Zechariah, Malachi*, p. 201.

[373]Although they do not mention it by name, 1 Kgs 11:7, 2 Kgs 23:13, and Ezek 11:23 probably refer to the Mount of Olives (cf. 2 Esd 13:6). On the Mount of Olives in the Old Testament, see John Briggs Curtis, "An Investigation of the Mount of Olives in the Judaeo-Christian Tradition," *HUCA* 28 (1957): 139-141. Josephus mentions the Mount of Olives by name in *J.W.* 2.262; 5.70, 135, 504; 6.157; *Ant.* 7.202; 20.169. The New Testament refers to the Mount of Olives in John 8:1; Matt 21:1//Mark 11:1//Luke 19:29; Luke 19:37; Matt 24:3//Mark 13:3; Luke 21:37; 22:39; Matt 26:30//Mark 14:26.

of Jerusalem for the glory of Yahweh on the way to Babylon (Ezek 11:23). Therefore, the depiction of Yahweh stepping on the mount signals his return to dwell in Jerusalem. Just as Ezekiel 43:7 portrays the temple as the place for the soles of Yahweh's feet and where Yahweh dwells, here the standing of Yahweh on the mount adjacent to the city boldly depicts Yahweh's presence in and for the city. Presumably under Yahweh's feet, the Mount of Olives **splits** (בָּקַע, *bāqaʿ*) **into two** parts, **forming** an east-west **valley** that cuts across the north-south range. Although the Old Testament depicts mountains quaking, smoking, blazing (Exod 19:18; Nahum 1:5), melting (Ps 97:5; Micah 1:4; Nahum 1:5), scattering, sinking down (Isa 40:4; Hab 3:6), and being removed (Job 9:5) in the presence of Yahweh, only this text speaks of the splitting of a mountain. The image is one similar to the Exodus tradition of the "splitting" (*bāqaʿ*) of the Red Sea (Exod 14:16,21; Neh 9:11; Ps 78:13; Isa 63:12). Moreover, this "splitting" of the Mount of Olives provides a way of escape for the inhabitants of Jerusalem like the Israelites who walk through the wind-split sea (Exod 14:21-22).[374]

**14:5** The newly created **mountain valley** allows the remaining inhabitants of Jerusalem an escape **to Azel**, a point of uncertain location. The people **flee** from Jerusalem **as** they have done **from the earthquake in the days of Uzziah king of Judah**. Amos 1:1 also refers to an earthquake in the reign of Uzziah (792–740 B.C.); otherwise the earthquake is unknown.[375] That the book of Amos is dated in reference to this natural phenomenon is unusual,[376] but it signals the earthquake's lasting impact, which the prophet uses to reinforce his prophetic message. Its mention here also speaks to its magnitude, where it appears as part of an instruction to take a specific action during a future crisis, comparable to actions taken during a

[374]Floyd, *The Minor Prophets*, p. 545.
[375]Josephus, *Ant.* 9.225, ostensibly connects the earthquake in Zech 14:5 and Amos 1:1 with 2 Chr 26:16-21, where Uzziah is stricken with leprosy for inappropriately entering the temple to make an offering. The Old Testament generally employs the image of an earthquake as a demonstration of divine presence or power (Exod 19:18; Ps 68:8; 77:18; 114:7; Isa 64:2-3) but more often divine judgment (Judg 5:4; Isa 5:25; 13:13; 24:18-20; 29:6; Jer 4:23-24; 10:10; Ezek 26:18; 38:19-20; Joel 2:10-11; 3:16; Micah 1:4; Nahum 1:5-6).
[376]Meyers and Meyers, *Zechariah 9–14*, p. 427.

past catastrophe in the days of King Uzziah. **Then** Yahweh **comes with all the holy ones.**[377] Yahweh's coming here answers the notion of Yahweh's going out in verse 3, highlighting Yahweh's role in providing rescue and security for the remnant of people.[378] In the Old Testament, "holy ones" refers to people (Lev 21:7,8; Num 16:5,7; Deut 33:2-3; 2 Chr 35:3; Ps 34:9; Dan. 7:18; 8:22,24), but it also designates angels or heavenly beings (Deut 33:2-3; Job 5:1; 15:15; Ps 89:5,7; Prov 30:3; Dan 4:13,17,23; 8:13).[379] The context, emphasizing divine action rather than human instrumentality, argues for the denotation here of angelic beings. Moreover, the designation "holy ones" may intimate that the holiness found within the heavenly realms becomes pervasive on the earth in the day of Yahweh; such all-encompassing holiness is imaged in the closing verses of the chapter (14:20-21).[380]

**14:6-7** Comprising the second of four episodes in the chapter, verses 6-7 envisage new temporal and luminary distinctions of the new creation. The metaphors of the diminution of **light** to signal divine judgment or the cataclysmic intervention of Yahweh are common in the Old Testament (Isa 13:9-10; 24:23; 30:26; Jer 4:23-27; Ezek 30:3-4; 32:7-8; Joel 2:1-2; 3:15, Amos 5:20; Zeph 1:15). That such apocalyptic language occurs in Jeremiah 4:23-26 for the destruction of Jerusalem in 586 B.C. warns the modern reader against taking this imagery as a literal depiction of the end times.[381] The final phrase of verse 6 in the MT is somewhat difficult, meaning something like "the splendid will congeal" (cf. KJV, NASB, and NET). The LXX reflects a different text, **no cold or frost**, which is followed by the ESV, NIV, NJB, and NRSV. Since the surrounding phrases in verses 6 and 7 focus upon illumination, a reading related

---

[377]On the allusion to Zech 14:5 in Matt 25:31, see Ham, *Coming King*, pp. 98-99; cf. Jude 14.

[378]Merrill, *Haggai, Zechariah, Malachi*, p. 350; McComiskey, "Zechariah," p. 1231.

[379]In the New Testament, "holy ones" may also denote angelic beings (1 Thess 3:13), but more often the New Testament uses the designation for believers (Matt 27:52; Acts 9:13,32,41; 26:10; Rom 1:7; 8:27; 12:13; 15:25, etc.). On this description of the believers' new relationship with Yahweh, see Stephen Woodward, "The Provenance of the Term 'Saints': A *Religionsgeschichtliche* Study," *JETS* 24 (1981): 110-111.

[380]Meyers and Meyers, *Zechariah 9–14*, pp. 429-430.

[381]McComiskey, "Zechariah," p. 1233.

to light is expected;[382] however, the sense of congeal may also play to this image. The verb "congeal" or "thicken" (קָפָא, *qāphā'*) appears in Exodus 15:8 to denote the cessation of the flow and surging of the waters of the Red Sea. Milk, when congealed or curdled, loses its liquid qualities and becomes cheese (Job 10:10), and wine left on its dregs solidifies (Zeph 1:12). The second line of verse 6 may then be a more poetic statement of the first. There is no light for the splendid things (possibly sun, moon, and stars) have congealed, and light no longer flows from them.[383] The NIV translates a Hebrew phrase "one day" (יוֹם־אֶחָד, *yôm-'eḥād*) as **unique day**.[384] The words *yôm-'eḥād* used in Genesis 1:5 conclude the description of the first day of creation. Taken with the following phrase (**without daytime or night-time**) and the following statement (**when evening comes, there will be light**), the verse then depicts a reversal of the first act of creation that marks the diurnal pattern of night and day (Gen 1:3-5); however, the absence of light results, not in darkness, but in continuous light.[385] This reversal underscores the unique quality of the day beyond human comprehension and known only to Yahweh. Although the affirmation that light exists in the evening (v. 7) appears to contradict the assertion that on that day there is no light (v. 6), the two statements may be designed to orient the reader to the first day of creation. At that time, light appears at God's command even though the sun is not created until the fourth day.[386]

**14:8** Verse 8 begins the third (vv. 8-12) of four episodes in chapter 14, which concerns the restoration of Jerusalem as the center of Yahweh's universal reign. The image of **living water**s flow**ing out from Jerusalem** brings to mind significant images in earlier biblical literature.[387] The notion of a river going out (יָצָא, *yāṣā'*) recalls the river that goes out (*yāṣā'*) from Eden to water the entire garden (Gen

---

[382]Ibid.

[383]Merrill, *Haggai, Zechariah, Malachi*, p. 351.

[384]Cf. "continuous day" in the NRSV, NJB, and NJPS, a rendering similar to "never-ending day" suggested in *HALOT*, p. 30.

[385]Meyers and Meyers, *Zechariah 9–14*, pp. 433-434; Sweeney, *Twelve Prophets*, p. 700.

[386]Baldwin, *Haggai, Zechariah, Malachi*, p. 203. Revelation portrays the heavenly Jerusalem as illumined by the glory of God (Rev 21:23) and without any night (Rev 22:5).

[387]Mason, "The Use of Earlier Biblical Material in Zechariah 9–14," pp. 184-187.

2:10). In Ezekiel 47, the prophet envisions water coming out (*yāṣā'*) from under the threshold of the temple; that water forms a river which no one can cross and which flows toward the Arabah and then into the Salt (Dead) Sea. The water of the sea then becomes fresh water, and the sea is filled with living creatures. Along the path of the river grow trees bearing all sorts of fruit, since "where the river flows everything will live" (Ezek 47:9). If Joel is indeed preexilic,[388] then the flow of living water in verse 8 may be similar to Joel 3:18, which portrays a fountain flowing out (*yāṣā'*) of the temple and watering the valley of acacias (or Valley of Shittim). Moreover, the image of living water links this text with the earlier image of the fountain opened for the house of David (Zech 13:1). The waters described in verse 8 are available **in summer and in winter**. The moisture from this river, presumably fed by a fountain (13:1), portends the security of the coming day as it makes the farmers of the region less dependent on the scant rainfall of the region.[389] **The eastern sea** refers to the Dead Sea, known as the Salt Sea in Old Testament times, and the **western**[390] **sea** refers to the Great Sea, later known as the Mediterranean Sea. These two seas and the places mentioned in verse 10 focus geographical attention on the old territory of Judah and on Jerusalem as the place of Yahweh's coming blessing.[391]

**14:9** Yahweh is frequently extolled as the king of the Israelites (1 Sam 8:7; 12:12; Ps 5:2; 84:3; 146:10; Isa 41:21; 43:15; 44:6; Zeph 3:15), but the Old Testament also boldly proclaims Yahweh as **king over** all the nations of **the earth** (Exod 15:6,7,11,18; Ps 9:7; 10:16; 47:8; 96:10; 97:1; 99:1; Jer 10:7,10; Mal 1:14). Three texts are especially suggestive for this context. Within the eschatological vision of judgment, Isaiah 24:23 affirms that Yahweh Almighty reigns on Mount Zion and in Jerusalem and punishes the kings on the earth

---

[388]For discussion of the date of Joel, see Dillard and Longman, *Introduction*, pp. 364-367; Harrison, *Introduction to the Old Testament*, pp. 876-879; and James E. Smith, *The Minor Prophets*, p. 35.

[389]Meyers and Meyers, *Zechariah 9–14*, p. 436.

[390]The word translated "western" is the word "behind" (Deut 11:24; 34:2; Joel 2:20), a notion that derives from the disdain of the Israelites for maritime activity. With their backs turned to the west, the Great Sea stood behind them.

[391]Meyers and Meyers, *Zechariah 9–14*, p. 437.

below. In the wake of the destruction of Jerusalem, Lamentations 5:19 affirms that Yahweh reigns forever and asks Yahweh to restore Zion. Among the nations whose gods are idols (Ps 96:5), Psalm 96:10 implores the nations to say, "Yahweh reigns." The ESV presents a more literal rendering of the concluding affirmation of verse 9, "On that day the LORD will be one and his name one." The wording clearly alludes to the Deuteronomistic creed, that is, the Shema of Deuteronomy 6:4, but it also suggests a cleansing from idolatry.[392] All the nations of the earth recognize that Yahweh alone is the master of the earth (אֶרֶץ, 'ereṣ) and render their worship to Yahweh. This pronouncement complements 13:2 that has asserted that "on that day" the names of the idols are cut off from the land ('ereṣ).

**14:10** The phrase **from Geba to Rimmon** indicates the extent of all Judah from north (2 Kgs 23:8) to south (Josh 15:32; 19:7). Geba is six miles northeast of Jerusalem and constitutes the northern boundary of Judah (1 Kgs 15:22; 2 Kgs 23:8); Rimmon (Neh 11:29) is approximately thirty-five miles southwest of Jerusalem at a point nine miles north of Beersheba where Judah's hill country merges into the Negev or south country. Geba (גֶּבַע, geba') means "hill," and Rimmon, meaning "pomegranate," resembles a word signifying "height" (רָמָה, rāmāh). The choice to use these terms may signal a play on words, suggesting that the hill country of the region is lowered to become like a plain or the great Arabah valley. It is not certain whether the whole land **becomes like the Arabah** or like an arid plain. The Hebrew noun עֲרָבָה ('ărābāh) may refer to any steppe (Num 22:1; Deut 34:1; Josh 4:13; Isa 35:1; 40:3; Jer 5:6), but it appears more frequently to designate the name of the rift valley that extends from the Sea of Chinnereth (Galilee) through the Jordan River valley and the Dead Sea to the Gulf of Aqabah (Deut 1:1,7; 3:17; Josh 3:16; 12:1; Jer 39:4; Amos 6:14). In either case, the initial focus of the verse is on the notion that the area surrounding Jerusalem is flattened like a plain.[393] This topographical transformation would be glad tidings to a Judean farmer who struggles to farm the hilly country round about Jerusalem, since plains are easier to plow and have richer soil quality. Thus, the depiction of eschatological blessings portrayed in the context uses imagery — climate (v. 6), light (v. 7),

---

[392]Mason, "The Use of Earlier Biblical Material in Zechariah 9–14," p. 188.
[393]McComiskey, "Zechariah," p. 1236.

water (v. 8), and terrain (v. 10) — related to the transformation of Jerusalem's agricultural economy from insecurity to abundance (cf. vv. 17-18).[394] More than the flattening of the area surrounding Jerusalem, the primary focus of the verse is the **raising up** of **Jerusalem** and the reestablishment of the city **in its place** (cf. 12:6).[395] Although Jerusalem is already elevated (1 Kgs 12:28; Ezra 1:3; Ps 48:2-3; 122:4; Isa 2:3; Jer 31:6; Micah 4:2), the prophet pictures the city more so (cf. the addition of the word "high" in the TNIV). The imagery of Jerusalem/Zion as an exalted city shares in the ancient Near Eastern conceptualization of a temple and its surrounding city constituting a cosmic mountain in which the earthly and heavenly conjoin (cf. Isa 2:1-4; Micah 4:1-4). Also in view here is a desire to portray Jerusalem as a sort of Sinai,[396] a place where the people of Yahweh have a direct encounter with their king which sanctifies them (see 14:20-21). The description **from the Benjamin Gate to the site of the First Gate, to the Corner Gate** represents the span of the northern wall of the city from east to west. The north to south expanse of the city is represented by the phrase **from the Tower of Hananel to the royal winepresses**. The Tower of Hananel (Neh 3:1; 12:39; Jer 31:38) is apparently a well-known landmark in Jerusalem both before and after the exile. The royal winepresses are mentioned nowhere else in the biblical text. Because the King's Pool (Neh 2:14) and the King's Garden (Neh 3:15) are located just south of the ancient city of David, it is likely that these winepresses are in the southeast corner of Jerusalem.[397]

**14:11** In verse 11, the prophet presents three descriptions of the security restored to Jerusalem. First, **Jerusalem** is **secure** for habitation. Other statements of this reversal of its depopulation at the time of the Babylonian conquest appear earlier in 2:3-7 and 8:7-8. Second, Jerusalem is militarily secure, never again doomed for destruction. Like most translations, the NIV follows the affirmation about repopulation with an assurance that Jerusalem is never again destroyed, but the NASB translates the noun חֵרֶם (ḥērem) as "curse" in the phrase, "and there will no longer be a curse." The word ḥērem

---

[394]Meyers and Meyers, *Zechariah 9–14*, p. 442.
[395]Mason, "The Use of Earlier Biblical Material in Zechariah 9–14," p. 189.
[396]Meyers and Meyers, *Zechariah 9–14*, p. 444.
[397]Ibid., p. 447.

occurs more than twenty times to signify a setting apart, usually for utter destruction (e.g., Josh 6:17-18; 7:11-13; 1 Kgs 20:42; cf. renderings of Zech 14:11 in the ESV and KJV). Several cities conquered by Joshua and the Israelite army are placed under such a curse (Deut 13:12-18; 20:16-18; Josh 6:21; 8:26; 10:28; 11:11). At issue here is whether Zechariah is making a statement about the city's future (**never again will it be destroyed** in the NIV) or is simply affirming that the curse that the ancestors have experienced is no longer in effect ("the curse of destruction will be lifted" in the NJB). The normal associations of *ḥērem* with destruction argue for the former option, but the latter option also plays a key literary role in the book (cf. Rev 22:3). Within the first night vision, the angel of Yahweh asks Yahweh Almighty, "How long will you withhold mercy from Jerusalem and from the towns of Judah, which you have been angry with these seventy years?" The remainder of the book, in essence, answers this question in various ways: the time of Yahweh's wrath on the sins of the ancestors has passed. Jeremiah 33 and Isaiah 43 also support this reading. Jeremiah speaks of a future cleansing of Judah and Israel from sin (Jer 33:8; cf. Zech 13:1; 14:8), a repopulation of the city (Jer 33:7,10-11), and the city dwelling in peace and security (Jer 33:6,16). These promises that reverse the calamity of the fall of Jerusalem and Judah (Jer 33:3-5,7) are connected with both the return from captivity and the arrival of the Branch (Jer 33:7,14-16; cf. Zech 3:8; 6:12). Isaiah 43:28 uses the term *ḥērem* to speak of the coming exile of Judah.[398] Third, Jerusalem is economically secure, the recipient of covenant blessings. The noun translated "secure" (בֶּטַח, *beṭaḥ*) connotes a sense of wellness and safety that is inherently linked to the covenant relationship between Yahweh and Israel (Deut 12:10; 33:12,28; Jer 32:37-38; Isa 32:17).[399] Leviticus uses it in parallel with concepts of having enough to eat (25:18-19; 26:5), a

---

[398]Baldwin, *Haggai, Zechariah, Malachi*, p. 204.
[399]Meyers and Meyers, *Zechariah 9–14*, pp. 448-449. John N. Oswalt, "בָּטַח," *TWOT*, 1:101-102, notes the significance for the context here of the use of the cognate verb בָּטַח (*bāṭaḥ*), meaning "trust," which appears some twenty times in the accounts of Yahweh's deliverance of Jerusalem from the Assyrians in the days of Hezekiah (2 Kgs 18:5,19-22,24,30; 19:10; 2 Chr 32:10; Isa 36:4-7,9,15; 37:10). The Assyrians challenge the worth of Hezekiah but Hezekiah trusts (*bāṭaḥ*) in Yahweh, and Yahweh vindicates that trust.

notion implied in the present context (see comments on 14:8-10 above). It describes the military and political security present during Israel's "golden age" under Solomon (1 Kgs 4:25) and the security that Israel and Judah experience in the days of the Davidic Branch (Jer 23:6; 33:6-16; cf. Ezek 34:25-28; Zech 3:8; 6:12).

**14:12** Yahweh assures the inviolability of the new Jerusalem by afflicting with **the plague** any peoples who fight **against Jerusalem** (cf. 14:15).[400] Verse 12 uses a construction consisting of a verb and its cognate noun to begin the description of the culmination of Yahweh's rescue of Jerusalem. Yahweh **strikes** (נָגַף, *nāgaph*) with a plague (מַגֵּפָה, *maggēphāh*) all those peoples who fight against Jerusalem. The noun *maggēphāh* elsewhere describes the destructive signs of Yahweh's power sent against Egypt (Exod 9:14) and those of Israel who sin in the desert (Num 14:37; 16:48-50; 25:8-9,18; 26:1; 31:16), the losses sustained by Israel during the days of Eli (1 Sam 4:17), the plague suffered by the Philistines after they capture the ark of the covenant (1 Sam 6:4), and the plague that comes upon Israel after David numbers the fighting men of Israel (2 Sam 24:21,25; 1 Chr 21:17,22). The NIV indicates that the plague strikes **all the nations**, but the phrase כָּל־הָעַמִּים (*kāl-hā'ammîm*) is more accurately translated "all the peoples" (cf. the ESV, NASB, and NRSV) Another phrase, כָּל־הַגּוֹיִם (*kāl-haggôyim*), meaning "all the nations" appears three times in this chapter (vv. 2,16,19). The use of *kāl-hā'ammîm* here highlights the universal scope of Yahweh's power. It also is a more personal term appropriate for reporting the suffering experienced by those individuals attacking Jerusalem. A similar interchange of "peoples" and "nations" for the same purpose occurs in 12:2-3. The plague itself is portrayed as affecting flesh, eyes, and tongues. The **flesh** of the people **rot**s away as **they are standing on their feet**. This constitutes a reversal of a covenant curse in Leviticus 26:39 where the verbal root here denoting rotting (מקק, *mqq*) appears twice. Should Israel violate the covenant of Yahweh and not carry out the commands, those who do not perish in the lands of their enemies languish or rot away in those lands. On the coming day of Yahweh, the tables are turned, and Israel's enemies rot away in the environs of Jerusalem. The mention of feet recalls the image of Yahweh's feet standing on the Mount of Olives (14:4), thus intimating Yahweh's superiority over the attackers. Also affected in

---

[400]Floyd, *The Minor Prophets*, p. 554.

the plague are the **eyes**, the organs of vision and comprehension, as well as the **tongue**, the instrument of speech communication, a distinguishing human characteristic.[401]

**14:13** The eschatological phrase translated in the KJV "and it shall come to pass in that day" (וְהָיָה בַיּוֹם, *wᵉhāyāh bayyôm*) marks the beginning of the last episode in the narrative description of the coming day of Yahweh in the chapter: verses 13-21 concern the universal worship of Yahweh as king. **On that day** Yahweh strikes people[402] (cf. 12:4) **with** a **great panic** (מְהוּמָה, *mᵉhûmāh*). When the Israelites enter the promised land, Yahweh promises to put the Canaanites into a confusion or panic before them (Deut 7:23), but a later covenant curse warns that curses, confusion, and rebuke await the Israelites if they do not obey Yahweh (Deut 28:20). The picture of **each** person **seiz**ing **the hand of another** and **attack**ing **each other** recalls when Yahweh causes the Midianites to attack one another as Gideon's army descends upon them (Judg 7:22). This representation appears also in 1 Samuel 14:20 in conjunction with the noun *mᵉhûmāh*. There, the Philistines attack one another with the sword as Saul and his men descend upon them with the ark of the covenant, and the Philistines are thrown into confusion.

**14:14** Ordinarily the preposition בְּ (*bᵉ*) following the verb "fight" (לָחַם, *lāḥam*) indicates the party against whom an attack is waged (Exod 1:10; 14:25; 17:9; Josh 24:9; Judg 1:9; 1 Sam 14:47; 2 Sam 12:26; Neh 4:8). One such instance describes an attack of the men of Judah against Jerusalem before David makes it Israelite territory (Judg 1:8). Nevertheless, the preposition may simply indicate the location in which an action takes place.[403] The close association of Judah and Jerusalem in the rest of the Old Testament and in Zechariah (12:2-7; 14:21; cf. Zech 1:12,19; 2:12) argues for this reading here (**Judah will fight at Jerusalem**) in the NIV[404] rather than "even Judah will fight against Jerusalem" in the ESV and NJB.[405] At

---

[401]Meyers and Meyers, *Zechariah 9–14*, pp. 453-454.

[402]The TNIV renders the masculine pronouns in the verse as plural pronouns.

[403]*HALOT*, p. 104; R. Laird Harris, "בְּ," *TWOT*, 1:87.

[404]McComiskey, "Zechariah," p. 1240.

[405]Sweeney, *The Minor Prophets*, p. 704. Ollenburger, "Zechariah," p. 838, contends that the notice in the previous verse that each man seizes the hand of his neighbor or fellow argues for adopting the reading "against."

first, the mention of Judah fighting seems out of character with the remaining text that emphasizes Yahweh's initiative and solitary action. Nevertheless, the Song of Deborah (Judges 5) is an example of an account of a miraculous intervention on the part of Yahweh (Judg 5:19-21) that does not preclude activity by the people (Judg 5:7,11,12,14-15,23). Also, Judah's participation in battle is required in order to set up the next image, the taking of spoils.[406] The second half of verse 14 lists a brief inventory of the plunder gathered from the **wealth of all the surrounding nations: gold, silver, and clothing**. The notion is similar to Haggai 2:7, where the collection of the nation's wealth accompanies the shaking of the heavens and the earth (see vv. 4-6). The listing of gold before silver in the catalog of spoil reverses the order found more frequently in the biblical literature[407] and earlier in 6:10-11. This shift within the book reflects the shift in the relative value of the precious metals that occurs in the mid to late fifth century B.C. as silver becomes more readily available.[408] Here clothing appears as an image of abundance (cf. 1 Kgs 10:5; 2 Chr 9:4).[409]

**14:15** Verse 15 indicates that **a similar plague** (14:12) engulfs the animals of the nations as well as their people. Here the equine motif extends the picture of divine judgment on the nations to include **the horses, mules,**[410] **and donkeys** as well as **the camels** and other **animals**. The mention of the horse is expected since it is the primary military animal. The additional animals add to the image as they comprise the corps of an army's pack animals.[411] The combined images of blind, deformed people (v. 12) and animals remind the

---

[406]Meyers and Meyers, *Zechariah 9–14*, p. 459.

[407]The order of "silver and gold" appears 59 times, but "gold and silver," 24 times.

[408]Meyers and Meyers, *Zechariah 9–14*, p. 460.

[409]*DBI*, p. 318.

[410]Mules, a hybrid produced by breeding a mare and a male donkey, are scarce in Israel due to the prohibition against crossbreeding animals (Lev 19:19). The Israelites circumvent this ban by importing mules at great expense from Phoenicia and Beth Togarmah (Ezek 27:14). Because of its strength, patience, and surefootedness, mules are used principally as royal mounts (2 Sam 13:29, 18:19; 1 Kgs 10:25; 18:5) and as beasts of burden (2 Kgs 5:17; 1 Chr 12:40). See Roland K. Harrison, "Mule," *ISBE*, 3:430; W.S. McCullough, "Mule," *IDB*, 3:456.

[411]Meyers and Meyers, *Zechariah 9–14*, p. 462.

reader that human and horse are but flesh (בָּשָׂר, *bāśār*) (Jer 17:5; Isa 31:3), and victory comes only through Yahweh and the Spirit of Yahweh (cf. 4:6).[412] The inclusion of animals mentioned earlier in the book invites reflection on those earlier texts. In the night visions (1:7–6:8), horses (1:8; 6:2,6,7) are instruments of Yahweh, and in 10:3 Yahweh vows to make Judah a proud horse in battle. A text similar to the present one speaks of Yahweh striking the horses of all the nations into a panic and blinding them (12:4). As Yahweh exercises universal kingship (14:9), the donkeys of the nations suffer a plague (14:15); Zion's victorious king, however, comes to Zion riding on a donkey (9:9).

**14:16** Verse 16 envisions a yearly pilgrimage to Jerusalem of **survivors** (יֶתֶר, *yāthar*) **from all the nations** conquered by Yahweh **to worship the King**, Yahweh Seba'oth (**the Lord Almighty**) by observing **the Feast of Tabernacles** (Sukkot). The verb *yāthar* appears earlier in 13:8 for those of Jerusalem who survive and are placed in Yahweh's refining fire that yields Yahweh's people. Now, in another instance of reversal and transformation within this chapter, the survivors of all the nations who have gathered to fight against **Jerusalem** (14:2) are now also included among those who go up to Jerusalem to worship Yahweh during the Feast of Tabernacles.[413] This depiction complements the earlier image in 8:20-23 of many from the nations coming to Jerusalem to entreat Yahweh Seba'oth ("the LORD Almighty"). Such a pilgrimage reflects the expectation in the ancient world that leaders of conquered nations make a journey in honor of a new king.[414] Here these survivors come to worship, paying homage or doing obeisance (שָׁחָה, *šāḥāh*) to Yahweh,[415] in a manner reminiscent of the eschatological theme of 8:18-23 and of the Zion tradition's depiction of Yahweh as a powerful and victorious

---

[412]Hahlen, "Equine Imagery," p. 258.

[413]In the words of Stuhlmueller, *Rebuilding with Hope*, p. 161: "Zechariah is extending the canopy of the sacred over foreigners. There is this proviso: everyone must worship Yahweh and join in Israel's traditions of the Exodus out of Egypt and the settlement of the land of Canaan, at least symbolically, by celebrating the Feast of Booths. The Jerusalem temple is beginning to reach out and consecrate the rest of the world."

[414]Ollenburger, "Zechariah," p. 838.

[415]See Gen 43:28; Ruth 2:10; 1 Sam 24:8; 2 Sam 14:4; 1 Kgs 1:31; 2 Kgs 4:37 for noncultic uses of the verb.

warrior-king. Verses 16-17 append the title "King" to the name Yahweh Seba'oth ("the LORD Almighty"). The combination of king (מֶלֶךְ, *melek*) and Yahweh Seba'oth (see on Zech 1:2-3 above) in these verses is unique in the Old Testament, although the terms appear in close proximity in Psalm 24:10 and Malachi 1:14. Noteworthy also is Isaiah 37:16 for its affirmation that Yahweh Seba'oth, the God of Israel, alone is God over all the kingdoms of the earth by virtue of the divine act of creating the heavens and the earth. The opening verse of this section of Zechariah (12:1) identifies Yahweh as the one who stretches out the heavens and who lays the foundation of the earth; now the close of the section presents Yahweh as king over all the earth. The word *melek* occurs often in the Old Testament in conjunction with the names of kings of Judah, Israel, and foreign nations, but in those places the king's personal name appears before the title "king" (e.g., Cyrus king of Persia). At this point, however, the title *melek* appears before the name, emphasizing the kingship of Yahweh Seba'oth. This emphasis is significant in a time in which the title "king" is reserved for the Persian kings Cyrus, Darius, Artaxerxes, and Xerxes who hold sway over the postexilic community (Ezra 1:1,7; 4:11; Esth 1:1).[416] Furthermore, the added title "King" makes explicit the notion of kingship implicit in the name Yahweh Seba'oth. Yahweh Seba'oth who is enthroned between the cherubim (1 Sam 4:4; 2 Sam 6:2; 2 Kgs 19:15; 1 Chr 13:6; Ps 80:1; 99:1; Isa 37:16) still reigns as king even though the ark of the covenant is not present in the postexilic era. This renewed use of the name Yahweh Seba'oth in the postexilic period also calls attention to the kingship of Yahweh and keeps hope alive for a restoration of the Davidic monarchy.

Beginning on the fifteenth day and ending on the twenty-first day of the seventh month (Exod 34:22; Lev 23:33-43; Num 29:12-39; Deut 16:13-15), the Feast of Tabernacles (also known as Booths or Ingathering or Sukkot) is one of the three great annual festivals, celebrating harvest at the close of the agricultural year, recalling Yahweh's provision during the wilderness wanderings, and renewing the Mosaic covenant (Neh 8:14-18). It celebrates not only the entrance into the promised land, but also the lessons learned in the forty years of desert sojourn during which the entire generation

---

[416]Meyers and Meyers, *Zechariah 9–14*, p. 467.

leaving from Egypt die. The nations now also have learned the consequences of rebelling against God, and they observe the feast that commemorates that learning experience.[417] Its association with the completion of harvest makes it an especially apt image for the inclusion of the Gentiles in the worship of Yahweh. Also significant for its mention in this context is its close association with the temple. Solomon's temple is dedicated in the seventh month, the month in which Tabernacles is observed (1 Kgs 8:2; 2 Chr 5:2-3), and it is in the seventh month when the altar of burnt offerings is constructed by the newly returned exiles under the leadership of Joshua and Zerubbabel (Ezra 3:1). The prophet Haggai delivers one of his four oracles on the final day of Tabernacles (2:1-9) in 520 B.C. Within that oracle, Haggai presents Yahweh Seba'oth saying, "In a little while I will once more shake the heavens and the earth, the sea and the dry land. I will shake all nations, and the desired of all nations will come, and I will fill this house with glory" (2:7).

**14:17-19** Yahweh withholds rain from those nations who **do not go up**. Because the Feast of Tabernacles precedes the beginning of the rainy season in mid-October, **no rain** is a suitable threat. More importantly, lack of rainfall is a standard covenant curse (Lev 26:19; Deut 28:22-24), and so the nations are seen now to be under the obligations of the covenant. The use of the noun מִשְׁפָּחָה (*mišpāḥāh*) in the Hebrew text, translated **peoples** by NIV, accentuates this connection to covenant for in Genesis 12:3, Yahweh promises that all peoples on earth are blessed through Abraham (on *mišpāḥāh* see 12:12-14 above). Because Egypt is watered primarily by the Nile rather than rainfall, the promised drought that afflicts those nations who do not worship Yahweh presumably represents no threat to Egypt. Therefore, the prophet portrays the people (*mišpāḥāh*) or family of Egypt as also suffering **the plague** for those who fail to acknowledge Yahweh at **the Feast of Tabernacles**. This prospect of plague for Egypt is fitting, given the formative experience of Israel with Egypt in the biblical narrative (Exodus 7–11). This interest in Egypt may reflect the prophet's awareness of the significant Israelite population in Egypt (Zech 10:10). Several factors explain the growth of this group. First, numerous political and economic refugees

---

[417]Gill, *Minor Prophets*, p. 374.

migrate to Egypt to avoid distress (Gen 12:10-20; 41:57; 46:1-7; 1 Kgs 11:18,40). Second, many from the northern kingdom flee to Egypt following the Assyrian conquest of Samaria in 722 B.C. Third, a large group escapes to Egypt near or after the fall of Jerusalem in 586 B.C. (Jer 24:8; 41:17-18; 43; 44). Fourth, beginning in the mid-fifth century B.C., the fortunes of Judah and Egypt are to a great extent intertwined. Threats in the western frontier of the Persian Empire and intermittent rebellion from Egypt cause the Persians to suppress both Egypt and Judah.[418] Fifth, a substantial collection of Aramaic papyri written by Jewish members of a Persian military garrison living on the southern Egyptian island of Elephantine in the sixth and fifth centuries B.C. shows their syncretistic devotion to Yahweh and other deities. What is more, these Elephantine Jews practice certain behavior denounced by the Old Testament prophets. Among these is their construction of their own temple dedicated to Yahu (a variant spelling of Yahweh).[419] Consequently, this text may be intended as a warning to the Jewish community in Egypt and any of their Egyptian neighbors who come under their influence to return to the normative Judaism represented in the Torah. Such failure to celebrate the Feast of Tabernacles on the part of Egypt or other nations is identified as "sin" (חַטָּאת, *ḥaṭṭā'th*), the principle term for human misconduct in the Old Testament (e.g., Gen 18:20; 50:17; Exod 34:9; 2 Sam 12:13), and deserving punishment (on *ḥaṭṭā'th* see 13:1 above).

**14:20-21** The final verses (20-21) envisage a redefined holiness displacing the old and artificial distinction between the sacred and the secular. Three images portray this new development **on that day**, a phrase that begins and ends the unit. Each image is part of a threefold portrait of redeemed creation and redeemed humanity:[420] holiness pervades public life (bells of horses), private life (every pot in the temple and the city), and religious life (no Canaanite in the temple). In fulfillment of the covenant ideal, holiness characterizes the entire nation (Exod 19:6).[421] First, the inscription **HOLY TO THE**

---

[418]Meyers and Meyers, *Zechariah 9–14*, pp. 475-476.

[419]"Elephantine Papyri," *TBD*, pp. 419-420.

[420]Meyers and Meyers, *Zechariah 9–14*, p. 480.

[421]Chisholm, *Minor Prophets*, p. 272; Petersen, *Zechariah 9–14 and Malachi*, pp. 159-160.

[422]The word for "bells" (מְצִלָּה, *mᵉṣillāh*) is used only once in the Old

LORD appears on the **bells**[422] **of the horses**. In the past, the inscription "HOLY TO THE LORD" appears only on the most sacred items (Exod 28:36; 39:30). It appears now even on the gear of creatures that have evoked fear in the Hebrews and have been evidence of their unwillingness to trust in Yahweh (Exod 14:5-12,23; Deut 17:16; 20:1; Josh 11:1-6; Judg 4:1-3; 5:4-5,19-22; 1 Sam 8:11; 2 Sam 15:1; 1 Kgs 1:5; 10:26-29). Throughout the book, Zechariah has transformed the stereotypically negative master image of the horse, a symbol for rebellion against and independence from Yahweh (Deut 17:14-16; 1 Sam 8:11-17), into a positive image by placing the horses in the service of Yahweh (1:7-17; 6:1-8); the book now closes with the horse appearing again as a redeemed character. Among those trees used to build the rough shelters needed during the Feast of Tabernacles are the myrtle (Neh 8:15; cf. Lev 23:37-40). The appearance of the horses in verse 20 thus contains a subtle echo of the book's beginning: the horse again is among the myrtles having been made holy under the dominion of Yahweh.[423]

Second, **cooking pots in the** temple (i.e., "the house of Yahweh") receive a status similar to **the sacred bowls in front of the altar**. "Pots" (סִיר, *sîr*) are used both for mundane cooking (Exod 16:3; 2 Kgs 4:38-41; Jer 1:13; Ezek 11:3) and for sacral purposes (Exod 27:3; 38:3; 2 Kgs 25:14). Specifically, these sacred bowls (מִזְרָק, *mizrāq*) are used to pour blood at the base of the bronze altar of burnt offering (Lev 4:18,25,30,34), to carry ashes from the altar of burnt offerings (Lev 1:16; 6:10), and to transport blood from the altar of burnt offering outside the temple proper to the Altar of Incense or Ark of the Covenant inside the temple building (Lev 4:7; 16:12-18).[424] Not only are the cooking pots used in the temple now deemed as holy as the sacred bowls, but cooking pots from the city also are even deemed fit for use in sacrificial rites.

Third, the **Canaanite** is now permanently excluded from **the house of** Yahweh Seba'oth (**the LORD Almighty**). English transla-

---

Testament, but its root צָלַל (*ṣālal*) indicates a tingling or quivering, making "bells" a probable rendering. Otherwise, *mᵊṣillāh* may refer to some part of the horse's trapping. If so, pictured may be a metal band on the bridle inscribed with "HOLY TO THE LORD" which, when stretched across the horse's forehead, is reminiscent of the high priests turban, according to Meyers and Meyers, *Zechariah 9–14*, p. 481.

[423]Hahlen, "Equine Imagery," p. 259.

[424]Meyers and Meyers, *Zechariah 9–14*, p. 485.

tions represent some uncertainty about the word "Canaanite" (KJV, NASB, and NIV), which other versions (e.g., ESV, NRSV, NJB, and NJPS) render as "traders." The question concerns whether the Hebrew word (כְּנַעֲנִי, *kᵉnaʿănî*) should be translated as a proper noun ("Canaanite") or as a common noun ("trader").[425] If the reading "trader" is assumed,[426] the image refers to the future absence of merchants who peddle sacrificial animals and gifts in the temple environs and make extortionate profits. However, the literal rendering "Canaanite" is preferred in the context of Zechariah 14,[427] which presents a series of images for pervasive holiness. Now the removal of the Canaanites, who in earlier texts are presented as an archetypal threat to the religious and political integrity of Israel (see Exod 34:11-16; Lev 18:2-5,24-30; 20:22-26; Deut 7:1-6; Ezra 9:1), assures the end of any threat to the holiness of Yahweh's temple and people.[428] The Hebrew text of Zechariah concludes with a seventh use of the phrase **on that day** (vv. 4,6,8,9,13,20,21). Since this seventh occurrence is not necessary to develop the content of the verse and the number seven is significant in Semitic thought, its use here may highlight the future orientation of the chapter, the section (chapters 12–14), and the book, not for the foreseeable historical fortunes of Jerusalem but for the eschatological hope of all humankind.[429]

---

[425]For examples of "Canaan" or "Canaanite" meaning "trader" or "merchant," see Job 41:6; Prov 31:24; Ezek 16:29; 17:4; Hos 12:7; Zeph 1:11 (see comments on Zech 11:7 above). Meyers and Meyers, *Zechariah 9–14*, p. 489, assert that New Testament references to buying and selling in the temple (e.g., Matt 21:12-13; Mark 11:15-18; Luke 19:45-46; John 2:13-16) should not be used in support of *kᵉnaʿănî* being translated "traders" in Zech 14:21.

[426]Baldwin, *Haggai, Zechariah, Malachi*, p. 207; Ollenburger, "Zechariah," p. 839; Petersen, *Zechariah 9–14 and Malachi*, p. 160, Paul L. Redditt, *Haggai, Zechariah, Malachi*, NCB (Grand Rapids: Eerdmans, 1995), p. 144; and Ralph L. Smith, *Micah–Malachi*, p. 292. Sweeney, *The Minor Prophets*, p. 706, suggests that the translation "trader" loses the possible double entendre from "Canaanite," which may intimate both the people and their profession.

[427]McComiskey, "Zechariah," p. 1244; Meyers and Meyers, *Zechariah 9–14*, pp. 490-492.

[428]Also possible is the notion that the Canaanites lose their identity with their integration into the people of Yahweh, for they too join with all nations in the worship of Yahweh.

[429]Meyers and Meyers, *Zechariah 9–14*, p. 492.

# THE BOOK OF
# MALACHI

# INTRODUCTION

## AUTHORSHIP

The name Malachi means "my messenger," and it may be a short-ened form of Malachiya, "messenger of Yahweh." The lack of any genealogical information for the prophet in the opening verse together with the appearance of "my messenger" in 3:1 and "mes-senger" in 2:7 have led some to assert that Malachi is not a person-al name but is rather a title for the prophet.[1] This notion has long standing. The LXX reads "by the hand of his messenger" (ἐν χειρὶ ἀγγέλου αὐτοῦ, *en cheiri angelou autou*), and one manuscript of the Aramaic Targum identifies the messenger as Ezra the scribe. Jerome, Rashi, and Calvin follow the Targum of Jonathan ben Uzziel in understanding Malachi to be an alternate name for Ezra, but 2 Esdras, a work in the Old Testament Apocrypha, lists among the twelve minor prophets, "Malachi, who is also called the messenger of the Lord" (2 Esd 1:40).

Indeed, other prophetic books identify the author in the intro-ductory header, so analogy argues for the plausibility that Malachi is indeed the prophet's name and not simply the title, "my messenger."[2] Although "Malachi" does not appear elsewhere in the Old Testament as a personal name, other names ending in the i-suffix ("my") such as Ethni, meaning "my gift" (1 Chr 6:41), and Beeri, meaning "my well" (Hos 1:1), do appear. Neither does the absence of any further description of Malachi as the "son of" someone or as "the prophet" argue against "Malachi" being a personal name. The

---

[1]See, for example, Graham S. Ogden and Richard R. Deutsch, *A Promise of Hope – A Call to Obedience: Joel and Malachi*, ITC (Grand Rapids: Eerdmans, 1987), p. 67.

[2]Robert B. Chisholm, Jr., *Interpreting the Minor Prophets* (Grand Rapids: Zondervan, 1990), p. 277.

superscription of Obadiah (1:1) lacks the same features. Further-more, the frequent use of the noun "messenger" (מַלְאָךְ, mal'āk) in the Old Testament (196×) argues that its appearances in the book need not be tied to the name nor the name to its appearances in the book.

Nor is it plausible that a later editor transposed the name "my messenger" from 3:1 to the beginning of the book, while collating three anonymous prophet texts, Zechariah 9:1–11:17, 12:1–14:21, and Malachi 1:1–4:6 (see comments on Authorship of Zechariah). Zechariah 9:1 and 12:1 as well as Malachi 1:1 all begin with the head-ing מַשָּׂא (maśśā'), meaning "burden" but translated "oracle" in the NIV. Several factors, however, show that the association of Malachi with the oracles in Zechariah is superficial. First, Zechariah 9:1 and 12:1 do not really function as full titles or superscriptions in the same way as does Malachi 1:1. Second, though the superscription of all three texts (Zech 9:1; 12:1; Mal 1:1) designates the following con-tent as a maśśā', the noun maśśā' is in the absolute form only in Malachi. Third, the oracle of Malachi is "to" (אֶל, 'el) Israel rather than "upon" (אַל, 'al) the land of Hadrach (Zech 9:1) and Israel (Zech 12:1). Fourth, the superscription of Malachi makes a simple affirmation that the word of Yahweh came to the prophet in a form common to other prophetic books (Ezek 1:3; Hos 1:1; Joel 1:1; Jonah 1:1; Micah 1:1; Zeph 1:1; Zech 1:1), and the syntax of the superscription of Malachi places "Malachi" (מַלְאָכִי, mal'ākî) after "by the hand of" (בְּיַד, bᵉyad). This construction ("by the hand of Malachi"), as in Haggai 1:1 ("through the prophet Haggai"), indi-cates the human instrument of revelation. Thus, the name Malachi appears in Malachi 1:1 where one would expect a personal name within a superscription, and the preponderance of the data does not argue against the assumption that the name Malachi is the prophet's personal name.[3]

---

[3]Modern commentators accepting Malachi as the prophet's personal name include B.S. Childs, *Introduction to the Old Testament as Scripture* (Philadelphia: Fortress, 1979), pp. 492-494; Robert L. Alden, "Malachi," in *Expositor's Bible Commentary*, ed. by Frank E. Gaebelein (Grand Rapids: Zon-dervan, 1985), 7:702-703; Andrew E. Hill, *Malachi*, AB 25D (New York: Doubleday, 1998), pp. 15-17; Pieter A. Verhoef, *Books of Haggai and Malachi*, NICOT (Grand Rapids: Eerdmans, 1987), pp. 154-156.

Little is known about the author himself. Talmudic legend places Malachi among those who return to Palestine from the Babylonian exile under the leadership of Zerubbabel and Joshua (*b. Zebah* 62a) and dates the beginning of his ministry in the second year of Darius (520 B.C.) (*b. Meg* 15a). The content of the book itself indicates Malachi has a strong interest in the temple, the priesthood, and the sacrificial system (Mal 1:6-13; 2:1-4,8-9; 3:3-4,6-11), but he appears to speak concerning it as an outsider.[4] Although a strong critic of the community, his opening and closing messages evidence passionate concern for the people.

# DATE

The oracles in Malachi lack specific historical dates as those found in Haggai and in Zechariah 1–8. Therefore, the book's date must be ascertained from other internal evidence. Several factors within the book clearly place Malachi in the Persian period. First, the Persian term for a "governor" (פֶּחָה, *peḥāh*) appears in 1:8. This term is used frequently for the Persian governor in Nehemiah (2:7,9; 3:7; 5:14,15,18; 12:26), and Haggai uses it for Zerubbabel (Hag 1:1,14; 2:2,21). Moreover, references to a fully functioning (though abused) sacrificial system (Mal 1:7-8) and to the doors of the temple (1:10) indicate a time after the completion of the temple in 516 B.C. The laxity with which the priests fulfill their duties (1:8-13) and the community's neglect of the tithe payment (3:8-10) may suggest a date further removed from the temple dedication when spiritual fervor has waned.

The latest possible date for the book is 180 B.C., since Sirach 49:10 refers to the "Twelve Prophets." Several parallels between Malachi and Ezra–Nehemiah point to a date in the fifth century B.C., but the exact relationship among the books and the three personalities is unclear. Ezra, Nehemiah, and Malachi refer to intermarriage with foreign wives (Ezra 9–10; Neh 13:23-27; Mal 2:11), failure to pay tithes (Neh 13:10-14; Mal 3:8-10), the covenant with Levi (Neh 13:29; Mal 2:4,8), and social injustice (Neh 5:1-13; Mal 3:5). However, Malachi does not refer to Sabbath abuse, a problem

---

[4]Hill, *Malachi*, p. 18.

with which Nehemiah is concerned (Neh 13:15-22). Malachi never mentions Ezra and Nehemiah, and neither Ezra nor Nehemiah mention Malachi. This mutual silence prevents placing the books in a definitive order.

A date around 420 B.C. would account for a lack of mention in the books of Ezra and Nehemiah, and the similar concerns among the three books would be explained by a failure of the reforms of Ezra and Nehemiah to bear lasting fruit. However, attempts to support a date around 420 B.C. by comparing the content of Malachi to that of the so called "Holiness Code" and "Priestly Code" (i.e., one of the sources postulated by the documentary hypothesis for the composition of the Pentateuch) fail on three scores. First, the existence of such codes as source documents for the Pentateuch is debatable.[5] Second, even if one allows for their existence, the date of the final form of those codes is a matter of conjecture. Third, the book of Malachi does not adhere any more closely to the content of one of the hypothesized codes as opposed to the other.[6]

A date sometime near Nehemiah's second visit to Jerusalem (Nehemiah 13) around 432 B.C. is advanced for three primary reasons. First, the existence of identical abuses in Malachi and Nehemiah related to tithing (Mal 3:8-10; Neh 13:10-14), mixed marriages (Mal 2:11; Neh 13:23-27), and oppression of the disadvantaged (Mal 3:5; Neh 5:1-13) suggests that the two works may originate from a similar time period. Second, the prominence of the law in both Malachi and Nehemiah suggests a time after Ezra's arrival in Jerusalem (458 B.C.). Third, the need for tithes to provide temple funds suggests a time after that of Haggai, Zechariah, and Ezra, when monies from the Persian royal treasuries are made available for the building of the temple (Ezra 6:15-17,20-24).[7]

---

[5]See T.D. Alexander, "Authorship of the Pentateuch," *DOTP*, pp. 61-72; Raymond B. Dillard and Tremper Longman III, *Introduction to the Old Testament* (Grand Rapids: Zondervan, 1994), pp. 38-48; G.A. Klingbeil, "Historical Criticism," *DOTP*, pp. 401-420; R.K. Harrison, *Introduction to the Old Testament* (Grand Rapids: Eerdmans, 1969), pp. 495-541.

[6]Rex A. Mason, "Malachi: Theology of," *NIDOTTE*, 4:927.

[7]Among those who support a date during the ministry of Ezra or governorships of Nehemiah are Gleason Archer, *A Survey of Old Testament Introduction* (Chicago: Moody, 1994), p. 440; Joyce G. Baldwin, *Haggai, Zechariah, Malachi: An Introduction and Commentary*, TOTC 24 (Downers Grove, IL:

Nevertheless, a date in the governorship of Nehemiah is far from certain. First, Malachi 1:8 seems to assume that the Persian governor would accept the people's offerings if they were worthy, but Nehemiah refuses to accept offerings (Neh 5:14-18).[8] Second, Ezra and Nehemiah make a continual distinction between priests and Levites, naming both in proximity to one another in at least twenty-three passages.[9] Malachi, however, never mentions priests and Levites together in the same passage (1:6; 2:1,7; 3:3). Since Malachi does not follow the practice of Ezra and Nehemiah, it may be that Malachi comes from a different milieu than Ezra and Nehemiah. The consistent distinction made between priest and Levite in Ezra and Nehemiah, moreover, seems to suggest that Ezra and Nehemiah work during a later time when the structures of authority have solidified in the community.[10]

That Malachi speaks of Israelite men marrying the daughter of a foreign god (2:11), but Ezra seems shocked and appalled to learn that Israelite men have taken daughters from the neighboring peoples as wives for themselves and their sons (Ezra 9:1-4) further implies that Malachi and Ezra are not contemporaries. If Malachi has earlier attempted to stop the practice of intermarriage with the neighboring peoples, both the degree of shock expressed by Ezra and the extreme measure (i.e., the sending away of the foreign wives and their children) advised by him to combat the problem (Ezra 10:3,9-11) would be explained.

A date early in the postexilic period nearer the time of Haggai and Zechariah may provide the more plausible context for Malachi's oracles. The defeat of the Persians at the battle of Marathon in 490 B.C. and its harbinger of change may have encouraged notions of the approaching day when Yahweh would "overthrow royal thrones and shatter the power of foreign kingdoms" (Hag 2:22), when Yahweh's name would be feared among the nations (Mal 1:11,14),

---

InterVarsity, 1972), pp. 212-213; Ralph Smith, *Micah–Malachi*, WBC 32 (Waco: Word, 1984), p. 298; and Verhoef, *Haggai and Malachi*, pp. 156-160.

[8]See Chisholm, *Minor Prophets*, p. 278, who dates the book after Ezra, but before Nehemiah.

[9]Ezra 1:5; 2:70; 3:8-12; 6:16-20; 7:7,13-24; 8:15,29-33; 9:1; 10:5; Neh 7:73; 8:9-13; 9:38; 10:28-34,38; 11:3-18; 12:1,7-8,22-24,27-30,44; 13:13,29-30.

[10]Joel F. Drinkard, "The Socio-Historical Setting of Malachi," *RevExp* 84 (1987): 387-389.

and when the nations would recognize the blessedness of Israel (Mal 3:12).[11] At such a time, the prophet Malachi calls the postexilic community to the repentance required before the arrival of the coming day of Yahweh (Mal 4:1-6).[12]

Other factors accord with a date around the turn of the fifth century for Malachi's ministry. King Artaxerxes' promise to Ezra of financial help from the royal treasuries of the province of Babylon (Ezra 7:12-24) indicates that similar financial aid extended to Sheshbazzar and Zerubbabel for the rebuilding of the temple and the renewal of the temple cult (Ezra 6:4,8-10) has been suspended between the time of the initial return (538 B.C.) and the time of Ezra (458 B.C.). This interruption of imperial funds during the interim period would make more devastating the lack of Israelite tithes (Mal 3:6-12). That Malachi speaks to other concerns found in the books of Ezra and Nehemiah (see above) but still does not refer to Sabbath abuse, a problem with which Nehemiah is concerned (Neh 13:15-22), suggests that the problems with Sabbath observance have not yet become problematic. The words of Malachi would provide a natural precursor to the work of the reformers. Therefore, the prophet's ministry ought to be assigned to a time before the reforms of Ezra and Nehemiah,[13] a date loosely supported by the Talmudic tradition that places the beginning of the prophet's ministry in the second year of Darius (520 B.C.) (b. Meg 15a).

Linguistic factors further substantiate a date near 500 B.C. The Hebrew of Malachi closely resembles the predominantly classical biblical Hebrew found both in the exilic books of Jeremiah and Ezekiel and in the early postexilic books of Haggai and Zechariah. It, however, lacks many of the characteristic elements of late biblical Hebrew found in Ezra, Nehemiah, and Chronicles, books clearly from the later postexilic period.[14]

---

[11]"Malachi, Book of" *DBI*, p. 529.

[12]Hill, *Malachi*, p. 55.

[13]Advocates of this date include Drinkard, "Socio-Historical Setting," pp. 387-389; William J. Dumbrell, *The Faith of Israel: Its Expression in the Books of the Old Testament* (Grand Rapids: Baker, 1988), p. 237; Otto Eissfeldt, *Old Testament: An Introduction*, trans. by Peter R. Ackroyd (New York: Harper & Row, 1965), pp. 442-443; Hill, *Malachi*, pp. 77-84; Eugene H. Merrill, *Haggai, Zechariah, Malachi*, WEC (Chicago: Moody, 1994), pp. 376-378; and Julia M. O'Brien, *Priest and Levite in Malachi*, SBLDS 121 (Atlanta: Scholars, 1990), pp. 113-133.

[14]Hill, *Malachi*, pp. 81-83, 395-400.

## HISTORICAL BACKGROUND

Internal evidence within the book of Malachi indicates that the prophet Malachi ministers after the completion of the rebuilding of the temple in 516 B.C. The use of the Persian term for a "governor" (פֶּחָה, *peḥāh*) in Malachi 1:8 indicates a time in which the Persian satrapy Eber-Nahara or Beyond the River (translated "Trans-Euphrates" in the NIV) has been subdivided into provinces (Ezra 7:21), such as Samaria, Ammon, Idumea, Ashdod, and Judah (called Yehud by the Persians), ruled by "governors" (Hag 1:1,14; 2:2,21; Mal 1:8). References to a fully functioning (though abused) sacrificial system (1:7-8) and to the doors of the temple (1:10) presuppose a completed temple.

Furthermore, since Ezra, Nehemiah, and Malachi refer to intermarriage with foreign wives (Ezra 9–10; Neh 13:23-27; Mal 2:11), failure to pay tithes (Neh 13:10-14; Mal 3:8-10), the covenant with Levi (Neh 13:29; Mal 2:4,8), and social injustice (Neh 5:1-13; Mal 3:5), Malachi likely works before or near the time Ezra the scribe comes to Jerusalem in 458 B.C. and the advent of Nehemiah as governor in 445 B.C. This period extending from the late sixth and fifth centuries B.C. witnesses key changes in the status of Persia among the nations and in Israel's postexilic community.

Just as rebellions on the fringe of the empire have occupied the attention of the Persian emperor Darius at the beginning of his reign (522–486 B.C.), trouble on the empire's frontiers engage the emperor in his closing years. In 499 B.C., the Athenians aid the Ionian cities of Asia Minor and Cyprus in their efforts to repel Persian authority. A Persian campaign against Athens in 492 has success in Thrace and Macedonia, but it then fails when a storm wrecks the Persian fleet off Mount Athos in the northern Aegean Sea. The Greeks then later rout Persia in the battle of Marathon (490 B.C.).

Possibly, their defeat at the hands of the Greeks in 490 B.C. leads the Persians to take preemptive action to avoid rebellion on the more vulnerable western fringe of the empire. One such measure may have been the appointment of non-Davidic governors in Judah. Lacking a governor with a Davidic pedigree would help squelch sentiment for rebellion based on messianic expectation. A more powerful priesthood and scribal class would also emerge in the Jewish community from such a transition of power away from the Davidic family into the hands of non-Jewish or non-Davidic persons. Political purges by Darius may also explain Malachi's lack of attention to individual leaders in the community as it becomes evident that human leadership is transitory.[15]

Xerxes, also known as Ahasuerus in other versions (e.g., the ESV, NASB, and NRSV), succeeds Darius in 486 B.C. and rules the empire until his death in 465 B.C. This monarch who takes Hadassah, a Jewish woman also known as Esther, as queen (Esther 1–2) oversees a series of setbacks for Persia. Although the Persians defeat the Spartans at the Pass of Thermopylae in 480 B.C. and occupy Athens later in that year, they suffer a crushing defeat in a monumental naval battle at Salamis. Once again, in 479 B.C., the Persians fall to the Greeks at Plataea and Mycale, and all hopes of expanding the empire westward die.[16]

Xerxes is assassinated in 465 B.C. and is succeeded by his son Artaxerxes I (Longimanus). During the reign of Artaxerxes I, the Greeks support a rebellion by the Egyptians against Persia. Although suppressed in 446 B.C., this revolt indicates that the Persians' hold over their empire is more precarious than in earlier times. In order to ensure payment of tribute and loyalty from local leaders in the event of border wars,[17] Artaxerxes sends Ezra the scribe to Jerusalem to instruct the Jews in the law of God and to support the Jews' temple in 458 B.C. (Ezra 7:6-9,21-26) and his cupbearer Nehemiah to the city to act as governor and to rebuild the city's walls in 445 B.C. (Neh 1:1,11; 2:5; 5:14).[18] After the death of Artaxerxes I in 424 B.C., Persia is ruled by a rapid succession of emperors who face rebellion. The chain of Xerxes II, Artaxerxes II, and Artaxerxes III culminates in Alexander the Great conquering the weakened state and control of the region passing into Greek hands by 330 B.C.[19]

A decline in the spiritual state of Israel during this era matches the decline of the Persian Empire outside the borders of Israel. As the presence of the rebuilt temple in Jerusalem does not bring about

---

[15]Hill, *Malachi*, p. 76.

[16]R.E. Hayden, "Xerxes," *ISBE*, 4:1161.

[17]Jon L. Berquist, *Judaism in Persia's Shadow: A Social and Historical Approach* (Philadelphia: Fortress, 1995), p. 26.

[18]P.R. Bedford, "History of Israel 8: Postexilic Community," *DOTHB*, p. 490.

[19]A. Kuhrt, "Persia, Persians," *DOTHB*, p. 776.

a new, autonomous, and prosperous Jewish kingdom ruled by the Davidic house, religious fervor begins to wane in the community. Promises made earlier by Haggai and Zechariah, having been wrongly understood, now seem to be a cruel mockery.[20] The laxity of the priests in fulfilling their duties (Mal 1:8-13) as well as the community's neglect in paying the tithe (Mal 3:8-10) evidence a waning spiritual fervor. This diminished commitment to Yahweh and the law is exacerbated when, as in the days of the conquest under Joshua, those Hebrews emigrating to Palestine encounter non-Hebrew residents in the land (Ezra 10:2; Neh 13:3,23; Mal 3:5) and strict obedience to the law comes into conflict with movements toward assimilation with Gentile culture.

The period of Ezra and Nehemiah is one in which two walls are built.[21] Readers readily recognize Nehemiah's wall built to protect the postexilic community from its enemies among the Gentiles, but one may also identify a second wall, Ezra's wall, consisting of the Torah which forms a spiritual boundary between Israel and all other people. This law would create a holy people fit to live within a holy city surrounded by Nehemiah's walls. Indeed, the account of Ezra's activities in Ezra 7:1–10:44 appears in the midst of accounts of the rebuilding of the temple and the city walls (Ezra 3:1–6:22; Neh 1:1–6:16). This literary positioning reflects the larger message in Ezra–Nehemiah that only the people's separation from the nations through adherence to the law of Moses would allow for rebuilding the house of Yahweh.[22] Depending on the chronological relationship among the ministries of Malachi, Ezra, and Nehemiah (see Date above), the words of Malachi either prepare for or reinforce the building of "Ezra's wall" and call the community to remember the law of Moses given to Israel at Horeb (Mal 4:4).

---

[20]Douglas Stuart, "Malachi," in *The Minor Prophets: An Exegetical and Expository Commentary*, ed. by Thomas Edward McComiskey (Grand Rapids: Baker, 1998), 3:1254.

[21]Douglas Green, "Ezra–Nehemiah," in *A Complete Guide to the Bible*, ed. by Leland Ryken (Grand Rapids: Zondervan, 1993), pp. 207-209.

[22]Ibid., pp. 207-209.

## LITERARY FEATURES

Like the Hebrew text of Haggai, Malachi does not contain the short "lines" one might expect in poetry. The frequency of various Hebrew particles (e.g., the relative pronoun, the sign of the direct object, and the definite article) in Malachi indicate the book is written in prose[23] rather than in the rich lyrical poetry that characterizes the majority of the prophetic writings. That elevated prose, however, uses limited parallelism and occasional strong imagery, features often associated with biblical poetry.[24]

The book of Malachi exhibits a hortatory style characterized by direct address. Forty-seven of the book's fifty-five verses appear in first person addresses by Yahweh through the prophet. These first person addresses, moreover, are a product of the disputation structure that characterizes the book. Although the disputation genre is found throughout the prophetic literature (Isa 40:27; 47:5-11; 49:3-4,14-18; Ezek 18:1-4,25-29; 20:15; and throughout Haggai), Malachi makes more pervasive use of the genre among the prophetic corpus. The disputation structure has three major segments. For example (1:2-3), an opening statement presents a truth claim by the prophet ("'I have loved you,' says the LORD") answered with an (hypothetical) audience rebuttal ("How have you loved us?"). The prophet then gives a rejoinder reasserting the original premise and presenting supporting evidence for its claim ("I have loved Jacob but I have hated Esau; I have made this hill country a desolation").

The book begins with a superscription that identifies the book as an "oracle" and "the word of the LORD." As an oracle, it asserts Yahweh's involvement in the historical situation, clarifies any previous prophecy about the situation, and provides a basis for an appropriate response. The further identification of the oracle as "the word of the LORD" gives the content a sense of urgency as well as authority and reliability.[25]

---

[23]Hill, *Malachi*, p. 24.

[24]Robert Alter, *Art of Biblical Poetry* (New York: Basic Books, 1985), pp. 10-11; Alden, "Haggai," in *Expositor's Bible Commentary*, ed. by Frank E. Gaebelein (Grand Rapids: Zondervan, 1985), 7:573-574; Harrison, *Introduction*, p. 947; Leland Ryken, *Words of Delight: A Literary Introduction to the Bible*, 2nd ed. (Grand Rapids: Baker, 1992), p. 159.

[25]Hill, *Malachi*, pp. 140-141.

Six disputations (see above) comprise the majority of the book (1:2-5; 1:6–2:9; 2:10-16; 2:17–3:5; 3:6-12; 3:13–4:3).[26] Three of the disputations are directed against the people of Judah as a whole (1:2-5; 2:10-16; 3:6-12), one against the priesthood (1:6–2:9), and two against skeptics within the community who doubt Yahweh's justice (2:17–3:5; 3:13–4:3). The final passage (4:4-6) summarizes the two main themes of the book: the need to keep the law of Moses (the primary focus of the first three disputations), and the need to prepare for the coming day of Yahweh (the focus of the final three disputations).[27]

The oracular formulas "this is what the LORD Almighty says" or "says the LORD Almighty" appear some twenty-one times in the book. Very rarely, however, do they appear as they normally do in other prophetic books as boundary markers for oracles. The formulas instead add emphasis to various assertions within oracles. Especially notable are instances in which the phrases appear in clusters in successive verses (1:8-11,1:13-14; 2:7-8; 3:10-12).

The use of questions placed on the lips of Yahweh is a standard literary device employed by Malachi. Not all the questions in the book are of the same type. Some are rhetorical with a self-evident reply (1:2,13; 2:10,15), others accuse (1:6,8; 2:10), and others move forward the author's argument by raising issues for clarification (1:2,6,7; 2:14,15,17; 3:2,7,8,13).

A variety of other rhetorical and literary features occur in the book. The description of the ideal ministry of the priest (2:6-7) is an encomium, a praise of an abstract quality or meritorious character trait. Hyperbole is found in 2:13 ("you flood the LORD's altar with tears") and 4:1 ("Not a root or a branch will be left"). There is a paronomasia between the prophet's name "Malachi" (*mal'ākî*) in 1:1 and the reference to "my messenger" (*mal'ākî*) in 3:1. The prophet satirizes the community's actions by challenging them to offer the inferior gifts they are presenting to Yahweh instead to their governor (1:8). Metonymy, the substituting of a word or phrase for a similar expression, occurs in 1:2-3 as the ancestors Jacob and Esau come to represent the Israelites and Edomites and in 2:11 where "the daughter of a foreign god" represents idolatrous, foreign wives.

---

[26]See Hill, *Malachi*, pp. 26-34, for a summary of alternative proposals concerning the structure of the book.

[27]Stuart, "Malachi," p. 1249.

The author utilizes rich imagery. A prominent familial motif emerges as the prophet uses the siblings Jacob and Esau and their descendant nations Israel and Edom (1:2-5) to communicate the depth of Yahweh's covenant faithfulness to his people, and the father-son relationship becomes an image of Israel's covenant obligations to Yahweh (1:6-14). The affirmation in 2:10 that the community has one father may refer to the patriarch Abraham or Jacob (see comments on 2:10 below). Violence done to covenant relationships is exemplified by the statements about divorce in 2:10-16.

The cavalcade of images in the book includes a series of anthropomorphisms, the ascription to Yahweh of human qualities, in chapter 3. Yahweh sits as a refiner at a crucible whose heat melts away the dross from the ore to reveal the purified silver (3:3), and Yahweh acts as a witness against evildoers (3:5; cf. 2:14). Yahweh promises to open the windows of heaven if Israel brings their tithes (3:10). Similes abound. Yahweh is like a refiner's fire or a launderer's soap (3:2) and sits as a refiner or purifier who refines the Levites like gold and silver (3:3). Israel claims they have acted like mourners before Yahweh (3:14). The coming day of Yahweh burns like an oven (4:1). In that day, the righteous skip like calves released from the stall (4:2). Metaphor appears in 4:3 to describe the fate of the wicked on the day of Yahweh ("they will be ashes under the soles of your feet").

The prophet effectively combines concepts from Israelite culture and the surrounding Persian culture to construct powerful images. The "book of remembrance" in which the names of the faithful are recorded (3:16) parallels not only the "book of life" spoken of elsewhere in the Old Testament (Exod 32:32-33; Ps 69:28; Dan 12:1) but also the Persian "book of the remembrance" referred to in Esther 6:1[28] or royal memorandum referred to in Ezra 6:2.[29] Moreover, the "sun of righteousness" which rises "with healing in its wings" (4:2) combines the associations of the sun with Yahweh in Psalm 84:11 and the winged sun-disk of Persian art to depict Yahweh as the one who blesses and protects.

---

[28]John H. Walton, Victor H. Matthews, Mark W. Chavalas, *The IVP Bible Background Commentary: Old Testament* (Downers Grove, IL: InterVarsity, 2000), pp. 486, 489.
[29]David C. Deuel, "Malachi 3:16: 'Book of Remembrance' or Royal Memorandum? An Exegetical Note." *MSJ* 7 (1996): 107-111.

The prophet uses allusion to highlight the love of Yahweh, the errors of Israel, the prospects of the nation, and their responsibility to the covenant. The opening disputation (1:2-5) recalls Yahweh's choice of Jacob over Esau. Yahweh's "covenant of peace" with the Levite Phinehas (Num 25:12-13) forms the backdrop for the critique of the priests in 2:1-9. The opening of the floodgates of heaven recalls both the torrential rains of the Noahic flood (Gen 7:11; 8:2) and the miraculous abundant provision for the people of Samaria during an Aramean siege (2 Kgs 7:2,19) to describe the copious blessing that ensues should Israel bring the whole tithe into the storehouse (3:10). The conclusion of the book (4:4-6) invokes the name of Moses, the mediator of the covenant at Horeb, and the name of that covenant's later champion Elijah as it calls the reader to faithfulness to Yahweh.

## THEOLOGY

The book of Malachi concludes the section of the Hebrew Old Testament known as the *Nevi'im* or the Prophets. It is therefore appropriate that Malachi reiterates and develops important themes of earlier prophets. Likewise, the book rests solidly on the foundation or constitution of the covenant, the Torah or law upon which the prophetic office and corpus is built.

The influence of Deuteronomy pervades every section of the book. Deuteronomy and Malachi are the only Old Testament books to begin with an address to the entire nation of Israel. Malachi refers to Horeb (4:4), the term for Sinai in Deuteronomy (Deut 1:2,6,19; 4:10,15; 5:2; 9:8; 18:16; 29:1). A collection of classic covenant vocabulary found in Deuteronomy permeates Malachi. The noun בְּרִית (*bᵉrîth*), generally translated "covenant," is found twenty-six times in Deuteronomy and appears six times in Malachi (2:4,5,8,10,14; 3:1). Israel is Yahweh's "treasured possession" (סְגֻלָּה, *sᵉgullāh*) (Deut 7:6; 14:1-2; 26:18; Mal 3:17). The election of Israel is described as Yahweh's love (אָהַב, *'āhab*) for the nation (Deut 4:37; 7:8,13; 10:15; 23:5; Mal 1:2) and Yahweh's sanctuary (Mal 2:11), and father-son imagery is used to speak of Yahweh's relationship with Israel (Deut 1:31; 32:6; Mal 1:6). Each of the book's disputations contrasts the faithfulness of Yahweh with Israel's unfaithfulness. The love of Yahweh requires a response of fear and love from the people (Deut 5:10; 6:5; 11:1,13; 30:15,19-20.). Israel is called to observe or keep (שָׁמַר, *šāmar*) Yahweh's commands and decrees (Deut 4:2,6,23,40; 5:32; 6:17, etc.; Mal 2:7,9,15,16; 3:7,14) in order that Israel may be blessed (Deut 7:13-14; 26:15; 28:1-12; Mal 3:10). Because Israel has not kept Yahweh's commands, they are threatened with curse (אָרַר, *'ārar*; מְאֵרָה, *mᵊʾērāh*; חֵרֶם, *ḥērem*) (Deut 7:26; 13:17; 28:15-20; Mal 1:14; 2:2; 3:9; 4:6).

Leviticus and Deuteronomy describe a variety of covenant curses that would ensue should Israel fail to keep covenant as well as restoration blessings that would occur after Yahweh has sent rehabilitative punishment upon Israel. A high proportion of each appears within Malachi. Israel encounters the anger or rejection of Yahweh (Mal 1:9; cf. Lev 26:17,24,28,41; Deut 4:24-25; 29:19,23,26-27), rejection and destruction of temple worship (Mal 1:10; 2:2,12; cf. Lev 26:31), desolation (Mal 4:6; cf. Lev 26:31-35,43; Deut 28:51; 29:22), fiery destruction (Mal 3:2; 4:1; cf. Deut 28:24; 32:22), decimation and infertility (Mal 2:3; cf. Lev 26:22,36; Deut 28:18,51,59,62), death and destruction (Mal 2:12; 3:2; 4:6; cf. Lev 26:36,39; Deut 4:26; 28:20-22,45,48,51,61), and curse and vengeance (Mal 1:14; 3:5,9; cf. Lev 26:41,43; Deut 28:16,20-21,27; 30:19). On the other hand, Israel's repentance leads to a renewal of Yahweh's favor, loyalty, and presence (Mal 3:1,7,17; cf. Lev 26:42,45; Deut 4:29,31; 30:3,9), the restoration of true worship and the ability to be faithful to Yahweh (Mal 1:11; 3:3; cf. Deut 4:30; 30:6-8), agricultural bounty (Mal 3:10-11; cf. Lev 26:42; Deut 30:9), general prosperity, well-being, and wealth (Mal 3:12; 4:2; cf. Deut 30:3,5,9; 32:39), power over enemies and aliens (Mal 1:5; 4:3; cf. Deut 30:7), and restoration (Mal 3:17; cf. Lev 26:44; Deut 30:6; 32:39).[30] Malachi thus emphasizes Israel's need for fidelity to the covenant Yahweh made with her at Horeb and the ramifications of keeping or breaking the law of Moses.[31]

Within the book appears a creative reworking and integration of major covenant themes that inspired earlier prophets.[32] Malachi emphasizes the internal attitudes of the people over external ritual-

---

[30]Stuart, "Malachi," pp. 1261-1262.

[31]Ibid., p. 1261.

[32]Eileen M Schuller, "Malachi," in *NIB*, ed. by Leander E. Keck (Nashville: Abingdon, 1996), 7:846.

ism (Mal 1:9-13; 2:2-3; 3:16-18; cf. Amos 5:12-15,21-24; Micah 6:6-8). The visitation of blessing or curse is contingent upon personal and corporate obedience to Yahweh. Like the preexilic prophets, Malachi admonishes the community to repent as a condition for Yahweh's return to the community (Mal 3:6-7; cf. Jer 24:6-7; Hos 6:1-3; Joel 2:12-14; Zeph 3:11-13). Also present is a concern for the disadvantaged and wronged (Mal 3:5) that characterizes the great eighth-century prophets (e.g., Isa 1:16-17; 3:14-15; 10:1-2; Amos 4:1; 5:11-15,24).

Postexilic prophecy did not share with preexilic prophecy a focused concern on idolatry (see, for example, Isa 41:7-8; 44:12-20; 57:8-9; Jer 7:31; 13:25; 32:30-35; Ezekiel 8; Hos 13:2; Zeph 1:4-6). The exile had, in essence, cleansed Israel of that sin. The concerns of Malachi and his postexilic colleagues, Haggai and Zechariah, are elsewhere. The book of Malachi criticizes the people for a lack of sincerity in their faith. They are not ardent in covenant worship and life. His criticism is founded in the Torah. The admonition to the priests in 2:1-12 indicates that they especially have failed in teaching the people and modeling for them devotion to the demands of covenant (Lev 10:11; Deut 17:8-11).

The books of Haggai, Zechariah, and Malachi each focus on the temple, but Ezekiel's vision of the eschatological temple does not have the same influence on Malachi as on his postexilic colleagues. Haggai and Zechariah encourage the postexilic community to rebuild the temple. Zechariah expands that message by focusing on the need for the community to repent so that their worship in the temple is acceptable. Ministering after the construction of the temple, Malachi then seeks a reform of temple worship, a cleansing of the priesthood, and an awakening from spiritual apathy.[33]

Eschatological concerns also align Malachi with the other postexilic prophets, Haggai and Zechariah. The book raises issues of theodicy (2:17; 3:14-15), and the solution is eschatological. Though Malachi does not directly refer to "the day of Yahweh," his affirmation that "the day is coming" (4:1) indicates that Malachi shares with earlier prophets the anticipation of such a day. In that day, Yahweh avenges wickedness, remembers those who fear Yahweh, and shows faithfulness to those who serve Yahweh (Mal 3:1-5; 3:16–4:3). With

---

[33]"Malachi, Book of," *DBI*, p. 530.

Zechariah, Malachi pictures the coming day as one that refines and purifies the faithful (3:2; 4:1; cf. Zech 12:6; 13:9) and effects repentance (3:7; cf. Zech 10:9-12). Zechariah envisions this purified remnant surviving the judgment that comes upon the nations and those of Jerusalem not included among Yahweh's people (13:8–14:9). In the day of Yahweh, the remnant will not experience the "destruction" (חֵרֶם, ḥērem) of the day (14:1-2,11). Malachi, however, heightens the call to repentance by closing the book with a threat of the curse (ḥērem) on the land (4:6) rather than with images of future blessing like those that conclude Zechariah (14:20-21).

Whether the coming figure called "my messenger" in 3:1 is to be identified with "the messenger of the covenant" in the same verse (see comments on 3:1) remains uncertain, but the arrival of this figure (or these figures) is clearly associated with covenant. The anticipation of a messenger recalls the angel or messenger who appears in Exodus 23. There the community is charged with listening to the angel and obeying his commands so that Yahweh's blessings may come upon them (Exod 23:21-26). The covenant God of justice executes justice against those who violate justice and covenant relationships (Mal 2:17; 3:5). The purified community then is able to bring righteous offerings to Yahweh and the community's relationship with Yahweh is restored (Mal 2:4).

The notion of a "book of remembrance" (Mal 3:16) is an original contribution to Hebrew eschatology. This image parallels the "book of life" spoken of elsewhere in the Old Testament (Exod 32:32-33; Ps 69:28; Dan 12:1) and the Persian "book of the remembrance" in Esther 6:1[34] or royal memorandum referred to in Ezra 6:2.[35] Furthermore, this "book of remembrance" may have encouraged later references to books of judgment, deeds, and life in intertestamental apocalyptic literature[36] and the "book of life" used to distinguish the righteous from the wicked in Revelation 20:11-15.

Malachi addresses a set of special themes. Though Malachi is greatly concerned with temple affairs, he rejects the notion that proper dispensing of ritual is sufficient. Malachi would rather one shut the

---

[34]Walton, Matthews, Chavalas, *IVP Bible Background Commentary*, pp. 486, 489.

[35]Deuel, "Malachi 3:16," pp. 107-111.

[36]*T. Ab.* 12.6-7; *Mart. Ascen. Isa.* 9.19-23; *Jos. Asen.* 15.2-5.

doors of the temple than for shallow, unaffecting worship to persist (Mal 1:10). The payment of tithes and aspects of temple worship have significance only as they indicate the community's desire to return to Yahweh so that Yahweh might return to them (3:7). The people of Yahweh must act in faithfulness toward one another if they are to expect the continued blessing of Yahweh (2:13-16).

Linked to Malachi's concern for sincere worship is his attention paid to the priesthood. Malachi makes explicit reference to a covenant between Yahweh and the priesthood that is implied elsewhere (e.g., Jer 33:21), and Malachi refers to priests as "the messenger of the LORD Almighty" (Mal 2:7). The context of 2:4 does not clarify whether Malachi is rejecting the priesthood in favor of a more general covenant with Levi.[37] In fact, the alternation of "priest" or "priests" (2:1,7) and Levi (2:4,8) indicates Malachi is not attempting an unambiguous distinction between the two but is speaking to their complementary ministries.

The prophet draws attention to the integral role of the nations. The future honoring of Yahweh among the nations stands in dramatic contrast with Israel's failure to give Yahweh proper reverence and obedience (1:6-11). Nevertheless, should Israel return to Yahweh, then all the nations call Israel blessed (3:7-12).

Although the prophet does not speak extensively about social injustices, he shows special concern for marriage. Malachi's high regard for the institution of marriage reflects its exalted position in the Proverbs (Prov 5:15-20; 6:23-29; 31:10) and anticipates the words of Jesus directed against easy divorce (Matt 19:1-9; Mark 10:1-12).

The theme of covenant renewal underlines the entirety of the book, and the notice of the return of Elijah at the close of the book (4:5-6) accentuates that theme.[38] The reminder to keep the law of Moses (4:4) and the anticipation of the coming of Elijah before the great day of Yahweh (4:5) places the Prophets on the same level of authority with Torah. Whether the closing verses of the book (4:4-6= MT 3:22-24) represent a later editorial addition intended as a conclusion to both the Book of the Twelve (Hosea–Malachi)[39] and the

---

[37]Dumbrell, *Faith of Israel*, p. 238.

[38]Ibid., p. 237.

[39]Both Sirach 49:10 and Josephus (*Ag. Ap.* 1.40) evidence an early grouping of the Twelve Prophets.

larger unit of the *Nevi'im* (Joshua–Malachi),[40] they remind the people of Judah that they, like their ancestors, remain under the authority of the Mosaic law. The mention of Elijah alongside Moses links the Latter Prophets (Isaiah, Jeremiah, Ezekiel, and the Minor Prophets) with both the Torah (Genesis–Deuteronomy) and the Former Prophets (Joshua, Judges, Samuel, and Kings).

The threat of curse in the book's final verse gives it a dark conclusion, and attempts have been made to soften the ending. Some LXX manuscripts move verse 4 to after verse 6, while the NJPS reflects the synagogue practice of reading verse 5 a second time after verse 6. This aversion is unnecessary, since the warning only serves to highlight the mercy of Yahweh spoken of in the heart of the section (4:5-6a). Yahweh sends Elijah to cause the turning of the people's hearts so that Israel may be the treasured possession of Yahweh (3:17) and may enjoy healing from the sun of righteousness (4:2). Moreover, such an ending is not totally unique among the prophetic writings. The concluding verse of Isaiah contains an implicit curse on those who rebel against Yahweh (66:24). Indeed, prophetic ministry primarily warns the people of the coming day of Yahweh's wrath so that they might experience salvation rather than judgment.

The ordering of the Old Testament books in English Bibles follows the ordering of the LXX rather than that of the MT. The canonical ordering of the MT with its conclusion in Chronicles and the Writings rather than in the Prophets and Malachi may complicate the characterization of Malachi as the natural introduction to the New Testament. Nonetheless, the mention of Moses (4:4) and Elijah (4:5), the two individuals who appear with Jesus in the transfiguration (Matt 17:4; Mark 9:5; Luke 9:30), in this section does anticipate the coming of Christ about whom the Law and the Prophets testify (John 1:45; Luke 24:27; Acts 26:22; 28:23; Rom 3:21). Likewise, early Christian authors regard the book as a significant theological bridge between the old covenant Scriptures and those of the new covenant. For example, both Tertullian (*Adv. Jud.* 9) and Origen (*Comm. Jo.* 2.17; 6.13) read Malachi 4:2-6 (=MT 3:21-24) as a direct foreshadowing of John the Baptist as the messenger of Jesus Christ.

The book of Malachi is quoted directly five times in the New

---

[40] Hill, *Malachi*, p. 45.

Testament. Quotations in the Gospels serve to define Jesus as the messiah by identifying John the Baptist as the prophetic precursor to the messiah. Matthew 11:10, Mark 1:2-3, and Luke 7:27 each quote Malachi 3:1 with Mark conflating this quotation with wording from Isaiah 40:3. Luke 1:17 contains a loose quotation of Malachi 4:5-6, and the disciples' question about the coming of Elijah (Mark 9:11) reflects the content of that same passage. Paul quotes Malachi's affirmation of Yahweh's choice of Jacob over Esau (Mal 1:2) in his discussion of God's election (Rom 9:13). Whereas Malachi uses the names to refer to their descendant nations, Paul focuses on the individual ancestors.

The soteriological and eschatological roles of Jesus and John also are the objects of allusions to the text of Malachi in the Gospels. John's question carried by his disciples to Jesus, "Are you the one who was to come, or should we expect someone else" (Matt 11:3; Luke 7:19), and John's denial that he is not the messiah but is one sent before him (John 3:28) indicate that John recognizes Jesus to be the promised "messenger of the covenant" while John is one whom Yahweh designates "my messenger who will prepare the way before me" (Mal 3:1).

## MESSAGE

The preaching of the second temple period focuses on the person of Yahweh, Yahweh's covenant relationship with Israel, and the pressing need for complete obedience to Yahweh in both national and personal life. Malachi especially stresses the covenant between Yahweh and Israel and the other covenants that arise from it. He specifically mentions the covenant with Levi (2:4-5), the covenant of the fathers (2:10), and covenant of marriage (2:14), and the messenger of the covenant (3:1). Each of the book's disputations contrasts the faithfulness of Yahweh with Israel's unfaithfulness in covenant. The faithful love of Yahweh requires a response of fear and love from his people (Deut 5:10; 6:5; 11:1,13; 30:15,19-20).

This love should be evidenced in worship that involves the spirit as well as ritual form. The prophet asserts that Yahweh would rather one shut the doors of the temple than for shallow, unaffecting worship to persist (1:10). Yahweh desires and demands to be loved as a person rather than to be manipulated as an abstract divinity.[41] The postexilic community has dedicated the rebuilt temple with fervent joy (Ezra 6:16-18), but now only defective sacrifices are being offered by disinterested priests who act on the behalf of stingy, uncommitted worshipers. The payment of tithes and aspects of temple worship have significance only as they indicate the community's desire to return to Yahweh so that Yahweh might return to them (3:7). The people of Yahweh must act in faithfulness toward one another if they are to expect the continued blessing of Yahweh (2:13-16). The Haggai–Zechariah–Malachi corpus presents a spiritual history of the postexilic community that culminates in Israel standing at the brink of covenant failure. Malachi now calls Israel to complete her worship and obedience of Yahweh just as they have completed the construction of the temple urged by Haggai and Zechariah.[42]

Throughout the book, Malachi uses vocabulary associated with covenant, allusions to the patriarchal covenants, and allusions to covenant curses and blessings (see Theology above) to remind the postexilic community of the wondrous election of Israel by Yahweh and the conditions Yahweh has placed on the nation for their continued exaltation. As Leviticus 26 and Deuteronomy 28 emphasize, the community's obedience leads to blessing, but its unfaithfulness results in curse. Yahweh has been faithful to his word; however, Israel has breached covenant (3:6-7). Even a cursory reading of Malachi reveals Israel's need for fidelity to the covenant Yahweh made with Israel at Horeb and the ramifications of keeping or breaking the law of Moses.[43] The people of Judah, like their ancestors, remain under the authority of the Mosaic law (4:4-6=MT 3:22-24).

The prophet also addresses those who have been faithful to Yahweh but now find themselves waiting in frustration for Yahweh to act. The coming of the day of Yahweh has been delayed, but Yahweh reaffirms the certainty of its promised coming. Yahweh, in time, distinguishes between the righteous and the wicked (2:17–3:5). Nevertheless, on that day, the faithful righteous escape the destruc-

---

[41]Hill, *Malachi*, pp. 41-42.
[42]Ronald Pierce, "Literary Connectors and a Haggai/Zechariah/Malachi Corpus," *JETS* 27 (1984): 277-289; idem, "A Thematic Development of the Haggai/Zechariah/Malachi Corpus," *JETS* 27 (1984): 401-412; Hill, *Malachi*, pp. 14-15.
[43]Stuart, "Malachi," p. 1261.

tive wrath of God and are purified by Yahweh's refining fire (3:2-4). Only through and after that purification does Israel experience restoration in the day of Yahweh that the coming of Elijah heralds (4:1-5=MT 3:19-23).

# OUTLINE

# SELECTED BIBLIOGRAPHY ON MALACHI

Alden, Robert L. "Malachi." In *Expositor's Bible Commentary*, vol. 7. Ed. by Frank E. Gaebelein. Grand Rapids: Zondervan, 1985.

Baldwin, Joyce G. *Haggai, Zechariah, Malachi: An Introduction and Commentary*. TOTC 24. Downers Grove, IL: InterVarsity, 1972.

_____ . "Malachi 1:11 and the Worship of the Nations in the Old Testament." *TynBul* 23 (1972): 117-124.

Blomberg, Craig L. "Elijah, Election, and the Use of Malachi in the New Testament." *Criswell Theological Review* 2 (1987): 99-117.

Coggins, Richard J. *Haggai, Zechariah, Malachi*. OTG. Sheffield: Sheffield Academic Press, 1987.

Glazier-McDonald, Beth. *Malachi: The Divine Messenger*. SBLDS 98. Atlanta: Scholars Press, 1987.

Graffy, Adrian. "Malachi." In *The International Bible Commentary: A Catholic and Ecumenical Commentary for the Twenty-First Century*. Ed, by William R. Farmer. Collegeville, MN: Liturgical Press, 1998.

Hill, Andrew E. *Malachi*. AB 25D. New York: Doubleday, 1998.

Klein, George L. "An Introduction to Malachi." *Criswell Theological Review* 2 (1987): 19-37.

Mason, Rex A. *The Books of Haggai, Zechariah, and Malachi*. CBC. Cambridge: Cambridge University Press, 1977.

McKenzie, Steven L., and Howard N. Wallace. "Covenant Themes in Malachi." *CBQ* 45 (1983): 549-563.

Merrill, Eugene H. *Haggai, Zechariah, Malachi*. WEC. Chicago: Moody, 1994.

O'Brien, Julia M. *Priest and Levite in Malachi*. SBLDS 121. Atlanta: Scholars Press, 1990.

Ogden, Graham S. "The Use of Figurative Language in Malachi 2:10-16." *BT* 39 (1988): 223-230.

Ogden, Graham S., and Richard R. Deutsch. *Joel and Malachi: A Promise of Hope, A Call to Obedience*. ITC. Grand Rapids: Eerdmans, 1987.

Petersen, David L. *Zechariah 9–14 and Malachi: A Commentary*. OTL. Philadelphia: Westminster Press, 1995.

Redditt, Paul L. "The God Who Loves and Hates." In *Shall Not the Judge of All the Earth Do What Is Right?* Pp. 175-190. Ed. by Paul L. Redditt and David Penchansky. Winona Lake, IN: Eisenbrauns, 2000.

——————. *Haggai, Zechariah and Malachi*. NCB. Grand Rapids: Eerdmans, 1995.

Schuller, Eileen M. "Malachi." In *NIB*, vol. 7. Ed. by Leander E. Keck. Nashville: Abingdon, 1996.

Stuart, Douglas. "Malachi." In *The Minor Prophets: An Exegetical and Expository Commentary*, vol. 3. Ed. by Thomas Edward McComiskey. Grand Rapids: Baker, 1998.

Taylor, Richard A., and E. Ray Clendenen. *Haggai, Malachi*. NAC. Nashville: Broadman & Holman, 2004.

Verhoef, Pieter A. *The Books of Haggai and Malachi*. NICOT. Grand Rapids: Eerdmans, 1987.

# MALACHI

## I. TITLE (1:1)

¹**An oracle: The word of the LORD to Israel through Malachi.**ᵃ

ᵃ*1 Malachi means my messenger.*

**1:1** Malachi begins with two labels that identify the book as an **oracle** and **the word of the LORD**, a specific combination found only here and in Zechariah 9:1 and 12:1. However, the title of Malachi is more comparable to the titles in Nahum and Habakkuk than these two sections in Zechariah, since only in Nahum and Habakkuk does the word "oracle" (מַשָּׂא, *maśśāʾ*) also stand at the beginning of an entire prophetic book. The word *maśśāʾ* (translated "prophecy" in the TNIV) generally indicates a particular type of prophetic pronouncement.[1] The oracle answers those in the Israelite community who may doubt or wonder about Yahweh's intended action in a particular historical situation. Specifically, an oracle asserts Yahweh's involvement in the historical situation, clarifies any previous prophecy about the situation, and provides a basis for an appropriate response. As a *maśśāʾ*, Malachi displays these three elements. In view of a corrupt priesthood (1:6–2:9) and an unfaithful people (2:10–3:15), Yahweh clarifies through the prophet the implications of the Pentateuch (i.e., Torah) for "those who feared the LORD" (3:16) and exhorts them to remember the law of Moses given at Mount Sinai (4:4).[2]

---

[1]Richard D. Weis, "Oracle," *ABD*, 5:28-29; Michael H. Floyd, "The מַשָּׂא (*maśśāʾ*) as a Type of Prophetic Book," *JBL* 121 (2002): 401-422.

[2]Regarding the function of Malachi as a *maśśāʾ*, Floyd, "מַשָּׂא," pp. 416-418, asserts that the book encourages a covenant fidelity in accordance with the provisions of the sacred writing (3:16) as opposed to oral instruction given by a corrupt priesthood.

The message of the book is further described as "the word of the LORD," a common introductory phrase among the prophetic books (Jer 1:2; Ezek 1:3; Hos 1:1; Joel 1:1; Jonah 1:1; Micah 1:1; Hag 1:1; Zech 1:1; Mal 1:1). The titles of Hosea, Joel, Micah, and Zephaniah all describe their contents as "the word of LORD," and the titles of Jeremiah, Jonah, Haggai, and Zechariah assert that "the word of LORD came to [the prophet]." Here, the introductory phrase "the word of Lord" appears without a verb (cf. 2 Chr 35:6) and is expanded with two prepositional phrases **to Israel** and **through Malachi**. The preposition "to" (אֶל, *'el*) is used instead of the preposition "concerning" (אַל, *'al*), which appears in the similar formula found in Jeremiah 14:15, 46:1, and Zechariah 12:1. The use of *'el* minimizes the role of Malachi and portrays the message as coming directly from Yahweh to the people.[3]

The word of Yahweh comes "to" Israel (see also 1:5; 2:11,16; 3:22). Although, in Malachi, the people addressed are also called Judah (2:11; 3:4), Jacob (2:12), and descendants of Jacob (3:6), the comprehensive term "Israel" here denotes the covenant nation. Moreover, the book's content indicates that the eschatological Israel will both exclude unfaithful Jews and include Gentiles who acknowledge Yahweh.[4] In Isaiah, the term "Israel" takes on such a theological nuance that it is no longer purely national or geographic, but refers rather to the faithful people of Yahweh (Isa 4:2; 10:17-23; 14:1; 56:8). Deuteronomy is the only other Old Testament book addressed to "all Israel" (Deut 1:1). The address to Israel in Malachi 1:1, therefore, aligns the book even more closely to Deuteronomy whose theology often is reflected by Malachi (e.g., 4:4). Most immediately, the term sets the stage for the discussion of the election of Jacob in verses 2-5.

The word of Yahweh comes "through Malachi." The word "through" translates the Hebrew idiom "by the hand of" (בְּיַד, *b⁰yad*), a formula also used in Haggai (1:1,3; 2:1) to identify the prophet and elsewhere as a marker of intermediate agency (Exod 9:35; Lev 8:36; Josh 20:2; 1 Kgs 12:15; Neh 8:14; Esth 1:12; Zech 7:7). However, the

---

[3]Richard A. Taylor, and E. Ray Clendenen, *Haggai, Malachi*, NAC (Nashville: Broadman & Holman, 2004), p. 243.

[4]For use of "Israel" as a title for the eschatological people of Yahweh, see Joel 2:27; 3:2,16; Amos 9:9,14; Zech 9:1; 12:1.

word "Malachi" (מַלְאָכִי, *mal'ākî*), which means "my messenger," presents a certain ambiguity about whether it is a name or a title (on the word "Malachi," see the comments in the Introduction above). This uncertainty exists even among the ancient translations and paraphrases. The LXX reads "by the hand of his messenger" (ἐν χειρὶ ἀγγέλου αὐτοῦ, *en cheiri angelou autou*), and one manuscript of the Aramaic Targum identifies the messenger as Ezra the scribe. But 2 Esdras, a work in the Old Testament Apocrypha, lists among the twelve minor prophets, "Malachi, who is also called the messenger of the Lord" (2 Esd 1:40). The word "Malachi" may be borrowed from 3:1, where it is translated in most versions as "my messenger"; however, its presence in 1:1 signifies that Yahweh now speaks through someone other than the priests, who no longer offer the people true instruction (Mal 2:6).

## II. PROPHETIC DISPUTATION ABOUT YAHWEH'S CLAIM TO LOVE ISRAEL (1:2-5)

[2]"I have loved you," says the LORD.

"But you ask, 'How have you loved us?'

"Was not Esau Jacob's brother?" the LORD says. "Yet I have loved Jacob, [3]but Esau I have hated, and I have turned his mountains into a wasteland and left his inheritance to the desert jackals."

[4]Edom may say, "Though we have been crushed, we will rebuild the ruins."

But this is what the LORD Almighty says: "They may build, but I will demolish. They will be called the Wicked Land, a people always under the wrath of the LORD. [5]You will see it with your own eyes and say, 'Great is the LORD -even beyond the borders of Israel!'

Malachi 1:2-5 contains a prophetic disputation about Yahweh's claim to love Israel, perhaps an assertion not self-evident to those who have survived the exile. The genre of prophetic disputation serves as a kind of public debate to counter popular opinions; the disputation does not record an actual exchange between debaters, but it reflects such an exchange (cf. Isa 40:27-31; Jer 7:1-15; 8:8-9;

26:1-7; 28:1-11; Ezek 11:14-21; Micah 2:6-11; Hag 1:2-11).[5] Thus, verse 2a presents Yahweh's claim to love Israel ("I have loved you") and Israel's uncertainty about that claim ("How have you loved us?"). To reverse this public skepticism, verses 2b-5 present Yahweh's response in support of the claim that Yahweh loves Israel. This response compares Yahweh's treatment of the two descendants from Isaac who represent the peoples of Israel and Edom. Yahweh has rejected Edom (v. 3) and will deny them any possibility of restoration (v. 4). This divine judgment upon Edom witnessed by Israel will cause Israel to acknowledge the universal sovereignty of Yahweh (v. 5). Therefore, 1:2-5 attempts to convince Judah that, in spite of the conditions of the postexilic period, Yahweh continues to love Judah who will soon witness Edom's permanent demise.

**1:2** In verse 2, the prophet constructs a kind of dialogue between Yahweh and the people (see also Mal 1:6-7; 2:14,17; 3:7-8,13; cf. Jer 13:11-12; 15:1-2). Yahweh claims to love Israel (**I have loved you**), but Israel remains uncertain about that claim (**How have you loved us?**). The NIV translates **But you ask** a term (וַאֲמַרְתֶּם, *wa'ămartem*) that appears eight additional times in Malachi to introduce human responses that dispute claims made by Yahweh (1:6,7,13; 2:14,17; 3:7,8,13). Yahweh responds to the people's skepticism with a comparison of Yahweh's treatment of the two descendants from Isaac who represent the peoples of Edom and Israel (**Was not Esau Jacob's brother? Yet I have loved Jacob**). Esau stands for Edom (Gen 36:1,8; Deut 2:4-12; Jer 49:8-10), and his brother Jacob, for Israel (Num 23:7; Ps 14:7; Isa 41:8). Thus, the story of Yahweh's election of Jacob over his twin Esau (Gen 25:19-34) and the perennial conflict between their descendants forms the backdrop of this section.

Even though this dialogue may not record an actual conversation per se, it does reflect the concerns of the community toward Yahweh. At issue is a perceived distance between the theological affirmation of Yahweh's love (Deut 7:7-8,12-13; 10:15; 23:5) and the experience of the postexilic community. The glorious expectations of the people for a restored kingdom and renewed greatness (Zeph 3:20; Hag 2:7-9,21-23; Zech 1:17; 2:4,9; 6:15; 8:12-13) have not transpired. They remain under Persian rule (1:8), and they still experience agri-

---

[5]Michael H. Floyd, *Minor Prophets: Part 2*, FOTL 22 (Grand Rapids: Eerdmans, 2000), p. 638.

cultural failures regarded as covenant curses (3:11-12). These hardships following the exile have apparently caused doubt about Yahweh's love for the people. The language of love (אָהַב, *'āhab*) appears extensively in ancient near eastern treaty and covenant texts to speak of a suzerain's choice to enter into a relationship with a vassal nation.[6] A theological adaptation of this language appears extensively in Deuteronomy (7:8,12-13; 10:15; 23:5) and in Jeremiah (31:3) to speak of Yahweh's choice of Israel, a theme also articulated in the first book in the Book of the Twelve (Hos 3:1; 9:15; 11:1,4; 14:3-5). Moreover, just as loyalty to the suzerain is demanded from the vassal, Israel's choice as Yahweh's people obligates them to show evidence of their love for Yahweh (Deut 5:10; 6:5; 7:9; 11:1,13,22; 19:9; 30:16,20). In Malachi, the failure of Israel to recognize Yahweh's covenant love for them leads to their failure to demonstrate covenant love toward Yahweh (1:6–2:9) and others (2:10-16).

**1:3** The assertion (**but Esau I have hated**) draws upon the theme of sibling rivalry between Esau and Jacob (Gen 25:28) and the role reversal in which Jacob receives the greater blessings over Esau (Gen 27:1-41).[7] In this way, the Genesis narrative anticipates the contemporary experience of both nations.[8] Both the descendants of Jacob and of Esau experience judgment and defeat, but only the descendants of Jacob endure. The remnant community has been restored to the land that has been promised to Abraham, Isaac, and Jacob. Some sixty to seventy years after the temple is rebuilt along with much of Jerusalem, Nabatean raiders ransack Edomite territory and force its inhabitants to seek refuge in the Negev region south of Judah. Later the Maccabeans conquer the Edomites (1 Macc 5:3,65; 2 Macc 10:15-23), and John Hyrcanus compels them to be circumcised.[9]

The language of "love" and "hate" in verses 2 and 3 should not be interpreted simply in the sense of "more" or "less."[10] Even though

---

[6]William L. Moran, "The Ancient Near Eastern Background of the Love of God in Deuteronomy," *CBQ* 25 (1963): 77-87.

[7]Other examples of a younger sibling receiving a greater blessing than the older one include Abel over Cain (Gen 4:4); Seth over Cain (Gen 4:25); Isaac over Ishmael (Gen 21:12-13); Judah over Reuben, Simeon, and Levi (Gen 49:8-12); and Ephraim over Manasseh (Gen 48:17-20).

[8]Marvin A. Sweeney, *The Twelve Prophets*, BerOl: Studies in Hebrew Narrative and Poetry (Collegeville, MN: Liturgical Press, 2000), p. 724.

[9]Josephus, *Antiquities of the Jews* 9.257.

[10]Verhoef, *Books of Haggai and Malachi*, p. 200.

the notion reflects the contrast of preferential treatment within the family structure (Gen 29:31-33; Deut 21:15-17; 1 Sam 1:2-5; cf. Luke 14:26), the idea fails to convey Yahweh's consistent and determined opposition to Edom (Isa 34:5-17; 63:1; Jer 49:7-22; Ezek 25:12-14; 35:15; Joel 3:19; Amos 1:11-12; Obad 10-16). The same language later appears in Romans 9:11-13. There Paul quotes Genesis 25:23 ("The older will serve the younger") and Malachi 1:2-3 ("Jacob I loved, but Esau I hated") in support of his assertion that the election of Israel does not arise because of human merit ("Yet, before the twins were born or had done anything good or bad—in order that God's purpose in election might stand: not by works but by him who calls"). Paul asserts that God has directed Israel's history without regard for the deeds of Israel or Edom. This assertion stands in contrast to an alternative interpretation within Judaism that Yahweh's election of Jacob over Esau indeed relates to Edom's actions: "God loved Jacob, but he hated Esau because of his deeds."[11] If Romans 9:13 appropriates the citation from Malachi 1:2-3 regarding God's election of Israel, the context of 1:2-6 evidently emphasizes the rejection of Edom. Yahweh has indeed "loved" Jacob, but what is more, Yahweh has "hated" Esau. The word "hate" (שָׂנֵא, śānē') here conveys "not so much an emotion as a rejection in will and deed"[12] (cf. the NET's "yet I chose Jacob" and "rejected Esau" or the NJPS's "yet I have accepted Jacob and have rejected Esau").

Such rejection ultimately results in Edom's destruction, the effects of which are portrayed with the images of **wasteland** and **jackals**. Esau's **mountains** (translated "hill country" in the ESV, NRSV, NLT, and NJPS) most likely refer to the hill country of Seir (Gen 36:8-9; Deut 2:5; Josh 24:4). The image of these mountains turning into a wasteland implies disaster and desolation that result from divine judgment.[13] Instead, Esau's inheritance is left to the

---

[11]Ps. Philo, *Biblical Antiquities* 32.5. Though no cause for Yahweh's condemnation of Edom in Malachi 1:3 is given, Obadiah 10-14 describes Edom's violence done to his "brother Jacob" and how Edom had stood aloof and gloated over Judah in the day of their distress. Edom had entered Judah and looted her and cut off fugitives. These may recall the aftermath of the Babylonian conquest of Jerusalem in 586 B.C. or some earlier time in which Edom took advantage of a military loss in Judah's history.

[12]Otto Michel, "μισέω," *TDNT*, 4:687.

[13]*DBI*, p. 927; Hermann J. Austel, "שָׁמֵם," *TWOT*, p. 937.

**desert jackals** (Jer 9:11; 10:22; 49:33). Such an image occurs elsewhere in a curse of desolation on a city (Isa 13:22; 34:13; Jer 9:11; 10:22; 49:33; 51:37; Lam 4:3).[14]

**1:4-5** Even if Edom attempts to rebuild, Yahweh will demolish whatever Edom rebuilds. Edom's statement, **we will rebuild** is literally "we will turn and build." The verb "turn" (שׁוּב, *šûb*) commonly signifies repentance. Its appearance with that sense in Malachi 3:7 and 4:6 is significant in comparison with 1:4. Edom vows they will turn, but cannot. Israel is called to turn, but will they? If they refuse to repent, they too will suffer curse.[15] Edom's permanent devastation is further evidenced in Edom's new name **the Wicked Land**, a name that further emphasizes the abiding wrath of Yahweh at Edom's wickedness.[16] While the word **under** can portray protection (e.g., Ps 91:4), it can convey divine judgment (e.g., Ezek 20:37-38).[17] The term used to denote the **wrath of** Yahweh (זַעַם, *za'am*) may, as in Numbers 23:7-8 and Micah 6:10, designate curse.[18] If so, this is the first occurrence in the book of words signifying curse. Other words include אָרַר (*'ārar*) in 1:14, 2:2(3×), and 3:9(2×) and חֵרֶם (*ḥērem*) in 4:6. Thus the opening section of the book begins with a notice that Edom will be accursed forever by Yahweh and ends with a warning of curse if Israel fails to repent. In between come notices of the present accursed state of Israel with the implied call to repent. This complexity of curse vocabulary also bolsters the covenant motif within the book.

The name "the LORD Almighty" (יהוה צְבָאוֹת, *YHWH ṣᵊbā'ôth*) appears twenty-four times in Malachi.[19] It appears once in the messenger formula **this is what the LORD Almighty says** (1:4), three times in nonformulaic expressions (2:7,12; 3:14), and the remainder in the phrase, "says the LORD Almighty" (1:6,8-11,13-14; 2:2,4,8,16;

---

[14]*DBI*, p. 580.

[15]Taylor and Clendenen, *Haggai, Malachi*, p. 254.

[16]Adrian Graffy, "Malachi," in *The International Bible Commentary: A Catholic and Ecumenical Commentary for the Twenty-First Century*, ed. by William R. Farmer. (Collegeville, MN: Liturgical Press, 1998), p. 1201.

[17]*DBI*, p. 905.

[18]Robert P. Gordon, "זעם," *NIDOTTE*, 1:1129.

[19]On *YHWH ṣᵊbā'ôth* elsewhere in the Old Testament, see Nahum 2:13 above. The divine name is also translated as "the LORD of Hosts" (ESV, KJV, NASB) or "Yahweh Sabaoth" (NJB).

3:1,5,7,10-12,17; 4:1,3). These uses each appear in contexts high-lighting some aspect of the name's association with the presence of Yahweh signified in the ark and/or the temple, with Yahweh's iden-tity as the enthroned God, or with Yahweh's power as the Lord of the Armies. Moreover, the title is found in each of the seven major sections that comprise the book.[20] The single use of the formula "this is what the LORD Almighty says" occurs in the first section of the book (1:2-5) in which Yahweh defends the assertion, "I have loved you" (v. 2). The military connotations of the name emerge as *YHWH ṣᵉbā'ôth* asserts the demonstration of love for Israel in the demolition of Edom if she builds. Doing so will validate the divine choice of Jacob and exhibit the greatness of Yahweh beyond Israel's borders (v. 5). The use of a unique messenger formula may highlight the thematic significance of the section for the book: Yahweh is eager to demonstrate love for Israel, and Israel **will see it**.

When Israel sees the devastation of Edom, Israel will acknowl-edge Yahweh as **great** over Israel. The repetition of the noun גְּבוּל (*gᵉbûl*) in verses 4 and 5 focuses on the contrast between Edom as "the Wicked Land" (v. 5) and the greatness of Yahweh over the "boundaries" or "land" **of Israel**. A play on sounds highlights the greatness (גָּדַל, *gādāl*) of Yahweh's name over the "land" (*gᵉbûl*) of Israel. The Hebrew preposition מֵעַל (*mēʿal*) means "over," "above," or "upon" rather than **beyond** found in NIV and most modern translations.[21] The concluding declaration thus concurs with the sec-tion's central theme of Yahweh's love for Israel by affirming that Yahweh's greatness overshadows Israel. Subsequent statements expand the theme to speak of Yahweh's greatness beyond Israel's borders among the nations (1:11,14).

[20]Mal 1:1-5; 1:6-14; 2:1-9; 2:10-16; 2:17–3:5; 3:6-12; 3:13–4:6[MT 3:13-24]; See Hill, *Malachi*, pp. xl-xlii, for a division of the book into six, rather than seven, major sections.

[21]G. Lloyd Carr, "עָלָה," *TWOT*, 2:669; *BDB*, p. 759; *IBHS*, pp. 657-658; Hill, *Malachi*, pp. 145, 161-162; Schuller, "Malachi," p. 855; Verhoef, *Books of Haggai and Malachi*, p. 194. For a defense of the rendering "beyond," see Taylor and Clendenen, *Haggai, Malachi*, p. 259.

# III. PROPHETIC DISPUTATION ABOUT THE PRIESTS' CONTEMPT FOR YAHWEH (1:6–2:9)

Malachi 1:6–2:9 contains a prophetic disputation about the priests' contempt for Yahweh (on the genre of prophetic disputation, see comments on 1:2-5 above). This section, the longest in Malachi, is addressed to the priests (1:6; 2:7), while the following section (2:10-16) shifts to the first person plural ("we") and introduces a new concern for the observance of proper marriage. The present section consists of three smaller units (1:6-8,9-14, and 2:1-9), two of which display characteristics of other prophetic forms. The first unit of the section begins as the previous one (1:2-5) with a supposed exchange between debaters, this time between Yahweh and the priests. The disputation is extended by an additional question and response (cf. 3:6-12). Yahweh asserts that, as the father and master of Israel, Yahweh deserves honor and respect, and the priests ask for specific evidence of their failure to honor Yahweh (1:6). Then Yahweh responds that the priests have placed defiled food on the altar, and the priests ask how they have defiled Yahweh (v. 7a). Then Yahweh replies that the priests have done so by offering injured, crippled, or diseased animals (vv. 7b-8).

The second unit of the section (vv. 9-14) begins with the emphatic adverb "now" (עַתָּה, *'attāh*) and elaborates on the accusation against the priests (vv. 6-8). In this way, this unit combines with the previous one as a kind of prophecy of punishment (cf. Zeph 1:2-6; 2:4-15), containing its two major features: accusation of offense (vv. 6-8) and announcement of punishment (vv. 9-14).[22] The priests are commanded to entreat Yahweh for favor (v. 9), but no one among the priests will stop these improper offerings, so Yahweh will not accept offerings from the priests (v. 10). The basis for this rejection, introduced by the particle "for" (כִּי, *kî*) not translated in the NIV, is that Yahweh receives pure offerings from the nations (v. 11) but contemptible sacrifices from the priests (vv. 12-13). Thus, Yahweh curses those inside Israel who offer improper sacrifices, for the name of Yahweh is to be feared even by the nations outside Israel (v. 14).

The third unit of the section (2:1-9) also begins with the emphatic adverb "now" (*'attāh*) and with an admonition addressed to the

---

[22]Floyd, *Minor Prophets*, p. 595.

priests (v. 1). However, the admonition is not clearly stated (as in
1:9) but rather implied in Yahweh's intention to punish the priests
if they do not turn from their practices and show honor for Yahweh
(v. 2). The priests will experience the consequences of rebuke and
defilement (v. 3) and of contempt and humiliation (v. 9) unless the
priests demonstrate the true instruction and the impartial practice
required of them in the covenant of Levi (vv. 4-8). The unit then
specifically urges the priests to reverse their improper practices
through a description of the potential disastrous results that will
happen if they do not follow Yahweh's admonition. As such, the unit
may be seen as a prophetic call to repentance (e.g., Zeph 2:1-4; Mal
2:13-17).[23] Therefore, Malachi 1:6–2:9 attempts to persuade the
priests that they should honor Yahweh properly by offering appropriate sacrifices; otherwise, they risk incurring the curse of Yahweh.

[6]"A son honors his father, and a servant his master. If I am a
father, where is the honor due me? If I am a master, where is the
respect due me?" says the LORD Almighty. "It is you, O priests,
who show contempt for my name.

"But you ask, 'How have we shown contempt for your name?'
[7]"You place defiled food on my altar.

"But you ask, 'How have we defiled you?'

"By saying that the LORD's table is contemptible. [8]When you
bring blind animals for sacrifice, is that not wrong? When you sacrifice crippled or diseased animals, is that not wrong? Try offering
them to your governor! Would he be pleased with you? Would he
accept you?" says the LORD Almighty.

[9]"Now implore God to be gracious to us. With such offerings
from your hands, will he accept you?"-says the LORD Almighty.

[10]"Oh, that one of you would shut the temple doors, so that you
would not light useless fires on my altar! I am not pleased with
you," says the LORD Almighty, "and I will accept no offering from
your hands. [11]My name will be great among the nations, from the
rising to the setting of the sun. In every place incense and pure
offerings will be brought to my name, because my name will be
great among the nations," says the LORD Almighty.

[23]Floyd, *Minor Prophets*, p. 600.

¹²"But you profane it by saying of the Lord's table, 'It is defiled,' and of its food, 'It is contemptible.' ¹³And you say, 'What a burden!' and you sniff at it contemptuously," says the LORD Almighty.

"When you bring injured, crippled or diseased animals and offer them as sacrifices, should I accept them from your hands?" says the LORD. ¹⁴"Cursed is the cheat who has an acceptable male in his flock and vows to give it, but then sacrifices a blemished animal to the Lord. For I am a great king," says the LORD Almighty, "and my name is to be feared among the nations.

**1:6-7** The first unit of the section (1:6–2:9) begins as the previous one (1:2-5) with a supposed exchange between debaters, this time between Yahweh and the priests. Yahweh asserts that, as the **father** and **master** of Israel, Yahweh deserves honor and respect. The verb **honor** (כָּבַד, *kābad*) deals with acknowledging one's "weight," that is, one's importance, authority, or position.[24] If a proper assessment of a father's position elicits appropriate honor, so too should Israel, Yahweh's firstborn **son** (Exod 4:22-23; Deut 1:31; 14:1; Jer 3:19; 31:9; Hos 11:1), honor Yahweh. Like a master, Yahweh also deserves from Israel "fear" (ESV, KJV) or "respect" (NASB, NET, NRSV, NLT). Such respect (מוֹרָא, *môrā'*) is rightly rendered to one's parents (Lev 19:3), to holy places (Lev 26:2), but most importantly to Yahweh (Ps 86:11; 112:1). In several passages, the concepts of "fearing" Yahweh and "obeying" Yahweh's commands are nearly synonymous (Lev 19:14; 25:17; Deut 17:19; 2 Kgs 17:34). Perhaps fearing Yahweh becomes synonymous with obedience, since fear provides a motivation for righteous living. The call in the closing words of the book to remember the Law of Moses (4:4) highlights this connection between knowledge of Torah and the fearing or honoring of Yahweh.

The two rhetorical questions (**If I am a father, where is the honor due me?** and **If I am a master, where is the respect due me?**) assert that Yahweh does not receive proper honor or respect. The concluding speech formula (**says the LORD Almighty**) establishes Yahweh as speaker; it appears ten times in this disputation about the priests' contempt for Yahweh (1:6–2:9). In this way, the God whose name is associated with the Ark of the Covenant expresses disgust

---

[24]Verhoef, *Books of Haggai and Malachi*, p. 211.

with those who offer defiled sacrifices and treat Yahweh's **name** with **contempt** (cf. Isa 1:2-4) rather than reverence (Mal 2:5). One's name (שֵׁם, *šēm*), like one's honor (*kābad*), designates one's nature, character, and reputation.[25] The word "contempt" (בָּזָה, *bāzāh*), translated here in other versions as "despise" (ESV, KJV, NASB, NRSV, NLT, and NJB), appears more than forty times in the Old Testament to signify an undervaluing or an accounting of little worth.[26] "Contempt" (*bāzāh*) also stands in contrast with "honor" (*kābad*) in 1 Samuel 2:30 and Psalm 15:4. This description of the priests' failure (**It is you, O priests, who show contempt for my name**) corresponds with the priests' punishment for their offense in 2:9 ("So I have caused you to be despised and humiliated before all the people").

The priests offer two hypothetical objections, requesting specific evidence of their failure to honor Yahweh (**How have we shown contempt for your name?** and **How have we defiled you?**). To the first objection, Yahweh responds that the priests **have placed defiled food on** the **altar**. Here "food" refers to the animal offerings (Lev 21:8,21). The implicit allegation suggests that the animals have not been properly selected nor properly prepared as stipulated (Lev 22:17-25 and Deut 15:21), a sense represented by the NET's rendering, "You are offering improper sacrifices on my altar." To the second objection, Yahweh replies that the priests have done so **by** offering **contemptible** sacrifices on **the LORD's table**. The expression "the LORD's table" occurs only here in the Old Testament. Its near parallels in Ezekiel 40:39-43 and 44:16 as well as the mention of animals in verse 8 may indicate it refers collectively to tables used for the slaughtering of sacrificial animals,[27] but the phrase is more likely a metaphoric designation for the altar of burnt offering (see Ezek 44:15-16) arising from associations of sacrifices with food and with meals connected with the sacrificial system (Lev 6:24-30; 7:11-15,28-36).[28]

**1:8** Two rhetorical questions aim to establish the guilt of priests

---

[25] Walter C. Kaiser, "שֵׁם," *TWOT*, 2:934.

[26] Michael A. Grisanti, "בזה," *NIDOTTE*, 1:628.

[27] Baldwin, *Haggai, Zechariah, Malachi*, pp. 225-226.

[28] Merrill, *Haggai, Zechariah, Malachi*, p. 396; Verhoef, *Books of Haggai and Malachi*, pp. 216-217. At work may also be an extended metaphor in which Yahweh is the host at the meal, the altar is the table, the sacrifices are the food, and the priests are the servants serving the food, according to Taylor and Clendenen, *Haggai, Malachi*, p. 268.

and insist on the need to present **animals** without defects **for sacrifice**. The conditions of **blind**ness, lameness, and sickness all point to defective offerings and render animals unacceptable for sacrifice (Lev 22:17-25; Deut 15:21). To offer such a sacrifice brings one under the curse of Yahweh (Mal 1:14). Two other rhetorical questions challenge the priests to present such sacrifices to their **governor** and demand that they offer as much respect to Yahweh. The noun translated "governor" (פֶּחָה, *peḥāh*) usually designates a representative of a foreign ruler with some level of authority over a group. This "governor" may be a foreigner (Neh 5:15) or, like Zerubbabel (Hag 1:1,14; 2:2,21) or Nehemiah (Neh 5:14; 12:26), be a member of the governed people.

**1:9** Verses 9-10 elaborate on the charges made against the priests in verses 6-8. The temporal adverb **now** (עַתָּה, *'attāh*) gives verse 9 a note of immediacy. In addition to its temporal meaning, when combined with a conjunction (not translated in the NIV, but rendered "and" in the ESV and NRSV), it has an emphatic use. It denotes the next stage in an argument. In the prophets, the adverb *'attāh* often introduces the imminent actions of Yahweh either in blessing or in curse (e.g., Isa 33:10; 43:19).[29] In this instance, the adverb anticipates the curse pronounced in verse 14. The prophet's voice intrudes with the language of repentance (**implore God to be gracious to us**), but in the context of the command in the previous verse ("try offering them to your governor") this wording is clearly ironic. The priests may implore the favor of Yahweh, but this action is to no avail, since they have already insulted Yahweh with defiled offerings. In other contexts, the invitation to entreat the favor of Yahweh is accompanied by genuine repentance (Dan 9:13; Zech 7:2). Both "implore" and **accept** translate Hebrew idioms involving the noun "faces" (פָּנִים, *pānîm*). That noun and the verb "be gracious" (חָנַן, *ḥānān*) appear in Numbers 6:24-26 as part of the blessing prescribed for the priests to pronounce over the people. Malachi may allude ironically to that blessing here. Even though the priests and people may seek the gracious turning of Yahweh's face toward them, it will not happen.

**1:10** Yahweh will not accept the priests, nor will Yahweh **accept** their **offering**s (cf. Lev 26:31; Isa 1:15; Jer 14:12; Amos 5:22). Yahweh longs for someone to **shut the doors** to the temple and to stop these

---

[29]Allan Harman, "Particles," *NIDOTTE*, 4:1031.

defiled sacrifices.[30] The dual form of the noun "doors" refers to a set of double doors. These double doors may have given access to the temple from the court of priests (2 Chr 4:9) or access to the inner court where the **altar** of burnt offerings is located (1 Kgs 6:31-36). Ahaz king of Judah shuts the temple doors before leading Judah in the worship of false gods (2 Chr 28:24). Malachi may be implying the priests' present actions are no better than Ahaz's idolatry.[31] The prophet's objection is not that the temple ritual is meaningless in itself, but that it becomes useless when issuing from those who are not committed to Yahweh.[32] The term "useless" (חִנָּם, *ḥinnām*) may, because of its similar sound, play on the word "be gracious" (*ḥānān*) in verse 9. The concluding speech formula (**says the LORD Almighty**) appears twice in verses 9 and 10, establishing Yahweh as speaker (on the divine name "the LORD Almighty," see on 1:6 above) and emphasizing Yahweh's refusal to accept the priests' offerings. Here the royal associations of the divine name come to bear, after the challenge to the priests to offer lame and diseased animals to their governor in a bid for acceptance. Rather, Yahweh's name should be honored as a father and a master (vv. 6-7) and as great among the nations (v. 11).

**1:11** If verses 9-10 elaborate on the accusation against the priests (vv. 6-8) and announce the punishment against them (that is, Yahweh will not accept their offerings), then verses 11-14 describe the basis for this rejection: Yahweh receives pure offerings from the nations (v. 11) but contemptible sacrifices from the priests (vv. 12-13). Accordingly, the unit is introduced by the particle "for," (כִּי, *kî*) not translated in the NIV (cf. ESV, KJV, NASB, NET, NRSV, and NJPS). The word "name" (שֵׁם, *šēm*) appears often in Old Testament texts as

---

[30]Sweeney, *Twelve Prophets*, p. 727.

[31]Taylor and Clendenen, *Haggai, Malachi*, p. 272.

[32]The Qumran community cites this verse to reject the validity of the sacrificial system in the Jerusalem temple in the *Damascus Document*: "None who have been brought into the covenant shall enter into the sanctuary to light up His altar in vain; they shall 'lock the door,' for God said, 'Would that one of you would lock My door so that you should not light up My altar in vain' (Mal. 1:10). They must be careful to act according to the specifications of the Law for the era of wickedness" (CD VI, 11-14). Citation from Michael Wise, Martin Abegg, Jr., and Edward Cook, *The Dead Sea Scrolls: A New Translation* (New York: HarperCollins, 1996).

a substitute for the person of Yahweh (see on v. 6 above). Two special uses of "the name" appearing in Deuteronomy provide significant background for two themes in Malachi: the abuse of prescribed
worship and the negligence of the priests. First, frequent mention is
made in Deuteronomy of the place where Yahweh will choose for
Yahweh's name to dwell (Deut 12:5,11,21; 14:23-24; 16:2,6,11; 26:2).
Second, Deuteronomy indicates that the Levites have been chosen
to minister in Yahweh's name and to pronounce blessing in it (Deut
10:8; 18:5,7; 21:5). The three uses of "name" (*šēm*) link this passage
with the double use of "name" in verse 6. There, contempt is shown
for Yahweh's name. The four references to Yahweh's name in the
rest of the chapter (vv. 11,14) indicate this improper stance toward
the character and reputation of Yahweh will be reversed.

The repetition of the profession (**my name will be great among
the nations**) brackets the promise (**in every place incense and pure
offerings**[33] **will be brought to my name**). The area traversed **from
the rising to the setting of the sun** is an image of Yahweh's universal reign in Psalms (50:1; 113:3) and Isaiah (45:6; 59:19). Earlier
prophets have laid the foundations for Malachi's declaration of the
greatness of Yahweh's name among the nations. An assumption of
Yahweh's universal sovereignty is evident in Amos's words of judgment against the nations (Amos 1–2; 9:7). The prophets demonstrate their understanding that Israel and Judah are part of a family
of nations who answer to one God by delivering both oracles of
judgment against Israel and Judah and against the nations (e.g., Isa
30-31,34; Jer 22–27, 47–51; Ezek 21–32). Moreover, other prophetic
texts anticipate the day when the nations come to know Yahweh (Isa
2:2-4; 42:6; 55:5; 56:3-8; Ezek 36:23; 37:28; 38:23; 39:7; Jonah; Micah
4:1-3; Zech 8:23; 14:16). The Hebrew verb tense in verse 11, however, gives no clear indication of the timing of this day. The statement
may refer to a future time, "my name *will be* great" (e.g., ESV, NASB,
NET, and NIV), or to a present reality, "my name *is* great" (e.g.,
NRSV, NJB, and NJPS). The latter option ("my name *is* great")

---

[33]The adjective "pure" (טָהוֹר, *ṭāhôr*) is not elsewhere used to describe
offerings. Its use here may set up the subsequent use of its cognate verb
"purify" or "refine" (טָהֵר, *ṭāhēr*) in 3:3 where the refining and purification
of the Levites will result in Judah and Jerusalem bringing righteous and
acceptable offerings to Yahweh. The NT uses the image of offerings to
describe Christian worship and good deeds (Heb 13:15-16; 1 Pet 2:4-5).

would refer to the worship of Yahweh among pagan nations, Jewish proselytes, or Diaspora Jews. Two factors, however, argue against this reading. First, evidence is lacking for extensive proselytism among the exiles. Second, the prophet would probably not have viewed pagan worship of his day as acceptable to Yahweh. Any acceptable worship of Yahweh among the nations without some mediation of Israel would contradict the very purpose of Israel's election to be a means through which Yahweh's salvation comes to the nations. Thus, the former option ("my name *will be* great") is more likely: the prophet envisions future worship rendered to Yahweh among the Gentiles (cf. Isa 2:2-4; 19:19-21; 24:14-16; 42:6; 45:22-24; 66:18-21; Micah 4:1-3; Zeph 3:8-9; Zech 8:20-23, 14:16).[34] This anticipated reverence contrasts sharply with Israel's present disregard for Yahweh and Israel's profane worship (1:12-13).

**1:12-13** Verses 12 and 13 repeat the accusations against the priests (vv. 6-8) in contrast to the offerings that will be made by the nations (v. 11). The priests profane Yahweh's name, calling the altar **defiled** and its **food contemptible** and announcing with a gesture of contempt how wearisome their service seems (cf. Isa 43:22-24). Leviticus contains several warnings against the priests or people profaning (חָלַל, *ḥālal*) Yahweh's name (18:21; 19:12; 20:3; 21:6; 22:2,32). Leviticus 22:2 is especially noteworthy, since it warns the priests against profaning Yahweh's name by failing to treat with respect the sacred offerings (cf. the behavior of Eli's sons in 1 Sam 2:15-17). The image of **sniff**ing **at** Yahweh's name **contemptuously** is expressed in a more modern idiom in the NET: "You turn up your nose at it." The NRSV takes the antecedent of the pronoun "it" as Yahweh's name rather than Yahweh's table, that is, "you sniff at me" (cf. NJB). The adjectives used to describe the offerings here (**injured, crippled, or diseased**) are identical to those in verse 8 with the exception of "injured" (גָּזוּל, *gāzāl*) rather than "blind" (עִוֵּר, *ʿiwwēr*). The "injured" (*gāzāl*) animal actually refers to one which has been seized with violence.[35] While possibly referring to an animal stolen from another Israelite (Lev 19:13; Deut 28:31; Job 24:2; Ezek 18:12,16,18; Micah 2:2), the context may indicate that the animal has been stolen

---

[34]Verhoef, *Books of Haggai and Malachi*, pp. 227-231; Schuller, "Malachi," p. 860.

[35]*HALOT*, p. 186.

and mutilated (perhaps by another animal) and thus rendered unacceptable (Exod 22:31). In verse 8, the word "pleased" (רָצָה, *rāṣāh*) intimates the governor's displeasure with a flawed gift; here *rāṣāh*, translated **accept** in the NIV, signals the rejection of these blemished sacrifices.

**1:14** Verse 14 ridicules the hypocrisy of one who possesses an **acceptable** animal but **sacrifices** a blemished one to Yahweh. The specific example given in the verse relates to a sacrifice that accompanies a voluntary **vow**, for which Leviticus 22:16-23 prohibits the offering of **a blemished animal** (for additional instructions on this vow, see Lev 27:9-10; Num 30:2; Deut 23:21-23). One who makes such a vow with a defective animal is called a **cheat** and is thereby **cursed**. The word translated "cheat" (נָכַל, *nākal*) connotes conspiracy and deception (Gen 37:18; Num 25:18; Ps 105:25). In Numbers 25, the Midianites seduce the Israelites into worshiping the Baal of Peor. Phinehas turns away Yahweh's wrath from Israel, and Yahweh makes a "covenant of peace" with Phinehas (Num 25:12-13), to which Malachi 2:4-5 refer. The verb "cursed" (אָרַר, *'ārar*) appears first in Malachi here and later in 2:2(3×), and 3:9(2×). The word *'ārar* recalls the cultic curses the Levites announced on Mt. Ebal and to which the people give their assent (Deut 27:15-26); the Levites charge the people to obey Yahweh and follow Yahweh's commands by reciting various curses the people would suffer for failing to do so.

The causal conjunction **for** (כִּי, *kî*) may refer to what follows it rather than what precedes it. The statement, **I am a great king**, would then explain why Yahweh's name is to be feared rather than explaining why the cheat is cursed. The concept of Yahweh's universal kingship appears throughout the Old Testament (Judg 8:23; 1 Sam 12:12; Ps 10:16; 24:7-10; 84:3; 95:3; Isa 6:5; 33:22; 43:15; 44:6; Jer 8:19; 10:10; Zeph 3:15; Zech 14:9). The affirmation that **the LORD Almighty** (*YHWH ṣᵊbā'ôth*) is a great king approximates the unique divine title "the King, the LORD Almighty" found in Zechariah 14:16-17 (cf. Jer 48:15; 51:57). The title "great king" refers to the suzerain in ancient Near Eastern treaties.[36] Thus its use here accords well with the covenant imagery in the book.[37] Also, the portrayal of Yahweh as

---

[36]*ANET*, pp. 202-203; *ANESTP*, p. 529.
[37]Steven L. McKenzie and Howard N. Wallace, "Covenant Themes in Malachi," *CBQ* 45 (1983): 557-558.

a great king is especially moving in the postexilic context in which Israel lacks the monarchy. The concluding statement in the section, **my name is to be feared among the nations**, evokes the use of "fear" in verse 6, where the same root (יָרֵא, *yr'*) is translated "respect" (see comments on v. 6 above). It also amplifies the sin and peril of the postexilic community. Verse 11 has twice affirmed the coming greatness of Yahweh's name among the nations. Now, Israel is called to align themselves with the anticipated reverence of the nations.

[1]**"And now this admonition is for you, O priests.** [2]**If you do not listen, and if you do not set your heart to honor my name," says the LORD Almighty, "I will send a curse upon you, and I will curse your blessings. Yes, I have already cursed them, because you have not set your heart to honor me.**

[3]**"Because of you I will rebuke**[a] **your descendants**[b]**; I will spread on your faces the offal from your festival sacrifices, and you will be carried off with it.** [4]**And you will know that I have sent you this admonition so that my covenant with Levi may continue," says the LORD Almighty.** [5]**"My covenant was with him, a covenant of life and peace, and I gave them to him; this called for reverence and he revered me and stood in awe of my name.** [6]**True instruction was in his mouth and nothing false was found on his lips. He walked with me in peace and uprightness, and turned many from sin.**

[7]**"For the lips of a priest ought to preserve knowledge, and from his mouth men should seek instruction—because he is the messenger of the LORD Almighty.** [8]**But you have turned from the way and by your teaching have caused many to stumble; you have violated the covenant with Levi," says the LORD Almighty.** [9]**"So I have caused you to be despised and humiliated before all the people, because you have not followed my ways but have shown partiality in matters of the law."**

[a]*3 Or cut off (see Septuagint)*     [b]*3 Or will blight your grain*

**2:1** Like Malachi 1:9, verse 1 begins with the conjunction **and** and the temporal adverb **now** (*'attāh*). The adverb *'attāh* often introduces the imminent actions of Yahweh either in blessing or in curse (e.g., Isa 33:10; 43:19);[38] here obviously it is the latter. No specific

---

[38]Allan Harman, "Particles," *NIDOTTE*, 4:1031.

**admonition** (the TNIV reads "warning"; the NRSV, "command") is given, but the context makes the admonition clear: the **priests** should honor Yahweh properly by offering appropriate sacrifices and demonstrating the true instruction and the impartial practice required of them in the covenant of Levi. The word "priests" appears rarely in the Old Testament in the form of direct address; when it does occur, it does so in a context of judgment (Hos 5:1; Joel 1:13; Mal 1:6).

**2:2** Yahweh threatens the priests with punishment, if they do not listen and if they do not set their heart to honor Yahweh's name. The consequences of failing to honor Yahweh's name (for "honor," see on 1:6 above) are here expressed in a conditional statement. The two stated conditions (**If you do not listen, and if you do not set your heart to honor my name**) are reinforced by the concluding speech formula (**says the LORD Almighty**). The expression to "set the heart" (the TNIV has "resolve"; the ESV, "take it to heart") is similar to the phrase translated "give careful thought" in Haggai 1:5,7 and 2:18. The idiom demands serious reflection and a determined change of attitude and action. The NIV indicates that Yahweh **will send** "a curse," but the Hebrew text actually reads "the curse" (cf. the renderings of the ESV, NASB, and NRSV), a likely allusion to the covenant curses of Deuteronomy 28:15-68 ("the curse" appears elsewhere only in Deut 28:20). Yahweh will also make their **blessings** become curses; this wording is reminiscent of the contrast between blessing and curse based upon the peoples' obedience to Yahweh's commands (Deut 4:1; 5:1; 6:1-9; 28:1-68; 30:15-20). These cursed blessings may be past blessings that Yahweh has bestowed upon the priests or present blessings that priests pronounce over the people (e.g., Lev 9:22-23; Num 6:23-26; 2 Chr 30:27).

**2:3** The NIV and NRSV do not translate the interjection "behold" (הִנֵּה, *hinnēh*) that begins verse 3, but it does appear in other versions (e.g., the ESV and NASB). The grammatical construction of *hinnēh* plus a participle (here "rebuking") also appears in Malachi 3:1(2×), 4:1, and 4:5; each time it denotes an imminent event, one whose coming is certain.[39] The Hebrew text speaks of **rebuk**ing or cutting off the "seed" of the priests. This may refer to a

---

[39]GKC, pp. 359-360; *IBHS*, p. 627; Ronald J. Williams, *Hebrew Syntax: An Outline*, 2nd ed. (Toronto: University of Toronto Press, 1976), p. 39.

judgment on their **descendants** (as in the NIV),[40] or to a diminished
harvest (as in the NIV margin).[41] The following threat of removal
(**you will be carried off with it**) probably favors the first option. The
covenant curses of Deuteronomy speak of judgment visiting the offspring of those who violate covenant (Deut 28:18,32,41,53,55,57).
The perpetrators' actions negatively impact not only themselves, but
others. The NJB ("I am going to break your arm") follows the wording of the LXX, implying that the priests will no longer be able
either to raise their arms to offer a blessing or to perform their official duties at the altar.[42]

Moreover, Yahweh will defile the priests with the **offal** ("dung"
in the ESV, KJV, NRSV, and NJPS) **from** their **festival sacrifices**.
"Offal" (פֶּרֶשׁ, *pereš*) refers to the entrails and feces of a sacrificed animal that the priests would carry outside the camp of Israel to be
burned (Exod 29:14; Lev 4:11-12; 8:17; 16:27). The offal comes from
the "festival sacrifices," those offered at the three great annual festivals: Passover and Unleavened Bread; Harvest, Weeks, or Pentecost;
Ingathering or Tabernacles (Exod 23:15-16; 34:18-22; Deut 16:16).
The connection of these offerings with covenant feasts sets up the
ensuing discussion of covenant violation (Mal 2:4-8). This shocking
image conveys Yahweh's disgust with the failure of the priests to
honor Yahweh and their disqualification from offering sacrifices at
Yahweh's altar. The concluding statement ("you will be carried off
with it") continues the earlier image: Yahweh will carry off the
priests for disposal in the refuse heap outside the city, removing the
priests from their office in disgrace and humiliation (cf. v. 9).

**2:4-5** The intended consequence of the priests' bitter experiences depicted in verses 2 and 3 is the continuation of Yahweh's
covenant with Levi. Thus, the purpose of **this admonition** is that the
priests repent and thereby preserve this covenant. Levi, Jacob's third
son (Gen 29:34), is the ancestor of Israel's priestly families (1 Chr
6:1-48). Malachi apparently uses the name Levi (v. 4; cf. "Levites in
3:3) as an equivalent for the ideal or exemplary "priest," in a way
similar to the use of Jacob for Israel (1:2-5; 2:12) and Esau for Edom

---

[40]Graffy, "Malachi," p. 1202.

[41]Sweeney, *Twelve Prophets*, p. 729.

[42]C.F. Keil, *Minor Prophets*, in *Biblical Commentary on the Old Testament*, by
C.F. Keil and R. Delitzsch, trans. by James Martin, repr. (Grand Rapids:
Eerdmans, 1988), 10:645.

(1:2-4).[43] The Old Testament does not make specific mention of the **covenant with Levi**, though Jeremiah 33:21 and Nehemiah 13:29 presuppose it. The "covenant with Levi" may refer to Yahweh's choice of the Levites (Num 3:12). It may refer to the "covenant of salt" Yahweh made with the Levites in order to provide permanent provision for them (Num 18:19). Or, it may refer to Yahweh's "covenant of peace" with Phinehas, Aaron's grandson (Num 25:12-13). In Numbers 25, the Midianites seduce the Israelites into worshiping the Baal of Peor. Phinehas turns away Yahweh's wrath from Israel, and Yahweh promises Phinehas and his descendants a lasting priesthood. The occurrence of the word "peace" (שָׁלוֹם, *šālôm*) in Malachi 2:5 favors the last of these three options.[44] By rewarding the actions of Phinehas, Yahweh implicitly establishes those actions that Phinehas is known for, that is, he is zealous for Yahweh's honor among the Israelites (Num 25:11-13), as the conditions for the preservation of the covenant. However, the priests are now subverting the actions that have elicited this blessing of peace from Yahweh. They are treating the service of Yahweh with contempt (1:6,12) and are causing many to stumble through their failure to instruct the people properly (2:7-8). Yahweh grants life (perhaps an image for the lasting priesthood of Phinehas) and peace in return for **reverence** and **awe**. Indeed, **life and peace** are the natural outcome of complete commitment to Yahweh (Deut 4:40; 6:2; 30:15-20; Prov 3:1-2). Now the promise to Phinehas is in jeopardy, since the priests' disloyalty stands in the way of the covenant with Levi continuing.[45] Moreover, this admonition given to the priests anticipates the one given to the nation in the book's conclusion. Malachi warns the priests so that Yahweh's covenant with Levi might be preserved. He later warns the nation to remember the law of Moses lest the land also be cursed (4:4-6).

**2:6-7** Whereas Malachi 1:6–2:3 focuses on the priests' abuses in their sacrificial duties, Malachi 2:6-7 stresses their responsibilities as teachers. In their sacrificial duties, the priests represent humanity before Yahweh; as teachers of **true instruction**, they represent the

---

[43]For a full discussion of the relationship between Levites and priests in the Old Testament, see Verhoef, *Books of Haggai and Malachi*, pp. 258-261; Taylor and Clendenen, *Haggai, Malachi*, pp. 293-295.

[44]Against this conclusion, see Chisholm, *Minor Prophets*, p. 283.

[45]Merrill, *Haggai, Zechariah, Malachi*, p. 407; Schuller, "Malachi," pp. 860-861.

will of Yahweh to the people (Lev 10:11; Deut 17:9; 20:9-13; 2 Chr 17:8-9; 19:8; Ezra 7:6; Neh 8:9; Jer 2:8; 18:18; Hag 2:11).[46] The word "instruction" translates the Hebrew word תּוֹרָה (tôrāh). The noun is most often translated "law" in reference to the law of Moses (Exod 24:12; Deut 30:10; Josh 1:7-8), but tôrāh, which derives from the verb יָרָה (yārāh) meaning "to point," possesses broader applications through the Old Testament. Thus, the NIV renderings of "instruction" and "matters of the law" (2:6-9) in place of the more common "law" are appropriate in this context, especially so in 2:8 where the priests' tôrāh causes people to stumble. This tôrāh is described as true (אֱמֶת, 'ĕmeth), an adjective indicating genuineness, reliability, and trustworthiness. Psalm 119:142 and Nehemiah 9:13 describe Yahweh's tôrāh as true. It is not **false**, wicked, or unjust (עַוְלָה, 'awlāh), an attribute profoundly adverse to Yahweh (Job 6:30; 13:7; Ps 119:3; Zeph 3:5,13). True instruction and **knowledge** should remain in the **priest**'s **mouth** and **lips** so that the people might **seek instruction** from them. The obligation to walk before Yahweh **in peace and uprightness** connotes covenant loyalty. The word translated "uprightness" (מִישׁוֹר, mîšôr) or "fairness" (Ps 45:6; 67:4; Isa 11:4) generally refers to a level place or plain (Ps 26:12; 27:11; Isa 40:4; 42:16; Jer 21:13; 48:8,21; Zech 4:7); here mîšôr anticipates the critique, in verse 9, that the priests show partiality. Verse 7 highlights the instructional responsibilities outlined in verse 6 by indicating they originate from the priest's role as Yahweh's **messenger** (מַלְאָךְ, mal'āk). This Hebrew word, most often translated "angel," provides the basis for the name "Malachi" (see comments on 1:1 above). The designation is applied elsewhere to the prophets (e.g., Hag 1:13), but here is the only place in the Old Testament where it refers to a priest rather than a prophet.[47]

**2:8** Verse 8 begins with **but you**; the aversive conjunction and emphatic pronoun heighten the contrast between the description of priestly ministry in verses 5-7 and the charges made against the priests in the present verse. Thus, the focus of verses 8-9 turns from past obedience of Levi to the contemporary disobedience of the priests. Both the reintroduction of direct second person address in

---

[46]Verhoef, *Books of Haggai and Malachi*, p. 258.
[47]Rex A. Mason, *The Books of Haggai, Zechariah, and Malachi*, CBC (Cambridge: Cambridge University Press, 1977), p. 147.

these verses and the divine speech formula **says the LORD Almighty** emphasize this disobedience. Specifically, verse 8 levies three charges against the priests: turning from the way, causing others to stumble through their teaching, and violating **the covenant with Levi** (cf. Jer 2:8; Ezek 44:10-14). These charges reverse the normative description of priestly ministry in verse 6. Instead of teaching what is true, the priests have **caused** others **to stumble** in sin through their **teaching** (cf. Hos 4:6; Micah 3:11). Instead of walking with Yahweh (i.e., maintaining covenant fidelity), the priests now have **turned from the way** and **violated** (other versions read "corrupt," including the ESV, NASB, NRSV, and NJPS) their covenant with Yahweh. The verb "violate" (שָׁחַת, *šāḥath*) appears in Genesis to speak of the corruption of the earth (6:11-12) that leads to Yahweh's destruction of the earth by the flood (6:13,17; 9:11,15) and the destruction of Sodom by fire (Gen 13:10; 18:28,31,32; 19:13,14,29). Malachi uses *šāḥath* in 1:14 to describe the blemished animals brought for sacrifice and in 3:11 to speak of pests devouring or spoiling crops. The priests have so corrupted the covenant that it is ruined, inoperative, and destroyed. The only hope for the covenant is Yahweh's provision for purification and forgiveness (see Mal 3:3).

**2:9** Within a covenant relationship, the failure of one party to fulfill obligations could lead the other party to enact punitive or disciplinary steps. Yahweh now describes the penalty the priests have incurred for their violation of the covenant. By using forms of the verb בָּזָה (*bāzāh*) in both the description of the priests' failure in 1:6 ("show contempt") and their penalty in 2:9 (**despised**), Yahweh has matched the priests' punishment with their offense. What has been their offense has become their punishment. The causal statement (**because you have . . .**) identifies two reasons for such punishment. The priests do **not follow** the **ways** of Yahweh (cf. v. 8), and they are guilty of **show**ing **partiality in matters of the law**. The idiom used for showing partiality is "to raise the face," a phrase which indicates the showing of favor, respect, acceptance (1 Sam 25:35) or to show partiality and favoritism toward either the poor or the rich (Lev 19:15). The wording is similar to the expression used for "accept" in verses 8 and 9 (see on 1:8-9 above). Here the idiom may suggest the inconsistency of the priests to practice and teach torah.[48]

---

[48]Sweeney, *Twelve Prophets*, p. 731.

## IV. PROPHETIC DISPUTATION ABOUT JUDAH'S
## UNFAITHFULNESS IN MARRIAGE (2:10-16)

[10]Have we not all one Father[a]? Did not one God create us? Why do we profane the covenant of our fathers by breaking faith with one another?

[11]Judah has broken faith. A detestable thing has been committed in Israel and in Jerusalem: Judah has desecrated the sanctuary the LORD loves, by marrying the daughter of a foreign god. [12]As for the man who does this, whoever he may be, may the LORD cut him off from the tents of Jacob[b] —even though he brings offerings to the LORD Almighty.

[13]Another thing you do: You flood the LORD's altar with tears. You weep and wail because he no longer pays attention to your offerings or accepts them with pleasure from your hands. [14]You ask, "Why?" It is because the LORD is acting as the witness between you and the wife of your youth, because you have broken faith with her, though she is your partner, the wife of your marriage covenant.

[15]Has not ⌊the LORD⌋ made them one? In flesh and spirit they are his. And why one? Because he was seeking godly offspring.[c] So guard yourself in your spirit, and do not break faith with the wife of your youth.

[16]"I hate divorce," says the LORD God of Israel, "and I hate a man's covering himself[d] with violence as well as with his garment," says the LORD Almighty.

So guard yourself in your spirit, and do not break faith.

[a]10 Or father   [b]12 Or [12]May the LORD cut off from the tents of Jacob anyone who gives testimony in behalf of the man who does this   [c]15 Or [15]But the one ⌊who is our father⌋ did not do this, not as long as life remained in him. And what was he seeking? An offspring from God   [d]16 Or his wife

Malachi 2:10-16 contains a prophetic disputation about Judah's unfaithfulness to Yahweh (on the genre of prophetic disputation, see comments on 1:2-5 above). This section shifts from addressing the priests directly (1:6; 2:7) to the people in general with the first person plural pronoun ("we"). In this disputation, the exchange begins with three questions (2:10), but the expected reply from the disputants, in contrast to the previous sections (1:2 and 1:6-7), is delayed until verse 14. The section itself consists of two smaller units (2:10-12 and 13-16), both of which display characteristics of other prophetic forms. The first unit of the section (2:10-12) presents a kind of prophecy of punishment (similar to 1:9-14).[49] It begins with an accusation of offense, presented in a series of rhetorical questions (2:10), and a general description of Judah's infidelity. This offense is evidenced specifically in the marriage of Jewish men to foreign women who worship other gods (v. 11). The unit concludes with an announcement of punishment, the deprivation of the legal and religious benefits from participation in the community (v. 12). The second unit (vv. 13-16) is linked to the previous one by the phrase "Another thing you do," but the unit treats a different subject dealing with marriage. It presents a brief prophetic call to repentance (similar to vv. 1-9), exhorting the people to maintain fidelity in marriage.[50] The unit begins with a description of the present situation in which people recognize the rejection of their offerings by Yahweh (v. 13), and then it describes the reason for this rejection: Yahweh's reaction to their practice of divorce (v. 14). This practice does not bring about a faithful generation of offspring (v. 15) and is one which Yahweh hates (v. 16); for these reasons, the people should exercise care in maintaining the covenant of marriage. Therefore, 2:10-16 urges the people to abandon the two practices related to marriage, the intermarriage with women who worship other gods and the divorce of couples already married, by showing proper concern for fidelity in their own marriages.

**2:10** Verse 10 begins with three questions, but the expected reply is delayed until verse 14. Here the prophet strengthens the rhetoric of the section by including himself in the question, **Have we not all one Father?** The NIV capitalizes "Father" and thus identifies the father as Yahweh (cf. the ESV, NJB, and NJPS). The second question (**Did not one God create us?**) and the previous characterization of Yahweh as father (1:6) supports this identification. Isaiah 64:8, moreover, characterizes Yahweh both as creator and father.[51] However, other versions (e.g., the NASB, NET, and NRSV) translate the word with the lower case. If this is correct, the prophet's question may well refer to the patriarch Abraham or Jacob. Old Testament texts explic-

[49]Floyd, *Minor Prophets*, p. 605.
[50]Ibid., p. 609.
[51]Hill, *Malachi*, p. 224; Merrill, *Haggai, Zechariah, Malachi*, p. 414; Verhoef, *Books of Haggai and Malachi*, p. 265.

itly identify both Abraham and Jacob as Israel's father (Josh 24:3; Isa 51:2; 58:14), and Israel is identified as the "sons of Jacob" (1 Chr 16:13; Ps 105:6). The repeated mention of Jacob in Malachi (1:2; 2:12; 3:6), especially later in this context (2:14), may argue for identifying the father as Jacob.[52] If so, the question "Did not one God create us?" complements the first question rather than paralleling it. The three questions in the verse reflect the two sides of the covenant relationship. The first and third refer to the patriarchs, whereas the middle question refers to God. The third question indicates that yet another covenant has been profaned (on **profane**, see 1:12 above), **the covenant of our fathers**. Malachi 2:4-5 refers to Yahweh's covenant with Levi and Yahweh's promise to Phinehas; here the covenant is likely the one made when Yahweh brought Israel out of Egypt (Exod 19:5; 1 Kgs 8:21; 2 Kgs 17:15; Jer 31:32). The wording of the NIV obscures the emphasis in the Hebrew text that the breaking of faith with one's fellow results in the profaning of covenant (cf. the reading of the NRSV: "Why then are we faithless to one another, profaning the covenant of our ancestors?"). The verb **breaking faith** (בָּגַד, *bāgād*) appears five times in Malachi, all in this section (2:10,11, 14,15,16). The Old Testament normally uses this verb, which signifies betrayal or treachery within a relationship calling for loyalty and service (Judg 9:23; Job 6:15; Ps 78:57; Isa 24:16), to speak of Israel or Judah breaking faith with Yahweh (Ps 73:15; 78:57; Jer 3:8,11,20; 5:11; 9:2; Hos 6:7). Malachi uses *bāgād* to speak of a broken human covenant, in a way similar to Exodus 21:7-11, a passage providing protection for a Hebrew woman purchased as a slave by an Israelite man who subsequently breaks faith with her.

**2:11** Judah's breaking of faith is characterized as תּוֹעֵבָה (*tôʿēbāh*), an abomination (ESV, NASB, NRSV), **a detestable thing** (NIV), or an unspeakable sin (NET). This word designates horrible acts certain to result in Yahweh's wrath upon the perpetrator. These acts include immoralities practiced among the Canaanites, such as homosexuality, prostitution, child sacrifice, witchcraft (Lev 18:22; Deut 18:9-12), and idolatry (Deut 7:25-26). Deuteronomy 17:1 labels as an abomination an action of the priests mentioned earlier in Malachi, namely, the offering of defective animals for sacrifice (Mal 2:8,13-14). The reference to **Judah**, **Israel**, and **Jerusalem** indicates

---

[52] Baldwin, *Haggai, Zechariah, Malachi*, p. 237.

the belief that the remnant community is the heir of the ancient covenant promises and obligations,[53] but it also highlights the extent of the detestable practice in a way similar to Zechariah's use of the three terms to describe the completeness of the persecution and scattering of the nation (Zech 1:19).[54] In verse 11, the people profane the covenant of their fathers; here Judah has profaned (translated **desecrated** in the NIV) **the sanctuary** Yahweh **loves**. Malachi 1:12 uses the same word (חָלַל, *ḥālal*) to speak of the desecration of Yahweh's name by those priests who call the altar defiled and its food contemptible. The NIV, like most modern English translations, understands the adjective "holy" (קֹדֶשׁ, *qōdeš*) and the phrase "the holy [thing] of Yahweh" (קֹדֶשׁ יהוה, *qōdeš YHWH*) to refer to a holy place or the "sanctuary." However, the specific denotation of "holy" is difficult to identify with certainty. The adjective may refer to the divine attribute of holiness (cf. KJV and NJPS). If so, then the actions of Judah are an affront to Yahweh, the one and only God.[55] More likely, *qōdeš* refers to Israel,[56] recalling Yahweh's choice of Israel from among the nations as a holy people, a treasured possession (Deut 7:6; 14:2; cf. Dan 11:28,30). Accordingly Psalm 114:2 states, "Judah became God's sanctuary (*qōdeš*)."

Finally, verse 11 states the means by which Judah has profaned itself as the *qōdeš* of Yahweh, namely, **by marrying the daughter of a foreign god** (or as the TNIV renders, "by marrying women who worship a foreign god"). Although this "abomination" may be understood as a general reference to idolatry (e.g., the NET renders the clause, "has turned to a foreign god"), it probably denotes the actual marriage of Jewish men with foreign women who are identified with a foreign god (Neh 13:23-27). Ezra 9:1-2 indicates the priests have led the way in this error of intermarrying with pagan nations.[57] Even though, before the giving of the law, both Joseph and Moses marry foreigners (Gen 41:45; Exod 2:15-22; Num 12:1) and, after the Mosaic law is in effect, David himself marries a foreigner

---

[53]Ibid., p. 238; Verhoef, *Books of Haggai and Malachi*, p. 268.

[54]Merrill, *Haggai, Zechariah, Malachi*, p. 415.

[55]Hill, *Malachi*, pp. 221, 230.

[56]Keil, *Minor Prophets*, p. 650.

[57]On the reasons why Jewish men would marry foreign women during the postexilic period, see Sweeney, *Twelve Prophets*, pp. 732-734.

(1 Chr 3:2), the Old Testament generally forbids Hebrews from marrying those outside the covenant community. Such intermarriage would inevitably lead to the worship of foreign gods (Exod 34:15-16; Deut 7:1-4; 13:6-11; Judg 3:6-7; 1 Kgs 11:1-6).[58]

**2:12** Verse 12 pronounces the punishment for those of Judah who have broken faith: the deprivation of the legal and religious benefits from participation in the community (v. 12). Furthermore, those who break faith are liable to destruction, even though they offer sacrifice to Yahweh. The Hebrew text for the verse is difficult. The NIV translates as **whoever he may be** a phrase which means literally "the one who is awake and the one who answers," a phrase expressing totality by listing two opposites.[59] Such an idea is expressed in the NET: "every last person who does this."[60] Yahweh cuts off every such transgressor from the covenant community, **the tents of Jacob** (cf. Jer 30:18). To **cut off** is a standard phrase to describe exclusion from the covenant community (Exod 12:15,19; 31:14; Lev 7:20,21,25,27; 20:18; 22:3; Num 9:13; 15:31; 19:13,20). Especially significant for this context are Leviticus 18:29 that commands the cutting off of those who do "detestable things" (תּוֹעֵבָה, *tôʿēbāh*) and Leviticus 19:8 that demands those who desecrate what is holy to Yahweh be cut off from the people. The form of the verb **bring** (נָגַשׁ, *nāgāš*) implies repeated or continuous action.[61] Those breaking faith exacerbate their sin by continuing the charade of bringing **offerings to** Yahweh. The appearance of the name **the LORD Almighty** in verse 12 highlights the seriousness of the issue in the postexilic community.

**2:13-14** A second charge is added in verses 13 and 14 (**Another**

---

[58]Such intermarriage, however, is discouraged because of religious objections rather than racial or nationalistic ones. Many other people come out of Egypt along with the Israelites (Exod 12:38). Provision is made for non-Israelites to celebrate Passover with Israel and to become part of the community (Exod 12:48; Num 9:14), and specific regulations make it possible for Israelite men to take wives from among foreign captives (Deut 21:10-14). Indeed, the family tree of David and Jesus includes two women who are not Israelites, Rahab and Ruth (Matt 1:5; cf. Josh 6:25; Ruth 4:13-22).

[59]Verhoef, *Books of Haggai and Malachi*, p. 271; Merrill, *Haggai, Zechariah, Malachi*, p. 419.

[60]The KJV translates the phrase, "the master and the scholar," a reading that implicates both the priests (i.e., master) and the people who are their students (i.e., scholars).

[61]*IBHS*, p. 625.

**thing you do**). The community weeps over Yahweh's apparent inattention toward to their offerings. Generally prolonged weeping is regarded as a demonstration of repentance (2 Kgs 20:5; Ezra 10:1; Ps 6:6-9; 39:12; 42:3; Isa 38:5; Joel 2:12,17). Here, however, it reveals a lack of remorse from those seemingly oblivious to the reason for Yahweh's displeasure: the men of Israel have **broken faith** with the wives of their youth. The relationship between the marriage to the daughter of the foreign god and the breaking of faith with the wife of one's youth is uncertain. The repetition of the verb "break faith" (*bāgād*) throughout this section (vv. 10-16) suggests some connection. The desire to marry foreign women may have led some Israelite men to terminate the marriages with their Israelite wives. Nevertheless, the passage never makes an explicit connection between intermarriages in verses 11-12 and the divorces of verse 14, suggesting that other motivations may also have prompted these divorces.[62] Yahweh's role as witness is more than merely observing the divorces that the Israelite men consider to be private acts. Just as Yahweh is called to witness the covenant between Jacob and Laban, such that they would not seek to harm one another (Gen 31:40-53), Malachi portrays Yahweh as the witness, guarantor, or protector of the marriage covenants made between the Israelite men and the wives of their youth.[63] The previous use of second person plural forms ("Another thing you do" and **You ask**) changes to second person singular forms when the prophet states that Yahweh has become **witness between you and the wife of your youth**. In so doing, Yahweh makes the charge more personal. The reference to the wife as the **partner** in the **marriage covenant** is the fifth use of "covenant" (בְּרִית, *bᵊrîth*) in chapter 2. The first three deal with the priests' disregard for the covenant with Levi (vv. 4,5,8). The last two connect the marriage covenant (v. 14) with the larger covenant with the nation's ancestors (v. 10).

**2:15** The grammatical structure of verse 15 is problematic.[64] At least four options appear in how to treat the word "one" (אֶחָד, *'eḥād*)

[62]Taylor and Clendenen, *Haggai, Malachi*, p. 343.
[63]Verhoef, *Books of Haggai and Malachi*, p. 274.
[64]For extended treatment of the various issues of Hebrew grammar, syntax, and vocabulary within the text, see Taylor and Clendenen, *Haggai, Malachi*, pp. 349-357; Merrill, *Haggai, Zechariah, Malachi*, pp. 420-425; Verhoef, *Books of Haggai and Malachi*, pp. 275-280.

among the different translations. One, is *'eḥād* an adjective describing what Yahweh has made the husband and the wife to be (cf. Gen 2:24)? For example, the NIV reads, **Has not ⌊the LORD⌋ made them one?** Two, does *'eḥād* modify a missing noun for Yahweh to describe the one God who creates the wronged wife of verse 16 as well as her husband? For example, the NRSV reads, "Did not one God make her?" Three, does *'eḥād* go with the next phrase to describe the perpetrators of the unfaithfulness? For example, the NASB reads, "But not one has done so who has a remnant of the Spirit." Similar is the NET: "No one does this who has even a small portion of the Spirit in him." Four, does *'eḥād* allude to the patriarch Abraham (see Isa 51:2; Ezek 33:24) whose wrongful efforts to secure a godly offspring lead him to enter a surrogate relationship with Hagar without putting away Sarah, the wife of his youth (Gen 16:1-16)? This notion is reflected in the marginal reading of the NIV, "But the one *who is our father* did not do this, not as long as life remained in him. And what was he seeking? An offspring from God," and in the NET, "What did our ancestor do when seeking a child from God?" Of these, the fourth reading is least likely, since the remainder of the verse does not clearly indicate the prophet is using a past event as an example. Moreover, if "father" in verse 10 does not refer to Yahweh (see 1:10 above), the repeated mention of Jacob in Malachi (1:2; 2:12; 3:6) may argue that the implied father of verse 15 is Jacob rather than Abraham. More probable is one of the first two options. The second option renders the wording in a sense similar to questions in verse 10. The first option understands the wording in a way that follows logically from the mention of the marriage covenant in verse 14. Nonetheless, the import of the second half of the verse is quite clear: one should guard his **spirit** and remain faithful to his **wife**. The verb translated **guard yourself** (שָׁמַר, *šāmar*) appears six times in Malachi (2:7,9,15-16; 3:7,14). Three times (2:7,9; 3:7) the word appears in statements indicating the failure of one obligated to exercise care with Yahweh's knowledge and ways. One time (3:14) the word appears in a statement questioning the usefulness of keeping Yahweh's requirements. In verses 15-16, the community is called to reverse this pattern of nonobservance.

**2:16** The admonition to **guard** oneself **in spirit and** not to **break faith** (vv. 15,16) brackets the declaration of Yahweh's disdain for divorce. The NIV omits translating the causal conjunction (*kî*) that

links the call not to break faith in verse 15 with a motivation statement in 16. The MT of verse 16 contains a third person form "he
hates" rather than a first person form ("I hate"). This reading is followed by the majority of the ancient versions and the ESV ("For the
man who hates and divorces"). This reading, however, seems out of
line with the prophet's preceding concerns and may represent an
attempt by later scribes to bring Malachi into line with Deuteronomy 24:1 which permits divorce under some circumstances. A third-
person reading also requires that one read the following infinitive of
the verb "send away" or "divorce" as a third person verb ("divorces")
rather than as a verbal noun ("divorce"), the normal syntax of the
infinitive.[65] Moreover, the word "hate" (שָׂנֵא, śānē') may be understood as a participle and thus render the reading "'For hating
divorce (am I),'" says Yahweh."[66] The verb "send away" (שָׁלַח, šālaḥ)
is commonly used for "divorce" (Deut 22:19,29; 24:1,3,4; 1 Chr 8:8;
Isa 50:1; Jer 3:1,8). Papyri from the Jewish colony in Elephantine
during the Persian period indicate that the verb "hate" may have
been a legal term for repudiating a wife by divorce.[67] If so, Yahweh's
statement **I hate divorce** may be an ironic expression: Yahweh is
divorcing divorce. The unmitigated affirmation that Yahweh hates
divorce is the strongest statement on the subject in the Old
Testament. Nevertheless, one should not view it as an innovation.
Earlier texts protected married women from various abuses that
could occur in divorce (Exod 21:7-11; Deut 21:10-14; 24:1-4), and the
words of Malachi here indicate the motivation for those earlier laws.
The use of כָּסָה (kāsāh), translated here as "covering," complements
its earlier use in verse 13, where it is translated "flood." To flood or
cover (ESV, NRSV, NJPS) the altar with tears is senseless, at the
same time Israel also covers themselves with violence. Whereas the
NIV uses a comparison to speak of one **covering himself with violence as well as with his garment**, a more natural reading occurs in
the NRSV, NASB, ESV, and TNIV, all of which identify violence,
wrong, or injustice as that which covers the man's garments (cf. Ps
73:6).[68] The pairing of **the LORD God of Israel** with **the LORD**

[65]*IBHS*, pp. 598, 600; Williams, *Hebrew Syntax*, pp. 35-37.
[66]Hill, *Malachi*, pp. 249-250.
[67]Schuller, "Malachi," p. 866.
[68]Baldwin, *Haggai, Zechariah, Malachi*, p. 241.

**Almighty** reinforces the statement about divorce, and this repetition of these formulas serves to authenticate the message since Malachi has introduced a more stringent approach to divorce and has equated it to violence.[69]

## V. PROPHETIC DISPUTATION ABOUT YAHWEH'S JUDGMENT AGAINST THE WICKED (2:17–3:5)

Malachi 2:17–3:5 contains a prophetic disputation about Yahweh's judgment against the wicked (on the genre of prophetic disputation, see comments on 1:2-5 above). The section begins with a structure similar to previous disputations in the book (esp. 1:2-5 and 1:6–2:9). Malachi 2:17 presents a claim that the people have wearied Yahweh with troublesome speech, the people's uncertainty about this claim ("How have we wearied him?"), and a rebuttal in support of the claim ("By saying . . ."). This rebuttal reflects an attitude among the people that questions divine morality ("All who do evil are good") and divine justice ("Where is the God of justice?"). Malachi 3:1-5 then answers these questions with an announcement about coming judgment. Yahweh will send a messenger to prepare the way for Yahweh so that the covenant may be enforced (3:1) and to purify the Levites so that they will present acceptable offerings (3:2-4), and Yahweh will come for judgment against the wicked (3:5). Therefore, Malachi 2:17–3:5 seeks to disabuse the people of their attitudes about the prosperity of the wicked and the ineffectual justice of Yahweh with the announcement of coming purification and judgment.

> [17]**You have wearied the LORD with your words.**
>
> **"How have we wearied him?" you ask.**
>
> **By saying, "All who do evil are good in the eyes of the LORD, and he is pleased with them" or "Where is the God of justice?"**

**2:17** This section (2:17–3:5) begins as others in Malachi with a supposed exchange between debaters. First is a claim that the people have **wearied** Yahweh **with** their **words** (cf. Isa 43:24). Second is a request for clarification about **how** the people **have wearied** Yahweh. Third is a rebuttal that contains statements purportedly

---

[69]Hill, *Malachi*, p. 253.

made by the people challenging divine morality (**All who do evil are good**) and divine justice (**Where is the God of justice?**). The people's doubts about moral expectations may have resulted in part from their experience of hardships following the exile (1:8; 3:11-12) and from the failure of the priests to ensure impartiality among the people (2:9). The people's doubts about the justice of God, however, seem ironic in view of the preceding section (2:10-16). Even though Israel is guilty of breaking faith with one another and thereby profaning the covenant of their fathers, the question implies that Yahweh has broken the covenant with Israel. The following section answers these doubts with the announcement about the coming of Yahweh's messenger and judgment.

¹**"See, I will send my messenger, who will prepare the way before me. Then suddenly the Lord you are seeking will come to his temple; the messenger of the covenant, whom you desire, will come," says the LORD Almighty.**

²**But who can endure the day of his coming? Who can stand when he appears? For he will be like a refiner's fire or a launderer's soap. ³He will sit as a refiner and purifier of silver; he will purify the Levites and refine them like gold and silver. Then the LORD will have men who will bring offerings in righteousness, ⁴and the offerings of Judah and Jerusalem will be acceptable to the LORD, as in days gone by, as in former years.**

⁵**"So I will come near to you for judgment. I will be quick to testify against sorcerers, adulterers and perjurers, against those who defraud laborers of their wages, who oppress the widows and the fatherless, and deprive aliens of justice, but do not fear me," says the LORD Almighty.**

**3:1** The announcement that a **messenger will prepare the way before** Yahweh signals a response to the question of 2:17, and the transition from third person reference to Yahweh in 2:17 to first person speech by Yahweh in 3:1 heightens the gravity of the content of the following verses. The interjection **see** (הִנֵּה, *hinnēh*) followed by a participle (also found in Mal 2:3; 4:1; and 4:5) emphasizes the imminence and certainty of the future coming of the messenger.[70] Yahweh's

---

[70]GKC, pp. 359-360; *IBHS*, pp. 627-628; Williams, *Hebrew Syntax*, p. 39.

announcement about the sending of the messenger (מַלְאָךְ, *mal'āk*) may allude to Exodus 23:20 where Yahweh promises to send an "angel" or "messenger" (*mal'āk*) in front of Israel in the journeys to Canaan. Furthermore, the call to prepare the way for Yahweh may also allude to the call in Isaiah (40:3), a text which the Gospels relate to John the Baptist (Matt 3:3; 11:10; Mark 1:2; Luke 1:76).

Important for the verse is the identification of **my messenger** and **the messenger of the covenant**. The use of the first person pronoun "my" in the verse and the description of his task to prepare the way before the Lord distinguishes "my messenger" from Yahweh.[71] Also, the sending of the messenger excludes the possibility that Malachi is referring to the priests who earlier are identified as the "messenger of the LORD Almighty" (2:7). Rather, the same sentence structure (that is, the interjection "see" [*hinnēh*] with the first person pronoun **I** and the participle translated **will send**) reappears later in Malachi 4:5 and thus links "my messenger" with the prophet Elijah whom Yahweh will send. The title "messenger of the covenant" should be identified as Yahweh, here referred to as **Lord** (אָדוֹן, *'ādôn*). This is corroborated by the mention of "**his**" temple and by the parallel construction[72] in the Hebrew text of the verse (**the Lord you are seeking will come . . . the messenger of the covenant, whom you desire . . . will come**). The title "messenger of the covenant" is an appropriate title for Yahweh as the one who enforces the covenant. In addition, the title recalls the earlier identifications of Yahweh with the divine angel or messenger (Exod 3:1-22; 23:20-23; 32:34; 33:14-15; Isa 63:9) and the use of Angel as a name for Yahweh in Genesis 48:16. The coming of Yahweh in the

---

[71]See Chisholm, *Minor Prophets*, pp. 286-287; Verhoef, *Books of Haggai and Malachi*, pp. 288-289; Taylor and Clendenen, *Haggai, Malachi*, p. 385; for arguments that equate "my messenger" with "the messenger of the covenant," see Merrill, *Haggai, Zechariah, Malachi*, pp. 429-430, 432.

[72]This parallel construction is more clearly indicated through a chiastic arrangement of the Hebrew text. A word-for-word rendering of the Hebrew reads: "suddenly he comes to his palace the Lord whom you seek, and the messenger of the covenant whom you desire behold he comes." The construction begins and ends with an interjection/adverb and the verb "he comes"; in the middle are two noun phrases, each modified by verbs of longing.

person of Jesus, the messenger of the new covenant, may be understood to fulfill this promise of Yahweh's coming.[73]

Malachi's use of "Lord" (*'ādôn*) to designate Yahweh (**Then suddenly the Lord you are seeking will come to his temple**) rather than the covenant name Yahweh (יהוה, *YHWH*), may stem from Israel's violation of the covenant relationship with Yahweh (the NIV renders the covenant name *YHWH* as **LORD** with small capital letters). The people who have neglected their covenant obligations experience Yahweh apart from any covenant mercy (i.e., they experience Yahweh as Lord rather than LORD). The description of Yahweh as the one "whom you desire" is probably ironic, since the verb translated "he is pleased" in 2:17 comes from the same root (חפץ, *ḥpṣ*). Yahweh is not pleased with those who do evil, nor do the people desire the sudden coming of Yahweh to the temple. Yahweh comes suddenly (פתאם, *pith'ōm*), an adverb which appears almost exclusively in contexts of judgment (e.g., Isa 29:5; 30:13; 47:11; 48:3; Jer 4:20; 6:26; 15:8; 18:22; 51:8). One notable exception in 2 Chronicles 29:36 speaks of the speed at which, in the days of Hezekiah, the temple is purified from defilement and the priests, Levites, and people are again consecrated to Yahweh. The context here may also combine the notions of judgment and purification.

**3:2-4** Two rhetorical questions **But who can endure the day of his coming? Who can stand when he appears?** convey the impossibility of standing against Yahweh (cf. 2 Chr 20:6; Ps 5:5; 76:7), whose coming presents an unexpected challenge for those who are seeking or desiring Yahweh. While the coming of Yahweh brings salvation, it also brings judgment. Isaiah 40:1-2 speaks of judgment preceding the preparation for the coming of Yahweh (40:3-5). In particular, the phrase "the day of his coming" resembles the frequently appearing Old Testament concept of the imminent day of Yahweh (e.g., Isa 13:6,9; Ezek 30:3; Joel 1:15; 2:1,11; Obad 15; Zeph 1:7,14; Zech 14:1).

Two images illustrate that the purpose of Yahweh's coming for the covenant people is not to destroy but to purify. The first of these images (**a refiner's fire**) is expanded in verse 3 (see below). The sec-

---

[73]See Walter C. Kaiser, Jr., *The Messiah in the Old Testament*, Studies in Old Testament Biblical Theology (Grand Rapids: Zondervan, 1995), pp. 227-229, on the identification of the angel/messenger in Exodus 23, 32, and 33 with both the messenger of the covenant in Malachi 3:1 and Jesus.

ond image (**a launderer's soap**) adds to the first. The term "launderer's" is a participle form of a verb to wash (כָּבַס, *kābas*) that is never
used for washing one's body. Instead, it generally refers to the washing of clothes (Exod 19:10,14; Lev 6:27, etc.), usually in order to
remove ceremonial defilement from leprosy or a bodily discharge
(Lev 11:25,28,40; 13:6,34,54-58; 15:10-11). Priests are instructed to
wash their clothes when inducted into office (Num 8:7) and when
sacrificial blood spills on their garments (Lev 6:27).[74] This is significant in the larger context of this text in Malachi. The one who
divorces the wife of his youth covers his garments with violence (Mal
2:16) and needs cleansing from that defilement. The associations of
the "violence" (חָמָס, *ḥāmās*) with bloodshed accent this connection
(Judg 9:24; 2 Sam 22:3; Jer 51:35; Hab 2:8). The priests also have
been defiled (Mal 2:3,9) and are in need of cleansing. Soap in the
ancient world comes from decomposing oil (usually olive oil) with
alkali derived from burning certain plants.[75] The word for soap (בֹּרִית,
*bōrîth*) is similar to that for covenant (בְּרִית, *bᵉrîth*) in verse 1 (also
2:4,5,8,10,14). Perhaps there is an intended wordplay; the messenger
of *bᵉrîth* is coming to purify the covenant people as with *bōrîth*.

The first image ("a refiner's fire") originates from the craft of
metalworking, in which through intense heat a metal is isolated in a
purer state. Such language is often used in the Old Testament for
Yahweh's punishment of Israel as a means for purging impurity and
producing purity (e.g., Isa 1:25; 48:10; Jer 6:29; 9:7; Ezek 22:17-22;
Dan 11:35; 12:10; and Zech 13:9). Here, however, the Levitical priesthood rather than the people as a whole are to be refined **like gold
and silver**. Once purified, the **Levites** can make an offering **in righteousness** that is acceptable to Yahweh. This outcome, of course,
stands in contrast to the earlier indictment of the priests who offer
blemished and unacceptable sacrifices (Mal 1:6–2:9). The Hebrew
actually contains the singular form of "offering." The NIV (cf. NJPS)
understands this as a collective noun designating sacrifices made by
the people and translates **the offerings of Judah and Jerusalem**. The
ESV, KJV, NASB, NET, NRSV, and NJB, however, retain the singular, and, in doing so, retain a possible double nuance. The purification of the Levites not only leads to the **acceptable** sacrifices offered

---

[74]Elmer Martens, "כבס," *NIDOTTE*, 2:593.
[75]H.N. Richardson, "Soap," *IDB*, 4:394-395; R.J. Way, "Soap," *ISBE*, 4:558.

by the community but also to the acceptable offering of the community itself. By saying that the offerings acceptable to Yahweh are offered **as in days gone by, as in former years**, the prophet anticipates a renewal of Israel's direct dependence on Yahweh immediately following the exodus (cf. Jer 2:2-3).[76]

**3:5** Verse 5 satisfies the complaint of the people about divine justice in 2:17, since Yahweh **comes near to** Israel **for judgment** against all who do evil.[77] The people have asked, "Where is the God of justice (מִשְׁפָּט, *mišpāṭ*)?" Now Yahweh comes near to them for judgment (*mišpāṭ*) and comes **quick**ly **to testify** (עֵד, *ʿēd*) or to be a witness (cf. the ESV's "I will be a swift witness") against evildoers. This word is related to the "witness" (עוּד, *ʿûd*) used in 2:14 where Yahweh acts as a witness between the husband and his wife. The designation of Yahweh as a witness involves more than Yahweh's mere observance of a thing. It also connotes the vindication of wronged parties and the judgment of the wicked (e.g., 1 Kgs 21:10,13; Ps 50:7; Jer 42:5-6; Amos 3:13; Micah 1:2).[78] Those listed for judgment (**sorcerers, adulterers and perjurers . . . those who defraud laborers of their wages**) are frequently censured (Exod 20:7,14,16, 22:18,21-22; Lev 19:11-13; 20:9-27; Deut 5:11,18,20; 18:9-11; 22:22; 24:14-15; 2 Chr 33:6; Isa 47:8-15; 48:1; Jer 7:9; 27:9-10; Zech 5:3-4). The indictment against those **who oppress the widows and the fatherless, and deprive aliens of justice** reflects the frequent reminder of Israel's obligation to treat properly widows, orphans, and aliens (Lev 19:10,33-35; 23:22; Deut 14:29; 16:13-15; 26:11). As a result, Israel remembers its former alien status in the land of Egypt (Exod 22:21; 23:9; Lev 19:34; Deut 10:19) and its present alien status as tenants living on Yahweh's land (Lev 25:23). The list of those against whom Yahweh testifies culminates with those who **do not fear** (יָרֵא, *yārē'*) Yahweh. This is the third of four uses of the verb *yārē'* in Malachi. The first two appear in statements contrasting the fear of Yahweh's name among the nations (1:14) and the memory of the priesthood's past reverence for Yahweh's name (2:5) with Israel's present disobedience and disregard. Yahweh's judgment now comes upon those who by their actions show no fear of Yahweh (3:5) in a day characterized by fear

---

[76]Baldwin, *Haggai, Zechariah, Malachi*, p. 144.

[77]Graffy, "Malachi," p. 1204.

[78]Robert B. Chisholm, "עוד," *NIDOTTE*, 3:337.

or dread (4:5). The concluding speech formula (**says the LORD Almighty**) establishes Yahweh as the speaker of this section (cf. 3:1) and emphasizes Yahweh as the one who comes near for judgment.

## VI. PROPHETIC DISPUTATION ABOUT THE PEOPLE'S ROBBERY OF YAHWEH (3:6-12)

[6]**"I the LORD do not change. So you, O descendants of Jacob, are not destroyed. [7]Ever since the time of your forefathers you have turned away from my decrees and have not kept them. Return to me, and I will return to you," says the LORD Almighty.**

**"But you ask, 'How are we to return?'**

[8]**"Will a man rob God? Yet you rob me.**

**"But you ask, 'How do we rob you?'**

**"In tithes and offerings. [9]You are under a curse—the whole nation of you—because you are robbing me. [10]Bring the whole tithe into the storehouse, that there may be food in my house. Test me in this," says the LORD Almighty, "and see if I will not throw open the floodgates of heaven and pour out so much blessing that you will not have room enough for it. [11]I will prevent pests from devouring your crops, and the vines in your fields will not cast their fruit," says the LORD Almighty. [12]"Then all the nations will call you blessed, for yours will be a delightful land," says the LORD Almighty.**

Malachi 3:6-12 contains a prophetic disputation about the people's robbery of Yahweh (on the genre of prophetic disputation, see comments on 1:2-5 above). Like the first and second disputations (1:2-5 and 1:6–2:9), this section begins with words of Yahweh. Like the second disputation, this one is extended by an additional question and response. Malachi 3:6 is linked to the previous section with the conjunction "for" (כִּי, *kî*), even though it is not translated in the NIV, and in some way continues the announcement of Yahweh's coming to judge the wicked (3:5; cf. 4:1-3). Perhaps the people see in their present situation the prosperity of evildoers (2:17) and wonder if this results from a change in Yahweh's commitment to the covenant. Instead, this section begins with the assertion that Yahweh does not change, evidenced by the reality that the descendants of

Jacob have not been destroyed (v. 7). Yahweh exhorts the people to return, and then Yahweh will return to them (v. 7). The people request clarification about Yahweh's claim ("How are we to return?"), and Yahweh replies that they rob Yahweh. Again the people request clarification ("How do we rob you?"), and Yahweh replies that they rob Yahweh in tithes and offerings (v. 8). Because of this, the whole nation is under a curse (v. 9). Yahweh commands them to bring in the whole tithe (a single stipulation likely signifying the entire covenant) and to test Yahweh who will bless them abundantly (v. 10), removing covenant curses and fulfilling covenant promises (vv. 11-12). Therefore, 3:6-12 urges the people to return to a faithful observance of covenant norms, by contributing fully to the support of the temple.

**3:6** Like the first (1:2-5) and second (1:6–2:9) disputations, this one (3:6-12) begins its exchange between debaters with the words of Yahweh. Even though the ESV, NASB, NET, NRSV, and NJPS translate the connecting particle כִּי (*kî*) as a causative ("for" or "since"), an emphatic sense of "behold," "truly," or "indeed" suits the following statement (the particle is not translated in the NIV).[79] In this way, *kî* signals the beginning of this section and highlights its key assertion: **I,** Yahweh**, do not change**. The perfect tense verb "change," however, would be better translated "I have not changed" (as in the NJPS), a rendering that reflects the notion of Yahweh's continuing reliability from the past through the present (cf. Ps 89:34). Specifically, Yahweh has been faithful to the covenant, remaining true to its promises and not destroying Jacob (cf. the reading in the NET: "Since, I, the Lord, do not go back on my promises, you, sons of Jacob, have not perished"). This is the third use of **Jacob** as a name for the people in Malachi, and each instance involves a notion of covenant: Yahweh has loved or chosen Jacob (1:2), Yahweh cuts off from the tents of Jacob those who break faith (2:11), and the faithfulness of Yahweh accounts for Jacob's continued existence. This last use of the name together with the affirmation that Jacob is **not destroyed** alludes to the book's opening passage. Only the enduring love of Yahweh (1:2; 3:6) can explain Jacob's continued existence in contrast to the destruction of Edom (1:4; 3:6).

[79]GKC, pp. 471, 498; *IBHS*, pp. 665-667; Verhoef, *Books of Haggai and Malachi*, p. 299.

**3:7** Nevertheless, the people replicate the infidelity of their ancestors. This unfaithfulness is stated positively (**you have turned away from my decrees**) and negatively (**and have not kept them**). The word translated "decrees" (חֹק, *ḥōq*) in the NIV refers to something engraved, but attempts to distinguish *ḥōq* from other nouns denoting that laws and commandments (e.g., Exod 15:25; 18:16; Josh 24:25; Ezra 7:10; Mal 4:4) have been ineffective;[80] consequently, different versions offer varying translations of the word: "statutes" (ESV, NASB, NRSV, NJB), "commandments" (NET), and "laws" (NJPS). The command here to **return** (שׁוּב, *šûb*) to Yahweh is matched by the command to bring the whole tithe in verse 10. Bringing the full tithe demonstrates the community's repentance. The accusation and demanded response in this verse frequently appear in Jeremiah who accuses Israel of turning away (סוּר, *sûr*) from Yahweh (5:23; 6:28; 17:5,13) and calls for their return (*šûb*) or repentance (3:12,14,22; 4:1; 15:19; 18:11; 35:15). The same two words ("turn away" and "return") appear together elsewhere in 1 Samuel 7:3, 2 Chronicles 30:9, and Jeremiah 4:1. The prophetic call to repent is followed by Yahweh's pledge to turn toward Israel. Such language is similar to Zechariah 1:3 ("Therefore tell the people: This is what the LORD Almighty says: 'Return to me,' declares the LORD Almighty, 'and I will return to you,' says the LORD Almighty"), except here in Malachi 3:7 the concluding speech formula (**says the LORD Almighty**) only concludes the call to repent. The question **How?** appears six times in Malachi (1:2,6,7; 2:17; 3:7-8). Each time, with exception of 3:7, involves an incredulous response to an accusation by Yahweh. In 3:7, the question challenges the command to return to Yahweh. Perhaps the postexilic community supposes that the return from the Babylonian exile is sufficient evidence that Yahweh has accepted their repentance as complete or sufficient (Deut 4:25-31; 30:1-3; 1 Kgs 8:33-34,48).

**3:8** The exchange between debaters continues into the next two verses. Yahweh asserts that the people **rob God**. This verse contains the first use in the book of the divine name "God" (אֱלֹהִים, *'ĕlōhîm*) without the covenant name Yahweh (יהוה, *YHWH*) in the same verse. Elsewhere *'ĕlōhîm* appears without יהוה only in 3:15 and 18. Whereas יהוה characteristically bears connotations of the deity's immanence

---

[80]Jack P. Lewis, "חָקַק," *TWOT*, 1:317.

and availability to the worshiper and of the deity's covenant relationship with Israel, *'ĕlōhîm* connotes the deity's creative power,
supremacy, and transcendence.[81] In this verse, the implications of
*'ĕlōhîm* as creator are especially significant in contrast with "man" or
"human being" (*'ādām*). God is the transcendent creator upon whom
Israel depends as creature.[82] How dare Israel rob the divine creator?
The people request clarification (**How do we rob you?**), and Yahweh
replies that they do so **in tithes and offerings**. The verb "rob" (קָבַע,
*qāba'*), appearing three times in this verse, may be an intentional
wordplay on the name Jacob (יַעֲקֹב, *ya'ăqōb*) earlier in 3:6, since the
two words contain the same three letters. If so, the play on words
reminds the people of Jacob's vow to present a tenth of what
Yahweh gives him (Gen 28:22). "Tithes" means tenths. The account
of Abraham giving a tithe to Melchizedek (Gen 14:18-20) and
Jacob's vow to give a tenth to Yahweh (Gen 28:22) indicate the practice of giving a tenth of one's possessions to a superior is an ancient
custom. More importantly, the law acknowledges that a tenth of
Israel's produce belongs to Yahweh and is set apart as an offering to
Yahweh (Lev 27:30).[83] This tithe also supports the Levites and priests
in their sacred work, but even they must offer to Yahweh a tenth of
what they received (Lev 27:30-33; Num 18:21-29; Deut 14:22-29;
26:12-15).[84] "Offerings" are portions of sacrifices that are set aside
for the priests (Exod 29:27-28; Lev 7:32; Num 18:8,11,19,21-24).
Together "tithes and offerings" may refer to a "general tithe" stored

<hr>

[81]William Dyrness, *Themes in Old Testament Theology* (Downers Grove, IL:
InterVarsity, 1979), pp. 45-46; Walther Eichrodt, *Theology of the Old
Testament*, OTL (Philadelphia: Westminster, 1961), 1:186-187, 190-191;
Edmond Jacob, *Theology of the Old Testament* (New York: Harper and Row,
1958), pp. 43-44, 52; Horst Dietrich Pruess, *Old Testament Theology*, OTL
(Louisville, KY: Westminster/John Knox, 1995), 1:139-142, 147-149.

[82]Hill, *Malachi*, p. 304.

[83]The Pentateuch insists that the land belongs exclusively to Yahweh, who
has given it to Israel (Lev 25:23). Thus, Israel is a tenant on Yahweh's land,
and all the wealth the land produces rightly belongs to Yahweh. All material prosperity that the individual, family, or nation possesses is Yahweh's gift
and not solely the product of human strength and cunning (Deut 8:17-18).
For more on the theology of land in the Old Testament, see Christopher
J.H. Wright, *God's People in God's Land: Family, Land, and Property in the Old
Testament* (Grand Rapids: Eerdmans, 1990), pp.; 22-23, 116.

[84]See Verhoef, *Books of Haggai and Malachi*, p. 304, for a summary of the
various tithes prescribed in the Old Testament law.

in regional storehouses and the "tithe tax," funds sent to Jerusalem for support of the priesthood (cf. Neh 10:36-39; 12:44).[85] The accusation that Israel is robbing Yahweh in the tithes and offerings indicates that the people have rejected Yahweh as the nation's benevolent provider (Deut 6:10-12) and have repudiated the worship of Yahweh financed by the tithe (Num 18:21-29).

**3:9** This accusation that **the whole nation**[86] robs Yahweh in tithes and offerings fits the historical context of Malachi's ministry. Nehemiah 13:10 indicates that the people's failure to bring the tithes is an act that forces the Levites to leave their ministry and work in the fields to support themselves. Such neglect of the tithe is tantamount to robbery and has resulted in a curse. The rendering of the NIV (**You are under a curse**) does not translate the force of the Hebrew text, where the verb "curse" appears with its cognate noun. The NRSV approaches a more exact representation ("You are cursed with a curse"), but the Hebrew text is still more emphatic ("You are cursed with the curse"). "The curse" (see comments on Mal 2:2 above) is a likely allusion to the covenant curses of Deuteronomy 28:15-68 ("the curse" appears elsewhere only in Deut 28:20). Among these curses are agricultural disasters, which are the result of the disobedience of the postexilic community (Hag 1:4-6,10-11; 2:16-17).

**3:10** Verse 10 presents Yahweh's proposal that the people **bring the whole tithe into the storehouse** so that they may **test** what Yahweh does in response to their obedience.[87] Such obedience must

---

[85]Hill, *Malachi*, p. 306; David L. Petersen, *Zechariah 9–14 and Malachi*, OTL (Louisville, KY: Westminster/John Knox, 1995), p. 216.

[86]The use of the noun "nation" (גּוֹי, *gôy*), which usually refers to the non-Jewish "nations," suggests that the covenant nation is acting no better than the pagan nations.

[87]It is inappropriate to use the promise of Malachi 3:10 as some sort of "investment strategy" in which one obligates God to increase material prosperity in response to the payment of tithes. First, the promise is made to the nation as a whole, not to individuals. Second, the treatment of the promise as a means toward gaining wealth reverses the principles upon which the tithing laws are given. The Hebrew people tithe in response to what Yahweh has already provided, not to coerce or ensure provision. Third, the promise of abundant provision represents only a restatement of the promises given to Israel in anticipation of their entrance into Canaan (Deut 28:4-5,8,11-12; 30:9). In this way, the promise is merely a reminder that Yahweh provides

precede the experience of Yahweh's blessings.[88] The *whole* nation (v. 9) is to bring the *whole* tithe into the storehouse, suggesting complete obedience. Deuteronomy 14:28-29 also speaks of bringing in "all the tithe," that is, the whole tithe. This collection, taken at the end of every three years, would ensure that the Levites, aliens, fatherless, and widows are able to eat and be satisfied. In response, Yahweh blesses Israel in all the work of their hands. The word "storehouse" translates the Hebrew phrase "the house of supplies," perhaps a building in or near the temple complex that consists of numerous rooms or cubicles for the storage of grain, wine, and olive oil, the staples of Israelite agriculture.[89] In the eighth century, Hezekiah prepares storerooms in the temple (2 Chr 31:11-12), and, after the time of Malachi, Nehemiah testifies to their use and administration (10:38-39; 12:44; 13:4-5,12). Usually Yahweh is the subject of the verb "test" (בָּחַן, *bāḥan*) (Ps 7:9; 11:4-5; 17:3; 66:10; 139:23; Jer 11:20; 17:10; Zech 13:9); in only three texts (Ps 95:9; Mal 3:10,15) is Yahweh the object of testing. Other texts, without using *bāḥan*, however, describe the willingness of Yahweh to be tested (Exod 4:1-9; Judg 6:36-40; 1 Kgs 18:22-46; Isa 7:10-17). Once more, the prophet employs the messenger formula **says the LORD Almighty**; here the

---

Israel with what it needs. Fourth, the promise is less a guarantee of prosperity than it is an assurance that the one who trusts Yahweh with the tithe is also able to trust Yahweh for provision.

The New Testament does not renew the tithe command in as many words. Nevertheless, it reflects principles within the tithing laws of the Old Testament. First, giving should be proportionate in keeping with one's means (Acts 11:27-30; 1 Cor 16:1-2; 2 Cor 8:11-12). Second, giving shows concern for the poor or those in need (Acts 4:34-35; 11:27-30; Rom 12:13; 15:26-27; Gal 2:10; 2 Cor 9:12-13; Eph 4:28; Jas 2:16; 1 John 3:17) and for the provision for those who minister to the church (1 Tim 5:17-18). Third, giving acknowledges that the believer is a steward of God's possessions (Matt 6:25-32). Fourth, giving generously on the basis of faith in God provides all that the giver needs (2 Cor 9:6-11). Fifth, giving results in "many expressions of thanks to God" (2 Cor 9:12-13), just as tithing in the Old Testament results in the satisfaction of those in need (Deut 14:28-29). Since New Testament texts contain these parallels to principles in the Old Testament tithing laws and since tithing is a pattern for giving even before the Mosaic law (Gen 14:20; 28:22), one may consider the tithe or tenth an initial guideline for giving according to the New Testament.

[88]Mason, *Books of Haggai, Zechariah, Malachi*, p. 156.

[89]Hill, *Malachi*, p. 310.

formula marks this speech as the most prominent part of the paragraph, making more solemn the charge for the nation to test Yahweh in the tithe (3:10). If the people do so, Yahweh promises to **throw open the floodgates of heaven and pour out** an abundant **blessing**. The idiom of opening the floodgates of heaven may refer to the outpouring of judgment (Gen 7:11; 8:2; Isa 24:18) or blessing (Deut 28:12; 2 Kgs 7:2,19; Ps 78:23-24). Here the idiom depicts the reversal of the covenant curse (Mal 3:9) with covenant blessing (Deut 28:12; 30:9)

**3:11-12** Likewise, **pests** represent an example of covenant curses (Deut 28:39-40) that are now reversed (Deut 30:9). The NIV translates as "pest" what other versions render "devourer" (ESV, NASB). This may refer to a **devouring** insect like the locust (NRSV, NJB, NJPS) or some crop-destroying plague (NET). **Crops** (or "the fruit of the ground") represents the grain harvest, and **the vines of the fields**, the total fruit harvest. The verb in the promise that the **fields will not cast their fruit** appears in contexts speaking of fetal miscarriage (Gen 31:38; Exod 23:26; Job 21:10; Jer 50:9). Here, as in 2 Kings 2:19-21, its figurative extension describes the failure of the land to produce a harvest.[90] Nevertheless, Yahweh promises to change these conditions of agricultural devastation. When the surrounding nations witness the resulting agricultural prosperity, **the nations call** Israel **blessed**, a complement to the ancient promise that all the nations are blessed through Abraham and his descendants (Gen 12:3; 18:18; 22:18). The assurance that Israel is **a delightful** (חֵפֶץ, *ḥēpheṣ*) **land** represents a reversal of the situation in 1:10 where the same verb is used to express Yahweh's displeasure with the people. The prophet uses the messenger formula, **says the LORD Almighty**, twice more. Here, and in verse 10, it makes prominent Yahweh's promises of agricultural abundance and blessing.


## VII. PROPHETIC DISPUTATION ABOUT YAHWEH'S REMEMBRANCE OF THE RIGHTEOUS (3:13–4:3)

Malachi 3:13–4:3 (3:13-21 in the MT) contains a prophetic disputation about Yahweh's remembrance of the righteous (on the

---

[90]Victor P. Hamilton, "שָׁכֹל," *TWOT*, 2:924.

genre of prophetic disputation, see comments on 1:2-5 above). As in previous disputations, the section begins with a premise ("You have said harsh things against me") and a request for clarification ("What have we said against you?" v. 13). The rebuttal cites statements evidently made by the disputants themselves about the futility of serving Yahweh and the prosperity of the wicked (vv. 14-15). Following this exchange, the focus of the section shifts to those who fear Yahweh and their conversations which Yahweh hears and remembers (v. 16). Yahweh assures them that they are a treasured possession and that they will see the clear distinction between the righteous and the wicked (vv. 17-18). The wicked will be destroyed, but the righteous will be healed and triumph over the wicked (4:1-3). Therefore, Malachi 3:13–4:3 shows that some of the people have responded positively to Malachi's previous calls to repent (esp. 2:10–3:12) and report that Yahweh will act on behalf of them and against the wicked.

¹³"You have said harsh things against me," says the LORD.
"Yet you ask, 'What have we said against you?'

¹⁴"You have said, 'It is futile to serve God. What did we gain by carrying out his requirements and going about like mourners before the LORD Almighty? ¹⁵But now we call the arrogant blessed. Certainly the evildoers prosper, and even those who challenge God escape.'"

¹⁶Then those who feared the LORD talked with each other, and the LORD listened and heard. A scroll of remembrance was written in his presence concerning those who feared the LORD and honored his name.

¹⁷"They will be mine," says the LORD Almighty, "in the day when I make up my treasured possession.ᵃ I will spare them, just as in compassion a man spares his son who serves him. ¹⁸And you will again see the distinction between the righteous and the wicked, between those who serve God and those who do not.

ᵃ17 Or *Almighty, "my treasured possession, in the day when I act*

**3:13** Like previous disputations (1:2-5; 1:6–2:9; 3:6-12), this one (3:13–4:3) begins its exchange between debaters with the words of Yahweh. As in 2:17, the prophet portrays Yahweh as countering misperceptions about God's justice. The similarity of the charges in 2:17

and 3:13-15 indicates that the speakers in both instances are probably identical. Yahweh addresses the people with the statement, **You have said harsh things against me**. To describe the "harsh words" (cf. the TNIV's "arrogantly") of the people, the prophet uses the same word (חָזַק, ḥāzāq) used to describe the hardening or stubbornness of Pharaoh's heart (Exod 4:21; 7:13,22; 8:19; 9:12,35; 10:20,27; 11:10). When followed by the preposition "against," ḥāzāq may describe an act of violence or subjugation (Exod 12:33; 2 Sam 24:4; 1 Chr 21:4; 2 Chr 27:5; Dan 10:21). In the same way, Jude 14-15 speaks of the Lord coming to judge the ungodly of "all the harsh words ungodly sinners have spoken against him."

**3:14** Verses 14-15 specify the charges made in verse 13. Malachi generally uses the divine name אֱלֹהִים ('ĕlōhîm) to refer to God as an abstract universal creator deity (on 'ĕlōhîm see 3:8 above).[91] Here the speakers of the harsh words say, **It is futile to serve God.** This statement minimizes the covenant relationship and responsibility between Yahweh and Israel; thus, their use of the name **the LORD Almighty** (YHWH ṣᵉbā'ôth) at the end of the verse takes on a sarcastic tone. The speakers allege that serving God is "futile" (שָׁוְא, šāw'), a noun meaning without substance, without result, or without truth and thereby deceptive (Exod 20:7; Job 15:31; 35:13; Ps 119:37; 127:1-2; Jer 2:30; 4:30; 6:29; 46:11; Ezek 13:6). They claim that serving Yahweh profits them nothing and, therefore, the disobedient are the truly blessed ones (Mal 3:15). The noun for **gain** (בֶּצַע, beṣa') intimates the hypocrisy and motives of Israel. Its twenty-three uses designate personal advantage, usually ill-gotten gain, derived from some activity.[92] They have hoped that covenant obedience would be a means for wealth and prosperity. The verb translated **carry out** (שָׁמַר, šāmar), meaning to exercise great care or diligence over, appears with its cognate noun translated **requirements** (מִשְׁמֶרֶת, mišmereth). This phrase (cf. the ESV's rendering, "our keeping his charge") is used to speak of tasks and obligations given to Levites (Ezek 44:8), priests (Lev 8:35; 22:9; Ezek 44:15-16; 48:11), the high priest (Zech 3:7), and the people as a whole (Lev 18:30; Num 9:19,23; Deut 11:1; Josh 22:2-3). That the phrase generally refers to priestly service at the temple may implicate the priests themselves as

---

[91]Hill, *Malachi*, p. 265.
[92]John N. Oswalt, "בֶּצַע," *TWOT*, 1:122.

being among those who doubt Yahweh's justice and power.[93] The image of **going about like mourners** may refer to acts of fasting or penitence such as those associated with the Day of Atonement (Lev 16:29-31); the expression here reflects the delusion that their outward worship is genuine and warrants divine reward.[94] The arrogance of their contention is highlighted with the occurrence of the divine name "the LORD Almighty" (יהוה צְבָאוֹת, *YHWH ṣᵊbā'ôth*), also translated as "the LORD of Hosts" (ESV, KJV, NASB) or "Yahweh Sabaoth" (NJB).

**3:15** As unsettling as the assertions in verse 14 may be, the adverbial phrase **but now** (וְעַתָּה, *wᵊ'attāh*) signals a more direct accusation: the speakers declare that **evildoers prosper** and even escape the judgment of God. The verb translated "prosper" is a passive form of a verb normally translated "build" (בָּנָה, *bānāh*).[95] It appears earlier in 1:4 where the Edomites boast that they intend to rebuild their ruins. Yahweh, however, asserts that any attempt to rebuild will be demolished. Its use here then represents another repudiation of the book's initial affirmation of Yahweh's love for Israel (1:2-5). The word for "challenge" here is identical to the word in 3:10 translated "test" (בָּחַן, *bāḥan*). Yahweh instructs Judah to test the faithfulness of Yahweh to extend covenant blessings in tithes and offerings, but instead they test Yahweh through their complaining, rebellion, and unbelief (cf. Exod 17:2-7; Num 14:22; Deut 6:14-18; Ps 78:17-19,40-42,56-58; 95:8-9; 106:6-29).[96] The statement that **those who challenge God escape** (cf. the TNIV's "when they put God to the test, they get away with it") draws attention to the distorted thinking of Israel, in which it is asserted that the evildoers handily escape the judgment of the God (*'ĕlōhîm*), the transcendent one. Yahweh provides an escape or deliverance (מָלַט, *milaṭ*) for the righteous (Prov 28:26; Job 22:30) who call on Yahweh (Joel 2:32); those who sin, however, cannot escape (1 Kgs 19:17; Amos 2:14-15).[97]

**3:16 Those who feared the LORD** names a new group of people that should be distinguished from those speaking the harsh words of

---

[93]Sweeney, *Twelve Prophets*, p. 746.

[94]Keil, *Minor Prophets*, p. 661.

[95]Wisdom writers speak often of the apparent prosperity of the wicked (Job 9:24; 12:19; 21:7,13; Ps 37:1; 73:2-14; Eccl 8:14).

[96]Taylor and Clendenen, *Haggai, Malachi*, p. 423.

[97]G. Lloyd Carr, "מָלַט," *TWOT*, 1:507.

verses 13-15.[98] Perhaps the phrase refers to those who respond to the message of Malachi (cf. the report of Haggai's ministry in Haggai 1:12-15).[99] In general, translations take the statement **and the LORD listened and heard** as the action that follows the conversation of those who fear Yahweh, but the statement may indicate the content of the conversation of those who fear Yahweh, in which they console one another about the affirmation of Yahweh's attention to them ("those who feared the LORD talk with each other, 'The LORD listened and heard'").[100] The prophet affirms Yahweh's love and care for the people. Yahweh listens (קָשַׁב, qāšab) to those who fear him. The verb qāšab appears forty-five times in the Old Testament. It occurs mostly in poetry and denotes paying close attention or heeding. It is used to speak of Yahweh's listening to pleas for help (Ps 5:2; 10:17; 17:1; 55:2; 61:1; 86:6; 142:6), and to describe the attention a son must pay to a father's instruction (Prov 4:1,20; 5:1; 7:24). The contexts of the other two uses of qāšab in the postexilic prophets (Zech 1:4; 7:11) speak of the failure of the ancestors to pay attention to the warnings of the earlier prophets. The reference to **a scroll of remembrance** draws on administrative imagery associated with ancient Near Eastern practice of a private memorandum preserving the details of an administrative decision regarding some future action,[101] an idea reflected elsewhere (Exod 17:14; 32:32-33; Ps 40:7; 56:8; 69:28; Esth 6:1-2; cf. Dan 7:9-10; Rev 3:5; 17:8; 20:12). In this context, that future action regards the sparing of the righteous (Mal 3:17–4:3), those who fear and honor Yahweh. The context to this verse indicates that the fearing of Yahweh (see comments on 1:6 above) refers to more than a reverence and awe. It also connotes righteous and obedient behavior in contrast to the disobedience (evildoers who challenge God) or feigned obedience ("going around like mourners") of the speakers of harsh words against Yahweh (3:13-15).

**3:17-18** Yahweh's words do not address the people as a whole in the second person. Instead, Yahweh speaks of those he will spare and honor in the third person. The verse begins with Yahweh's per-

---

[98]Verhoef, *Books of Haggai and Malachi*, p. 313; Schuller, "Malachi," p. 872.
[99]Mason, *Books of Haggai, Zechariah, Malachi*, p. 157.
[100]Verhoef, *Books of Haggai and Malachi*, p. 320.
[101]Deuel, "Malachi 3:16," pp. 107-111; Verhoef, *Books of Haggai and Malachi*, p. 320.

spective regarding the righteous ("They will be mine") and continues with Yahweh's promise to protect the righteous on the day when Yahweh acts on their behalf and against the wicked. The NIV translates the opening assertion, **They will be mine . . . in the day when I make up my treasured possession**, and most translations have similar wording (e.g., ESV, KJV, NASB, NET, NJB, and NJPS). However, the NRSV (cf. the marginal reading in the NIV) reflects a different reading of the Hebrew text ("They shall be mine . . . my special possession on the day when I act") and one also evidenced in the TNIV ("On the day when I act . . . they will be my treasured possession"). The difference between the two renderings is the translation of the word עֹשֶׂה (*'ōśeh*), which can mean "to do," "to make," or "to act," and the placement of the word "treasured possession" (סְגֻלָּה, *s⁰gul-lāh*). The NIV takes *s⁰gullāh* as the object of the verb *'ōśeh* ("when I make up my treasured possession"), but the NRSV takes *s⁰gullāh* in apposition to "mine" ("They shall be mine . . . my special possession"). The renderings in the NRSV and TNIV are favored based on the analogy with the appearance of the original occurrence of the word *s⁰gullāh* in Exodus 19:5 ("you will be my treasured possession")[102] and the reappearance of the phrase "on the day when I act" (בַּיּוֹם אֲשֶׁר אֲנִי עֹשֶׂה, *b⁰yôm 'ăšer 'ănî 'ōśeh*) in Malachi 4:3 (cf. ESV, NIV, NRSV, and TNIV).[103] Hence, the phrase in Malachi 3:17 likely refers, not to the making of Yahweh's treasured possession, but to the action of Yahweh on the day in which the righteous are spared and the wicked are punished.

Moreover, the use of the word "day" (יוֹם, *yôm*) and the phrase **says the LORD Almighty** supports Yahweh's reassurance to those who fear him, for they are the treasured possession of Yahweh who now acts on behalf of the righteous.[104] The secular use of "treasured

---

[102]In Exodus 19:5, the Hebrew reads, "you will be to me a treasured possession;" likewise, the Hebrew in Malachi 3:17 reads, "they will be to me . . . a treasured possession."

[103]Keil, *Minor Prophets*, p. 467. The phrase "when I make up" or "when I act" (אֲשֶׁר אֲנִי עֹשֶׂה, *'ăšer 'ănî 'ōśeh*) appears in at least seven other texts in the Old Testament, and these texts indicate that the phrase is generally followed by a preposition, e.g., "to," "for," or "with," (Exod 34:10; Isa 5:5; Jer 29:32; Ezek 22:14) or by no object at all (Gen 18:17; Isa 66:22; Mal 4:3).

[104]Christopher J.H. Wright, *Walking in the Ways of the Lord: The Ethical Authority of the Old Testament* (Downers Grove, IL: InterVarsity, 1995), p.

possession" (*s⁽ᵊ⁾gullāh*) refers to personal treasures a king may esteem above his entire kingdom (1 Chr 29:3; Eccl 2:8). More importantly, it describes Yahweh's election of Israel (Exod 19:5; Deut 7:6; 14:2; 26:18; Ps 135:4). Here, it denotes the righteous remnant of those who fear Yahweh.[105] The New Testament reiterates this theme in describing believers as a people belonging to God (Eph 1:14; Titus 2:14; 1 Pet 2:9). The anticipation of the day in which Yahweh acts answers the question in Malachi 3:2, "Who can endure the day of his coming?" and contrasts the fate of the arrogant and evildoers on the coming great and dreadful day of Yahweh (4:5) that burns like a furnace (4:1).

Unlike Zechariah 14, in which Judah endures the judgment of Yahweh against the nations, Malachi here portrays the righteous as being spared from that judgment.[106] The verb **spare** (חָמַל, *ḥāmal*), found twice in verse 17 (cf. the ESV's "I will spare them as a man spares his son who serves him"), designates the compassion the daughter of Pharaoh felt for the baby Moses (Exod 2:6). Just as Moses is spared from the death other Hebrew infant boys experience, those who fear Yahweh do not experience the wrath coming on the wicked in Israel. Furthermore, the image of Yahweh's **compassion** for Israel as that of a father for **his son** reverses the earlier image of Israel as the rebellious son of Yahweh (Mal 1:6). The return to the second person in verse 18 makes clear that not all of Malachi's audience is among Yahweh's treasured possession. In essence, Yahweh answers the speakers of verses 13-15. The action of Yahweh (3:17; 4:3) makes clear this **distinction between the righteous and the wicked, between those who serve God and those who do not**. In an ironic turn, verse 18 capitalizes on the transcendence connoted with the divine name *'ĕlōhîm*. The powerful judge of the universe calls to judgment the evildoers.

[1]**"Surely the day is coming; it will burn like a furnace. All the arrogant and every evildoer will be stubble, and that day that is coming will set them on fire," says the LORD Almighty. "Not a root or a**

---

284, notes that the action of Yahweh removes the need for the wronged sufferer to seek vindication.

[105]Hill, *Malachi*, p. 342.

[106]Mason, *Books of Haggai, Zechariah, Malachi*, p. 158.

**branch will be left to them. ²But for you who revere my name, the sun of righteousness will rise with healing in its wings. And you will go out and leap like calves released from the stall. ³Then you will trample down the wicked; they will be ashes under the soles of your feet on the day when I do these things," says the LORD Almighty.**

**4:1** Verse 1 begins with the causative particle "for" (כִּי, *kî*), not translated in the NIV (see ESV, NASB, NET, NJB, and NJPS), and *kî* indicates that 4:1-3 (3:19-21 in the MT)[107] reinforces the preceding two verses (3:17-18). The interjection **surely** (הִנֵּה, *hinnēh*), which other versions translate "see" or "behold," is here followed by a participle (found also in Mal 2:3; 3:1; and 4:5); the construction emphasizes the imminence and certainty of the coming of the **day** of Yahweh (3:2; 4:5).[108] The previous images of a refining or purifying fire (3:2-3) now give way to images of a destroying fire. **Furnace** (תַּנּוּר, *tānnûr*) refers to a relatively small cylindrical oven, used for baking breads and basic foods (Lev 2:4; 7:9; 26:26), rather than a large kiln. Malachi's use of *tānnûr* rather than כּוּר (*kûr*), the word for a larger metal smelting furnace (Deut 4:20; 1 Kgs 8:51; Prov 17:3; 27:21; Ezek 22:18,20,22), may reflect the presence of bakeries in the northwest area of Jerusalem guarded by the Tower of the Ovens (Neh 3:11; 12:38).[109] Malachi's use of *tānnûr* may reflect the word's association with divine presence and judgment. In Genesis 15:17 a smoking oven (*tānnûr*) and blazing torch in Abraham's vision represent Yahweh's theophanic presence. In other texts (e.g., Ps 21:9; Isa 31:9), an oven (*tānnûr*) is used as an image for Yahweh's anger and judgment. The verb to **set on fire** (לְהַט, *lāhaṭ*) is used to describe the burning of Korah's followers (Ps 106:18; 16:1-50), the anger of Yahweh in burning the foundations of the mountains (Deut 32:22), the enveloping in flames of sinners in Israel (Isa 42:25), and the blazing fires of the day of Yahweh (Joel 2:3). The **arrogant and evildoers**, earlier described as prosperous and able to escape God (Mal 3:15), now burn like **stubble** (Exod 15:7; Isa 5:24; 47:14; Joel 2:5; Obad 18; Nahum 1:10) such that none are left. The last clause of the

---

[107]Those verses designated as 4:1-6 in English translations correspond to 3:19-24 in the MT. The versification of English versions follows that of the LXX and Vulgate.

[108]GKC, pp. 359-360; *IBHS*, pp. 627-628; Williams, *Hebrew Syntax*, p. 39.

[109]Ronald F. Youngblood, "תַּנּוּר," *TWOT*, 2:974.

verse, **Not a root or branch will be left to them** is similar to other curse imagery that portrays the ruin of root and fruit (Hos 9:16; Amos 2:9) or root and flower (Isa 5:24). The present formula depicts complete destruction, since without root or branch a plant cannot survive (cf. Ezek 17:8-9).[110]

**4:2** Verses 2 and 3 describe the benefit of Yahweh's actions for the righteous, who are now addressed in the second person (**But for you who revere my name**). The prophet uses the image of **righteousness** (צְדָקָה, ṣᵊdāqāh) as the rising **sun** that appears to dispel darkness and bring **healing**. Ancient near eastern art, especially in the Persian period, frequently depicts the **sun** as a winged disk, and the image here may be an adaptation of the practice of connecting solar deities with justice (cf. Ps 84:11).[111] In this context, the coming righteousness likely refers to the vindication those who fear Yahweh (Mal 3:16-18) experience when Yahweh's judgment comes to restore justice in society.[112] At least three translations overtly emphasize the motif of vindication or justice by translating ṣᵊdāqāh as "vindication" (NET), "justice" (NJB), or "victory" (NJPS). Both Isaiah and Psalms use ṣᵊdāqāh in contexts speaking of Yahweh's salvation, deliverance, or vindication of the people of Yahweh (Ps 51:14; 65:5; 85:9-11; Isa 1:27; 42:6; 45:13; 46:13; 51:5-6). The reference to the sun's **wings** probably depicts the sun's rays (cf. NJB and TNIV) that bring healing to those they touch. David uses the rising sun as an image for blessing on the righteous (2 Sam 23:4), and Isaiah speaks of sunlight seven times brighter (than normal) shining on a day when Yahweh binds up bruises and heals wounds inflicted on the people by Yahweh (Isa 30:26). The image of **calves** being **released from the stall** conveys joy, satisfaction, and victory (2 Sam 22:34; Ps 18:33; Isa 35:6; Jer 50:11; Hab 3:19).

At least two translations (KJV and NKJV) support the supposition that "Sun of righteousness" be regarded as a messianic title. Early Christian interpreters often identify Jesus as the Sun of righteousness.[113] The early Christian understanding of Malachi 4:2 as a mes-

---

[110]Sweeney, *Twelve Prophets*, p. 748.
[111]Walton, Matthews, and Chavalas, *IVP Bible Background Commentary*, p. 811.
[112]Chisholm, *Minor Prophets*, p. 289.
[113]E.g., Clement of Alexandria, *Protr.* 11; Origen, *Cels.* 6.52; Origen, *Comm.*

sianic prophecy may have contributed to the celebration of Christ's nativity on December 25, since the title "sun of righteousness" is identified with *sol invictus,* "the unconquered sun," a deity whose birthday is celebrated on December 25.[114] Later, John Calvin adopts a messianic reading of the image.[115] The main arguments for reading the "sun of righteousness" as a messianic title include the association of light with the coming of the messiah in Isaiah 9:2, 42:6, and 49:6 and the possible allusions to Malachi 4:2 in Luke 1:76.[116] Nevertheless, the first argument is too general to be persuasive, and the second argument is too tenuous, since the possibility remains doubtful that the "rising sun" that comes from heaven in Luke 1:78 alludes to the full title "sun of righteousness." More importantly, the context of Malachi 4:2 does not uphold the notion of a messianic title, since the verse regards righteousness itself as a sun.[117] Any correlation of the English words "sun" and "son" is profoundly misleading since the two Hebrew words have completely different spellings: "sun" (שֶׁמֶשׁ, *šemeš*) and "son" (בֵּן, *bēn*).

**4:3** Generally images of the day of Yahweh portray Israel's victories over the nations (Isa 11:14; Amos 9:1; Zeph 2:9) and their receiving praise from the nations (3:19-20), but here the righteous are victorious over the wicked among the covenant community. Even though some in the community have alleged that evildoers prosper (3:15), a distinction between the righteous and the wicked becomes complete when those who revere the name of Yahweh **trample the wicked** like **ashes under the soles of** their **feet.** Placing feet on (the necks of) enemies and crushing an enemy underfoot are common biblical images for victory and mastery (Josh 10:24; 2 Sam 22:39-40; 1 Kgs 5:3; 2 Kgs 19:24; Ps 18:39; 47:3; 110:1; Isa 60:14; cf. Matt 22:44; Mark 12:36; Luke 20:43; Acts 2:35; Rom 16:20; Heb 1:13). The image of ashes complements the image of the fire of Yahweh's

---

*Matt.* 12.37; Eusebius, *Dem. ev.* 7.15; Jerome, *Jov.* 2.25. For others, see Jack P. Lewis, "'Sun of Righteousness' (Malachi 4:2): A History of Interpretation" *SCJ* 2 (1999): 89-110.

[114]Ogden and Deutsch, *A Promise of Hope,* p. 113.

[115]John Calvin, *Institutes of the Christian Religion* 3.11.12; 2.9.1; 2.10.20; 3.25.

[116]James E. Smith, *The Minor Prophets* (Joplin, MO: College Press, 1994), p. 650.

[117]Keil, *Minor Prophets,* p. 662.

judgment that leaves nothing (Mal 4:1). Nonetheless, this vindication comes only after **the LORD Almighty** (*YHWH ṣ'bā'ôth*)[118] acts on behalf of the righteous. The love of *YHWH ṣ'bā'ôth* for Israel has been questioned in Malachi 1:2-5 but now is decisively defended.[119]

## VIII. CONCLUDING EXHORTATION
## AND ANNOUNCEMENT (4:4-6)

[4]**"Remember the law of my servant Moses, the decrees and laws I gave him at Horeb for all Israel.**
[5]**"See, I will send you the prophet Elijah before that great and dreadful day of the LORD comes. [6]He will turn the hearts of the fathers to their children, and the hearts of the children to their fathers; or else I will come and strike the land with a curse."**

Malachi 4:4-6 (3:22-24 in the MT) contains a concluding exhortation and announcement. The verses do not include any assertions or counterassertions. Although the three verses may merely conclude the previous section,[120] more likely they form a conclusion to the entire book of Malachi with an appeal to two ideal figures in the Old Testament.[121] The admonition to remember the Law of Moses (v. 4) embodies the appeal made throughout the book to honor Yahweh. The announcement of Elijah's coming (vv. 5-6) refutes the

---

[118]On *YHWH ṣ'bā'ôth* elsewhere in the Old Testament, see Nahum 2:13 above.

[119]Hill, *Malachi*, p. 355.

[120]Floyd, *Minor Prophets*, pp. 622-626.

[121]Baldwin, *Haggai, Zechariah, Malachi*, p. 251; Childs, *Introduction to the Old Testament*, p. 495; Verhoef, *Books of Haggai and Zechariah*, p. 338. Possibly Malachi 4:4-6 also comprises an editorial postscript to the entire collection of prophetic books intended to link and append the Latter Prophets to the Torah which has earlier achieved canonical status, according to Hill, *Malachi*, pp. 45, 364-366, 370, and Ogden and Deutsch, *A Promise of Hope*, p. 114. The canonical ordering of the MT with its conclusion in Chronicles and the Writings rather than in the Prophets and Malachi makes problematic any characterization of Malachi as the natural introduction to the New Testament. The mention of Moses (4:4) and Elijah (4:5), the two individuals who appear with Jesus in the transfiguration (Matt 17:4), does anticipate the coming of Christ about whom the Law and the Prophets testify (John 1:45; Luke 24:27; Acts 26:22; 28:23; Rom 3:21).

previously expressed view about the prosperity of the wicked, for only a united community who returns to a proper observance of the covenant will avoid divine curse.

**4:4** The book's final command uses Deuteronomic vocabulary to call the community to covenant faithfulness. The verb **remember** (זָכַר, *zākar*) connotes an active reflection upon the past so as to create appreciation, commitment, and action (Exod 20:8; Josh 1:13; Esth 9:28; Ps 103:18).[122] In Deuteronomy (5:15; 7:18; 8:2,18; 9:7,27; 15:15; 16:3,12; 24:18,22; 32:7) the word "remember" repeatedly appears in commands for the people to recall Yahweh's acts of deliverance, and Joshua uses the same word to implore the two and a half trans-Jordanian tribes to remember the command of Yahweh (Josh 1:13). Nehemiah's prayer for the postexilic community indicates that a failure to remember Yahweh's commands given through Moses has resulted in the ultimate curse, the scattering of Israel among all the nations (Neh 1:8; cf. Deut 28:63-65).

**The law of my servant Moses** is a unique identification of the torah, but the term "law of Moses" appears thirteen times in the Old Testament (Josh 8:31,32; 23:6; 1 Kgs 2:3; 2 Kgs 14:6; 23:25; 2 Chr 23:18; 30:16; Ezra 3:2; 7:6; Neh 8:1; Dan 9:11,13), and the "book of Moses" four times (2 Chr 25:4; 35:12; Ezra 6:18; Neh 13:1). Moses is called the "servant of Yahweh" some forty times in the Old Testament. Its use here may reflect the exhortations in Joshua to "be careful to obey all the law my servant Moses gave you" (1:7) and to "Remember the command that Moses the servant of the LORD gave you" (1:13). The tandem of חֹק (*ḥōq*) and מִשְׁפָּט (*mišpāṭ*), translated by the NIV **the decrees and laws**, further identifies the torah. Other renderings of the pair include: "statutes and ordinances" (NASB and NRSV), "statutes and rules" (ESV), "statutes and judgments" (KJV), "rules and regulations" (NET), and "decrees and rulings" (NJB). The noun *ḥōq* is derived from a verbal root "to scratch" or "to engrave" and reflects the common practice in the ancient world of engraving laws on stone slabs or upon metal in order to display them publicly (see 3:7 above).[123] It appears with the verb *zākar* also in Deuteronomy 16:12, where Israel is told, "Remember that you were slaves in

---

[122]Leslie C. Allen, "זָכַר," *NIDOTTE*, 1:1101-1106.

[123]Jack P. Lewis, "חֹק," *TWOT*, 1:317; Allan Millard, "חֻקָּה," *NIDOTTE*, 2:251.

Egypt, and follow carefully these decrees." The noun *mišpāṭ* ("laws") appears some four hundred times in the Old Testament with an abundance of nuances.[124] Here, it refers to judgments or ordinances associated with the torah (see also Exod 21:1,31; 24:3; Lev 5:10; 9:16; 18:4,5,26; 20:22; 25:18; Deut 4:1,5,8,14; 5:1,31; 6:1,20). Significant for this passage among the thirty-six pairings of *ḥōq* and *mišpāṭ* in the Old Testament are its thirteen appearances in the covenant contexts of Deuteronomy (4:1,5,8,14,45; 5:1,31; 6:1,20; 7:11; 11:32; 12:1; 26:16) and the four occurrences in Ezra and Nehemiah (Ezra 7:10; Neh 1:7; 9:13; 10:29), passages that link these words to the law given through the hand of Moses at Sinai. Malachi further emphasizes that Yahweh rather than Moses is the ultimate source of the torah by characterizing the decrees and laws as being given by Yahweh to Moses at **Horeb**, an alternate name for Sinai (Exod 3:1; Deut 4:10; 29:1; 1 Kgs 19:8). Horeb forms a geographical link between Moses and Elijah. Yahweh meets with Moses and establishes his covenant with Israel there (Deut 4:10-14), and there Elijah also encounters Yahweh (1 Kgs 19:8).

**4:5** The interjection **see** (*hinnēh*) followed by a participle, as in 3:1 and 4:1, emphasizes the imminence and certainty of the coming event described.[125] Frequent use of this interjection in the Haggai–Zechariah–Malachi corpus (Hag 1:9; Zech 1:8,11; 2:1,5,7,13,14; 3:8,9; 4:2; 5:1,7,9; 6:1,12; 8:7; 9:4,9; 11:6,16; 12:2; 14:1; Mal 3:1; 4:1,5) is a feature the postexilic prophets share with Jeremiah and Ezekiel (e.g., Jer 6:19; 18:11; 50:9; Ezek 7:10; 33:33), but not with the remainder of the Book of the Twelve (see Date above). Moreover, the interjection with the participle form of "send" (שָׁלַח, *šālaḥ*) appears also in 3:1 ("See, I will send my messenger"). There Yahweh announces the sending of the messenger; here Yahweh announces the sending of the **prophet Elijah**. The similar structure in the announcements supports a reading that understands the coming Elijah to be "my messenger" in 3:1 (see on 3:1 above).[126] The expectation of the return of Elijah is rooted in both the Torah and the Former Prophets. Moses

---

[124]For a listing of thirteen separate uses, see Robert D. Culver, "שָׁפַט," *TWOT*, 2:948-949.

[125]GKC, pp. 359-360; *IBHS*, pp. 627-628; Williams, *Hebrew Syntax*, p. 39.

[126]Graffy, "Malachi," p. 1205; Hill, *Malachi*, p. 383; for other understandings, see Verhoef, *Books of Haggai and Malachi*, p. 340.

promises that Yahweh will raise up prophets like Moses whose words Israel must heed (Deut 18:15), and Elijah's ministry concludes as he ascends into heaven without suffering death (2 Kgs 2:1-11).[127] The prophet is sent as a precursor to the day of Yahweh. Although the phrase "day of the LORD" appears thirteen times in the Old Testament (Isa 13:6,9; Ezek 13:5; Joel 1:15; 2:1,11; 3:4; 4:14; Amos 5:18,20; Obad 1:15; Zeph 1:7,14), **the great and dreadful day of the LORD** appears only here and in Joel 2:31. Malachi, like Joel, warns of approaching judgment on the day of Yahweh that only Israel's authentic repentance may avert.

**4:6** The task of Elijah is to **turn the hearts of the fathers to their children, and the hearts of the children to their fathers**. Implied here may be a priestly function on the part of the prophet, since the causative form of the verb "turn" (שׁוּב, *šûb*) links it to a similar use in 2:6, where true instruction from the upright priest turns many away from sin, and in Numbers 25:11, where the actions of Phinehas turn away the anger of Yahweh (see comments on 2:4-5 above).[128] Elijah's coming brings reconciliation between the generations ("fathers to their children . . . children to their fathers"), which is paradigmatic for justice among the postexilic community as a whole. Furthermore, this reconciliation includes a renewal of the covenant between Yahweh and the people in their return to the covenant obligations originally given their ancestors. Earlier the prophet accuses the nation of profaning the covenant of the fathers by breaking faith with one another (2:10), and of turning away from Yahweh's decrees since the time of the fathers ("forefather" in the NIV). Also, Malachi invokes Jacob's name to speak of Yahweh's love for Israel and Israel's obligations to Yahweh (1:2; 2:12; 3:6). In this way, Elijah joins ancestors ("fathers") with their descendants ("children") through mutual covenant devotion to Yahweh.[129]

---

[127]In the New Testament, John the Baptist denies that he is the coming Elijah (John 1:21), but this indicates only his humility or his lack of insight into the full impact of his ministry. He clearly understands that a time of fiery judgment is coming (Matt 3:11-12), and Jesus plainly identifies John the Baptist as the second Elijah (Matt 11:14; 17:12-13) who is the messenger of the Lord (Matt 11:10; Luke 7:27).

[128]Both Jeremiah and Ezekiel are prophets from a priestly background (Jer 1:1; Ezek 1:3), and John the Baptist is born into a priestly family (Luke 1:5).

[129]The announcement of Gabriel to Zechariah of the coming birth of John

The **curse** (חֵרֶם, *ḥērem*) of verse 6 refers to the curse of 4:1-3, which is the culmination of the curse (מְאֵרָה, *mᵊʾērāh*) of 3:9.[130] The **strik**ing of **the land with a curse** no doubt alludes to the series of curses pronounced in Leviticus 26 and Deuteronomy 28 on a disobedient Israel. The noun "land" (אֶרֶץ, *ʾereṣ*) may designate the earth itself (Gen 1:1-26; Ps 8:1; Isa 48:13), a geographically specific territory on the earth (Gen 12:5; 13:10-12; Deut 3:8; 7:1), or the material of which the earth is made (Gen 18:2; 19:1; 27:28,39; Deut 15:23; Ps 7:5). The land plays a pivotal role in the covenant between Yahweh and Israel. Israel's faithfulness or unfaithfulness while living in the land determines Yahweh's response to them in the land. Their faithfulness results in agricultural abundance and political security. Unfaithfulness, on the other hand, results in agricultural failure and, ultimately, the loss of the land.[131] The word signifying the curse (*ḥērem*) striking the land occurs more than twenty times to signify a setting apart, usually for utter destruction (e.g., Josh 6:17-18; 7:11-13; 1 Kgs 20:42). Several cities conquered by Joshua and the Israelite army are placed under such a curse (Deut 13:12-18; 20:16-18; Josh 6:21; 8:26; 10:28; 11:11). Zechariah, however, foresees a day when Judah is secure from the threat of such a curse (Zech 14:11).

The book's final phrase concludes the book with the dark threat of curse. Efforts to soften this ending to Malachi include the movement of verse 4 to follow verse 6 in manuscripts of the LXX and the synagogue practice of reading verse 5 a second time after verse 6 (cf. NJPS). Such alterations are unnecessary, since such an ending is not unique among the prophetic books. The concluding verse of Isaiah contains an implicit curse on those who rebel against Yahweh (Isa 66:24). For Malachi, the warning serves only to highlight the mercy of Yahweh spoken of in the heart of the section (4:5-6a). Yahweh

---

(Luke 1:17) may concur with this reading. Gabriel tells Zechariah that his son John will "turn the hearts of the fathers to the children." The text alludes to Malachi 4:6 but, instead of citing the next phrase from Malachi ("and the hearts of the children to their fathers"), Gabriel's announcement contains the words, "and the disobedient to the understanding of the righteous." This parallelism links the disobedient with the descendants of Israel ("children") and the righteous with their ancestors ("fathers"), according to Taylor and Clendenen, *Haggai, Malachi*, p. 463.

[130]Chisholm, *Minor Prophets*, p. 291.
[131]Christopher J.H. Wright, "אֶרֶץ," NIDOTTE, 1:518, 523.

sends Elijah to cause the turning of the people's hearts so that Israel may be a treasured possession (3:17) and may enjoy healing from the sun of righteousness (4:2). Nonetheless, only a united community devoted to the observance of torah can avert the curse, whose placement at the end of the book provides its final motivation.